From Vintage to Classic to Amphibian

INCLUDING THE WORLD'S FIRST HIGH SPEED AMPHIBIOUS VEHICLES

By David A. C. Royle

Published by Cardox Limited. Copyright © David A C Royle. ISBN 978-0-9569355

DEDICATION

This book is dedicated to my wife Johan, 'Jo-Jo', for her wonderful support and patience down the years, without which I would probably not be here. I also want to include our two boys, Jeremy and Nicholas and their families Claire, Camilla and Jonny and Helen, Alfie and 'B' respectively, for letting me be 'out of circulation' whilst putting this book together. A task with which Jeremy became closely involved and who put up with the ever changing and growing number of subjects and pages to finally create the 'Royle' book!

SPECIAL THANKS

I must begin by thanking Her Majesty The Queen and The Duke of Edinburgh for their kind support which has helped to maintain the morale of just one of their millions of admirers when times were difficult.

Nearer to home, I would also like to thank Roger for his many years of service and help with the history of Royle's and my secretary, Irene Harris for all her work and latterly for translating my scrawl into the neatly typed early sections of the book. My brother John Royle for encouraging me to write it, Alan Theakston and Peter and Pauline Weegram were most kind for reading through the early draft copies, Michael Ware, who was the Curator of The National Motor Museum and is a well known motoring Journalist, has been most helpful, as was Frederick Forsyth the author and Fred Barter, whose marine publications are well known. Their advice and help in trying to keep me on the right track, has been invaluable and greatly appreciated.

ACKNOWLEDGEMENTS

Naturally, I have been involved with a number of the specialist motor clubs and I would like to thank them for all the fun and pleasure which they have given me down the years. I also would like to mention and thank them for the many editorials about our work and motor cars which they have kindly included in their club magazines. There are too many to list here, but those with whom we regularly kept in touch are:

The Alvis Owners club, The Aston Martin Owners Club, The Bentley Drivers Club, The Bugatti Owners Club, The Delage Section of the VSCC, The Lagonda Club, The MG Owners Club, The Rapier Register, The Rolls Royce Enthusiasts Club, Teesside Yesteryear Motor Club, The Vintage Sports Car Club.

I would also like to record my thanks to the many people in the Press and motoring journals, along with both the BBC and commercial television companies who have reported our projects. We have seen a great deal of support from many people in the media. I would especially like to mention and thank the following publications:

A.M. Aston Martin Magazine
The Autocar
The Autocar and Motor
The Automobile
Automobil Revue (Switzerland)
Blandford Press
Brooklands Books
Bus and Coach Buyer
Coach and Bus Week
Business Review
Classic & Sportscar
Classic Cars
Classsic Car Mart
Classic Car Weekly
Dagbladet (Norway)
The Daily Telegraph
The Darlington & Stockton Times
The Darlington & South Durham News
Emap Automotive
Engineering
Enjoying MG
Enterprise North East
Eureka Innovative Engineering Design
Eurofile
Fawdingtons
The Guardian

Kit Car
Inventors World
Markt Klassische Auto (Germany)
Motor Sport
The N.E. Club For Pre-War Austins
The Newcastle Journal
The News of the World
North East Business
The Northern Echo
The Observer
Portrayal Press
Practical Classics
Royal Institute of Mechanical Engineers
Ship and Boat International
Small Ships
Subsea Diving
The Sun
The Sunday Herald
The Sunday Times. Tec Talk
Technisch Weekblad (Holland)
The Teesdale Mercury
The Times
Waterways World
The Wharfe Valley Times
Workboat International
The Yacht Report

CONTENTS

FOREWORD 7
INTRODUCTION 8
1. ROYLE FAMILY BACKGROUND 12
2. THE FAMILY IN WARTIME 19
3. MOTHER TAKES OVER 25
4. NEW SCHOOL AND FREEDOM 30
5. BIKES AND BOATS 36
6. MOTORING, THE LEARNING CURVE 43
7. JOBS IN THE 1950'S & 1960'S 54
8. LAGONDA DAYS BEGIN 60
9. THE GRAND TOUR 65
10. THE BACHELOR COTTAGE 68
11. JOBS & RESTORATION 76
12. THE OLD SCHOOL WORKSHOPS AT STAINDROP 81
13. A NEW ERA BEGINS 85
14. VINTAGE MOTOR SALES 97
15. THE WORKSHOPS TODAY 103
16. CONDITION & COSTS 111
17. MAULE'S COACHWORKS 1825 - 1933 116
18. THE ROLLS ROYCE DRUG CAR 121
19. VISITS AND TALKS 125
20. THE ROLLS ROYCE FRUA PHANTOM VI 130
21. THE TROUBLES BEGIN 150
22. EARLY WORRIES 155
23. DELIVERY UP & SKULDUGGERY 158
24. A WELCOME BREAK 165
25. 1996, UPPING THE STAKES 172
26. THE HIGH COURT HEARING, APRIL 1996 176
27. THE THIRD WEEK 182
28. THE JUDGEMENT 186
29. AFTER THE HEARING 187
30. THE OTHER AGENDA AND COLLUSION 190
31. SEEKING JUSTICE 193
32. THE LEGAL OMBUDSMAN AND PARLIAMENT 197
33. UNDERSTANDING LEGAL CORRUPTION 201

CONTENTS

34.	THE CHALLENGE	205
35.	PARLIAMENT AND NESTA IN 2000AD	208
36.	THE LAW SOCIETY CRITICISED IN PARLIAMENT	212
37.	LEGAL ADJUDICATORS AND OMBUDSMEN	220
38.	LEGAL AND GOVERNMENT MALPRACTICE PROVEN	226
39.	SUMMING UP	235
40.	VEHICLES RESTORED AT ROYLES WORKSHOPS - PART 1	238
	VEHICLES RESTORED AT ROYLES WORKSHOPS - PART 2	288
41.	THE START OF COVELINK MARINE LTD	560
42.	UNIQUE AND VALUABLE EXPERIENCE	569
43.	FIRST TEST OF MK 1 PROTOTYPE	576
44.	CHANGE OF DIRECTION	582
45.	THE MK III PROTOTYPE	586
46.	GOOD PROGRESS	592
47.	THE MARK 1V PROTOTYPE	599
48.	JET ENGINES AND SUPERCHARGED SUPPORT	605
49.	1996, ANOTHER EVENTFUL YEAR	609
50.	RESUMPTION OF THE MK IV STORY	619
51.	DESIGN METHODS AND PHILOSOPHY	624
52.	PATENTS & IPR	630
53.	SALES AND MANUFACTURING	636
54.	THE FIRST CONTRACT	643
55.	STARTING PRODUCTION	650
56.	BW CONTRACT CONTINUES AFTER WHEEL OPENS	658
57.	AUTUMN 2002, HERE WE GO AGAIN	667
58.	TWO YEARS OF REMARKABLE ACTIVITY	675
59.	BACK TO THE FUNDING STORY	680
60.	FACTORY PROGRESS INCREASINGLY DIFFICULT	691
61.	EXTREME FUNDING EFFORTS	700
62.	DESTRUCTIVE DISHONESTY	706
63.	2005, NEW DEVELOPMENTS	711
64.	THE NEW REGIME	722
65.	THE LAST POINT OF CONTACT	726
66.	MEANWHILE BACK AT ROYLES	728
APPENDIX		743

FOREWORD

From childhood David Royle, my younger brother, has been fascinated by motor cars and boats, a characteristic he inherited from our father, a gifted artist and designer, who was also a talented engineer.

During his formative years David channelled this interest, appraising quality of styling, construction techniques and engineering methods, especially as seen in vintage motor cars and handmade boats. Like his father he derived much pleasure from driving and sailing such cars and boats. However, it was through his other inherited attributes that he found greatest satisfaction, in exercising the craftsmanship and skills required for their restoration, which became the primary focus of his interest for a lifelong commitment.

Following valuable early commercial and practical experience in the business world, David established one of this country's best known specialist motor car restoration companies. He gathered around him a team of highly skilled and committed craftsmen and engineers, in whom he inculcated an ethos of the highest standards, which few other companies could match. Indeed, such was the quality of workmanship that the very name of his company, Royle's, became synonymous with excellence; and with success, as many of the hundreds of cars shown in this book went on to win trophies all round the country.

This book is an extraordinary record of one man's endeavours, facing many challenges, some involving great risk and demanding immense patience and determination. His work has attracted the attention and support of some of Britain's leading designers, scientists and academics; and many others, a few holding the highest and most powerful positions in government and the state.

David's book sets out the pleasures and problems of running a highly specialised business and how, later, he developed the most advanced high speed amphibious vehicles in the world. It presents a wide ranging variety of subjects and remarkable stories, some funny, some serious and some disclosing unexpected and surprising twists; I am sure the reader will find all of them fascinating.

John Royle
(Colonel John A.N.R. Royle, MBE, DL)

INTRODUCTION

A LIFETIME SPENT WITH MOTOR CARS, BOATS, AND AMPHIBIANS

If you are interested in vintage and classic motor cars then you are likely to know the name "Royle". This is due to my life's work of restoring many wonderful and exciting motor cars having been publicised for many years in the press, the motor car clubs and motoring magazines.

I have been blessed with a wonderful wife and family and with many good friends, far too many to include them all in a book which was not intended to be an autobiography. None-the-less, the book has finished up not unlike one and some friends are, of course, mentioned, especially those who were involved with my business and our motor cars. The stories are generally in chronological order so that there is some structure to it, but it is really a conglomeration of events and subjects which I hope you will find interesting. Some of them are funny, others are very serious and penetrate the very structures of our legal and government's organisations.

I have been very fortunate in having met, through my work with old motor cars and Amphibians, many wonderful people. I am hoping that you and many other enthusiasts and interested parties will buy this book, enjoy the stories in it, and then learn from the dreadful facts which, later on, I uncovered during the course of my activities. Hopefully, one or two of you might even be in a position to help me to do something about it all!

Having been involved with all manner of motor vehicles from my teenage days, some of them quite ordinary, others of very high quality and some extremely valuable and historic, I found that all of those people who own and run them, enjoy them for what they are. Whether a little Austin 7, a Morris 8, a racing car or a luxurious Limousine, they appreciate the quality and pleasure of owning them and want to see them being maintained to the highest standards.

When I decided to try to make a living with the many interesting challenges and rewards involved with this work, I was confident that there would be enough people who would understand the nature and the costs involved to keep me busy and this has generally been true. I did not expect to make big profits or want to be a trader, it was the work itself and satisfaction of a job well done, which appealed to me.

Buying and selling vintage cars, as such, did not appeal to me as a way of life, but our customers wanted us to provide this service, so this type of business did develop as time went on. It was great fun dealing with all the different types of cars, but there was always a conflict of interest between the two businesses, so we developed a separate company to trade in our specialist motor cars.

I think that I have been very lucky to have grown up and worked in the North of England. Where better to be, than in the beautiful and unspoilt countryside of the Dales, in my case Teesdale, where the roads are quiet and where most of the people whom I met are not moving around the country, or the world, during their lifetime. This stability gives me great comfort and is missing in so many spheres of activity these days.

When I Started 'Royles' as a business in 1972, I naturally first advertised in 'Motor Sport' and still do to this day. At the time, this was the only specialist magazine which, not surprisingly, focussed on motor sport! It covered all the racing events and was the sports car and the vintage motor car enthusiasts 'Bible' and it was well known as such.

Subsequently, we advertised in the growing range of motor magazines which expanded to include a number of the now well known Classic Car publications. The first notable new one appeared on the news stands in October 1973, Thoroughbred & Classic Cars. The word 'Classic' being adopted as a general term used mainly in America, it covers pretty much any motor car which was considered to be outstanding in some way.

There are motor vehicles of all kinds included in this book, alternatively, if you enjoy sailing and motor boats, then there are also sections of it which will interest you, even amphibians, which link the two different kinds of transport together.

I also describe the story behind the creation and development of the world's first commercial High Speed Amphibious Vehicles. My designs resulted in a new technology incorporating new theories and mechanical ideas. Royles small, but highly skilled team of engineers and craftsmen, then built various prototypes to test the many innovative designs incorporated in them.

I am neither a natural entrepreneur nor someone who likes to jump onto any new money making bandwagon. When I started my own business, I wanted to follow my heart and head and be free to spend my working life doing the work which interested me most. There obviously has to be a commercial aspect, so that I can support my wife and family and I have been very fortunate in being blessed with the best of these that one could wish for, and they have supported me all down the years. They are mentioned in some of the stories of course, but it is the wonderful motor cars, boats and amphibians which I expect will most interest those who will want to read this book.

I wanted people to benefit from the high quality which I have always aimed to produce but, in my innocence and trusting nature, what I didn't foresee however, was that some people would go to unexpected lengths to steal the benefits of our work for themselves. I couldn't just stand by and watch whilst this was going on, so did all I could to protect our interests. In doing so, I was exposed to a series of the most extraordinary and corrupt activities where you would least expect to find them. The first time it happened resulted in a major hearing in the High Court in London facing a multi-millionaire. I include the story of this later in the book.

The famous author, Frederick Forsyth, told me that legal actions are not good material for books. He explained that there are usually so many people involved that the reader has difficulty remembering who is who. Because it is part of a story, already in the book, about a £2 million Rolls Royce, you the reader, will already be familiar with the people involved. This being so, I hope that you will persevere since the events leading up to, and following it, and the far reaching effects which are still continuing as I write, are quite remarkable.

Another later chapter focuses upon my second important battle. This was when there were the most upsetting series of events imaginable for a person like me. This was after spending seventeen years designing, building and testing innovative new amphibians. I was laying down the principles which are now accepted as being the most advanced for this specialised form of transport.

I am writing this book because I want people to know what can happen to an ordinary, but determined 'man in the street'. One who greatly enjoyed his work, but whose efforts opened up one or two big 'cans of worms'. The events are quite remarkable.

As well as the few devious people who caused the trouble I have, down the years, also met many wonderful people in all walks of life. I hope you will excuse the fact that you will read about some quite famous people, some with titles, whom I mention because they played an important part in supporting my work and in the development and continuation of my small company despite critical economic and market conditions (It may sound like 'name dropping', but I want you to be able appreciate how genuine and helpful they are.)

These days, the old families are undervalued and even mocked by the Press and thus, by some of the general public as well. They are often an easy target because of their gentle nature and desire to keep a low profile. Now devoid of power, we are seeing how Parliament is falling apart without them.

I have been privileged and have had the honour to meet and know a number of these exceptional people and I want to take this opportunity to emphasise how important they are to this country. The majority are highly intelligent, well educated, have valuable and specialised knowledge in many spheres of activity; business, agriculture and politics. Their removal from Parliament is a grave loss to us all. Indeed, they and ultimately The Royal Family themselves, continue to set the highest standards of service and duty to the country. This is in such contrast to the self serving and unscrupulous practices of so many people who are now in positions of commercial and political power.

Nobody has seen more clearly than me, how dishonesty and corruption is destroying the fabric of our legal system and Parliamentary democracy. The 'old families' are often made scapegoats and are used as a distraction to hide the abuse of power so clearly demonstrated by many of this country's big companies, and organisations like the Banks who are taking advantage of the power they wield at huge cost to the public.

EXPLANATION OF TERMINOLOGY RELATING TO CARS

It may be worth clarifying here, the terms used to describe various categories of old motor vehicles. In America, the term 'Classic' is used to describe all period Motor Cars.

In the UK we have been more specific about the age and period of construction as follows: The pre 1905 vehicles are 'Veterans', 1905 to 1914 'Edwardian'. Some of these were pressed into service during WWI along with the expanding range of military and commercial machines. From 1918 to 1930 was known as the 'Vintage' period. Outstanding motor cars built between 1930 and 1939 were known as 'Post Vintage Thoroughbreds'. A Classic Car in the UK is generally one which was manufactured after the second World War.

QUOTES AND SAYINGS BY PEOPLE IN THIS BOOK

"The only really good artist is a dead one"

SOURCE: my father, Cyril. N. Royle, to me as a boy talking about painting pictures.

"If you reveal the Prince's name you will not see the light of another day"

SOURCE: unknown telephone caller when drugs haul was discovered in a Rolls-Royce.

"If it has wheels or wings don't touch it with a barge pole"

SOURCE: City saying by investment organisations quoted by me to Sir Eddie George at the Bank of England as a warning against bad risks.

"Don't turn out of the wind"

SOURCE: shouted from 200 ft above lake Ullswater by Captain de Boulay to Sir Waverley Wakefield (Castrol) who was driving a powerful Chris craft speed boat towing him in an experimental 12ft rotor blade autogiro boat... This was shortly before the captain and the auto giro boat plummeted into the lake, (he survived.) Needless to say Sir Waverley did turn out of the wind, (circa 1958)

"Drive me over to that little boy in a wheelchair",

SOURCE: instructions from Harry Secombe in the middle of a RT 999 parade in Darlington, the little boy was as thrilled to talk to him as I was.

"Quickly come to the window, the Germans are strafing the town" (Including the Police Station in Northgate in Darlington)

SOURCE: father to my brother John and me during the war 1944. (mother not happy about it, but we still saw it.)

"It's alright for you, but I've just been disembowelled"

SOURCE: DR jokingly to surgeon Mr Menzies-Gow in the Princess Grace hospital in London.

His reply - "It's a lot more skillful than that". Actually, I felt marvellous, it was a brilliant piece of surgery.

"Do the roof panels usually end up on your passengers lap when you land?'

SOURCE: DR to ageing air hostess in Boeing 747 as it landed in San Francisco in 1986 just before the Boeing company itself collapsed.

INTRODUCTION

"Let me describe you - balding, fat and fifty".

SOURCE: Jazzman Chris Barber on the telephone after discussing a pre-war Hudson Straight 8 car which he bought from me when he discovered that I was a fan of his Jazz band.

"What a lot of gubbins you've got in there"

SOURCE: Windermere Lake policeman looking into our Mk 'I' prototype wheel boat - during a break in the first high speed tests on Tuesday 1 2 June 1990 at Windermere Racing Boat Club.

"If you force the sale and I lose my house - I promise that you will lose yours as well, I will burn it down".

SOURCE: DR to 'Nimble' Thompson, a senior partner in Eversheds law firm who was threatening to force the sale of our Old Vicarage if I did not stop reporting the facts to Parliament after winning a High Court action. The solicitors refused to obey the court orders and pay us our £70,000 awards.

"I've spent £120,000 on amphibians, I am not wasting any more money, I will buy a boat and trailer"

SOURCE: Alan Gibbs to me before spending £60 million, according to press reports, to build 'Aquada' after detailed discussion with me following the failure of his own designs.

"You'll be alright in there"

SOURCE: hotel receptionist pushing me into an empty, but commodious ladies loo in smart restaurant near the Albert Hall in London. I was trapped in there for ages. (I had colitis at the time) the room filled up the minute I entered the cubicle. The 'Ladies', not the loo!

"You don't need to impress anybody, David"

SOURCE: Duke of Hamilton to author when joining a formal party given by the attractive and elegant daughter of Mr Rockefeller. We were in tweed jackets, all the other guests in dinner jackets, I was concerned at being underdressed.

"We will take care of all your business support needs"

SOURCE: Government leaflets and advertisements running for years when author had to appoint administrators for Covelink's Amphibious project in October 2004 through lack of funding for production. The government did not do as it said.

"Don't underrate yourself, I have never known you not to have a good answer to any question in any meeting"

SOURCE: Sir Alex Smith at Gainford after a meeting with Mayflower directors, two years before their company folded, I was not feeling confident at the time.

"No, we want you to be in the photo as well"

SOURCE: Vanessa Redgrave to author when she was filming 'Agatha' in Harrogate. She wanted a picture of her children sitting in my old Lagonda which I was driving in the film.

"Die Strasse ist stinke und bucherliche"

SOURCE: German girl commenting on a drive to Croft in the Lagonda when I was expecting her to have enjoyed it. (Stressholme was a sewage works in those days, not a golf course!)

"Well, have we got the money?"

SOURCE: The Duke of Edinburgh at a Buckingham Palace garden party in 2006. He is most supportive of the "Roylecraft Amphibious Project."

CHAPTER 1:
ROYLE FAMILY BACKGROUND

It might be helpful to give you a brief outline of my family, some of their past activities and the events which have shaped my nature and outlook.

The first notable family event in history is recorded in 1612 when my grandmother, Olivia Nutter's forbears, who were yeoman farmers in Lancashire, were involved with and suffered as a result of the last major witch hunt in England. A full report of the court hearing and the story is recorded in the London Library and also some interesting information is included in Volume 1 of the four volumes of Edward Baines, "The History of the County Palatine of Lancaster, Published in 1836 by Fisher, son & Co. A more readable version is in 'Mist over Pendle', a soft back book first published by Arrow Books in 1951.

By a most strange coincidence, when sitting on the plane on our way to Ibiza for our honeymoon in 1968, my wife Johan, Jo-Jo, took out a book from her handbag. I asked her what it was about and when she told me that it was 'Mist Over Pendle' and that she had picked it up in the Airport, "It was because it looked interesting" she said. I was amazed and explained that it would be more interesting than she thought, because she had just married the great, great etc, etc, grandson of Alice Nutter who was imprisoned in Lancaster Castle and then hung for witchcraft.

Briefly, what happened apparently, was that Alice Nutter took pity on the group of "poor, wretched old women" who met in an old building on Pendle Hill in Lancashire, called Malkin Tower. They were very poor and she used to take food to them. Alice was considered to be 'well to do' and lived at the family home which still stands, Roughlee Old Hall not far from St Mary's Church, Newchurch, by Pendle hill. Alice is reputed to have been buried in the family grave at St Mary's.

The story goes that the old women grew Deadly Nightshade and would threaten to cast spells and poison people if they would not help them. The impression is that they were destitute beggars and would use every possible means to feed themselves. The best known are Old Demdike and Old Chattox (chatterbox) and their 'families'. At the time, King James 1st troops had been organised to carry out, what became known as, The Last Great Witch Hunt in England.

When the King's troops arrived at Malkin Tower, Alice had the great misfortune to have just brought them some food and was arrested along with the 'Old Hags' and taken with them to the prison at Lancaster Castle. Nineteen persons were tried at the assizes at Lancaster in the Autumn of 1612, with the crime of 'Witchcraft'. The evidence is reported by Baines to be "a mass of absurdities". One having said to have mounted her spirit," took flight through the air and became invisible". Commentators at the time noted that with such powers they could "easily and invisibly have conveyed themselves from the bar of the castle at Lancaster".

Alice protested her innocence, but was hung on the gallows erected on the moor for the purpose, along with nine others. Tough old days!

This newspaper article refers but a bit late in the day!

An earlier story of the events than' Mist over Pendle' was published in 1884 by George Routledge & Sons entitled 'The Lancashire Witches' by W.H.Ainsworth, 'A Romance of Pendle Forest'. Inside the front cover of this book, the introduction says;- "To remember the many women who were wrongly accused of witchcraft in 17th century Lancashire". A BBC play a few years ago, depicted Alice as a decent woman, which as a relative of mine, I am sure she was, obviously!

Moving into more recent history, the 1860's onwards are far less dramatic, there are many letters and photographic records of the family. These show the family in the late 19th and 20th century and up to the first world war. The oldest are of my great grandparents Annie and John Royle.

Annie Royle.
Born 14 July 1868.

John Royle.
Born 11 January 1845.

The later ones were taken by my grandfather Albert, with his Plate Camera. They are on glass slides to be shown with our 'Magic Lantern'. I still have the original projector. Later, the photographs are printed on card to make normal early photographs. These record the family into the 1920's, after which there are also 9.5mm movie films. These take us up to 1960 and then 8mm film cameras are used to take us up to the late 1990's. After this, various BBC films on video and of course many black and white and coloured photographs from the 1920's up to the present day.

Whilst, to my knowledge, there has not been a written record of the family history, during the latter half of the 19th century, the Nutter family seemed to have a small woollen mill and there are some excellent old photos of it. The Royle family were running a number of retail shops in and around Manchester and Warrington. They were also manufacturers and sold clothing, jewellery, hats, hosiery, umbrellas and were also Pawnbrokers.

Amongst the boxes of early glass lantern slides, I still have one which was used for advertising. Although cracked, it is still clear that 'ROYLE'S FIT WELL TROUSERS', cost 7/11d to 9/6 d. a

The author's 'Great Grandfather's Mill'

pair, shirts from 4/6d. This shop was at 18 Brynn Street in Manchester. As well as being a business man, my Grandfather, Albert Royle was also a gifted artist and used to spend his holidays around the turn of the century touring and motoring in Wales and I still have a few of his pictures and a collection of the small china Goss models which were such popular memento's during that period.

Albert was obviously successful in business and twelve years after marrying Olivia Ann Nutter on 24 June 1896 they commissioned the Builders, Contractors and timber merchants A. Bywater & Sons of Wigan, (Est. 1864), to built a substantial and lovely new house for them. This was built on Newton Road, at Lowton, St Mary's near Newton le Willows in 1908 and

Royle's Fit well Trousers advert on a lantern side.

was called "Brantwood", No 83. I still have the bills for this work. The style is mock Tudor which was so popular at that time, especially in Wales and the lake district. The name 'Brantwood' originating from the house of the famous John Ruskin, the artist and poet.

Although the war in 1939 uprooted my father and soon after, my mother as well, from the

Olivia Ann Nutter married Albert on 24 June 1896.

family house, my aunt Evelyn retained the remaining furniture along with paintings and most of the early family's records. These include both her and her brother, my father, Cyril's writing cases along with a great many early postcards,

The Royle family circa 1908. Albert, Olivia, Cyril and Evelyn.

Brantwood. The house where my brother John and I were born, built by my grandfather in 1908.

photographs and bundles of old family letters dating back to the mid-19th century, fortunately, I still have these. They have never been carefully read or sorted out, but looking through them, one of the letters to Evelyn from a friend stood out from the others.

This letter dated 8 February 1921 tells the story of how her friend Kathleen's father, RT Dixon JP. of Dunlavin, Co Wicklow, had been shot and killed with a revolver after two men, who were "disguised and wore slouch hats", came to the house after midnight and demanded money. The letter describes in detail, that there was a fight when Evelyn's friend and her father fought one of them with sticks in the hall, whilst her brother and her aunt battled with the other. Included with the letter are two paper cuttings, these explain that Constable W.Mitchell. RIC. was executed for murder and the other accomplice, Constable Hardy, had "shot himself with a service revolver" whilst under arrest in Dunlavin Barracks.

Some earlier family letters are quite different, they show that Olivia and Albert were very affectionate to each other and are very redolent of the way of life in the late 19th century. I am looking forward to putting them all into chronological order and building up a more complete picture of the family all those years ago.

From our large family bible I see that my father Cyril Nutter Royle, was born on 27 May 1902, 4½ years after his sister Evelyn Elizabeth in November 1897. The name Elizabeth being that of her mother, my great grandmother, Elizabeth Royle who died "at the home of her eldest son, Albert "on 13th May 1919 aged 75, meaning that she was born in 1844.

After the house was finished, the family lived at Brantwood from 1908 until 1939. My father inherited Albert's artistic skills and his love of photography. In the early days, he had a hand wound camera for home 'movies' which were so new and fashionable in the 1920's and 30's. I have his early films which are a fascinating record of those days. I have had them transferred onto DVD and now they can so easily be shown without the film breaking ,etc.

From an early age, my father was also artistic, very practical and enjoyed all things mechanical. Amongst his pictures, I have a charming little watercolour which he painted at the age of eight and a glass lantern slide showing him at

Newton Road, Lowton. Brantwood on left.

CHAPTER 1: ROYLE FAMILY BACKGROUND

Cyril Royle. Playing with his train in Brantwood garden.

Outside the gates at Brantwood. Cyril on belt driven 1914 Rex Motorcycle circa 1919.

the age of twelve playing with his 'O' Gauge clockwork model railway engine on a track laid around the lawn in the garden at Brantwood. The slide is labelled "BSG" 1914. I am fortunate in still having this well made model engine.

My father attended Manchester Grammar School, whilst his sister Evelyn, went to Fairhaven High School in 1913 near Lytham St Annes. Early films show her to be a petite and refined lady who loved music and the finer things in life. Amongst the many postcards is one which shows, "The young Ladies" on a walk along a country lane in crocodile, dressed in typically Edwardian long flowing dresses with wide brimmed hats covered with flowers and feathers. Subsequently she became a Spiritualist and there were many letters from around the world thanking her for her help which we found after she died in 1972 Her work had evidently helped a lot of people.

Father, Cyril in his schooldays.

Cyril left school at the age of 18 and his artistic talents led to him being employed as an artist at Salford Royal Hospital. There are two interesting sketches drawn by him dated 1920 and Feb 19th 1921, showing surgical operations in progress in the theatre there. His job was to sit in on the operations and paint, in great detail and in colour, the subject of attention and the internal organs of the patient which were revealed during the operation. I also have a number of these wonderful examples of his work. They were used to instruct students training to be doctors and surgeons. They are incredibly fine and no doubt, they would have to be most accurate and technically correct. There was of course, no coloured photography in those days, so they had to rely on the skills of an artist.

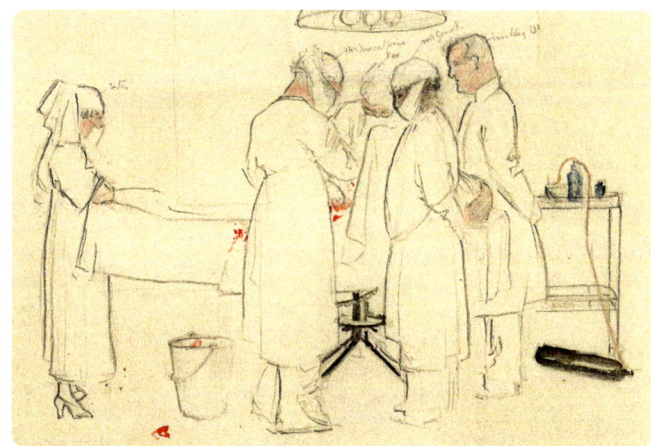

Operation in progress. Salford Royal Hospital circa 1920.

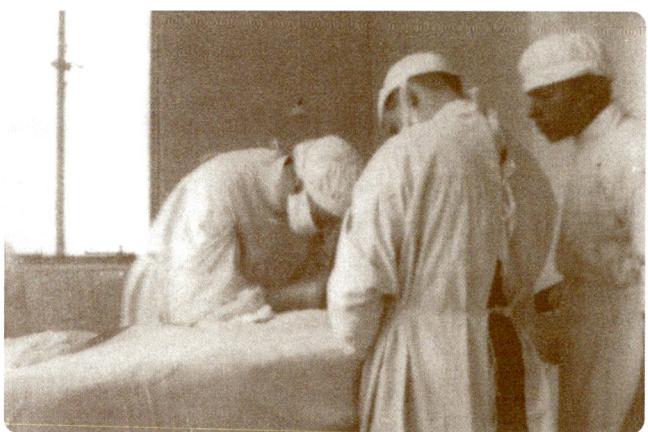

Surgical photograph.

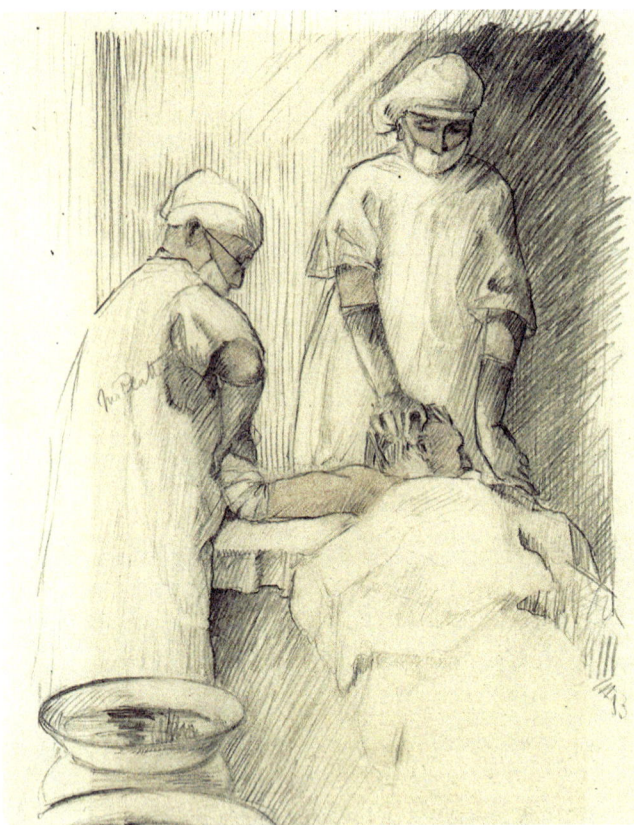

Cyril's surgical drawing.

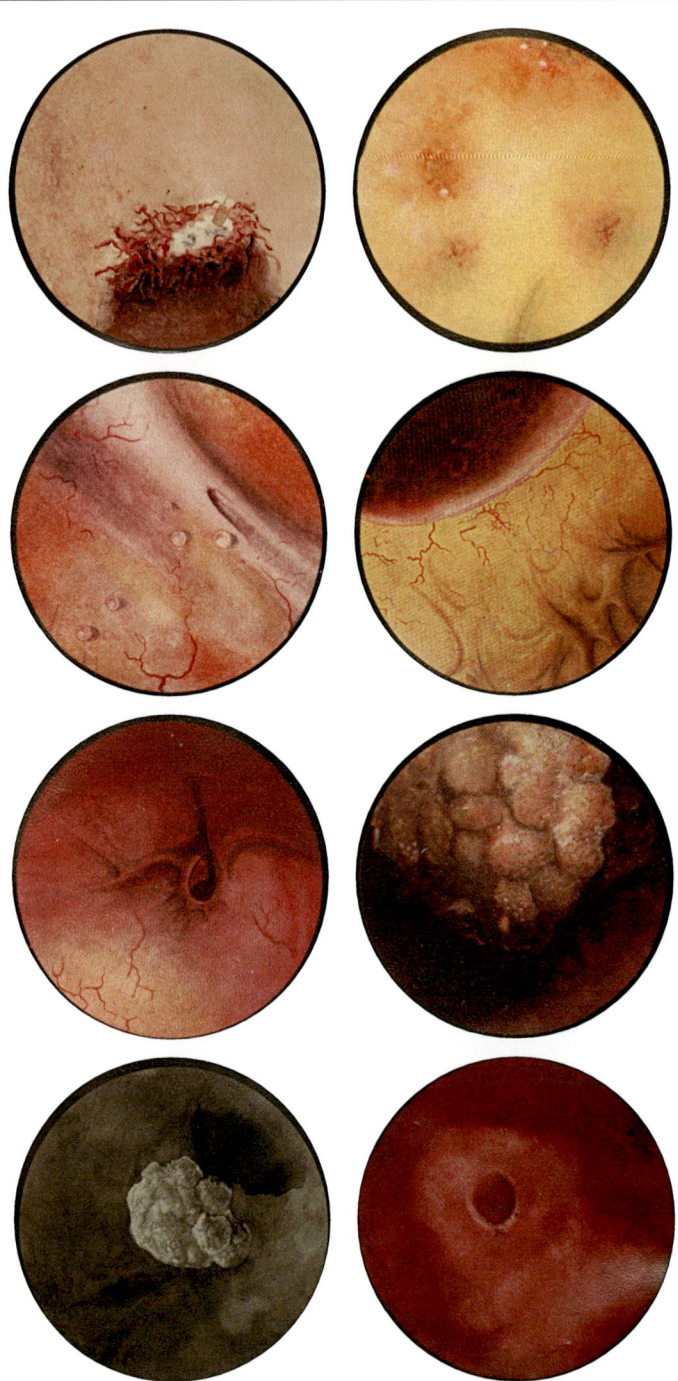

Cyril's surgical paintings.

After two years of being so closely involved and seeing, at first hand, what I imagine to be some fairly unpleasant surgical sights, he felt he needed a change. With one of his father, Albert's, businesses being a "Gold Medal Hatter, Hosier and Umbrella " business in Warrington, 'C. Mounfield,' he decided to become involved in the manufacture of Umbrellas. His trade name was 'Pluvious', 'we shall have rain', and in 1925 he Patented, what I believe, is the sliding fitting we see on all umbrella's today. The story goes that he sold the patent in 1926 for £5,000, quite a large sum of money in those days.

He continued to enjoy painting for its own sake, but knowing as he used to say, that "the only 'good' artist is a dead artist", he decided to apply his artistic talents and paint items which he could then sell at a reasonable price. He decided to produce hand painted, electric table lamps and shades to meet the expanding market for them and he

Pluvius umbrella business advert using self-portrait.

Manchester shop given to Cyril by Albert. Circa 1925.

CHAPTER 1: ROYLE FAMILY BACKGROUND

Cyril sketching in the garden sitting on a leopardskin coat.

formed his own business, C.N.Royle & Co Ltd, but that was later on in 1934. His company was therefore, involved with the manufacture of both electric lamps as well as umbrellas.

Cyril N. Royle. The author's father.

He married Dorothy Read, my mother, on 25 April in 1936 and my brother John was born on 6 April 1938 and eighteen months later, I came along on 7 October 1939. The company traded until the second world war intervened. After the war, he resumed his work with his company and was employing a team of artists and men selling his hand made lamps and shades all over the country when he died and we lost him on 18th November 1949 when he was only 47 years old. He had sclerosis of the liver.

Over twelve years later, in 1962, my mother remarried an old friend of theirs, the Rev Tom Grinham, a most entertaining and charming man who appears on some of the early family films. She sold our house in Darlington and with brother John being away in the army, I was determined to look after all the remaining family furniture and fathers pictures which mother didn't take with her. They came with me to the cottage at Headlam which is a delightful, rural hamlet, ten miles west of Darlington near to Gainford in Teesdale, County Durham. Not having a name, I called it Brantwood Cottage after my grandfather's house where I was born.

When it comes to fathers paintings and drawings, my brother and I still have quite a few of his works in the family. Not surprisingly, most of his paintings are in a style redolent of the late 19th and early 20th century period. They are in a romantic style, in some respects similar to that of Edmond Dulac and Aubrey Beardsley. One picture, which is especially interesting, is quite large and being oils on canvas, remained rolled up for many years on top of some high wooden shelves in the packing shop at the Aycliffe factory. Blowing the dust off, I unrolled it once or twice in the late 1950's and 1960's to have a look at it. The style looked strange and unusual to me at the time, so I rolled it back up again, but kept an eye on it.

It was only after Jo-Jo and I had moved to the Old Vicarage in 1977, that we had the ideal place to hang it in our dining room. Being 10 ft by 6ft, it needed a special frame onto which we could mount and fit the canvas, so with the help of Harry Pickles, we made a frame to suit it.

I would mention here that Harry joined us soon after we had a garage built over the stable yard in front of the old coach house. He was working for Charge Bros, the long established family building firm in Gainford, but asked if he could work for me at Royle's Workshop at Staindrop. He was an excellent builder and previously had been an engineer in the Yorkshire mills. Watching him work, it didn't matter what he did, he made an excellent job of it. He stayed with me until he died in 1993 and was a most skilled and helpful man.

When finished and stretched on its new frame, for the first time since before the war, my father's picture could be properly seen in all its glory, and glorious it is. This unique work is such a beautiful and colourful painting and we were so impressed by it, that we redecorated our Regency dining room to reflect the colours father used when he painted it. I'm pleased to say that this has worked very well.

The picture was painted in 1933 and the date is visible. Three figures are depicted, a princess flanked by a soldier and a student, and they are almost life size. The princess's cloak becomes

*Dorothy Royle.
The author's mother.*

her throne and the unique style is unmistakably 1920's. Mother told me that it took father 300 hours of work, mainly by candlelight, which he preferred. This is featured in the painting itself by showing the smoke from two large stylish candles, curling over the 'frame' which he also painted onto the canvas. I know that father illustrated one or two books, sadly, I do not know the story being illustrated on this large canvas, but other pictures which I have, relate to the 'Tinderbox Soldier' and other fairy stories. I am so pleased that I kept this big painting which, I gather, originally hung in the Midland Hotel in Manchester until it was taken down just before the war for safe storage.

By the time I was born, both of my grandparents had died, so my father and mother were living at the family home at the outbreak of the war.

My mother told me that I had a lucky escape when I was a few months old and still living at Brantwood. She was washing me in the hand basin of an upstairs bathroom, had dried me, put my vest on and turned away to pick up some more of my clothes. When she returned, I had disappeared. I inadvertently, had crawled out of the open window.

Wondering where I had gone, mother searched the room and eventually looked out of the window and saw me hanging by my vest from the thorns of a rosebush below! No harm was done and I think it must have been this exploit which led to me not to be overly concerned about heights. Whenever I am involved with rosebushes in our garden and catch myself on the thorns, I may curse them, but without them, I probably wouldn't be here!

10 x 6ft painting by Cyril N. Royle in 1933. It took 300 hours by candlelight - hence candles are seen to be smoking over the painted border or 'frame.'

CHAPTER 2:
THE FAMILY IN WARTIME

From his war time note books, it is clear that during the war, my father was closely involved with a number of Royal Ordnance Factories(ROF) around the country. Firstly to the ROF at Risley as Process Tool Controller and then in 1940 to ROF Aycliffe in county Durham. His notes show that he also visited various suppliers such as ICI at Wilton and Standish in Lancashire and also the ranges where munitions were tested, eg Holcombe, Whalley etc. He was fortunate to have motor car expenses which was a great privilege in those difficult times.

It seems that his work was highly technical and that he was a manager and controller, not only involved with production and machinery, but also with improving the efficiency and performance of Large as well as Small calibre bullets. His meticulous notes show that he was working with Armour Piercing, Flame Tracer as well as 303 and a range of other sizes. There are notes recording outputs and delivery of Small and large calibre munitions. The planned increase in output is remarkable;-

SMALL CALIBRE totals in November 1940 was 750,000, in June 1941 it was to be 6,000,000.
LARGE CALIBRE totals in April 1940 was 25,000 In August 1940 was 970,000. There were 16,000 people, mainly women, working in three shifts over a 24 hour period.

In his notebooks, there are handwritten details of the chemical make up of propellants including cordite, Nitro-cellulose, Nitro-glycerine etc, plus Velocity, Pressures, Hangfires, Trajectories and the like. He also has formulated notes and instructions for the handling of explosives, safety procedures and the methods of transportation.

This highly specialised and dangerous engineering was a step change from being an artist in a surgical operating theatre, then designing and manufacturing umbrellas and then hand painted electric table lamps and shades. His talents for these and for manufacturing must have been appreciated however, and judging from his note books and other files, he was obviously very good at what he did.

THE MOVE TO DARLINGTON

When it became clear that my father's activities were going to be centred at the (ROF) at Aycliffe for most of the war, to be near my father, my mother took my brother and I to live in a house in Darlington in 1940. My aunt Evelyn, my father's sister, remained in Brantwood for a while, but eventually moved to Wales where my grandparents had spent many holidays. It seems that Brantwood was then rented for a while, but was later sold and became the Lowton Labour Club which it still is to this day. My mother later told me that my grandmother would turn in her grave if she saw the dreadful state that her beautiful Parquet flooring had got into after the war!

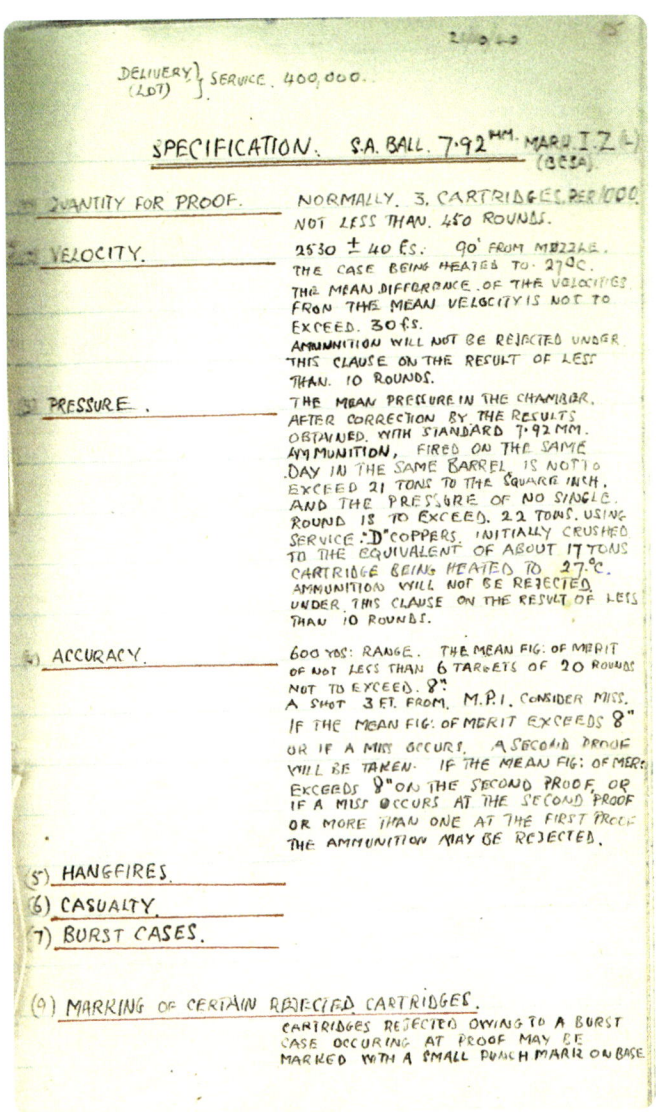

A page out of his pocket notebook, one of many with reports on ordinance of many types.

Our Darlington house was quite spacious, it was the upper two floors of quite a large house which was built of red brick, like Brantwood. Facing South, it stands at the end of Woodlands Terrace and in those days, overlooked a small field in which hens were kept. Nearby was a large Nunnery which stood at the top of a short, steep hill called Boyes Hill. This was aptly named as it was an excellent road for sledging in the winter! With a good sledge, we could easily run past the house and down the 'black path' well beyond the end of our garden, a good distance, two or three times the length of the hill itself!

Looking back, although only 5 years old when the war ended, I have fond memories of being there. For our parents it was a different story. There was always the constant fear that Britain would be invaded. There were many good targets for the Germans in the North East, Aycliffe munitions factory where father worked, is only 7 miles away, the docks at Teesside and many airfields, mainly used as the bases for bomber squadrons. With the regular drone of aircraft overhead, especially at night time, the thought of invasion by German parachutists was never far away.

My memories of the war are like a number of snapshots:

One night, I can remember mother objecting strongly when father excitedly called my brother, John and I to look out of the high, East facing window on the second floor. " Quickly, come to the window, the Germans are strafing the town". We could clearly see the outline of a German plane strafing the town with tracer bullets. The pock marks remained clearly visible on the old stone built Police Station for years. It was on the south side in Northgate on the corner of Chestnut Street, until it was demolished in more recent years.

On another occasion, I thought that it would be great fun to ride down the main staircase on my three wheeler 'trike'. I ended up in a heap at the bottom of course. Hearing the yells, I was picked up by Iris Oakey who was a secretary working on the ground floor of the house. The door to her room, the office, was at the foot of the stairs. A quick cuddle and I was fine. She was always very kind to me and used to encourage me to sing when she was 'baby-sitting' for my mother.

Just recently, I was passing the house and stopped. The field with the hens had gone, it is now a row of new houses. Boyes Hill was still there of course, but the Nunnery at the top of the hill had also gone, it has been demolished to make way for more new houses. A new proper road now passes in front of the house, so the 'black path' has gone along with the row of pollarded Poplar trees which ran alongside it. I can remember as a boy, climbing into these trees in the summertime and listening to the leaves 'rattling' in the breeze, they must have been very 'waxy' to make this sound. A fond memory.

The house in which we had lived had hardly changed. The low wall round the garden was still there on which we used to have our own miniature 'wars' using the toy armoured Tanks which were made out of clay from the field by a kindly teenage neighbour called Jim Booth. Jim's elder brother Tom, was a most gifted Engineer and we occasionally were allowed to visit his small workshop where he was building, what I now know is a 7¼ "Gauge, scale model Locomotive, "The Royal Scot". To see this beautifully engineered large working model of a Steam Railway Engine, even then as a child, was a great thrill. Little did I realise that Tom and Jim would be doing specialist work for me in the years to come and that, 30 years later, I would be closely involved with his magnificent Royal Scot model again.

Painting Tom Booth's 'Royal Scot' steam engine in the 1970's.

Standing in front of our old house, I couldn't resist walking up the path and pressing the bell to ask if the present owner would allow me a quick glimpse inside. I explained that our family had spent the war there and he very kindly invited me in to look round. The staircase was not as big as I remembered, but it was still fairly imposing and steep! I told the owner my trike story, but now there wasn't a door at the bottom of the stairs. I began to doubt my memory until he told me that it had been blocked up when the ground floor had been properly divided from the upstairs accommodation after the war. Otherwise, the internal layout was, like the outside, still virtually unchanged and fascinating to see it all again after sixty years.

Towards the end of the war, we accommodated a Canadian Bomber crew who flew from Middleton St George or Goosepool, as it was known in those days. They were a friendly bunch and spoilt John and me with sweets which they must have brought with them from Canada, a great luxury in this country during the war. It was commonplace for us all to stand outside and count their Halifax bombers as they flew out in the evening and then count them in again when they came home from their raids over Germany. This was how we knew how many planes had been shot down or lost. I am pleased to say that, unlike the thousands of brave aircrew who died, 'our crew' survived the war and they used to call in to see us long afterwards. Sad to say, I can only remember the name of one who was known as 'Doc'.

One last memory which is as clear today as it was near the end of the war, was on Christmas morning 1944. John and I woke up to see what we thought was Father Christmas laid on top of the old oak chest which was at the other side of our bedroom. When we removed the cover, there was the most magnificent sledge we had ever seen. It had red runners with shiny varnished wooden planks mounted on a red frame, well above the runners. There was also a steering bar with a rope to pull it along. Father had painted our names in white on the red steering link bar, "John and David Christmas 1944".

The Bomber crew, realising how marvellous it would be for Boyes Hill, had bought the sledge in Canada and flown it across the Atlantic in their bomber especially for us. It proved to be as fast as it looked and it held the record for the furthest distance run after speeding down the 'hill'. The design is light, strong and very cleverly conceived and I know that these sledges are, today, considered to be a classic. I am pleased to say that after giving 60 years of excitement and fun, I still have it and do, of course treasure it. It will soon be onto its third generation of the family and it still performs as well as it has always done!

THE END OF THE WAR

In 1945, as the war was ending, Father took John and I to visit the ROF munitions factory at Aycliffe. To get in, we had to pass through high barbed wire fences and security gates with armed guards. Father showed his High Security Passes, which I still have, and we saw that it

Father's high security wartime passes 1941. Front and reverse.

covered a huge area. There was a network of railway lines with sidings which connected various areas and buildings. I particularly remember being taken into the Magazines, these low buildings were stacked to the roof with Artillery shells, high explosives and munitions of every description. They were surrounded with grassy embankments up to the height of their flat roofs and there was a concrete lined entrance to each building. If one of the magazines exploded, they were designed to limit the collateral damage. The whole place was a sight to behold for two small boys! We also went to see the Railway Steam Engine and the offices where father worked. Offices in which I also was eventually to work, twenty years later.

Altogether, there were hundreds of low buildings of all shapes and sizes where the thousands of people worked. Connecting the various buildings, for safety, were black covered, asbestos lined water heating pipes elevated on poles running from remote boilers. These often ran parallel to the 'cleanways', which were walkways with very smooth tarmac surfaces. These were regularly washed down to prevent accidental explosions and were, in places, elevated above the ground. Father explained that in spite of this, at night time, you could see the cordite flashing as people's shoes hit the smooth surface as they walked along. It was a dangerous place to work.

Interestingly, it seems that the Germans didn't know that this large munitions establishment existed and Newton Aycliffe didn't exist in those days. We had the occasional bomb dropped around Darlington, but these were usually the German Bombers jettisoning their unused bombs and bullets after attacking the ship yards at Barrow in Furness on the west coast, as they headed for home out across the North Sea.

It was only after the war when father joined the Croft Flying Club, that I was able to see Aycliffe from the air that I saw how cleverly

Darlington and District Aero Club membership card 1947/48

camouflaged it was. The club had a few light aircraft including a Miles Magister trainer and an Auster Autocrat and they were, of course, able to use the runways which had seen so much service during the war. I can remember the thrill of being flown in the open cockpit of the Magister and flying low over Aycliffe, I simply could not see it. The grassy mounds and camouflage cleverly combined to blur any features.

Numerical List of Competitors

No.	Entrant & Driver	Car	c.c.	Town
SPORTS CARS				
1.	T. A. Twaites	Lotus 23.b Ford	1093	Dewsbury
2.	M. West	Lotus 23.b Ford	1098	Hull
3.	J. Nicholson	Lotus 23.b Ford	1098	Glasgow
4.	B. A. Moore	Lotus 23.b Ford	1098	Hull
5.	P. Fattorini	Elva Mk. 6 Climax	1098	Ilkley
6.	J. I. Payne	Elva Mk. 6 Climax	1098	Giltbrock
10.	R. Forester-Smith	Lotus XI Mk. 2	1200	Edinburgh
11.	R. W. Knight	Lotus 23.b Ford	1630	London
12.	G. A. Taylor	Merlin Ford	1500	Bury
14.	R. Scott	Elva Mk. 7 B.M.W.	1991	Aberdeen
15.	M. J. Wayne	Elva Mk. 8 B.R.M.	1930	Leeds
16.	J. Bridges / B. T. H. Redman	Lotus Brabham B.M.W.	1991	Preston
17.	J. Scott Davies	Lotus 19 Climax	2700	Ormskirk
CLUBMAN'S SPORTS CARS				
22.	D. Buller-Sinfield (Driver : G. Silverwood)	Lotus 7 B.M.C.	997	Mirfield
23.	G. P: D. Bellerby/ P. Mossman	Lotus 7 Ford	997	Morpeth
24.	R. A. A. C. Hilling	Mallock U.2 Ford	997	Leeds
25.	I. D. MacAlister	Mallock U.2 Ford	997	Edinburgh
26.	S. P. Rowstron	Mallock U.2 Ford	997	Sunderland
27.	M. J. Smith	Mallock U.2 Ford	997	Whalley
30.	Miss J. Hutchinson	Terrier Mk. 2 Ford	1500	Newcastle
31.	I. A. B. Harris	Mallock U.2 B.M.C.	1390	Glasgow
32.	B. Joell	Mallock U.2 Ford	1500	Sheffield
33.	G. Duncan (Driver : J. S. Obank)	Mallock U.2 Ford	1498	Leeds
34.	H. Burgin	Lotus 6 Ford	1172	Scunthorpe
36.	J. Lumsden-Taylor	Lotus 7 Ford	1498	Herrington
37.	P. Marran	Lotus 7 Ford	1498	Newcastle
38.	M. Bartram	Lotus 7 Ford	1498	York
39.	J. Holtyrd	Lotus 7 Ford	1498	Leeds
40.	R. G. Turnbull	Lotus 7 Ford	1498	Middlesbrough
41.	J. Love	Lotus 7 Ford	1498	Barnsley
42.	R. Cochran/ M. Cochran	Lotus 7 Ford	1500	Burton on Trent
43.	R. E. Dale	Lotus 7 Ford	1498	Stocksfield
44.	J. Epton	Mallock U.2 Ford	1498	Canwick
SPECIAL SALOON CARS				
48.	A. I. Robertson	Hillman Imp	998	Kirkcaldy
49.	A. Barton	Morris Minor 1000	998	Newcastle
50.	P. Suppan	B.M.C. Mini	850	Chesterfield
51.	L. Kirk	B.M.C. Mini	998	Stockport
52.	D. Huntley	B.M.C. Mini Cooper	998	Sunderland
53.	K. Wright	B.M.C. Mini Cooper	997	Batley
54.	G. Carr	B.M.C. Mini Cooper	997	Durham
55.	H. M. Waddingham	B.M.C. Mini Cooper	998	Newcastle
56.	R. J. S. Haining	B.M.C. Mini Cooper	997	E. Lothian
57.	G. Wood	B.M.C. Mini Cooper 'S'	999	Grimsby
58.	Vitafoam Developments (Driver : G. Goodliff)	B.M.C. Mini Cooper 'S'	970	Littleborough
59.	Vitafoam Developments (Driver : H. W. Ratcliffe)	B.M.C. Mini Cooper 'S'	970	Littleborough

NUMERICAL LIST OF COMPETITORS—continued

No.	Entrant & Driver	Car	c.c.	Town
SPECIAL SALOON CARS				
63.	R. Storey	B.M.C. Mini Cooper 'S'	1070	Blackpool
64.	L. E. Little	B.M.C. Mini Cooper 'S'	1275	Aberdeen
65.	A. Blenkin	B.M.C. Mini Cooper 'S'	1275	Spennymoor
66.	W. Jacques	B.M.C. Mini Cooper 'S'	1275	Wirral
67.	J. Dryden	B.M.C. Mini Cooper 'S'	1293	Dundee
68.	D. Forsyth	B.M.C. Mini Cooper 'S'	1293	E. Lothian
69.	M. Caulton	B.M.C. Mini Cooper 'S'	1293	Stockport
70.	D. J. Muter	B.M.C. Mini Cooper 'S'	1293	Bedlington
71.	D. N. Smith	B.M.C. Mini Cooper 'S'	1293	Bowness
76.	E. J. Heron	Ford Anglia	1440	Stocksfield
77.	P. J. Finney	Ford Anglia	1588	Bradford
78.	P. Hawthorne	Ford Anglia	1650	Wombourne
79.	A. Wright	Ford Anglia	1650	Whitley Bay
80.	J. R. Blanckley	Austin A.40	1665	Durham
81.	D. Wood	Ford Cortina	1498	Aberdeen
82.	K. G. Hubbard	Sunbeam Rapier	1500	Nuneaton
SPECIAL GRAND TOURING CARS				
88.	D. D. Carmichael, Jnr.	M.G. Midget	1149	Edinburgh
89.	D. Cullen	Ginetta G.4 Ford	997	Glasgow
90.	A. Barton	Marcos Mini	1293	Newcastle
91.	R. G. Smith	Marcos Mini	1293	Windermere
92.	G. K. Hadfield	Lotus XI G.T. Climax	1098	Newcastle
93.	J. Mackay	Lotus XI G.T. Climax	1097	Thurso
94.	J. Mackay, Jnr.	Lotus XI G.T. Climax	1097	Thurso
95.	B. A. Moore	Lotus XI G.T. Climax	1148	Hull
97.	J. Blades	Ginetta G.4 Ford	1598	Whitley Bay
98.	S. McCracken	Lotus Elan	1600	Glasgow
99.	G. Durham	Lotus Elan	1600	Yarm
100.	E. J. Bird	Lotus Elan	1600	Gerrards Cross
101.	J. N. Cuthbert (Driver : W. N. A. Dryden)	Lotus Elan	1598	Galashiels
102.	G. Machin	Lotus Elan	1594	Darlington
103.	T. E. Blackadder	Lotus Elan	1594	Falkirk
104.	J. A. Lepp	Lotus Elan	1594	Hale
106.	A. E. Liddle	Porsche Carrera	1788	Stocksfield
107.	E. M. Nickell-Lean (Driver : M. F. Nickell-Lean)	M.G. 'B'	1798	Huby
108.	R. Baldwin	M.G. 'B'	1798	Burnley
109.	J. R. Ballantine	T.V.R. Mk. 3 B.M.C.	1800	W. Lothian
110.	F. J. G. Gill/ Dr. I. W. Williams	Jaguar XK. 120	3442	Herrington
111.	J. Lumsden-Taylor	Jaguar 'E' Type	3781	Herrington
112.	G. M. F. Humble	Jaguar 'E' Type	3791	Lancaster
114.	Lord Cross	A.C. Cobra Ford	4727	Itchenor
115.	J. N. Cuthbert (Driver : E. J. Liddell)	Ford G.T. 40	4736	Galashiels

CROFT AUTODROME SPORTS CAR RACE MARCH 27th 1966. LIST OF COMPETITOR

List of competitors at Croft Aerodrome Sports Car Races 27 March 1966, when cars became more evenly matched.

Some years later, Croft was used for motor racing. Local amateur enthusiast Bruce Ropner with his friend Keith Schellenberg and other friends, bought 180 acres of the airfield from the Air Ministry in 1962. After successfully appealing following a refusal by the local planning authority, they were able to organise their first race in March 1964 and these continued for some years. We greatly enjoyed attending most of these amateur race meetings.

The variety of cars lining up for the start was a delight. There were such cars as an Allard, a Fraser Nash Le Mans Rep, the Barnato Hassan Bentley, a number of 'XK', 'C' and 'D' type Jaguars, Ford Specials, lotus etc, etc and even a brand new big MK IX Jaguar saloon which, I remember, was borrowed without the knowledge of the drivers father. The loose grit on the circuit 'shot blasted' all the paint off the front of the car, so a very urgent paint job was called for! Every type of motor car imaginable, wonderful sport.

In those days, there was no Armco Barriers, just straw bales and if you went through those, the flocks of sheep which grazed nearby on the old airfield, would scatter far and wide. I don't ever recall one being actually hit, so the sheep were obviously faster than the cars!

In more recent years, another old friend and my best man, when Jo-Jo and I were married, Jimmy Wilson, along with Trevor and Kate Chaytor-Norris, took over the circuit and instigated an ongoing programme of upgrading the facilities and safety standards. It has now become an even more popular circuit hosting important national competitions. Trevor and Kate have kindly let me use the circuit for road testing the Roylecraft Amphibious prototype Jet-Buses which are described later in this book. It is so good to have the help and support of old friends when needs must.

But I digress, After the war, my father reopened his lighting and lampshade business, C.N.Royle & Co Ltd. Initially, he occupied the first floor above Williamson's Garage in Darlington and then returned to the same ROF buildings which he had occupied during the war. They were on 'Street 4', but this is now called Burtree Road. He was one of the first people to establish manufacturing on what was becoming known as Aycliffe Industrial Estate.

Lampshade factory team circa 1947.

At the end of the war John and I, as five and seven year olds, were part of a small group attending Mrs Wilds little primary school, 'Clareville' in Carmel Road North. I still have my first report dated January 31st 1945 which shows my marks were remarkably good, 86 out of 90. She said that I had made a "splendid start", if only they were the same for the rest of my schooling! My only memory is of trying to knit with needles as thick as a fireside poker. I think she was trying to encourage us.

In those days knitting was common practice for many people, my mother was very good at it and knitted many good clothes and jumpers for all the family. Father was apparently a wizz at knitting socks. Looking at our family films taken at the end of the war on 9.5 mm film, I can see that my first swimming trunks were also knitted wool. When wet, the weight of water made them sag, but my smart 'Snake' belt saved the lot from slipping down to the floor. We were lucky to have anything in those days, everything was in short supply.

It was at this time that we moved from the house by Boyes Hill and we bought No 278,

Darlington trolley buses.

Coniscliffe Road, opposite Elm Ridge Gardens. This is on the road which heads west out of Darlington towards Barnard Castle. In those days it was a broad, quiet, tree lined road with the Trolley buses trundling in and out of town. This house is semi detached, has big bay windows and facing south, was always bright and sunny.

Just for the record, we then attended the Arthur Pease Junior School which, from memory, had around 120 pupils. This was also a happy place to be, with its long veranda overlooking a big field in which we could play. Our school adjoined the Teacher Training College with the Queen Elizabeth I Grammar School gymnasium and big playground running along the eastern wall of our playing field. As a boy, seven or eight years old, I didn't like the look of that school at all. The big boys were loud and rough and always seemed to be fighting amongst themselves and

Arthur Pease Junior School. Circa 1949.

whistling at the nearby High School girls. In the winter, there were regular snowball fights with the boys from St Peters, the Roman Catholic School, which was further up Abbey Road, as it was appropriately called. I thought the QEGS boys were a thoroughly bad lot!

Display of C. N. Royle & Co. Ltd lamps in Binns shop window, Darlington.

'Royle' table lamp with oriental shade.

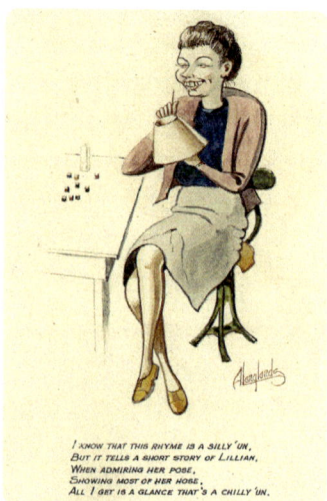

A few of the excellent charactures of the staff painted by Bert Langlands. A gifted artist, standing next to Father on the steps in the photo taken in 1947.

CHAPTER 3:
MOTHER TAKES OVER

After the war, when father resumed production, materials for consumer products of all kinds were in very short supply, consequently, my father focussed upon materials which were available. He had patented a special decorative plaster which added a unique finish to the range of lamps which we were making. Our Royle Lamps were therefore made of traditional materials, wood and parchment and were selling well in all the major stores in London and all over the country.

Having seen success with the lamp business growing at Aycliffe, father was looking to start a similar enterprise in Iceland where there was another untapped market. He was spending his time between Iceland and the UK when he became very ill with Sclerosis of the liver. Like most people, once the war was over, father was able to resume a more normal social life. Both he and my mother enjoyed parties and inevitably, he also enjoyed a drink. Sadly, it gradually began to affect him badly and he became an alcoholic. Just one drink would go straight into the blood stream with the inevitable dreadful results. I sometimes wonder if he had not spent so much time in Iceland, mother might have seen his illness developing and been able to do something about it.

Towards the end, when in hospital, mother wouldn't let John and I see him because he had lost a lot of weight and she wanted us to remember him as he had been, a rounded jolly person. Treatment at a specialist hospital in Dumfries failed to make him better and he died in 1949 aged just 47. Fortunately, we had all the old pre and post- war 9.5mm movie films and earlier slides and photographs taken by father and all the projectors to show them on. We also still had grandfather's Magic Lantern, so as boys, we could still see him and all the family. We used to show them on the silver screen which he had set up behind curtains in the dining room. The screen had the words "MOVIEROYLES CONGLOMERATED" printed in large letters underneath it.

I have mentioned that these films are now on DVD, so now, we don't have to stop and keep splicing them whenever the film breaks as it used to and also we now have the benefit of being able to see single frames if we want to. Previously we were having to repair and splice the film each time, since if you paused, the film would burn from the heat of the powerful bulbs. As a result, we have now been able to see details which I had missed in the past.

Having altogether, a total of 4500 feet of film readily available which records 90 years of the family and the fun we've all had from the 1920's onwards, is most valuable. We still have to resort to the Magic Lantern if we want to see my grandfather's Glass slides which date back to the 1880's, but I have had some of the most interesting ones enlarged and framed so we can enjoy them every time we walk up and down the hall stairs here in Gainford.

BOARDING SCHOOL

After father died, naturally mother wanted to keep the Factory running which was quite unusual for a woman to do just after the war. She realised that trying to look after her two boys at the same time would be too demanding, but needs must, so with a heavy heart, brother John and I were sent off to board at Pinner Schools near London in Middlesex. This school was founded in 1845 and was linked to the Royal Commercial Travellers Association, an organisation with which father had been closely involved and which he had actively supported for many years.

Parting with her two boys was naturally quite a wrench, so on our very first day of term, to soften the blow and take our kit, mother drove us down to London in father's Wolseley 14. It was a long journey down the Great North Road, as the A1 was called in those days, so after that, we always went to school on the train.

To make the trip south to Kings Cross as enjoyable as possible, we would go on the Pullman , but before climbing in, we would run up the platform to the front of the train to see which of the magnificent steam engines was pulling us. These were the famous engines of

The Flying Scotsman like the Sir Nigel Gresley and of course, the Royal Scot. At the ages of 9 and 11, seeing these engines was most exciting and standing alongside the huge driving wheels, the smell of oil, coal smoke and steam under pressure, is unforgettable. An impressive sight, especially for boys of our age. Darlington is, of course, famous for its railway history having been the first to provide a public passenger service in 1825.

Sitting in the dining car of the Pullman in the late 1940's, I can still remember the small table lamps, (of course!), the crisp white linen, the antimacassars and napkins. Sitting next to the window, as ever, I would watch the droplets of condensation gathering together, then trickling down the inside of the windows with specs of soot in them. They formed small puddles on the narrow, varnished mahogany window sil cappings. I can also remember that I would put my finger into a little puddle and taste the sooty flavour of the cold water drops.

The boarding school stood in its own grounds. The large traditional Victorian red brick buildings were relieved with some stonework. The main building with dining hall, dormitories, bathrooms, lavatories and prefects rooms was divided internally by a large Mahogany door, 120 boys on one side, 120 girls on the other.

There was a separate building nearby, the Elliot Hall, a handsome building which housed the large, panelled Assembly Hall with its

The Elliot Hall at Pinner Schools.

impressive organ at one end. The classrooms ran off it along each side, the boys to the Left and the girls to the right, each with its own high masters desk on a plinth. The centre isle again divided the girls from the boys at morning assembly and prayers. Another building, running parallel to the hall, was separated by a gently sloping yard, down which ran shallow furrows. I later saw how these had been formed over a great many years. In this smaller building was a rather old Edwardian style swimming pool. This facility also had lavatories which were divided by ¾ length slate slabs, but they did not have the luxury of being fitted with doors. 'Old school practice'!

It was like going back to Dickensian times. Not a sign of home comforts anywhere. The only reminder of the mid twentieth century was the sound of the nearby London Underground railway which ran 'over ground' not far away.

It was quite a shock, at the age of nine, to be away from home for the first time, especially knowing that it was 250 miles away. The only time to yourself was when you were in bed in the dormitory at night. The older age groups were in 30 bed 'dorms' which was not so good, whereas we eight and nine year-olds, had smaller dormitories with just 12 beds, which wasn't too bad. Never the less, the first night or two was awful being surrounded by sobbing boys who were away for the first time. I can't and don't want to remember if I joined them, but I probably did, it is infectious. Like all regimes, you soon get used to it and begin to feel better after a day or two.

In the mornings it was always a mad rush, running up and down stone flights of stairs and down long stone flagged corridors, 30 hand basins, or 10 baths at once, and then dress rapidly and down to the Dining Hall. We were always very hungry and sat at long tables each with its own white enamel tea jug, called 'Booze' and there was porridge most mornings. Occasionally there was a rasher of bacon, or an egg, but never toast. We did have a bread bun once a week on a Friday, with a 'round' of butter ¼" thick. The bun had white icing on it, so was a special treat.

The smell of toast did permeate down the dormitory landing sometimes however, this was when the prefects were making it in their room. It is a particularly delicious smell, especially when you can't have it. We young ones would gather in a small group outside the door sniffing that lovely, distinctive smell. Suddenly the door would open and one or two slices would be tossed out onto the floor where we would scrabble about like animals trying to grab a morsel for ourselves. Pretty cruel really.

There were funny events of course. The porridge always seemed to have been made the night before and one morning, my white porcelain bowl slipped out of my hand and smashed to pieces on the stone-flagged floor. Such was the solid consistency of the porridge that I was able to pick it up in one piece by its edge, brush the broken bits of crockery off the porridge and then fit it neatly into another bowl which was handed to me. The boys nearby laughed as they enjoyed my practical demonstration of how to avoid wasting food. We were always hungry.

Early on, I noticed that the high ceiling of the dining hall was a blotchy mess of all colours, the boys explained with a smile that it was a mass of butter 'rounds'. Some, they said, dated back to the last century and I could well believe it. There were ones which were black with age and some were covered in green mould. When the top table was distracted by something , the boys would flick them up on the end of their knives. Funny what you find entertaining when strict controls are constantly exercised.

Thinking about food and always being very hungry, we thought about it pretty much all the time. There were many amusing incidents associated with it, some which come to mind are:

The first day I went out onto the football pitch, I was most impressed by the obvious enthusiasm for the game, the way everybody eagerly ran out onto the playing fields, I had never seen such a display. But no, to a man, or boy, they all then spread out and promptly threw themselves to the ground and began crawling around on all fours. It was only when I looked carefully that I realised what they were doing. They were searching for and eating raw mushrooms, they were tasty and very welcome, it was common practice.

If it was popularity you wanted, all you needed to do was to wait for your birthday Tuck Box to arrive. Mine was full of home made cakes and Pies and a few sweets, they were still on ration. There was fruit, biscuits and all kinds of FOOD. (I still have it! The box that is!) Suddenly, you were the most popular boy in the school— for twenty minutes. If you were able to save 10% of it for yourself, you were doing well.

There were times, however, when we were prepared to forgo some of it, if there was a really good cause. Two occasions spring to mind:

The first was the 'Bacon Strike'. One morning, some of the older group of boys started it when they refused to eat, what had become, one tiny piece of bacon which sat alone on their large breakfast plates. The top table were aghast, but the evidence sat before them. Us younger boys quickly followed suit and also refused to eat our diminutive rashers. This was a serious rebellion. The entire school then turned to face the prefects table. This was to be the crucial test, there was a silent pause and then they all noisily stacked their plates with the bacon uneaten. The entire dining hall broke into a round of applause and cheers, we had won! The next morning we made up for this serious loss of food with plates full of bacon and eggs!

Two days later breakfasts were back to normal and the afternoon sports were delayed, as usual, as all the boys were on their hands and knees, searching for mushrooms. Hunger it seems, was a school tradition.

There was the time when we fondly believed that we could start a plague. We saw mice coming out of a small hole in the old disused fireplace next to our table. We spent a few weeks putting down crumbs and morsels of food by the hole, but the number of rodents didn't seem to increase so we gave up. Another more aggressive and carefully planned scheme occurred a year or so later after I had been transferred to a big 30 bed dormitory.

We were repeatedly kept awake at night by a cat which howled outside on the gravel path well below our third floor dorm windows. Our plan was put into force the following night. We laid in bed until the howling began, groups of four boys were stationed at each of the four windows, and on the count of three, it was "go", the windows were thrown open and our treasured breakfast egg 'grenades' rained down on the noisy animal below. The plan which we had so carefully 'hatched', was a great success, the cat did not come back. Not surprisingly, questions were asked as to how the path came to be 'littered' with eggs! Luckily, we got away with it.

I have explained how the boys and girls were kept separate. The only time when we boys could meet girls was at morning break and then only for a few minutes. If you had struck up a friendship with a girl, you were permitted to walk up and down the sloping yard together by the swimming baths which I mentioned earlier. This had been common practice for so long that it had worn furrows in the yard. We also had to use the same yard for regimental drill or 'square bashing'. It was quite amusing when the master would order us to march along the yard, rising and falling, trying to avoid tripping and stumbling as we crossed over the furrows.

Boxing was another activity which was intended to toughen us up. We all had to practice the 'noble art', but every time I went into 'the ring', I was confronted by Evans. He was a friend, but turned out to be one of the best boxers in our year. Although I have always been fairly agile, I could not avoid being punched and sooner or later, he would hit me on the nose, fair and square. Whenever this happened, it would bleed profusely and the blood would run down and spread across my chest. Actually, he was doing me a favour. The effect must have been quite dramatic, because the fight would be stopped so that I could be cleaned up.

As a young, fit lad and a gymnast, I have never known a sport which takes so much energy in such a very short time. Like all experiences in life, there are lessons to be learnt and this confirmed that I am not aggressive by nature, I much prefer to enjoy people and have plenty of fun.

In less 'painful' games and sports, I am perfectly happy to let people win if losing upsets them. It may be that I am lazy, but I know that when push comes to shove, I have reserves which I can call upon. I have been very lucky in many ways and have gifts and an average sort of body which has now served me very well for the last seventy years. I have no objection to people who enjoy knocking seven bells out of each other, but I can think of many better ways to pass the time.

Actually, the School masters were generally pretty good. I didn't come in contact with the Headmaster very often which, probably, was no bad thing, if his nicknames were anything to go by. He was known as "Dodger, Bomber, Cracker, Fot", this was because he would dodge about, bomb down on you, he was crackers and had only one eye, the school word for that was 'fot', we all kept clear of him.

When it came to academic work in class, it was however, difficult to avoid punishments in one form or another. They were very much according to the masters choice, some of which would not go down well these days. Two which come to mind, if we ignore the carefully aimed wooden blackboard dusters often hurled across the classroom, involved the use of rulers. (No, not Kings or Presidents as we were repeatedly told!) If caught talking in class or whatever, you would be summoned to the front where you would place your hand, palm down, on the elevated masters desk. Pivoting the end of a 12" wooden rule between his finger and thumb, he would effortlessly lift it and allow it to fall, edge on, across the knuckles of your fingers.

As he reprimanded you, the rule would rise and fall repeatedly, effectively emphasising his words. Try it a few times and you will see how painful this simple punishment is. After a while a row of black bruises appear across the top of your fingers. The second punishment was more dramatic and less imaginative. It was a two - foot steel rule applied hard across your bent - over bottom. Extremely painful and not good, but it kept control and we are all still here!

The idea of a schoolboy threatening a master with litigation, as happens today, would have been beyond all reason and truly incredible in the true meaning of the word, the opposite extreme. No wonder there is a breakdown in certain areas of our society nowadays. I really do feel sorry for today's school teachers.

Much of the foregoing was typical of pre-war schooling and not uncommon in our school days just after the war. Possibly the worst aspect of school life at the RCTS was that after 4pm each day, the masters left the school and the Prefects took over total control of the boys. The fagging was not too oppressive, but cleaning their shoes or whatever, further restricted the little time you had in the mornings. The memories about the prefects which don't fade are the punishments which they doled out to us younger ones.

We all had to address them as 'sir' and it was very much the same regime as in the book, 'Tom Browns School Days'. Like most of the boys, I suffered various punishments, there was no escape or redress, they had total power until class the next morning. God help anybody who would risk reporting any abuse to a master.

One of the worst incidents which I saw and was involved with, was the result of a particularly nasty practice which was commonplace in those days. When somebody was caught talking in a dormitory after 'lights out'. The prefects would hide in the corridors to catch us and the minute anybody spoke, they would rush in and all 30 boys would be woken up if asleep. We all had to sit up in bed, incline our heads to the right, whereupon two or three prefects would go from bed to bed slapping each boy in turn, as hard as they could, across our face. My clearest memory was when, on one of these occasions, one of the prefects, who were all aged 16 or over, slapped a boy of ten or eleven so hard that he broke his own arm doing it.

Talk about mixed emotions, upon seeing the 'Priggy's' arm hanging down and him howling in agony, the boy who was being slapped, laughed out loud and although we were also suffering the slapping as well, we all joined in. It was something to see and experience. The prefects arm was in a sling for the rest of term.

Because we were never allowed out of school, except in a crocodile on Sundays for church, not surprisingly, we used to refer to the school as 'prison'. Like any of the good wartime prisons, there was an 'escape committee'. Less formal than that in Stalag Luft III perhaps, but boys would save whatever food and any money they could, in order to make a break for it. The only one to my knowledge, that had a 'home run' was my brother John. Being older than me, he was in a different dorm, so I don't know what finally triggered it, but he found his way through London and got as far as York, not bad for a youngster!

At the time, it caused an awful rumpus at the school, but I was kept pretty much in the dark about it all, I don't think it happened very often. I stayed on for a while, but later, against the wishes of the new Headmaster, Mr Lowe, I also left the school. Mother obviously thought that John and I should stay together, so I came back home to Darlington. I imagine that there will have been an investigation into the whole affair by the RCTS and it may be, that some of the less savoury aspects of the school were revealed, since it was not long afterwards that Pinner Schools were closed down. The main building has apparently been demolished, but the Elliot Hall and its adjoining classrooms and the swimming pool building still exist.

Unlike me, John had taken and passed his 11+ exams before he went to Pinner so, although 4 years late, he was automatically admitted into the Queen Elizabeth 1st Grammar School. I was too young for the exam when I left Darlington and too old when I came back, so couldn't sit it. When I came home, mother must have spoken to the Education Authorities. With father having died and mother wanting us to stay together, it seems that John's successful 11+ was helpful because, after taking some tests, I also was admitted to the Grammar School, the very school which had seemed to be so awful when I was four or five years younger.

CHAPTER 4:
NEW SCHOOL AND FREEDOM

After the RCTS at Pinner, the Queen Elizabeth Grammar school in Darlington and the boys who seemed to be such a loud and rough lot to me as an eight year old, was now my idea of heaven! How wrong I had been and how my perspective had changed. It was absolutely marvellous, the majority of the boys were great fun and going home every evening on my own bike, to my own bed, was the height of luxury, not to mention being at home all weekend!

Queen Elizabeth Grammar School, Darlington.

The Headmaster, Dr Arthur Hare was a large, tall and most imposing man and highly respected by all. Being acutely aware of punishments, I quickly found out that he had a leather Cat O' Nine Tails and a 'Black Book' in which to record misdemeanours. Apparently, it was used sparingly and only by the Masters. I was told that it didn't hurt that much, it was having your name in the book that counted.

I quickly discovered when they laughed at me, that you didn't address the prefects as 'sir' and that there was no 'prefect rule'. What a godsend! The prefects were senior boys and had some authority, but it was at a sensible level.

The masters were first class, again, often with military as well as academic backgrounds. They enjoyed the respect of the boys and really knew how to teach us. They had control without the need of two-foot steel rules. There was a great spirit and lots of fun as well as getting down to the serious work.

Unlike Pinner, where the pupils came from far and wide and you knew little of the boys families or backgrounds, the Grammar School was very different. With them all being local and living at home, and with being able to visit them on my bike and enjoy their company in the evenings and at weekends, I found that they were from a wide range of backgrounds. One or two did not even have a proper pair of shoes and buying sports kit was a problem for their parents. At the other extreme, some of the other boys would come to school in smart motor cars. It was a real mix of people and was all the better for it.

It is difficult to imagine all the differences in the way of life between the two schools. In Darlington, life at home played a much more important role. John and I had a proper radio in our bedroom, rather than the home made crystal set like some of us had at Pinner Schools. These homemade radios were built into in a cigar box with a 'cats whisker' to tune them and were used with ear phones. Later on mother gave us a proper portable radio with a lift-up lid. As soon as the prefects at Pinner Schools found it, it was confiscated. Television was just coming to the North of England at that time, but the radio was still our prime source of entertainment at home.

In those days there was absolutely no swearing in the media, or at home, even 'damn' was not a good word to use and nothing which could be construed as being rude was permitted. The outstanding radio programme for us teenagers on Tuesday evenings was 'The Goon Show'. These programmes were a rich and unconventional mixture of sufficiently rude and novel humour, all with a military flavour, to make us laugh until we literally cried. We used to gather around the radio each week and without fail, we would roar our heads off, marvellous!

Unlike comedians today, 'The Goons' had the great benefit of having a 'clean sheet' to work with. We were part of a prim and proper society with a media to match, one which was a wonderful basis and counterpoint for their unique wit and fun. This so clearly emphasised their fresh, brilliantly clever and original military and schoolboy humour, that it became so deep rooted that even just to think about it would set us off in uncontrollable laughter.

In a biology lesson one day, my good friend Ian Hunter and I picked up on something 'Goonish' which the master had said. The more we tried to control our laughter the worse it became until we were sent out of class and told not to come back "until we had stopped". We walked around the school for half an hour still convulsing with laughter, we couldn't stop even when we returned and stood outside the classroom door. The bell went, but we weren't seriously reprimanded. It turned out that the biology master was a 'Goon fan' as well!

Dicky Bird our art master and 'Sully' by DR.

Our English master Mr Osborne, an ex military man, is still talked about today by my old school friends. As was the case with most lessons, we were often set homework to do. The only one which comes to mind, because he enjoyed it, was when we were asked to write a poem. With the ever present wartime and military influences around us, and with unavoidable National Service being ever present in our minds, I wrote a schoolboy poem very much in the style of, Cyril Fletcher's 'Odd Odes'. These were poems which he read on the popular TV personality, Cliff Michelmore's 'Tonight' programme in the 1950's. He used various accents and over emphasised the words which helped to bring his poems to life. My poem is about 'Bill', a fictional lad who was 'called up' for military service, as was still a requirement for all boys in those days when they left school. From memory, it goes something like this:

'OUR BILL'

Our Bill to National Service went,
and down to Catterick Camp was sent.
One day when on the rifle range,
something happened rather strange.
Sighting down along the groove,
the target suddenly began to move,

But alas - alack it was too late,
the bullet grazed the Colonels Pate.
The colonel bellowed out in rage,
"Take him along to the Sergeant Maje"
Whereupon it was plain to see,
our 'Bill' had seven days 'CB'.

Short and simple, yes, but I read it out in the same manner and style as Cyril Fletcher and everybody laughed. Strangely enough, I find that stringing words together is fun and over the years, have written a few more poems. These are longer and I have to say, a little more carefully contrived and they are usually aimed at a particular audience. I find that it is easier than making speeches and if I can make them humorous, then all the better. I will include one or two of them later in this book, including one about 'the little man in the street 'which has a very serious message.

An example of the happier and more relaxed attitude of our masters was exemplified by 'Dicky' Bird our art Master. He was delightfully vague and genuinely 'Arty' and we always enjoyed his classes. One afternoon, another great school friend of mine, Edward 'Neddy' Keighley, decided to call in to see me during one of Dicky's classes, as you do! Being older than me, Neddy had been left school for a couple of years and was working at the SMT in Edinburgh. He was training as a motor engineer to go into his father's long established garage business in Darlington.

"Ah, Keighley", said Dicky loudly as Neddy walked in, "I haven't seen much work from you lately, sit down and get on with your work boy". We all thought this was marvellous knowing that Neddy had left school a long time ago. What made it all the funnier was that he was wearing a flashy striped bow tie, a loud pink shirt and the latest fashionable flecked jacket. About as far removed from our traditional school uniform as you can get!

Normally, Dicky was fairly tolerant of me because I had the wonderful gift of being able to draw and paint without difficulty. No doubt handed down from my parents, a gift which was to prove to be so useful in so many ways in the years to come. In fact, I often won the school prize for art which seemed to be so unfair for others who would strive so hard to create good work. It goes without saying that, sooner or later, I would overstep the mark and sure enough Dicky was sufficiently annoyed with my fooling about one day, to send me to the Head Master to get the Strap and Black Book. I had to wait for some time outside the Heads study door. When I returned to the art room, Dicky was busy with one of the boys and didn't notice me coming back in, so I quietly sat down and got on with my work for the rest of the period, Nothing was said so, hiding the dreaded strap and black book under my jacket, I surreptitiously returned it to the headmasters study. Was it luck, or was Dicky being craftier than we thought?

OUTSIDE SCHOOL

Enjoying the freedom of being able to travel around on our bikes and always on the lookout for fun, we were lucky that we didn't get into more serious scrapes than we did. Another good school friend, Fred Lucas, whose father had been posted out to India and had married an Indian lady in Peshawar, used to joke about his exploits as a child, 'Plodging' in the river Ganges. Nothing so common as us messing about paddling in the nearby river Tees. Like Ian Hunter, who won the Victor Ludorum, Fred was also a great sportsman at school and one evening, with me being a bit of a gymnast, we decided to see if we could climb the school tower and hang a bike frame on the ornamental finial.

We donned Black jumpers, woollen hats and black gym shoes and headed off on our bikes towards the school. On the way, we passed a biggish old detached house which was up for sale. Knowing that it was empty, I suggested that we should explore it. Quietly putting our bikes in the bushes round the back, we found a small open pantry window and climbed in. As expected, there was no furniture, but it was dark and interesting and I can remember the loose floor tiles rattling noisily in one of the upstairs bathrooms as we walked on them.

We came back downstairs and were standing in a big, empty sitting room when we suddenly heard voices and a torch flashed. Being bare of furniture, the only place to hide was to lie along the skirting board immediately below the windowsill. It was the Police, they shone their torch into the room, but the beam couldn't quite reach us. We waited until they went round to the front of the house, with hearts beating, we hastily climbed out of the little window and hid in a garden shed when we heard them coming round again. They opened the shed door which we were hiding behind. The torch shone, not seeing us, they went out and closed the door behind them.

We breathed a sigh of relief and went to look out of the shed window. "Have they gone?" asked Fred, "No" came the loud reply from the 'Rozzer' (to use a proper criminal word!) as he smartly opened the shed door again. He didn't say "your nicked" which was a bit disappointing, but we were. We were driven back to the Police Station on the corner of Chestnut Street in Darlington, the one which still bore the pock marks of the German Tracer bullets. After interrogation, they realized that it

Pen and ink wash of Fred Lucas by the author.

was all an innocent jape, and instead of arresting us for housebreaking, they took us roaring round the town in their smart Mark II Jaguar Police Car. They showed off mercilessly and we loved it. We collected our bikes and rode home. It was getting late and we'd had enough excitement for one night.

We never did put the bike frame on the tower, looking at it today, we would probably have killed ourselves.

GUNS

Whilst on the subject of illegal activities, it was at the age of 14, that I took a keen interest in and started to collect bayonets, swords and firearms of every description. I think that this was as a result of all the cowboy films, war films and those fashionable films of the Chicago underworld. It all began when a boy at school whose father was a policeman, offered to swap a Colt 45 revolver for my Bow and arrows. I jumped at the chance to move up from the 17th century into the 20th. Actually the gun dated from the first world war, so was almost an antique, the 'blacking' had worn off, but it worked well.

Normally, it would be difficult for a boy to be allowed and able to collect firearms, especially one whose father had an intimate knowledge of the dangers associated with munitions and had always discouraged us from having anything to do with guns and the like. After his death in 1949, his influence had faded and mother obviously had confidence that we would not come to any harm. Good old mother, luckily she was right! As the months passed, it was not difficult in those days, for me to find all sorts of weapons. They were readily available and by asking relatives, friends and becoming known as a collector, people would come up to me in the street and it was not long before I had over fifty weapons in my collection.

There were so many that my dressing table drawers eventually collapsed under the weight. There were some rare and interesting pieces as well as one or two which were dangerous, not necessarily to anything or anybody standing in front of them, but to the person firing them! One which caused a problem was an American snub nosed 44 revolver, it was typical of the kind used by gangsters during the Prohibition in America. The barrel was just over an inch long and the chamber held only five bullets. This was designed to keep it as compact as possible, but to have a big bore. The handle was decorated with dancing girls and the like, the real 'McCoy' from Chicago.

It was obviously cheaply made and I didn't risk firing it. Later on, I swapped it for another gun and the next time I saw the enthusiast who took it, Bob, his thumb was bandaged. He had ignored my concerns about it and tried firing it. The whole thing exploded and it nearly blew his thumb off.

There were in fact, some wonderful guns in my collection including a superb Flintlock Brass bound Horse Pistol and various single and double barrelled Percussion Cap pistols and shot guns, Hammer guns, 410 and 12 bore Shotguns, .22 rifles, poachers guns, and two first war German Very Light pistols. Like the swords, African and oriental hunting knives, bayonets, Gurkha knives, etc, they all have a part in history and have stories to tell. Some, of course are for dress purposes and others are, or were, serious weapons.

Today, such a collection in the hands of such a young person would be looked upon in horror, dangerous in the extreme. The obvious conclusion being that I was some sort of killer criminal. To an enthusiast like me however, the thought of this never entered my mind. As a young teenager, being able to actually handle them and having the open country in which to fire them, was a valuable experience. I was quickly able to appreciate the dangers and firepower of the different kinds and periods of weapons. In fact, later on, it led to me being able to enjoy years of wonderful small game shooting.

Starting with vermin and then rabbits and hares for the pot, I eventually graduated to shooting pheasants and grouse on the moors. Like all hunting, it goes back to our earliest forbears and nowadays, in this country, it is a great and traditional sport which is misunderstood by many. Often, those who vote against it, live in towns and simply do not understand the nature or the care and knowledge exercised by those who are involved with the sport. Without most of our country sports, much of our wildlife would not exist. It is conservation balanced with the world around us. The concern shown by city dwellers for wildlife is understandable, but it is the huge numbers involved in the mass production of animals for food, which should be the focus of their attention.

Returning to my collection, and what I did with it. I would usually go with a friend when firing and testing the guns. Michael Stephenson, 'Stivvy', was a friend and also an enthusiastic collector. We would each take a licensed shotgun over our shoulders in a proper carrying case to legitimise the shooting noises and would also fill our bike saddlebags with various pistols. We had a friendly farmer who kindly let us use a suitably safe and isolated wood where we would set up tin cans and targets and then blast away with revolvers, flintlock pistols and shotguns. Besides experiencing the thrill of firepower, the lessons learnt are most valuable.

The kick from a Colt 45 revolver is something to experience. With flint locks and early guns, we were lucky that none exploded, but we used to limit the charge for reasons of safety. We were always impressed by the skill which people who used them, must have had. The delay with a flintlock mechanism for example, is such that the trigger has to be pulled before the target is in its perfect position. Swinging to shoot game birds must have been a true art. Another interesting fact which we learnt was that shooting from the hip is a perfectly viable and accurate method. If you just hold a stick or a gun by your hip and, looking at the target, imagine firing a shot at it, you will see that you are pointing right at it.

You may be wondering what happened to my collection. When my shooting friend Stivvy returned from the cinema one evening, he found a policeman standing on his doorstep. He was taken to the Chestnut Street Police Station where he was shown into a room with a long table which had his whole collection of guns, swords, military helmets and other wartime memorabilia laid out on it. Apparently he had bought two rifles which turned out to have been stolen from a local gun shop by a certain 'Panchy Dannet'. This thief had been caught and had told the police that two of them had been sold to Stivvy. His entire collection was confiscated.

When he told me about this, I immediately approached members of the local Rifle club and sold my collection to one of the people there. I was sad to part with them, but I had learnt a lot from my experience of shooting and handling them. I sold them for ten shillings (50p) each so the buyer got a bargain, but as they had cost me so little, I was still into pocket. I used the money to buy a proper drum kit.

TRAD JAZZ

At the time, traditional Jazz was de rigueur, and Humphrey Littleton gave us all a lot of pleasure and fun. Lonnie Donnegan, who was in Chris Barbers Band, was introducing another popular variation at the time which became known as Skiffle. This was the 'Rock Island Line' and the like, it was all lively and good fun to dance to. We teenagers in Darlington, all used to meet in Louis Dipalo's coffee bar in Post House Wynd in those days and decided, one day, that we should form our own Jazz Band and Skiffle group.

I happened to know an elderly Welshman who had a lovely vintage square tank BSA motorbike which he used it to ride every year, to go to the Eistedford in Wales. I used to listen to a popular welsh radio programme at the time called, 'We'll Keep a Welcome in the Hillsides' and talking to him about music one day, I told him that we were thinking of forming a Jazz band. To my delight, it was then that this 'vintage' pensioner told me that he could help us if we needed any musical instruments. Confirming that we did, he went on to explain that he collected muscial instruments and invited us all to his house to see them, saying that he was happy to sell us whatever we needed.

On the appointed day, our group of aspiring musicians turned up at his large Victorian terraced house just off Coniscliffe road, in Darlington and we were led upstairs to the attic. This formed a long gallery and entering in to it, beheld a remarkable sight. All we could see were instruments wherever we looked. There were literally dozens of violins hanging in bunches from the beams and ceilings like bananas, there was every sort of instrument imaginable. They were stacked around the walls and covered most of the floors. Trumpets, trombones, glockenspiels, harps, saxophones, mandolins, guitars, cornets, xylophones, cellos, French horns and all manner of other stringed and wind instruments, including even a serpentine, an instrument made out of some sort of root. An amazing sight, there were hundreds of them!

We were like children in a 'sweety shop'. Only my brother, John, had played any sort of instrument previously, this was when he had practised the cello for the school orchestra, but he fancied the trumpet, so bought one. Each of us chose and bought what we fancied. We finished up with a base trombone, a guitar, saxophone, banjo, clarinet and two trumpets. Sadly there wasn't a drum kit which is what I wanted to play, so I bought the only drum he had, a 'gong drum' which was like a one sided base drum, it was better than nothing

It was essential that we had the right sort of environment for the band, we needed a cellar. It turned out that my girl friend, Heather Barwick, had one under her house and her mother would let us use it for practise. Marvellous! So the 'Downtown Seven' as we called ourselves, started to meet there every week.

I acquired a foot pedal for my gong drum, then made some more drums by converting empty paint tins with some strong man-made fabric stretched tightly over them. These worked reasonably well, but after selling my gun collection a few months later, It was most satisfying to have a proper drum kit complete with a side drum, tom-toms, cymbals and a 'high hat'. I also made a 'String Base' out of a tea chest and broom stick which was standard practice for a Skiffle group, as was having an old fashioned wash board which Neddy used to play.

We practised every week and had tremendous fun, especially when we hit upon a tune which suited all of us. We reached a bearable standard, but it was interesting to see how two of the group soon displayed the most remarkable natural talent. Within a matter of only two months, the guitarist and trumpet player were playing as well as any professional. The guitarist ended up playing in an orchestra in Harrogate and the trumpeter, Campbell Finlay, playing in the top London night clubs and finally becoming the MD of Porsche motor cars in England.

Before leaving this enjoyable activity however, I must mention the arrival of Bill Haley on the music scene. Following my father's love of music, especially classical, I followed his habit of listening to music on the radio whenever I could. Indeed, before he died, he had wired up the whole house with loudspeakers so that we all could enjoy his records and the radio in every room.

In 1955 I heard Rock and Roll for the first time. It was an astonishing sound, Bill Haley's Rock Around The Clock hit every teenager like a thunderbolt. The 'Downtown Seven', had to try it. We had a reasonable line up of instruments, so we practised the Bill Haley sound and we got away with the first few bars to a reasonably satisfactory standard. Although we were excited by it, we didn't really want to be rock and rollers, or pop stars. Our group were really just 'Trad jazz' purists and played music for our own pleasure.

Somehow we were asked to play at the local technical college dance, so on the appointed night, we climbed onto the High Stage. There were around two hundred teenagers. We started the be-bop and Jive dancing with a mixture of Trad Jazz and skiffle and then just for fun, announced "Rock Around the Clock". It was too late, when they all cheered, we realised that we might have a problem. We struck up with our well rehearsed intro and the first few bars, the crowd WENT MAD, we soon reached the end of the rehearsed bit, so we stopped and then announced that " No, it's not as good as Trad Jazz", But before we could play another note, they stopped dancing and screamed for more. We couldn't give them any more, so had no choice but to rapidly leave the building to save our skins. So much for the Downtown Seven !

Thinking back, had we really wanted to become a pop group, we were in at the very start of Rock and Roll and could have put a full band together without too much difficulty, but were just doing it for fun, and we had plenty of that and, anyway of course, we were still at school.

CHAPTER 5:
BIKES AND BOATS

By now you may be thinking that I was growing into some sort of 'wild child', but not really. With mother being busy running the factory and not having the controlling hand of a father, my brother John and I, certainly had more freedom than most teenagers. After boarding school, we had a lot of catching up to do so, albeit within severe financial constraints. We greatly enjoyed finding out about anything which interested us.

Looking back, there is no doubt that the knowledge we gained through the practical experience of being closely involved with all sorts of activities in our spare time, was tremendously valuable. With the quiet roads and 'track bikes' which we built for ourselves, inevitably mainly by visiting scrapyards. We were then able to spend time exploring the dales and wonderful countryside around Darlington on our bicycles. The 1950's were a good time to be a young teenager.

As John was 18 months older than me, when he was 16 his interests had turned to motor bikes, no, not of the trials variety or the high revving modern Japanese bikes of today, but what, even then were considered to be old machines. A pre-war 500cc 'sloper' BSA and a Velocette come to mind. These were heavy and powerful machines and were readily available at £5 each. Once again, we could play with these away from the main roads and have some thrilling rides. Push starting could be a problem and I can clearly remember John being dragged round a field in circles one day, when the BSA fired up before he had the chance to sit in the saddle. After this, he bought an old Austin Seven saloon, took the body off and drove it around with just its bonnet and bulkhead. It was his 'sporty motor'.

We also spent a lot of time down by the river Tees in those days. It is a beautiful river with miles of unspoilt river banks and open rolling countryside. It's nature changes from its rocky, tumbling waters of upper Teesdale, where there is the famous and impressive High Force waterfall, down to smoother waters below Blackwell near Darlington where it levels out and further downstream, in the 1950's, it was still tidal at Yarm. In more recent years, with the new Barrage built below Stockton, this is no longer the case and it is now navigable all the way up to Yarm and has passenger boats operating on it.

On one of our bike rides in 1953, 'Stivvy' and I cycled to Yarm and were exploring the old disused warehouses and buildings beside the river, when we discovered an old canvas canoe sitting up in the rafters of one of the old buildings covered in a thick layer of dust. It had obviously been there for a long time, so we enquired about it at the nearest house and were told that the owner had died during the war and that we could have it if we wanted it. We couldn't waste such a great opportunity, so we climbed up and brought it down. It turned out to be a two-man canoe around 18 feet long. A great bonus was that it was, effectively, two 9ft units with flat transoms which bolted together in the middle. We had a boat each! We undid the bolts which held them together, quickly dusted the two halves down and pushed them back to Darlington resting them on our bike handlebars and saddles.

Two boys, two boats and two bikes.

With father having died, the family no longer went to the 'Hut' on the river Weaver in Cheshire. This is where we had 'Gleam', our pre-war motor cruiser and where we had spent so many happy holidays as boys, messing about in boats at the end of the war. Our old 9.5mm movie film is a good reminder of these days, so the thought of now having my own little boat which I could use on the Tees, was a great thrill.

After giving it a good clean, checking it for leaks and giving it a coat of paint, I was able to take it to Blackwell on my handlebars. Stivvy and I spent a lot of time in 1954 canoeing for miles up and down the river. There were many 'rapids' and pools to keep up the excitement, and one day, just like the river Severn, we did have a 'bore' come down the river, fortunately it was not as big. We usually paddled a mile or so upstream which could be hard work as we were often heading into the wind as well as the current. We would go as far as the weir at the Broken Scar Water-Works on the outskirts of Darlington and then turn round and have an easy and faster trip home with the current helping us along.

Hearing about the canoe, presumably from mother, my aunt Evelyn sent me a little book on canoes by Percy Blandford for my birthday. This explained how to build a 'PBK' canoe and also how to build a sailing dinghy. Reading about how sails worked, I thought it would be fun to see if I could rig up a mast and fit a sail onto my canoe. Joining two broom handles together by fitting them into a short length of tubing, I made the mast and also made a mounting bracket for it on the coaming of my canoe. Then, using another broom handle, rigged it up as a gaff onto which I lashed the 'sail'. This was one of mothers bed sheets which I cut at an angle to suit and make a proper looking Gaff Rig. I was now ready for our next expedition on the river.

Stivvy came round the next day, and as usual, we wheeled our canoes down to the Tees on our Bikes. Whilst launching them, I noticed that we would, as usual, be heading into the prevailing westerly wind, so I tucked the mast and sails inside the canoe and as ever, we paddled upstream. Reaching the waterworks, I rigged up the sail, turned round and we headed downstream. The wind filled the sail and with the slender hull of the canoe and the current under me, as well, I immediately picked up speed and I was thrilled that it worked so well. Stivvy was paddling hard to keep up. I quickly found out how to steer with the paddle and the journey home was tremendous fun and a memorable experience. I began to appreciate the power of the wind and importantly, for me as a school boy, it was free!

Looking again at the drawings in Blandfords little book, I noticed that the sailing dinghy was only 12ft long, only three feet longer than my half of the canoe. In his book, he provided instructions on how to build it and I thought that I should be able to do it, after all, it didn't look very big in the book. As I had enjoyed being on the river so much in the summer and with the winter months coming on, being 1954 my 15th birthday was on the 7th October which gave me an excuse to ask my mother if she would buy the timber for it as my birthday present and she agreed!

The timber was ordered and we went to Browns Sawmills in Darlington on Tuesday 30th November to collect it. We bought our timber from Browns for making the lamp bases at the factory and it was there I met Philip Brown who was given the job of putting our order together. I can remember that it consisted mainly of Parana Pine for the frames and resin bonded BS 1088 ¼"plywood for the skin. From memory, I think it cost £25, quite a lot of money in those days, so mother must have had confidence in me.

Rather than build it in the garage at home, where the car was kept, mother 'pulled a few strings' and as there were still plenty of empty wartime buildings at Aycliffe, I was allowed to use one which was next to our factory. This was about 100 feet long by 30 feet wide and had thick brown linoleum on the floor. This lino was used in many buildings during the war, its smooth surface could easily be kept clean for safety, with there being so much explosive material everywhere. It was also ideal for me because, following Blandford's instructions, I was able, with chalk to draw out the lines of the boat in full scale on this dark, smooth surface.

It was good having all this space, but a bit eerie at night with the low, round metal wartime lights and especially with the noise of the wind, which always seems to blow at Aycliffe, rattling the doors around this big empty building, especially when there was nobody about and in the winter.

Not having much pocket money, and not wanting to scrimp on quality, I had to scout around for my needs. I didn't want to ask mother for more money after she had already paid for the wood. The hull was supposed to be partly screwed and partly nailed together with glue between the joints. I didn't like the idea of using nails very much.

Thinking about this, I remembered that there was an old single seat, wooden aircraft fuselage lying in a ditch at the back of Croft airfield three or four miles from Darlington, near where the old bomb dumps had been. I had seen this on one of my bike rides when exploring these old perimeter areas. It was quite an exciting find, even though it was incomplete. The tail plane, wings and instruments had gone, but it still had the old joystick. More importantly, I had remembered that it was fastened together with brass screws, hundreds of them.

Taking a good screwdriver with me, I cycled back to the same ditch, it was still there and carefully unscrewing a few, I found that they were exactly the right size and type, ¾" brass countersunk, perfect. I don't know the actual number, but the joke was that I retrieved (stole!) 2000 screws, and when finished, the boat would be entirely screwed together with them and be a strong, first class job! Some years later, I met and became quite friendly with Bill Chaytor who owned most of the land around Croft including the airfield and I confessed to my crime. I don't think he knew that the old aeroplane fuselage was there, so he hadn't missed the screws and gracefully forgave me!

Working in the evenings, at weekends and in the holidays, I 'roped in' any friends who would help and on one occasion, even one of the school masters kindly joined us. It was the man who was the Goon Show addict and very kind of him! Occasionally I would get a lift from my mother, but normally we would cycle the seven miles to Aycliffe, which could be pretty cold in the winter.

I started by making the hull frames to the drawings on the floor. I cut the pieces to length, then cut the correct angles for the joints, set them up and then screwed and glued them together with ply corner brackets. Using laths and setting the frames up on the lines, I was able to screw the plywood skin to them. I was thrilled to see it all coming together, but it was so much bigger and heavier than I thought.

It looked so small in the little drawing in the book, I realised that I wouldn't be able to take it down to the river on top of my bike! When complete with its decks and seats, or more correctly, thwarts, as I learned to call them, I was amazed that I had been able to construct a real sailing boat.

There was no possibility of buying the correct marine fittings, so I had to use whatever would do the job. For mounting the lifting rudder, I used the gudgeons and pintles for hanging garden gates. A local engineer cut out the steel centre-board plate for me. I then went to see Philip at the Sawmills again, who by now, was becoming a friend. He suggested that the mast, gaff and boom could be made out of staircase hand rails. These were of kerewin, a wonderful long lasting, if rather heavy, wood, but they were fine. The pulley blocks and thimbles which are used to lift old fashioned clothes driers up to the kitchen ceiling are galvanised and were fine for the sheets.

A pulley wheel from a sash window frame made a good masthead roller. For the halyards, the sheets themselves and the rigging, I used window frame sash rope which I knew lasts for years in situ. It proved to be difficult for my purpose though, because it has a sisal core with a waxed woven outer covering. This can slide over the sisal if not really tightly bound together, but it did the job.

Being a standing lugsail design, I used a pair of normal curved front bicycle forks as the gaff jaws which worked very well. When finished, I varnished the spars and painted the hull of the boat pale green with white Quarter decks and coamings which looked very smart at the time. I don't know why I chose this colour, probably because we had some of this paint. The work had taken around six months, but I still had to make the sails. Whilst I was doing this, we had to have a road trailer made, so some old vintage Daimler motor car road wheels were used and a friend of mothers welded up a steel frame to fit the shape of the hull so that it could be towed behind the car.

I knew that traditional canvas sails rotted easily if put away wet which was a real pain and that the latest sailing boats were using modern synthetic materials. So scouting about, as ever, I discovered that the Faverdale Chemical works in Darlington were throwing away some large chemical bags which were made of terylene or nylon. It was certainly a synthetic cloth, so I was able to beg some of these. I washed them and opened the seams which gave me pieces of cloth which were long enough to sew together to create the Jib and Mainsail. I knew that boat sails aren't flat, so put a radius on the seams as I tacked them together. I then ran the seams through mothers Singer treadle sewing machine a few times to make them strong. Hand stitching the rope edges and eyes where necessary for strength.

This last job caused a stir when I had to tell my friends that I couldn't join them, because I had to stay at home to do my sewing!

1955. 12 foot 'PBK' sailing dinghy finished.

PLEASURES OF SAILING

The boat was ready for the water. Although still tidal at that time, I knew that the river below Yarm was wide and deep, so decided to launch it there. It was the nearest stretch of water. In the morning, before taking the boat and to be sure it would be OK, mother drove a friend, David Birch and I, to the field below Yarm at Ingleby Barwick which was used by the Tees Sailing Club and where I was told we could launch it. When we found the right field, there was nobody about, but a few sailing dinghies were parked there. Sure enough the river was beautiful, it was broad and slow moving, ideal for our first proper sail.

We drove home, attached the trailer to the car with my 'spanking' new boat on top. I then lashed all the spars, sails and my smart new varnished paddles to the thwarts for the journey. The paddles were a final, 'finishing touch', which I had bought from F. Collar and sons of Oxford. I still have the receipt dated 29th July 1955 for One Pound, Five Shillings. After lunch we drove back through Yarm to the field and reversed to be near the river bank. When we got out of the car, the scene was very different! I was absolutely astonished to find that the river was now just a murky stream perhaps 20ft wide with steep muddy banks sloping down to it. I had no idea that the tides would drain so much water out of the river. A valuable lesson!

Not daunted, I didn't want to waste all the trouble and this first opportunity for the 'big launching' and the boats 'maiden voyage'. So, we pulled the boat off the trailer onto the edge of the mud with her bows pointing towards the middle of the river, or what was left of it. As I moved round towards the stern of the boat to see if I could start to move it, David climbed in to undo the lashings, but before I could do anything, his weight must have caused the boat to set off. It shot down the steep slippery mud and went in like a lifeboat. The bow wave was most impressive and the boat certainly had a 'big launching', but I wasn't aboard to share the moment, at least it floated!

There were shouts from David who got rather a shock, but was safe enough because the boat looked fine. The snag now was that he was slowly floating down the river, to use the classic line- 'without a paddle'. They were still lashed down! I ran along the river bank to get ahead of him and stepping off the grass I began to realise how deep the mud was. I was able to make progress, but the mud was filthy black and when disturbed, it stank horribly. Although up to my thighs, fortunately I didn't fall over and when I reached the water, it wasn't too deep. I managed to intercept the boat and washing off my black legs as best I could, climbed in and helped David to untie the paddles and rigging.

We paddled back upstream and realising that it would be some time before the tide would be high enough for us to come ashore with the boat, I called to mother on the bank who kindly agreed to come back later to collect us. The boat turned out to be stable in the water and becoming familiar with it, David and I managed to step the mast and sails and with only part of the centreboard down, we started to make progress upstream. All in all, the dinghy was a good boat and we sailed up to Yarm and started to enjoy ourselves. As the tide came in, unlike the upper reaches of the Tees, where we had spent so many good years paddling, swimming, canoeing and generally enjoying its clean waters, the water here was dirty and not at all inviting. We passed floating rubbish including a sack which, when we bumped into it, the smell was really awful. It must have had a dead, rotting animal inside it.

On the way home, later that day, mother agreed that we should find more salubrious sailing waters and she kindly agreed to tow the boat over to the lake district for my summer holidays. We agreed to go to the nearest lake which was Ullswater.

The summer of 1955 turned out to be a wonderful summer for sailing. Taking a friend from school, Fred Lucas, we took a heavy duty canvas tent, sleeping bags and a small tent and Primus stove for cooking. We took plenty of food and planned to camp across the lake from Glenridding at the head of Ullswater.

Preparing to launch the boat for the first time, we had driven down the track from Glenridding to the steamer pier. We had parked the car and trailer near to the beach when we were approached by a man who was clearly intent on discouraging us two boys from spending their time sailing on lake Ullswater.

He started off by telling us that the lake was polluted from the nearby stream which ran through Glenridding from Greenside Lead Mine in the hills behind the village. Believing (correctly) that we were not old enough to drink and enjoy beer, he said that everybody had to drink it to avoid being poisoned. He then went on to say that the lake was very deep and bitterly cold and that many people had drowned in it. Fortunately, he did say that he couldn't stop us from launching the boat.

Our camp site with cooking and sleeping tents.

Sensing that his intentions were so obvious, and the place so beautiful, I was confident that we would be OK. Luckily, mother agreed with me, so as soon as he drove away, we carried on and launched it anyway. We sailed across the lake and pitched our tents on the other side.

Learning the ropes. 'Sea boots' and all.

So began a wonderful, five week holiday which was blessed with fine sunny weather. The boat was our sole means of transport, so any journey to the village or exploring the islands and shores of this long and impressively beautiful lake, involved the boat in one way or another. So much better than a bike or a bus!

Ullswater is a wonderful place to learn to sail and my sturdy boat sailed well. The hull design was ideal for the lake with its fluky winds. It was hard chine with a shallow 'V' which was

On board the 'Lady of The Lake', with Ann and her friend from Glenridding.

stable and was strong enough to allow me to sail straight up onto the beach, so that we could step out without even having to get our feet wet, great fun! Being only ¼ decked, there was plenty of room to carry friends for swimming parties and the like.

We became friends with the local teenagers in Glenridding who, of course, knew the area well and it was through them that we learned, for example, that the best spot for swimming was at the very head of the lake. This was especially so in the evening when, after a sunny day, the water here is comfortably warm because it benefits from the shallow and heat absorbing nearby Lake Brotherswater. This drains down via the connecting stream and where it comes into Ullswater, the bottom is like a grass 'lawn', so it is even comfortable to walk on.

When talking to our local friends, I discovered that the person who had tried so hard to dissuade us was no other than Sir Waverly Wakefield of Castrol Oil fame. He had many interests in the lake district and Ullswater in particular. He was obviously following in the footsteps of William Wordsworth when, in 1848, he had opposed the coming of the railway to Windermere. Sir Waverly also was trying to prevent the 'unwashed ' invading the lake district!

Sailing with Malcolm. Campbell's Bluebird in the shed in the background.

That summer, Donald Campbell was testing Bluebird on lake Ulleswater and broke the world speed record in July 1955 at 203 mph. Bluebird was kept in the corrugated iron shed which is visible in the background on one of the little photo's. This was built near the steamer pier and often landing there, I had the opportunity to talk to Leo Villa his engineer about it.

For many years afterwards, long after Donald Campbell had his fatal accident in 1967 trying to beat his own world record on lake Coniston and long after the shed had gone, I could still see blue paint on part of the concrete foundations where Bluebird's sponsons had been sprayed to cover up areas where they had been scraped.

Climbing up Place Fell, which was on the same side as our tent, across the lake from Glenridding, we had magnificent views of the surrounding mountains and the lake itself of course. One day, Fred and I were near the top when we saw, for the first time, some speedboats on the lake twisting and turning making patterns on the water. In those days, we usually had the lake to ourselves. There was no sailing club and no speedboats, so this was a real thrill. We scrambled back down sliding on the scree, as quickly as we could and then sailed across the lake to watch them.

By the time we arrived and drew nearer, we could see that they were now towing water skiers. I had only ever seen this before on one of fathers old 9.5mm films which was taken in America. It turned out that they were the British Water Ski Team in training and what a wonderful sight it was for us young lads.
I would have been even more excited if I had known that, ten years later, I would be Water Skiing from the same boathouse on the same stretch of Ulleswater with a young man called Fenwick Purvis.

Fenwick's racing speed boat at the workshops in Staindrop.

Fenwick is the most brilliant expert on Water Ski's , he was capable of some remarkable trick skiing and was a delight to watch. He had the support of Major Len Wood who let us all enjoy the fun after he bought out Simmons, the well known speedboat manufacturers. He kept two of them in the large and splendid green boathouse which was in the garden of the annex to the Ullswater Hotel, which he used to rent.

Later on, Fenwick became a most enthusiastic and successful motor boat racer and he kept in touch and recently we carried out some improvements to his Delta speedboat at our Staindrop workshops. After this, he invited me to join him for a day's testing on lake Windermere. To say it was thrilling would be an understatement, I was amazed at the superb performance and how well the boat handled at high speed, especially on the slalom course. I couldn't help but shout to him that it reminded me of the 'old days' at Ullswater forty years ago.

Looking back, the holiday in 1955 was the beginning of a long and very happy relationship with this magnificent lake with its unspoilt and wonderful scenery. The independence and freedom of having our own boat for transport also meant that whatever we were doing, was fun.

CHAPTER 6:
MOTORING - THE LEARNING CURVE

Let me explain how I came to own my first motor car, let alone a vintage one. In the last chapter, I explained how I built my first boat, a 12ft sailing dinghy which I launched on the River Tees and then sailed on Lake Ullswater. This was in 1954/55 when I was a lad of fourteen, going on fifteen. Eighteen months later I realised that if I could find a motor car with a tow bar, I could tow it to new sailing 'grounds' without having to trouble my mother, which would be a real boon.

Although not old enough to drive, quite a few friends were keen on motor cars and I see from my diary, that Neddy Keighley and I went to the Earls Court Motor Show on 23 October 1954 catching the 10.35pm train home so was interested.

To give you a flavour of the car showrooms in 1954 I include one of Jimmy Blumer's photographs of

This photograph of Sherwoods Jaguar Garage Showroom in Darlington 1954, taken by Jimmy Blumer, a popular local character and motor racing driver, reveals that the XK models are Left hand drive and were for export. The showroom itself had obviously been a workshop and still has the beam to carry the chain lift for moving engines and heavy components.

Officer Cadet Royle with Mohamed Bin-Hashim in the Standard Avon Special.

Sherwood Bros. in Grange Road, Darlington that year, most Jaguars were left hand drive for export.

At this time my brother, John, was now in the army and had sent me a photograph of his sporty looking car, it was a Standard Avon Special. This turned out to be a ten horsepower Standard chassis with a special 2 seat open sports body by Avon Coachworks. A handsome little car with Marchal headlamps, importantly, it also had a strong tow bar!

John was not overly keen when I said that I wanted to buy it from him, but being a penniless Officer Cadet, he needed the money, so we agreed that I would pay him £40 for it. My total savings of £20 would be the deposit and I would also pay him £1 per month for twenty months. My pocket money, at that time, was five shillings (25p) a week. In the 1950's old motor cars were not valuable, but sporty ones fetched more than the £10 which pre-war family saloons were selling for at that time.

Because John was stationed at Aldershot at the Mons Officer Cadet School, we agreed that I should come down and meet him at nearby Farnham to collect it. As I had just started to learn to drive and didn't yet have a license, I asked another of my school friends, Derek 'Dingo' Richmond, if he would drive it home for me. He was seventeen, had a licence and said he would be very pleased to do it for me. Somehow we travelled down to Farnham where we met my brother who showed us the Avon and the controls. This done, we excitedly set off to drive my 'new' car home.

Once on the 'Great North Road', heading towards Darlington, I began to realise why brother John was hesitant to sell the 'Avon' to me. On the slightest gradient, we found that the car slowed down to around 10mph and this was with Dingo's foot 'down to the floorboards'. This old motoring term was not really appropriate in this case, because there weren't any floorboards! We rested our feet on the brake cross shaft.

On a slight hill, somewhere near Peterborough, a boy from school was thumbing a lift. We were going so slowly that I had time to tell him that we couldn't do it because we would come to a complete standstill with the extra weight, if we did. Later on, he cheerfully waved to us as he scorched by in a new Ford 10, doing at least 50 mph.

After sleeping for an hour or two by the canal at Ferrybridge during the night, we finally made it home the following day. This was eighteen hours after setting off! At least the old car got us home, but I realised that, in its present condition, it could hardly propel itself along, let alone be able to tow a boat. To put it in the present day vernacular, this 'Avon' was 'calling' for an overhaul!

Remembering that I had been allowed to use an empty building at Aycliffe to build the boat, I asked mother if she would ask the trading estate people again to see if there was one which I could use to sort out the mechanical problems with the Avon. I was delighted when, this time, I was offered a much smaller, garage sized building, which was empty. So began my relationship with the 'innards' of old motor cars.

As the autumn of 1957 passed and winter approached, we had the usual mix of cold, wet and snowy weather. There was no heating in the garage of course, but full of enthusiasm with now having been taught to drive by my mother and friends and having a driving license, I didn't notice the cold. When winter really set in however, the 'garage' flooded and the water was two or three inches deep. I went 'soft' and acquired some duck boards which were just above the water level and managed to maintain good progress.

As before, when working on the boat, I sometimes got a lift from home, at other times I would cycle from Darlington on my excellent, but low geared 'track bike'. The roads were quiet in those days and it was no problem.

When taking the engine out and lying under the car on the duck boards, Although, just to say above the water level, it was not much fun. It was particularly annoying when the spanners, small parts or nuts and bolts dropped through the gaps in the boards. With little daylight and two dim wartime bulbs in the evenings and cold fingers trying to locate them in the black cold water, I soon learned how cursing and swearing relieves the tension!

Once I had removed and stripped the engine down, I discussed the problem with my friends and found that one of the reasons for the lack of power was that the exhaust valves were burnt oval and not round as they should be. There was hardly any compression, so not much power being transmitted to the crankshaft.

As you do, I went to our local Standard Motor Car agents in Darlington, the Cleveland Car Company. This was an old garage which had beautiful 'GARAGE' lettering chiselled in stone over the doorway and was partly Mock Tudor in style. I went up the steep wooden stairs and asked one of the store men in his brown dustcoat (what else!) for a set of valves for a 1930 Standard Ten. "No problem" he said, shouting to a trainee "Aisle No 7 part No XYZ" and within two minutes they were on the counter, - "four shillings and eleven pence". I was looking at them carefully when the storeman said, "it's alright sonny, they are correct and not spurious". A lovely word which has stayed with me ever since. They must have been in stock for over twenty-five years - marvellous, but bang went another week's pocket-money!

I can't remember all the jobs which I did to the car, it is 53 years ago, but I remember making some floorboards and comfortable seats. The Avon had two small racing screens which were good in the summer and legally didn't need windscreen wipers or washers. It didn't have a hood, but such things were luxuries for me. I did fit a 'straight through', side mounted exhaust however, - like the racing cars. With the doors having previously been sealed up, this was practicable, but It sounded a bit like a tractor. Still, I thought it was a really smart, sporty feature.

I also fitted new king pins and shackle bushes and made and fitted some smart aluminium supports and stone guards to the mudguards. I also made dummy 'knock-ons' to act as dust covers for the wheel hubs and painted the wheels silver. The spoked wheels were an attractive feature of the car which was, of course, painted British Racing Green.

In those days there was a good, old fashioned engineering firm in Darlington called Thekla, which was run by the father of one of my friends. I had the engine block bored out, the crank ground and the main and big end bearings white metalled. I fitted new pistons and the new Valves, and reassembled the engine. I do remember however, that I had to strip it all down again when the oil pressure disappeared soon after starting it for the first time. I found that I had not cleaned out the machinings and swarf from the engine block and oil ways and they blocked as soon as I started the engine. This was most upsetting, but fortunately, because I was watching the gauge, it didn't do any damage.

I had no choice, but to strip down the whole engine again and carefully clean the entire unit including all the oil pipes and galleries. I wanted to make sure it was right this time. It is all part of the learning curve, doing it the hard way! Talking of gauges, reminds me of one of the unusual features of the Standard Avon which sticks in my mind. This was that the fuel gauge was chain driven. There was a fine chain running up a small curved tube from the top of the bulkhead mounted petrol Tank. This chain went into the back of the dashboard and then rolled round a small spring loaded drum in the petrol Gauge itself. As the float moved up and down with the petrol in the tank, the chain turned the needle on the dashboard petrol gauge. Marvellous straight forward engineering!

When the work was finally complete, the Avon looked very smart and ran beautifully. I could well understand why Sir William Lyons is reputed to have stopped the Avon brothers on the road one day, to ask them who had designed and built their car, or so the story goes. The early SS Jaguars had Standard engines.

After driving a Ford Squire for a couple of years mother bought a Morris 1000 'Woody Estate' in which I learnt to drive.

So it was in 1958, that I then had the thrill of going into Bull Wynd in Darlington where the local vehicle licences were issued and I was able to present my documents to get my first Tax Disc. This was a major psychological step for me and all us young motorists who, at the age of 17, were taking that important step of becoming more of an adult rather than a boy. Somehow, walking up to the high wood panelled desk with the log book and first Insurance Certificate for "Third Party only" insurance, was the last and the most important stage of having my own car.

After having passed the driving test on our parents cars, would they issue us with the Tax Disc? When that little round disc of paper was handed over, I knew that, from then on, I would be able to enjoy the freedom of having my own open, two seater sports car and be able to tow my boat to Ullswater or go anywhere I wished, providing I could afford to buy the petrol of course. As it turned out, it was not only the beginning of what was to be a most enjoyable and interesting experience, it would be one which would influence my whole future.

GOOD OLD MOTORING

I had great fun with the old Avon. It was not that fast by modern standards, 70 mph flat out, the cable brakes were poor, but it was a reliable car. It wasn't too thirsty and the Salutation Filling Station petrol bill shows that it cost, in old money, 5/7d a Gallon which is approximately

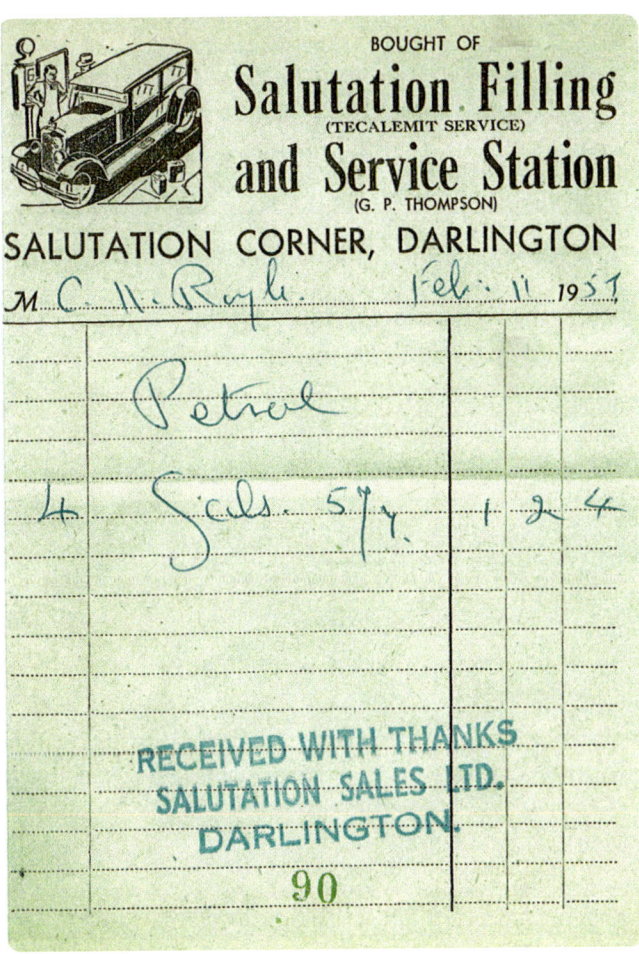

Salutation Filling and Service Station receipt.

6 new pence a litre in todays money.

Although a pound had value in those days, it still wasn't too costly, especially if I could 'fiddle' a bit on my mothers account! Sitting behind the large, red, sprung, Brooklands steering wheel, with just two racing screens and the long bonnet in front of you, was a most exhilarating experience. The wind is all around you, but not in your face, which is an absolute delight in fine weather. Even being stoic and becoming a true 'Vintage' man, it could still be difficult to look cheerful however when, not having a hood, the rain would be dripping onto my lap off the

1930 Standard Avon Special. My first motor car.

pointed 'Hawthorn' peak of my cap, especially when held up by traffic lights in town!

Altogether, motoring in the 1950's and 60's was far more pleasurable and easy going than it is today, especially for young drivers. Most family cars and even sports cars were much slower than today, especially those which we youngsters could afford. Many of which were only capable of 70 or 80mph at 'full chat' as the motor-bike boys used to say. With few people aspiring to own a car and few accidents, one important benefit was that the insurance companies were happy to simply add the youngsters names to their parents policy, so the cost was minimal, especially for third party cover.

There were some problems of course, for example, vintage size tyres were quite difficult to obtain, so we would go raking round old country garages and scrap yards for suitable pre-war sizes, 18",19",20" and 21" inch. These had been out of production for some years, especially during the war. With there being no MOT tests in those days, we could at least run on second hand tyres until they were bald with the cords showing. This sounds dangerous, but we were well aware of the risks of a blowout and with slower speeds and less traffic, we learnt how to cope with the consequential lack of grip and the 'dreaded side slip' as it was called in the early days of motoring, With poor brakes, good grip wasn't that important anyway!

In the snowy winters, so frequent in those days, we learnt to drive within the capabilities of the cars. This gave us a keen awareness of speed, braking distances, under steer in wet conditions and the techniques of driving in snow. All this may sound rather blasé', but the roads were much quieter in those days of course. With much less traffic, you didn't stop driving when there were a few inches of snow. In fact, it was a great challenge to see if you could get to the pub or wherever you wanted to go and then get home again afterwards, despite what the weather was like.

Instead of being told by the media not to drive when there is any snow, you carried on and learnt how to maximise traction and keep the car moving in all conditions, especially for example, getting up as much speed as possible to get up a hill. If you were ever in any difficulty, most motorists would stop and help, unlike today, when people will just drive by. Inevitably, we did have accidents of course, going through the odd hedge backwards or 'losing it' occasionally, but most were not too serious and we had to sort out the problems for ourselves. When accidents did occur, it was the price we had to pay for our freedom, it was our choice to take risks.

BOWES MOOR & CARTER BAR

Jumping ahead slightly - Bowes Moor was often a challenge in the snow. It was only closed when the Lorries themselves closed it by becoming snowed up or locked into drifts of up to 6 to10 feet. The A66 was a single carriageway in the 1960's and I have had some very exciting drives heading for home in fresh, deep, drifting snow over that bleak, exposed moor. On one occasion, in an MGB GT coming back from a trip to see a customer near Penrith, there were diversion signs to the M62 at Brough. This is a very long detour south and it was becoming dark and snowing, but I still thought it worth the risk of trying the short route home over the moor. There had been little snow that morning, so it would all be fresh and soft and I was on my own, so there would be no risk to anyone else.

I reached the sheltered lay-by just before the

moor itself, I pulled in and parked next to a council van in about a 9 inches of fresh soft snow. Speaking to the driver, I asked what conditions were like over the top. He explained that there were some deep drifts, but a large snow plough had just contacted him and was expected soon and if I followed behind him, he was returning east across the moor, back to Bowes, which is not too far from home. He thought I should be able to make it OK. Standing in deep snow, I asked him how he was managing in the van, "OK" he said, pointing into the back where there must have been at least a ton of kerb stones!

Sure enough, a few minutes later, a huge snow plough roared into view. It's plough was at least ten feet high and the wheels were huge and knobbly, "just the job" I said to myself. The van driver told him of the plan and the driver of the plough asked me to follow him as he climbed up into his cab. We soon reached the higher ground and fortunately he kept his foot down, because the plough was set with a ground clearance of perhaps four inches which left me driving over semi compacted, but heavily 'stirred up' and rutted snow. Keeping my speed up was vital if I was to keep going, he must have known this and my narrow tyres were a great help.

All I could see were two six foot walls of snow on either side of me left in the wake of the plough and also its tail lights were visible in the confused maelstrom of disturbed and falling snow. It was not long before we were thundering past a line of snowed up, west bound lorries with drifts up the sides of their cabs. An impressive and awesome sight against the darkening grey sky. We had just cleared them all when the plough lurched to the left, the lights tilted over as it slid into what must have been a hidden ditch at the side of the road. I had to make a rapid decision, the wall of snow looked a lot softer than a ten tonne snow plough, so I accelerated and headed straight at the curving wall as it tried to lead me into the back of the plough.

As it turned out, the low profile bodywork of the MGB was ideal for punching its way through drifts. The wind screen was suddenly a blank wall of snow and I could see nothing, but at least the glass screen held and didn't collapse with the weight of snow. I was steering slightly to the right and kept my foot down in order to penetrate the snow wall and keep going. At the same time, heading towards the centre of where I thought the road should be. Driving completely blind, It seemed like ages, but in fact was only a few seconds before a gap appeared in the windscreen and I found myself on a short stretch of road with intermittent tarmac and low drifts. It seemed that the wind, which was almost horizontal, was blowing the snow off the smooth surface in some places. I stopped on a clear bit of road, left the engine running and quickly checked around the car, clearing the snow from the clogged radiator grill and the windscreen.

It was all OK, so knowing that the plough driver had a radio and I couldn't go back to reach him anyway, I decided to press on. I was now quite optimistic, knowing that it had been the snow building up against the lorries which had caused some of the deep drifts. Although it was almost a 'white out', I had the benefit of the snow poles and the rest of the journey over the moor was mainly a question of accelerating hard between the drifts to maintain a good speed so that the momentum carried me through them. They were not much more than 3 or 4 feet deep and fortunately were interspersed with areas of clear black road. It was most satisfying and thrilling to be making such good progress.

Eventually, I made it safely to Bowes where there were two police cars blocking the road and although in the fading light, there were queues of vehicles as far as the eye could see. I explained the situation to the policeman and was able to drive the rest of the way home in the much less snowy conditions. Listening to the radio, the road remained blocked for four more days. It was perhaps, slightly fool hardy, but was a memorable and thrilling challenge.

I had another similar experience, heading North over Carter Bar, going up to Scotland on the A68. This time I was driving a 1934 Daimler Light 15 to deliver it to a customer. Bill Keighley was following in my Scimitar GTE to bring me home. Climbing up towards the summit, with heavy snow falling and about ten inches of snow, I was able to maintain a good speed up the incline. Being a pre-war model with 'thin' tyres and a pre-selector gearbox, I was penetrating the soft snow, but I had to

The Scimitar GTE brochure. Same colour as the author's.

A 'van' for all weathers.

keep as much speed up as was sensibly possible to be able to maintain the momentum.

Behind me, Bill was really struggling to keep up with the old Daimler. The Scimitar's modern broad tyres and high revving, powerful engine was not at all good in these conditions. Never the less, with some difficulty and a few broadsides, he managed extremely well and we both made it over the top and down the other side into Scotland where we found ourselves going through the 'Road Closed' signs from the wrong direction!

We didn't always make it home and on another snowy occasion, Bill and I did end up having to spend the night in the staff quarters of a restaurant when, after rounding a bend on a country road in the Scimitar, we punched into a snow drift which was more solid than previously. Being about 6ft high and blocking the road, it brought us to a standstill. The A1 was blocked and Leicester was cut off on this occasion and we were trying to find a route north. Fortunately, the Scimitar wasn't damaged, so we dug it out the following morning!

After the Scimitar, I bought an 'E' type 4.2 Coupe, the car shown on the cover. This served me very well, as every day all year round transport. I found it to be especially useful because the rear platform behind the front seats was ideal for carrying engines. By lifting the big glazed 'boot lid', it was easy to crane in big 4.5 litre Lagonda engines, for example. In those days, the late 1970's and early 1980's, I used an excellent machine shop in Edinburgh for cast-on-white metal boardings, in-line boring etc and the 'E' type was ideal as my fast company 'van'. Surprisingly, a con rod snapped and came out through the side of the sump one day, but I was able to drive the last mile home because the big end remained in one piece. It was an excellent machine and I acquired a case full of suitable eight track stereo tapes to entertain me on long trips.

Whilst the 'E' Type was not ideal for snowy conditions, the cars of today are worse as soon as there is any snow on the roads. This is mainly due to the wide, low profile tyres fitted to most modern motor cars. The tyres sit on top of the snow, rather than penetrating down to the tarmac. Combine these with the more powerful engines and higher gear ratios and many drivers are faced with vehicles which are not at all suited to motoring in winter.

When it comes to driving in more normal weather, especially on dry roads and motorways, they are of course, excellent. They are economic, reliable and give years of comfortable, reliable transport, Ironically, the problem for young drivers is too much traffic and the lack of quiet roads where young drivers can familiarise themselves with the limits of tyre adhesion and learning at what stage the car will lose grip on the road.

Improved tyre performance and suspension design also permit much higher speeds and cornering ability, far in advance of pre-war cars and tyres.

All this advanced technology puts the young drivers of today, at greater risk. Travelling much faster, in dry or wet conditions and with much more traffic, if the car starts to drift or lose adhesion, there is less time and space to correct it before hitting something. With the comfort, sound insulation and efficient air conditioning of modern motor cars, young drivers have very little conception of the physical speed at which they are travelling.

THE OPEN ROAD

Returning to the early post war days of motoring again and to give you a better idea of the situation with old cars at that time, the situation was very different, in many other respects. The shortage of raw materials and loss of many good men during the war held up the production of new motor cars in the years immediately following the war. This resulted in a demand for any motor vehicles which were roadworthy. In the late 1940's and early 1950's all motor cars which would run, were useful and needed and had value, however, with the gradual re-establishment of motor manufacturing in this country by the late 1950's, new cars were becoming available and the value of old pre-war vehicles dropped to very low levels.

Old motor cars were at their lowest price in the 1950's and 1960's, for example a mid range 1920's and 1930's family saloon car could be bought for as little £5 to £10. Although 26 years old, the 1930 Standard Avon Special cost me £40 in 1957. This was an above average price because it was a stylish open Sports 2 seater, but still only a 10 hp car. The earlier motor cars of the Veteran and Edwardian periods built prior to the 1914-1918 war, were not really practicable as everyday transport, so unless they had specific history and were considered to be museum pieces, they had very little value. The Veteran Car Club existed, but with few members, many of these lovely and interesting old vehicles were still being scrapped in the 1950's and 1960's.

There is little doubt that we were in the right place at the right time and were very lucky in many ways when it came to having a motor car. The attitude of the general public was still that they were a luxury form of transport, not a necessity. The average working man wouldn't consider owning one, he could easily cycle to work. With no Hire Purchase or bank Loans available to buy cars, the demand for them was consequently, very limited. This meant that they were readily available and cheap and being relatively simple in their design and construction, a young man like me could, with a lot of enthusiasm and not much money, have his own motor car and start motoring.

Whilst I was out of circulation overhauling my car, a few of my school friends and others who were over 17 were, by one means or another, also managing to acquire motor cars. Obviously, the wealthier families in the area were able to buy their youngsters new motor cars and one or two had some really exciting machines. With most of us however, it was a case of saving pocket money, just as I had done when buying

Catterick Speed hill climb with John Ginty 1959.

Some of the lads. Peter, Nobby, Mart, Dicky and Terry.

the 'Avon' from my brother or begging and borrowing from parents, relatives etc,

With there still being few cars on the roads and with being able to visit all the lovely country pubs in the dales and nearby villages, not surprisingly, it was not long before all those of us who were fortunate enough to have a motor car, began to see more of each other. We would also visit the local amateur racing circuits on the disused airfields like Croft and Thornaby and at the speed hill climb at Catterick. Some of our friends parents had Motor Garages which enabled them to turn up, occasionally, in pretty smart, modern vehicles borrowed for the day. On the whole, we had a most interesting assortment of cars and whilst my car was a rare machine, other friends had equally interesting vehicles.

Brother John in Austin 7.

John at speed.

My brother started with old motorbikes, then had a stripped down Austin 7 and moved on to having a Three Wheeler Morgan Aero. This had good acceleration and was a most exciting machine, but after a while, it was replaced with a 1930's Austin Saloon for about £10 and later with a rare, Aerodynamic HRG Sports, quite an interesting car. This was after I had bought the Standard Avon which is when I came into the picture. Some of these cars are shown here.

Triumph Roadster in the Dales.

Not surprisingly, we met many of the young farming crowd who had to have transport and so were able to get to the pubs, Hunt dances and parties which we all enjoyed so much in the countryside in North Yorkshire and Durham. Many would have pick-ups and vans and some would have more interesting machines.

My old friend John 'Robbo' Robinson started with a Sunbeam Talbot saloon, but then acquired a very smart P 1800 Triumph Roadster with a Dicky seat. This was great fun and he went to the trouble of designing a removable hood for the back seat which was quite ingenious and made life much more comfortable and fun, especially when in the 'dicky' with a young lady!

It was not only the boys who had interesting vehicles. One of our keen young motorists was Heather who turned up one day in a very neat

Gainford Drama Club's 'Bunny Girls'. Ann, Pam, June and Pauline with Robbo and the author 'inspecting' the team.

late 1930's Talbot Ten pillarless saloon. I seem to recall that she rescued me from a close encounter with the local police one day in this neat and attractive car. Her friend Ann, also acquired a car, this was an Austin 7 Chummy. I remember painting the wheels a delicate shade of yellow for her!

Inevitably, there was a sprinkling of early MG's. These always were popular and tended to command a higher price than some sports cars of the period. My old friend Brownie had an MG TC as did another school friend Martyn Stephenson.

I was introduced to the Gainford Drama Club

CHAPTER 6: MOTORING - THE LEARNING CURVE

Playing Harry Simpkinson in 'Mountain Air'.

by my friend 'Robbo', where for many years, I acted in many hilarious plays and I helped to write a few of our own shows as well. We had great fun and thanks to the dedication of Enid Burdon and Robbo, it is still a very successful village theatre and always plays to full houses. Acting on the stage in 1959 playing Harry Simpkinson in 'Mountain Air', I met Wendy, who became a steady girl friend. She used to drive her fathers very sporty Healey Tickford saloon which had a most beautiful exhaust note. She also drove a rather tired 'L' type Magna MG for a while

Wendy's Healey Tickford.

Wendy with Andy the dog and brother John's Aerodynamic HRG the Avon Special, the Healey and a modern Standard Vanguard parked across the road. A peroid shot of motoring in the late 1950's.

which smoked heavily (like most of us!) Later an MGA came on the scene! Her father, Alan Hare, was a most kindly man and ran the local garages in High Coniscliffe and Gainford. One of his excellent engineers was Jim Cobb, an ex-Bugatti mechanic. He was extremely thorough and was always pleased to help me and any of us who had a problem.

Another good old friend and MG owner was Alan Wynn-Williams whose activities could always be traced by the pools of oil left wherever he parked his old MG. Being an old railway town, in fact the first to have a public rail transport system, the Darlington to Stockton line. His father, like others in Darlington, was in the Railway industry and was, like his son, also an enthusiastic motorist and I remember him taking Alan and me to Aintree for a Grand Prix in his MK II Jaguar. Quite a thrill in those days.

Another member of our 'crowd' and one with whom I spent some very happy times at school and afterwards, was my good friend Ian Hunter. He was one of those who was lucky enough to be bought a new car, an Austin A30. Today they look so small, but at the time a new car was a great luxury and as such, was highly rated. One incident which comes to mind was driving back one wet night after a 'boozing session' in the Imperial Hotel in Darlington, which was very popular in the late fifty's. Ian and I decided to have a race home along Coniscliffe Road, I got away first, but Ian soon overtook me and then another car shot passed, ringing its bell as it did so. Yes, In those days the Police cars had bells! I hadn't seen that it was the Police, because my 'interior' mirror was wet with the rain.

Soon after he passed me, giving chase to Ian, I switched off my lights and turned sharp right and parked by some tennis courts. Quickly covering the Avon with my tarpaulin (which I always kept handy, having no hood). Being only a quarter of a mile from home, I walked down Coniscliffe Road to where poor Ian was being questioned and 'booked' by the police. I couldn't resist walking past Ian and said "hello" to him as I did so. He nodded, but thankfully said nothing. I was just in time to hear them telling him that they would "catch the other speeding driver" as I walked past. After the police car drove away, I ran back to Ian and we watched them from my bedroom window, driving round and round for a couple of hours looking for me. It was after one o'clock in the morning before they finally gave up. I retrieved the car the following day!

Fortunately the police were quite sympathetic to us youngsters in those days, but we obviously avoided contact with them if at all possible. If we had an 'incident', we would move the car as quickly as possible. An example of this was

Neddy's Big Seven with replacement 'sporty' front mudguards.

1923 Minerva as 'found' with 'estate' working rear bodywork.

when another car, featured in my collection of old photographs, the Austin 'Big 7' belonging to my old school friend, Neddy, was damaged

Neddy's Healey Silverstone.

when rounding a sharp hairpin bend coming back home from a pub one night. We had slid off the road sideways up a steep banking when the car literally "fell over." We crawled out through the sunshine roof, which conveniently was open and became like a door. We quickly pushed it back on its wheels ready to drive home.

Our main concern was that a king pin had fallen out and rolled across the road. This was quite disconcerting until we discovered that it was a spare one which had been kept in a tool box under Neddy's seat which he didn't know was there. The engine was OK, so we drove home. Neddy soon made some new, simple, but smart, sporty aluminium mudguards and was back 'in business'. You can see these in the photograph.

Later on, Neddy had acquired a splendid Healey Silverstone which we all thought was the 'bees knees'. It had a superb exhaust note and was a delight to drive. Strangely enough, many years later, I bought the very same car from the Midland Motor Museum, a fun machine and one of two Healey Silverstones which I was fortunate enough to own and drive.

Another old school friend, Terry, whom we also saw a lot of, was one of those who's father, 'HPR', as I used to cheekily call him, was also in the Railway industry. His father had a very smart Rolls Royce Silver Wraith with a Chauffeur and this car was kept at the company's offices at Mowden Hall in those days. Terry was showing me round one day when I saw an ancient motor car parked in one of the company's garages. This turned out to be a 1923 Minerva which had a Knight sleeve valve

Terry took this photo of the 1923 Minerva when we were going up to Scotland, after the back of the bodywork had been re-built in the original style.

engine, As we looked around it, I could see that the back of the bodywork of this fine vintage motor car had been modified. Terry explained that its previous owner, Sir Graham Esplin, had adapted it to be used as an estate vehicle.

Minerva's are very handsome and were built in Belgium to the highest quality, so I was delighted to 'find' it and straight away started to encourage Terry to restore it and get it running. I am delighted to say that he set about doing this and when it was finished, it was back to its original two seats configuration and when running, being sleeve valve, the engine was as smooth as silk.

Terry and I subsequently had a lovely trip up to Scotland in this superb vehicle when we went to the First Sale of the Sword Collection in 1962. There were over 200 vintage and other rare cars which we saw there. Knowing Mr Frew, the man in charge, we were given the key and allowed into the second Hangar which was full of cars, packed so close, that we could only see them by moving through the actual cars themselves and walking along the running boards. These vehicles were sold at a later date in 1965. I am pleased to say that Terry is a most enthusiastic Vintage motorist and has gathered about him some lovely motor cars since these early days.

Thinking about interesting visits, I have mentioned that visits to scrap yards was a regular practise for us in those days. This was in the constant search for tyres and spares. It was always interesting as well as being necessary. Importantly, it was also a low cost way of keeping our cars on the road.

On a holiday tour of France, Switzerland and Northern Italy in 1959, with Robbo, using the excuse of 'running in' his mother's new Standard Pennant, we ended up on the Mediterranean coast, the Cote d'Azur. When in Nice, we could not resist seeking out the local scrap yard cum car lot at the back of the town. Thinking back today, we beheld a remarkable sight. There was an aeroplane or two and all sorts of continental pre-war motor cars standing out in the open. The most memorable being a type 35 Bugatti with grass growing through it and a 2.3 Super-Charged Alfa Romeo with very stylish and special coachwork similar to the style of Zagato of the period. Although they were very desirable, we were not 'in funds' at the time so didn't even ask the price! Such is life! But we met some pretty French girls, so I include a snap of Robbo with them.

Robbo with French girls on the Promenade des Anglais - Nice.

CHAPTER 7:
JOBS IN THE 1950's & 1960's

After leaving school in 1958, before I started work at our family's lamp factory, C.N.Royle & Co Ltd, I wanted to see what other jobs were like. I had the luxury of knowing that a job was always waiting for me at Aycliffe, so I was able to test the jobs market. Believing that if I found one which was sufficiently interesting then, subject to mother being OK at the factory, I thought that I would be able to stay with it. I have always enjoyed a wide variation of activities and was keen to see and experience different types of jobs.

I first applied for and got the job as a trainee manager for Woolworths. This was thought to be a good, solid career in the 1950's. After a few weeks however, I began to see aspects which didn't please me at all. Being one who placed a high value on time spent with personal projects like building track bikes, boat building and vintage motor car work, my evenings and weekends were sacrosanct.

The retail business was bad enough for a young man, often working until 7pm in the evenings and all day on Saturdays, but when I was given a huge packing case with hundreds of different sizes and colours of plimsoles to unpack and sort at 6pm one Saturday and then to be told that I couldn't go home until it was finished, was the last straw! Going home at 8.30pm walking past everybody going out for the night was too much. I was already perturbed by having seen a particularly nice, elderly female member of the staff, fall down the concrete back service stairs when carrying a large box. This was unfortunate enough, but not only were the stairs very dimly lit by a single small bulb, the stairs adjoined the goods lift which she wasn't allowed to use in order to save electricity! That was the end of Woolworths for me.

Other jobs included a stop gap job, working for the Darlington Council in the 'Forestry Dept'. This involved laying lawns on newly built council estates as well as forestry jobs. It was hard work, "Get your backs bent lads" was the order of the day, but I *was* working with my old friend, Stivvy and we saw some kindly and funny things. One was when chopping down a large tree the foreman, a tough, burly character, stopped the work and climbing up the tree, carefully extracted a nest full of chicks and put it safely in a nearby bush. "I thought I heard something" he said, "Right-o, carry on lads". Another memory was one Friday, half an hour before 'clocking off', we were due to roll a newly laid lawn. The roller was the type which you fill with water, there was no time to do this, so the foreman said we should pretend to roll it with an empty roller.

Being 'Goon' fans and with me being a member of the Gainford Drama Club, this was a wonderful chance to show our brilliant 'acting skills' . We made a huge play of heaving and pushing the roller and couldn't help laughing when instead of rolling a small pebble it into the soft ground, the roller would be lifted and be kicked up over the top of it. The foreman then announced "home time", the pretence stopped and we lifted the heavy roller onto the truck with one hand, marvellous fun!

Not surprisingly, in 1959, I ended working in the family business, helping mother at father's old factory. This business was established in 1933 by my father, but was suspended in 1939 at the outbreak of the war and remained so until after the war when production started again. He was eventually able to take over the buildings which he occupied during the war at Aycliffe. It had been Street 4, when an ROF, but was renamed Burtree Road when under the control of English Industrial Estates. Father died in 1949 and Mother had been running it since then and later on, wanted me to help her and after the other jobs, I was quite happy to do this.

Because I had changed senior school twice, I was older than most of the boys in my form, I had six 'O' levels, but didn't want to stay on, or go to college. One or two boys did of course, but the majority of my school friends went straight into their family businesses, so when I finally did, it didn't seem unusual for me to do it.

WORKING AT C.N. ROYLE & CO LTD

Starting work in a family business can be difficult, the 'bosses son' often being labelled by the other employees as being pretty useless. In my case, I was lucky, because we employed mainly women and they were a happy bunch most of the time and I was not doing the same artistic hand painting work which they did. Also, as is often the case with family businesses, they were paid much more than me, because I was learning the business, so the pay was very 'nominal'. This was the same for most of my friends, so it wasn't a problem, but there were perks, like the odd few gallons of petrol and the use of the company van.

In my case this was a Morris 1000, painted Royal Blue of course! I can remember my first speeding offence in July 1961 for exceeding 30mph on the OPEN ROAD travelling to work from Darlington to Heighington. The fine was £3. In those days, all commercial vehicles were limited to 30mph maximum. Difficult to imagine today, but some heavy wagons were limited to only 20mph, even on major trunk roads like the A1. How times have changed.

I learned some interesting skills at the factory, like woodturning for example. We employed one of Browns Sawmills old wood turners, Tom. He was a highly skilled man and to watch him work was a delight. To start with he showed me how to make my own hand tools, the special chisels which are used.

'WOOLIES' & WOOD TURNING

So often, nowadays, I see wood turning on television when the tools are not as they should be. When working with blocks of wood for the lamp bases, especially those of up to 9 inches in diameter and even more, up to 15 or even 16 inches diameter for Standard Lamp bases, ordinary chisels will not do. The handles of the chisels need to be 16 to 18 inches long. They have a knop on the end to tuck comfortably under your armpit and are then tapered and shaped up again to make it easy for the turner to have a firm grip on the tools with both hands. The handle is then reduced in diameter to take the ferrule which supports the tongue on the end of the chisel blade itself, which is a tight fit into the handle.

Using a tool of this design, it is possible to turn down hardwood blocks smoothly, efficiently and with great control. With well seasoned Sycamore or Beach for example, the turnings come away in a continual 'string' of turned wood which builds up around you 3 or 4 feet high, which crumbles when you press gently down on it. It is wonderful to see it done properly. Interestingly, one might think that it would have no application with motor car restoration, but for my first commercial job, the 'baby' Railton, I needed to manufacture a set of polished aluminium Ace type wheel discs. To do this I needed a hardwood pattern upon which to spin and form the aluminium. Using top quality Marine plywood, I laminated up the big disc and turned it up on the lathe to the desired shape. The actual aluminium discs themselves, were then spun over my pattern by a local man and the excellent results can be seen on the Railton wheels.

At our factory, I shovelled tons of coal and stoked the big boiler and in complete contrast, I also designed new lamps and spray painted the turned Lamp bases. In this way, I became proficient at getting a good cellulose finish. Other jobs included setting up displays at the

Some of the artists who painted the lamps and shades.

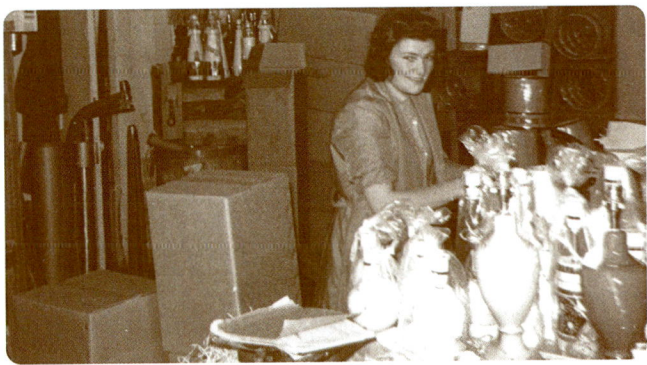
Packing the Royle lamps and shades. A tricky job with them being so fragile.

Commercial Fairs around the Country where our sales Representatives and Agents would gather to meet all our buyers. These could be quite fun and sometimes led to exciting drives in the van coming home in winter with heavy snowy conditions.

Although Aycliffe Industrial Estate is a bleak place, it was expanding after the war and with many new companies developing, there was a positive atmosphere. Mother was always a lively and popular figure with most of the Company Directors on the Estate and was the first (and only?) lady Chairman of the Aycliffe Club. This was a lively and busy social club and meeting place for all the directors and businessmen at Aycliffe.

The club was located in an wartime timber building at the South Gate, facing the then Police Headquarters on the other side of the road, which was also just a large wartime timber hut. The policemen often would call in for drinks at the bar in the club. In fact, later on, I had my 21st birthday party there, when, in those days, we all wore DJ's on these occasions. Being the 'birthday boy', the drummer in the band let me have a go and let me play his drums. My party piece was a short, noisy solo which reflected the style of the popular 'show drummers' at the time. Anything to attract the girls!

The new town called Newton Aycliffe, was also rapidly growing. It had been just a few Prefabs on the North side of the railway line immediately after the war, but was rapidly becoming a modern town with all the facilities. I still have the invitation to mother and I for tea in the Marquee. This was when Her Majesty the Queen and the Duke of Edinburgh came on the 27th May 1960 to celebrate the creation of this new town. It was good to see the 'Royals' so close.

The local newspaper, the Northern Despatch, produced a humorous 'Coat of arms' for 'New Aycliffe' in 1948 which is shown here. On it, can be seen some local dignitaries with the products which were being manufactured on the adjoining trading estate. Amongst them are our Table lamps which are shown on the upper left side of the cartoon.

ON, IN AND ABOVE THE WAVES

Looking back, in my late teens, I was a very lucky young man. I had my own sailing boat and a splendid two seater vintage sports car. Admittedly they represented a lot of work and what little money I had, but when the weather was good and now working with a little more money in my pocket, I was able to drive over to the beautiful Lake District towing my own sturdy little 12 foot dinghy behind the handsome Standard Avon. Whenever I went sailing on Ullswater, I took various friends with me. There was Richard Jeary and also 'Neddy' Keighley, Wendy and later on, Terry Leonard joined me when I was having a few days sailing on my own.

With Richard Jeary.

With Neddy at Ullswater.

Although Ullswater is possibly the most awe inspiring of all the lakes with an impressive beauty of its own. When I first sailed from Glenridding in the mid 1950's, there were only a few rowing boats for hire from Mr Flint and

Proposed Coat of Arms for New Aycliffe.

the two Lakeland 'steamers', to keep me company. There was one other sailing boat, a lovely gaff rigged, clinker built, day boat which was moored nearby on the lake. The reason for there being so few boats on Ullswater for example is, I believe, that the fluky, gusty and variable winds demanded constant vigilance when sailing.

The mountains and valleys play tricks which can easily 'upscuttle' a small sailing boat. Unlike Windermere, where the winds are steadier when sailing, on Ullswater you could tack into the wind in one direction and have to do the same in the opposite direction, all in one afternoon, or if you were lucky, simply run before it both ways! Small water spouts are also not unusual on the lake and if you saw one coming, you had to be sharp if you didn't want your mainsail wrapped around your mast!

Having such a magnificent stretch of water to myself was delightful and generally, except for bank holidays, there were very few visitors and tourists. Because I knew the local teenagers in Glenridding, the atmosphere was like that of any village rather than that of a tourist centre.

To give you an idea of the wonderful attitude of people in those days, on a particularly fresh and fluky, windy day when sailing my second boat, a 16ft 'Wildcat', on the lake, I was not quick enough to avoid one of the flooky and unexpected strong gusts and over she went. The steamer 'The Lady of the Lake' was passing at the time and changed course to come and help me to right the boat. The passengers hung over the rail to watch this unexpected bit of action! After sorting me out, I thanked the captain, whose name was Capt de Boulay, for his great kindness and so I was able to continue to enjoy sailing back to Glenridding. I wonder if someone would do such a kindly thing today. Probably not, because of some ridiculous legal or insurance regulation.

The next time I saw him was on another unforgettable occasion a few weeks later. I had sailed over to Glenridding village, which is at the head of the lake, and there being a strong wind, was just putting on my war surplus Mae West lifejacket to sail back, when I noticed a small, lightweight, aluminium dinghy by the pier. What attracted my attention was that it had a large aerial rotor blade mounted on a rigid frame two metres high, which was fitted to the hull. Not having seen such a machine before, I went over to investigate.

Standing nearby, was the indefatigable Captain de Boulay, obviously preparing to fly this interesting machine off the lake. I was just saying hello when I heard the roar of a powerful engine and a very smart varnished Chris Craft speedboat appeared from the other side of the pier, another unusual sight on Ullswater in those days. The captain explained that it was being driven by Sir Waverley Wakefield of 'Castrol R' fame. Yes, the same man I had met on my first trip to the lake. With not having its own engine, this autogyro boat had to be towed to make it fly. A rope was thrown to the captain who secured it to the bow of the little machine and then launched it onto the water and quickly jumped in.

I sprinted back to my boat, raised the sails and headed out into the middle of the lake to have a good view of this demonstration. It was apparently its maiden 'voyage'. The Chris Craft headed down the lake which was down wind, passing me and the island, paying out a lot of rope as they did so, towing the autogyro boat. Turning into the wind, Sir Waverley took up the slack and pointing the speedboat back towards Glenridding, throttled up the engine. I was just thinking what a tremendous sport de Boulay is when I remembered that the Lakeland steamers belonged to the Wakefields, so the gentlemanly captain probably felt obliged to be the 'test pilot', he worked for them.

As the speedboat accelerated, the rope, which must have been all of 200 to 300ft long, became taut and the little boats bow wave appeared as its speed increased. The Chris Craft engine, now working hard, emitted a powerful roar and de Boulay gently pushed the control 'T' bar forward. The rotor turned faster and faster and as they passed me, the little boat and de Boulay rose gracefully into the air. The boat was flying! It was marvellous to see the captain sitting in this tiny boat climbing higher and higher above the lake.

Tacking into the wind in my boat, I couldn't possibly keep up with them, even though the strong head wind and drag meant that they were not making that much speed over and through the water. In any event, as they were now approaching the head of the lake, being downwind I could hear a shout from above the lake. It was de Boulay repeating the call "don't turn out of the wind", - "don't turn out of the wind" but, being up wind and over 100 feet below and ahead of the gyro-boat with the Chris Craft engine still bellowing, Sir Waverley could not hear this desperate call and needless to say, he did turn out of the wind. The brave Captain De Boulay, in his little 'flying boat', pirouetted as he plummeted down into the lake. By now, Sir Waverley, noticing the lack of tension on the rope, throttled back, but it was too late.

By the time I had sailed back to Glenridding pier, there was no sign of Sir Waverley or the good Captain. Although uncertain, I believe and hope that he had survived the rapid descent, all that there was to be seen was the crumpled wreck of the 'rotor' boat. A wonderful and whimsical idea, but I have heard no more of the captain or of the special boat, or if any more were even built.

VINTAGE JAZZ TRIP

Looking at my Diaries, we were always going somewhere and we were all enjoying our cars. In July 1960, we went to the Jazz Festival at The Motor Museum at Beaulieu in the grounds of Princess House, Lord Montague's home. Terry Scott and I discussed having a week's holiday to visit the Museum, take in the Jazz Festival and have a few days touring in the South.

As luck would have it, Terry's father let us use their lovely Sunbeam Talbot 90 Drop Head Coupe. We set off on the 28th July with the hood down and with no speed limits, we were cruising on the A1 at around 70 to 80 mph, we were really enjoying the drive and were just saying what splendid cars these Sunbeams are, when we had a very near scrape. We were well south of Doncaster on the A1 on a piece of single carriage way, when an oncoming wagon suddenly jack-knifed straight in front of us. It had braked hard behind another wagon heading north, effectively completely blocking our southbound lane with smoke pouring from its back tyres. Terry slammed the brakes on, but there was no way we could have stopped in time. As luck, or skill would have it, the on-coming lorry driver released his brakes and his trailer unit swung back in to its own lane, literally, a second or two before we would have gone into, or under it! We were very lucky, as we had nowhere else to go.

I offered to take the wheel for a while and I think Terry was pleased to have a break. Thankfully, the rest of the trip was uneventful and I was able to enjoy my turn at driving. We spent the next day looking around the museum and were fortunate in having the chance to meet and to have a chat to Lord Montague. We returned again on Saturday the 30th for the Jazz Festival. People were descending on the Palace House grounds from every direction, some even carrying their bundles of clothes above their heads as they swam across the lake! The place was inundated.

It all started well enough, then somebody leant down from the roof of Humphrey Lyttleton's bandstand and literally took his trumpet out of his hands when he was playing. Looking around, People were climbing on everything. even the trees were full of people. I'll quote from my diary, " Good at first, but developed into a chaotic shambles. TV lights and camera scaffolding collapsed, stage mobbed, people climbing all over the place, one on top of the Manor". This man was performing a mock tight rope walk along Palace House roof. We quietly walked away when the music stopped.

We continued with our grand tour visiting Lymington, Torquay, Paignton, Exeter and Plymouth. It had been a good trip with each of us seeing who won the daily competition to choose the meals which turned out to be best on the menu at each stopping place. With it being late one evening, we decided to sleep in the car for the night, so drove into a field. We were woken early next morning when we found that the farmer had been going round us making hay and we were left on an 'island' of long grass. We apologised and remembering that there was a Drama Club committee meeting that night, decided to see if we could be back in Gainford in time for the meeting. We were home by 5pm so must have made good time, because motorways were few and far between in those days. It had been a most interesting trip.

Three days later on the 5th August 1960, I was sleeping in the car again. This time it was the Avon after its rear axle 'cracked up' at Yanwath coming back from Ullswater after seeing Wendy at Ambleside on Windermere where we had arranged to meet. This was the only time the Avon seriously let me down. This time I had to sleep in the car in a lane near the bridge next to the railway line. It was the differential which, after 30 years, must have failed due to the extra load of towing the boat. Anyway, Wendy came over the next day in the Healey and rescued me. We towed the Avon into Penrith to Kaisers Garage where we left it for 'repairs'.

A fortnight later, the garage rang to say the car was ready for collection. I see that I got up at 4.30am, (difficult to believe these days!) and I caught an early train from Darlington to Penrith. At the time, this line was one of many country railways which was soon to be Axed by Beeching, the transport minister who closed down so many of our local railway lines.

Looking out of the window, as the train headed West on its single track up beautiful Teesdale, I saw that most of the old stations were falling into disrepair. As It crossed and re-crossed the river Tees over the splendidly built stone bridges and then puffed its way over the bleak Bowes Moor, I noticed that the paint may have been peeling on the buildings, but the flower boxes on the platforms were still in full bloom. The railway men still had some pride in their work.

Arriving in Penrith at 8.40 am, I found that Kaisers Garage had been able to locate another differential in the local scrap yard. The cost of finding and fitting it was £10/15/- fortunately, I could afford this and was delighted to be able to be driving the old Avon home. The only problem was that the replacement differential now had a lower Final drive ratio, so top speed was nearly 10 mph slower. Perhaps the Sports Avon had been fitted with a higher Ratio diff' than the Standard saloon models. It was good to have it back again, though.

CHAPTER 8:
LAGONDA DAYS BEGIN

As the late 1950's became the early 1960's, the social scene really got under way. There were more and more parties, especially 21st birthdays, I was 21 in October 1960. There were Drama Club parties, Hunt dances, Round Table events and big barbecues, often with well known bands and groups playing. They were mainly held in the country and in some wonderful houses, so having your own car was essential. Of course we could drink without worry and when driving home at unearthly hours of the morning, we had the roads to ourselves.

As ever, we were very lucky with having motor cars, we were meeting people all the time and our expanding group of friends included a lot of good farming people of our age, also there were motor racing, shooting and boating friends and It was difficult to organise any function without having 300 or more invitations to send out.

After my father died and being on her own for fourteen years, one my father's oldest friends, the Rev T.W.E 'Tom' Grinham, asked mother to marry him and go to live in Cheshire with him. Tom's dear wife had died after having been in a wheelchair for many years, during which time Tom had nursed and looked after her. Mother asked me what I thought about it all and I said that I thought it was an excellent idea, he was great fun and good company and they had known each other for years, in fact he appears on some of my father's pre-war 9.5mm films. Mother was worried that I would have nowhere to live if she sold the house in Coniscliffe Road, I wasn't at all concerned, so the house was sold and I was comforted to know that the proceeds from the sale would give her a nest egg for the future.

So, early in 1963, mother did get married again and Tom wrote a delightful letter nine weeks later, to tell me to how much he was enjoying life with his new wife. I was so pleased for them both. None of us realised that he would only live for two more months, but he did, at least, enjoy the last few months of his life. After many years on her own and having made the break, mother decided to stay in Tom's old house in Cheshire and was already involved in the Church and had made many new friends, so decided to 'stay put'.

In her wisdom, she had decided to give me £250 as a belated birthday and going away present. This was a wonderful gift and she said that I could spend it on whatever I wanted, but made it clear that there would not be any more! I had organised some lodgings, so this money opened up the opportunity to buy a really splendid motor car.

In the early sixties there were some really interesting vintage motor cars at this sort of price, and by now, I had driven quite a varied selection of those which my friends had owned, but my dream car was a Vintage Bentley, a Lagonda or an Alvis speed 20. I realised that I would need to keep down to 3 litres or the petrol consumption would have been too high. I obviously asked my friends if they knew of anything which might suit me.

The first interesting motor car I heard about sounded to be just the ticket. It was Terry who came up with it. He had been speaking to his father 'HPR', who's co-director, 'Tommy' Summerson, was thinking of selling his 3 Litre Vintage Vanden Plas Bentley. I have already mentioned that their company, Summerson Holdings, had garages at Mowden Hall on the outskirts of Darlington. This is where I had first seen the Minerva which Terry had put back into good shape. It turned out that this is where the Vintage Bentley was also kept.

So on the appointed day, Terry and I turned up at the company's garages to be greeted by the owner's chauffeur who was smartly dressed in green livery with a smart peaked hat. He was standing by the Bentley which had already been driven out of the garage and was every bit as handsome a motor car as any young man could wish for. He opened the small rear door and directed us to sit in the back, so we stepped onto the running board, over the high door sil and sat in the typically deep leather seat. The leather matched the colour of the bodywork which, naturally, was British Racing Green. The chauffeur climbed into the driving seat and started the engine. With that typical rich Bentley exhaust note, we were driven in great style as he took us on a tour of the local country roads. An absolute delight.

I wrote to Mr Summerson asking what price he wanted for the Bentley, but he replied by saying that it wasn't on the market. Still very keen to buy it, a month later, I offered him £300. I must have been planning to borrow £50, since I only had the £250 which mother gave me. This time, he replied saying that he would only "consider a substantially improved offer". Naturally, I was very disappointed but somehow, I was able to increase my offer to £355, but he turned this down as well. I had no choice, but to resume my search elsewhere for another vintage car which would appeal to me and this time, one which would be within my price range.

I had heard that that there was an open 1933 Speed 20 Alvis not far away, at Ayro Cars at Marske by the Sea, so drove over to see it in the old Avon. It seemed to be in reasonably good condition, but Mr Ayrton was asking £275 for it, which I thought rather high for an Alvis at that time, so continued my search.

Naturally, the Motor Sport magazine always had a really good selection of interesting sports cars and desirable vintage cars. As is usually the case, most of them were in the South, which meant a long journey to go to see them. I then spotted an advert in Motor Sport for a 1930 Special 3 litre Lagonda Tourer which was down in Wootton Basset in Wiltshire. I rang the owner, the price was £250 and he told me that the engine had recently been overhauled. Wendy agreed to drive down with me in the company's Morris 1000 van, so we could drive the Lagonda back, if we bought it.

After an uneventful journey in the van, we inspected the Lagonda, and it was certainly very original and was a most handsome motor car. It had a 3 litre engine which was the size I was looking for and interestingly, it also was fitted with a strong, but nicely made tow bar, so, like the Avon, I would be able to tow the boat with it. It had an all steel body painted BRG, which was in sound condition. The Front mudguards turned with the wheels which was a feature of these Lagonda's which I particularly liked.

Priming the twin carburettors with the Ki-Gas pump on the dash board, which leaked slightly, the engine started straight away and we had a short test drive round the block, it ran smoothly with good oil pressure and looked to be a very genuine machine.

I paid the owner and with Wendy driving the Morris van, we set off to drive cross-country, heading for the A1. Keeping a close watch on the gauges, the oil pressure was good and hardly moved and the water temperature only increased very slowly. Like the Standard Avon, it had the typical vintage foot pedal arrangements with the throttle pedal in the middle between the clutch on the left and the foot brake on the right. The crash box gear lever was in a gate on the right hand side of the seat alongside the handbrake, which was of the fly-off type for use as a secondary brake when driving. There was also a clutch stop to assist with gear changing.

Once on the Great North road, we headed North to Darlington. It certainly handled well, but seemed big and heavy after driving the Avon for so many years. Cruising at 50 to 60mph on the A1, still keeping an eye on the instruments as ever, I saw that the cooling water

DR checking engine oil of Lagonda.

temperature slowly climbing from around 70 towards 80°c. At the same time, I noticed the oil pressure was slowly dropping back from around 50 psi as the miles rolled past.

When I became familiar with the car later on, I learned that normally, with having 3½ gallons of oil in the sump, and around 2½ gallons of water in the cooling system, it does take some time to heat up all this liquid before reaching its normal running temperature.

After Doncaster, I could see that the oil pressure continued to fall, so I slowed down to around 45-50mph, by now the pressure was down to 25psi.

Nearing home, almost in sight of Scotch-Corner, the oil pressure was still falling and down to 10 to 12 psi, so I throttled back down to 25mph and pulled into a lay by near a wood. As I did so, I heard the big ends begin to rattle. At the same time the pointers on the speedometer, the rev counter and the oil pressure gauge all fell together down to zero. A miserable sight;

So much for the engine having been overhauled.

Wendy pulled in behind me in the van, but such was my confidence, that I had not even taken a tow rope in the van which she had so patiently been driving all the way back for me. We looked in the back, but could only find a length of strong sisal string about 15ft long. We tied this to the Lagonda's front cross member and with the lightest of clutch and throttle control, Wendy gradually pulled me back onto the road, past Scotch Corner and down the A68 towards Piercebridge. Doing this with a short length of string was no mean feat, bearing in mind that the Lagonda weighs over a ton and a half!

It was a brilliant piece of driving by Wendy, especially bearing in mind the fact that it is the vehicle which is being towed which is the one which is supposed to do all the braking for both vehicles. This is to keep the tow rope taught to avoid braking it! No matter how delicate we were, the string still snapped a few times. By the time we made it home, the van and the Lagonda were only five feet apart on a very short length of knotted string, but at least we made it.

Once back home, I was soon able to examine the engine. Compared to the simple side valve Standard ten, it was a magnificent piece of machinery. As with most high quality Vintage engines, it is beautifully engineered, well built and very much an example of practical, straight forward engineering with none of the electronic complications of modern motor cars. Despite the overall weight of the car being 31 cwt, the petrol consumption for the 250 mile journey home, was around 20 mpg, which I thought very good for such an early design. Its Twin Bronze carburettors ran rich at low revs which was helpful when starting the engine from cold, especially with it not having any choke, but once cruising at 60 to 70mph, the exhaust was grey showing a correct mixture.

I was naturally upset to have to start stripping the engine down, especially when I had been told that it had been overhauled, so I did talk to my solicitors but, as I delved further into the car, I realised that it was so good in so many ways that I didn't take it further. It was very original and was going to be worth the trouble of sorting out the engine problems.

THE SPECIAL 3 LITRE LAGONDA ENGINE

Turning the large knurled knob mounted on the heavy Nickel Silver oil filler cap, I was able to withdraw the dip stick from the cylindrical alloy sump extension which houses the wire mesh filter. Examining it, I could see that the engine oil had emulsified, so water was somehow getting into the lubrication system. There could be a number of reasons for this, some of which could be serious and costly to rectify. It looked as if I had little choice but start stripping down the engine.

Wendy's father, Alan Hare very kindly offered me the use one of the pits at his garage. Jimmy Cobb, his expert mechanic was, of course, very interested and it was good to have his advice. Not wanting to take up any more of his valuable time than was necessary, I soon started to strip it all down to find the root of the problem. After removing the magnificent P100 headlamps, bonnet boards, the bonnet, the stone-guard and disconnecting the hoses, I could remove the heavy radiator. Next, the front seats came out, I could then lift the floor and remove the toe boards which gave me access to the pedal mountings, the drive shaft, starter unit and gearbox.

The engine was now exposed and readily accessible. I stripped off all the external pipework, oil lines and filters and took off the aluminium side plates. Disconnected the twin exhaust Manifolds, removed the rocker cover and carburettors and then was able to remove the cylinder head. This is a heavy and solid casting and was found to be undamaged which was good. I then drained off all the emulsified oil by undoing the large brass lock nut which holds down the oil release plunger on the tapered alloy sump extension. This plunger is a strongly made device which, if misused, can do a lot of damage to the big sump casting. Fortunately, it had been treated with respect and was in good condition.

After undoing the many nuts and bolts supporting it, I was able to remove the large finned sump. Whilst cleaning it out after emptying all the oil, I was able to carefully examine the bottom of it for traces of white metal and any other unwelcome materials. Regrettably there was quite a lot of white metal which meant that the big end bearings had 'picked up' on the crankshaft, consequently the whole engine would have to be stripped down and overhauled.

The root of the problem turned out to be that a 'dry' cylinder liner had been fitted and left protruding above the machined surface of the cylinder block. We guessed that some work had been done to the engine and one of the pistons must have seized and a new liner fitted, but not properly ground off. This had prevented the cylinder head seating properly on the head gasket. Water had gradually seeped into the oil in the sump and it had been emulsifying on the journey North. If there had not been such a large reservoir of oil, we would not have been able to drive as far as we had done before the bearings failed.

It is worth mentioning that working on the 3 litre engine, even when still in the Lagonda chassis, was very convenient when compared with many of the motor cars built at this time. This is because the Cycle Type front mudguards are so neatly fitted to the front axle and so compact, that there is plenty of room to stand 'inside' the front wheels right next to the chassis and engine. It was therefore a pleasure to be able to work on an engine which is so readily accessible without having to lean over large front wings.

I set about stripping the remaining engine components so that the various parts could be attended to and the specialist machining work carried out. Accordingly, I removed the clutch, flywheel, crankshaft, connecting rods and pistons and all the valve gear. The timing chest and the block itself was then removed from the chassis. There was quite a lot of work to be done by specialist engineers. I knew the local engineering firm, Theckla, would do the machining for me, including casting the main and big end white metal bearings, in-line boring, etc.

Whilst the car was off the road and the engine being machined, I took the opportunity to improve various other aspects of the car. I have found my list of the various jobs carried out in 1963 including having the Magneto overhauled, re-upholstering the front seats and making new carpets. I also improved the paintwork, soldered new mesh onto the radiator stoneguard, which I had re-chromed along with other small fittings.

I stripped down the handsome, big P 100 headlamps, the reflectors, the magnifying 'bullseye' glasses, frames and the side lamps and stalks and took them down to the Darlington Chrome Plating Co in Haughton Road. One day, when I called in to check on progress, I had the misfortune to see a new man who had been taken on as a polisher, have a nasty accident. As with most plating work, it is the preparation which is an important part of the process.

The metal must first be cleaned, the old plating stripped off and then be carefully polished prior to re-plating. This is a particularly dirty and unpleasant, yet skilled job, so employing the right people can be difficult. After plating, the chrome, nickel or silver needs to be carefully polished again if the final result is to be correct. With vintage lamps and reflectors being made of spun brass, the metal is very thin, so whilst polishing must be thorough, it must be done with great care or damage is done to the delicate components.

The polishing mops can easily wear away the details and make the metal so thin that it loses all its strength. The lamp reflectors were electro-plated with real silver in those days and when complete, are a delight to behold. After preparation, the longer the items are in the electro plating tanks, the thicker is the plating, so when the parts are in the tanks, I used to keep the owner talking, not difficult for me! All the time knowing that I had plenty of microns of silver and chrome building up on these impressive lamp components.

I was doing this when the new man came into the office. He looked very pale as he took off his thick leather gloves and as he did so, blood splashed onto the floor. He had tried to slow down the polishing wheel with his gloved hand. These are turning at around 2000 revs per minute and have fine abrasive coatings applied which remove the surface metal. The polishing wheel had removed the leather and all the skin from his hand which looked like an anatomical specimen with all the veins, tendons and muscles clearly visible. I left straight away, so that the owner could take the man to hospital.

Side view of Lagonda with red 18" wheels.

Thinking about this awful accident, one which would put the unfortunate chap out of work for quite a long time, reminds me that I very nearly put myself in a worse position at that time. Working under the Lagonda in the garage pit, is so much more convenient and better than crawling around underneath when the car is on its wheels or jacked up on stands. All chassis components are visible and can easily be inspected and checked. I thought it was a good opportunity to drain off the petrol tank and wash it out. This is a job which is often neglected with old cars and deposits or rust and dirt can lead to fuel supply problems. There wasn't much petrol in the tank, so I took a funnel and gerry can down into the pit to drain off the remaining fuel.

I undid the central hexagonal drain plug, but before I could put the funnel under the drain hole, petrol poured out so quickly and in such a thick stream that the funnel couldn't cope. I was drenched from head to foot. Although there was not much showing on the gauge, it is a 20 gallon tank and there is a reserve tap, so there was a lot more fuel in the tank than I expected. Standing underneath, I had to quickly drop the gerry can, so that I could screw the plug back in as quickly as I could. With petrol pouring down on me, I was soon drenched from head to toe, all it needed was one spark! I shouted to Jim who ran over to me and told me to take all my clothes off. I put on some dry overalls and he then helped me to mop it all up.

The old joke is that cigarettes are difficult to light when wet, this was not the time to find out! The learning curve was ongoing and I was lucky to get away with it.

After all the machining to the engine and its components was finished, but before assembly, I made sure this time, that all the oil ways, galleries, oil pipes and the engine block itself was scrupulously clean inside and out and whilst the engine block was bare, I decided to paint it pillar box red and also paint the wheels to match. I thought this looked really smart and when fully assembled with all the aluminium, nickel silver, copper and brass-work brightly polished, the engine bay under the bonnet, looked very smart indeed.

All the work was finished by the end of August and I had promised Brownie that the minute the Lagonda was ready, we would have a 'grand tour' before the summer was out.

CHAPTER 9:
THE GRAND TOUR

With the Lagonda having been off the road for quite a few months and not having been road tested, I wanted to keep the first day's journey fairly short, so Brownie and I decided to start with a visit to the Old Church Country Club on the shores of Ullswater. This was a very special place which we greatly enjoyed visiting. The owner, Mr Wood, always made us feel very welcome, the food was excellent and with a limited number of members, it was a delightful place to stay and sail from. He maintained it as a private club to the highest standards in every respect. The Old Church was built as a beautiful private house with well kept lawns sloping gently down to the water's edge.

The drive over Bowes Moor to the Old Church went well, the Lagonda was running beautifully and after we had settled in to our rooms and had dinner, we thought it would be a good idea to drive up the road, beside the lake, to the Ullswater Hotel at Glenridding for a little fresh air and a late evening's drink. The plan was to head South the following morning with a good, long drive down to Devon and then into Cornwall. Brownie's parents, Alan and Marney had very kindly offered to treat us to a few nights at the Bristol Hotel in Newquay.

Without realising it, we were to have a little excitement first. It was a pleasant evening and we hadn't gone far along the twisting lakeside road when I had to make an involuntary stop on a small gritty promontory by the lake.

THE CLIFFHANGER, BROWNIE SAVES THE DAY

For God's sake let out the clutch" shouted Brownie. Although it was dark, I could see the top of his head outlined against the lake as he pulled hard on the headlamp bar in front of the vintage Lagonda's tall chrome radiator. The car moved forward as he pulled hard going backwards towards the 20ft drop into Lake Ullswater, I needed to be sure that we had enough forward momentum to ensure that we had a 'fat' spark from the Scintilla magneto, so I was waiting until the very last moment, It was critical if the engine was going to start.

You may wonder why he was not pushing the car more safely from the back. The problem was that the little lay-by had a loose grit surface and Brownie could not get a grip on it. In these circumstances by pulling the car, the downward thrust gave him sufficient grip with his shoes to move the ton and a half of well-built vintage motor car.

After another desperate shout from Brownie when he was rapidly approaching the edge, I let out the clutch, the magneto sparked, the engine fired up, I immediately pushed in the clutch pedal and then jammed on all the brakes, hard. 'Brownie', by this time, was literally right on the very edge of the little vertical cliff and would have fallen into the lake if he had let go of the bar. The fact that it had started was a great relief to both of us.

What had happened was that all the lights on the Lagonda had gone out as we drove towards Glenridding. Thinking that I might be able to quickly detect the fault, I switched off the engine, but after checking round, realised that I would need to remove the seats, floorboards etc. Because the fault was the main feed to the switchboard and the starter motor, which, like the lights, had no power to it. Not a simple job in the dark. Fortunately these cars have magneto ignition so can be push started. It is just a question of a good push, or in our unusual circumstances, a good pull.

Lesson number one, when checking the wiring on a car, do not leave that one important connection unchecked which is so hard to get at when the car has been re-assembled.

The small gritty lay-by was a convenient place to stop, but a little on the short side for 'jump starts'. The thought of leaving the Lagonda parked right on the edge of a 20ft drop, all night, did not appeal to me at all. Now that the engine was running, but still with no lights, I was able to reverse back from the edge so that Brownie could let go of the bar and come round from between the front wheels and jump back into his seat. By now we had adjusted to the dark and could, just to say, see where we were going, so headed back to the club without any lights.

The next morning we removed the front seats, carpet and floor board and I was pleased to find that the fault was where I thought it might be, so it was soon rectified. With this job done, we set off and headed south.

This incident occurred on my Lagonda's first day's outing following an overhaul of the engine which, due to pressure of time, had to be its test run. It was the first days run and the beginning of a 1,000 mile round trip drive to Cornwall and back. This was in 1963 when motorways were few and far between, so Cornwall was a long run of over 450 miles.

The following day the Lagonda ran beautifully and we made very good time and by the middle of the afternoon, we found ourselves driving into Devon. Being a lovely day and following the coast road we came across, or rather were confronted with, Porlock Hill. Not long before this, we had picked up two rather 'dishy' girls who were thumbing a lift. To be companionable, one girl sat in the front seat next to me, whilst 'Brownie' squeezed into the back seat with the other girl and all the luggage, refastening the tonneau cover over the pair of them as he did so. This left only their heads and shoulders visible as they sank down to protect themselves from the wind, he said! Although, to be fair, anybody who sits in the back seat of open vintage touring cars, will know, that the blast of the air can be more than exhilarating after a few miles at a good speed!

Not being familiar with Porlock, we approached the bottom of the hill in top gear, we were soon into third, then another double de clutch and down into second. The hill seemed to go on and on and so, as ever, my eyes were focussed on the temperature gauge. As it climbed up from 75 to 85° centigrade, I had the impression that the temperature was also climbing up in the back seat! I then had no choice, but to change down yet again to bottom gear, not an everyday event in a 3 litre Lagonda. The temperature was now nearly 90° and still climbing and we still had not reached the top of this long steep hill.

As it was the first really long trip in the car after many weeks of work burning the midnight oil, I regret to say that my attention was distracted away from the pretty girl sitting next to me towards my other and rather older lady - the Lagonda!

The gauge now showed 100° and the engine was boiling. Carrying all the weight of four passengers and all our luggage, especially when we were still 'running in', I decided that something had to go and I didn't want it to be my engine.

We still had a lot of hill to climb, so as they say nowadays, I made an 'executive decision', regrettably the girls and their luggage had to go. Because of the slow progress up the hill, the sunshine, the consequential lack of a headwind and mostly hidden under the tonneau cover, unlike the car, 'Brownie' and our rear guest had been getting along fine, so I'm afraid that the forced disembarkation did not go down at all well!

After some difficulty and much 'manoeuvring' under the tonneau cover, the young ladies and their luggage were reluctantly extracted. With a none too happy 'Brownie' climbing back into the front seat, we waved goodbye. With the lighter load, it was not too long before we reached the top of the hill and the old lady was able to cool down. Fortunately, Brownie is essentially a practical person, so had realised that it was better not to 'pull' the birds, rather than have to 'push' the car!

We now had the long descent down to Lynmouth which you may remember suffered the serious flooding disaster in 1952 (showing my age again!). This long downhill run into the village, cooled down the engine marvellously, but it was the first time that the brakes had been used continuously for so long and under such pressure, so they got very hot. Although they are superbly efficient on the Lagonda's, I had painted the drums with what I thought was heat resistant paint. It could not stand up to such prolonged use however, and when we pulled up in the middle of the village, poor old 'Brownie' was embarrassed yet again with dense palls of smoke rising from each corner of the car. The big brake drums were smoking furiously. A small crowd gathered expecting the car to burst into flames at any moment. Fortunately it did not, but the smoke was intense and it must have looked pretty impressive.

Other than for the Ullswater 'lights out' event and this last 'hiccup', the Lagonda ran beautifully for the rest of the holiday. We had a lot of fun with trips to Lands End and other

CHAPTER 9: THE GRAND TOUR

Brownie at the wheel with Janet in Cornwall.

jaunts, we also enjoyed our stay at the Bristol Hotel where there were some very pretty girls, but that is another story.

On the way home, we unfortunately did get stuck going over a Bailey bridge in Faringdon where a sewer had burst in the middle of the town. The long wheelbase on the Lagonda caused the car to 'ground' on the apex of the angular bridge. As luck would have it, three policemen appeared from nowhere, half carrying, half dragging a drunken chap who they dumped across the back of the car, they then helped 'Brownie' to push us off the bridge.

The action being in the town centre, there were plenty of shoppers who greatly enjoyed the fun. Needless to say 'Brownie' is not one who likes to be at the centre of this sort of 'circus' and, as always, seemed to lose out when things happened, but he put a brave face on it as we eventually drove off to a round of applause. This was after having returned our 'extra' passenger to the supportive arms of the Law. Looking back I have to smile.

CHAPTER 10:
THE BACHELOR COTTAGE

After mother moved to Cheshire to live with her new husband, the Rev Tom Grinham early in 1963, I lived in digs in Darlington for a while until Wendy's father, very kindly offered to let me stay with them at Prospect House in High Coniscliffe which is on the road to Gainford from Darlington. This was much appreciated and I enjoyed staying with them, but I did want to be independent.

Towards the end of 1963, knowing that I was looking for somewhere to live, my good friend John Robinson , 'Robbo', offered to rent to me one of the cottages in the pretty little village of Headlam, which is also not far from Gainford in Teesdale, It is really just a hamlet and is where his family had farmed since the late 1920's. As it turned out, number 5 The Green, became vacant at this time.

Headlam is a delightful, rural place with hardly any passing traffic on the narrow country lanes. I had always enjoyed the many visits and time I had spent there, so I knew the village quite well. I had stayed with the Robinson family sometimes, especially if we were late back from a party. I also used to go shooting there and had a lot of happy and memorable experiences, including riding his horses. The Zetland Hunt is very active in South Durham and a lot of our friends were hunting people, so not surprisingly, along with others, Robbo tried to encourage me to improve my riding skills so that I could join in the fun.

He had a big Hunter called 'Lucky' which was 17.2 hands and every time I was 'on board', as soon as I encouraged him to canter, it would be difficult to stop the animal going at full gallop. Inevitably, it was a thrilling ride, but I couldn't control it. The horse knew it 'had me' and would, with ease, clear any fence, ditch or stream which we came to. That is until I would eventually pull myself out of the saddle trying to stop it. Inevitably coming off at full gallop and would end up rolling down the field. I gave up after a while, and fortunately didn't come to any harm, even though we would only wear a tweed cap on our heads in those days. Hard hats were only worn when hunting. May be that is why the hunter was called 'Lucky'!

The Robinsons had another horse called 'Starlight' which was entirely the opposite to 'Lucky'. This was a dapple grey Percheron, a heavy working horse which was fully trained and taught me just how wonderful these animals are. Climbing onto its incredibly broad back without a saddle, was an experience in itself. Using the words of command and leg movements to control it which had been explained to me, the horse would go in any direction, forwards, sideways and backwards. It was a gentle, but powerful giant and I could well understand how our agricultural system had benefitted so much from having such well trained, docile but strong animals in the early days before tractors.

At one of the many Drama Club parties, we rigged up hoops and a tarpaulin onto an old four wheeled farm cart and made a proper covered wagon. In large letters, we wrote 'Pancho's Beer Wagon' on the side. Robbo hitched 'Starlight' into the shafts, we loaded it up with all the drinks for the party and we drove it the two miles down the main road to Gibson's Farm where we were having the barbecue. Everybody enjoyed such a novel delivery and it was great fun. 'Starlight' behaved impeccably of course and the 'rig' turned a few heads when we drove it back the following day.

Generally, the hunters I rode knew that they were in control of me, not the other way round, which is a great shame, because it is a wonderful

Another hunter which I fell off trying to stop it at full gallop. This time, my friend Ann Boyd's horse - too many oats!

sport and I know that I would have really enjoyed hunting. I think that I am too gentle with them.

Back to the cottage, No. 5 and the adjoining house, No. 6, date back many centuries, certainly before the window tax laws which were introduced in 1696. This was confirmed later, when we subsequently uncovered larger windows which had been reduced in size. We discovered this when we were carrying out structural alterations a few years later. The cottage has beamed ceilings, open fireplaces and beautiful views looking south west towards the Dales, with a walled private garden at the back. Adjoining it on one side is No 4, the old Irishman's cottage. This is a one room dwelling which was used in bygone days by the casual labourers during harvest time, but had been empty for many years. On the other side, the adjoining house, Number 6, was occupied, at the time by Dennis Tallentire, who was the village blacksmith at nearby Ingleton.

With the help of Brownie, Robbo and other friends, we set about making various improvements to my 'new' home. There was a large high stone fireplace surround with an enamelled 1930's 'cottage' range set into it which had probably replaced an earlier black range. We removed this and opened up the original complete fireplace. I asked Dennis, next door, to make me a large fire grate for logs on his forge and also make a fire hood for me. He did this and I mounted a cast iron oval plaque onto it which, from memory, bore the heraldic crest of the Lords Barnard with the words "Nec Temere nec Timide" around the edge. This was part of an old cast iron oven door which I found in the Irishman's cottage.

Whilst some of the village is privately owned, including Headlam Hall, which is a large and most impressive Elizabethan house, most of this area of Teesdale is part of Raby Estates. The Vane family bought the land from the Crown after it had been taken from the ancient Nevilles after the Northern Uprising in the 16th century. It was a serious affair in those days and the reprisals included hanging two people from each of the villages which, including Headlam, had supported the Nevilles at the uprising. The Vane family still have around 50,000 acres here in South West Durham I believe, along with its many farms and villages. The present Lord Barnard, John Vane, lives in the magnificent Raby Castle which is now partly open to the public. This fortification dates back to King Canute, as do parts of Staindrop church.

The improvements we made to the cottage included planking out part of the kitchen. Pinewood planking was just becoming

No 5 & 6 The Green with Sunbeam Alpine.

fashionable and Brownie said that he had piles of knotty pine which was put aside as 'seconds' at the sawmills in those days. So, for a relatively low price, we built in a neat six seat dining area with high traditional seat ends in 2" pine to match. Because the kitchen only had a tiny North facing Yorkshire window, we also had to build in a lot of lighting. Mother gave me some furniture for the other rooms and as it had concrete floors, I had carpets fitted which helped to make it comfortable. All in all, the cottage made a great 'bachelor pad' and when finished, I had lots of parties and fun there. I called it 'Brantwood Cottage' after the house which my grandfather had built, the house in which I was born.

The Wheel House garage with the work finished.

Just along the green in Headlam, was the Goose House and the Tithe Barn. These were very old, disused buildings which included some old stables. At the back, was a traditional, stone built Wheel House and knowing that I would need to have somewhere to keep the Lagonda, Robbo very kindly offered to let me use this as a garage if I did certain work to make it weatherproof and secure.

The wheel house had not been used for many years and had open sides and rafters and no doors. I began by concreting the old earth floor which still retained the circular furrow formed years ago, by the work horses walking round and round to power the mill wheels which ground the corn. I also fitted folding doors and windows and panelled in the open sides, I fitted hardboard panels to the low roof beams so that it would stop the pigeon's from roosting. The gaps in the old pantiles on the roof are far from being wind proof and as I would be keeping my cars in there and probably working on them, I wanted to keep the place draught free and clean. When finished, it was well lit and with a good workbench and my various tools, it made an excellent rural garage.

By this time, with my Lagonda having been seen around the area, I was told of another Lagonda which had been laid up locally for many years. This turned out also to be a 'Special 3 litre' model, but this time it was a saloon, registration No, PJ 4399. Being in need of restoration, I was offered it for £25, so I acquired a second Lagonda. I then also bought the 'bones' of another similar car. This time, it was only the chassis, engine and various parts. When the 'new' garage was finished, being 25 feet wide and 23 feet long, there was enough space to house the two complete Lagonda's and all the other parts.

The wheelhouse opened onto a walled yard which provided me with a pleasant and secluded area. This enabled me to work in private on my cars, outside in the summertime. With the building facing north and being dark inside, I needed to fit plenty of lights, so I ran an extension power cable from the cottage along the top of a wall bordering the field at the back. This was fine, but being covered with soft rubber, the cows eventually chewed through it! I replaced it with a less 'tasty' cable which had a hard plastic covering.

THE FACTORY CHANGES HANDS

After working at the factory for seven years, the last three of them as manager for Crookston Royle & Co, I left on the 31st March 1965.

The Lagonda parked by the factory in 1963 when I was managing it for Crookston Royle & Co. Ltd.

This was partly due to a clash of personalities with the accountant who Mr Crookston appointed to oversee the factory when he was in Cairo. Like me, he was a director, but it annoyed him, especially at the exhibitions and trade shows, when our customers would focus their attention on me rather than him. With my name being Royle, they had known my father and would ask after my mother and he didn't like this, so my directorship ceased and our relationship deteriorated.

I should explain that father's old company and the factory had previously been taken over by Andrew Crookston & Co. This gentleman's Egyption Railway company had been nationalised, along with the Suez canal, when Nasser came into power in the mid 1950's. With the money which he received from the government for his assets in Egypt, Mr Crookston bought a number of small companies, C.N.Royle & Co Ltd was one of these. Henceforth the company was known as Crookston Royle & Co and our head office was then in London, at 38, Grosvenor Gardens.

In the 1950's the factory buildings at Aycliffe were all rented from English Industrial Estates. So when mother found trading conditions difficult in the late 1950's she had no assets to support bank facilities. The result of this was that the business was sold and this London based company eventually stepped in and I became the manager of the factory just before she remarried. This was a salutary lesson and I promised myself that if I ever started a business, I would make sure that I owned the premises.

Soon after I left in 1965, the company changed hands again and came under the control of Tony Jackson. He was a charming man who had been an agent for our company for many years and lived just outside Leeds. He already owned other lamp manufacturers, so ours joined his other businesses in Leeds.

Not having a job suited me fine, I was always busy and it was an excellent opportunity to get on with all my other interests. I found the process of overhauling and improving my sports tourer GG 8071, to be so satisfying that I turned my attention to the 3 litre Lagonda saloon, 'PJ'. Having taken the purist approach to the restoration and conservation work required on the Tourer, I thought it would be fun to overhaul and rebuild 'PJ' as well. This time because the saloon bodywork was in a such a poor state, I thought it would be interesting to design and build my own body and make it a relatively lightweight 2 seater 'sports'. With PJ then being non-original, I planned to risk using it for competitive hill climbs and other competitions.

With 'GG' now in really good running order and in regular use, I had plenty of time to design and build the body onto PJ and then overhaul the engine and running gear later on. In the coming months, I made a start and removed the rotten saloon bodywork, carefully storing all the components for future use. Over the next year or two, whenever I had time, I built the framework and later on, discussing the problem of forming the double curved aluminium body panels with Robbo, he offered to use his wife, Anne's, new Austin 1100 to roll the side panels in a sand pit which we had scooped out to the desired shape. Using the front wheels, Robbo repeatedly drove forwards and backwards and it worked very well. The panels took the desired shape with smooth double curvatures, but we burn't out the clutch doing it, so it was not the most economic way of shaping panels!

As it turned out, when the body was eventually finished, it would not be until the spring of 1972 that I would be able to properly tackle the mechanical overhaul. This was when I had been again 'fired up' after completely stripping

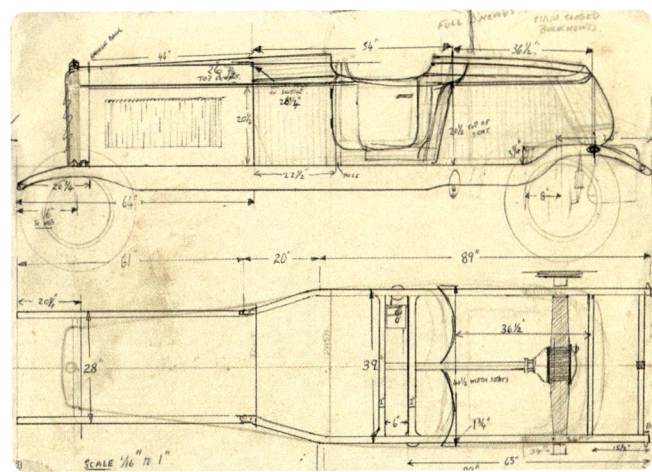

Outline drawings for a two seater 3 litre Sports Lagonda.

 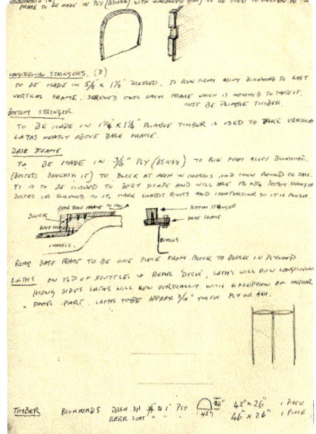

'PJ' Lagonda rough sketches. *'PJ' Lagonda restoration notes.*

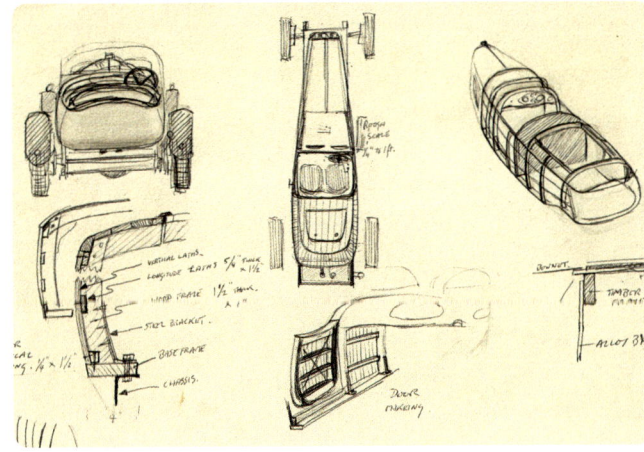

'PJ' Loagonda rough skethches of body ideas.

and this time, carrying out a full and detailed restoration of GG 8071, a most satisfying job!

A few months after leaving the factory, I met a chap in a local pub in August, who offered me his sales job. This was with Kolok, part of the Ozalid group, a London firm who supplied hundreds of shops and print houses with papers, inks, typewriter ribbons, carbon papers and other printing materials. It was well paid,

Rebuilding No. 2 Lagonda at Headlam 1971. The bodywork is finished.

but he said he was fed up with driving 60,000 miles a year covering the North of England, Scotland and Ireland.

I wasn't too keen on spending so much time away from my 'new' home, but when he said that the company would share the cost of buying whatever sort of car I wanted, I thought it would be interesting and might be fun. He arranged for me to have an interview and as I had been invited down to St Mawes in Cornwall by Jimmy Wilson and his family, I drove into London first on the way south. The interview went well and I was given the job and we agreed that I would start working for them in early September, after the holiday.

When on holiday, the Lagonda always adds to the fun, so I drove down in it and after the interview, carried on down to Cornwall. The car ran beautifully all the way, despite the good days run of over five hundred miles. Jimmy's father, Bob Wilson, kindly met me at the lane end, just past St Austell, to guide me down the narrow Cornish lanes to their cottage in St. Mawes. It was dark by the time we met, he was driving his new Mini Cooper 's' and we set off at a good pace. Whilst the Lagonda was running beautifully after such a long journey, when thoroughly hot, it would sometimes backfire on the overrun and in the narrow lanes where the trees meet overhead forming tunnels, I could see that the flames coming out of the three inch copper exhaust pipe, were lighting up the entire road. This egged me on and when we reached St Mawes, Bob said he couldn't get away from me. I am sure that he was being kind, but I was really enjoying myself!

The holiday was a great success, the Wilsons were most kind to me and I ended up staying with them for three and a half very enjoyable weeks. Jimmy, Robert, his brother and I, crewed and sailed in a most interesting range of boats, one of which was 'Sabrina' a slender wooden Tumlaren keel boat which belonged to John Whitton whom we met in the 'Riser', the Rising Sun pub in St. Mawes, our local.
I crewed for him in one or two races, then he very kindly put the boat at my disposal when he returned home to Leicester. We all went sailing almost every day and it was the beginning of a long and happy relationship with the Whittons and St Mawes.

After another good journey home, I put the Lagonda into the old wheelhouse garage and patted the bonnet like an old friend. Once again, it had been very reliable and made the holiday and round trip of a thousand miles, an absolute pleasure and lots of fun.

Once back at home, I started work for Kolok and found that I had the use of a pink and cream Chevrolet which the previous salesman had bought and kindly allowed me to use whilst I found a car for myself.. It was surprisingly good. It had a flexible, six cylinder engine, soft suspension and very low geared steering. It was a bit 'Flashy' for me and not being British, it wasn't really my sort of car in those days. I wanted a modern open sports car and fancied a Sunbeam Alpine, so bought a smart red one with wire wheels. In those days the first motorways were just opening and there were no speed limits, so I could sit at 90mph all day in overdrive-top and really cover the ground. It was a first class car and gave me excellent reliable motoring and was a delight, with or without the hardtop, which came with it.

As is the case with all the jobs I have had, there is always lots to learn and especially with this one, covering much of the country and visiting many towns which I had not been to before. When in the Leeds area, I used to stay at a small private club called the Carlton Club in Bradford. There were some very enthusiastic vintage car members and in time, through them, I met people like Peter Black who was putting together quite a large collection of early motor cars.

Another chap, Brian Waddilove was a keen motoring enthusiast as was Peter Hepworth. His family were famous for their 'Hepolite' Pistons and Jet Engine Blades. He had branched out on his own however, to supply the specialist Vintage market. Some years later, in 1982, we were to join forces when we established Royle Hepworth and created our smart, vintage motor car sales Showrooms at Poole in Wharfedale near Leeds. This is described a little later on in the book.

After a while, the pleasure of driving every day began to wear 'thin', whilst staying in hotels all the time, had the opposite effect, I was rapidly putting on weight and getting fat. Not surprisingly, I also missed not being at home where there was always so much useful work to be done. I was earning a good salary and commission, but never the less, I resigned in July the following year in 1966, with a good reference.

THE INEVITABLE HAPPENS

Shortly after this, on a fine day in the summer of 1966, I was sailing with Brownie at the Old Church Club on Ullswater when, on coming ashore, I noticed two pretty girls sitting on the lawn. The winds were light and I wondered if they would like to come for a sail. One of them June, whom I knew, wasn't too keen, but the second girl said she would like to come, so off we went. It turned out that she was called Johan. I later discovered that this is an old Scottish name and is pronounced 'Jo-Ann'. It was a lovely sunny day, not always the case in Ullswater and without going into the romantic details, we both seemed to 'know' and a few hours later, driving home, I asked her to marry me and she said "yes".

People are surprised when they hear that this happened on the first day we met, but it didn't seem strange to us. Looking back it was, in some ways, easier for me to ask this than it was for Johan to accept. This was because I didn't have a family at home to confront with this unexpected news like Jo-Jo did, as I have called her ever since. I wrote to my Mother to tell her about it and I still have her reply expressing how surprised and pleased she was, I say this, but I also should have been surprised myself because, up until then, I was a confirmed bachelor.

I had been greatly enjoying my independence and had been fortunate in having some wonderful girlfriends. I was also very active in various organisations; the Gainford Drama Club, the local Conservative Association and also in Darlington Bondgate 999 Round Table, (of which I was a founder member). Along with these, I was also kept busy, as ever, with the work on my motor cars and boats, so much so that, until then, marriage had not even been on the horizon!

Living in the North of England, there is so much going on and the social life is marvellous. Looking through my old diaries, there were a never ending series of parties, dances and events, all tremendous fun.

Jo-Jo and I were engaged straight away and I wanted to buy her a decent engagement ring, so, in March 1967, I put my MK II Sunbeam Alpine up for sale in Motor Sport at a price of £425. Before it was in print however, my old friend Jimmy Blumer offered to sell it for me. Jimmy was one of the older local motor racing fraternity in this area. He had raced all sorts of machines including Austin Healey's at Le Mans. His description of this race was that it was boring! His biggest problem, he said, was being able to hide his cigarette below the door each time he passed the pits!

Jimmy was running a car showroom in Yarm at the time, but sadly, had to close it down shortly

MK II Sunbeam Alpine.

afterwards. He sold the Sunbeam however, and paid me out just before liquidating his business. Like Jo-Jo, he must have known that it was important for me to be selling such a good motor car and that I was serious! Despite the recent extreme anti-smoking campaigns, he still smokes like a chimney and whenever we meet is always good company when we share a 'fag' or two.

I soon heard that Jo-Jo's mother and father, Wheatley and Margaret Wilson were, to put it mildly, not at all thrilled at the engagement of

Jo-Jo extreme right at meet of the Zetland Hunt at Redwell Inn.

their on daughter to that 'dreadful playboy' Royle man. Some of the stories going the 'rounds' were as imaginative as they were untrue. As her parents are a well known farming family going back many generations, I think they were hoping for a son in law with a similar background. The idea of a person who seemed to spend most of his life with old cars, boats, and acting on the stage, was not their idea of the ideal husband. Actually, of course, part of our family were also from a farming background, but that was in the 17th and 18th centuries!

Jo-Jo's brothers, Ken and John, were always fine with me. Unlike me, Jo-Jo was most experienced with ponies and horses and enjoyed a good days hunting. She often instructed at pony club and has won many trophies for eventing. Her brother Ken was also an expert rider and won many point to point races. After a couple of years, Jo-Jo's parents must have decided that the situation could be worse and that I might not be that bad after all. Eventually 'Wheat' and Margaret 'came round' and bravely accepted me.

They generously gave us a wonderful wedding two years later, on 4th June 1968 when, with the blessing of Lord Londonderry, Jo-Jo and I were married at his private family chapel at Wynyard Hall. It was a lovely sunny day and the many guests came from all over the country. In the fullness of time, Jo-Jo's parents came to realise that I wasn't such a bad lot after all! (Sadly, neither of them were alive to see us celebrate our 40th wedding anniversary two years ago.)

Some people still think it surprising that we were engaged the first day we met, but we never doubted each other for a moment. It goes without saying, that Jo-Jo has been with me and supported me right down the line and has been wonderful. A great partner, standing by me through all sorts of events down the years. Some of which are included in this book.

With Brantwood Cottage, No. 5, The Green, being fairly small and a rented property, I was keen to find a house with a bit more room which we could buy. I wanted the security of owning our home, one which Jo-Jo and I could live in after we were married. We looked at one or two interesting houses in the area, especially those which needed renovating and would be relatively inexpensive. At the time however, our next door neighbour Dennis, had vacated No 6, the adjoining house to Brantwood cottage. Naturally the subject came up when I was talking to Robbo and he thought that it might be possible for me to buy both 5 and 6 along with No 4, the small Irishman's cottage which adjoined them. These happened to be part of Lord Barnard's estate which were originally hind's cottages occupied by the Robinson's farm men.

After further discussions with Robbo and Mr Pardoe, the Raby Estates agent, we were able buy all three, which overlooked The Green at Headlam and we planned to make them into one detached house. This was good, because I enjoyed living at Headlam and the local planners subsequently allowed us to make various improvements. It was when knocking through the intervening walls and making larger, south facing windows, that the local builders, Kendal and Moreland Charge, found that the size of windows which I wanted were already there, but had been filled in. Presumably it was because of the window tax in the late 17th Century.

CHAPTER 10: THE BACHELOR COTTAGE

The little Pack Horse bridge in Headlam with Brantwood cottage at the top of the Green still to be finished after the alterations.

When an upstairs wall was removed we found that the floor boards ran through the dividing walls between the two cottages, so it became clear that the two had originally been one house. Together they produced a four bedroom, two bathroom house with a good sitting room and dining room, a kitchen and 'snug'. We linked the two north facing wings at the back to form a utility room which overlooked their private walled garden. Not surprisingly, the cottage walls were damp in some places. The foundations were simply large boulders and there were no damp courses. So, in the sitting room, after the builders had finished their work, I panelled the walls with marine plywood (to BS 1088 specification I remember). Then, cutting into long lengths of specially rebated timber mouldings made for me by Brownie at the sawmills, I cut hundreds of mitre joints and created properly formed panels all round the room which I painted white. This brightened up the room considerably.

I then had a plain Tudor style stone fireplace made for me at nearby Dunhouse Quarry which was set off with a most handsome open fire grate with dogs which, as previously, our old neighbour Dennis made for me on his forge at Ingleton. The open beamed ceiling and double doors opening onto the dining room, made for a house full of character.

Brantwood cottage finished as one house.

Jo Jo

Jo-Jo after a good day on Foxtrot

CHAPTER 11:
JOBS AND RESTORATION

Returning to the subject of motor cars, my old Lagonda's and the wheel house garage in Headlam. By the late 1960's, after the building work was finished and Jo-Jo and I had refurbished Brantwood Cottage, I had been steadily progressing with the bodywork on 'PJ', but decided that I should carry out a complete restoration of 'GG' the special 3 litre Lagonda tourer. After six years of reliable and enjoyable motoring, I felt that the 'old girl' deserved to be fully restored. It was good to have the space in which to do the work, so I set about stripping it down to the bare chassis, so that I could thoroughly overhaul and restore all the components of the entire vehicle.

By this time I had sold the sunbeam Alpine, but had a company car, a Ford Cortina which had replaced the Ford Anglia supplied by RMC, the concrete supply firm, so I did have transport whilst working on the Lagonda. I should explain that this was due to the fact that Jo'Jo's parents had not been happy when, soon after I first met her, I had handed in my notice to Kolok in London. Through an old boyfriend, she had organised an interview for me with RMC, as they were looking to employ somebody to look after the contracts for 2 or 3 of their concrete supply plants near Durham.

I was successful at the interview and found myself closely involved with the construction of the dual carriageway which is the Durham Bypass and with all sorts of jobs and contracts, including regaining the contract for the supply of concrete to the nuclear power station at Hartlepool. Civil engineering was not really a subject which was close to my heart, but as with all jobs, there are interesting aspects and there is always much to learn. I produced some good figures and stayed with RMC for four years before leaving them and joining and working for my friends, the Wilsons in Darlington.

I had told Jimmy and his father Bob, that RMC were wanting me to move up to Northumberland which, although it is a lovely part of the world, would have meant Jo-Jo and I would have to leave Headlam, which we were not prepared to do and I left soon afterwards in February 1971.

Not long afterwards, Bob asked me if I would like to run the warehouse side of Walker & Wilson's in Darlington. This branch of their company supplied, from memory, around 1200 retail shops. It stocked all the stationary and other items which every newsagent's shop normally sells along with the Newspapers and magazines. Once again, a step change in the type of work which I had been doing, but after Kolok, I was not entirely ignorant of the retail business and so, on 22 March 1971, I set to with a will, to do my best for them. I am pleased to say that the systems I applied worked very well, and the turnover and profitability increased considerably.

But I digress, the restoration work to the Lagonda was, as ever, most interesting and as I stripped it down, the quality and design of the components again reminded me of just how well built these motor cars were. It was no effort to work every spare hour that was available. I found that hooks screwed into the conveniently low beams and ceiling of the wheelhouse, were ideal for hanging all the many freshly painted components where they could safely dry, without being disturbed or marked.

I would come home from the office, bathe and change into overalls and happily work on late into the night and at weekends. Most satisfying, especially knowing what a great motor car it is. I was able to examine all the components and could see why the steering and brakes are so good. For example, the handbrake always surprised those who tested the car for the MOT. It could easily lock up the wheels when many modern cars had hopeless handbrakes.

Remembering that the gearbox was a challenge on these Lagonda's, I also was able to inspect it and the Clutch Stop which was incorporated to help the driver. Once you knew the ratios and the technique, with practice and a gentle touch, you could actually change gear without using the clutch or the clutch stop, by 'feeling it in' with the correct engine revs.

Later in the book, there are a wide selection of photographs which effectively show what is involved with this sort of work, so I won't go into detail here, other than to say I found the car to be extremely original in virtually every respect. Even when rubbing down the body, after it had been removed from the chassis, I found that the original paint was still there and still in sound condition. After flatting it down, I simply applied two or three finishing coats over the top.

The complete 'ground up' restoration work took over two years, but the results were well worth it. The Lagonda was now in absolutely 'as new' condition and drove better than ever. Knowing every detail of any car is most comforting and in 1972, I enjoyed many more miles of first class motoring, attending rallies and events all over the country. Being such a handsome car and now in splendid condition, the car won many awards and it was a great pleasure to drive it.

Lagonda 1930 Special 3 litre after full restoration.

Cheshire Life Trophy, Oulton Park 1972.

One of the first 'jobs' was when I was asked by my Round Table to drive Harry Secombe in the Darlington Carnival Parade on 1 May 1971. This was a great thrill as he had given me years of fun in The Goon Show. I was able to chat to him for 2 or 3 hours sitting next to me in the Lagonda - marvellous.

Harry Secombe at Darlington parade 1 May 1971.

I was delighted with these events and to see 'GG' being such a success at the rallies which I was attending and this gave me the incentive to finish the work to 'PJ', the two seater sports Lagonda, and put it back on the road. This car had been steadily progressing before I focussed on 'GG' and restored it after completely stripping it down to the bare chassis.

Although 'GG' had taken hundreds of hours of work, I hadn't noted down what I had done or the time taken. This time, I decided to properly record all the jobs I was going to do, along with the hours of work needed with 'PJ'. Looking at the many pages of notes in my notebook, I can see that the work began in May 1972 and was finished in August 1974. As previously, I was usually working every evening after my 'day job', plus every available weekend, (except for parties too of course!). The total time spent over this period was 2,281 hours. I see that the MOT test was passed on 3rd September in 1974 and with various improvements to the engine and lighter body, when driving PJ, I found that it had better acceleration than 'GG' and performed very well. Because the car incorporated all the parts from the original saloon, it looked like a Lagonda, albeit a 'specially bodied' one.

At this time, I had been successfully running the warehouse for my old friends, the Wilsons, in Darlington for four years. Their company was in the process of some reorganisation, and I thought that if I was ever going to establish my own business, this would be the time to do it. I was now 33 and was keen to see if I could make a living out of restoration work which I found to be so interesting. I discussed the idea first with Jo-Jo of course and then with the Wilsons, who were reorganising their businesses and relocating. I explained to Jo-Jo that I didn't think we would make a lot of money out of it, but that hopefully, we might have sufficient to live on.

PJ and GG outside Brantwood cottage.

As ever, she had sufficient confidence in me to support the idea, so late in 1973, I placed a small, single column width advertisement in what we used to call 'the Bible', the 'Motor Sport' magazine. I wanted to see what the response would be. It was quite a decision for us to make, especially when there would no longer be a monthly salary cheque coming in and as our son, Jeremy was, at that stage, still only a babe in arms.

Because I had won quite a lot of trophies around the country with GG 8071, my car had become quite well known which I also thought might help, so the advertisement explained that I would be pleased to restore other people's vintage motor cars to the 'same standards as my own'. I was delighted by the positive response. I had enough enquiries for work which would keep me busy for four years! Altogether, It was a most encouraging result from such a small advert.

In those days, there were a few dealers in sports and vintage motor cars and one or two engineers who overhauled engines and did mechanical work, but very few people who set out specifically to provide a comprehensive restoration service. My aim was to set up fully equipped workshops, so that I could carry out high quality work and cover virtually every aspect involved with motor car restoration. I could see that by doing all the work 'in house' meant that it all would be under my control, rather than much of it being subcontracted, as was the often the case, and still is, with other restoration firms.

To start the ball rolling, I arranged to leave the Wilsons at the end of July 1974, finish 'PJ' and then, utilising my wheelhouse garage workshop in Headlam, I decided to begin the business by restoring the 1938 'Baby' Railton which belonged to Ken and Irene who lived not too far away in North Yorkshire. It was an ideal 'Job No 1 ' because it was a small, coach built motor car, based upon a Standard 10 hp chassis with which I was familiar. My old Standard Avon Special had a similar engine and running gear.

Working at the bench in the old wheelhouse workshop at Headlam.

Being a smaller car and less complicated than higher quality cars like Lagonda's, I estimated around £2,000 as the possible cost. When complete, including materials of £870.00, the actual cost was more than double the estimate. At £2.50 per hour, the charge rate in 1973, this was 1760 hours work. 500 hours less than the time taken with 'PJ' Lagonda. Incidentally VAT was 8% in those days, so the total cost was £4,752. Having visited me and followed the work as it progressed, they saw what was needed and appreciated what had been done. They have remained firm friends ever since and throughout the work, always brought with them a lovely tray of eggs for Jo-Jo and I. They went on to own some magnificent motor cars including some built before the first world war. We could not have wished to work for a better No. 1 customer!

1938 'Baby' Railton, the first commercial restoration carried out at the Wheelhouse Garage, Headlam. All photographs were taken outside due to not having a camera with flash or time exposure facility. Hence none showing (indoor) mechanical work-engine, axles etc.

1938 'Baby' Railton. Still like new 14 years later.

CHAPTER 12: THE OLD SCHOOL WORKSHOPS AT STAINDROP

The Lagonda with a brace of Jaguars at Raby Castle near Staindrop.

Although the workshop in Headlam had been fine for working on my own cars and the Baby Railton, it was clear that I would need more space to be able to run a professional business. I didn't want to be on an industrial estate, so I made various enquiries in order to find a suitable and secure building and found that there was an old disused school in Staindrop village which is only six miles from Headlam here in Teesdale.

It turned out that, originally, it had been a Sunday school built in 1841 by the Duke of Cleveland for the benefit of the village children. The north facing part of this Georgian style building is across the main street from St Mary's Church which dates back to the 11th century. Apparently, the early part was built by King Canute as does one of the towers of nearby Raby Castle I believe.

The Sunday School was extended in 1926 to the South, at the same time taking in the garden of the adjoining house. This provided space for extra classrooms to accommodate older children, also with space for a playground. It then became the village school. There are separate boys and girls lavatories and a cookery and domestic science building on the southern boundary. In the early 1960's a new school had been built nearby, leaving the old buildings empty.

When I first saw the Old School in 1974, it had been neglected for nine years. The whole place was in a sorry state. Although in the middle of the village, its high stone boundary walls concealed the vandalism and devilment of the youngsters who, it seems, had taken their 'revenge' for all the homework which they had to do. Many of the small multi-paned windows were smashed. The slate roofs had also been damaged and in places, the ceilings had been holed and school books were strewn all over the floors.

I asked my old friend, Bill Keighley if he would like to have a look around to see what he thought of the place. As we made our way through the classrooms, he stopped me, "have you noticed how uneven the floors are?" adding, "It is not entirely the hundreds of old books which we are walking on". The parquet floors beneath the holes in the roof and ceiling had absorbed the rain which had leaked through the holes. The wooden blocks had expanded causing them to lift. In places they were 5 to 10 inches off the concrete floor beneath. Bill, being ex RAF, was amused to think that "We are walking on air", but this was only for a few seconds before the blocks would collapse and a section of the hardwood blocks drop to the solid concrete floor beneath, taking us down with them.

Although the place was a dreadful mess, we could see the stonework was excellent. Looking into the various roof spaces and after examining all the buildings, we could see that, in fact, the school was well built and structurally as sound as a bell and would make wonderful workshops.

As the property was part of Lord Barnard's Raby Estate, I contacted the agent, Mr Pardoe, with whom I dealt previously when buying the cottage at Headlam. He was pleased that these derelict buildings might be put to good use once more. Lord Barnard himself is no stranger to vintage cars. He told me that, as a young man, he drove a vintage Bentley down through Africa, so was not averse to having vintage motor cars restored in the old school buildings.

When I approached the planners for change of use and the banks for facilities, however, neither of them were too sure about the idea. With the restoration of vintage cars, as a business, being in its infancy at that time and not understood, the former thought the old school might end up being a scrap yard, whereas the latter needed persuading that it would be a viable business. When I pointed out to the planners that the last thing I intended to do, was to scrap vintage cars and when I told the bank that there is no Capital Gains Tax on them, they both finally agreed to help me. A price was agreed with Mr Pardoe and so I was able to buy the Old School it in 1974.

Having given up my 'day job' in July 1974 and completed the restoration of the Baby Railton by August 1975, I was then able to apply myself to sorting out the old school buildings on a full time basis. Bill and other friends helped me with clearing away all the rubbish, broken glass, and piles of old school books.

Whilst the school buildings are not listed, they are quite handsome, so I kept the external

Starting work on the Old School after removing the rubbish.

alterations to a minimum. The planners were pleased about this, but I needed to create an access for the vintage motor cars so, as ever, Charge Brothers of Gainford, adapted two of the glazed classroom petitions to make the large double doors for access to the south facing buildings which overlooked the old walled-in play ground. They also enlarged the entrance gate off the back lane and fitted doors to the cookery and Domestic science building at the top of the yard. At the same time, they helped replace the many broken windows, mended the roof slates and repaired the holes in the damaged ceilings.

The classroom petitions proved to be most useful, as they could be relocated inside the building or removed as necessary, to provide us with different sizes of workshops wherever they were needed. The interior layout was therefore easily adapted as required, as the years passed.

One of the necessary jobs in the yard was bashing down the internal brick division walls in one of the school lavatory blocks. These were literally as tough as the proverbial brick 'miss and hit' house. This building was then ideal to accommodate the shot and bead blasting cabinets used for cleaning the rusty and corroded components. A good friend from Cornwall, St John Whitton, was roped in for this job on one of his visits up north, just the ticket for a Marlborough educated lad! Once the business was up and running, we restored his Speed 20 Alvis Tourer which is a most handsome motor car and which he still has and uses to this day.

Although the classrooms had very high ceilings, we retained and used the old school coke stoves for heating for quite a few years. Along with coke, we would be able to burn the off cuts of new ash timber and scrap rotten body frames to help with the heating. Ash timber is, of course, the 'Rolls-Royce' of timber for burning.

Sorting out the parquet floors.

Once all the building work had been done, we could see that the hardwood Parquet floors could be re-used and as they are excellent for working on, I wanted to restore them. This turned out to be a big job. As mentioned, most of the wood blocks were loose, so I set about lifting them all, hundreds of them, as I did so, I found that they had been laid on black bitumen which, with age, had turned to powder. They all had to be cleaned which was a big and dirty job and took ages, during which time, I was black with dust from head to toe. When this was done, I re-laid them all with the help of Hewitsons of Hull, the flooring specialists. This job alone, took us three weeks.

When they were all firmly back in place, I had them sandpapered down and I re-lacquered them which brought out the rich colour of the hardwood. Later on, I invited the Factory inspector to see the workshops and make sure that we had met the regulations. His first comment was to ask if we were planning to have ballroom dancing! The floors did look smart.

THE KEIGHLEY FAMILY

I would like to mention Bill Keighley again, he continued to be a great help to me and being retired, he spent a lot of time working with me helping to clear the whole place out, burning the rubbish, and helping with the painting and glazing. Bill, in fact, is a most knowledgeable motor engineer, his family had been one of the earliest motor dealers in the North of England. His father joining George and Jobling's motor business which was established in Newcastle in 1904 and was subsequently responsible for setting up one of the first garages in Darlington and Bishop Auckland, here in the North East.

Before the first world war Bill's father was the Main Agent for a number of important manufacturers;- Ford, Wolseley, Angus Sanderson, Argyll, Morris and even Blackburn Aeroplanes. In fact, after joining his father's firm, Bill became an aeroplane pilot in the 1930's before the second world war. Having already joined the Royal Air Force, he was flying at the outbreak of the war in 1939.

In 1941, he was returning from a raid over Germany in his Blenheim bomber when he was hit by anti-aircraft fire over Holland. He was losing oil pressure on one of his engines and Bill's rear gunner was badly hit and losing blood fast, so Bill turned round over the North sea and returned over the Dutch coast. He successfully landed the plane back in Holland in a cabbage field in the hope of saving his rear gunners life. Despite this, sadly, his crew man died and Bill spent the rest of the war in the German POW camp, Stalag Luft III. He survived the war and returned to join the family business, Keighley's Garage in Darlington. The business continued to be very successful and the company was sold in the 1960's.

Winter 1940-1941 POW 'Baltic Camp'. Photograph taken by hidden camera provided by John Whitton who was also a POW at Stalag Luft III like Bill. They poured water on the ground for the ice skating. The photo was given to me by his sons, St John and Bill Whitton.

Following in his father's footsteps, Bill's son, Jeremy, also took up flying as a career. He was a most enthusiastic and respected young pilot when, at the age of 22 and still under training, he was involved in this country's worst air disaster at that time. He was the Second Officer of the Trident 'Papa India' on 18th June 1972 when, only two minutes after take-off from Heath Row heading for Brussels, the plane crashed near Staines. He was killed along with all the passengers and crew on board. Not surprisingly the press was full of it and Bill, his wife, Dorothy and Jeremy's sister, Sue, suffered dreadfully as a result of all the publicity with people ringing up accusing Jeremy of killing their family and friends. This was long before the results of the investigation were known when the full circumstances which led to the accident became known and it was clear that the Captain, the Pilot in control, had suffered a heart attack on take-off.

Like my parents before me, we have been friendly with the family for many years and whilst he is over twenty years older than me, Bill and I have had many enjoyable trips involving my work with all the rare and wonderful motor cars which we have restored and dealt with. I like to think that this helped to fill the void left after the loss of his son. I still see Bill who is now 94 years old and is a dear friend, as is his daughter Sue and his nephew, Edward. As previously mentioned, I went to school with 'Neddy' Keighley who also has been in the motor trade for most of his life, and with whom I have had many interesting exploits!

Altogether the work to the old school took six months and it adapted well for the purpose of vehicle restoration. The domestic science building was divided and became our trimming department and paint shop. Adjoining it is a small building which had a concrete roof, this had been a cold store for food which turned out to be ideal as a licensed paint store for all our paints, flammable liquids and materials.

After the dark north facing Wheelhouse at Headlam with its cold concrete floor, I was looking forward to moving into the freshly painted workshops with their splendid shiny parquet floors. The south facing rural aspect of the buildings and the private yard with its high walls would make for an excellent, bright and cheerful working environment.

Over the years, I had been collecting together the machinery for the specialised work and continued to buy suitable machines whenever I could. These included wheeling, swaging, and powered weld crushing machines, also rolling, welding, folding, sewing and cutting machines. Shot blasting cabinets with dust extraction units, air compressors and many more were added as the years rolled by. As the heavy machinery was being moved in with a tractor, the last job we had to do was to make some robust work benches using timber which was laid around, these are still in use today.

CHAPTER 13:
A NEW ERA BEGINS

Needing money towards the cost of buying the old school, I had little choice, but to sell my second Lagonda PJ 4399. I arranged to do this by driving it down to the auctions which were then so popular at Alexandra Palace in London. It sold well making £4.300 on 21 November 1974. Bearing in mind that it had been a very thorough restoration, but with my own, non-original design of two seater body, this was still quite a good price. My plan to enjoy using it for competitions, rather than as an original restoration, had to go by the board to help with the cost of setting up a properly organised business.

I had made outline plans for the layout of the buildings and for the location of the machines. In fact, with around 6000 sq feet, I had more space than I thought I would need, but within a few months, the Old School soon filled up, from then on, we were always short of space!

The Old School comes back to life.

Wanting some sort of trade name and logo, I chose the obvious title of Vintage Motor Car Restoration, (VMCR) and registered it as a business name using a simplified impression of my Lagonda as the logo. The idea being that our work was sufficiently unique, at that time, to be able to use this as a trade name as well as describing what the business was all about. I dropped it later on however, because it was too 'wordy' and formed a limited company in 1983, David A. C. Royle & Co Ltd., emphasising the ROYLE name for adverts etc, which is short and has a certain 'ring' about it. It became known as 'Royles'.

The VMCR logo.

In January 1975 with the sun shining through the large school windows, I had the great pleasure of starting work in the freshly restored school buildings and of seeing them filling up with a wide range of marvellous and interesting motor cars. They were predominantly vintage and pre war vehicles and were to be the first of hundreds of fine motor vehicles to come into my 'new' workshops in Staindrop. Later on however, we also worked upon many post war sports cars and some more up to date, high quality machines. A complete list is included later in the book.

I had previously mentioned my ideas to Roger Tyrrell whom I met at the Gainford Drama Club. He is a vintage car enthusiast and used to come and help me with the restoration work at the old wheelhouse in Headlam. He was keen to come to work for me once the 'new' workshops were ready, so shortly after VMCR opened, Roger joined me.

We didn't have an office, just a telephone on one of the windowsills in the newly decorated and restored south facing workshop. To provide a finishing touch, I had a red carpet running in front of the long workbenches. With the polished parquet floors, high ceilings and large windows, it was a wonderful place to work and was the first space to be occupied. It was a real treat for me after the dark wheel-house.

Life in the 'new' workshops was good and as the year progressed, I had settled into the daily routine of driving to Staindrop and was enjoying the work and visiting customers to inspect their motor cars for potential new jobs. It was a much more interesting and rewarding way of life than being employed by others. Without thinking about it, I was working many hours a day and often arriving home late, but Jo-Jo happily put up with it and is an expert at keeping our supper fresh and hot, no matter how late it gets.

FILMING WITH MGM

Only a few months after settling in, during the summer of 1975, I had a telephone call from

Filming James Herriott's 'All Things Bright and Beautiful'. Eric Till directing Colin Blakely, John Alderton and Raymond Francis.

MGM. This well known film company wanted to use my Lagonda for a film they were making. It was based upon one of James Herriot's marvellous books about his experiences as a vet in Yorkshire. It turned out, not surprisingly, that they were filming locally, in the beautiful Yorkshire dales and were making 'All things bright and Beautiful' which was written the year before. They explained that they were filming during August, September and October and wondered if I would be available during October.

The idea of this appealed to me enormously, it sounded like a lot of fun and would be very interesting to see a film being made, especially being involved with one which is going out on general release. Now working for myself, I was free to decide what to do and, fortunately, I could nicely fit it in without upsetting the work which was going through the workshops. I was also going to be paid for it, which was helpful. I rang them back and told them that I would be pleased to bring the car and do whatever I could to help them.

The first day for me began early, as is often the case when making films. I was asked to drive into Darlington to pick up Raymond Francis from the Railway station. Ray, as I came to know him, was playing the part of Colonel Bosworth in the film and was best known for his part in the very successful, long running 1960's TV series, 'No Hiding Place'. This was when he played Detective Superintendent Lockhart of Scotland yard. The minute I saw him, he was immediately recognisable and I looked forward to working with him. Sitting next to me in the front seat, I had the opportunity to chat to him as we left Darlington and drove West towards Richmond and the dales. The early morning mist was clearing as we drove up the quiet roads in Swaledale and as we came to the higher ground, the sun came out in a clear blue sky on this lovely October morning.

Filming with Raymond Franicis in the Lagonda, 1975.

Ray was good company and kindly commented on how well the Lagonda was running. At times like this, the pleasure of driving such a splendid old motor car with the its rich exhaust note rumbling along behind, takes some beating. We wound our way up the valley until we reached Downholme, the appointed location where the filming was taking place. On the way, Ray told me that the reason for collecting him was that the Lagonda was to be 'his car' in the film. The Director wanted him to familiarise himself with it, so was killing two birds with one stone.

Funnily enough, we know Downholme quite well because Richard and Sue Calvert, who's farm it was, are old friends of ours. As we drove into the farmyard with its old stone buildings, we were confronted with a typical outdoors film set. There was a hive of activity with all the paraphernalia concerned with filming assembled in the farmyard. There were cables running everywhere with big lighting units and sound and other equipment being set up and quite a crowd of engineers, actors and other people who were involved. They all turned to see who was driving in and as they did so, Ray told me not to stop, but to drive into the middle of the 'circus'. As we did so, the entire crew began to sing the well known background theme music of Ray's 'No Hiding Place' TV series. There was a round of applause for him and it was a marvellous start to what everybody said was a most happy film. Apparently, this is not always the case.

One of the benefits of working with old motor cars is that I often found myself in some remarkable and most interesting situations. Not only looking on, as it were, but actually being closely involved and, as in this case, finding that I am being treated as one of the team. I went on to have four very enjoyable weeks with them all. The principle Actors along with Ray Francis, were John Alderton of TV fame, as James Herriot, Lisa Harrow as his wife, the famous Shakespearian actor Colin Blakely as Siegfried, Bill Maynard as Hinchcliffe and John Barret as Crump. I had plenty of time to chat to most of them and to members of the crew, especially on the rare occasions when it was raining. This was when we all retired to the caravans, always provided for the purpose when shooting at outdoors locations.

John Barrett for example, is a man who has been in so many films and plays that he is instantly recognisable. When I asked him why he appeared in so many supporting roles rather than the lead, he explained that he would not move from Manchester to live in London. He went on to tell me that he was content not to be a star when continuity of work and travel could be a problem. As I had seen, he was in constant demand and always working, playing character roles in film after film, a life which he enjoyed. He was a delightful person to pass the time of day.

After a mixed start as a footballer, coalman and salesman, Bill Maynard developed his career on the stage at working men's clubs, summer shows and the holiday camp at Skegness. By the 1950's, he had became famous as a marvellous comedian on TV and was extremely successful. I had come into contact with him before, in the early 1960's when, as ever, my friend Ian's father, John Hunter 'of the North', had asked me to drive him when he opening another of his chain of hairdressing shops. At that time, Bill had told me how hard work it was for him wherever he went. This was, he explained, because everybody expected him to be constantly funny. It was no surprise therefore, to see him again in the mid 1970's focussing upon his acting. A career in which he has been very successful and continues to be in demand with leading roles and with TV work. Again a most interesting and entertaining man.

I continued to spend quite a lot of time with Ray of course. He was trying to master the different layout of the controls of the Lagonda. As mentioned, the hand brake and gear lever, which operates in a 'gate', are on your right, the foot pedals are also different to all modern cars with the accelerator in the middle. The brake pedal is on the right and clutch pedal on the left. When shooting, I invariably had to set him off by standing on the running board and then

John Alderton with John Barrett.

running round behind the camera out of shot, so that I could jump on the running board again and help him come to a stop!

He was good fun to be with and on one occasion when we went to the Black Bull in Reeth for a lunchtime drink, I saw a wonderful example of his technique to ensure privacy. He was dressed in a tweed jacket which was not dissimilar to my own and we were standing at the bar with a couple of beers, when a chap from a nearby table came up and asked "Aren't you Raymond Francis?" Ray casually turned round and said, "funny you should say that, you are the second person that has said that today", "I must look like him". The chap apologised and went back to his friends at the table.

Another amusing occasion which comes to mind was when I was watching the second unit filming the scene. This is when a horse gallops off around a field which has more than its fair share of cow pats in it, with a stuntman being dragged behind it, hanging on to the Halter. In the film, it would be Herriot who is supposed to be covered from head to foot in cowshit, but after three takes, the horse was missing the cowpats every time and the poor man arrived back relatively clean , but rather bruised I imagine. For the fourth 'take', the man in charge of the animals, David Parker, offered to see if he could do it, so he grasped the halter and as before, one of the crew gave the horse a sharp smack on its rump and off it went again at full gallop. This time, we saw a remarkable demonstration of animal control as David was dragged through plenty of cowpats. He arrived back covered from head to foot in cowshit to the applause of the assembled crew. It was wonderful to see!

Then there was the day when Jo-Jo joined us all in Downholme itself. This was when the crew were filming Ray driving up the village street in the Lagonda. She had Jeremy with her and was watching the action from behind the camera when in the middle of the first 'take', a cloud masked the sun and there was the usual shout of 'CUT', the light had changed. There was a pause until the sun reappeared followed by shouts of 'camera turning', 'sound on' and the director called 'action!' and off we went again. This time there was the rumbling sound of a big Jet aircraft as it flew overhead - 'CUT' said the director Eric Till again. The period depicted by the film was just before the war in 1938, so big passenger jet planes had not been invented and I also noticed, whilst we waited for silence to return, that all the TV aerials had been cut off down the street. They certainly worked hard to keep the details right!

After ten minutes or so, 'Camera, sound, action !' again and this time things were progressing very nicely with a quiet conversation which we could barely hear behind the cameras, taking place around the Lagonda in the main street. This was until the quiet was broken by a loud sneeze, 'CUT', "who was that?" shouted the Director, Jo-Jo raised her hand like a naughty school girl, it had been Jeremy who had sneezed loudly, "off my set Please". The fourth 'take' then went smoothly, but at least Jo-Jo and Jem had seen a bit of the filming.

I could go on to relate more stories, but there is one final, little event which occurred at the "end of shooting" party at the Scotch Corner Hotel on the 6th November. I was in the 'gents' standing next to a man whom I had occasionally seen, but not spoken to, "What connexion did you have with the film" I asked, "nothing much" he replied, "I just wrote the books". It was Herriot himself, or more correctly, Alf White the vet who had actually written all the story's. As it happens, he was Jo-Jo's vet for many years when she was very active with the Hurworth Hunt Pony Club and she confirmed that he is indeed, a most unassuming and charming man.

Before leaving the subject of MGM and filming, I should mention that I was also fortunate in being asked to drive the Lagonda in the making of 'Agatha' in Harrogate. This was when Vanessa Redgrave and Dustin Hoffman were playing the lead roles in the film which was a fictional story of the time when Agatha Christy, disappeared. Unfortunately, with the action taking place within the confines of a busy town environment, there was not the same opportunity to spend as much time with the Actors and crew as when we were working in the remote areas of the dales.

I did have the opportunity to meet Vanessa and her children however, who were also there at times. One day, outside The Old Swan Hotel where they were shooting, Vanessa asked me if she, her daughters Natasha and Joely Richardson along with, whom I believe was her son, Carlo Nero (the son of the actor, director Franco Nero) could have their photograph taken in the Lagonda, "Of course" I said and

The author with Vanessa Redgrave and family in 'GG'.

told them to climb in.

Once they were all sitting down, I closed the doors behind them and was just starting to walk away when she called me back saying that she wanted me to be in the car with them as well, so I climbed into the front passenger seat next to young Carlo who was 'the driver'. Within no time at all, a 'wall' of photographers appeared, it was obviously the photo opportunity they had all been waiting for. The photograph included here, records the event with me enjoying the 'reflected glory' of it all. Actually, it is an interesting record of the family who went on to become so well known in their own right. Sadly, Natasha died in a skiing accident in 2009.

LEAVING HEADLAM

After we were married, we had happily lived in Headlam for ten years when Jo-Jo spotted a 'For Sale' sign outside the Old Vicarage which faced onto the village green in the nearby village of Gainford. After the years of alterations, building work and the filthy job of sorting out the Old School buildings, I was not very keen to start all over again and I was, by now, very busy at the time, with the restoration business in Staindrop, but Jo-Jo pestered me until I would go with her to see it. It was a large, old stone building which we had last visited when we had arranged to have our Banns read out at St Mary's church which stands next to the house. We made an appointment to view the house and were greeted by the Rev Hugh Defty who was having the new modern vicarage built in the vegetable garden, this was why the old vicarage was being sold. As we walked in, I was amused by his opening remark when he asked us why we were interested in such a "dreadful, cold barn of a place."

Looking round, it certainly was in need of a lot of work and some TLC, but had the tremendous attraction to me, as a vintage motor car enthusiast, of having all its original features. There were the handsome marble and slate fireplaces, lovely ceiling mouldings, original Georgian panelling and door furniture. Historically, it turned out that there had been a building on the site since the 12th century when the first incumbent, Bernard de Balliol, lived here. He later left Gainford to build himself a castle further up the valley, now known as Barnard Castle.

The north facade of the present building is Georgian and dates from the early 18th century, but the house has been enlarged with substantial Regency and Victorian additions. These provide the house with rooms which vary in scale from the beautifully proportioned, high ceilings of the elegant Regency Drawing and Dining rooms with their large south facing, multi-paned windows, to the north facing rooms with open fireplaces in the earlier parts of the house. The features which let it down were the lack of a proper kitchen, a primitive, but original Victorian bathroom to serve its many bedrooms and the fact that the north facing Georgian sash windows had been replaced with later, plain, four paned sash windows which didn't suit the house at all.

Virtually the whole of the interior had brown varnished woodwork and the walls had been covered with lining paper which had turned brown with age. Some of the fireplaces had been filled in with coke stoves fitted and others, with tiny, tiled fireplaces. It must have been impossible to heat as there was no central heating or carpets. The vicar's desk sat in isolation on the bare wooden floor in the centre of what is the drawing room, one of the larger spacious rooms. There were four wires leading to it from different corners of the room, each with an electric fire at the end of it. It was a depressing sight, as was the whole of the interior of the house. This was the case from the ancient wine cellars up to the old servant's bedrooms on the top floor, making four floors in all. Despite this, we were both excited by the wonderful opportunity it presented for us, but it would be a lot of work.

In what had been the stables in the old, adjoining coach house, I couldn't help noticing that there was a pit, for working underneath motor cars, sunk into the cobbled floor. There also were some outhouses including the old harness tack room with its early fireplace, set pot and wooden hooks for the harnesses. There was also a small workshop which would be useful. We were then shown into the garden which faced south and overlooked the Tees valley. It had been neglected and the gravel paths had become so overgrown, they were barely discernable from the un-mown lawn.

There was the trunk of a large dead tree standing near the house, but It was when we strode down to the end of the walled garden that any doubts were cast aside.

There before us, was the most beautiful stretch of the River Tees glistening in the sunlight as it tumbled over its rocky bed to a deep pool below us. The final decision- making process was complete. There was no doubt that the garden and the house could be restored and would make a most wonderful, practicable and elegant place in which our growing family could live very comfortably.

The Old Vicarage was to be auctioned at the Kings Head Hotel in Darlington a fortnight later. I spoke to Charge Bros the Gainford builders who knew the house well, their family firm having worked in the village for a hundred years. They told me that the only structural fault was a rotten beam in the cellar. I then spoke to my building society, who told me that a mortgage for such a property would be impossible. We were in a period then known as 'doom and gloom' and they also explained that their refusal was due to part of the building being let. The Blythe family had been occupying the west end of the house since 1947. I rang three more building societies, but the response was the same. Whilst this was bad news, I thought that it might actually have a silver lining, that is if I was prepared to take a risk.

I didn't have any time to put our own house on the market, but It meant that the number of potential buyers for the old vicarage would be very few indeed, so I asked a friend who was involved with finance, who said that he would lend me the necessary money if I needed it. I then spoke to the well known local auctioneer, Peter Bainbridge, who had been instructed by the church commissioners to sell the house and he, like the vicar, asked why we should want to buy such a terribly depressing place. Finally, I asked my old friend Barrington Wearmouth, who was also dealing with all sorts of properties, what chance would I have of selling Brantwood Cottage and would he like to take it on for me? He said that I should easily be able to sell it myself, because it had so much charm and character, so I immediately put an advert in the local press.

We duly arrived at the auction on the day of the sale and my first assumption proved to be completely wrong. There must have been over 150 people there, including local developers who knew that there was planning permission to convert the old Vicarage into three houses. The bidding started very low and was increasing by £2000 each time, but I refrained from joining in. It soon stalled however, still at a very low figure. The church Commissioners repeated the description of the property, but there were still no increased offers, so the auctioneer, Peter Bainbridge, then repeated the particulars all over again and this time, when he had finished, looked very pointedly at me.

By now I was standing on my own by the double glazed doors along the side of the hotel ballroom where I could see who was bidding. Jo-Jo had to go out because our little boy, Jeremy, who was just a babe in arms, was being noisy. She could see my back through the glass door and when Peter looked at me, all I had to do was blink and this time, instead of going up in steps of £2000, he added just £1000 to the existing bid and after asking around once more, he promptly knocked it down to me. There was a roar and applause in the hall and Jo-Jo, not having seen me flinch, came in and asked why I hadn't bid for it. She was astonished when I said that I did and that the house was ours! A broad grin spread across her surprised expression.

It turned out that the previous offer to mine was only £1000 below the reserve which the Church Commissioners had agreed with the auctioneers, which was why Peter was happy, with my bid he could complete the sale.

We paid the deposit immediately after the auction, but the new Vicarage was not quite finished, so the vicar asked if he could continue to live in the old house for another two or three months. This suited us as well, since it gave us time to sell Brantwood Cottage. As luck would have it, the mini 'Doom and Gloom' period in 1977 disappeared within a matter of weeks and we sold the cottage for £3000 more than we had paid for the old Vicarage. We were obviously meant to have it and my building society eventually provided me with a mortgage after all. All-in-all, we had been very lucky.

As soon as the Rev Defty moved into his new house, we set about the rewarding experience of restoring this most interesting old vicarage. We began with those rooms which would be likely to be left until the end and possibly never done, those at the very top of the house. As the work proceeded, we gradually moved from room to room moving down from the top floor. Jo-Jo was painting and decorating solidly for the first twelve months. We had lots of help from 'Pips' our marvellous 'daily' and from many friends, I was very busy with business matters but was decorating all the high and risky parts, like the hall and top windows, balancing on triple extension ladders with planks and the like.

As the work progressed, it was wonderful to see the house coming back to its former glory. The coke stoves and small, tiled fireplaces were carefully removed, central heating installed and I carefully cleaned the marble fireplaces. The newly decorated rooms then had carpets fitted for the first time and the atmosphere of the house changed completely. Visitors to the house were surprised how it had become such a homely and cheerful place and realised just how elegant the rooms were.

After the initial work, we carried on down the years refining and improving it all. One summers day, before the north facing four pane windows were removed and replaced with correct twelve pane Georgian ones, I was mowing the lawn overlooking the village green. I had my usual old clothes on when a passer-by presumed me to be the gardener (which I am!), asked me who lived in this "dreadful looking" house, adding that it looked like an institution of some sort. I agreed with him and said "it must be awful", he walked on.

In fact of course, we have greatly enjoyed living here for over thirty two years as I write and during this period, we have added a splendid conservatory and continued to improve the house. We were extremely lucky to have been able to buy such a wonderful place and at the right time and price.

As this part of the story has developed into events about personal matters, I will include a few more snippets about our two boys, Jeremy and Nicholas, who are now in their thirties. Beginning with Nick still laid in his pram when we were decorating, the edges of which are still ragged where he chewed them with being so bored. They grew up in the Old Vicarage and as children, they would swim in the river with me and we even had a punt made with which we

Barney boys smoking in school lavs.

could explore the various beautiful reaches of the Tees. They also shared in all the fun with the old motor cars and living with us on board the boats during the holidays. As they grew older, they were a great help to me and Jo-Jo, crewing when we were sailing and helping with the jobs around the house. They have lots of friends and were good at sports and enjoyed their life at Barnard Castle School, probably too much at times! Jeremy became quite 'famous', firstly as an unofficial school potato crisp supplier. This 'business' eventually failed when there was a serious litter problem at the school with all the empty crisp packets. He actually ended up by being made Head Boy, and went on to study at Bristol.

Nick was better known for being a bit of a renegade. He used to smoke in the school lavatories and was also known for his motorcycle exploits, including riding in competitions like The Scott Trial and the 'Scottish Six Day' events. And later motor cycle racing with his Enduro competition bike in one or two of the big national and European events. After helping me at the workshops with various jobs including some of the R&D work, building the amphibious prototypes, Nick worked in Australia for a year and then came back to run the amphibious project at our new 'starter factory' near Winston. I tell you about this project later in the book. It was good having him there and I was delighted with the efficient methods he employed. He is popular with all the people who know him.

Both boys have been free, like I was, to follow their own interests and in due course, have gone their own way in life, but Jo-Jo and I are

Richard Brown with quadruple SU Carbs off his Straight Eight Delage.

pleased that each of them has now settled down within a few miles of us and they have given us four wonderful grandchildren, so although I am trying to wind down, life seems to be busier than ever! They all call in regularly and 'the boys' will always help me with anything which needs a bit of muscle power.

BACK TO THE WORKSHOPS

Not long after opening up, Richard Brown came to see me. He was an experienced motor engineer and a keen vintage motoring enthusiast. He was a great character, was always entertaining and a friend whom I had met at various rallies and functions and who later joined me filming in the dales when they wanted one or two more vintage cars. He was also a well known local publican and was always full of fun and can best be described as looking exactly like Father Christmas. He had a large white beard, rosy cheeks and a rotund figure to match.

Over the years, I had seen him driving various vintage machines and It turned out that he had a small collection, some of which he regularly drove and obviously much enjoyed. Richard offered to come and work for me, without payment, on condition that he could bring some of his cars and use some of my facilities to work on them. We had plenty of room and I thought it was a good idea. Using some of the glazed partitions, we set up a small machine shop near the double doors for him and whilst he would not be there every day, he worked on our cars as well as his own. He was fun to work with, he was a knowledgeable man and I was happy to have his help and to be able to accommodate him and his cars.

The old school classrooms in this part of the building were nearly 6 metres high, So there was sufficient height in this long workshop to install a large 'shelf' on which we could store bodywork whilst working on other parts of the cars. This was hung from the strong rafters in the roof by scaffolding tubes. In the fullness of time, we also installed a Four Post Bradbury Lift by the main doors, next to Richards machine shop.

From the time we opened up at Staindrop, Roger and I had been kept very busy with plenty of work ahead of us and still coming in. One day we were, as usual, sitting next to the coke stove one lunchtime, discussing the work, when we agreed that we could really do with another man to help us. By sheer coincidence, the following day, a young man called Dick Francis walked into the workshop, he had married a local girl and had come to ask if we had any vacancies. He was very much the typical Londoner and told us that he had been working in London with all sorts of motor cars, mainly repairing the bodywork. I don't know how he found us, but I thought I should give him the chance to prove himself, so employed him on a three month trial basis.

He was enthusiastic and enjoyed doing body work. He could weld thin sheet steel and aluminium, was keen to learn and I was able to impress upon him that we were aiming to work to the highest standards. Working alongside him, I showed him the techniques of traditional coach building with wooden framework and how to use various wheeling and swaging machines. Machines which are not normally used nowadays with modern monocoque bodywork. Dick has a lot of natural aptitude and as time passed, he picked up and became skilled with the wide range of jobs which our kind of work involves. Like most of the people who joined us, he was to work with me for many years. With his typical cockney accent, he became known by the men as 'Cocky Dick' and whenever photographs were being taken, he would often be there in the foreground, posing as if he had done all the work to the cars himself, typical!

Some years later, after our old friend, Richard Brown had sadly died, the machine shop was relocated to the front of the building where Allan was able to gradually upgrade the machinery. Allan is a gifted man who came to work for me at Staindrop in October 1979. He had a great deal of experience with light and heavy engineering work and had a broad spread of knowledge, including electrical work, steam engines and all aspects of motor car work and engineering. He also enjoyed boating as a hobby which was helpful later on. He brought his small lathe with him and helped to set up the new machine shop. This workshop adjoined the trim shop which was also relocated to the front of the building. Both were partitioned off from the long central workshop.

As more people were gradually taken on, not surprisingly, the workload in the office increased, so we had a small office built into the little enclosed yard which was linked to and convenient for the main workshop. This was fine for a while, but as we gradually expanded, by 1979 we needed some help in the office, this is when Judith joined us. Judith proved to be a wonderful, reliable and conscientious secretary and a great help to me in many ways. She also helped Roger with the books and was always popular with the staff and our customers.

Judith.

As we became busier and gradually took on more staff, more space was required and we realised that we could replace the body 'shelf'

DR and the team.

with a full width, strongly built mezzanine floor. On this we would also be able to park complete vehicles. So we employed Mechtool of Darlington, who constructed and installed a free standing, sturdy, steel floor which would support the weight of 150 tonnes.

We had previously installed a Bradbury lift which, as well as being used for working underneath and servicing the cars we could, by using two removable, sloping, steel ramps from one end of it, just manage to push or drag vehicles up onto this new floor. This method worked, but was rather risky, because the lift wouldn't reach the height of the new floor, so vehicles would often have to be hauled and pushed up the sloping ramps.

With wide gaps around the lift and the ramps, any of us could easily have fallen through, but fortunately didn't! Not even Don, who by now had joined us along with his long standing workmate, Jim, in the paint shop, had not done so. Don is an excellent engineer, is gifted and did a lot of wonderful work, but tended to be accident prone. Never the less, with just over two metres clearance under the roof beams, by using this method, this new floor was capable of accommodating up to twelve cars.

The steel floor was later extended to meet a screw type garage lift which we acquired and was much needed. This was because it would reach high enough to line up properly with the Mezzanine floor. It was much safer and a great improvement and at the same time, enabled us

Irene. 1989 in the new, unfinished offices.

to enlarge the steel floor to create even more storage space, some of which was partitioned off and made into a good tea room.

At times, this upper floor has also been used as a workshop, especially by the men who were not too tall. Neil was one who, after he joined us and was working in the main shop for quite a long time, also made himself a good little workshop up there for a while, He was an excellent motor engineer and a devoted enthusiast and enjoyed working on the wide range of cars which came to us.

Although the values of Vintage and Classic motor cars had been climbing steadily in the 1970's, there was a real boom in their values during the 1980's and with Royles having become established and well known by then, we were in a good position to take advantage of the additional business. I increased the workforce to 19 staff during this decade, so I needed and was able to afford to further improve our facilities and the amount of working and storage space for the men and cars.

This was all to the good, but we were now very cramped and short of space in the office and with all the workshop dust and dirt which seemed to accumulate, we needed to improve our conditions.

It is ironic that, by 1988, with the company continuing to expand, the staff were the ones who were now enjoying the bright sunny workshops and we were working in this dark and grubby little room. Not surprisingly, I was keen to improve matters and make life more pleasant for the 'office workers', but will tell you about this later on.

As a result of the restoration work, our customers would sometimes ask if we could store their cars, others asked if we could supply them with cars, or buy or sell theirs. Whilst this was not what I had aimed to do, this side of the business developed and I bought the old Methodist Chapel on the south side of Staindrop Green and also arranged storage facilities with friends who had secure space available. These were at a farm near Winston, another at Headlam and some garages at Streatlam Park. Altogether, we were then able to accommodate around 60 motor cars, all under cover of course.

Harry Pickles on the right, with John Harding who was his assistant.

One of our growing team of skilled men was Harry Pickles who worked for the local builders. Knowing what my business was, when

Building the paint shop at Staindrop.

he was building a garage for us at home in Gainford, he had asked me if he could come to work for me. Harry lived locally and had previously been employed as an engineer in the mills in Yorkshire. Having seen how he tackled the problems associated with the stonework on our listed property, including a stone roof which stands as a tribute to his skills with masonry, I was pleased to offer him a job. He joined us in 1983 and proved himself to be as competent an engineer as he was a builder.

As the company developed during the 1980's and early 1990s, Harry was to play an important role in all the further improvements which were carried out at Staindrop. I had asked the excellent Teesdale architect, Norman Pooley, to draw up plans for a new building to adjoin the old Domestic Science department which was by then, as mentioned, divided, and being used as our paint and trimming shops at the top of the yard. This new building was to accommodate the large, new and specially built Dolby Paint Booth and Bake Oven. Harry was pleased to do all the building work and happily set about it with the help of an assistant John Harding, whom we took on to share the heavy work.

Working in the roof.

The support beams go in.

The offices take shape.

The new building was finished in good time, complete with under floor filter chambers and overhead ventilation ducts. The Dolby booth was a great improvement and was to provide us with a marvellous facility for synthetic enamels, cellulose painting and baking modern two pack and isocyanate paint finishes. This is when Jim joined our company, his reputation went before him as one of the most skilled painters in this region and it was he who recommended that we improve our painting facilities. He worked to the highest standards and proved himself to be as good as anybody in the country.

During this time, I had also asked Norman Pooley. to draw up the plans to build new offices in the roof of the main building. There was plenty of room up there and by utilising wall thickness and working within the roof trusses, we could create some spacious South and North facing offices. With very careful design and use of space, there was just enough room to incorporate two staircases giving access to the offices from both the front and rear entrances of the buildings. This is an important feature as I didn't want visitors and delivery people walking through the workshops.

Working with stone, Harry, helped again by John, built up and altered the South facade in such a way, that it was hardly noticeable when compared with the original walls adjoining his work. He removed the large windows and built in smaller ones to suit the new offices. The alterations to the roof itself were so complex that Norman was concerned about it, but Harry took them in his stride and they have never leaked since he built them. The two new staircases were made in Pine, were varnished and were set off nicely with two Parana Pine poles which Harry incorporated into the hand rail on the upstairs lobby. The leather hides used to be rolled round these poles when delivered to us. A neat link with our restoration business, which I liked.

When finished, we had three good offices with windows facing South over the yard and North to the front gate. We had agreed that Harry should insulate the office floors against noise with three inches of sand, he did this and it worked well. Harry also opened up a door from the new upstairs lobby, onto the steel Mezzanine floor and it was then that he also built in a tea room and storage racks for parts. He also created a doorway from the steel floor for access onto the original front stairs which went to the upper

Edna in the trim shop.

floor of the original Sunday school building which face the church across the main street.

When this work was finished in 1989, most of the main buildings were two storeys and we had a lot more office space as well as workshop and storage space for the cars. I now had my own office, and Roger and Irene occupied the central main open office area with the north facing room being used as Royle Cars sales office. By this time, Piers Leigh had joined the company to run this side of the business and occupied this new room. At last, we had bright, clean and more efficient offices which were looked after by Edna, who had originally joined us to help in the trimming department. As time passed, she and Irene took control of the domestic side of the business. She was popular with the customers and visitors and would look after them and try to control the men and keep the tea room tidy. They shared the vacuuming and she would help out in our trimming department and wherever she was needed.

Soon after the new offices were finished, Irene left us to have her baby daughter, Katy, so was only able to enjoy the new, clean environment for a few months. Naturally, we were very sorry to lose Irene after so many years. In the fullness of time however, she was to come back and resume her work with the accounts, my correspondence, my diary and looking after our customers and visitors. She also was involved typing out some of the early chapters for this book.

Roger continued with the daily records and other aspects of the accounts. He also shared with Allan, the work of maintaining stocks and materials and was involved in the constant search for rare and special components, materials and everything the men needed to progress the increasing number of jobs passing through the workshops. Whilst I was the main contact for all our customers, later on, Roger also shared some of this work with me and was popular with them all.

When visitors to the office were taken to see their cars, we would often walk across the lobby onto the steel floor where they were surprised to find motor cars 'upstairs', there being no obvious means of getting them up there!

CHAPTER 14:
VINTAGE MOTOR SALES

With the increase in business, and with other restoration firms setting up, mainly further South, the 'VMCR' title, registered in July 1974, did not clearly identify us any longer. So it was, that exactly nine years later, the restoration business was registered in July 1983, with Companies House, as David A. C. Royle and Co. Ltd., more commonly known simply as 'Royles'. At this juncture, I think that I should also explain the story behind the formation of Royle Hepworth and later, my other company, Royle Cars Ltd, both of which were registered at Companies House. They were involved in the entirely separate activity of specialist motor car sales rather than restoration work.

From the beginning, I derived great pleasure from seeing a car being restored to 'as new' condition. When VMCR was established, my aim was to focus on top quality work with profit not being the principle aim. My philosophy was that high quality would always attract customers and to minimise hassle, the company would be run with an open books system, so that customers would know what was done and that the charges were fair and reasonable. I wanted to continue to enjoy the work and the quality of life in rural Teesdale.

Not being involved with sales, meant that there was no need, and I had no desire, to move into a large conurbation to become a trader in old motor cars. There is also a serious conflict of interest between smartening up a car to make it look its best in order to sell it for a profit, as against proper, in depth, restoration work.

I felt that It was important for people to understand the nature of my principal business so, early on, I had registered David.A.C.Royle & Co Ltd with the Museum and Galleries Commission and later, with the United Kingdom Institute for Conservation.(UKIC) The linkage with museums opened the door to the rare and wonderful machines in their charge. When we carried out restoration and conservation work for them, we naturally had to conform with their requirements which included keeping detailed records. We were doing this anyway, so it wasn't a problem. Their work was especially interesting but, like the majority of our work, it was not very profitable, if at all.

Our customers respected our close and in-depth involvement with Vintage and early motor cars and later, also with Classic cars. They expected and were always given, an honest appraisal of their market values. I could not contemplate the idea of taking advantage of people who trusted me, not to under value their motor cars when I was buying them and then charge more for them and make a profit when I sold them at a higher price. It may be commercial practice, but it was against my principles and did not sit comfortably with the restoration business.

As the business grew however, some of our customers would ask me to buy or sell their cars for them. I wanted to help and indeed with our small margins, we really needed to have additional sources of profit. Normally therefore, rather than buying the cars, I would offer sell them for the owners on a commission basis. It then remained an 'open books' relationship which suited my mentality and my business. It also minimised my bank borrowings of course. Over the years the amount of sales business increased, so I was always on the look-out for additional storage space.

ROYLE HEPWORTH

After seeing my ongoing sales advertisements in most of the specialist motor car magazines, my old friend Peter Hepworth of Piston 'Fame', asked me to meet him early in 1982 to discuss his ideas. He was thinking about setting up a vintage and classic car sales business near Leeds and wondered if I could give him some advice. I had met Peter through my Yorkshire friends in the early 1960's and whilst Royles were in regular contact and obtaining all our pistons from him, it was good to see him again. We had various meetings and agreed to join forces and decided to call the business 'Royle Hepworth'. This new business was beneficial to both of us, it was to be near to a heavily populated part of the country, it would transfer the sales cars away from the restoration work at Staindrop and Peter would have the time to run it and we could share the profits.

We found an ideal empty building at Poole in Wharfedale which backs onto the river and is near a junction of the main road to Harrogate from Leeds. We cleaned out and decorated the buildings and had the benefit of attractive and

Royle Hepworth, Poole in Wharfedale.

spacious offices upstairs. Peter moved into these offices full time, with his secretary, Joan, to run the new company, along with his Piston Business, on a day to day basis. I also had a desk there and we agreed that I would visit the showroom regularly and advise Peter and help him to keep a good supply of suitable period motor cars to fill the showrooms.

Joan at Royle Hepworth, Peter's secretary.

To make them attractive and furnish them, we had paths laid and then spread white gravel between them, on which we parked the cars for sale. I brought down some proper old Museum Display Cases along with some period display items and some large photographs and vintage petrol signs to add some 'colour' to the show rooms. Outwardly, there were no large showroom windows of course, since passing trade is not a likely source of much business and with some valuable vehicles in stock, security is always foremost in our minds. Those who are seriously interested in buying, make appointments or knew where we were. Also on the ground floor, was a useful

Royle Hepworth. D.R. and Peter with various displays of fine motor cars.

separate preparation area which was where a friend of Peter's, Jake, worked to test, check and prepare the vehicles for sale. Any specific mechanical work required was carried out at Royles workshops in Staindrop.

Importantly, I was able to bring a good selection of desirable veteran and vintage motor vehicles to stock the new showroom whilst Peter began to tap into his many contacts in the area and around the country. We opened up with a good

The Lotus Eclat.

display of vehicles, twenty three motor cars altogether and had a Grand Opening Party when the local press gave us good coverage. At the time I was looking for another interesting motor car for personal transport and asked Peter to see if he could find something for me. The result was a Lotus Eclat complete with 'go faster' stripes. This was a fast and interesting machine with remarkable road holding. Jo-Jo wasn't overly impressed, but it was a good machine.

The company ran well and after two years, Peter wanted to buy me out. Although we got on well together, all the driving around the country to inspect motor cars, plus the trips down to Poole and back every week, was all rather time consuming, especially as we were also very busy at Royles. We agreed a figure and parted company after an interesting and amicable working relationship.

I continued to send him my contacts and information about suitable motor cars for the 'RH' showroom but, like me, I don't think he had sufficient time for all the travelling which is necessarily involved in following them up. He eventually closed 'RH' down a couple of years later to focus on his Piston business which like Royles, also continued to be very busy, but we still keep in touch.

ROYLE CARS LTD

Because restoration work is so time consuming and despite minimising the rates charged to our customers, it is still a very costly exercise when the work is done properly. It was important therefore, that I kept looking at ways to try to expand and create additional business and profits. I wanted to utilise the skills and equipment in our core business, so to broaden the base of our activities, I had the idea of building first class, accurate, half-scale, driveable cars for children. In Allan Barkley, we had just the man to build the prototype, he is a clever engineer and enjoys a challenge. Allan runs our machine shop and like many of my team, is multi-skilled and with his hobby having been building model steam locomotives, he was ideally suited to build the prototype of a large scale model.

Well known Lagonda club members visit Royle Hepworth soon after opening.

After careful consideration, I thought that a model of an 1920's Austin Seven Chummy would be an ideal subject to start with. These were to be not so much a toy, but more of a motor car in miniature. They were to be well built and accurately scaled and drivable by children who would be using normal brake and accelerator pedals as well as a scaled down steering wheel. A youngster would then become accustomed to driving, and from an early age, know how to drive a real car.

They had a proper steel chassis, a sealed aircraft battery powering a 12 volt electric motor. It would have rack and pinion steering, electric brakes, a GRP body with working headlights and a horn. Also fitted was a removable bonnet, a cast alloy Radiator, inflatable tyres with a spare wheel, a wind screen and a folding canvas hood. When finished this lovely little car really looked 'the business'. Even an adult could just get in to drive it.

When finished, the Prototype was wheeled out into the yard for the first time, the men gathered round to watch its very first 'road test'. Allan, who is no lightweight, proudly squeezed into the little seat, switched it into forward drive, (it also had reverse), took his feet off the brake pedal, pressed the little accelerator and sure enough, it pulled away in great style. He had only gone just a few feet however, when the front axle parted company. The little car scraped to an abrupt halt and Allan fell out and ended up lying in the yard. We couldn't help laughing as we had just witnessed the smallest car accident anybody could have! It was a case of out with the welding gear and then further testing. Allan's work is good, but like the rest of us, he is not perfect!

In fact, when finally finished, it was a fine, handsome and well built little machine. I made contact with British Leyland who owned Austin at that time and when they saw what a splendid and accurate model it was, they granted me permission to call it an 'Austin', so we put proper, scaled down Austin badges on it, quite a compliment! Plans were then made to start a limited level of production, so in 1985, I registered another company, Royle Cars Ltd to be a separate business from the main company and deal with the sales of our own products.

Nick road testing the childrens Austin 7 Chummy prototype.

Shortly afterwards, I took the first little Austin home for a proper boy, my younger son Nick, to test it. He was nine years old at the time and he drove it up and down the little road outside the house next to the village green. The BBC took some film of it which I still have. I also 'launched' it at a dinner party one night at home. Putting out all the lights in the room, I squeezed into the little seat and drove it from the Drawing room, across the inner hall and into the Dining room with its little headlights 'blazing'. Well, it is not every day that you can drive a car in the house!

The ideal person to build these small motor cars was Harry Pickles who, with his engineering skills, was perfectly suited to this refined assembly work. He had worked in the Yorkshire woollen mills as an engineer and always being conscientious in whatever he did, I knew he would make a good job of them. I didn't want to have them being built alongside the real cars in the main workshops, so Harry set about creating what must have been the smallest 'car factory' in the North. He converted the Old School girls lavatory block into his workshop!

The smallest car factory in the country!

A second version of our Royle Cars model followed the actual history of Austin sevens in that the original Austin cars had also been built under licence in Germany before the war. They

The BMW version.

Small scale production of Royle cars.

were 'badge engineered' to be the BMW version of the 'Chummy'. We built this version ourselves of course and painted the BMW models white and these were sold through the BMW main dealer in Newcastle upon Tyne.

We also built a few Austin Chummy Vans, the roof lifted off these, so that youngsters could sit inside to drive them like the cars. In all, over

Little to Large, Austin 3½, Austin 7 and Austin 20.

thirty Austin models were built and sold by various organisations and agents. I wanted them to be top quality and properly engineered, but being built to such a high specification, they were costly. I was originally aiming them at people in the Professions, many of whom ran Austin 7's as students. At around £3,000 each they, were too costly for this market, never the less we sold over 30 of them. Some were sold via motor dealers and some through Harrods and other stores in London.

Children did drive them, but quite a number of them ended up in museums and private collections. I had planned to extend the range of model cars on the same scale, with an MG TC being the next one, but other work for Harry intervened and a local man who said he

Fits like a glove! Well known motorist, Stewart Skilbeck on commercial business.

was going to be an agent for Royle Cars, set up his own workshop and built the MG himself. He also found them to be expensive and sold very few I believe. The original intention was that it would tap into another market and gamefully employ Harry when he did not have building and other work to do, so it satisfied the need and helped to maintain cash flow when he was between other jobs.

THE CHAPEL SHOWROOM

After Peter closed the Royle Hepworth showroom at Poole, old car values continued to increase and as previously mentioned, the opportunity arose to buy the Methodist Chapel in Staindrop. This would provide more space to store and sell our kind of motor cars. Harry carried out the necessary alterations to enlarge the entrance to enable motor cars to be driven into the building. Typically, in this part of the world, it is built of stone and the work was done so that it suited the existing architectural style and with having no showroom windows, when finished, it looked as if no alterations had been made. The building would accommodate twelve vehicles and was a great help to us.

Shortly after this, Piers Leigh joined us to run Royle Cars Ltd and was appointed as the Sales Director. He was enthusiastic and very competent and he helped to make Royles profitable during the late 1980's. We sold a great many motor cars covering every aspect of those dating from the early Veterans and Edwardian vehicles, right through the Vintage period to post war classics and racing cars. He enjoyed his job and stayed with us until the mid 1990's. I will return to Royle Cars Ltd and Piers later on, as the story develops.

CHAPTER 15:
THE WORKSHOPS TODAY

Walking into Royles workshops in Staindrop today, a rich mixture of smells greets you. These are a heady mix of old cars, of leather, oils, sawn timber, old petrol, occasional exhaust fumes, glues and welding smoke. These, combined with the cacophony of noises produced by the craftsmen and engineers and the occasional roar of the engines of the cars themselves, make for an unforgettable atmosphere. An atmosphere charged with enthusiasm and dedication, both vital to meet the many challenges involved in this highly specialised and demanding work.

It is now over fifty years since I worked on my first motor car. A far cry from the beginning when I had my first 'hands on' experience in 1957 as a schoolboy working on my first motor car, the 'old' 1930 Standard Avon Special.

When I think back to those days and the primitive conditions working in that dark, cold, flooded and exposed little garage building at Aycliffe and compare it to the facilities which we have at the Old School today, the contrast could not be greater. Walking from one warm, bright workshop to another, it is wonderful to see the array of sports, racing, touring and saloon cars of the veteran and vintage periods. These being complimented by later classic sports and racing cars which were built after the second world war through into the 1960's and 70's, it is no wonder that it still gives me a great thrill. There is something of interest for everybody to see, an absolute delight to every motoring enthusiast or 'petrol head' who visits us.

Let me take you on a tour of the workshops: Turning right through the green door marked 'Staff Only' we enter into the workshop which I first worked in. The first job we can see in, what is still, the coach-building workshop, is a rare 1939 Lea Francis. Paul is making a first class job of rebuilding this sports 4 seat open tourer which has an attractive ash framed, aluminium panelled body by Corsica. As is often the case with pre-war British coach built motor cars which have been used in our climate, the wooden body frame has suffered through rot caused by water and dampness.

Whether it be as a result of standing outside, or being used in wet weather conditions, once water is trapped between the outer body panels and the inner trim panels, It takes a long time to dry out if the car is not stored in a well ventilated garage or one with a de-humidifier.

Depending upon the amount of damage done, in some cases, we find that the body structure is sometimes only held together by the metal body panels themselves which are nailed onto the wood frame. The only satisfactory solution, when this is so, is to carefully strip down the entire body into its component parts, or what is left of them. Looking at the pile of rotten timber and decayed panels after disassembly, one would think that they were of no value at all. Far from it, with the benefit of our shot and bead blasting facilities and our detailed photographic record taken as the body is stripped down, we can then proceed with the restoration, knowing that it will come together exactly as it did when first built and using as many of the original parts as possible.

Paul joined Royles after working in a local body shop. Although modern car monocoque bodies are very different in construction in many respects to pre-war motor cars, the experience is never the less valuable. Like all of our men, he has much natural ability and with guidance from me and the team, he is sufficiently skilled to develop them. Coachwork involves working not only with aluminium and steel panelling, but also with ash timber used for the body frames. It is good to see a younger man capable of doing this specialised and skilled work. The satisfaction of restoring and conserving as much of the original body in this way, is enjoyed and appreciated by both the craftsman and owner alike.

After this has been done, all the other necessary work can be carried out to the chassis, the engine, the trim and all the associated components. As the work proceeds, they are carefully cleaned and repainted and the bright work re-plated and the entire vehicle is then progressively re-assembled. The Paintwork being extremely important, not only in its appearance, but especially in the preparation of all the surfaces of the metal and wood before top coats are applied. This ensures a long lasting, protective coating and the final result is then a superb motor vehicle down to the tiniest detail.

I have already mentioned Jim who has worked at Royles for over twenty years and has the necessary attributes for his job. This includes a great deal of patience along with the technical knowledge of the chemical make-up of the various different types of paints themselves. As well as these, he has a great eye for colours which, when combined with his considerable practical skill gained from over forty years experience, makes him one of the country's finest and most experienced painters. When we were working closely with the people from Rolls-Royce at Crewe and with their Mulliner Park Ward factory and service centre at Hythe Road in London for example, they saw techniques of painting at Royles which they had not seen before, which impressed them greatly. The finish achieved is always to the highest possible standards.

SPECIALIST SKILLS & COSTS

Due to the labour intensive nature and high standards of restoration work which is carried out at Royles, we have always kept the charge-out rates to the minimum. These equate to around half, or less, of those charged by garages which deal with modern motor cars. In spite of this, the total costs can still be thought of as being high. In some cases, with motor cars of low commercial value, the cost of restoration can easily be more than the market value of the car itself. To some, this may seem to be nonsensical, but to those who enjoy their particular motor car or have a sentimental attachment to it and plan to keep it indefinitely, then the value of the work is in the 20 or 30 years of reliable use and pleasure which it will give in the long term.

In today's world of mass production, manufacturing costs have reduced the price of cars and most other complex assemblies, to levels so low that, to my generation, they seem to be incredibly cheap. This is especially true when efficient methods of production are combined with the low labour costs of the developing countries. The imbalance in their costs when compared to European and Western developed nations is now such, that the cost of repair is not viable for many everyday items, hence we have become a throw-away society. Whilst this is not yet true of complete motor cars, it has been so for their components for many years. Cost effective, yes, but a most wasteful system for the raw materials and the labour used to make the products. These go against all the principles which I was brought up to value.

The work which we have been doing for years at Staindrop, although not directly comparable, could certainly now be called 'green', although this was not a phrase used when I started restoring motor vehicles. Nowadays, the increasing level of mass production on a large scale and the huge requirement for raw materials and metals and then the waste of it all is, at last, being recognised.

I have also seen how there is a noticeable lack of understanding of skilled labour and workmanship in this country. As the East develops and their costs inevitably rise, especially with this increasing demand for raw materials, we will hopefully soon see the return of a more common sense approach to manufactured goods. If a fault appears or as fashions change. everyday items will again be valued and maintained and not be thrown away at the drop of a hat. This in turn, will encourage an appreciation of skilled workmanship by the general public and will, once again, create a demand for practical skills and experience. Academic qualifications on paper are fine, but are proving to leave many service industries without the people who are able to do the work.

In my own case, being brought up in a wartime environment, being conscious of and avoiding waste, it is not surprising that I found the gift of having the practical skills of being able to work with my hands, to be so beneficial and satisfying. These and a small amount of money, enabled me to have my own boat and motor car by the time I was seventeen. This valuable experience and the fun I had as a consequence of having done it, led me on to devoting my life to restoration and other creative work. This close involvement and the knowledge gained through all this practical work with hand-made motor cars and boats and the wide range of

CHAPTER 15: THE WORKSHOPS TODAY

Looking into Aladdin's cave at night time.

materials and components incorporated in them, later on after many years experience, enabled me to design and develop the first high speed planing amphibious vehicles.

But I am jumping ahead again. When contemplating restoration commercially, being so labour intensive, I realised that it would not be a big profit maker, but I thought that if it would provide my wife, Jo-Jo and me, with a living, then I could not wish for a more interesting way of life. So, bearing in mind that the final cost of doing any job properly still seems high to most people and that the cost of it may exceed the market value of the car, you may wonder how it is that my workshops have been kept so busy ever since I started my business in 1974.

The fact is that there are a growing number of people who are not only great enthusiasts, but who also have grown to appreciate the quality and craftsmanship inherent in early motor cars and which is needed in order to maintain them. Most owners want to retain the original details of construction and of the mechanical design. This is not only for the sake of the visual appearance, it is also important because of the pleasure derived from driving, maintaining and owning an historic vehicle. They can experience the techniques, the foibles and practice the driving skills necessary to get the best out of them. This is particularly true of veteran and vintage machines.

Post-war classic cars, with their improved performance, narrow tyres and period suspension, require different skills from the earlier motor cars, but also have distinctive characteristics of their own. Some sports cars, of course, do have excellent performance, but need to be treated with respect. They are a great thrill to drive however, and handle very well with experience and knowledge of their capabilities

It is the comfort of knowing, down the years, that my principles have been firmly established with my team of men which has ensured that the work is to the highest standards. We also focus on originality, roadworthiness and a high standard of finish. All this gives the owners of fine motor cars the confidence to trust me with one of their most prized possessions. It is these principles which have attracted so many people to come to me with their motor cars since 1973.

ROYLE'S SYSTEMS & RECORDS

Whilst we all live in a 'fast buck' society, most of my customers can see the value of a 'slow buck' investment. Those who focus entirely on fast profits are missing out on the long term pleasures and benefits of owning a good, historic motor car which is in tip-top condition. If they plan to sell their car after a Royle restoration, they are simply giving the benefit of all the work to somebody else.

Naturally, there are exceptions to the rule, the foregoing economic discussion is based upon the restoration of the low to middle value range of sports, touring and saloon cars. These include the type of motor cars which, broadly speaking, were built in quantity and would sell, at auction, for prices which are similar to the modern day family or sports car. When period vehicles of high quality or performance are involved, then much higher values influence the thought process.

For example, rare touring, sports, or racing cars can sometimes command a price well into seven figures, as can a desirable high specification limousine or saloon. This is especially true of specific ones which won important races or ones with stylish and exotic coachwork, silver fittings, inlays or historic links with famous people. In such cases, whilst the restoration/conservation work may take 3,000, 4,000 or even 5,000 hours of work, and the costs may well run up to £500,000 or even more, their value will easily absorb these sums and still leave the owner with an immediate potential for profit, if that is what he or she seeks, subject to market conditions of course.

Because of the possibility of high costs, I should mention that the systems we created and established at Royles, reflected the need for Vintage Motor Car owners to be comfortable with, and satisfied that the costs involved are correct. This is particularly important due to the fact that accurately estimating the cost of an in-depth restoration is impossible. I realised from the outset, that if the work was to be thorough and done properly, a fixed price was not possible or indeed desirable. Knowing that hundreds of components would be involved and that the variation in cost could be wide, I knew that I would have to work on a 'time and materials' basis, despite the bad reputation which such contracts have in some activities..

In recent years, I have seen a widespread increase in sharp practise, not only in some small organisations, but also in large and previously honourable institutions like the banks and some big commercial and legal organisations. From the outset, it was essential and important to me that I established and developed a system which would conclusively prove that our charges were fair and reasonable.

As the work is so labour intensive, I knew that the restoration business would not be very profitable, financially speaking. Knowing this, I was perfectly happy to establish an 'Open Books Policy' from the start. For example, we have our full 'Terms of Business' on the front of our Estimate Forms. They are not hidden away in tiny print and used as a means to apply extra charges, or take advantage of our customers in other ways, as is common practice with some organisations. I wanted to ensure that my new business would not be "tarred with the same brush".

Our Open Books Policy includes the provision of copies of the actual worksheets for our customers. These are filled in by the men each day and give details of the work done and hours spent and are sent along with records of materials and photographs of the work progressively, on a regular basis, as it proceeds. This prevents any subsequent 'doctoring' of the costs by altering the figures. This can occur when this information is provided when the work is finished. I am aware that this happens in certain other 'industries' and in some of the professions.

Whilst all this may sound rather like a 'Royle promotion' it is fact. I mention it so that you can understand how we do all we can to reassure 'our' owners that, not only is the work done properly, they can see and know what is being done progressively and have their own comprehensive record and written file of it at the end of the work. Down the years, it seems that most other restoration firms in this country have adopted our methods and it now has become an established, common practice.

We also have created and maintained our own comprehensive and detailed records. As previously mentioned, being formerly listed by the Museums and Galleries Commission and now, as members of the UKIC we are, in any event, obliged to maintain our archive. This now contains tens of thousands of photographs and records of all the vehicles which have been restored by Royles, approaching 900 to date. A most interesting and wide-ranging selection of motor cars, horse drawn vehicles and boats. The complete list of customers vehicles, from these files, is included later in this book.

MEANWHILE, IN OUR WORKSHOPS

Along with the Lea Francis in the coach building workshop, is a racing car which belongs to Sir Stirling Moss. This is a Maserati Osca of 1958. Sir Stirling's engineer of long standing, Don Haldenby, has carried out the necessary mechanical overhaul, but he wanted Royles to restore, rework and planish the aluminium body work panels. This is not a wooden framed body, being post war and designed specifically for racing, it is very light in weight. In order to be so, it relies upon its double curvature panels and light metal tube framework to give it the strength. Once again, we are retaining the maximum amount of the original metalwork in this car, only shaping, wheeling and seam-welding in new alloy panels, where necessary, to maintain the shape and structural integrity of this original, lightweight racing car body.

Stirling Moss's 1958 OSCA FS372.

Moving through into the long central workshop, a 1939 LG 6 Lagonda saloon is on the lift with Ron working underneath it. Ron joined us three years ago and is a very gifted and experienced engineer. Although compared to many of our long served staff, Ron is relatively new to Royles, he is highly skilled and his intimate knowledge of quality and performance cars is quite exceptional. Having worked with Lotus, Ferrari, Rolls Royce, Bentley and other world famous vehicles, he is most experienced in every aspect of the mechanical work and is particularly good with engine tuning.

Lagonda LG6 saloon.

The superb Lagonda motor car which he is working on, was completely restored by us twenty years ago and is with us again for one of its regular services. This vehicle has been in the same Yorkshire family since new, the Shaw family. Having been finished in midnight blue, a subtle colour which is only discernable in bright sunlight, combined with cream leather upholstery and royal blue carpets, the overall effect is stunning. When it came to us in late1987, the original engine had been replaced with a Perkins diesel engine and the car was fitted with a heavy duty, strong tow bar. The car had worked very hard during its life, and was originally painted black.

Stripping this Lagonda down to the bare chassis, a correct 4.5 litre Lagonda engine was found and overhauled and every component of the vehicle was stripped, examined and overhauled. Nikolas Shaw, the present family owner, enjoys driving it and uses it extensively in the summer, returning it to us every year for servicing and general maintenance. The engine bay is a delight with its polished aluminium air intake, carburettors, bulkhead and other components. Externally, the flowing lines of the bodywork by the Lagonda's famous designer, Frank Feeley, are set off by the large R100 headlamps. The photographic record of this comprehensive restoration is shown later in this book.

All in all, a most stylish and impressive driver's saloon and the last of the pre-war Lagonda's. The mechanical design work is by W. O. Bentley who joined Lagondas after his contract with Rolls-Royce came to an end in 1936. In one way or another, the engineers, designers and people who have been involved with the wonderful world of automotive transport, are often linked. In this case, Rolls Royce and Walter Owen Bentley, "WO", the original creator and designer of the Bentley marque.

Standing next to the four post lift and the LG 6 Lagonda and looking down the long central workshop. there are some large sheet metal working machines and a special solid steel bench which Nick made for working metal. There are also a number of racks with a wide range of different sizes of nuts, bolts and washers to fit vehicles of all types including BSF, UNF, Metric, Whitworth and American sizes. These are convenient for the three work stations and readily available for everybody working in this long workshop where there is room for five or six motor cars.

Amongst a number of vehicles on the steel mezzanine floor above the long workshop, is a 1933 Austin Seven Saloon. This motor car has been restored and is the treasured possession of Alex Birkbeck. Since its restoration, although a small car, it has attracted much attention and is admired by all who see it. The bodywork is dark green with black mudguards and a black fabric covered, sliding sunshine roof. The interior is a mid green colour and is correct in every detail and compliments the green of the bodywork. The whole vehicle is a delight to see. Job 717.

Before describing the work done, I can do no better than quote the following copy written for the Classic Car magazine by Michael Ware who was, at the time, the curator of the National Motor Museum at Beaulieu. This extract gives a brief description of how the Austin came to our workshops:

"Some thirty years ago Alex Birkbeck was driving his new Austin Cambridge in a street in South Gosforth on Tyneside. There, on the side of the road, was a 1933 Austin Seven Box Saloon with a 'For sale' notice on it. Alex had owned a number of Austin Seven Rubies when he was a student and always wanted an example of an earlier model. In the end, his wife bought it for him for the proverbial (in those days) £25. Its condition was, however, was not as good as they had anticipated. After 12 months of trying to keep it legally on the road, WP 3343 was put away in the garage. The ten-year test sticker from that period, now in itself a collector's item, is still on the windscreen of the car".

"Family and business commitments then took precedence and only in 2001, did the car stir again when Alex consigned it to David Royle of Staindrop for complete restoration. After 40 years in the restoration business and having completed over 700 cars, many of which were far grander than the Austin, David knows that this will be a challenge. He told us that "I want to get it exactly right for its period and I will do my utmost to see that it is not over-restored". (End of Mr Ware's article.)

Once in our workshops, the owner drew particular attention to the sunshine roof which needed to be properly restored and put into working order. Both before and after the war, many cars were built with a sliding sunshine roof, even the smaller cars like this Austin 7. The owners wanted to have the relative comfort of a saloon car in the winter so, even though there were no heaters or windscreen washers before the war, these small popular motor cars still had the luxury of being able to have plenty of fresh air in the summer by sliding open the sunshine roof.

The bodywork of the Austin was first stripped to bare metal for examination. It was found to be, generally, in better than average condition for its age. Not surprisingly, there was some rotten wooden framework and some rust in parts of the steel panelling. Earlier in the life of the car, the sunshine roof must have leaked, like many of them did. Fortunately, it seems that the whole roof had then been covered early on, to prevent further leaks. With it having been neatly done and waterproof, it had fortunately, protected the main structure of the body before serious, widespread damage was done.

It is often the case that sliding roof panels cannot, in themselves, be sealed satisfactorily to the roof to prevent against the ingress of water. This means that when it rains or when the car is being washed, the water runs under the edge of the sliding panel and then down internal roof gutters inside the bodywork. The water then runs through tubes which are neatly concealed within the structure of the wooden body frames, draining away the water onto the road.

With the passage of time, leaves, dirt and other material can block these small drain tubes which, as a result, cause the water to run down inside the actual framework and body panels. In time, this causes wet and dry rot which often seriously weakens the entire body structure. The modern day owner can then be faced with the high cost of rebuilding the complete body, not just the sunshine roof. The total cost of doing this will then depend upon the size and method of construction.

As ever, explaining to owners the potential for added cost is a constant problem facing today's restorers since the extent of rot is invisible and thus the amount of work needed is impossible to estimate. Not only is the work hidden from view before it has been done, without a fully detailed and photographic record, it is also invisible after the bodywork is finished. The cost of overhauling saloon cars which have suffered in this way, can easily be 50% or more of the total restoration cost of a complete motor car. If the bodywork is found to be in sound condition, then the cost will be very much less. This is another example of why it is not practicable to try to encompass and estimate the wide variation in potential costs to a customer.

In the case of this Austin 7, the roof covering was removed and sliding roof examined. Fortunately, the fittings and guttering were all still present which was most helpful and saved cost. Sufficient of the original framework also remained, so the sliding roof could be reconstructed exactly as original. Neil made new timber fames and shaped the double curvature steel panels. He made the entire new sunshine roof assembly, using the original fittings. To do this took three full weeks which is over 130 hours and then it had to be covered, as original, with weatherproof fabric externally and finally trimmed with headlining to match the refurbished interior. So, here was a major element of cost in only one part of the body, but one which is important for its future well being and one which will give the owner much pleasure when the weather is fine.

It is worth mentioning here, that the risk of damaged body frames as a result of wet and dry rot and rusty and corroded panelling, is higher with saloon cars than open touring or sports cars. The reasons for this are that past owners will have been more content to use a saloon car in wet weather and also would not be so concerned about leaving their cars standing outside, rather than garaging them. Bearing in mind also, that once rainwater or condensation is present within the structure, the enclosed bodywork prevents it drying out. There are rarely any facilities within coach built bodies for ventilation of the internal structure itself.

The main structure of the Austin 7 body was then tackled and found to still have a number of sound wooden frames. The rotten or broken frames were renewed and as ever, where practicable, the sound wood and metal was retained to maximise the cars originality. Then new metal was beaten and wheeled to shape and invisibly seam welded into place. The net result is a body which, once painted, is as good as it was when new. The refurbishment only obvious by the excellence of its condition, both internally and externally, in much in the same manner as when the vehicles were built.

We have developed special techniques whereby seam welding, when joining new replacement or part panels to the original panels, is carried out without the usual heat distortion. The joint may then be planished and lead loaded or modern fillers used for an invisible finish. If spot welding was the original method used for joining panels, as on later cars, then any joints which are replaced or re-made, follow the same original method of manufacture. Once again the finished job is correct for the period of the motor car being worked upon and the new metal is virtually invisible.

When the bodywork structure was finished, the chassis, running gear, engine and gearbox could be attended to. The chassis and components are examined and then bead and shot blasted as necessary, and then repaired and overhauled in the same way as the body. Wherever possible, the original parts are overhauled and retained.

In recent years, many of the clubs and enthusiasts have made correct replacement parts and if this is the case, then these are used to minimise the cost of making one-offs. Once back into sound condition, the chassis can be primed and painted and all the parts can be correctly refinished and re-assembled. In the case of the Austin 7, a good number of parts are available which is helpful and keeps the costs down for the owner.

The interior trimming was usually in 'leatherette' in the Austins, but leather was also used, particularly in the larger cars; the pre-war 10, 12, 16 and 20 hp Austin models for example. Although considered, in their day, to be of average cost, the standard and quality of some of the models was remarkably high. In the 1920's, some saloons had deep buttoned, leather upholstery with well made Mahogany door cappings and dash boards with nickel silver fittings, good carpets and a high standard of finish all round. Furthermore, the performance of the Austin 20hp, for example, was considered by some, to be better than the 20hp Rolls Royce of the period!

1925 Austin 20hp Tourer.

CHAPTER 16:
CONDITION & COSTS

Before leaving the subject of damage through wet rot, I would like to tell you briefly about two examples which I came across some years ago. The first was a pre-war Rolls Royce Wraith which was painted white and was being used as a wedding car. We had carried out the jobs which the owner had requested towards the front of the car and afterwards, we were cleaning and preparing it in readiness to return it to its owner, when I happened to pull out one of the rear arm rest ash trays. Inside it, I was surprised to see some white, wriggling worms. There was obviously something going on behind the rear upholstery!

The owner asked us to look into it and as we removed the rear cushion and squab, a strong mouldy smell wafted out. Inside, lurked some large, dark and evil looking 'mushroom-like' growths living on the ash framework and spreading onto the metal panels. We were asked to attend to this wet rot and had to make and replace some of the wooden framework which supported the rear of the body. We also attend to the trimming and then refitted it all afterwards.

This happened not long after moving into the old school and was one of our first few jobs. When the work was finished, the owner said he would pay for the extra work if we let him have the car back to earn the money to do it. I believed him, but was never paid for this work which, from memory, cost about £2,000 and this was over 30 years ago!

The second story was some years later, when I was asked to visit an estate in Scotland to examine another Rolls Royce, also a Wraith, from memory. This time, it was with a view to buying it. This motor car had been completely overhauled by the factory, shortly after which, the owner was unfortunately hospitalised and was unlikely ever to be able to use it again, hence the reason for selling it.

Driving up the long private road with my friend David Reid of Edinburgh, who had been asked to contact me, we came to a large, handsome and typically Scottish country house with pointed towers. The house was surrounded and protected by a high wire fence with barbed wire. Inside the fence, running free, were some very big and fierce dogs, all barking furiously.

We were met by the estate Factor who took us to a well built stone garage which, fortunately, was outside the fence. The building had a Clerestory roof and typically, had those heavy wooden doors which are mounted on small cast iron wheels which run on rails. 'Sliding' them open, we walked into the garage. Inside, it was a bright and spacious building with plastered walls and could have accommodated four vehicles. In the centre however, was just one car, the Rolls Royce, it was standing on blocks with just a covering of dust. The Factor explained that the car had stood here for 16 years. The tyres still had the small 'bobbles' on the tread which showed that they were new and unused.

The car looked to be in good shape, but rather dull with no shine on the chrome or the paintwork. I asked if I could look inside and with a little effort, opened the driver's door. As I did so, my eyes were drawn to some movement on the inside of the door. The leather door panel slid down and collapsed onto the floor like a cow pat. Looking into the car, the whole of the interior was brown and looked as if it was covered in a deep pile brown carpet, including even the leather seats.

Spreading my fingers, I put my hand onto the driver's seat cushion and with a little pressure, I found that I could move it down through the brown 'carpet', through the leather beneath and even through the springs themselves. The whole interior had that familiar foisty smell and the 'carpet' was, in fact, an even covering of mould which collapsed when touched, it crumbled under the slightest pressure.

Being late 1930's, the dashboard was plywood. This had de-laminated and had 'opened' up like the pages of a book with its 'spine' running along the lower edge. Where instruments had been, the holes for each one penetrated each layer like sections of a tunnel. Not surprisingly, I found that the engine was seized as were many of the mechanical parts and fittings.

We have all read the stories in books and magazines of 'barn finds', when the 'Four litre 'Lagbentatty' fires up as soon as the plugs were cleaned, a little petrol added and a battery fitted. This doesn't happen to me. Before inspecting the car I thought this time however, that it might. All the signs were good, but no, even a vehicle which had been overhauled by Rolls Royce themselves, stored in a well built 'Motor House', and hardly turned a wheel since, was in a seriously bad condition.

Analysing the reason for this, further examination showed that the garage was so well built with the walls being plastered and everything, including the clerestory windows, were beautifully made and fitted. With not having been used, the doors had moss growing around the edges. The result was that there was no air circulation at all and with no means of ventilation, the car had suffered 16 years of condensation. Every time the outside temperature was warmer than the inside, the moisture had gradually seeped into the every part of the fabric of the vehicle and had never properly dried out.

Returning to 'Barn Finds', these days, they are the speciality of the aforementioned Journalist and author, Michael Ware, who often writes a column about them. He is well known in motoring circles around the world and was the leading light as the Curator of the National Motor Museum for many years. In fact, a draughty old barn is actually a good place for ash framed motor cars to be stored. Vehicles can survive very well for long periods of time as long as the barn roof is OK and not too many chickens have roosted on, or in them!

Before leaving this subject and returning to the tour of the Royle workshops, I would like to proudly record the fact that I believe that I am the originator of a phrase which is now in common usage. A good friend of mine from just north of Staindrop, who lived in Weardale, Toddy, asked me to sell an old motorcycle and sidecar for him which had been in his barn for many years. It was an early square tank Royal Enfield. We pulled it out of the building and I included it in our advert and without thinking, described it as being "Barn Fresh". Not long afterwards, I saw this phrase being used in the smart brochure of one of the London Auction houses. I had made my mark on the global vintage motor world!

The 'barn fresh' Royal Enfield motorcycle.

THE WORKSHOP TOUR CONTINUES

Moving on, at the north end of the long central workshop is the trim shop. All the seats, trim panels, linings, carpets, and finishers are dealt with in this department. In here are a wide range of stuffings, padding, cotton wool wadding, springs, hides and rolls of various trimming materials. Our trimmer is Dave who, like me, has been restoring and trimming motor cars most of his life. He was apprenticed to one of Darlington's best known motor vehicle trimmers, Clifford French, who worked at the Cleveland Car Co, after the war. This, you may remember, is the garage where I bought my valves in 1956 when restoring my Standard Avon Special.

When I was working on 'GG' my first Lagonda in 1963, Clifford came to help me with the trimming work. Over the years, he continued to help and was a most popular and charming man. His favourite story was when he 'fought' Rommel with his sewing machine in the desert campaign in North Africa. He explained that he was in great demand, making awnings to attach to the tanks and war vehicles as sunshades. The

Clifford French working on job number 2.

photograph shows him helping me with job No 2, the Brooklands MG, when he was making the tonneau cover. When 'Cliffy', as he was affectionately known, died some years ago, there were hundreds of people at his funeral. This is an indication of the popularity of the man.

As well as being a very good trimmer, Dave is multi-skilled and can tackle virtually every aspect of the work involved when restoring vintage and classic motor cars. This is very helpful because an understanding of the inter-relationship between the bodywork, the chassis and the trim components which are attached to them, is important and helpful. Trimming is another example of a frequently misunderstood skill.

Once again, estimating costs is extremely difficult. It is not only the condition of the leather, headlinings and trim, it is the interior panels, frames, cappings and seats to which they are attached, which is equally important, as is the nature of the trim itself. Furthermore, depending upon whether the trim is to be retained, conserved or restored, the work is quite different, as are the costs involved.

VALUES & COSTS = QUALITY, TIME & MATERIALS

Because Royles are established and located in the North East of England, there is a difference in the number and type of vehicles which are most numerous here when compared, for example, to London and the home counties.

With this region having been primarily industrial with heavy industries like shipbuilding and mining before the second world war, wealth was centred mainly upon a few very wealthy families with a relatively small number of middle income families. The consequence of this, historically, is that there are relatively few of the more valuable and costly vintage cars in this area, most of the pre-war vehicles being the more everyday family cars of the period.

Whilst generally, Austins and Morris motor cars for example, are less valuable than say, Bentleys or Lagonda's, the owners never the less, still have a strong sentimental attachment and enthusiasm for them and want to have them properly restored. When considering having work done, they are usually well aware that they would not recoup the cost if they sold their car afterwards. The important point here, is that they have no desire to sell them anyway, but it is a drawback when costs are considered.

From our point of view, we like our customers to enjoy seeing their cars being restored and the costs in these cases, will normally be less than they would be for the more expensively built vehicles. Never the less, It is unsettling for them to know that the restoration of more valuable cars would have been more viable.

My philosophy has always been to work to a high standard, no matter what type of car is brought to Royles. All motor cars are stylish and have attractive features and of course, are powerful and if not in good working order, can ultimately be dangerous machines, so a high standard of workmanship a first class finish is expected and is maintained. The hourly rate which we charge is generally the same for all the vehicles. The overall cost of any overhaul and restoration is therefore entirely dependent upon the amount of work which is necessary and/or instructed. Our aim is and has always been, to please our customers.

Generally speaking, a car which was more expensive when new, is invariably going to be more costly to restore than a smaller and more economically built vehicle. This is due, not only to the physical size of the car, but also to the number and quality of the components used in its construction, each being very different to the other in most respects. Both types of vehicles may well serve their purpose as reliable transport, but the cost of an overhaul and restoration will be markedly different.

In some cases however, there are exceptions which prove the rule. The costs involved in bodywork restoration alone, using in this case, examples of a vintage Austin tourer and a VDP open vintage Bentley tourer, can in fact, be very similar. This is because they are of relatively simple bodies and use the same method of construction. An ash timber frame mounted on bottom boards with aluminium or steel or fabric panelling nailed on to the frame. There can be the same number of frames and a similar number of panels and doors, so the cost of restoration can also be very similar even though the market values of the cars themselves, are miles apart.

The same can also apply to more recent motor

cars of the post 39/45 war period which are of monocoque construction. If the panels are not available, then the cost of making a body panel, by hand, for a Ferrari can be very similar to making a panel for a Morris.

The mechanical components however, being very different in quality, size and complexity, are likely to vary considerably.

I have already explained that one of the main problems for our customers is that estimating the cost of a complete restoration is impossible. Often people will say, "David, surely after having restored hundreds of motor cars, you can provide me with a pretty good estimate of the cost". If the work to be done involves just a few components, then it may be possible, but if it is involves the hundreds of components which are involved in all the mechanical assemblies and also the overhaul of a complete body, then it is simply not possible.

I can well understand the owner of an old motor car wanting to have the comfort of a fixed price and I have seen cases when an owner has accepted a fixed price from another workshop. The result is predictable, with profit being their motivating factor, it is then too easy for them only to carry out the work which is visible, leaving other jobs not done. The owner subsequently discovers this and then comes back to us for the rest of the work to be finished and any poor workmanship put right. This can end up costing the customer more than it would have done originally, because some of the work may now have to be done twice.

In simple terms, if the work is done properly by dedicated engineers and crafts-men and the time also properly recorded, as has always been the case at Royles workshops, everybody knows where they stand. With our charge out rate being kept to a minimum, half that of most modern garages, our margin for profit is small, but our customers enjoy the benefits of well equipped workshops and a highly skilled and motivated workforce.

Of course, there are times when problems do arise and when there are bad debts for example. Regrettably, these do occur and I have not always been able to draw a salary, but that's the price I've had to pay for being conscientious and doing my utmost to provide a first class service at the lowest practicable cost.

It is only after a great many years of restoration work that I have been able to build up our reputation as an honourable and diligent company. This is vital if the owner is to benefit from a thorough job. In a world of increasing sharp practice, I can see that some people will find it difficult to believe that I am unable to give them a reasonably accurate estimate. To give you an actual example of a customers faith in us, the following story of what happened when we completely restored two identical Lagonda's, illustrates what I mean.

The motor cars involved were two LG 45 Drop Head Coupe 4.5 litre Lagondas, they were identical in virtually every respect and each had been in their respective families from new. Built in 1936, both were over sixty years old at the time of restoration and each had been well used during its long lifetime of motoring. Both needed a complete overhaul including the engine, gearbox, the chassis and running gear, the bodywork, upholstery, hood and trim, instruments, wiring, In each case, the entire vehicle.

The first Lagonda from start to finish took 3,200 hours of work, the second, with the same engineers and craftsmen, took over 5,000 hours. 1,800 hours more work than the first. The difference in cost, including parts and materials was in the region of £50,000, This gives you some idea of just how much variation there can be when two identical motor cars are completely restored. The nature of the wear, the faults and the deterioration was different in each car, but they looked to be in very similar condition.

From the outset we explained to the second customer, that we had just finished an identical car a few months earlier, so we had shown him the file, explained the history and the costs involved of restoring the first car. Naturally, the figures were used to provide the customer with a guide price. When the second Lagonda was finished two years later, despite the substantial additional cost, when compared to the previous job, our customer was most gracious in his appreciation of the work and afterwards, he generously went on to recommend Royles to other owners.

To sum up, although we have restored forty-four Lagondas to date, one of these two identical

LG45 cars cost nearly 60% more than the other. Both were restored efficiently and sensitively by the same team of men and both needed a complete overhaul and both have gone on to provide many years of reliable service.

AVON STORY

Talking of motor cars which have been in families for a long time and which have sentimental value, we have been involved with many of these down the years. Although a different subject altogether, these cars often remind me that I always thought how unfortunate it was, that my own first car, the old Standard Avon Special, had been scrapped.

After buying the Lagonda, I sold the Avon, in 1963, to a chap in Darlington. The last I heard of it, was that it was parked in a back lane and had then been scrapped. I always thought that it was ironic that a person who spends his life renovating other peoples treasured cars, had lost his own first car.

One evening, a couple of years ago, at around 7.30pm, I was finishing off one or two jobs at Staindrop when a chap came up to the office and said that he had something to show me. I followed him down stairs and there, in the yard, was a little pale green sports car. It took me a second or two to realise what I was looking at, I could hardly believe my eyes. Being side-on to me, I couldn't see the number plate, "it's not MG 861 is it" I asked. "Yes" it was, he said. My own 'Avon' still existed after all! He then went on to tell me that he had spent 20 years restoring it back to its original condition. I was delighted, amazed and thrilled to see this splendid, sporty car again, I never thought I would.

The owner had stripped the car down, re-opened the sealed doors, he had retained the Marchal lamps along with the spot lamps which I had

A recent photo of my old Avon Sports MG861.

fitted. The racing screens were still there, the wheels were now red, but the car was still green, although it had now been repainted a pale green, which is the period shade of BRG. Its proud owner, Mr Wilson, took me for a drive around the village and it ran as sweetly as a sewing machine. Even the dash board was just the same.

I could hardly believe that it still existed and it looked so good. Even my original tax disc was still there and in its original holder along with my old AA badge. They were fitted where they always had been, on the front headlamp bar. It immediately brought back memories of the local AA man who, on his yellow motor cycle and sidecar, would always grin broadly and give me the formal pre-war 'AA salute' whenever we met on the road. Happy days! Mr Wilson lives in Millom, Cumbria and soon afterwards, he very kindly sent me a framed picture of the Avon which is hung near to me as I write these notes.

CHAPTER 17:
MAULE'S COACHWORKS 1825 - 1933

Occasionally, you may have seen the name Maule appearing in various automotive publications. From the earliest days of the motor car, their stylish coachwork adorned the chassis of those built by the highest quality motor car manufacturers in Europe.

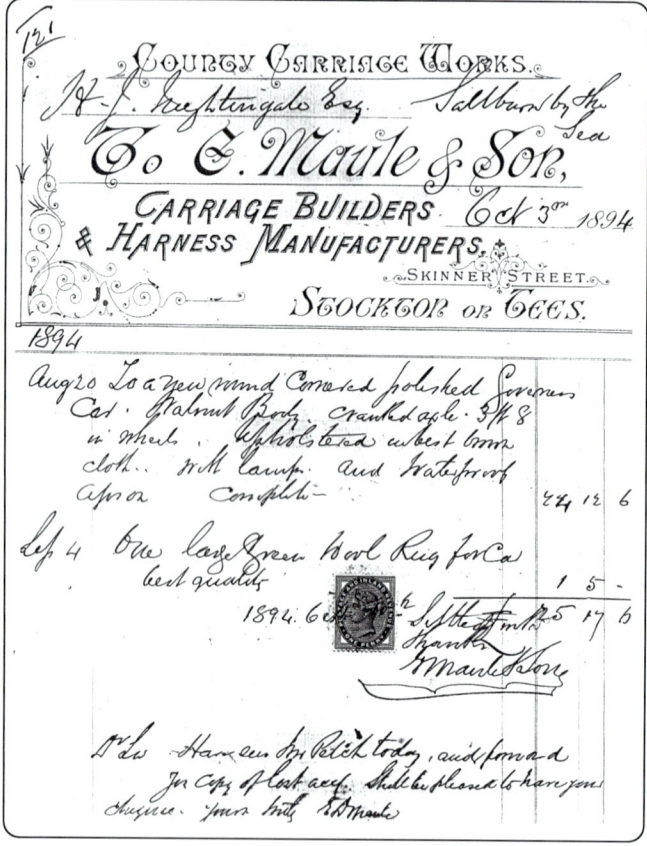

Maules bill dated 1894.

The family began as traditional horse drawn carriage manufacturers in 1825 and from the turn of the twentieth century, benefitting from their wealth of experience, went on to design and build some of the very finest motor car coachwork. The skills were handed down through the Maule family and their designs and craftsmanship were sought after by some of the most eminent motorists in the country.

Although I obviously met some of Jo-Jo's relatives at our wedding in 1968, I didn't realise that one branch of her family had been coach builders. It was some years later, after her father had died in 1977, that I was to come into more regular contact with Kyle Maule when he was to become my step father in law. This is when he married Jo-Jo's mother, Margaret, in May 1980.

Kyle was a regular visitor to Gainford, he was a jovial and interesting chap and we got on well together. Born in 1914, he had been a Captain in the Royal Artillery, the 21st Army Group, during the 1939/45 war and was honoured by being mentioned in despatches by Field Marshall Montgomery. Actually this is not untypical of the Maule family, their military history is remarkable.

When Jo-Jo's mother was due to be married to Kyle, I happened to be in Scotland and mentioned it to my ducal friend Angus Hamilton. His knowledge of Scottish history is,

Bernard Maule. Kyle's father.   Kyle Maule.

Kyle Maule at Maule Works, Stockton.

not surprisingly, very extensive and he knew the name of Maule straight away. He went on to tell me about some of the family's illustrious historical connexions with Scotland. Later on, Kyle presented us with a bound volume which

CHAPTER 17: MAULE'S COACHWORKS 1825 - 1933

records the family history and this confirmed what Angus had told me.

Going right back, his family have an illustrious military history in France, long before the Battle of Hastings. One of Kyle's forebears fought as a General in the French army against the King of England in 1048 and then played an important role in the Norman Conquest in 1066 with William the Conqueror. His family went on to gain a remarkable record of success and fame in Scotland, notably during the time of Robert the Bruce, but there is far too much to tell here.

Returning to more recent times and the subject of the family's connexion with coach building. This was first explained when Kyle visited Royle's workshops in Staindrop in the November of 1979. I could see that he was fascinated to see all our restoration work going on, especially the coach work. Kyle then told me about the Maule family's carriage and coach building businesses during the 19th and 20th centuries.

Kyle was descended from Alex Maule who was a professor at Edinburgh University around 1700. One of his sons became a school master in Alnwick and it was his grandson William James Maule, born in 1804, who became a Carriage Builder in the town. He is listed in Slater's Directory of 1854 as being at Howick Street and being a "Coach and Harness Maker". He lived to a great age and eventually died in 1897.

It was one of his three sons, Edwin Davidson Maule, born in 1837, who moved from Alnwick to Stockton on Tees in 1876, where he carried on the successful carriage building business and established E. Maule & Son at 20, Skinner street. The company were forward thinking and were happy to develop their skills and experience and progressed from building their attractive horse drawn vehicles, in order to satisfy the growing demand for purpose built bodies for motor cars.

Kyle explained that, regrettably, his father Bernard was the last member of his family to run their old established firm. They were in business for 108 years until, in the early years of the depression in 1933, the company finally closed down. At that time, it had been operating in Stockton on Tees for over fifty years.

Sadly, Kyle died in 1990, but before doing so, he entrusted Jo-Jo and me, with the bound volume of the Maule family history and with various documents and other treasured family belongings. Amongst the interesting artefacts which he presented to us included a number of early wooden coach building hand tools, stamped with the name Maule, which he knew we would treasure.

At this juncture, I would like to mention and thank Michael Ware of Beaulieu Motor Museum and Beryl Turner of Potto, for the research which they carried out into the Maule coach building business. Whilst briefly recording the history of Maule's, the information which they provided has added much to the stories which Kyle had told me about, so I would like to include it here.

The first record they found was in the 1848 'Royal National Commercial Directory and Topography'. This showed that William Maule was listed as a Coach and Harness maker and Post Horse Master at Howick Street, Alnwick. Similarly, he was listed as such, in Slater's Directory of 1854. By 1881, the British Cencus records that William had retired and Frederick.T. Maule and family were coach building at the same address, so is likely to have been his son. Interestingly, the same year, Edwin.D.Maule is listed as a Master Coach builder in the census and with his large family of three sons and three daughters, was living near here, in Stockton on Tees.

In the 1887 edition of Kelly's directory, Edwin Maule & Son are now also shown as being carriage builders and employing 14 men and 8 boys in Skinner Street, Stockton, and again in 1894, by which time their home address was Wickliffe house in nearby Norton.

By 1906, Kelly's Directory shows that they are now building Motor Car bodies as well as Carriages, so they are really moving with the times and were one of the earliest into this new form of automotive transport. As the 20th century progressed, the Maule family increased in number and Bernard Maule is listed as living in Stockton in the 1914/15 edition of Wards Directory. Bernard was apprenticed to a 'London coachbuilder' and then joined his father's coach building business. Bernard is Kyle's father.

As mentioned, the business continued until

1933 when, presumably, the depression must have adversely affected the business and the company closed. The 1934 edition of Kelly's lists only Mrs Agnes Maule as living in the area, but by 1938, there is no entry for the Maule family here. It seems that they may have moved to Sheffield, since that is where Kyle was living prior to marrying Jo-Jo's Mother.

Amongst the documents which Kyle gave to us is an original Maule Publicity booklet entitled;- "LUXURIOUS TRAVEL". "E.Maule & Son, Designers and builders of High Class Automobile Bodies suitable for any Chassis. Exclusive Designs." Tel Stockton 353".

The cover of the booklet is printed on dark brown card and incorporates 24 Plates showing some of their wide range of styles and designs

Mors chassis.

Hispano Suiza.

Sadly, the booklet is not dated, but refers to the fact that "Our Principal, Bernard Maule will be in attendance at the Olympia Motor Show... Nov 7th to 15th... on the Auster Stand No

Daimler, to Lancia, Austin, Hispano Suiza, Arrol Johnson and others.

which they had built. I have included a few of them here. Their splendid designs include Semi-Pullman Limousine, Torpedo, Cabriolet coupe', Phaeton saloons and others mounted on vehicles ranging from Mors, Rolls Royce and

Muales coachwork on what appears to be a Renault.

CHAPTER 17: MAULE'S COACHWORKS 1825 - 1933

Streamlined body on Rolls Royce.

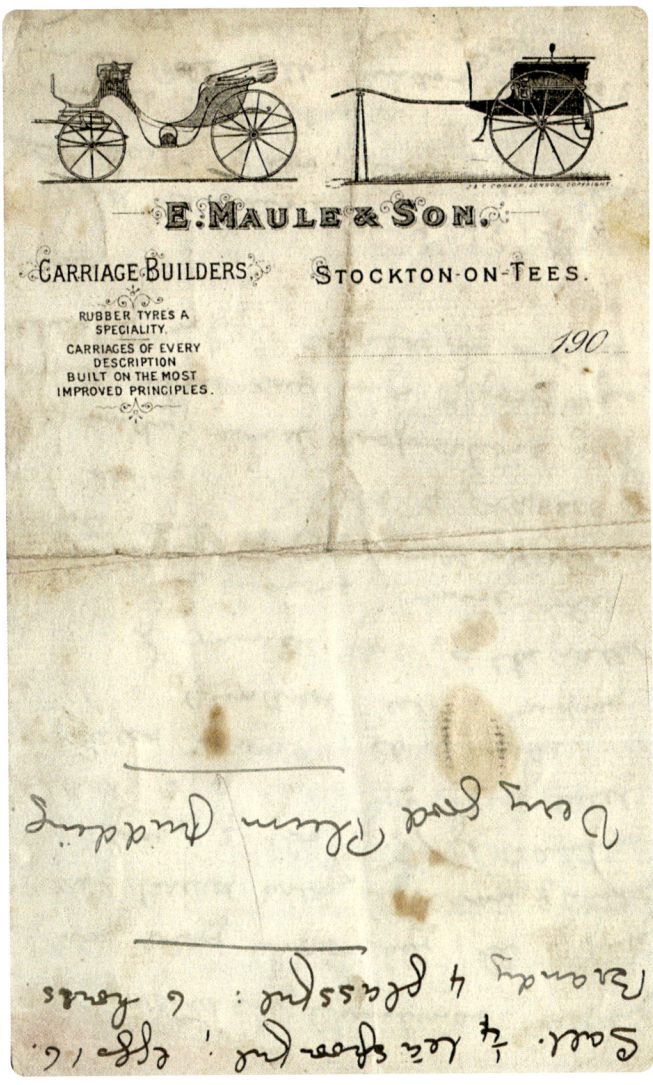

Letter heading.

245, Gallery. Judging from the body styles, my guess is that it must have been just after the first world war. Auster used to supply a range of well made windscreens to the motor trade, so probably supplied Maule's as well.

Some of the original photographs and letterheads illustrated here are, I'm afraid, showing their age. The letterhead with the elegant horse drawn vehicles for example, has Mrs Maule's instructions for making a "very good plum pudding" on the back. Others show a cyclecar with an enthusiastic driver and young passenger whilst the radiator is topped up with water, and another with Kyle Maule as a 5 or 6 year old boy, coyly holding up a hinged interior door panel to reveal a neatly concealed side screen for the Drop Head Coupe' body in which he is standing. I imagine that both photographs will have been taken at Skinner Street. Another is a postcard dated 26th November 1913, which shows a handsome body on what appears to be a Mors chassis.

Because most of the well known coachbuilders were located in London and one or two in the midlands, I particularly wanted to include Maule's story in this book. Although it is relatively brief, I hope that there is enough information to give you some idea of Maule's business. For over a century, this highly respected family firm was operating in Scotland and the north east, providing first class coachwork built for horse drawn and the developing motor car markets during the 19th and 20th centuries.

Not surprisingly, Maule's handsome and exclusive designs attracted a number of well known and wealthy motorists and so there are bound to be one or two examples of Maule's work surviving, it is a great pity that I didn't come across one of their vehicles during all my years of involvement.

It was most interesting however, that I was to be rebuilding, restoring and actually designing and making motor vehicle and horse drawn bodywork in the same styles and to the same specification as was seen 100 years earlier locally in nearby Stockton on Tees, here in County Durham. Not only were our businesses very similar in many respects, but it was a remarkable coincidence that I should become related by marriage, to the direct descendent of the last traditional coachbuilders in this region.

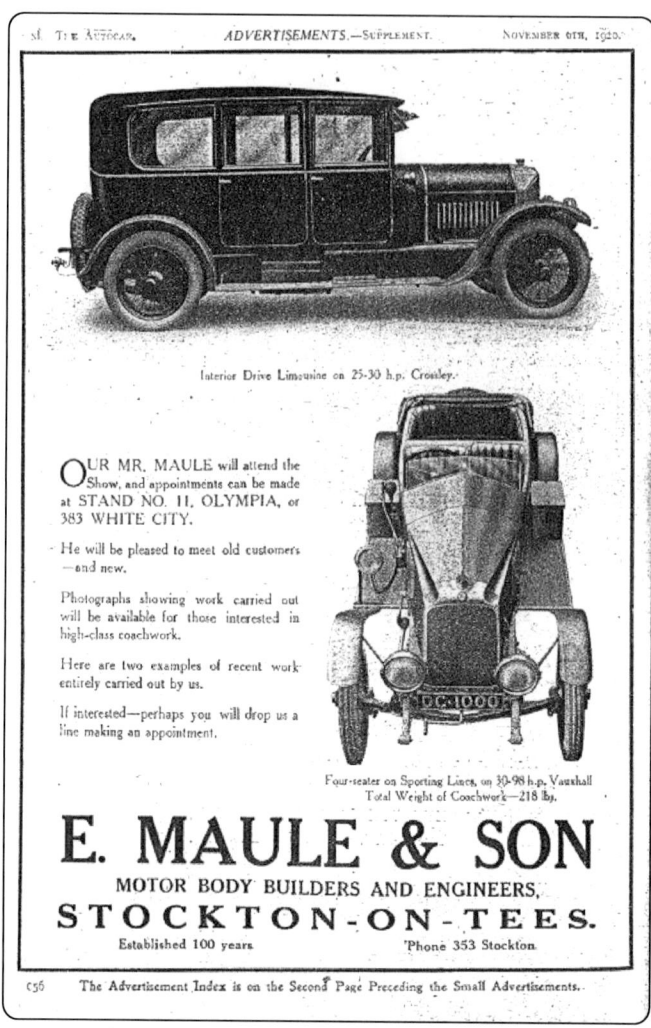

1920's advertisememnt in Autocar journal.

CHAPTER 18:
THE ROLLS ROYCE DRUG CAR

Walking towards the office along the narrow walkway from the front street, came two scruffy looking individuals with long, unkempt hair, jeans and ' T ' shirts. The pair looked as if they had just left some third rate pop festival, not the normal Vintage car owners I see in the North of England. In fact, they were undercover officers from the Drug Squad.

The year is 1980 and it was the 8th October, the day after my 41st birthday and we had just started work on a four year old, left hand drive, Silver Shadow Rolls Royce which, although not very old, had come in for re-trimming work. The number plates were Arabic and although, by our standards, the car was fairly new, even a brief examination revealed that the interior was scruffy and the vehicle had a number of visible faults which one would not expect to see in a modern Rolls Royce.

Because our reputation for good quality work was spreading, we were seeing more of these fine Motor Cars coming to us. The interior leather upholstery and trim was a pale champagne colour which set off the rich Regal Red colour of the bodywork. We had made a

The 1976 Rolls Royce Silver Shadow.

start stripping out the interior dash board, door panels, wiring and all the components involved with interior trim of this luxurious car, when Dick, who was doing the work, came to the office to ask me if I could help him. He explained that he could not remove the front seats or even slide them along their tracks.

After examining the problem, I saw that the tracks and slides were clear, but the seat itself was so hard up against the deep pile Wilton carpets which covered the centre transmission tunnel, that it couldn't be moved. It was a case of both of us pushing and pulling until, between us, we eventually managed to remove both front seats. Such extreme effort not being a normal requirement for such a modern car of this quality.

Dick then set about removing the Wilton carpets and underlay from floors and the transmission tunnel. These vehicles have particularly large, automatic Gearboxes, so the tunnels have to be large to accommodate them, but in this case, it was bigger than usual. We then saw what was causing the trouble. The reason for this was because, closely packed all around the outside of the tunnel, under the carpets, were heavy packages of a dark brown material tightly wrapped in polythene. Although I had not seen the like of it before, it was obviously drugs of some sort.

The word went rapidly round the workshops and Peter, a young trainee, rushed in and after opening up a corner of one of the many packages, sniffed it and with the air of a knowledgeable expert, enthusiastically declared that it was "Moroccan Sunset", Cannabis. Then, as if we had hit the jack-pot, excitedly said that it would "fetch a lot of money" in nearby Bishop Auckland. I also sniffed the stuff and had to admit that it had a rich and appealing aroma, rather like a cross between cigar tobacco and some other sort of herbs.

It was early days of drugs coming into the UK and I had never come across it before. I enjoy smoking the odd cigar and cigarettes which I find sufficiently satisfying not to feel the need to add a new dimension, especially one which seemed to create serious problems for the users. Not having planned to broaden the company's 'trading base' in a direction which was so far removed from our 'core business', as the consultants would say, profitable though it might be, I rang the Police!

At that time, drugs were a fairly new problem in Britain and were the focus of media attention and the response was immediate. Various police officers quickly arrived, closely followed by the aforementioned undercover Drug 'Specialists'. After quickly assessing the situation, they wanted to take the Rolls Royce away immediately. This was difficult because of its partially stripped out condition. The wiring looms were hanging out in bundles and all the seats were out, so it took two hours of feverish work to make the car drivable. The car, the Police and their drug entourage then disappeared leaving us with an empty trim shop and me with a problem as to how I was going to explain the disappearance of one Regal Red Rolls Royce to our customer.

The man with whom I was dealing was, in fact, not the owner of the car, but a local man whom I knew. He was acting as an agent for a member of the Saudi Royal Family.

After he regained his composure when I had explained what had happened, he then told me that he had bought the Rolls Royce at an auction of second hand cars in London. It was bought on behalf of the 'Prince' whom he knew personally, and being Left Hand Drive, was to be used in Europe. He had no idea that there were any drugs in the car and was as surprised as we were, which gave me some comfort.

After the car was taken away, it disappeared for many months. We pressed the Police for its return and the owner's agent rang me periodically to find out when it was coming back. It turned out that it was now in the custody of Customs and Excise (C & E) and there was the question as to whether it would come back at all, since all vehicles used in drug smuggling are usually confiscated and then sold by C & E. The owner, if guilty, loses his car and his freedom too, I gather!

I am pleased to say that the car was, in fact, eventually returned to us for the owner who had not, of course, been involved with drug smuggling. This was so that we could carry out the work originally intended. Twelve months had been taken, as indeed had the Flying Lady Mascot and the heavy duty battery, whilst in the 'care' of C & E. It was never the less, good to have it back and be able to make progress with the refurbishment work. We had just re-started the work when, one morning, the phones went mad and never stopped ringing for two days. The cause was that the Annual County Durham Chief of Police Report had just been published and the story of the Drugs in a Rolls Royce was in it. The Cat was out of the Bag!

We had three telephone lines, so all three of us, myself, Irene and Roger were under pressure, non-stop on the 'phones until I had a call from Reuters. The voice on the other end said "are your phones busy?" I explained that every newspaper imaginable was on the lines. "Give me the story" he said "and life may return to normal pretty soon". I told him what had happened, but like all the previous callers, he was pressing me to tell him who owned the car.

Who was this Rolls Royce owner who used his car for drug smuggling? It was a real life James Bond story and the press were keen to have it. I did not answer the question.

It was not entirely because of our normal customer confidentiality, importantly it was also because by then, I had taken a telephone call from a well spoken man who also had specifically asked to talk to me. Speaking in measured and unhurried tones, the caller made it lucidly clear that if I revealed the Royal Princes name to the Press, then I "would not see the light of day". My comfort zone had evaporated, and what made matters worse, was that I subsequently, had two more calls from other well-spoken men saying exactly the same thing. They all obviously meant it!

In the middle of all this, Jo-Jo rang up to say that the birth of our second baby, Nick, was now imminent, so she was going over to her mothers. I told her that things were a 'little difficult' at the time and that I would join her later. In the event, it all happened very quickly and I didn't get there in time, but all was well thank goodness. Nick was keen to 'get out' and there was no need for assistance as in Jeremy's birth, 18 months earlier.

As soon as the first of these calls was received, I immediately had the registration number plates and the Rolls Royce Engine and Chassis Plate in the engine bay removed. Either of these could have been used to trace the owner of the car via the DVLC records and possibly Rolls Royce themselves. This event occurred not long after there had been a lot of publicity in the press known as the 'Princessa' affair. This was when an eastern princess was reputedly put to death for some sort of scandalous behaviour. Had it been the case that the Royal owner of the car was involved with drug smuggling, the consequences could have been most serious, in fact fatal.

THE STORY

Talking to C & E people afterwards, it seems that whilst the Rolls Royce was in their care, the history of it was traced back. The Cannabis which we found, turned out to be 4 kilo's, which apparently, had been missed, and was only a small part of the much larger consignment.
The chassis of the car along with most of the other spaces in the structure of the car had been opened up, filled with the packages of drugs and resealed. The total amount was not revealed to me, but It must have been over 50kg or more, a considerable amount at the time. No wonder the interior and leatherwork was scruffy!

It seems that, after being loaded in Morocco, the Rolls Royce was put into a container and shipped to London where the drug smugglers would unload the consignment and check it against a delivery note. I was told that this delivery note is normal practice, they are, after all 'trading in merchandise'.

At this point, my imagination takes over and I like to think that the story was as follows:

I picture the receiving party in some dark, back street premises, probably under some railway arches in London. The Gang have successfully shipped it to London, stripped and unloaded the car, but on checking the delivery note, the boss finds that there are a number of missing packages. The boss gruffly questions 'Bert', the man who has just unloaded the 'goods' (not the most expert in the trade!) "Alright Bert" says the boss, "what have you done with the missing 4 kilo's of drugs?" 'Bert' replies in a strong cockney accent, "Honest guv, I haven't pinched any of the stuff, I gave you every arnce of it that I farned in the motor, honest!" The boss gives him a rough time, but still doesn't believe him.

The story moves on, 'Bert' quickly puts the Rolls Royce back together and it is sold at auction to the Princes Agent. Upon seeing the poor state of the interior, and knowing that David Royle will make a good job of it (I like that bit!) drives it North to Staindrop. This is where Royles, doing a thorough job, as ever, soon find the missing cannabis.

The Customs boys take the car away, investigations continue and they trace it back to the 'boss', Bert and the whole drugs gang, who are now so confident after their success with the 'Roller', that they are planning a much bigger shipment of the 'stuff'. This time it is coming in by boat, half a ton of it, into Felixtow. This time, the Customs boys have staked out the harbour and are waiting for them.

Success! The shipment of drugs are found and the whole Gang 'nicked' and are now languishing in the local cells where the C & E boys tell them how Royles found the well hidden, 'missing' cannabis and how their boys traced it back to Morocco. On hearing this, Bert grumbling turns to the Boss telling him that it's all his fault. "your trouble guv, is that you aint got no integrity, I told you that I didn't nick the stuff art of the Roller".

BACK TO REALITY

Meanwhile, back to reality at Staindrop, where the work to the car has been resumed. There are still sporadic attempts to find out who was the Royal owner of the car. The most amusing one was when a very tall and glamorous 'lady', dressed to kill and dripping in diamonds, walked into the office saying that she was a motor enthusiast.(not the most likely 'petrol head' I had come across!) She explained that she wanted to have her Rolls Royce restored and could she see one to show the standards of our workmanship.

Thinking that she just might be genuine and to put her to the test, I said I would be pleased to do so. I walked with her across the yard to the 'top shop' where we were working on a 1926 Rolls Royce Shooting Brake. This was a lovely vintage machine with a typically vintage, square body with varnished external wood frames.
I had bought this fine car in Scotland from an old colonial Gentleman, but that's another story. Her face fell when she saw it, "Oh no" she said disdainfully, "my car is much more modern than that, don't you have a more up to date Rolls Royce to show me?"

Rolls Royce shooting brake.

As if surprised, I said "of course". She smiled as we walked back down to the main buildings and then past various other interesting vehicles which she ignored until we reached the trim shop where 'The Car' was. Opening the door, "Yes" she said excitedly, "this is the sort of car I am talking about". I watched her very carefully as we entered, her eyes immediately went to where the front number plate would be. It had been removed of course. There was a flicker of disappointment, but she quickly recovered her composure saying how beautiful the leatherwork was, having hardly looked at it. "I also love engines" she said, "can I see the engine?" I lifted the bonnet, her eyes immediately focussed on the bulkhead where the chassis plate is normally fitted. It too, had been removed, just two small holes remained where it had been fixed. At that point her enthusiasm evaporated, there was no further attempt at being polite, she wheeled round and was gone.

The Arabic Number plate remained in the upstairs stores where I had hidden it for many years. It was only recently that I went to find it, but it had disappeared, I wonder who had taken it? I also sometimes wonder if the prince, who wasn't actually involved, never the less appreciates the confidentiality which we uphold for our customers. Admittedly, not normally a life threatening affair, but this time it really was.

CHAPTER 19:
VISITS & TALKS

Whilst discussing the subject of restoration generally, on a number of occasions down the years, I have been called upon to speak about the techniques which we have developed and which we practice to overcome the wide variety of challenges associated with our work.

Being one of the first firms to be set up specifically to deal with virtually every aspect of vehicle restoration, people are keen to know what has been involved when creating an unusual business like ours. In effect, our workshops are like a factory in miniature, I have had to gather together the specialised machinery and equipment needed for a machine shop, timber work and joinery, metal working and fabrication, shot and bead blasting, steam cleaning, paintwork and bake oven facilities, sewing and trimming dep't, parts store and early books for design and research. With Roger's help, we even had to develop our own special accounts systems. All important when dealing with such a wide range of the parts and materials incorporated in the construction of early motor cars.

I then had to bring together experienced craftsmen and engineers whom I could train in those skills which have not been practised since the first half of the last century. Quite a challenge, particularly so, when carried out on such a small scale, especially considering the problems associated with vehicles which can be over 100 years old.

These talks have been given when clubs and organisations have visited the workshops and also at more formal events, when I have been asked to present a paper to assembled audiences. These include invitations by various organisations; The Institute of Mechanical Engineers, The National Motor Museum at Beaulieu, Newcastle University and The World Forum for Motor Museums when they gathered together at Stuttgart in Germany in 1999.

These have all been very interesting events and as ever, I could write at length about them as I could about other fascinating trips I made abroad. The size of this book is growing however, so I will just mention one or two to give you a flavour of them.

The talk which I gave in November 1979, in a large lecture theatre at Newcastle University, was to a good audience and particularly memorable for me when I brought it to a noisy conclusion by starting the engine of the pre-war Brooklands Racing MG, (job number 2), which we restored for Norman Hart. Norman found this single seater racing car, a most desirable machine, near Durham where he lives. He was clever to 'see through' the 1960's style GRP body which covered this exciting original racing motor car. Included in the comprehensive restoration work, we made a straight through exhaust system to the original design, complete with a fish tail as was originally fitted. The sound it made was wonderful when it burst into life in the university's main entrance hall and echoed up and down the main staircase, Marvellous!

Another memorable occasion was when Michael Ware, the Curator of the National Motor Museum at Beaulieu, asked me to present a paper on restoration. Also speaking that evening was Nick Mason, of Pink Floyd fame, who's subject was classic motor car racing. We were also joined by a gentleman speaking about vehicle restoration work carried out by the Science museum in London. Altogether, a most interesting event.

My hosts at the Royal Palace in Seoul, South Korea. The people are, from the left: Byung-Hyo Bae. Assistant G.Manager Prototype Manufacturing team Hyundai. Dr Chang-ho Kim. Ph.D. Chief Research Engineer. Hyundai. I.W.Lee. (Ivan) Gen.Manager, Prototype Manufacturing Team, Hyundai. Ullsan. DR., Kang sun Hyong. Office of Cultural Properties. Seoul.

As a result of a request made to the National Motor Museum for them to send over an expert to South Korea, I was asked if I would be prepared to represent them. The Hyundai Motor Company, acting on behalf of the Korean government, needed to have their 1911 Daimler and 1918 Cadillac motor cars evaluated and a report prepared upon their condition. These two early Royal vehicles had belonged to the Empress and Emperor of Korea, respectively, and had been stored in the garages of the Royal Palace in Seoul since 1918.

When I flew over to see them in May 1997, the cars had been taken from the palace to Hyundai's Research and Development centre, a few miles outside the city. My job, after inspecting the cars, was to advise them on their restoration. I found these fine old vehicles to be in very original, sound and complete condition, only the seat cushions were missing. The Daimler didn't have any means to record the mileage, but the Cadillac did and only had 400 miles on its gauge! It is always a delight to see 'special' motor cars which are substantially original and have important historical connexions.

Fortunately, all my hosts spoke English and were also most kind to me. I found them to be good company especially when, on social occasions, I poked fun at them. Being a lone European figure surrounded by them all, they took it as it was intended, as pure fun and returned the compliment. We had some highly amusing times. They generously showed me round some of their superb and extensive R&D facilities, where they employ around 1000 engineers I believe.

Their plan was to open a museum in Seoul so, as well as having their two cars restored, they wanted to send over a group of engineers to Staindrop to learn about restoration. Having seen how time is of little consequence to them and how hard working they are, I thought that I should make due allowance for the fact that our customers cars would, almost certainly, have to take second place. So, when estimating restoration costs, I made a substantial allowances for this.

The Korean minister and some of my Hyundai hosts visited us in Staindrop. I booked them in at nearby Headlam Hall, my friend Robbo's popular hotel which so many people praise for its pleasant atmosphere. They loved the place and the gardens and once again, we had some fun, especially when Jo-Jo plied the minister with wine at dinner. His formality disappeared and he ended up dancing around the dining room with a glass of wine on his head!

When all came to all, I wasn't surprised when they thought my estimate was very high and another firm was awarded the contract. They told me that they were disappointed to have to tell me this, because they said that they also had enjoyed working with me.

A few months later, I received an urgent telephone call from "JH" in Korea. "JH" Kim was the man who had been detailed to look after me whilst in Korea. He rang to tell me that the restorers had walked off the job leaving the cars all in pieces, and could I help them. I said that
I would, of course, be pleased to do so and told him that we often had to take over half finished restoration projects. The problem was eventually sorted out however, and the work was completed. It is my guess that the difference in expectations would be the root of the trouble.

When talking about interesting trips, I cannot leave out the two visits I made to California, these were in 1986 and 1987. The first was when my old globe-trotting, motoring friend Martyn Stephenson and I flew over to America carrying one of our Half-scale Austin 7 Children's Cars as hand luggage. Hearing that this was possible, we fitted four rope handles and had some fun at the airports, especially when asked what was inside our big box.
We were honestly able to reply that it was an "Austin motor car". The customs officials at San Francisco were greatly amused when the airport staff happily carried it through for us and were delighted when we showed it to them. A car as hand luggage, wow!

Because it was my first trip to America, I wanted to get into the spirit of things and fly by an American company, so we had booked and flew over with Boeing. As we were boarding at Heathrow, Martyn counted the top windows on the 747 and commented that it was an old plane. His judgement proved to be correct when we had a bumpy landing at San Francisco and two large roof panels collapsed on top of us.

As we struggled to push them off, I was able to

call to the ageing air hostess who was sitting on the jump seat near to us, "Does this often happen"? Peering underneath them to speak to us, "No", came the weary reply, "not too often". After she had helped us to lift them off, we could see up into the black void of the fuselage above us. It was filthy black and reminded me of the underground railway tunnels in London. We could see all the air ducts, bundles of wires and other conduits hanging down from the frames where they had been tied up with, what looked like, old string. It amazed us that the plane would fly. I was not at all surprised to hear that the Boeing company closed down a few months later.

In fact the rest of the trip went very smoothly. There is far too much to tell here, but suffice to say, we rented a car and visited some of the Californian restoration companies and other interesting Rolls Royce, Ferrari and classic car dealers. Importantly, we met a good contact, Gordon Keller and his wife Betty, who lived in the Bay area in San Francisco. They worked with us for some years, buying classic motor cars for us, up and down the west coast. These were shipped over to Staindrop to be checked and serviced and then shipped or driven out to Geneva

Gordon Keller, our man in California" standing next to black XK 120.

where Martyn lives. Being left hand drive, they were suitable for the European market and many of them were sold in Switzerland.

We had arranged to meet the Vice-Consul, Greg Hoppe, who was most helpful and introduced us to some good contacts and people who were involved in the old car world as well as the market for our little Austin Children's Cars. We were entertained at some of the excellent restaurants in the fashionable places like Beverly

Martyn and me with Austin 3½ in Beverly Hills.

Hills, where some of the diners were well known personalities in the 'movies'. It was great fun to see the places which one hears so much about. As we motored south via Los Angeles towards San Diego, we had the pleasure of meeting many interesting people, one of whom was Briggs Cunningham at his museum in Costa Mesa.

The following year, I went over again. I took Jo-Jo with me and this time, I focussed on visiting many of the big car collections in California in the hope of picking up some restoration work. When my old friend, John Bentley, heard that I was planning to return to America, he recommended that I should visit some of his friends over there. John, like me, employed a skilled restoration team and had built up a well deserved reputation for his highly skilled engineering work.

We had an uneventful flight, except that Jo-Jo felt she should report a red distress flare which had been fired up into the sky, well below us, as we flew over Greenland. Hopefully it might have helped somebody. This time we travelled with normal hand luggage and again rented a car. It is always strange when first driving out onto the wide US highways on the 'wrong side', but I soon get used to the wide expanses of Concrete. The most notable feature which struck me, (no not physically!) was that there are virtually no road works anywhere, despite all the traffic.

Once again, there is far too much to tell you, but we saw some remarkable sights and the collections of motor cars amazed me, both in quality and quantity and John's friends couldn't have been more hospitable. Whilst in the San Francisco area, we made the short flight to

Reno to see what remained of the huge Harrah collection which had consisted of around 1450 classic motor cars, Although now much reduced in numbers, there are still many motor cars there, even the airport reception hall had a good

Harrah car transporter, USA style.

display of them.

Our first night in the hotel at Reno was made interesting when the chandeliers began to swing and it felt as if the hotel was built on a fluid 'rice pudding'. It was an earthquake, but nobody took any notice. Whilst in Reno, we also were shown a remarkable collection of period speed boats, some of which take part in the nearby, beautiful Lake Tahoe Classic Boat show. They belong to a friend of John also called John, and have all been restored to superb condition. With their gleaming, richly varnished mahogany hulls, they are a delight for any boating enthusiast.

Returning to San Francisco, we found a fire engine parked near the hotel at Fisherman's Wharfe. It turned out that it had been on fire,

Jo-Jo with 'our' fire engine in San Francisco.

but we saw no sign of it.

We had appointments to visit a number of people and their collections. One of many memorable trips was when, at San Ramon, we met and were

Jo-Jo, like a little pea in a big pod, enjoying the sun in the Cadillac Eldorado.

driven in a pink and white Cadillac Eldorado by Bill Bernbrock, to see the Blackhawk Collection. We set off from the classic car showroom (with its carpet pile so deep you nearly tripped over it), down a dual carriageway heading towards some mountains in the distance, not unlike the distant view of the lake district, seen when heading west over Bowes Moor.

After a while, I turned to Bill and asked, "how far is it to your 'Bosses' place", as he called him. His reply was that we were already in it and that the Dual carriageway belonged to his boss, as did the mountains ahead of us. Well, what can you say when this is the answer! We eventually had to stop at what looked like a border control across the motorway. Bill flashed what must have been a security pass and said "Mistrun Mizzes Royle from Lunnon England to see the cars". It was good to have him looking after us and he was most kind.

The Barrier lifted and we soon found that we were on a smaller winding road leading up into the hills which we had seen in the distance. The road was lined with houses of every style imaginable, each with its own laid out gardens and small lakes and ponds. There was then a neat central area of smaller houses with shops and then we were driving up higher into the hills, past a very large steel framed building development which Bill told us was to be the new Motor Museum. We then reached a small plateau where we pulled in so that Bill could show us the Bosses new 'bungalow' being built. Bill said that it was going to be 40,000 square feet which, by now, seemed perfectly reasonable and in scale with everything else.

We then continued upwards until we finally reached rows of low buildings which can best be described as resembling an army camp. These were surrounded by triple, high, barbed wire fences and again, we passed through security. We parked the Cadillac in the centre of the 'camp' and entered the first low building.

As we did so, Bill explained that this was temporary storage for the collection until the new Museum complex had been finished. For the next three hours, he patiently took us from one building to another and showed us the most remarkable collection of Motor Cars which I had ever seen and am ever likely to see. Bill, knowing that I was very much involved with classic cars', as the Americans call them all, very kindly, answered all our questions and let us open doors, lift bonnets and generally let us look at all the cars which we asked about. We sat in the Mercedes which Hitler used on his parades complete with its Swastika Flags. Bill flipped open the rear armrests, there were the Luger Pistols which Hitler obviously felt he might need. There were also two Bugatti's which had belonged to Coco Chanel and her sister. There were hundreds of wonderful vehicles, so many of them with a fascinating history.

We also visited the Nethercut collection in the magnificent marble hall at San Sylamar and again saw a breathtaking collection. This time, not only of cars, but also of Historic musical instruments, orchestrons and radiator mascots. We also were entertained and listened to the most magnificent, computer controlled Wurlitzer organ which, in traditional theatre style, rose up through the floor. The sound was excellent.

We visited many other wonderful collections and interesting places whilst we were in California, but I had better draw a line, or I

A few of the many magnificent motor cars in the Blackhawk Collection.

CHAPTER 20:
THE ROLLS ROYCE FRUA PHANTOM VI

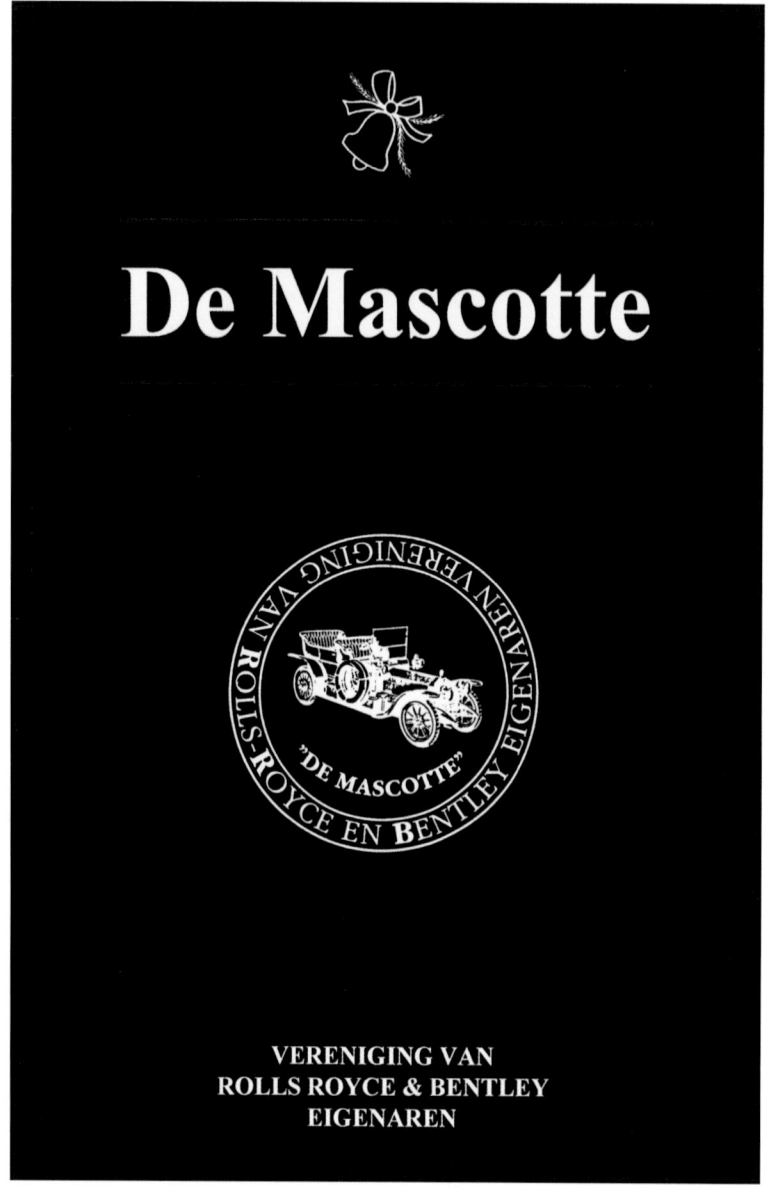

De Mascotte cover. Rolls Royce Frua.

THE STORY OF THE PHANTOM VI RR BY FRUA

Hierna volgt een artikel in het engels van dhr Royle, de bouwer van de "Frua-Phantom VI", welke hij ons toezond, n.a.v. het eerder geplaatste artikel "Zonder blikken of blozen", in ons blad van oktober 1995.

Het verhaal over deze wel zeer bijzondere Phantom VI, welke op de salon van Geneve in 1993 aangeboden werd voor FL 6.500.000, en daarmee een der duurste Rollsen uit de geschiedenis werd, willen wij U niet onthouden en drukken het af in het engels om de essentie ervan niet te verliezen.

In totaal duurde het 20 jaar voordat de Phantom afleveringsklaar was......

CHAPTER 20: THE ROLLS ROYCE FRUA PHANTOM

THE STORY OF THE PHANTOM VI RR BY FRUA

BY DAVID ROYLE

This remarkable motor car started life in the tradition of all the earlier Rolls Royce models as a rolling chassis ordered by a private individual who lived, in this case, in London. He wanted to have a body built to his own specification by a coachbuilder of his choice. The chassis was sold through Jack Barclay of London, chassis number PRH 4643 in June 1971 to Mr Buchanan Michaelson. Initially, Tom Karen of Ogle designs was asked to provide the designs for this one-off Phantom and the enclosed drawings were produced by him. The styling is not at all like those produced at the Mulliner Park Ward factory in London which normally adorned these impressive chassis.

The chassis was shipped out to Italy to the studios of Frua in Turin. Pietro Frua was well known for the prototypes and show cars he had designed for manufacturers and coachbuilders around the world, particularly in America and Europe. In England he was well known for his beautifully designed AC 428 sports cars which were built in the late 1960s. In Switzerland some attractive coachwork was designed and built for Bentley and Rolls Royce chassis.

In 1972 the owner of PRH 4643 suffered a setback when the property market slumped. The chassis remained in Frua's studios without any developments until it was

THE STORY OF THE PHANTOM VI RR BY FRUA

bought by the well-known American Rolls Royce collector, James Leake. At that time he was reputed to have 150 Rolls Royce motor cars and this impressive Phantom VI chassis provided him with a rare opportunity to build one of the world's most interesting, stylish and exotic coachbuilt motor cars of the post-war period. Mr Leake and Frua designed a cabriolet body with graceful, yet uncomplicated lines which were very much 'de rigueur' in the 70s. The Ogle designs were not proceeded with.

Jumping ahead in the story, it is interesting to note that this styling was much admired at the 1993 Geneva Motor Show by Riccardo Majocchi, the Technical Manager of Pininfarina, a fellow countryman, who said that he liked Frua's work and longed for a return to the less contrived designs of the period. He was most complimentary about the overall finish and luxurious interior which Royles had designed and incorporated into the Frua bodywork.

So around 1974 the work began on the construction of this one-off motor car. The chassis was returned to Rolls Royce to be converted to left hand drive and the chassis number amended to PRX 4643.

The length and width was increased as the work progressed which caused considerable extra work and problems for Frua, but he soldiered on for nine years. The final product was 21 ft (6.45 m) long and 6.6 ft (2.02 m) wide. Regrettably, Frua died before the work was finished, in 1983, I believe. A friend of his told me that it was partly the result of the stress and pressure resulting from the work involved with this enormous and complicated motor car.

The Story of the Phantom VI RR by Frua

The vehicle was shipped to London where little was done and it remained in store until inspected by David Royle in 1987 for the American owner. Once again, nothing was done until it changed hands yet again and was bought by a Swedish businessman, Kaj Kjellqvist, and it was then transported to Royle's workshops in Staindrop in the North of England in 1989 for the design work of the interior and completion of the entire motor car.

This Phantom VI incorporated a remarkable number of variations in its exotic and adaptable design. It was described by one of MPW's managers as a 'state cabriolet' which is a traditional and elegant title for what, in 198x, was a rare example of modern styling, yet incorporating a host of novel features, some traditional, some more modern.

This Phantom has a long, broad, stately bonnet with a steeply raked windscreen. There is a driver's compartment separated from the rear passengers by a fixed division, with a powered retractable glass partition. It has four doors, the roof is divided, the front is a rigid yet removable targa top which, with the partition glass rai sed, forms a self-contained driver's compartment which incorporates its own luxuriously upholstered seats each with twin armrests and independent air conditioning. The rear part of the roof is a fabric-covered, folding powered hood. With the driver's compartment closed and the rear open, it forms a landaulette and the division beam incorporates a plaited leather hand rail for state occasions.

With the hood in closed position, the targa top removed and the front windows lowered, the motor car becomes a Sedanca de Ville.

The rigid front roof, or 'targa top', is clamped in place but when removed is fitted into special retaining brackets under the boot lid where it is safely stored until it is needed again. The supporting gas struts are designed to cope with the varying loads put upon the boot (or trunk) lid. With both the driver's compartment and rear passengers compartment open, the division beam can be removed from the door pillar tops. This substantial component is also stowed in the boot area in a neatly designed swi nging tray into which it slides then swings out of sight beneath the hood and back seat area. There is a specially adapted refrigerator which fits into the boot for picnics or sporting occasions.

THE STORY OF THE PHANTOM VI RR BY FRUA

CHAPTER 20: THE ROLLS ROYCE FRUA PHANTOM

THE STORY OF THE PHANTOM VI RR BY FRUA

We now have an open topped cabriolet with or without the glass partition. Power this down out of sight, lower the side windows and rear quarter lights, all power operated, lift the hinged burr walnut top flaps on the division and by releasing two catches by the front seats, the door pillars fold away into the centre division and are concealed when the top flaps are closed. We are now looking at an elegant, yet modern open touring limousine and the luxurious interior is in full view.

The luxurious upholstery is a pale champagne colour and is complimented with carefully selected American burr walnut veneered panels, cappings and finishers. These are set off with tastefully inlaid stirling silver stringing. The doors are panelled taking full advantage of the intricate sap wood features and designed carefully to reflect the style and forms of the interior. The carpet was specially woven and has a shaped border to match the leather upholstery.

Incorporated into the folding centre rear armrest is a drawer which conceals and contains built-in remote controls for the many facilities incorporated into this motor car. Sitting in the back seat with the armrest drawer extended, one is looking at the beautifully veneered division. A centre panel lifts at the touch of a button and the six Royal Doulton crystal glasses come into view. Each is underlit and is retain-

The Story of the Phantom VI RR by Frua

ed in a fitted polished tray. Another button operates the concealed rotating drinks cabinet which contains three Royal Doulton decanters, a specially designed ice box with silver tongs, all set into a polished retaining tray. At night this internally lit cabinet literally sparkles with the multi-faceted polished mirror interior and crystal glass.

Between the decanters and glasses is a cupboard with inlaid doors concealing a colour television and video, also remote controlled. Framed on either side are folding picnic tables and occasional seats which also fold away into the centre division. In the heel board are a Davidoff Humidor cigar box and a matching silk-lined lady's companion, these boxes are also burr walnut veneered. There are also facilities for a telephone, and there are ash trays with cigar lighters. The rear compartment also has its own separate air conditioning. All in all a most sumptuous and tasteful interior.

The motor car is painted a medium metallic red with matching hood and roof panel and the bumpers are chromium plated. The engine compartment incorporates built-in tool boxes with a comprehensive set of the best quality tools, the jack and standard Rolls Royce equipment and spares also having their own neat tool boxes. There is a further box containing the flag poles which fit into special sockets on the front

The Story of the Phantom VI RR by Frua

wings so that national flags can be flown.

This remarkable vehicle weighs 3.5 tonnes and is, of course, a most impressive motor car on the road. It was exhibited at the 1993 Geneva International Motor Show on the Royle stand and caused a sensation with the world's Press. Interestingly, there was some confusion, a large number of people could not understand why a 'new' Rolls Royce was being exhibited on Royle's stand, rather than Rolls Royce's own stand at the Show. The notion of an owner buying a chassis and having the bodywork built to the owner's requirements is not a concept which is readily understood today. This resulted in a most inaccurate and, to a certain extent, amusing article in Le Figaro the week before the Geneva Show.

Royles are, of course, one of very few motor car coachbuilders left in the world today. Their highly skilled team have been involved with specialist motor car work for 25 years, encompassing restoration, museum work and one-off motor cars of all ages, over 600 motor cars having been built or rebuilt in their well-equipped workshops. It must be remembered that a great deal of Royle's work is in the restoration and reconstruction of period Rolls Royce and Bentley motor cars where, typically the amount of

THE STORY OF THE PHANTOM VI RR BY FRUA

hours of work involved could be up to 2000 hours. This type of work is quite different in many respects to that involved with the design and construction of such a large, exotic and complicated motor car as the Phantom VI.

The Frua Phantom VI is, without doubt, the largest and most demanding vehicle we have worked on. We spent over three years finishing off the bodywork and designing and building the luxurious interior. There were up to ten people working on the car at times and it was a very big undertaking in terms of the time spent by Royles alone. From the time it left Rolls Royce to its appearance at the Geneva Show, twenty two years had elapsed. One important aspect of the work was to strip and replace all the perishable components of the chassis, although new and unused except for Rolls Royce pre-delivery chassis testing and further testing subsequent to its completion, this Phantom had only covered the normal mileage for a new Phantom motor car when it appeared at Geneva.

By the time this Phantom VI was finished, the last factory-built Phantom VI had already left the MPW works in London, the production of this model having ceased in 1992.

I would like to express my thanks to Rolls Royce Motors at Mulliner Park Ward and Crewe for their help

THE STORY OF THE PHANTOM VI RR BY FRUA

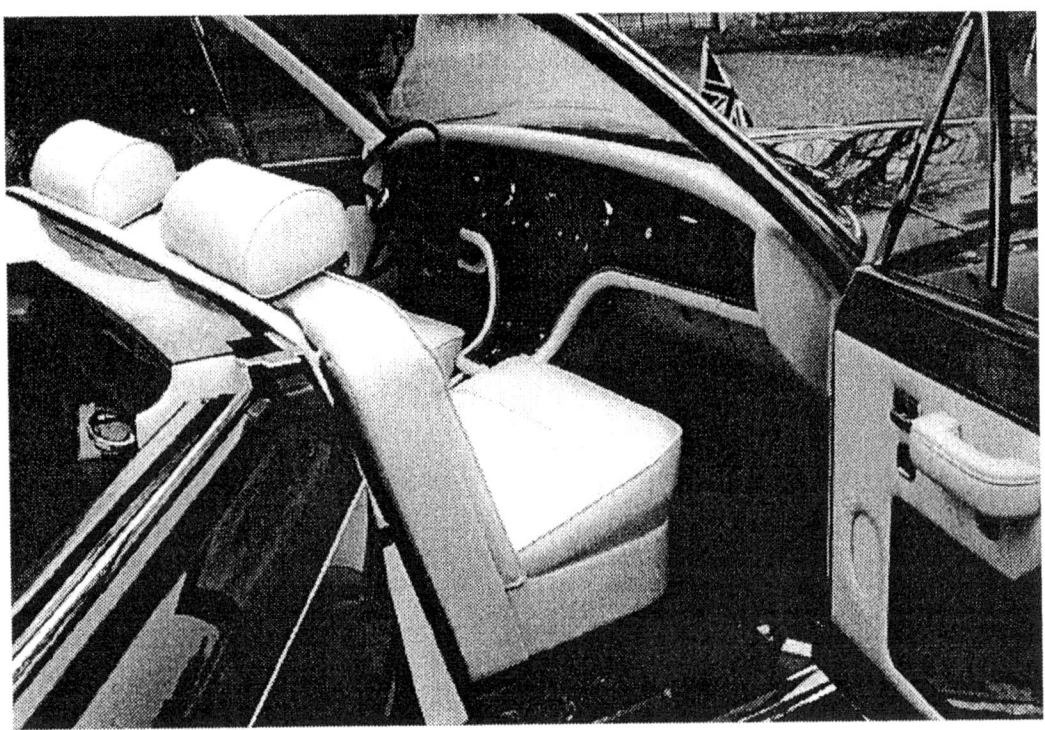

and support during the work to this car. Their advice and regular visits by their staff was greatly apprecia- ted and helped to make this Rolls Royce into one of the most remarkable vehicles built since the War.

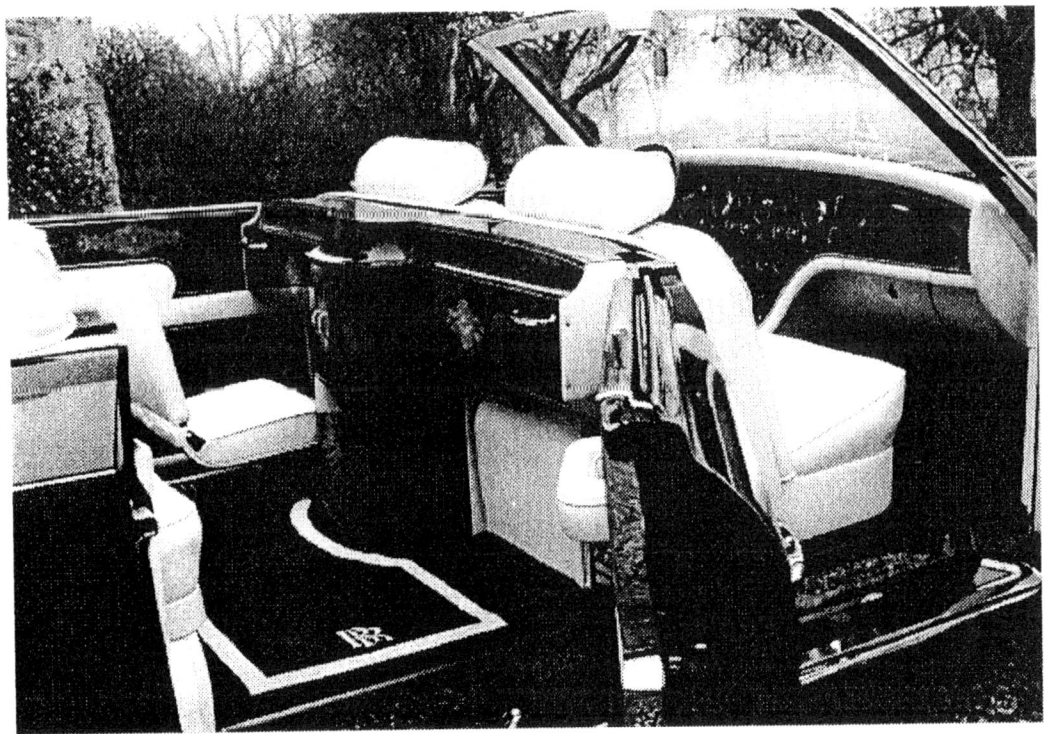

Mei 1997: Rolls-Royce opent een showroom in Peking en verkoopt direct drie auto's (krant: Sing Tao).

CHAPTER 20: THE ROLLS ROYCE FRUA PHANTOM

The last few pages briefly explain the story behind the last and most unusual coach built Rolls Royce to be finished on a new and unused Phantom VI chassis. This brief article appeared in the 1998 edition of 'De Mascotte', the club magazine of the Dutch Rolls Royce and Bentley Club. They had seen the Phantom VI at the Geneva Motor Show and had asked me if I would write it for them.

It is worth remembering that the chassis' of the Phantom series have been fitted with some of the most elegant, coach built bodies in the World. After the Daimlers in the early years, they have been used for transporting the British and many Overseas Royal Families throughout most of the 20th century. From memory, the last Phantom VI to leave Rolls Royce Mulliner Park Ward was a Landaulet in 1992 and being properly coach built, cost its owner in excess of £1million I believe.

To recap, the Phantom VI discussed here was a new, right hand drive RR chassis, sold by Jack Barclay in 1971. After various delays, it was transported to Italy. It was later shipped back to the UK to be converted to left hand drive by the factory. Returning to Italy, it was fitted with a unique, specially designed and coach built cabriolet body by the famous Italian designer Pietro Frua in his studio in Turin.

To help to clarify the story, it is one of frustration and many delays. The coachwork on the chassis actually began when it was three years old in 1974. Frua's styling was naturally, redolent of motor cars built in that period, so after nine years of his work and more delays, although a cabriolet, which was a rarity if not unique on the Phantom VI chassis, the styling was already becoming dated in 1987, when I first saw it.

It seems, from what I hear, that the length of time in Frua's studio occurred mainly as the result of a number of important changes to the specification instructed by the car's American owner. Changes which would not only introduce major technical problems with the, by then, existing new body and frame, but ones which also would have serious cost implications. I understand that the owner wanted to enlarge the bodywork to make it longer and wider. It seems that he wanted the biggest and most glamorous Rolls Royce P VI in the world.

Such changes would create a lot of extra work, especially with a body which was already one of the most complex post-war, one-off designs which I have ever seen. It is said that the frustration and pressure of this work and I imagine, the increasing costs of it, were the probable cause of Frua's death in 1983 and with it still being incomplete, I can well believe it.

Out of nearly 900 cars which have been restored and built at Staindrop, I have also designed and we have built a number of one-off motor cars. Having been charged with completing Frua's work to this particular car, I can understand the problems which he faced and as a result, the extreme stresses it created. It is the desire to please, which adds to the pressures.

When a person in his and in my position, is working for, and is reliant upon relatively few wealthy customers for his business and income, some of whom may have little or no knowledge of the amount of work and the problems and challenges associated with the creation of a one off motor car, let alone one which is as large and complex as the Frua car, then the pressures can be very considerable indeed. This is so, even when the work proceeds in a straightforward manner without design changes.

The only comparison which could be made, is to the work and costs involved when building prototype vehicles. Any motor manufacturer will tell you that the costs of this work are measured in £millions. In this case, there are teams of people involved, with ample funds set aside, not just one creative and gifted person, like Frua employing a few highly skilled engineers and craftsmen.

The specification for the Frua Car involved many unusual coachwork features. Having therefore, had to design, make and incorporate unique mechanisms into this specially designed, one off, complicated bodywork structure and then make, by hand individually, each of the external double curvature metal panels to achieve the desired shape, in this case, very long and gently flowing lines, the work is extremely demanding. When having done all this, if the owner then wants to make major changes to the overall size and shape of the car, the problems are likely to multiply to an extraordinary degree.

When changes of such a fundamental nature are demanded, especially to such a refined design of this size and complexity, then you have a recipe for huge cost increases. The problems then faced of trying to estimate costs and explain the technical and practical issues to a customer, can be insurmountable. The customer may believe that he is being taken advantage of, begins to mistrust the designer and the skilled men who are working on the car. From then on, the project can be a nightmare.

Those customers who have practical experience or have worked on old motor cars at the bench themselves however, know the problems involved and are usually most sympathetic and also pay their bills promptly. By doing this, they enjoy the best of good will of everybody, including the engineers and craftsmen, who always want to please.

I have been most fortunate with most of the people I have worked for. Ironically, my worst customers can be those who have made extremely large sums of money. It may be that they have made their money by being able to charge extremely high rates for their work or by being able apply good margins of profit, or by paying very low rates to their hundreds of workers. They probably think that they are now on the receiving end of a regime similar to their own! In our sort of work in the UK however, there are no big margins or quick profits.

In my experience, for most of the serious specialists in this country and certainly in my case, it is the pleasure and satisfaction of creating exciting and attractive motor cars which is the main reward for all the work. This is whether by restoring or by designing and building them. Dealers in classic cars can, at times, make good profits, but the labour intensive nature of our work, which must be thorough and properly done, precludes any chance of big or quick profits. In my case, as you know, making a lot of money out of this sort of work has never been the principal aim.

THE CAR STORED IN LONDON

My first involvement with the Frua Rolls Royce, was when the American owner, Mr Leake (Pronounced 'Lake') , rang me up in 1987 and asked me to fly down to London, where his driver would pick me up at Heathrow and take me to see the Frua. He wanted to know if I would like to do the job and the likely cost.

It transpired after the death of Pietro Frua, that yet again, there were further delays. It seems that two or three years had passed before the car had been shipped back to England to have the work completed. Some work had been done in London, but apparently, it was not to the satisfaction of the owner. Once again, there were difficulties, this time with the styling and/or the workmanship. My guess is that the owner was emphasising the amount of money which he had already spent and wanted to keep the costs down. This has happened to me on a number of occasions. I can understand how they can believe that their wealth will lead them to think that they will be overcharged. In my case, it didn't, I simply want to be paid for the work we do.

My first sight of the Frua car was when it was stored in a warehouse in London. By now the new and unused chassis was sixteen years old. The large, open bodywork was a bare steel shell which had been oiled all over for protection. The metal was dark in colour and had lost its shine long ago. Not surprisingly, it was very dirty and there were small areas of filler. The interior was cluttered with all manner of half finished work, unsuitable seat frames, ill fitting window frames, no glass, bundles of wire, unfinished mechanisms, unfinished linings, a poor dashboard, etc.. Altogether, a conglomeration of components which did not provide the basis for such an outstanding and luxurious Rolls Royce motor car.

Two more years passed before I heard any more. This was when I was asked by an existing customer of mine, Mr Kaj Kjellqvist ('KK'), to go to London to inspect it in 1989. He had bought it from Mr Leake and was then the third owner of this very special, but incomplete and unused motor car.

KK loved the quality of Rolls Royce motor cars and had a collection of them, all Phantoms of different ages. We were already working on two of his Rolls Royce motor cars and he was pleased with our quality of work. I explained to KK that I had already seen the car, so KK arranged for it to be delivered to Staindrop. Once it was with me, he could then describe what he was aiming to achieve. It was clear that

CHAPTER 20: THE ROLLS ROYCE FRUA PHANTOM

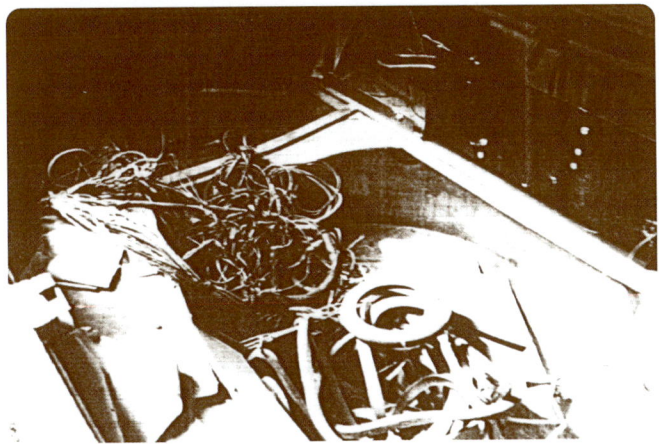

The Frua Phantom VI Rolls Royce when in store in London.

Looking back, it seems that bad luck was part and parcel of this very special Rolls Royce. Like the first owner in England, Mr Leake was apparently also now suffering financial difficulties in America. After Frua's death, he must have decided that the ongoing costs of the work to the car had to stop. The bodywork alone, of the Frua, was reputed to have cost £600,000.

KK was a most successful Swedish businessman who had many companies around the world. It seems that he and his family came to live in England to escape from the high levels of taxation in Sweden. He admitted that he was not popular in Sweden and told me that the press had hounded him out of the country.

He was a tall man with expensive tastes, loved good food and was very knowledgeable. It transpired that he spent £2000 a week eating out and his knowledge of good restaurants around the world was impressive. Jo-Jo and I frequented the well known Black Bull at Moulton near Richmond in north Yorkshire, in those days. When we first took KK, he was very surprised to find that the standards were as high as any he knew. Their fish dishes were renowned and he relished our visits to the 'Bull'. I particularly remember his astonishment when, one evening, I ordered Quails eggs which were soft boiled. He said he had never seen that before!

We got on well and I enjoyed working for him. His stories were most interesting and he and his wife Maj and daughter Asa, spoke good English and were good company. He enjoyed discussing the details of the designs and appreciated the high quality of work which we were doing for him. He was always concerned about costs, so I wanted him to know that we would do whatever we could to help minimise them. As time passed and as we came to know him better with his frequent visits to Staindrop, travelling 250 miles up and down from Sunninghill where he lived, it seemed sensible to save his ongoing hotel costs and maximise the time available to us. As a result, Jo-Jo and I invited him and members of his family, to stay at our home in Gainford. This continued for the next three years.

he wanted the vehicle to incorporate the most comprehensive luxuries, all made of the finest quality materials. The specification was to be the absolute tops.

I prepared coloured drawings and designs of my proposals for the interior, including details of the solid silver inlays, quarter cut veneers, a rotating drinks cabinet and other distinctive features. KK wanted it to be the most luxuriously appointed Phantom VI, and when these were combined with the exotic convertible facilities which Frua had planned, but not been able to finish, KK was hoping to have the most remarkable Rolls Royce to be built since the war. Not unlike his predecessor.

THE MULLINER PARK WARD FACTORY

When visiting him, we had some interesting trips to the Rolls Royce Mulliner Park Ward (MPW) factory and Service Centre in Hythe

Road, London, where the coach built RR motor cars were built. I had a good relationship with the managers at MPW who were always most helpful to me. I was able to see the techniques used when building the Phantoms and Corniche models and they were also able to supply some of their fittings which complimented the Rolls Royce and Frua's designs.

Sometimes, when visiting KK, I would stay with my old friends, Edward and Heather Carter in Windsor. You may remember that Heather was one of our original group of motoring enthusiasts. Edward was an airline pilot who enjoyed flying in all forms of aircraft and also motoring with high performance cars. We built a special Aston Martin sports car for them which I will tell you about later on in the book.

From the Carters at Windsor, I would drive over to Sunninghill in my faithful and excellent 3.6 Daimler Jaguar and take KK to the Factory at Hythe road. As I write, I still have this car eighteen years later with 178.000 miles on the clock. On other occasions, we would go in one of his cars. I remember one trip when travelling round the M25 in his Maroon Phantom VI with KK's driver at the wheel, we passed a police car at around 100 MPH. We were enjoying a gin and tonic at the time and didn't even slow down. This was because KK had his 'secret deterrent' in operation; a pair of Swedish flags mounted and flying from each front wing of this impressive Phantom VI Rolls Royce!

On another occasion, he wanted to show me the interior layout and veneers on another of his cars which he liked, so he arranged to collect me at Heathrow. As I walked out of the terminal, I noticed a chauffeur sitting in the driving seat of a large black Phantom VI, reading the paper. I didn't recognise the car, so was about to go in search of him when the Driver called to me. It was in fact KK, sitting in the driving seat in a dark suit, looking every bit like a chauffeur. He asked me to sit in the back, so that I could study the woodwork and veneers whilst he drove me over to the MPW Rolls Royce factory.

Arriving at the large gates, the uniformed attendant, believing KK to be a chauffeur, spoke to KK instructing him to take 'his master' to the door and then where to park the Rolls Royce. I had difficulty in suppressing a smile,

The Black RR PVI Limousine.

But KK took it well and didn't say a word until he had parked the car, but when he got out, he said that I could carry his brief case for him as a penance! The MPW factory was a fascinating place with all the 'Special Order' Corniche models lined up as they were being assembled. The range of colours and exotic trimming styles were an absolute delight to see.

A row of Corniche models at Hythe Road.

The hood and frame of a Corniche Rolls Royce.

Back at Royles workshops, as the work proceeded, KK was happy with my designs and our workmanship, but as ever, he wanted the very best materials and the most elegant and costly elements of design. As with all customers, KK was constantly pressing us to estimate costs. I did my best, but with a vehicle of this complexity and with so many unknowns and work being added as we went along, it was, as ever, impossible to estimate them and so we were working on our 'Time and Materials basis'. He was, by now, becoming familiar with our 'open book' systems, and as ever, had copies of the worksheets, detailed reports and photographic records which we always provide as the work proceeds. Indeed, he was sufficiently content to bring to us five of his Rolls Royce motor cars to work on.

Throughout the work, both KK and ourselves, had the benefit of help from two of MPW's managers, Peter Hand and Peter Goodall. They were closely involved with Phantoms and other vehicles built at Hythe Road, and helped and advised me of the details of construction of these coach built cars. Although the Frua Design was quite different to those produced by Rolls Royce themselves, as were my interior designs, they echoed the style and quality and they were able to provide some of the normal fittings used on Rolls Royce motor cars. Peter Hand visited Staindrop to inspect the work, not only for KK's benefit, but also for the Rolls Royce company, since it was still a 'new' and unused RR chassis and the classic RR radiator was its most pronounced feature.

Periodically, Peter Hand would travel up with KK in one of his RR motor cars and was also invited to stay with us at home. As the work progressed, it became clear why the bodywork had taken so many years. There were areas that had obviously been previously reworked and so much of the later interior work was not up to RR standards, so was scrapped. I enjoyed the challenge of starting afresh and designed the interior, the complicated division, the boot and under bonnet areas in a manner which reflected the RR quality, but which was unique to the car. I was complimented by RR for my designs which necessarily incorporated the individual features to meet the needs of this unusually complex coachwork.

At the time, traditional coach-building methods at MPW were coming to an end and the last of the Phantom VI series was being built whilst we were there. The photographs show what

The last Phantom VI. Built at MPW.

may well have been the very last one. I believe this was sold to a customer in Switzerland. This is a Landaulette and the original P. VI Buck can be seen in the background of the photographs.

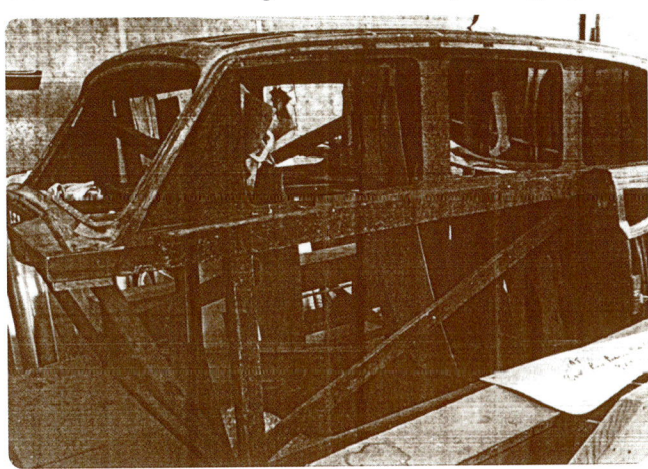

The Phantom VI Buck.

I understand that the regulations no longer permitted the use of wooden panels in motor cars due to the risk of splinters in accidents.

Meanwhile at Royles workshops, the work and input from all our staff was excellent, they had many challenges to deal with. Some of the interior folding components, occasional seats, and many other mechanisms and features were not only unique and difficult to make, they had to be of exceptional quality and at times, Don and the men were working within very close tolerances.

The specially designed equipment and mechanisms which we made, were compact and as with most Rolls Royce vehicles, had to be concealed. In certain areas, this was done with panels veneered with carefully selected, beautiful, quarter-cut American Burr Walnut complimented with the finest Swedish marquetry on the folding picnic tables. One of the unusual features which I had included in my designs, were panelled doors and each one was veneered and outlined with heavy solid silver inlays. The styling of the doors and interior ran through from front to back. Altogether, a most luxuriously appointed motor car.

The work took three years. At times there were up to ten men in different departments of our workshops involved at the same time. The cost of the work even at our low rate of £25 per hour, including materials, was nearly £440,000. The largest sum spent on a single motor vehicle at Royles at that time.

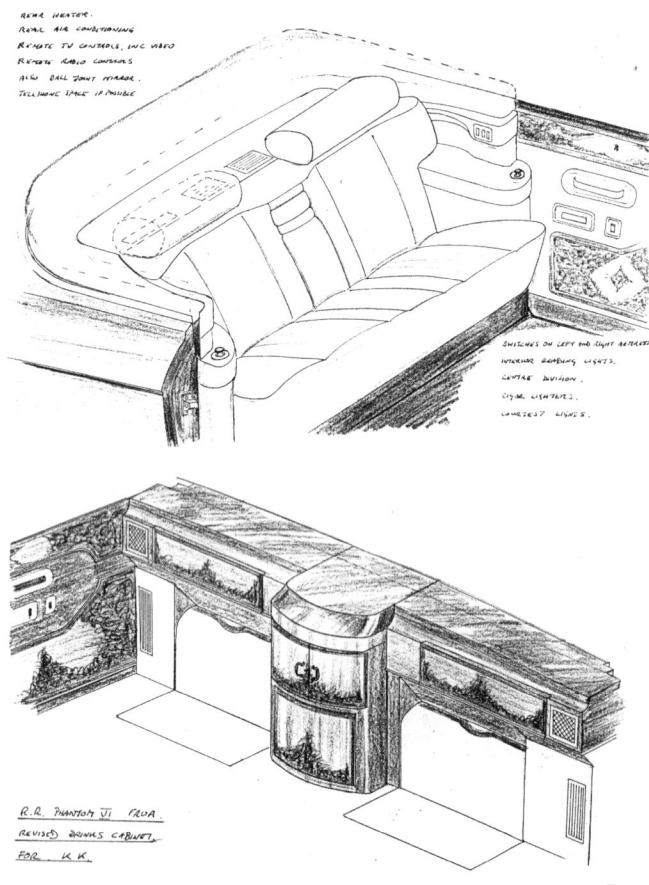

Two of DR's many sketches and drawings of the Frua Phantom VI, often coloured, provided to our customer 'KK'.

THE GENEVA SHOW

Coinciding with the period when all this work was being carried out, this country was suffering from a serious recession which began early in 1990. KK must have been affected by this since, Late in 1992, he decided not to keep the Frua car after all. He asked us if we would like to sell the vehicle for him and he decided that our sales company, Royle Cars Ltd, would put the vehicle up for sale and display it at the International Geneva Motor Show in the coming year.

Working at MPW, Peter Hand had been involved with many important Rolls Royce customers and was familiar with the costs and prices that new Phantom VI motor cars sold for. With its high specification, unique and complicated convertible open coachwork, it was unquestionably one of the most glamorous and exotic Rolls Royce PVI cars ever to be built. Peter proposed a figure of around two million pounds as a selling price. Not surprisingly, KK readily agreed to this profitable figure.

Not having ever exhibited at an international motor show, let alone what is probably the world's most important one, this was going to be a most interesting exercise. Piers Leigh, who was the Sales Director of Royle Cars Ltd and ran the company for me, immediately set about organising the stand and making all the necessary arrangements. Quite a challenge when we are such a small company and not known as motor car manufacturers.

Henri Scheidegger the general manager of the Geneva show, wanted to be sure of our credentials, so Piers attended to this along with the actual planning for the stand. The organisers were very thorough, especially as we were exhibiting for the first time and with, what was likely to be, the most expensive motor car at the show. Once satisfied, they were most helpful to us and we were allotted Stand No 42.02.

Being regularly in touch with the Rolls Royce company, we explained our plans to them and knowing that our work was to a high standard, they saw no reason to object to us exhibiting a coach-built Rolls Royce on the 'Royle' stand. Rolls Royce were, of course, already exhibiting at Geneva themselves as usual and were announcing the new Bentley 'R' model, so a one-off coach built RR vehicle on one of their

CHAPTER 20: **THE ROLLS ROYCE FRUA PHANTOM**

Frua's sleek styling and Royle's superb finish can be seen here on the Phantom VI Rolls Royce Cabriolet.

The luxurious interior, showing unique styling with burr walnut and marquetry veneers, panelled doors, solid silver stringing inlays. The rotating drinks cabinet with underlit glasses tray, and decanters and folding picnic tables.

The centre division at night showing the drinks cabinet lit up with the TV and video unit and occasional seats folded up.

Phantom chassis was not likely to be in conflict with their announcement. Furthermore, as production of the coach-built Phantom VI series had just come to an end at MPW, there wasn't a problem.

Although my Colitis was making life increasingly difficult for me, I was very much looking forward to exhibiting this luxurious motor car at the famous Salon International de L'Automobile de Gene've. Especially with such an interesting and impressive Rolls Royce Motor car. The quality of our work could not be better demonstrated than at the 63rd Geneva Show which ran from the 4th to the 14th March 1993. The 'News Release' Brochure was very smart in silver and described the car as a 'State Cabriolet'.

As it was the first time Royle's had exhibited at the salon, there was a lot of planning work, but with Roger and I helping when needed, the result was most satisfactory. Unlike most of the other exhibitors, we required special dispensation to have a protected stand. The organisers preferred exhibitors to have open stands with the cars open and available to the public. In our case, we had the most expensive car at the Price of £2.1 million, so they were happy to allow us to have it fenced in with a gate for controlled access.

It was a great thrill to see the 'Royle' name above the stand along with all the most famous car manufacturers in the world. The press had given the car a lot of publicity in the UK and also in 'Le Figaro' in Paris. The French journalist who had written the half page article, had obviously been confused by the various body styles which were possible with Frua's complex and convertible coachwork. He had produced a most creative 'piece' which, whilst being highly inaccurate, must have entertained Rolls Royce themselves as much as it amused us.

It seemed that the writer did not understand the tradition of English coach-building, and how one-off bodies were built to order, onto manufacturers Chassis. In his article, he accused Royles of building a number of different 'RR' vehicles and of falsely trading under the Famous Rolls Royce name, viz, "Royle's Royce", and saying that "nine lawyers" from Rolls Royce would be waiting for us at Geneva! It seems that he had misunderstood our brochure which describes how the Frua car converted into its various body styles! Not surprising really, I suppose, if his English was not too good and it was a most unusual motor car. It may just have been a bit of sensational journalese of course.

In fact, of course, RR had been working with us and their own stand was not far from ours. The MD at the time was Peter Ward, who came along for a friendly chat and to inspect our car. It was unlike any other coach-built RR and being open, looked very glamorous, especially with the many high pin-point lights which typify the Geneva show. I was on the stand at the time with Piers Leigh and Peter Hand was

Geneva Motor Show 1993.

also in attendance to deal with potential buyers, by this time, he had been made redundant from Rolls Royce MPW, who had transferred the coach-building work to their Factory at Crewe in Cheshire. Peter Ward kindly complimented us upon the standard of finish.

On the press day the Royle stand was surrounded with journalists, some were even standing on

adjoining display stands in order to see over the heads of the crowd. This was quite embarrassing, we were showing a one-off model when all the big manufacturers were doing their best to increase sales to survive the recession. It was of course the big price and the glamorous and unusual nature of it, which attracted their attention.

We had quite a number of overseas visitors to the stand during the show who were quite interested in buying the car, but in the final analysis, they were mainly members of royal families and statesmen who needed to have bullet proof cars. With it already weighing 3.5 tonnes and being an open cabriolet with a fabric roof, it was simply not practicable to make it an armoured vehicle.

One visitor was a young man whom, I would guess as being in his late twenties, was keenly interested. He was dressed in a brown 'T' shirt and jeans, he asked the price and specification and after showing him the features on the car, lifting his sleeve, he looked at his watch and left the stand. The watch was a bit of a give away, in contrast with his simple clothes, it was heavily encrusted with diamonds!

Not long afterwards, a most glamorous lady came onto the stand to ask if 'her Prince' could visit the stand. A tall elegant man duly appeared and after a while, politely asked if "his little friend" had been on the stand , I guessed whom he meant and I described the young man and his simple clothes. The prince confirmed that it was the same person and explained that he was a member of the Kuwait Royal Family. They were looking to replace their motor cars which had been taken when their country had been invaded by Saddam Hussain's Iraqi army.

Another interesting visitor asked if he could come onto the stand and be shown the car. After examining it, he was very complimentary about it all. He said he liked the Italian body styling and then asked who had designed the luxurious interior. After telling him, he complimented me on my work and said that it was very well done and obviously had "not been designed on a computer". Surprised by his depth of knowledge, I confirmed that this was so and asked him how he knew this. He explained that he was Riccardo Majocchi, the technical manager for Pininfarina Studios in Italy. A compliment indeed.

At the end of the show, we had failed to sell the car which was a great disappointment to us all, especially KK. The potential buyers were mainly from the Middle East where security is essential. When we quoted the price, some found it difficult to believe it was not lire or francs or whatever, the numbers were so big. In 1993, the recession was still affecting the market and it was a very costly vehicle indeed, so the Rolls Royce Frua Phantom VI State Cabriolet was unsold.

CHAPTER 21:
THE TROUBLES BEGIN

Before the show there was a lot of pressure to finish the Frua Rolls Royce and everything was done to expedite completion in readiness for Geneva. After the show I was becoming concerned because KK now owed us £73,000. Although he repeatedly promised that he was going to pay me, six months passed and he still had not done so.

Upon its return, the RR had been delivered to the workshops to remove all the protective coverings which we had used for the journeys to and from Geneva. I was pressing him to pay me, but he wanted to take the car away to sell it, but I refused to release it.

The recession was still adversely affecting Royles business in 1993 and the company overdraft was now approaching £100,000 and interest was accruing. I have always personally secured the companies banks borrowings and still do. I was seriously worried about the situation and my colitis was becoming more intense. I had no choice but to inform KK that we held a common law lien on the vehicle and that he could not have it back until it was paid for.

The result was that KK now declared 'War' on me, as he called it. He was threatening to take legal action against me and my companies and urgently wanted to have his car returned so that he could sell it, I could understand this, but after over three years, I was now seeing a side of him which I had not seen before. I realised that I may not be able to trust him. He had written to me in August saying that he was "sincerely" concerned about my health and had again promised to pay the "outstanding amounts", which he still had not done.

With MPW having ceased production at Hythe road and with Peter Hand now being redundant, It seems that he was being employed by KK. It transpired that he was helping KK to put a legal case together against Royles and me, so that KK could avoid paying the £73.000 debt. After working so closely with them for three years and with both of them regularly inspecting all the work, as well as having the fully detailed records of every hour spent from the outset, I was amazed that they would even consider such a thing. There were also around 250 photographs of the work being done.

It was especially hurtful, because Jo-Jo had gone to great lengths to look after and entertain them at home whenever they came North during the three year period of work. Jo-Jo is a wonderful cook and knowing KK's refined tastes, she took great trouble to create some delicious meals to please him. She was always most concerned, because she knew that he was an important customer. There also were a number of beds to make up in different rooms each time they came to stay with us at Gainford. We did have plenty of room, but with having little help in the house meant that catering for KK and his party was hard work.

What was really shocking was that KK would stoop so low when he knew how important the money was to us and he must have known that we would never take advantage of him.

THREATS & OFFERS

KK commenced Legal action in September 1993 claiming that he had been "overcharged and double charged" for the work. He said that he would take action through the High Court in London and that he would make it so expensive that I couldn't afford to defend my company or myself. Being open and honest as I am, he knew full well that I was in a dreadfully weak financial position and also that major surgical operations were imminent to remove my colon. After all, we had done evrything we could to please him and I found it difficult to believe that he would treat us so badly to save himself money when he seemed to be so well off.

Knowing how high legal costs are, and being so substantially overdrawn at the bank, I decided that it would be pointless for me to employ solicitors to defend ourselves. The cost of doing so in London, even if we won, would probably be more than the debt. On the other hand, I could not possibly write off the £73,000, especially with interest at around 12% and with the ongoing recession, I had no choice, but to defend the case myself, colitis or no colitis.

If I didn't, the company would be unlikely to survive.

At this time, in parallel, I had also made substantial borrowings for the Amphibious vehicle project. I was, by this time, confident that the demand for our amphibians was such, that it would be successful and far more profitable than our restoration work. This being so it would be able to reimburse Royles for all the development work and put the company on a firm footing in the coming years.

I was just resigning myself to have to tackle the defence without solicitors when Peter 'Nimble' Thompson, a friend and customer, offered me the services of his large legal firm Eversheds, saying that they would be more likely to win the case for me than my other smaller firm of solicitors which he obviously expected that I would turn to. I had told him about the debt on one of his previous workshop visits.

Nimble had inherited, from his father, a most handsome Continental Bentley S3 Mulliner Park Ward Drop Head Coupe'. This had given the family good service, but was now mechanically 'tired' and was showing its age with various problems, including seriously corroded bodywork. Actually, some of the work to the sub structures of this motor car can be seen in two of the photographs in our 'Royle' brochure. Nimble's Bentley was in the process of being restored at Royles workshops when the KK problems developed.

Having seen KK's work going on and with his Bentley having been built by MPW, Nimble was naturally interested and familiar with the work to the Frua Rolls Royce and also to KK's other valuable RR cars which were being worked upon in our various workshops. When Nimble offered his firm's services, he knew that KK had a number of overseas companies and he could see that KK was a very wealthy individual.

Being aware of all this and also, importantly, being very familiar with our work and our honest, straight forward 'open books' systems, Nimble felt confident in offering his legal services. He thought that if we had a fair hearing, we would win the action. He was also well aware that our detailed records, documentation and photographs would prove, in court, that we are an honest company.

I thanked Nimble for his kind offer, but declined to accept it. Knowing that Eversheds rates were about £150 per hour at the time, ours were £25 per hour! I explained that their legal costs would probably cancel out any benefits, even if we won.

THE REVISED OFFER

Nimble came back soon afterwards with a revised offer saying that, on this occasion, he was prepared to take a "punt", as he called it, on Eversheds getting their costs from KK, the opposition. He stressed that this offer was conditional upon us winning the action with the benefit of a Costs Order. I believed that he knew how important it was for us to have our bill paid and that there was no question of our defence being one of principle or simply an academic exercise. He had also seen my health deteriorating and I was sure that he was genuinely concerned about my predicament.

This revised offer was extremely kind and I gratefully accepted it. The agreement was that I would pay Eversheds costs if we lost the case. The risks were still such, that if we lost, they would be devastating on top of the existing borrowings. Nimble estimated that their costs would be approximately £25,000, which at the time, I thought, was likely to be low for litigation of this nature. Not having been in a court before, however, I had no experience of the cost of court proceedings. In return for his support, he asked me to pay as much as I could towards these costs as we prepared for the hearing. I was most grateful and despite my seriously over extended overdraft, I told him that I would do my very best to try to do this, but explained to him that it would be difficult, because of my financial position.

This support gave me much hope, but I was facing a veritable mountain of problems:

To begin with, whether in bed or at the office, my colitis meant that I had very urgent visits to the loo every 15 to 20 minutes or so, day and night. At the same time, I had a huge amount of preparation work to do putting together 3½ years of detailed documentation for the hearing. I was also starting a series of major surgical operations which were going to coincide with my first direct involvement in a court. Not just any court, but the High Court, defending myself and the company against an extremely wealthy and determined man in an action in the Royal Courts of Justice, on the Strand in London.

All this was bad enough, but with a reduced workload I also knew that I had to find the wages for my staff every week and was going to have to spend time in London, a city where I had no accommodation and where hotel costs are very expensive. All to be done with a seriously overdrawn bank overdraft.

If I failed in all this, Jo-Jo and I could lose the restoration and sales company, the amphibious project and possibly the house. You will understand why my focus and entire aim had to be to Win with Costs. If we did, Nimble said that our £73,000 "bill would be paid".

NIL BY MOUTH

I have included the story of my hospital operations here because they help to give you a more rounded picture of all the events surrounding the Rolls Royce and KK affair and of the relevance and nature of Colitis (described in my layman's terms!). It also explains how the operations and the time spent recuperating relates to the ongoing story.

By this time, in late summer 1993, I had suffered from Colitis since 1989 and despite my wish to try every possible drug which might have helped and avoided surgery, I was then taking 36 pills each day, but they had all failed. Every time I visited the loo, I could see that the internal bleeding had continued for three years and my local specialist was now recommending surgery.

With the Frua RR not selling at the Geneva show and with ever increasing pressure by KK to retrieve the car combined with the financial worries of my much extended overdraft, KK could see that I was now seriously unwell. Never the less, it seems that it was no coincidence that his lawyers started the action and increased the pressure on me in September, knowing full well that I was due to go into hospital for the first of a series of major operations at that time.

If the operations were to be carried out here in the North East, it seemed that I could be left with an Ileostomy bag indefinitely. This did not appeal to me one little bit. (This is similar to a Colostomy bag, but it drains the small intestine rather than the large one, the colon.) My old friend Brownie and his wife, Judy, strongly advised me to seek a second opinion, so I made enquiries.

At that time, we were working on a Low Chassis 4.5 litre Brooklands Invicta which belonged to an English doctor who was living in Canada. We were also working on a special bodied Rolls Royce Phantom 11, which belonged to another friend Terry Leonard who was living in Monte Carlo. It was interesting that both of these people lived far apart and in different countries and yet both recommended the same man, Dr Silk in Harley Street, London. This was a good sign, so on 25th August 1993, I followed their advice and went to see Dr Silk, (now Professor Silk), the highly respected specialist in Harley Street.

After he examined me, he advised me that the whole of my colon would have to be removed and that I now had so many ulcers that I should be operated on within ten days or it could be fatal. When asked about the long term effects, he said that the operation could be reversed and that I would only need to have a 'bag' for a few months. This was marvellous news!
He explained that the operations would best be carried out at The Princess Grace Hospital in London where similar operations were being done on a regular basis.

He stressed the urgency, but I was concerned that the cost of this London Hospital might be well above the BUPA level for which I was covered, but Dr Silk assured me that I would be OK and I was. Looking back, they admitted me very quickly, within ten days, I think that the hospital was fairly quiet, so I was being 'body snatched' to keep up the Princess Grace cash flow! They obviously had the expertise, so I was perfectly happy about this!

Needless to say, I returned home and made sure that the bank would support me and that all was in order, gave Roger all the firms Cheque Books and was admitted to the hospital in Nottingham Place, London on Sunday 5 September, ten days later on the dot!

It was a marvellous place with wonderful nurses and it was to be the beginning of some very interesting and, believe it or not, quite happy and memorable times. When you know that there is nothing you can do about what is happening, you might as well lie back, relax and let them get on with it. Because I didn't have cancer, I felt I was very lucky and had complete confidence in the Surgeon, Mr Menzies-Gow, who explained that I had a 90% chance of surviving the operation. I repeated this to the Anaesthetist Dr Walton, who assured me by saying that, "If anybody is going to kill you, it would be me", very comforting! We had established a good working relationship and I much enjoyed our conversations.

Without wishing to dwell on the subject, the first operation when my colon was removed, started with the inevitable trolley ride to theatre. As they administered the final knockout in the preparation room, I looked up and found myself surrounded by a remarkable mix of nationalities and can remember saying "it looks just like a meeting of the United Nations" just as I blacked out.

Coming round the following day in my room, with the surgeon and nurses bending over me, I told them that I felt absolutely marvellous. The surgeon said that this could be as a result of the anaesthetics. I said I wouldn't know about that, but explained that I had just awoken from the most comfortable and wonderful night's sleep, the best that I had had for three years!

At home, my major problem had been that I needed to visit the loo every 15 to 20 minutes, meaning that I averaged between 25 and 30 trips each night. The result was that, in the winter time, the loo seat was never cold and the bed was never warm! I was in a strange twilight zone for three years, but got used to it. Poor Jo-Jo, she never complained, we have always shared the same 4'6" bed and still do. Strangely enough, I had been able, with the constant interruptions, to carry on working during the day and all things considered, didn't feel too tired. It is amazing what the body can put up with.

Whilst in hospital and being in London, I had visits from many friends who were in town and popped in to say "hello" which I thought was very kind of them. Later on, it turned out, in reality, that they had called in to say "goodbye". Five days after the operation, I was able to manage without morphine and gradually was able to take food again. When I started to move around, I soon realized how weak I was, but felt fine.

There were many amusing incidents some of which are a bit too 'medical' to tell here, but one which still makes me smile was when the nurse came into my room one evening and asked if I had had an erection. Well, the nurses were all very slim and attractive girls, but my mind wasn't really working in that direction at this 'tender' time! She reminded me that Mr Menzies-Gow was sufficiently expert to know precisely where the nerve ran or whatever it is which activates this particular 'member', but I guessed that he wanted the nurse to check that all was in 'working order'. Strangely, I apologised for not being able to confirm one way or the other. She said she would come back later to check again! To use the hackneyed expression, my mind boggled!

Sure enough, she returned just after midnight and sitting on my bed, repeated the question. I apologised again and said quite coyly that I didn't know. At this point, she leaned over me and as I held my breath, her arm reached over me and taking hold of the TV remote control, which was on the bedside table, she switched the television on. Now sitting on the end of the bed, she tuned in to a rather sexy film and proceeded to enjoy it for a while. So, watching a pretty girl watching a sexy film sitting on the end of your own small bed, the answer to her question was not long in coming!

Another event which amused me was when the Stoma specialist, Liz Cheshire, called in and asked me if I would speak at the London Colitis Club meeting. I couldn't help but laugh at the thought of it and said that I would be talking to myself most of the time, because there would be more people in the lavatory than in the auditorium. At least in the loo, the acoustics would have been interesting! I do hope she didn't take it the wrong way.

A BUSY RECUPERATION

After two weeks in hospital, I felt fine if a little 'delicate', so I was invited to spend the first night after hospital in London staying with my good Swedish friends Nils and Lena Dalchvist at their lovely flat in Kensington. The following day, my old friend 'Brownie' kindly drove down to London in my comfy Daimler, picked me up and brought me home.

After hospital in London, it seemed strange to

be at home in the country again with Jo-Jo, the family and the dogs. I had to get used to having an Ileostomy 'bag' which wasn't much fun, but Jo spoilt me, as ever, and generally speaking, I felt fine. I called in at the office, but was not very strong, but was healing well and felt better steadily recuperating and doing my work in bed at home. I have always enjoyed a lie in bed in the mornings, so now I had a really good excuse! Never the less there was a lot to do and to think about.

I was seriously concerned about the worrying overdraft, the ongoing recession and also being confronted with all the work involved with preparations for the High Court hearing. I was also very busy with the ongoing design work for the Roylecraft Amphibious Vehicle Project.

Now that I've explained my intricate medical problems and you are aware of the relatively fragile state I was in at the time, I'll return to the court case.

During the next seven weeks, In order to minimise the legal costs, I was dealing with KK's London lawyers, Berwin Leighton, myself. Knowing that I was just out of hospital and no expert on legal matters, they were putting a lot of pressure on me. Long multi-page legal letters rolled out of our Fax machine on a daily and sometimes hourly basis, some reaching down to the floor. They demanded immediate responses and the release of the Frua Rolls Royce. Fortunately, I knew, under common english law, that I could hold onto it until it was paid for, so did not comply with their demands.

CHAPTER 22:
EARLY WORRIES

At the time, KK's lawyers kept demanding the name of my solicitor, I wanted to keep them guessing, but I finally told them that Eversheds solicitors were representing me. The faxes stopped, and all went quiet. From the start, Nimble had appointed another of Eversheds solicitors, Mr Coates, to deal with the day to day matters of my case. I soon began to have serious concerns about this man's allegiance to me, however.

My suspicions were first aroused when Mr Coates advised me not to hold onto the Frua Rolls Royce. He said that the court would not look favourably upon me, if I continued to prevent KK from having his car back and not being able to sell it. I was sufficiently confident to ignore this advice, since it was clearly against our interests. It would obviously have been foolish to give away our only security, especially when we had every right, under common law, to hold a lien on it.

It was not long however, before I was again becoming concerned about 'our' Mr Coates. Judging from ongoing events and the correspondence, it seemed that KK's lawyers knew a great deal more about our affairs than they normally should, matters which, certainly, should have been confidential.

This time I reported my concerns to Nimble, but he assured me that all was in order. Because I didn't want to appear troublesome to him when he was being so helpful to me, I needed some way to check on 'our' Mr Coates. To do this, I fed certain specific information to Mr Coates and to him only. Information which would certainly be useful to the 'opposition'. Sure enough, within two days, it came back to me from KK's lawyers. I explained what had happened about this to Nimble and again asked him to replace Mr Coates with another Eversheds solicitor, but Nimble still would not accept it and refused, this worried me a lot. Knowing what I now know, it is possible that they had no other work for him, as he had only recently joined the firm.

By now, I was fully occupied gathering together and compiling all the huge number of job sheets, time sheets, drawings, letters, photographs and other information. As advised by Eversheds, I was numbering them and putting them into bundles with descriptions of the events. This was a lot of work, because we had spent over three years and thousands of hours working on the Frua car and it was obviously important that all the aspects and information was given to Eversheds as evidence.

The years of work to the car had involved virtually all our staff at various times which meant that there were literally thousands of documents. As previously explained, we always retain all our records, so whilst it took me many months of work, It was especially worthwhile because I was also familiarising myself with all the evidence. The written documents which we needed to prove our case, were all there. Importantly, I also thought, at the time, that my work would help to minimise the solicitor's costs.

Fortunately, along with all the workshop documents, I had also written detailed reports to KK at regular intervals throughout the work. When these were read in conjunction with all our weekly job sheets and photographs, they provided a first class, comprehensive record of the huge amount of work done and the effort which had been involved in order to complete this outstanding and highly complicated vehicle.

Whilst doing all this, my second operation was becoming due. Before going back into hospital however, Dr Silk asked me to visit him at Harley Street in early November so that he could check to see if the first operation had properly healed. The condition of the long external incision down my front was, I learnt, a good indication of the healing 'within'. Although eight weeks had passed since the first operation, my first visit to Dr Silk proved, apparently, that it had not fully healed and so I was not quite ready yet. The doctor thought that I should wait another fortnight until the 21st November, when they would be opening me up again by cutting down along the same line. I had travelled to London by train and was there and back in the day, arriving home late in the evening.

Apparently, this would also happen again for the third operation, so jokingly, I asked if they could fit a zip fastener to save another Dr 'Silk-Cut'. Not very funny really, but strangely enough, talking of cigarettes, I was asked if I had given up smoking, which in fact I had done in 1989, not long before the colitis began. It could have been connected, apparently.

A few days before heading south to London again, for the second operation, I received the formal affidavit from KK. It was an astonishing 308 pages long, a full Lever Arch File. Knowing KK quite well by now, I could tell that he had not written it himself, this was because of its general tone and detail. My guess was that it had been written by the now Ex- MPW manager, Peter Hand. I presumed by its size and the accusations contained in it, that KK was trying to frighten me and dissuade me from defending my company's charges. He was showing that he meant business and had every intention to make the case a costly affair.

TO LONDON FOR THE SECOND OPERATION

The arrival of this long affidavit was, in fact, badly timed for KK. As far as I knew, at this stage, he may not have been aware of Nimble's offer of support and of our agreement and this seemed to confirm it. Also, I knew that I would be spending a lot of time in hospital, so I took the affidavit with me on the train and later, in my quiet, private room in the hospital and with all the drips and drains attached, I couldn't move much, so had a great opportunity to study this contrived and lengthy affidavit. As the days passed and I worked my way through the report, I could see that it included various statements which were blatantly untrue. I could also see that, in fact, it drew a veil over the truth and like any veil, it was full of holes !

Without wishing to dwell too much on medical matters, this second part of the surgical process turned out to be the major and most interesting, if risky, part of this Royle's bodywork 'Restoration'.

Being now without my colon, once eaten and having gone down the long, small intestine, the food then had nowhere to go, except into the external bag. In order to do away with this and eventually reconnect the top of the digestive system to the 'bottom', as it were, (which is the third operation,) the surgeon has to cut off a length of my long, small intestine. With this length of tubing, which is about 1 inch in diameter, he can reconnect the top to the bottom and construct a small 'pouch' part of the way along it to replace the colon. This major operation obviously involves very clever surgery and I owe my life to Mr Menzies-Gow.

When interviewing staff at the workshops, I like to look at their hands, so on my first meeting with the surgeon, I asked if I could look at the hands which would be delving into me. He kindly, but reluctantly, showed them to me and they were surprisingly rough, so I asked him what his hobby was, "tying flies and fishing" he replied. "Hmm" I thought, not a bad combination for this job.

After literally thousands of visits to the Loo during each of the previous three years, I asked Mr Menzies-Gow if he would kindly build me a nice big pouch, so that I would not have to go to the loo so often. "No, we have our limits" he said. I couldn't help having a little more fun, so told him that my company didn't mess about, if we had a problem, we would build a completely new body, not "fiddle around with a rotten old one". Fortunately, he took it the right way otherwise, I might not be here to tell the story!

I learnt that there is a lot of 'internal work' to do when rebuilding this part of the human anatomy and it certainly is important that the surgeon is very experienced. This operation is the most complicated of the three and takes many hours. Unlike the first, the aftermath turned out to be somewhat of a 'battle' for me. Looking back at my diary I was, never the less, able to get on with some of the affidavit work, but there was mounting concern, because I had lost three stones and nine days had passed since the operation and my stomach was rejecting all foods, even sips of water. Although I always felt fine, my situation was not good, my peristalsis had ceased to function.

Into the third week, after a determined effort to avoid another operation, one which I didn't like the sound of, I finally kept some milk down and started to feel better and was making good progress all round, both medically and with my work for the court.

When compiling my response to KK's affidavit, I soon realised that it could, in fact, be the key to his own downfall. He could well be hoisting himself up with his own petard. My affidavit dealt with the key points and finally ended up being 105 pages, so in comparison, was fairly 'brief'. The main difference being that it was all true and factual and I was able to provide plenty of references to written and photographic evidence. I was confident that, given a good hearing, it would undermine KK 's dishonest affidavit and his case against us.

At the end of the third week at the Princess Grace, I was considered well enough to return home, so this time, my good friend 'Lev' Kitching came down in my car to take me home. My Daimler Jaguar is a most comfortable car and it was extremely kind of my friends to rally round to drive me home. It was now the 12th December and the weather was foul with snow and slush and lots of traffic all the way home. As ever, Lev didn't mind this and got me home quickly and safely.

BACK HOME AGAIN

Once again, I needed to recuperate at Gainford whilst all my in-depth 'Repairs' healed up in readiness for the next operation, once again, I took the opportunity to do some useful work in and out of our comfortable old bed for the next few weeks.

Just after Christmas, on the last day of December, life became particularly difficult at home when Jo-Jo's back inexplicably seized up and she was in great pain if she moved at all. We both were now in bed and in a sorry state, the irony was that I was now the 'fittest' member of the two of us! It was particularly difficult because, in theory, I was not supposed to lift anything at all and also had to be careful that I didn't 'disrupt' the long row of stitches or the bag which I was still trying to get used to. We were like a couple of ancient pensioners with Jo-Jo rooted to the bed and me, literally crawling around the house on my knees trying to look after her. At least, I was able to move about and somehow we managed, with help, whenever we could get it.

After a week or so, Jo-Jo's back improved and as the weeks passed, I was healing up and as ever, was kept very busy with the ongoing legal preparation work of writing descriptions of the activities shown in the hundreds of our workshop RR photographs. I was also keeping the workshops busy and continuing with designing, building and as soon as fit enough, testing the Amphibious prototypes.

I continued to be increasingly worried about Mr Coates, our Eversheds solicitor. I was in great difficulty because I was loathe to give him any information which would help our defence, since there was the likelihood that it would be transmitted straight to, and be of value to KK's lawyers. It would therefore be self-defeating. What was so frustrating was that, at times, he gave the impression that he was working with us. Fortunately, I was soon to have further, definite proof of his allegiance to the 'opposition', KK and his lawyers, Berwin Leighton.

I delivered the photographic records to Eversheds Leeds office at a meeting held there on 7th February 1994 with Nimble and Mr Coates. I paid them another £750 towards their costs explaining how difficult it was for me and that it was all I could manage. I also said that I was becoming concerned about the increasing level of Eversheds costs and their constant requests for more money. I was told that we were still nowhere near being ready for the hearing and yet it seemed to me that I was doing most of the preparation work. I also mentioned at the meeting, that I would soon be due for my next, the third, operation.

CHAPTER 23:
'DELIVERY UP' & SKULLDUGGERY

At this time, still desperate to cancel our lien and get his valuable Frua RR Motor car back, I heard that KK was going to apply to the High Court for 'Delivery up' of the Frua Rolls Royce. To achieve this, the judge ordered that he was to provide a Bank guarantee of £90,000 to the court. This was imminent when my next trip to see Dr Silk was due on Tuesday 22nd February.

Having told Mr Coates at the Eversheds meeting that that my third operation was due fairly soon, as a matter of courtesy, I did mention a fortnight later on the telephone, that I was taking the train to London the following day. As ever, not wanting to reveal too much to him, I did not clarify that it was just a check up, but I didn't realise the importance of this omission until soon afterwards.

Not surprisingly, Mr Coates assumed that I would be in hospital for at least a week and would be well out of the way and not in the office. As previously, in fact, I was back that night by 11pm. No sooner had I arrived home when the phone rang. It was Roger to tell me that KK had been seen by one of our men in the vicinity in another of his Rolls Royce motor cars. So I was ready for him.

The next morning, I was waiting at the office for him to arrive. Sure enough, after what would, no doubt, have been a leisurely and enjoyable breakfast, his Rolls Royce drove into our yard at Staindrop. A few moments later, four people, including KK, burst straight into the office without knocking. I immediately confronted them, where upon KK blurted out saying "You are not supposed to be here, we thought that you were in hospital". So, for KK and his lawyers to be in Staindrop, 250 miles from London, they must have known exactly what my movements were within minutes of me telling Coates.

Even after such an obvious admission that information was immediately being passed from 'our' Mr Coates to KK's solicitors, when I told Nimble, incredibly, he still denied that there was collusion between them.

Looking back, having given Coates advance notice about my impending trip to the hospital in London, two weeks beforehand at the meeting, KK and his Lawyers had plenty of time to formulate a plan. They could make all the necessary arrangements to 'snatch back' the two million pounds Rolls Royce when I was in hospital and would not be there to stop them. So, the minute they heard that I was on the train and in spite of the bad snowy weather, the pre-arranged plan must have been immediately activated.

Without me knowing, when I was on the train heading south, the KK party, along with their transporter, must have passed me as they drove north up the motorway.

The party which burst into the office consisted of KK, his daughter Asa, Peter Hand, the ex RR manager and a fourth person, a man in a leather jacket and jeans whom I assumed to be the lorry driver. They immediately demanded the return of the Frua car and when I refused to hand it over, they threatened to telephone the police. They acted in a most threatening and authoritative manner, but I told them that they had no right to be on my premises and firmly ordered them out of the building.

Although having lost so much weight and not very fit or ready for this sort of confrontation, they could see that I was very firm and meant business. They immediately turned on their heels and as they went downstairs, I apologised to the 'lorry driver' for my abrupt behaviour, whereupon he told me that he was, in fact, KK's London lawyer! They then had no choice but to stand outside in the snow, which was about 6" deep at the time. Had Roger been on his own, it would have been very difficult for him to know what to do, and of course they knew this.

I then quickly telephoned Eversheds to check if the £90,000 Bank Guarantee was in place in the court. They rang back ten minutes later to tell that it wasn't. KK's cunning plan to 'snatch' the car back without the guarantee in place in the court had backfired!

I went downstairs to the yard and told them that my lien was still in place and that they most certainly had no right and could not take the Frua Rolls Royce away. Interestingly, KK's lawyer then told me that the application to the court for the guarantee was now out of time, so they would have to re-apply. Looking back, I now really don't know if this was true, but at the time, I believed him and was surprised that, under the circumstances, there actually had been an application.

After using his mobile phone, he told me that they would have the guarantee in place by noon the following day It then became clear that the Lawyer had telephoned the local policeman who then arrived. I quickly explained the situation which he rapidly 'took on board'. Seeing that I was not in the best of health and would appreciate some support, he then kindly offered to meet me the next day at the private estate where we had locked the Frua car away for safe keeping. He said he would ensure that the handover was properly carried out. I thanked him and asked the KK 'gang' to leave, which they did.

No appointment was made for the next day, but I had confirmed to KK that once Eversheds had assured me that the Banks guarantee was in place, we would drive over to the estate to release the Rolls Royce.

Accordingly, we had confirmation later the following morning, so we set off to release the Frua car. This time, to use an appropriate phrase, we were 'mob handed' with Roger and two of my men in the Daimler. As we drove through the village, we saw a solitary figure sitting alone on a park bench in the deep snow in the middle of the village green. It was KK's Lawyer.

Obviously, KK had blamed him for the trouble, the misinformation and the wasted opportunity, so was making him suffer for it. They had failed to 'snatch' the car and so he now had to keep watch and ring KK to let him know when we drove by. As we did so, I gave him a wave and they all duly arrived at the estate by which time the Frua car was out of its garage. They photographed it from every angle in the vain hope of finding something to criticise. Knowing what we were up against, we also recorded the fact that it was in perfect condition on our camera and then the local policeman arrived, which was comforting.

Whilst this was going on, I walked over to KK's Rolls Royce where his Daughter Asa, was sitting in the front passenger seat. I indicated that she should lower the window which she did and then I simply, but firmly, said "You should be ashamed of yourself". I didn't need to say more, she burst into tears and put the window up.

Soon after this, the vehicle was formally handed over and we drove back to the workshops leaving Peter Hand with the unenviable task of driving this valuable three and a half ton motor car along the smooth narrow estate roads in 6" of fresh snow. This entailed going down a fairly long, steep slope of about a quarter of a mile and then up an equally steep and longer hill out of the estate to the transporter. Not the ideal machine for these conditions, especially without any salt or grit and with KK breathing down your neck!

This entire affair was the most dreadful exhibition of a man who would trample on anybody and go to any lengths to get his own way. After all the years of work and care which all of us at Royles had taken to please him, including everything that Jo-Jo and I had done at home to save him money and make him, his family and Peter Hand comfortable, I have never witnessed such callous and unprincipled behaviour.

It later transpired that KK's lawyers, in spite of their dreadful sharp practice and threatening behaviour, apparently charged me with the costs for both of the court applications. Even worse, was that Eversheds were content to accept, without question, the £50,000 which they told me KK's Lawyers had charged for what was only a few hours work. It is important to note that a lien is Common Law and apparently, we should not be liable for any of their costs to override it. Later, I heard that Eversheds costs were around £1200 and that in any event, they would normally be similar to KK's lawyers costs for the application. Their £50,000 was blatantly dishonest.

There could now be little doubt that Eversheds, our own solicitors, were working with KK's lawyers and had their own agenda. One which was certainly not in our favour. It also seemed that both groups were creating and loading their 'costs'. At this stage, I found it difficult to accept that the legal profession would ever behave in such a dishonest and contemptible manner. My faith in our legal system was such that I still thought that there would be a satisfactory explanation in the fullness of time.

THIRD OPERATION

Four days after they finally collected the car, I was back in London again on Sunday 27th February 1994, but this time, I was properly in hospital. Being my third visit, I really felt at home. By now, I knew most of the nurses, they were good fun and I was always made to feel very welcome. When I walked in, the nurses asked me which room I would prefer, "the Blue or the Green room"? No wonder I had difficulty in thinking of it as not being a hotel. The hospital must still have not been too busy.

With the previous long external incision now being nicely healed again and still having the ileostomy bag, my first event was a trip to the X-ray room for a 'Pouchogram' to see if all was well. By now, I was accustomed to having various unidentified objects pushed up into my nether regions and was not particularly bothered about it. That was until I discovered that this time, admittedly after permission was given, I was to be used as the 'living demonstration' for what turned out be quite a large group of medical students of both sexes.

I was asked to lie on my side on a high 'bed' with my green gown split open so that the assembled group had a good rear view of me. Having always been told that I had quite a neat bottom and being a bit of an amateur theatrical and a 'show off', I was not too concerned about it. Then the camera was inserted, not a pleasant experience, but one which I was becoming accustomed to.

After a minute or two of the lecture, however, I felt very much left out of it all. There were constant references to my various internals and I wanted to see what they were looking at and talking about, so cheekily, I asked if I could watch all 'the action' as well. With the camera lead being flexible, they allowed me to roll over so that I could then see 'back to front' as it were. After all, it was my body and it was, actually, quite interesting. It is not every day that you can see your own 'inner tubes', as a true motoring man would put it!

Everything must have been in order, because the following morning, I was back to the 'real' theatre where, after the now familiar injection, I again experienced the strange coldness in my arm as I passed out. It later became clear that Mr Menzies-Gow, following the same familiar dotted line of Staple marks had, yet again, opened me up so that this time, he could reconnect the newly constructed internals to the bottom. When I came round, I was pleased to see that the 'bag' had been removed.

After a brief period of recovery in my room, it was suggested that I began to take some exercise, so later in the day, trying to stand up straight, which always seems difficult when you are stitched up the front, I put on my dressing gown and made for the door. Pulling along with me the high stand on its casters with my drips and drains still attached, I opened the door and was confronted by a man with a machine gun. "Where have you come from?" he firmly demanded. Being surprised by this unexpected confrontation, I meekly said that I was just going for my first short walk. Being at last, on the road to recovery, I didn't particularly want to be shot. Well, you don't expect to have this sort treatment in hospital, especially when all the work had been done!

The man with the gun explained that he was an armed guard for the patient in the next room who was Prince Carlo Abdullah, King Fahad's brother. I couldn't help wondering if he had a 'Regal red' Rolls Royce with champagne coloured upholstery. Not only did he have the adjoining room, he had a suite of them for his Royal entourage. His guard later explained that the Royal Prince had a dresser, his secretary, his hairdresser and his guards. It's a good job that I arrived early at the hospital or this 'Royle' might have been out on the street! Later on, I spoke to members of his staff who proudly showed me into his room. It seemed to me that there had been a competition to see who could give him the biggest bouquet of flowers, it was like a florists shop. Some of them reached from the floor to the ceiling.

After all this excitement, settling back into normality, I mentioned to my nurse that I hadn't seen beneath the large sticking plaster which was covering the place where the ileostomy bag had been attached to the side of my stomach. When she had pulled the plaster off, instead of a neat row of stitches or staples, we were both surprised to find a large round hole of about 4" diameter (10 cms). Concerned to see this, the nurse quickly brought the sister who also was quite surprised. We could see that my inner stomach lining was in place so nothing should fall out. It was however, a wide hole, but was only in the flesh itself and was only about half an inch deep.

In spite of this, I was still much relieved that the bag had gone. I must say that I really do have great sympathy and much admiration for people who have to live with these bags, they are a dreadful nuisance and do cause problems at times. (Not to be gone into here).

Back to 'the hole', after I had been 'servicing', changing and attending to the dressings of the bag at home for five months, I was now very familiar with it and I guessed what the problem was. As explained, the bag collects the food as it leaves the end of the lengthy small intestine. At this stage, it is still only four or five hours since the food was eaten and it is now impregnated with acids and all the solvents which dissolve it, which allows the body to extract all the goodness out of it as it travels down. With the end of the intestine 'tube', the ileum, protruding through the stomach wall, the food, now a thick brown liquid, pours into the soft bag which is stuck on to the skin of the stomach with self adhesive discs. Interestingly, I could still smell the food which I had eaten. The bacteria had not had time to affect it.

Previously, as the months passed, I had noticed that these acids and solvents do tend to leak out and attack the skin round the bag, making it sore. Plenty of creams were provided to give comfort, but looking at the flesh around the edge of 'the hole', it looked so ragged that I guessed that the acids had eaten it away leaving the surgeon with no firm flesh, or 'material' to sew it all together. This seemed to make sense and the nurses agreed and suggested that I take a bath to clean the wound whilst it was exposed.

Forgetting the terrible and constant threat of litigation which has so spoilt the quality of life for many people in this country, I pretended to be alarmed and jokingly said to them that with such a "big hole in me, if I jump into the bath, I will probably drown". Taking me seriously, they assured me that I wouldn't, so I then exaggerated the joke by pointing out that my bath would anyway, be in "dirty London water" so I would be poisoned and die. "No, No" said the nurses, by now realising that I was having fun, added that "it is only polluted with lead and other chemicals", followed by a firm "GET IN". I couldn't help smiling and was pleased that they had got onto my wavelength.

I did as I was told of course and they then had their 'revenge' by standing over me and giving detailed instructions to wash every crack and crevice and then watching me whilst I did it. Most embarrassing! At the same time, putting me in my place by saying that, anyway, it wasn't a 'big hole' and that I "should see the man in room four if I really wanted to see what a big hole looked like". Actually, I had met this chap who was an American, a Westinghouse director, a big man who had just had an enormous growth, the size of a football, removed!

It was now March 1994 and although the third operation was not as comfortable as the first, it was certainly much better than the second and I was pleased that it was to be the last of the series. In fact, all the operations had been a great success. During my various ups and downs, I had become friends with the nurses and eventually was enjoying the privilege of joining them in their dining room for some of my meals. They were a marvellous team and we had a lot of fun at times and they made the whole affair as pleasant as it could be.

As I write this, fifteen years later, other than for the occasional pain, I have been extremely fortunate and have Mr Menzies-Gow, Professor Silk and his team to thank for their skills and knowledge.

On the 9th March, I thanked everybody and said a final goodbye to all my friends at the Princess Grace Hospital. I was given a roll of adhesive dressing which was 6" wide (15 cms) as a farewell 'present'. This was for the 'Hole' in my stomach which was still there. My instructions were to pull the flesh at the top and bottom of the hole together until they met in the middle and then apply the sticking plaster. They were confident that I could do this and I was happy to do it myself.

This time, I was driven home by my old friend Glen Todd who, you may remember, had previously 'out of the Blue', so generously offered to lend me £60,000 when he heard that KK had let us down so badly. This was a huge help and I was gratefully accepted. As requested, I gave him security and was eventually able to repay it all, plus interest, with money from my mothers estate.

Thinking back, as we travelled North, I thought about all the operations and the many weeks spent in the Princess Grace Hospital. Although the removal and loss of my Colon is a serious affair which will affect me in some respects, for the rest of my life, I am very fit and extremely fortunate in having had the benefit and the expertise of the wonderful surgeons and nurses and the support of so many friends. The visits, flowers and cards were great morale boosters. A most memorable six month period of my life.

HOME AGAIN WITH PLENTY TO DO - MARCH 1994

It was good to be back home at Gainford even if, as ever, I was to be again confined to my bed for a while. With Jo-Jo looking after me as ever and with Spring in the air, my strength soon returned. I see from my diary that I was walking in the garden three days later and it was not long before the 'hole' healed up. I am still left with a crease across my stomach where it and the bag had been, plus a long vertical groove up to my chest where I wanted to have a 'zip fastener' fitted. All things considered, the 'old body' is working brilliantly well.

Talking of holes again, the week after coming home, we had gales which blew a hole in the roof of the Old Vicarage. I decided that this was one hole which I would not do myself, so I organised others to do the repairs for me. Although I have repaired a few broken tiles myself since then. Being in bed with the telephone is marvellous for getting on with all sorts of jobs as well as paper work and designing. I am away from all the household activities and could see visitors when I wanted to. By now, I was working on the drawings for the third prototype amphibian, the 22 ft general purpose and flood rescue version.

Having so much work for me to do, whether I was in bed, in hospital or during the weeks of recuperation after each of the operations, was a good thing. I had also finished collating the many hundreds of documents and photographs and had written the necessary reports for the solicitors in Leeds. They were now able to do their work using the information to plan for the defence and counterclaim.

I also see from my diary that I was sawing down a small tree in the garden three weeks after coming home, so was obviously feeling stronger. In May, after visiting Dr Silk in Harley Street and Mr Menzies-Gow for a check up at the Princess Grace Hospital, I was pleased to hear that they were both happy with my condition. As ever, there was a lot going on at Staindrop and it was at this time that I was also invited to Beamish Open Air Museum by John Gall who had asked Lord Montague to open John's recently completed Edwardian Motor car Garage.

There had been a huge amount of thought and

Job 511. Lord Montagu in the 'Royle Armstrong Whitworth' at the opening of the Edwardian Museum at Beamish.

time gone into building this challenging, new attraction and it is extremely well done. Once there, I was delighted to see His Lordship being driven in the 'Armstrong Whitworth' Open Drive Limousine which Royles had previously built especially for this popular and successful Open Air museum.

John Gall had wanted an authentic and a properly coach-built vehicle, but one which was easily maintained and serviced. Beneficially, we had previously restored the wonderfully original Armstrong Whitworth open, two seater model with 'dicky' seat, for the Science museum in Newcastle on Tyne, so we had already had the opportunity to study an excellent original example of this illustrious engineering firms work beforehand. It is on permanent display there and is a superbly built

CHAPTER 23: 'DELIVERY UP' & SKULLDUGGERY

This Leyland chassis was the basis of the Beamish car.

Modifying the chassis and patterns for the wheels for the 'Royle' Armstrong Whitworth open drive limousine.

vehicle and for its age, even built as long ago as 1911, it is wonderful to drive.

Enjoying the creative side of our work, it was a

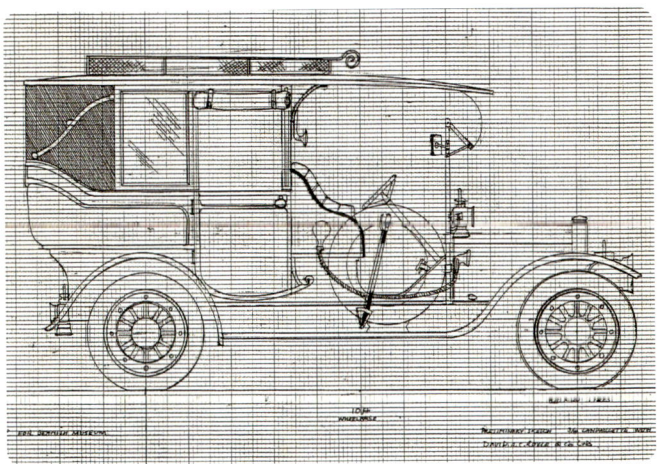

My first drawing of Beamish 'Armstrong Whitworth', the design was modified later.

most interesting project and I was pleased to have the opportunity to design a large, Edwardian Limousine body and one which would accommodate some of the many visitors to Beamish. For practical reasons, it was decided that we were to build and mount it on a new, commercial chassis. After some research, we selected a Leyland Daf for this which has proved to be most reliable and the vehicle seems to have been accepted by the public as being 'period' transport for everyday use. Some think that it is a genuine machine. It is a most impressive car and John Collins, who is a gifted craftsman and was then working for me at Royles, made a very good job of the coachwork. Allan did the mechanical work, he made patterns for the specially cast road wheels and Jim produced his usual high standard of paint finish. As is often the case, the cost was higher than the budget, but John Gall found some beautiful Lamps and other fittings in the extensive stores at Beamish which were ideal for the period and were a great help to us.

As is the case with many of our jobs, designing and building this car is quite a story in itself, but like many of the hundreds of vehicles with which we have been involved, it is too long to include here. I am pleased to say that this handsome motor car has been a great success. To date, it has been worked hard on unmade roads carrying huge numbers of museum visitors around the site and to date, has given 15 years of good service. A later adaptation was necessary due to the High Pressure tyres exploding and frightening the horses which haul various other forms of transport around the Museum.

As my health improved, I was able to spend more and more time at the workshops and in the office and was again, closely involved and busy with a wide range of activities. Val, who had taken over from Irene as my secretary, was always helpful and she had helped Roger to

With Angus, the Duke of Hamilton when I took an XK 120 to Elvington to join him when breaking the speed record for diesel engine motor vehicles at Elvington airfield. Near York with his innovative VM. Ibex car.

'hold the fort' whilst I was out of commission. Being in charge without me being there, I'm afraid that Roger had found it all to be very worrying. For six months, he had been much more directly involved with the day to day decisions of running the business and coping with the financial problems. He said that he was much relieved to have me back to take responsibility.

I was much heartened by having his help and also that given to me by some of our customer friends who could see how badly the ongoing recession and problems were affecting us.

Knowing that we were diligent and genuinely had their interests at heart, they offered to help in various ways. One example of this was Angus, The Duke of Hamilton, with whom I had been working for quite some time. He is a most charming man and as well as having been a test pilot in the RAF, was a highly qualified and knowledgeable engineer. Over the years, we became good friends and I always enjoyed his company.

For some time, Royles had been 'quietly' selling various motor cars and motor cycles from his interesting collection in Scotland. To help me with the recession and with our financial and legal problems, he sent down some more cars suggesting that when we had sold them. I should hold on to the money for a while to help us survive this difficult period. This most considerate and generous act was a great compliment from such an important person and the money was, of course, repaid when he requested it.

Another helpful and good friend was Jim Bidwell-Topham who lived in Paddock Lodge on the racecourse at Aintree in Liverpool. He also was a most knowledgeable man and like Angus, when visiting the workshops, he would come and stay with us at Gainford. He enjoyed telling ghost stories to our younger son, Nicholas, who would also make a fuss of him. Jim also had a wonderful collection of vintage and pre-war motor cars which he rarely spoke about. During this difficult period, he asked if we had plenty of work and when I explained the position, he kindly sent me three more interesting vehicles which needed repairs and restoration and which helped us to maintain our already slimmed down workforce.

Jim was always careful with costs, but was most kind to us. We enjoyed various times together and later on, we had a particularly enjoyable and memorable day at the Grand National when we were his guests at Paddock Lodge. It was the 150th Anniversary of racing at Aintree and it was amusing to watch the Horses in the parade ring just outside Jim's front window, or we could turn round and watch them on TV. I backed three, but as usual, they didn't come anywhere. Whenever I rely on 'Lady luck', I rarely win.

Jim's vehicles were a great help, we needed to keep as much work in the pipeline as possible to ensure that the men were kept busy to maintain our cash flow. Our margin for profit is very small, less than 10%, so we cannot afford to have anybody standing idle. As well as having the men working on the various Vintage and Classic motor cars, some were also kept busy building the High Speed Amphibious prototypes.

Overall, at this difficult time, the workload was less than it had been. With fewer staff and low overheads I was unable to draw a proper salary, but with the support of our good friends and customers, we managed to keep going when many other motor car restoration firms in this country were closing down.

CHAPTER 24:
A WELCOME BREAK

By now, spring was in the air and although there were financial difficulties, it was time to think about having my lovely old sailing boat, Meriva, put on her mooring in time for the family holidays in Cornwall. As with any of our luxuries, I had always followed the principle that if you want something, especially a luxury, you should wait until you can afford to buy it. Old fashioned, yes, but in times of difficulty, there are no ongoing hire purchase or lease payments to make and as in this case, I was able to continue to have the benefit of owning the boat and our mooring. Should it be necessary, it remained as a valuable asset to sell or to secure borrowings. In the meantime it was giving us wonderful family holidays for the cost of maintaining the boat.

The story of how I came to have such a wonderful boat as Meriva is explained in more detail later on in the book. Briefly however, being 43ft long and built of mahogany and pitch pine with a graceful counter stern and a powerful rig, she was the boat of my dreams. Going back to my earliest sailing days, I was an avid reader 'Yachting World' and 'Motor Boat & Yachting' magazines, in fact I still have some of them dating from early in 1955, I am loathe to part with them. These magazines are, of course, full of wooden boats and I would dream of owning one the many wonderful sailing Yachts which were illustrated in them. I was so enveloped in the stylish and high quality of them in my teenage years, that one of the biggest shocks was when, on one of my annual visits to the London Boat show, Instead of the marvellous sight and smell of varnished wood work, I was surprised by an entirely new range of boats which were made of plastic. They were accompanied by the all pervading, sweet smell of GRP which was also new to me. It came as quite a shock, it was the beginning of a revolution in the boating world.

Going back to wooden boats, after building my 12 ft Percy Blandford designed sailing dinghy and sailing it for seven years, I acquired a 16ft Wildcat ¾ decked dinghy which was a fast boat by comparison. In fact, it had a tall alloy mast and was really over-canvassed and not surprisingly, needed an agile and heavy crew in a strong wind, but it was thrilling to sail. It was at this time however, that Brownie was becoming more interested in sailing and asked me which of the up and coming sailing dinghies would be most enjoyable, if he was to buy one. I had always thought that the Osprey class were probably one of the most appealing and, in their day, also a high performance boat. Designed by Ian Proctor in the 1950's, they performed well, were comfortable to sail and had pleasing lines. Taking my advice, it was not long before we were scanning the adverts and soon afterwards, sure enough we found a good example and he suggested that whilst he would buy it, we could share it. I thought this would work well as it needed a two man crew and so it was that 'Sorella' appeared on the scene and we had many years of fun with this fine sailing dinghy.

She was eventually kept at the lovely Old Church Country Club on the shores of Ullswater and was, in fact, the boat in which I first took Jo-Jo for a sail. Early on, we realised that it would be beneficial to have a smaller mainsail made, so that we could still enjoy a day's sailing when there was a lot of wind or with a light crew. For my part, when it became necessary, I helped with the maintenance, painting and re-rigging her. On one holiday, my old friend Dicky Newhouse invited Jo-Jo and I to stay at his family's Villa in Javea. On this occasion, he and I trailed Sorella down to Spain behind Dicky's TR6. For this trip I had some white covers made for the side decks to avoid being burned when the varnish work became so hot that you couldn't sit on it. She was a delight to sail in Spain with the warm weather and the short choppy seas of the Mediterranean.

'Sorella' in the new Marina at Javea, Spain.

This trip was a complete break from our normal sailing holiday exploits in Cornwall, as mentioned, these were generally spent in St Mawes. For coastal sailing, it was clear that a good quality cabin boat with a deep keel was the answer, so I was keeping an eye open for a suitable boat which was not too costly and one which could be kept down there. It was in 1979 that my old friend, James Ferrier, rang me up to tell me about 'Ladybird of Rhu'. Briefly, she is 26ft long, is a well built Keel boat of GRP built by Camper and Nicholson in Gosport, Hampshire. She was for sale at a relatively low price because she needed a refit and overhaul. So it was that I soon became the proud owner of a proper, sea going sailing boat. Admittedly she was not built of wood, but beggars can't be choosers and she had a first class pedigree and was lined out with teak.

After spending nearly four years refitting and overhauling 'Ladybird' here in the north, she then became our 'home' in St Mawes with Jo-Jo and the boys living on board during the summer holidays.

At weekends, we still had the fun and the pleasure of driving over to the beautiful lake district in an open car, often in the Lagonda, not only sailing Sorella on lake Ullswater, we were fortunate in that some of our friends continued to spend a lot of their time there, especially on lake Windermere and we were able to join them and have some fun. The sailing boats were a Westerly which Stuart and Ann had and other friends John and Sue had a beautiful varnished Folkboat. These two were eventually to buy a larger boat and sail around the world. There was also always a speed boat or two for waterskiing and although I was by no means as proficient as Michael, Stuart and some of the others, I could, at least, manage to get up and have a good time on two ski's.

At the time, my friend Peter Hepworth and I were running the showroom at Pool in Wharfdale, 'Royle Hepworth'. After two or three years, Peter decided that he would like to buy me out and with all the driving up and down from Gainford, I agreed to his suggestion.

Our boys were growing rapidly and when back on board 'Ladybird' in the spring of 1985, we found that we kept banging our heads in the cabin, so with this additional money available, we decided to sell 'Ladybird' and look for a bigger boat . This is how Meriva came into our lives that year and what a splendid and comfortable boat she proved to be. She is a Holman and Pye design of 43ft. Built of mahogany and pitch pine below the waterline, she is a most beautiful wooden keelboat with a counter stern, a sleek traditional, yet low profile cabin and a Tall elegant 55 ft Mast.

I can think of no finer way to enjoy the sea than living on a boat. We had the company of so many good friends, many of whom we have known and sailed with in St. Mawes, for the last 45 years. Jo-Jo was one of very few wives who was prepared to live on a boat on moorings. In fact, we were one of very few families in St. Mawes to do so. Having Jo-Jo on board made it all the more enjoyable. In return, I did all I could to make her as comfortable as possible by installing a generator, a hair drier and with a lagged hot water tank , the spacious shower and a new cooker and fridge, she knew that I was doing my best.

In fact, Jo-Jo is really a 'country' girl who loved horses and had always been wary of boats and water, but she did enjoy the beaches and coastal environment around St Mawes and by living on board, she made the holidays an absolute pleasure for the family and friends who sailed with us.

Owning and maintaining a traditional wooden boat like Meriva is quite costly. There are laying up, overwintering, painting, mooring and other service costs every year, but when compared to holidays abroad, such as those enjoyed by many people in this country, it may not, in fact, be any more expensive. In times of inflation or when the value of the boat increases, as in the case of a beautiful, hand built boat like Meriva, the

Family and friends at the Lakes.

CHAPTER 24: A WELCOME BREAK

Meriva.

maintenance and running costs can be less than the increase in value. In our case we were very lucky when this proved to be true, some years later.

There is another important benefit, the more time you can spend on board the better value it is. I always enjoyed my holidays, so this appealed to me enormously and we would aim to have five weeks on board.

It was pointless to leave the boat laid up after the winter and sailing was such a satisfying way of getting fit again after all the time spent in bed. So, even with a much reduced salary of only £5,600, which turned out to be my last salary for three years, I was still planning to have Meriva varnished, painted and launched in May as usual.

We journeyed south as planned, and after a check up by the surgeon Mr Menzies-Gow at the Princess Grace hospital in London, we enjoyed staying with our old friends the Carters at Old Windsor on the way south, and then the following day with Malcolm and Ann-Marie Shaw at their cottage near St Mawes, who's boat was moored next to ours.

When we arrived at the boat yard, Mylor Yacht Harbour, to my disappointment the ongoing wet weather had delayed the paintwork and the planned launch date, so we spent a couple of days there and on the way home, called in to see our old friends Jonathan and Maggie Stirling. Although he is a busy and successful vet, he enjoys renovating old houses, so they had bought St Breock Place, near Wadebridge, another of his interesting restoration projects. He is always very thorough and ensures that the work is correct for the period. Maggie is very patient spending half her time living in a building site!

After returning home, the weather improved, so the work was soon done and the boat launched. As luck would have it, when we returned to St Mawes a fortnight later, the sun shone and we spent a glorious first week of the season on board in mid June. It was such a relief to be on our quiet mooring away from all the problems and be able to enjoy the sea air without telephones and all the day to day worries of the legal case and workshops.

Returning home there was, as ever, all the normal work to do. Thankfully, Val and Roger had kept everything going, which was a good job, because I had a very busy week ahead of

Nimble Thompson's father's DHC Bentley S3 after restoration.

me. To give you some idea of the variation, the week began with a workshop visit by the Jaguar Drivers Club on the Monday, on Tuesday, I went to the Workboat Show at Port Solent near Portsmouth in connexion with the amphibians and had a meeting with Michael Ware at the National Motor Museum at Beaulieu on Wednesday. On Friday Jo-Jo and I stayed with Nimble and his wife, Morven, and we all went down to a Bentley Drivers Club event at Blenheim Palace for the weekend. We were driven down in Nimble's very smart Drophead Bentley S III which we had recently restored.

Looking through my diary, the year continued to be filled with many varied and interesting events and trips. It was the constant variation in life which I loved so much.

On our trip to Cornwall in May, Jonathan Stirling and Quentin Batt – better known as 'Q', suggested that a trip to the Scilly Isles in Meriva would be a good idea during the summer. I was still not fully fit, but they were keen to go. 'Q' is an excellent navigator and skipper and Jonathon would help with the crewing, this can be heavy work with Meriva's big sail area. So it was that on Friday 22nd July, we set sail from St Mawes on the high tide at 05.40am. Making good progress in a fresh breeze, Jo-Jo went below to make breakfast at around 09.00am, but the timing was bad. No sooner had she made a start when we were in extremely turbulent waters with Meriva being tossed about. For the first time in all the years of sailing, the excessive movement of the boat had made Jo-Jo queasy. I persuaded her to come back up on deck for some fresh air.

Looking at the chart, it turned out that, to save time, the cause of the problem was that 'Q', who was navigating, had cut it fine by the Lizard where there are tidal rips and over-falls which cause a lot of turbulence. As soon as we cleared the headland, we were back into normal Channel seas and Jo-Jo was soon feeling fine, but this time, 'Q' went below and breakfast was soon served, he'd made amends.

Looking at the ships Log, we made excellent time and were abeam of Wolf Rock at 11.40am and were on the St Martins hotel mooring at 14.45 which 'Q' had organised. This mooring was a comfort to me as the tides and seas can be very 'impressive' on the Scilly's which, with its rocky outcrops, submerged reefs and craggy islands, is not the place to drag an anchor, or be adrift.

With the good breeze, we had enjoyed a wonderful sail. Meriva displaces over 13 tonnes and together with her deep draught of seven feet, she is most comfortable in a seaway. Like me, 'Q' and Jonathan love 'proper' boats, especially classic wooden yachts like Meriva. With 7 tonnes of lead on her keel and her large and powerful sail plan, she has a good cruising speed of around nine knots in a fresh breeze.

We spent a most enjoyable long weekend. With fine weather, we explored the Islands and Jo-Jo particularly enjoyed the gardens and flowers on Tresco and having dinner at the St Martins Hotel saved more work in the galley! A memorable sailing trip with another most pleasant and enjoyable sail back to St Mawes. As ever, it all passed too quickly and we were soon on the road back to County Durham.

A BUSY TIME

Once home again in Teesdale, there was the constant need for funding for developing the amphibious prototypes, which meant that I was meeting many interesting people. There were also ongoing meetings with the Department of transport, the County Durham Development Company and other Government agencies. I also visited Bob Armstrong the chief engineer at Vickers on Tyneside, where he helped me with technical advice as a result of the lessons learnt from the Challenger II tanks which they were building there. There were also trips to Rolls Royce at Crewe and we were continuing to test the latest High Speed Amphibious prototype at John Thompsons lake near Scorton.

In September, at the workshops, the men were very thrilled when the footballer Kevin Keegan unexpectedly called in for a look around. In the same month, I see in my diary that my old friend Jimmy Wilson, who was my best man when I married Jo-Jo, asked me if I would drive my old friend Bill Chaytor's daughter, Kate and her husband to be, Trevor Norris, to their wedding at Croft on 24th September. Trevor and Jimmy were running Croft Motor Racing circuit at the time and Trevor is most enthusiastic about all kinds of vintage and modern motor cars, and it was a pleasure for me to give the Lagonda an extra polish for this special occasion.

The following month, on 28th October, the Lagonda was pressed into service again for another wedding. This time it did the honours for John Thompson's son Graham who was marrying Sarah who lived near Simonburn in Northumberland. Afterwards, I was to drive them to the well known Gosforth Park Hotel. It was good to be able to do favours for them when they had always been so kind to me over the years.

Combining business with pleasure, I am reminded that Jo-Jo and I spent a few days in November staying with our good friends St John and Lou Whitton at their house at

Tickenham Hill near Bristol. Whilst there, I attended an interesting meeting at the Dep't of Transport offices in Bristol with Messrs Brayfield, Thompson and Perrot to discuss the certification of my new amphibians.

They were most helpful and enthusiastic, unlike those whom I had met at a previous meeting there when the negativity flowed! The following day, I called in 'on spec' to see Keith Bowley at his motor car restoration workshops at Ashton Keynes. Unfortunately, he was out, but I met Paul and John who kindly showed me round. The following day, on 25th November, Jo-Jo and I attended our eldest son, Jeremy's, graduation ceremony at Bristol Cathedral, rounding off an interesting and enjoyable three day trip.

There were plenty of good Christmas parties, but I found that my lack of 'internal equipment' meant that alcohol was not as appealing as it used to be, so I often ended up being Jo-Jo's driver which meant that she didn't have to worry about a drink or two, which was good. I began to see however, the drawback of not being able to join in and be silly and 'merry' with everybody else, like I used to be.

Had it not been for the constant worry of the court case, and the meetings with the Banks about borrowings for Royles and Covelink and the fact that Greta, our old Labrador and my shooting 'companion,' had died on the 4 July, it would have been an enjoyable year.

PARTING WITH ANOTHER OLD FRIEND

Back in the office after closing the workshops for Christmas, the only time of the year when we did, I was extremely busy with all the ongoing legal matters, the design work, Royles customers, meetings with Covelink's directors and the technical suppliers and advisers. We managed to have a week on the boat at the end of May, but there was so much to do, that we cancelled our next sailing holiday in June. I was also continuing with my ongoing efforts to raise funds for the amphibious company, Covelink's project. These were from my own personal resources, from new investors, from local government agencies and from interested parties.

As ever, it was important to keep Royle's and Covelink's financial affairs completely separate. Investors in the amphibious project needed to be sure that their money was entirely for the benefit of Covelink and whilst the work was subcontracted to Royle's, it was all carefully recorded and was done at cost and was therefore, beneficial to both companies.

At the time, I was also doing what I could to publicise Royle's restoration business and the Amphibious project, in the media. The recession was continuing to affect us in the North East and would do so, especially for those in the luxury trades, for most of the last decade of the 20th century.

To reduce the excessive borrowings and interest on KK's debt and with the constant ongoing need for money, I reluctantly decided to sell my old Vintage Lagonda. After 33 years of wonderful fun and reliable motoring, the money was now critical to keep the companies running. I knew that I would regret it personally, but I comforted myself by the change in attitude towards these splendid old motor cars.

To illustrate what I mean, when I bought it, boys on street corners would shout "how fast will it go mister?" nowadays they shout, "how much is it worth?" This change can also be illustrated by the fact that in the 1960's, I would quite happily park it for a few days and nights in the street in Soho without any worries!

Looking back over the years, after I had sorted out the internal engine problems, I found that the 'Special' 3 litre Lagonda is certainly a most refined, well designed and beautifully engineered vehicle. The brakes are superb and the steering is an absolute delight. I had two sets of wheels, 18" for local use and a set of 21" for long distance high speed motoring, she could cruise all day at 70mph.

Coming back from London with my old friend Brownie one day in the early 1960's, we were overtaken by a MK II Jaguar. He asked what the top speed was, I told him that the Lagonda was supposed to do over 90mph. He said, "go on then, put your foot down", and so I did. The speed soon built up to 96mph on the 'clock', which was pretty accurate. We were on the old Great North Road at the time, with no speed limits and little traffic, we were now flat out at her absolute maximum speed. The Lagonda was literally smooth as silk. There were no vibrations and she handled prefectly, she was directionally stable and even when I loosened my grip on the steering wheel, she continued in a dead straight line. We rapidly caught up with the Jaguar and the four men inside gave us a great cheer as we roared past. Great fun!

With the smaller 18" wheels, the actual top speed was slower, but the steering and cornering where much more positive. Acceleration was better of course, and the car would climb hills at faster speeds. In the 'sixties' the 18" tyres were more easily found, so I tended to use these for local driving. I would change the wheels round to suit the conditions for the journeys, using the 21" tyres for long distances. The centre throttle pedal needed to be borne in mind and the gearbox needed to be mastered, but once the ratios were understood, it was possible to change gear without using the clutch or the clutch stop.

Prior to me having bought and used this fine machine, quite a lot of people did not really know what the 'Special' 3 litre Lagonda was, they confused it with the 16/80 model which wasn't as fast or as powerful. Soon after restoring it and with it having won so many rallies and events, a lot more people in the Lagonda Club came to realise what a super motor car the 'Special' 3 litre model is.

After 33 years of wonderful, reliable vintage motoring, I was very sad to part with it, but sold it to a great friend and motoring enthusiast, Alan Wynn-Williams on the 4 April 1995. I was pleased to see it with a person who appreciated it. Later it was sold to another friend, Donald Fothergill, but I would love to have it back one day.

THE LEGAL STORY GOES ON

In April, I had been told that the court hearing would not be held until next year, probably in March of 1996. I had been pressing Eversheds to arrange for the court hearing to be as soon as possible, so this was not good news. All along, despite being substantially overdrawn at the bank as a result of KK's debt, and also because of Nimble's kind offer of support', I was trying to pay him as much as I could towards his original estimate of legal costs of £25,000.

In fact, it would be more than three years after the £73,000 debt was incurred before the action commenced in the High Court. During this period, with great difficulty I managed to pay just over £12,000. I explained at meetings with Nimble and other solicitors in Leeds, that any payments I made were a real struggle and that I was also becoming very concerned about the ongoing delays and the escalating costs.

Even by August 1994 the previous summer, I was told that the costs were £39,000 and that these were to collate the documents, correspondence and photographs. Work which, in fact, I had already done myself for Eversheds. Here we were a year later, still with nine months to go before the trial and I was being told that the costs were now £48,000. I could not understand what these costs could possibly be for. A revised written estimate of £80,000 was also now given as the likely total cost. This was more than three times Nimble's original estimate and we had not yet been to the court.

Something was obviously going on and although no longer on our case, I couldn't help but think that Mr Coates had something to do with it. I had done so much of the background preparation work to save coasts and yet I could not believe that Nimble would allow Eversheds to be loading their charges when he knew that it would completely cripple me if we lost the case. It didn't make sense, when he seemed to be so keen to help me at the beginning.

After I had finally persuaded Nimble to transfer Mr Coates off Royles case onto other work, I then discovered the facts about him. Apparently, he had only recently joined Eversheds in Leeds and had been working in London. I then found out that he had actually been working with Berwin Leighton, who were KK's lawyers and were the 'opposition'. So, not only was there a 'mole' in Eversheds Leeds offices, this mole was the very solicitor who Nimble had actually put in charge of our case! No wonder his advice and activities were against our interests, he wasn't working for Royles, he was still working for the benefit of his old colleagues at Berwin Leighton and KK!

The solicitor who Nimble appointed to replace Mr Coates was Mr Chamberlain who turned out to be a good and honourable solicitor. He continued to work with me up to and including the hearing in London and was most helpful.

In the meantime, Nimble said that it was very important that I found an expert witness, so I was making contact with various people I knew who were involved with high quality motor cars. The problem being, that most did not want to be involved with legal proceedings and I couldn't blame them! I was recommended to contact a Mr Dallymore who lived in Bristol and who dealt in Rolls Royce motor cars and so I visited him on the way down to Cornwall. He turned me down.

I then contacted Victor Gauntlett the Chairman of Aston Martin, who was a friend and knew that our work was good. He apologised and said that he strongly disliked litigation and kept well away from legal battles, but he said he would see what he could do to help. A few days later Louise Gaize rang me. He was Rolls Royce Motors company lawyer and asked me to drive over to the factory at Crewe to meet him at the RR offices to discuss the case.

This was another most interesting turn of events and gave me much hope. I went in my trusty old Daimler 3.6 and was embarrassed when, having parked this Jaguar based motor car in front of the Rolls Royce Head offices, a member of the staff nearly jumped out of his skin when, walking passed , the alarm went off. So much for my quiet, discreet approach!

I later found out that it was the automatic self-levelling suspension which caused it, so the alarm has been switched off ever since! I still have this good, but ageing motorcar after 19 years of reliable, comfortable use. It now has 178,000 miles 'on the clock' and has given me marvellous service. Sadly, the rust is taking its toll.

Mr Gaize's reputation went before him as the man who protected the RR logo all around the world, so I was looking forward to meeting him. I was shown into his large office at the front of the building and he listened patiently to the facts in this case. He then introduced me to Ian Rimmer who is an expert on matters of quality in Rolls Royce motor cars and whose knowledge of the problems and practical issues involved with one-off, high quality, coach built bodywork is second to none.

Ian's book, 'Rolls Royce and Bentley Experimental Cars', first published in 1986, is the authoritative record of these vehicles. He said that he was happy to represent us in court and we couldn't have wished for a more professional and expert witness. He was with RR for nearly forty years and subsequently became the Chairman of The Rolls Royce Enthusiasts Club.

The months rolled by with occasional meetings with Nimble, Mr Chamberlain and others at Eversheds Cloth Hall Offices in Leeds, and I also had the pleasure of meeting Ian Rimmer again when he kindly visited Staindrop. Obviously, the Bank was concerned about it all and were kept informed.

It soon was Christmas and it was good to meet old friends again, many of whom I had hardly seen in the last five years. This was mainly due to me having had Colitis from 1989 to 1993 and then all the months of hospitalisation. These, together with the financial problems, had not been conducive to much socialising.

LOOKING BACK

Few understand the implications of serious Ulcerative Colitis. This not only meant that drinking alcohol had been a problem, it was also the fact that it was essential to be very near to a decent loo at all times. For three years, I had only a matter of a few seconds to get there, otherwise, without going into detail, I needed a bath and a change of clothes. As ever, I got used to the in-'conveniences' of it all and then preferred to see the amusing side of it and have many funny stories of being trapped in Ladies Lavatories and being in various other 'wrong' places at the wrong time!

Looking back, the worst times were early on, when I would have an accident and when I didn't have a change of clothes, especially when I was on my own. I frequently worked late at the office after everybody had gone. Being tired, I might not be quick enough to run to my private little lavatory at the front of the building. On these occasions, I have to admit that I would occasionally sit there and the tears would flow. Fortunately, these occasions were rare, because I had so much to do and with the bleeding not being caused by the dreaded big 'C', I would normally be able to focus on the funny side of it all, when in company anyway.

I didn't use to broadcast it too loudly, but Sailing on board Meriva was so good because there was always the most wonderful 'convenience of conveniences', my restored and shining 'Baby Blake', my excellent marine loo, was within a few metres of me at all times. Even after the operations, this was a blessing, because I no longer had my 'internal storage' facilities for 'processed' food, this had been removed. Never-the-less matters have much improved and I now only need to visit a loo perhaps 10 to 15 times a day.

CHAPTER 25:
1996, UPPING THE STAKES

I continued to be very busy in January and as the hearing was now only ten weeks away, the number of meetings in Leeds increased with three in February. At one of them, Nimble asked me for some security as Eversheds 'costs' were still increasing. Although seriously concerned that this demand was made at all and also that it was made so late in the day, I had little choice but to give them something. With the importance of the money due to us from KK and after 2½ years of work and worry, I was under duress and had to go through with it. My first thought was to suggest Meriva, my afore-mentioned beautiful 43ft Sailing boat. "That will be fine" he said, adding that one of his partners was currently "on the look-out for a good boat". The way he said this implied that there seemed to be no doubt that his partner was going to have it, even before the hearing!

This worried me greatly.

As we approached the date for the hearing, my confidence in Nimble and Eversheds was rapidly evaporating. His optimism was gone, the implication now seemed to be that we were likely to lose the case. It was becoming clear that other influences were at work, since our evidence was as strong as it ever had been.

I was now seriously concerned to see the remarkable increases in Eversheds legal 'costs' and also the way in which they had accepted, without question, KK's lawyers £50,000 'costs' for a few hours work, when the attempted illegal 'snatch back' of the RR had failed. You will remember that the result of this was that KK's lawyers had to make two applications to the court for the 'Delivery up' of the Frua car.

There could be little doubt that the legal costs were not structured, but a 'movable feast' and that my £65,000 boat was there for the taking by one of Nimble Thompsons partners. Even now, 13 years later, I remember how upset I was at that time, to think that of all people, a solicitor and friend in whom I had put my trust and probably the future of my company, when he offered to help me, might be letting me down at this crucial time.

Not long afterwards, I met Simon Anderson at Eversheds Leeds offices. This solicitor was from their Manchester offices and was going to be in charge of the action in London. He was considered to be one of Eversheds leading litigation experts and I can remember going up in the lift when another solicitor commented that I was now 'in' with the 'strong arm boys'. At the time, I thought this might be a good thing, how wrong I was!

Nimble took more of a back seat as we approached the date set for the start of the hearing, the 16 April. After seeing the change of attitude towards me and how easily they were planning to take Meriva off me, I decided to withdraw that suggestion. In view of their continuing determination to have security in case we lost the defence action, I offered Simon Anderson our house, The Old Vicarage at Gainford. As explained, I was in no position to refuse them their demands for some security at this late stage, but knew that taking such a valuable asset from me would not be quite such a simple matter, politically, as taking a boat. It was a big risk, but one worth taking.

Bearing in mind that it was now three years since KK's debt had been incurred and after all the financial difficulties and waiting for so long to get to court, I was determined that I could prove our honesty in court and have our bill paid. Added to all this, Eversheds and KK's lawyers had now, allegedly, racked up costs of between £100,000 and £200,000. At least those 'costs' which they had told me about. I was also told that KK had 'upped the stakes' and was now accusing Royles of overcharging him by £200,000 for work to his Frua Rolls Royce.

By increasing the pressure on me and doing it so obviously, it looked very much to me as if they were still trying to frighten me off. Instead of doing this however, it made me all the more determined to see it through. After carefully studying KK's lengthy and dishonest affidavit and knowing that we had so much documentary evidence to prove our honesty and with KK's £90,000 'in' court, plus the valuable Frua Rolls Royce and KK's other monies to pay Eversheds costs, I was determined to have our case heard and prayed for a knowledgeable and interested Judge. Not having ever been in a court room and having already seen some dubious 'legal' activities, the hearing now seemed to be more of a risk, an all or nothing gamble, or so I thought!

After Mr Coates was taken off the case, our 'new replacement' Eversheds solicitor, Mr Chamberlain, was my contact throughout the remaining period of time when we were preparing for the hearing. It turned out that he was also going to sit next to me every day in court and continue to advise me throughout the court proceedings, which was reassuring. He seemed to be a genuine and considerate person and subsequently proved himself to be so.

BACKGROUND INFORMATION

Before starting to put this book together in 2007, I naturally discussed the idea with a number of friends, publishers and authors. Because of my years of involvement with vintage and specialist motor cars, both privately and commercially, I spoke, first of all, to my old friend Michael Ware. As the curator of the National Motor Museum at Beaulieu and one who has written books as well as being a well known motoring journalist, his advice was most helpful and valuable.

Another helpful man was Fred Barter of Bosun Publications. He specialises in boats and marine subjects and I spent a most interesting and enjoyable day in his company. This was when he took the trouble to travel up from London to Gainford to advise me of the 'pro's and cons' of writing and publishing books.

I also contacted Frederick Forsyth for whom I also have a great deal of respect. This is not only because he is such a successful and experienced author, but also because he speaks a lot of common sense on many subjects and he comes over so well on TV. As I was planning to include the events and stories about my legal battle with corrupt solicitors, I thought his advice concerning such events would be well worth having. I asked him if had heard any stories about corrupt solicitors, his comment was that he could "fill a library with them".

He kindly explained that the intricacies of most legal cases are so complex and with so many parties often involved, he said that it can be difficult to make these stories easily readable and sufficiently interesting, so he had kept clear of them.

This made sense initially. but was disappointing news, because this was an important element of the story which I wanted to tell in the book. After some thought however, with the legal events being so important and with me having already described to you, the reader, the remarkable Frua Rolls Royce and also introduced most of the characters in the story, I thought it worth the risk of including the rest of this unusual story here in the book.

The other factor was that this is not a fictional novel and therefore, with it being a true story of events which have had such far reaching consequences, if you will persevere, I think that you will find it to be remarkable in so many respects.

Bearing Frederick Forsyth's advice in mind however, I have avoided unnecessary complication and have purposely kept the number of people involved in this ongoing Rolls Royce story to a minimum in all the previous chapters. For the sake of simplicity for example, three of Eversheds solicitors were called Simon, so I have used only their surnames. Also, I have called Royle's legal people 'solicitors' and the opposing party, KK's legal people, 'lawyers' and not named any of the latter individually. In theory, therefore all the 'solicitors' are on my side, whereas the lawyers are with the opposition.

Whilst the story behind the unique £2 million Rolls Royce Frua Phantom VI is remarkable enough, the legal events following its completion introduced me to extraordinarily cunning and devious practices, the like of which I had never witnessed in 50 years of commercial business. They make for a story which is disturbing, but well worth telling.

THE STORY SO FAR

In a nutshell, this Rolls Royce has been the dream of three very wealthy individuals, each of whom in turn, wanted to create a most outstanding post war 'world class' motor car. The basis for this luxurious motor car, the new chassis of a Phantom VI, is the basis of the world's most prestigious models of this illustrious manufacturer. A motor car which has been used for ceremonial transport by Royal Families for most of the last century.

This particular vehicle:

1. Is the last coach-built Phantom Six to be finished and exhibited at an International Motor Show, in this case, Geneva in March 1993.

2. Is unique and an unusually complex, interesting and costly design.

3. Was eventually finished after 21 years, to the highest standards, but most who have been closely involved with it have suffered in various ways.

4. Has created problems long after the Geneva Motor Show, which have continued for me to this day, resulting in far reaching and extraordinary legal activities

The factor common to each successive owner has been the effect of a series of economic recessions. This resulted in each one of them changing their minds about their plans for this costly vehicle. Each of them seems to have suffered financial difficulties which rebounded on the people who were appointed to design and build this complex motor car. Additionally, the owner's lack of knowledge of the labour intensive and skilled nature of the work involved and hence the cost of it, exacerbates any problems which have arisen. There are few parallels where a customer is directly instructing work which is of the highest quality and yet is work which he cannot properly evaluate.

In my experience, as the costs of specialist work build up, the owner begins to mistrust the coachbuilder and suspects he is being taken advantage of. The work involved with constructing one-off coach-built cars which incorporate luxurious interiors, is very considerable indeed. Very few people understand it especially when, as in this case, it incorporates solid silver inlays, rotating cocktail cabinets, the finest veneers and all manner of fittings, all to the highest possible standards. A bespoke motor car is probably the ultimate and most costly form of road transport and this vehicle probably ranks as the most exotic of its kind built since World War Two.

Briefly, after buying the new Chassis in 1971 from the Rolls Royce Agent, Jack Barclay in London, Mr Buchanan Michaelson asked Ogle to design and build the coach-work for him. I understand that a fall in the London property market then caused him financial difficulties which prevented him from doing this and eventually led to the car being sold to James Leake, the wealthy American Rolls Royce collector. The new owner appointed Pietro Frua, the respected Italian designer, to create a most glamorous and complex cabriolet.

Later, when the work was already well advanced Mr Leake, I understand, wanted to enlarge the car by making it longer and wider and ordered Frua to do this. His instructions would necessitate very difficult and costly changes and I gather that the stress of this and I guess, the associated costs, allegedly led to Frua's death.

After shipping the partially built vehicle back to England and after yet another failed attempt to continue the work in London, the car was then bought by Kaj Kjellqvuist, a wealthy Swedish businessman. This gentleman asked me to design a most luxurious and unique interior and complete the whole car to the highest standards. This was done, but not without more serious problems.

The work, the 1990 recession and the demands led to me developing stress-related Ulcerative Colitis and I had to have a series of major surgical operations involving the complete removal of my Colon and the reconstruction of my intestinal tract afterwards. This was followed seemingly, by KK suffering financial problems as a result of the ongoing 1990 recession. No doubt on a different scale to mine, the net result has been the legal 'battle' which is described in this chapter. A most unprincipled and crude attempt to avoid paying for the refined work which he had instructed us to do.

Before relating what happened in court and the rest of the legal story, It might be helpful if I try to explain and clarify the high costs and nature of this kind of work by comparing it to those built before the war and earlier. After fifty years of working in this field, one way of illustrating just how wealthy those people were who employed coach-builders in the early years of the last century, is to relate the time and costs to wages, then and now.

It was only when early forms of mass production began in England in the mid 1920's through into the 1930's that the costs of buying a motor car and motoring came within reach of salaried, middle income families. Many of these retained the characteristics of coach-built vehicles including Ash timber body framework, but the designs and methods of construction had been simplified to minimise cost. Even so, the buyers still had to be comfortably off before they could afford any new motor car. I can remember here in the North in the late 1940's, for example, my brother and I being the only youngsters going to the junior school of 120 pupils by car. In the UK, some manufacturers were still building motor cars with timber frames right up to the 1950's, as in the case of some Rolls Royce and Humber limousines for example.

Going back to the early days of motoring, around the time of the first world war. It is worth remembering that a skilled motor engineer/mechanic would be earning between 25/- (£1.25p) a week, or £60 per annum. For him to buy even an average family motor car like a Morris in this period, the cost would be £150 to £200 before the war. This equated to three years wages for a working man. No hire purchase or easy payment schemes for motor cars in those days.

If we then look at the upper end of the market during the same period, say a Rolls Royce Phantom model, the 40/50. The cost of a complete car could be up to £1,500 depending upon the coachwork and style. A huge sum of money in those days, equal to twenty-five years of a working man's wages.

It is difficult to draw direct parallels today of course, due to the vastly different techniques involved in the work.

With all today's additional technology and refinement and the increase in the standard of living and men's wages, the last Rolls Royce Phantom VI to leave MPW, at over a million pounds is understandable and is not an unreasonable cost. This does have a bearing on the Frua Phantom which is far more complex than a standard design and hence much more costly.

CHAPTER 26:
THE HIGH COURT HEARING. APRIL 1996

From the time I knew that the hearing was going to be at the Royal Courts of Justice in the Strand and with my financial resources already drained, I was worried how I was going to afford to stay in London. This is when my friends Nils and Lena Dalchvist came to my rescue. You may remember that they invited me to spend the first night at their lovely flat in Kensington before travelling home after my first operation, which was most kind of them.

Knowing about the KK affair and when the action in the High Court was imminent, they very generously offered me the use of the flat for the duration of the hearing. This was marvellous news for me and solved one of my major worries. Strange how I was being sued by KK who is Swedish and yet here was I, being put up by a charming Swedish couple. We have always had a lot of fun with Nils and Lena here in the north where they also have had a house for many years. As it turned out, they were away in Sweden for most of the time, so my being in their flat didn't inconvenience them too much.

Arriving in London on Sunday 14th April, prior to the hearing, as soon as I had unpacked, I laid out and studied my files. I have already mentioned that our workshop and office records are very detailed and clearly record the three years of work involved with the Frua car. Studying these documents at every opportunity during the hearing, was to be standard practice for me, especially at weekends. It was imperative that I kept abreast of every aspect involved.

With having designed, instructed and been intimately involved with all of the work and regularly written reports to KK during the process, I did have a most detailed and thorough knowledge of this complex Motor car. By the time we were in court, the earliest records went back over six years, so it was beneficial to continually refresh my memory.

I was advised and kept detailed notes throughout the whole of the hearing, but will only mention a few of the events. These notes extend to over 150 pages and describe the questioning and the nature of the litigation.

I would like to tell you a lot more about the activities in the court and how it all progressed, but there is far too much detail for a book of this kind.

The following morning, the Monday, I took the tube to 'Temple' underground station and, for the first time, attended Keatings Chambers. Simon Anderson and Mr Chamberlain were there from Eversheds and I also met Nerys Jefford, our Barrister and her pupil. She was a petite young lady with whom I immediately felt comfortable. The Chambers were in Essex street, straight across the Strand from the imposing gothic archway entrance to the Royal Courts of Justice. They could not have been more convenient. At the meeting, we discussed the case and Nerys explained what would be expected of me.

THE FIRST DAY IN COURT

The next morning, Tuesday 16th April, again on the tube at rush hour, both in the morning and in the evening, I realised that I was experiencing the life of a typical Londoner. The IRA were very active during my time in London, so I saw, at first hand, the effects of bomb scares. A line would be closed, so double the numbers would crush into the remaining stations and trains. Sardines have it easy by comparison!

On one occasion, standing pressed up with my face only inches away from that of a portly lady, there was a most serious smell, to put it in the colloquial, some-body close by, had 'dropped one'. She promptly turned accusingly, to look at me. I was dying to tell her that I no longer had the equipment to create such things, but thought it not worth the explanation which I would have then wanted to provide! Yes, there are benefits for not having a complete set of 'internals', but annoying when accused, knowing for certain that I am innocent!

One evening, when Nils and Lena had returned from Sweden and we were dining together at their flat, there was a big explosion in the nearby square. I was most impressed by their complete lack of any reaction, they thought that it would be the IRA again and just carried

CHAPTER 26: THE HIGH COURT HEARING. APRIL 1996

on with supper. The following day they were proved to be correct, fortunately the house which was bombed was not occupied at the time.

When I met Nerys at her chambers that Tuesday morning, it was to be my first-ever day in court and it was all very interesting. For the first time, I saw Nerys' pupil with our barrow of documents as it was wheeled across the zebra crossing over the Strand. We then went up the well known flight of steps in front of the High Court where so often, we see on TV, the clamour of photographers when famous cases are in process. We then passed through the high gothic archway with its heavy panelled double doors and through security inside. Walking down the main hall, we passed the old court rooms on either side and turned right to walk down a long, wide corridor. Nearing the end we took the lift up to what was going to be 'our court' for the coming weeks, court 73, a modern court room towards the back of the building.

I found that we were sitting at the right hand of the front bench facing the Judge, with KK and his team at the opposite end (see sketch below).

Sketch by DACR during a quiet spell one day in court.

After we had taken our places and sorted out our documents, we were asked to rise as Judge Roger Cox, who was presiding in this case, came in and took his high seat with the Royal coat of arms on the wall behind him. He, like the barristers, was in wig and gown and the formality of it all impressed me.

Judge Cox began the proceedings at 10.30 am from his elevated position, by outlining the particulars of the case, the contract, the dispute and the pleadings and other issues were discussed with the barristers. Our counsel Nerys Jefford, opened by saying that the 'flavour' of the case needed to be clear. KK's Barrister responded by outlining the relevant facts in the dispute.

It turned out that KK's barrister also was a woman, Miss Ife, she was more solidly built than 'our' Nerys Jefford and in my view, didn't come over so well. She said that the cost of the work came to £437,000 a sum which, they claimed, was subsequently found to be excessive. Her client, KK, was reclaiming up to £170,000 . The Judge clarified the position by saying that £443,000 had been paid, but more was due which included the Geneva Motor Show costs. The discussions continued for the rest of the day, with an hour's break for lunch.

From the outset, it seemed that the judge had an understanding of the construction of motor cars. This became more apparent as the hearing progressed, which gave me much comfort. This was unlike the situation in Birmingham which, in the intervening period, had resulted in my Sales and Model Motor Car company, Royle Cars Ltd, being wound up. This was when the judge involved did not seem to understand the difference between a 70 year old 'vintage' motor car and a modern one.

All the parties attending the court had been supplied with their own copies of all the files (bundles) of correspondence, documentation and photographs. I could now see the benefit of all the ground work which I had done and how Eversheds had produced multiple copies of all the important documents for easy reference by all concerned in the court. They were neatly filed and packaged, but this work and the meetings with Eversheds solicitors still did not appear to correspond with the huge sums being charged for the costs of doing this.

At the end of the day's proceedings, we adjourned across the Strand to Keatings Chambers where Nerys analysed the discussions and we would plan the following days work. After our de-brief, Nerys suggested that we walk across the street to the 'Benjamin Stillingfleet' for a drink, this is the well known lawyers pub. I said that perhaps she, her pupil and Mr Chamberlain, might not want me, their client, to impose in their social life. She would hear none of it and so began what became another interesting and enjoyable routine. Being dressed in a pinstripe suit, I was taken as being another lawyer and had some interesting and revealing discussions. That is, until I clarified what I was doing there!

TEH NEXT THREE DAYS

On the second day of the hearing, KK was the first person in the witness box and with Bible in hand, he took the Oath. He was there for most of the next three days answering questions. I began to see how clever Nerys was as she went into more and more detail and as the hours passed, KK began to squirm. I was most impressed by the amount of information and detailed knowledge of the facts which Nerys had absorbed. Where appropriate, she would refer to the written evidence and photographs which I had provided, in order to prove her points.

On many occasions KK's replies were vague and he was finding it difficult to answer the questions, so he would try to 'charm' his way out of answering them. Sometimes, the Judge would have to intervene, demanding that he gave an answer to her detailed enquiries. This was markedly different to the times when KK was at the workshops when, if something didn't suit him, he would just walk away. Here in court, he was trapped in the witness box and spent the days in extreme and obvious discomfort. So much so, that I almost felt sorry for him! It became very clear that his knowledge of 'his' huge affidavit was poor. There can be little doubt that he never expected to have to go to court to support it.

Time and again, Nerys would lead him to a point where the conclusion was undeniably in our favour and then, just before 'spelling it out', she would suddenly change the subject and the course of questioning to focus on another point and then repeat the process all over again. Finally at the end of her cross questioning, she would reiterate all the points she had made and he was then confronted with a veritable 'bombardment' of evidence and conclusions which proved that most, if not all, of his accusations and statements were untrue and without foundation.

On one of these many occasions, I was pleased that my familiarity with the documents helped Nerys to satisfy the judge of my honesty. In his affidavit, KK had accused me, many times, of being dishonest and deceitful, this time, by charging him, behind his back, on our Frua workshop bills, for an expensive lunch at the Connaught in London, one which he said I was hosting.

In fact, it was he who was supposed to be the host. It was his idea to treat the two Rolls Royce MPW managers, Peter Hand and Peter Goodall and myself, to a splendid lunch at the Connaught. Not a place I could afford or would even consider. After we had finished lunch and the bill arrived, KK patted his pockets and gave the classic excuse saying, "Oh dear, I have forgotten my wallet" he then asked me to pay, saying that I should add the cost onto his Frua account. Fortunately, I had my credit card and settled the bill. £500 was a large sum to me and this was made worse when we returned to my Daimler to find that I also had a parking fine of £50 to pay!

As mentioned, KK loved good food and wines and his knowledge of them and of the finest restaurants around the world, which served them, was exceptional. The judge was openly astonished however, when he asked KK about his food bills, he told him that, on average, he would spend £2,000 a week eating out!

Returning to the subject of the expensive lunch, although Nerys referred to a fax which we had from KK's office giving details of the best table etc, implying that it was his 'treat', it was unsigned and in itself, the Judge thought was not conclusive proof. Peter Hand being a turncoat, had supported KK of course and annoyingly, a letter from Peter Goodall which confirmed the truth, arrived too late for it to be admitted as evidence. This Peter is a charming, honest and knowledgeable man, but was in hospital prior to the hearing, so his letter was delayed and could not be admitted in court.

A week or so later, when it was my turn in the Witness Box, the subject came up again and I was able to draw the courts attention to a letter which I had written to KK the week following the lunch. It was three pages long describing progress to the Frua and covering various other matters. The Judge commented that the court had already seen this letter, I agreed, but asked the court to turn again to the appropriate bundle and the same document. There was the usual rustling of paper, after which I drew attention to the last page. There was only one paragraph at the top of an otherwise blank sheet of paper. It was the closing paragraph which importantly concluded with me thanking KK for the "delicious lunch" at the Connaught.

It hardly needed me to explain to the judge that I would not be thanking KK for a lunch which, altogether, had cost me £550! "Quite right" said the Judge positively. Yet another dishonest accusation was proved to be so! Nerys kindly apologised to me later on for having missed it, but it was tucked away and I was pleased that I had remembered it and was able to contribute to her excellent work.

The questioning of KK went on until midday on the Friday then, after KK stood down, Peter Hands father was called as a character witness. By now, it was becoming clear, from the evidence, that KK's affidavit was untrue in many respects and that Royles were not dishonest. Although Hand senior was appearing as a character witness in support of KK, his accusation that I was a dishonest and an untrustworthy person could no longer be sustained so, in a complete 'U turn', Mr Hand senior, under oath, meekly agreed that we were decent people and stood down. This was a positive indication that we were indeed gaining ground.

Following this, KK's daughter, Asa, was put in the witness box. As a director and secretary of some of KK's international companies, she was asked details of various payments which she had authorised to be made to Royles from their different companies around the world. Once again, statements made in the affidavit were being shown to be untrue. She was not overly confident and it showed. I felt sorry for her because her father would be breathing down her neck! I am sure that she is a decent person, but had to support her father.

This was the end of the first week in the High Court. I felt that it was going well, but we were disappointed that our expert Rolls Royce witness Ian Rimmer, had failed to turn up in court as expected during this first week. Apparently, this was due to him being in America on Rolls Royce Business, but the Judge was not happy about this and the possibility of issuing a Subpoena was discussed. This worried me.

As ever, I spent the weekend studying the files, so was able to continue to pass messages on to Nerys via our solicitor, Mr Chamberlain, as the case proceeded. He was sitting with me in court all the time and was always helpful and I was pleased to have him there. Hardly ever in attendance however, were Simon Anderson or Nimble Thompson. As Eversheds two principle solicitors in this case, I thought that they were bound to be closely involved, especially Anderson as the Litigation expert. Once again, although unfamiliar with court procedures, I was uncomfortable about this apparent lack of interest by the two key solicitors, but optimistically, thought it might save costs.

THE SECOND WEEK

This began with Peter Hand in the witness box taking the oath. It seemed to me that the Oath meant very little to some people. Although now made redundant, he had worked for Rolls Royce at MPW and being KK's witness, he was on the stand for most of four days with many detailed questions from counsel and the judge.

As you can imagine, the 308 pages of 'KK's affidavit' introduced a huge number of complaints. Complaints which were intended to discredit me and frighten me sufficiently not to want to defend the action. My view from the start however, was that if they were properly investigated, then the truth would inevitably come out and we would have our work properly paid for.

After KK's poor showing in the witness box and despite Peter Hand being knowledgeable about RR coach building, I was becoming more confident, because counsel was again examining the accusations in the affidavit, this time in more detail. Both barristers and the judge were questioning Hand about costs and about all the criticisms which they had made about the quality of our work.

Nobody could ignore the fact that Hand had visited Royles workshops with KK, at regular intervals, for three years to inspect the work. It was undeniable that throughout all this time, neither he nor KK had made any serious criticisms of any consequence, about the quality of it. Hand had advised us all about the details incorporated in the Phantom Six and he had seen the work as it progressed and was satisfied with it throughout the whole of the three year period. So much so, that they were happy for us to exhibit the finished car to thousands of people at the world's most prestigious motor show in Geneva. This, you may remember, is where I heard Hand 'smarmily' and in measured tones, say to Peter Ward, the Managing Director of Rolls Royce at Crewe, who was admiring it, "good isn't it".

With KK's poor support for 'his' own affidavit, followed by the failure of Hand's father to follow through with his criticism of me and for the reasons mentioned above, it was becoming clear to the court, that most of their criticisms were not true and were, generally, without any real foundation.

On Thursday 25th April, Mr Dallymore took the stand as KK's Expert Witness. This was interesting, because you may remember, that this is the gentleman who had turned me down when I had approached him earlier on to represent me. Not surprisingly, representing KK, he criticised our standards of work and the costs of it, saying that he thought the number of hours of work we had charged for, was excessive. Nerys cross-questioned him on his estimates of time and costs and other details. It seemed that he was mainly involved as a dealer in Rolls Royce motor cars.

When the judge asked him about his practical experience of actually working on RR Phantoms, he replied disdainfully, saying that he certainly "didn't get his hands dirty", but he did oversee work done, often for his American clients. It was clear that he had not been involved with the design or construction of one-off coach-built Rolls Royce motor cars. I think this undermined much of what he said and I was relieved and pleased that he was not our expert witness.

At the outset, I was concerned that I was shown as being the defendant rather than the plaintiff, but was assured by 'our' Mr Chamberlain that this was to my advantage. Firstly, because they were on the stand before us, I would have the opportunity to see what KK and his team were claiming and secondly, being my first time in court, Mr Chamberlain would be able to point out to me the Do's and Don'ts as each person went into the witness box. He was quite right and we could clearly see the strengths and weaknesses of their case and the attitude of the judge as it progressed.

Jo-Jo came to London after the hearing began and visited the court on a number of occasions. Sitting at the back, she was able to see how the case was going. With me being near the front of the court, I was able to study the judge and his expressions as the questioning proceeded. It was interesting to watch him, particularly when strong and what might be dishonest statements, were being made against us. I sometimes followed his gaze when he would look to the back of the court to see what Jo-Jo's reactions were. He was not disappointed, she would show her exasperation and extreme annoyance whenever KK or his witnesses were not telling the truth. He was left in no doubt about her opinions of what she thought about their statements.

Towards the end of the second week, the Judge again asked why our Expert Witness, Ian Rimmer from Rolls Royce, was still not in court for this second week of the hearing. A voice behind me, I think it was Nery's pupil, explained that he had returned from America, but on arrival, he had discovered that his father had died and he had to journey north, because he had to identify the body.

To me, as the events unfolded, it was becoming more and more like a television drama, I had no idea what was going to happen next!

ANDERSON WANTS ME TO STOP THE HEARING

Although he rarely attended the court, I was approached by Simon Anderson later in this second week, saying that we should stop the hearing. I was surprised by this and I told him that we seemed to be doing quite well. He then reminded me that I had not been in a court before and didn't realise the risks I was taking. He said that we were likely to lose the case and that the court had only been booked for two weeks, so I should let him negotiate a settlement, so that I wouldn't lose my house.

Hearing this from one of Eversheds leading litigation solicitors was extremely worrying. It was becoming increasingly obvious to me, from what I had already seen and this reinforced my feelings, that there was something going on behind my back. I didn't know what to believe. Why stop now, especially when Nimble had originally been so confident in us winning and after all the detailed preparation, the 'costs' already incurred and waiting three long years for the hearing? I swallowed hard, repeated that I thought we were winning and said that we must continue. After all, so far, the court had only heard the criticisms of the plaintiff, KK and the witnesses who were supporting his charges against us. It was obvious that the judge would yet have to hear and consider our side of the arguments. I had not yet been heard, neither had our Expert RR Witness, Ian Rimmer nor any of my staff, who had also been called by KK as witnesses for the defence.

My decision to continue may seem foolhardy, but Anderson wasn't attending the court, so couldn't possibly be as familiar with it as I was. Furthermore, during the last three years of preparation, I had already seen some dubious activities carried out by one or two of Eversheds solicitors. I thought it safer to put my faith in what I could see was a formal and correct legal process, rather than rely on people whose intentions were certainly questionable.

I remembered how, after nearly three years to study the facts and evidence in our favour, it was only a few weeks immediately prior to the hearing that there was the unexpected demand from Nimble and Anderson for me to provide them with valuable security "in case we lost" and now here it was, already being used by Anderson as a lever to try to stop the hearing. It was all just too 'neat' to be a coincidence.

CHAPTER 27:
THE THIRD WEEK

This began with Mr Dallymore on the stand again. Our barrister Nerys, had previously asked him to produce some estimates, figures and other information which would support his previous statements, in court, that our time spent and our charges were excessive. It was interesting to see him endeavouring, but failing to explain his reasons and the difficulties he had for not being able to provide them. He obviously couldn't do it.

Although not expected, I noticed that Sir Alex Smith was in the courtroom. He was the chief scientist for Rolls Royce Aero Company and had been responsible for developing Radar, Nuclear submarines and the RB 211 jet engine. Although he wasn't directly involved with Royle's restoration business, he was obviously wanting to see how the case was progressing. He was the Chairman of my Amphibious Vehicle company, Covelink Marine Ltd. He was a fine and supportive man and a very good friend and I was pleased to see him there.

As it turned out, it was now my turn to be in the witness box and I was to be on the stand on Monday 29th April, Tuesday 30th and part of Wednesday 1st May. From the beginning of the hearing, as advised by Mr Chamberlain, I had noted down in long hand, in my file, all the discussions as they progressed day by day in the court. At the weekends, I was able to check these notes and find the appropriate letters, documents and photographs which related to the points raised and discussed.

This written and photographic evidence, which KK himself had also been provided with progressively, as the work proceeded at Staindrop by Royles, conclusively proved the facts and the truth and that they were fabricating their complaints. Nerys was familiar with this of course, but I was able to fill in whenever there was a gap.

Mr Chamberlain was right, it was certainly to our advantage to be the defendants and not be examined first. We had heard all the claims and the many untruthful statements which the plaintiff, KK, and his team had made and I had also seen how the court operated. The benefit of this, especially when I was in the witness box, was that I had two weekends to search and locate all the appropriate evidence which I needed to support my arguments.

This gave me confidence and I was able to provide the court, not only with the bundle and document reference numbers, but also was able to illustrate many of the points with the appropriate photographs. Each time I made references, there was a rustling of papers all round the court as their duplicate files were opened and as the appropriate photographs were examined.

Although I felt that we were making good progress, I was much relieved when our Expert Witness, Ian Rimmer, finally arrived. He followed me into the witness box on the Wednesday afternoon. His calm and confident professionalism shone through. It soon became clear that his position in Rolls Royce and his wealth of experience, made him the ideal person to represent us in a case of this nature. He explained that his work in the Rolls Royce motor car factory at Crewe, was as the Quality Control Engineer responsible for setting quality standards and enforcing them.

Whereas KK's witness, Mr Dallymore, said that the thousands of hours of work to the Frua car, were excessive, Ian Rimmer was quite happy to say that the number of hours which we had charged to produce a one-off Rolls Royce of this standard and quality, were normal and most certainly not excessive.

He drew parallels with other special and one off Rolls Royce motor cars which they had worked on in the factory. He drew attention to the Villiers Phantom III with which the Famous engineer, Amhurst Villiers was involved. In this case, he told the court that the time spent exceeded that which we had spent building the Frua car and the Villiers car had not even been completed.

As previously, in-depth discussions about KK's detailed complaints went to extraordinary lengths, but Nerys and the judge persevered, sometimes with humorous results. On one occasion KK's barrister, the indomitable Miss Ife, repeatedly pressed a criticism about a tiny crease in one of the car's leather seats. It went on for so long, that after 20 minutes, even the normally imperturbable Ian Rimmer, having pointed out that leather is not a smooth, man-made plastic material, but is a natural, flexible, animal hide, said firmly and loudly that "leather grows on cows", then looking across the court to the sturdy Miss Ife, he said "and madam, cows are cows". The whole courtroom burst into laughter and even the judge could not suppress a smile.

A DAY OFF

The following day, Thursday, was to be quite different for me. I was advised not to attend the court since all the members of my staff from Staindrop had been called, by KK, to give evidence. He obviously thought that they would be bound to give conflicting evidence which would be to his advantage. If I was sitting there, watching them, Mr Chamberlain explained that my staff might be uncomfortable and not feel able to speak freely.

Being in London for a day and free to do as I pleased, I decided to take advantage of this rare opportunity to visit St Pauls Cathedral in the morning and I also made an appointment to visit the Ministry Of Defence in Whitehall in the afternoon. After such intensive concentration in court, it was a refreshing change to be able to visit such interesting places and do something pleasurable and useful.

St Pauls is a remarkable building and I was able to climb right up into the dome where the impressive timberwork structure of the inner and outer dome can be seen and then look down through small central glass peephole into the cathedral far below, fascinating! After this, I walked down to Whitehall where I had arranged to meet one or two miltary people who were helping me with my Amphibious Vehicle development.

Upon entering the Ministry Of Defence main building, I was reminded of the need for high level security. This included two body searches and an X-ray. Once through this, I was met by my host, an army major, and taken round various departments where I was invited to show them details and pictures of the prototypes which we were building. The response was most heartening. They could see how useful our high speed amphibians would be for various military activities and were most enthusiastic.

Returning to court the following day, Friday, Mr Chamberlain told me that Royle's staff had been very good witnesses and came over very well. Roger had been on the stand first and had supported our figures by explaining our accountancy systems. Roger had always been extremely pedantic and accurate and I was entirely confident that our records and accounts would be in order. He was followed by each member of the staff from the workshops in Staindrop including Edna Hewitt who was originally employed in the trim shop, but would also look after me, the customers, the men, the tea room and other domestic duties keeping the place tidy.

Mr Chamberlain told me that the staff were very smartly dressed and professional. They were able to confirm that what I had said was true and prove that our systems are straightforward and honest. They helped to disprove the false allegations which KK and Hand had made. When Edna took the oath and the questioning began, it was clear that she was not closely involved with, or knowledgeable about the work to the Frua car and I can imagine that she would certainly feel even more out of place in a London courtroom than we did. I was later told that the judge had stopped the questioning and asked her to stand down when it became clear that Miss Ife, KK's barrister, was taking advantage of her. It seemed that KK was desperate to try to undermine our strong position by any means possible and the judge could see what was going on.

"STOP THE HEARING"

When the Friday's proceedings were finished, Simon Anderson appeared and once more tried to persuade me to stop the hearing. Yet again, he repeated his previous warnings and this time, more firmly emphasised the risks which I was taking by continuing with our defence. He repeated that we were likely to lose the case.

As before, with him not having been in court, his advice was less credible than it was the last time. I was even more confident that we were making good, steady progress. Now that our side of the story was being heard, it was becoming more obvious that it could only be to KK's advantage to stop what seemed to be a most successful defence. I repeated that I wanted to continue. He said that the costs were building up, which they would be, but I was still optimistic that we would win with costs and was even more suspicious about Simon Anderson's motives.

In the early days, long before the hearing, I had been given dubious advice and seen unacceptable levels of information passing freely between Evershed's solicitors and KK's lawyers. Now, Eversheds seemed to be determined to stop the hearing and by doing so, probably lose it. I was now sure that there was indeed another agenda, but I didn't know what it was. There was £90,000 guaranteed to the court and a two million pound motor car and plenty of money available for the costs as long as we achieved our aim to win 'with costs', as agreed with Nimble.

It is worth remembering that not even the £90,000 would have been available, if I had taken Eversheds solicitor, Mr Coates advice early on and let KK have his car back. It is difficult for me to describe how I felt about my extremely difficult situation. I was in the High Court in London for the very first time and was facing a millionaire opponent. It was becoming very clear that I couldn't trust my own solicitors, the very people in charge of our defence and counterclaim, who were now trying to prevent me from winning the case. Thank goodness for Mr Chamberlain, at least he was looking after our interests.

And so the third week in court drew to a close. I had been on the stand and our Expert Witness and the Royle team, had also now given evidence and we seemed to be gaining ground and on the right track. Being a long Bank holiday weekend, I thought it would be good to have a breath of fresh air, so headed home to catch up with some of the jobs such as mowing the lawns and weeding the gravel paths. It was a welcome break from London.

THE FOURTH AND FINAL WEEK

Travelling south by train to Kings Cross station, I arrived back at the Dalchvist's Kensington flat at 7.30 pm on Monday evening 6th May, I was able to spend a couple of hours checking my files to see where we were with the case in readiness for the fourth and last week in court.

The following morning, Tuesday 7th May, I resumed life in London with the tube to Temple and as usual, had a brief meeting in Essex Street with Nerys Jefford and Mr Chamberlain before going into the familiar High Court buildings. By now, I felt very much at home with the routine and was pleased to be working with and have the help and these two people. As ever, I had Mr Chamberlain at my shoulder with his advice and was looking forward to seeing what our barrister Nerys would be doing in court. She is a bright spark and we got on well. She was also good fun and I had great confidence in her abilities.

The day began at 10.30am as usual, this time with expert witness, Ian Rimmer in the witness box again. After each day's events in court, with more and more facts being revealed, there was the need for witnesses to be recalled to clarify and confirm particular facts. He stood down at 3.30 pm. I felt that our defence and the indisputable evidence which we had been able to provide, combined with the support of such an authoritative expert witness, had impressed the judge and that we did have a very good chance of winning the case.

The plaintiffs claims of being considerably overcharged for the work had resulted in endless discussions, going into minute detail about the quality of work and the costs involved. Hundreds of Royles time sheets, job sheets and pay records had been checked against each other by KK's team, but they had not found any discrepancies of any consequence. Out of the blue, at this late stage, Miss Ife asked if Royles men 'clocked' in and out, when they came to work. They did, so she immediately requested that these clock cards were produced for examination and to be cross checked against all the other workshop records.

Roger was now back at the office in Staindrop, so he bundled them all up, nearly two thousand of them, and sent them to the court. The cards covered a period of over three years and this last ditch attempt by KK's team to prove their case, indicated to me that they were becoming desperate to find any incriminating evidence.

When they arrived, the judge wearily asked Miss Ife to select a few sample clock cards at random. This was done and these were then compared to the equivalent time sheets, job sheets and pay records. Once again, there were no discrepancies, each one showed that the hours spent and charged out to KK was correct. Roger's book keeping was, as expected, perfectly correct down to the minutes. The judge obviously had had enough and said that he wished to see no more and said he was ready to hear the closing submissions from both the barristers.

Even at this late stage in the proceedings, Simon Anderson appeared yet again, for the third time. This time he bumped into me as I was walking across the zebra crossing on the Strand heading for Nerys's chambers for a bite of lunch. We stood on the small island in the middle of the road where, as previously, in spite of not being in the court, he tried to persuade me to stop the hearing. This time he was extremely assertive, saying that I was going to lose the case and probably my house as well. I again repeated that I thought we would win and that I was going to continue until the end of this final week. He was now being so forceful, and with our ongoing progress, I was even more sure that there was another agenda and whatever it was, it certainly was not for my benefit!

The rest of the week was taken up with counsels closing submissions. These were presented both orally to the court and formally in writing. They summarised the case for KK the plaintiff and for Royles defence. Interestingly, Nerys presented her submissions first, these took up most of the following two days, the Wednesday and Thursday.

Most of Friday 10th May, was taken up with KK's Barrister, Miss Ife's closing submissions on behalf of the plaintiff, these were also submitted in writing. When she sat down, there now only remained the judgement itself. Being the end of the day and of the week, an announcement was made that the Judges decisions would be given to the court on Monday 13th May.

Being my final weekend in London, Edward and Heather Carter invited me to stay with them at Windsor and so I spent an enjoyable weekend being spoilt by them. Whilst there, I had a good dose of fresh air in the open Aston Martin DB5 Sports which we had built for them at Royles (Job 398). This splendid one-off motor car is very much like that of a DBR2 and has now given them 18 years of superb high speed motoring.

CHAPTER 28:
THE JUDGEMENT

Monday dawned with me already back in Kensington and on my last underground trip to 'Temple'. As ever, the court rose as Judge Roger Cox entered and took his seat. His summing up and judgement took all morning. The formal typed copy of it extends to 76 pages.

Whilst summarising the principle arguments of this four week hearing, Judge Cox interspersed his remarks with the key judgements. These, when put together, were that he "finds in favour of David.A.C.Royle & Co Ltd", he "finds in favour of Royle Cars Ltd," He also "finds in Favour of Royles expert Witness, Ian Rimmer" and "in favour of David Royle himself."

The awards made and ordered by the Judge were £57,000, interest at 8% and with the all important benefit of 'costs', which were to be paid by the plaintiff, 'KK', we had all the important awards which I was aiming for. We would be paid for our work and Eversheds costs would be paid by KK.

You will remember that In 1993, the original debt owed by 'KK' was £73,000. With three years having passed before the hearing in 1996, three years of interest was due, plus the sum of over £12,000, which I had struggled to pay to Eversheds, piecemeal, for their costs before the hearing. This was nearly 50% of Nimbles estimated £25,000. When added together, the amounts awarded were in excess of KK's debt.'

'I have no doubt that Eversheds will have calculated the actual sum due to us, but they have never informed me of the total amount. What is certain is that, to put it in a nutshell, we won the case with flying colours! Our defence of the action had been a great success.

We had achieved our aims, we had proved beyond any doubt, that Royles are honest and our bills correct, importantly, as well as interest, we were awarded 'costs' which was pivotal to my agreement with Nimble and which was fundamental to Eversheds acting for us in this litigation. As mentioned, there was £90,000 guaranteed to the court and plenty of money and assets available from KK and his company to cover Eversheds costs, so I knew that I had satisfied all the requirements and that our house was safe.

I was extremely relieved that three years after the original debt and all the work done preparing for the hearing had been worthwhile and that I would now be able to repay most of the debts which had been such a worry. At last, I would see an end to the ongoing loans and bank interest which had been such a drain on me and the company for the last three years.

I caught the train home believing that I would be able to put the whole affair behind me.

CHAPTER 29:
AFTER THE HEARING

Following our great success in court, I allowed ten days to pass before I rang our solicitor, Simon Anderson, to ask when I would be receiving a cheque for the sums awarded. I was astonished by his reply completely ignoring the judgement, he actually laughed as he told me that we would not be paid any money because, "it had all gone in costs".

I was deeply shocked by this. After three years of serious financial difficulty and worry and having accepted Nimble's revised offer of support, when he promised that if we won 'with costs', which we now had done, then they would get their costs from the other side. I had no doubt whatsoever that, after all this we would, as Nimble put it right at the start, "have our £73,000 bill paid". In fact, we received no money whatsoever, following the hearing

Eversheds solicitors Simon Anderson and Nimble Thompson not only denied the existance of our agreement, they also completely ignored and paid no heed whatsoever, to the Judges awards including his 'costs' and 'interest' orders which were for our benefit. It transpired that they had immediately taken £57,000 of our award from the £90,000 guaranteed to the court by KK. Instead of looking after the interest of their own clients and obeying the judges orders and giving us this sum and other monies due, they chose to use our award money for the benefit of the losing party, the corrupt millionaire whose dishonesty had been repeatedly proved in court.

My solicitors did this, knowing full well that KK had ample monies to pay the awards and costs as ordered.

They had, in fact, reversed the high court judgement. They well knew how desperately we, their own client, needed the money and that we had originally worked hard to earn it and had proved it in the highest court in the land.

As well as the £90,000 court guarantee, there was ample money available from KK including the £2 million Rolls Royce, plus whatever other monies KK and his company had to cover the costs. (subsequently, an offer of £65,000 from KK proved that ample money was available).

As soon as we won, I had no doubt that the orders of the court would be carried out and was confident that I would, at last, be able to repay the bank and most of the other borrowings made to keep Royles running after the loss of £73,000 in May 1993. In fact, it transpired during the hearing, that KK had instructed his people not to pay the full amounts of our invoices. In this way, our overdraft steadily crept up in the three years prior the debt. So, by the time it came to court, we had actually been helping to fund his Rolls Royce work and had been paying increasing amounts of bank interest for six years, not just the three years awaiting the court hearing.

The award with interest and costs, as ordered, was worth over £70,000. Even with this, I would have still been out of pocket by having had to pay the interest on the difference between the £57,000 awarded and the actual debt of £73,000 as well as the interest on the £12,000+ which we had paid in advance, to Eversheds.

I mention this to emphasise the fact that although I was very pleased to have won, we would still actually be out of pocket by six years of interest charges and all the work preparing for the hearing, the loss of income with all the staff going to London as witnesses and the costs involved with train fares etc. This is why I desperately needed, at least, to have the awards paid as agreed with Nimble. In simple terms, the original £73,000 was money which we had earned for many hundreds of hours working on the Frua car at £25 per hour, together with the costs of the Geneva show.

I simply could not believe that Nimble Thompson, my own solicitor and a friend, working with Simon Anderson, the Litigation specialist of Eversheds, would not honour our agreement and would even completely ignore the Orders of the High Court, The Royal Courts of Justice in London.

Our entire defence and counter-claim action was entirely founded upon Nimbles proposal and this agreement. It was fundamental to the acceptance of Nimble's offer and the involvement of Eversheds in the case. Without this "punt" as he called it, there was no point what so ever, in having Eversheds costly legal firm involved and having stressed this at the outset, he was well aware of it. I would otherwise, have tried to defend the case on my own and do it alone. I really believed that Nimble was concerned for me, but with the benefit of hindsight, it looks very much as if he was, in fact seeking work for Eversheds expanding legal team, Mr Coates in our case.

When solicitors deny the existence of agreements and don't honour important promises and when they also ignore the orders of the High Court, they are self- evidently, not only dishonest, but seriously corrupt. As they come between the ordinary man in the street and the Law and Justice, then that 'ordinary man' is in a truly dreadful position, he is on his own.

The fact which struck me so forcibly, was that our years of honesty and diligence, both commercially and personally, had been proved beyond doubt by the Highest Legal Court in the country, yet we were being denied the benefits of this by dishonest solicitors. The very people who are charged with carrying out the law. It was incredible that the wealthy, losing party who had been proved to have been dishonest, under oath, time and again in court, should have the benefits accorded to us. It was a gross injustice.

The final insult occurs whenever there are any discussions with, or when I complain to third parties. Despite indisputable written evidence that Nimble and Anderson are dishonest and corrupt, their word is taken in preference to mine, their client. Why? Because they are solicitors and are presumed to be honest!

In any legal action, the solicitor is naturally completely in control. Whilst a solicitor will explain that he is 'instructed' by his client, any clients instructions can only be based upon the information and legal advice given to him by his legal expert, his solicitor. Therefore, a dishonest solicitor is easily able to manipulate a client and hence, the outcome of the case itself. He can choose what information he wishes to give, no matter whether it be true or not, and his correspondence can be framed to cover himself in the event that any malpractice is discovered later on. The advantage is therefore entirely with the solicitor at all times.

In this case, although I have little legal knowledge, I do have many years of business experience behind me, so I began to see early on, that some of the information and advice provided by Eversheds solicitors was dubious, to say the least. The collusion with KK's lawyers, the obviously inflated 'costs', the attempted 'snatch back' of the Rolls Royce, the increasing negativity as I provided the evidence and the last minute demand for valuable security, all progressively undermined my confidence in the people who were supposed to be helping me.

Increasingly, I had no choice, but to rely upon my own limited knowledge and common sense to judge whether I should accept their advice or reject it, rather than be manipulated for reasons unknown to me at the time. A most unsatisfactory state of affairs, especially as I was seriously ill and undergoing a series of major surgical operations prior to the High Court hearing in April 1996.

Unless you have been involved in a High Court action defending yourself with your home and business at risk, it may be difficult for you to understand the stresses of this. I had to summon up every ounce of determination to keep going and maintain a satisfactory relationship with my solicitors for the three years it took before appearing for my first time in court, knowing that once there, I would be facing a wealthy opponent and barristers who are trained for these proceedings.

Not being able to trust my own solicitors, the very people who's expertise I was supposed to rely upon for legal advice was bad enough, but then having to keep making important decisions, 'blind' as it were, was a terrible position to be in. I had to rely on my own judgement and snippets of information given to me. I could not possibly know what the legal implications of my decisions might be. Behind all of this however, I did have the comfort of knowing that we are honest and Royles business practices are straight forward and given a fair judgement in court, then we should win through.

CHAPTER 29: AFTER THE HEARING

When we won the case, I had not only proved that are we honest, but that there were indeed, very serious irregularities in Eversheds support for me, their client. For example Anderson's three separate, forceful appeals to me to stop the hearing saying that we were losing, were shown to be completely unfounded. This confirmed my previous suspicions, but the final proof that our own solicitors were not acting in my interests, was when they refused to give me our awards. I was astounded by this blatant disregard for our agreement, for honesty, for the High Court Judgement and for the Law itself.

After the hearing, at least I knew where I stood and could be fairly sure that whatever Nimble or Anderson said to me was likely to be untrue and probably against my interests. I had to face the fact that I may now be in an even worse position. Whilst technically, being my solicitors I was still entirely reliant upon them to enact the court orders, so somehow, I had to maintain a working relationship with them, even though it was now clear that they were looking after the interests of KK and his lawyers and had no concern for me, their client, or for my company.

CHAPTER 30:
THE OTHER AGENDA & COLLUSION

After the hearing and as the weeks became months in 1996, It was becoming clear that Nimble, working with Anderson, had no intention of honouring our important agreement or any of the orders of the High Court Judge.

A predicament which seemed to me not to be credible.

Bearing in mind that I had been previously involved with other partners and solicitors in Eversheds who were good people and who had been most helpful to me in the past, I then learnt from one of them, what the 'other agenda' was and what lay behind it all. For obvious reasons, I have not revealed the name of the man who told me what was going on behind my back. He knew me and obviously thought that I did not deserve the unfair and dreadful treatment which his colleagues were metering out to me. Now, with the benefit of hindsight, the elements which baffled me during this case, all fit neatly together.

KK'S INITIAL PLANS AND THEIR EFFECTS

During the three year period before the court hearing, KK's plan was to avoid paying his bill by frightening me off with high costs. When this was obviously failing, he must have become increasingly worried when he discovered that his huge 308 page affidavit had little effect, other than to be answered by my affidavit of 105 pages. His threats to make the case so expensive that I couldn't afford to defend myself also had little effect and even when he increased his claims of being overcharged by amounts of "up to £200,000" had not deterred me, he must then have had to consider the possibility of losing the "war" as he called it and the very high costs of doing so.

It must have been when KK discovered that the large legal firm, Eversheds, were going to act for me and defend the action, that he finally realised that his plans were likely to backfire. His lawyers were now seeing the bundles of our written documentary and photographic evidence which I had assembled, and how this evidence was likely to prove that his allegations were fabricated and were generally untrue.

If Royles won, KK could now see that It would be him who would be faced with the expensive legal costs. His own London lawyers, Berwin Leighton, would now be racking up high legal costs as they entered into long legal battles with Eversheds over KK's detailed and substantially dishonest affidavit. On top of these, he would also have to pay Royles original bill for £73,000.

THE CRUX OF THE MATTER

KK had to do something to try to protect himself from the mess and high potential for costs which he had created for himself. He apparently told his lawyers that if they couldn't win an action against such a small and inconsequential firm like Royles, then he certainly was not going to pay them if they lost the case!

With KK having many companies around the world which, no doubt, would provide a lot of ongoing and valuable legal work for his lawyers at Berwin Leighton, I think it is safe to assume that he would demand and expect them to carry on with this legal case regardless of not being paid, which they obviously did. This is when the collusion with Eversheds will have begun.

It seems that KK's lawyers then explained to Anderson that they would not be paid by KK if they lost the case. It must have been Anderson who then said that he would arrange things so that his professional colleagues would not be out of pocket with this case.

So began, what turned out to be, the most extraordinary demonstration of corruption and malpractice which I had ever seen in 50 years of business. The effects of which continue even up to the time of writing this, in May 2009, thirteen years later.

(Authors note: It is taking me much longer to write this book than originally anticipated, so I will leave dated comments such as that above, unchanged. Parts of this book already date back two years and as it is now summer 2010, I will leave them. This story is still ongoing and as I am still writing and dealing with matters I refer to, I will include a final update at the end, otherwise I will have to keep amending it and never finish it!)

OBSERVATIONS ABOUT OUR SOLICITORS

It might be helpful to briefly interrupt the story to provide some background about Nimble Thompson and Simon Anderson. Originally, I did think that Nimble's intentions were good and that he wanted to help me. He was a friend of mine, as indeed were his mother and father, friends of my parents. He seemed to be seriously concerned for my health and I believed that he understood how important it was for Royles to have their bill paid. He knew we were honest and that KK was a multi-millionaire and that there would be plenty of money to cover Eversheds costs if we won. Hence the "punt" as he called it, was a pretty safe bet.

It is also likely that Eversheds and Nimble were on the look-out for legal work. It is clear that Mr Coates was new to Eversheds and was obviously available for work. Whether it was simply because he was available or had just left KK's lawyers, I do not know, but he was certainly a 'mole' working closely with KK's lawyers.

The situation seemed to change when Anderson became involved, he was ambitious and was obviously prepared to do anything to further his career. I understand that his father was a very successful man in business and he must have wanted to impress him with his legal acumen! Being put in charge of our litigation by Eversheds, my guess is that when Anderson found that Berwin's were not going to be paid if Royles won, he saw this as an opportunity to ingratiate himself with Berwin Leighton's team and their wealthy client KK.

Being London lawyers with many wealthy and important clients, he must have thought that it could be beneficial for him, in the future, if he was able to help them. He would have quickly learned from Nimble and later on, from all the evidence, that Royles were honest and were likely to prove this and win in court. To prevent this, he needed to weaken my position in every possible way, so that he could manage the case for his own ends and for Berwin's lawyer's benefit. At the same time, keeping KK happy.

BACK TO ANDERSON'S PLAN

From the start, he had the help of Mr Coates, the 'mole' solicitor who had recently started work at Eversheds offices in Leeds and who provided Berwin's with details of our activities. He and Berwin's must have decided to load and inflate the costs on both sides, especially ours. This was mutually beneficial in any event and would probably also deter me from continuing.

Their next aim was to further weaken Royles position by advising me to drop the lien and return the Frua Rolls Royce to KK. This was to be done by their 'mole', our own solicitor, Mr Coates. With the car being our only valuable security and smelling a rat, I refused to do it. When this plan failed, they tried a more crude method when they tried to 'snatch back' the Frua car. This was when, more by luck than good judgement on my part, they thought that I would be out of the way in hospital and Roger would be on his own. In fact, I was back in the office and waiting for them.

The net result of this being that KK then had no choice, but to provide a guarantee to the court for £90,000, to get his car back, presumably so that he could sell it. Definitely a step in the right direction, one would safely presume.

The lengthy 2½ years delay in getting to court is also likely to be the result of Anderson's efforts. With all the problems I had, he would have no doubt that my serious illness, my hospitalisation and my financial difficulties, which they were adding to by their ever increasing and loaded legal 'costs'. Including the £50,000 'delivery up' and £200,000 'overcharge', would certainly maximise my worries and further weaken my position. So, the longer they could delay the hearing, the worse would be my misery and the more likely it would be that I would stop the hearing. Such is the dreadful nature of the people I was dealing with.

Using the passage of time as a legal 'tool', is probably the most unscrupulous and disgraceful technique employed by the legal profession. It allows them to steadily increase their costs and in this case, further debilitate people in my position.

At some stage in all this, Nimble must have had to make the choice between supporting me and honouring our agreement, or supporting Anderson, his professional partner in Eversheds. He obviously chose the latter.

Seeing that his plans were failing and that I was still determined to continue, Anderson then tried to persuade me to let him 'negotiate' a settlement with KK, but I was already well aware that I couldn't trust him, so insisted on going to court. Finally, just a week or two before the hearing, when he knew that he could still not control me, he demanded a valuable security from me, as a lever. The hearing was now imminent, so as previously explained, I gave him a charge on the Old Vicarage.

As soon as the Legal Charge was signed, Anderson again tried to persuade me to stop the hearing. He said that he would speak to Berwins to 'negotiate' a settlement and that he would do his 'best for Royles' and now, he would also try to 'save' my house.

This blatant and obviously contrived situation did no more than assure me that we were indeed, likely to win and that he was still trying to help Berwin's lawyers avoid the courtroom costs which were not going to be paid for by KK. Thus KK's lawyers would maximise their income from the existing loaded 'costs'. At the same time, he could also say that he had saved KK from having to pay Royles £73,000 bill.

CHAPTER 31:
SEEKING JUSTICE

After failing to stop the hearing in advance and not being in court himself, Anderson must have been told by Mr Chamberlain, who was there with me every day, that we were likely to win. Still determined to help Berwins and deprive me of the benefits of being honest and of the Law itself, Anderson became increasingly agitated as the 'court case' proceeded. He now had no choice and could not avoid, even more blatantly, demonstrating his determination by trying, on no less than three occasions, to stop the hearing. He knew that it would be much more difficult to look after Berwin's lawyers once we had won the action. He would have realised that he had no choice, but to ignore the Judges Orders, so that he could use our awards for the benefit of the losing party.

For such activities to be contemplated and actually take place before, during and after a formal legal action in the highest court in the land, illustrates the extreme level of confidence which is bred into these solicitors. To completely ignore their duty to their own clients and knowingly and purposefully cause them such serious physical and mental distress, as in this case, reveals a most extreme abuse of the power they wield to the detriment of another human being.

I was to discover and you will now find out for yourself as you read on, the lengths to which these solicitors would go, along with others in the legal fraternity, in order to control the legal system for their own benefit. The events which have occurred are truly remarkable, they are devious in the extreme and exhibit malpractice at levels which I wouldn't have believed could exist in a modern democratic society.

Ultimately, in this case, the solicitors effectively reversed the High Court Judgement for their own benefit and indirectly, for the benefit of the person who had been proved beyond doubt, under oath, to be dishonest. The person who made false accusations causing all the trouble in the first place, all to save himself some money. The action was then being used, simply as being a means to create an income for all the solicitors involved. Honour, justice and the Judgment of the High Court were of no consequence to them.

OPENING THE CAN OF WORMS

Believing that my experiences and that this travesty of justice must be an exceptional situation, I was confident that the legal complaints organisations would be sure to help me. I began by reporting the facts to the Law Society and the Solicitors Complaints Bureau (SCB) the month following the hearing on 27th June 1996.

The response from these organisations which are based at Leamington Spa, was sympathetic and they seemed to be very professional and to begin with, I really thought that I was going to be helped by them. They sent various official forms and literature to me.

At the time, I had no idea that that the Law Society controlled the legal complaints organisation, the Solicitors Complaints Bureau, (SCB) as it was then called. Nor that it does, in fact, work together, hand in glove, with any solicitor who is being complained about. This proved to be entirely for the benefit and to the advantage of solicitors. Some years later, this fact was highlighted by Ann Abraham in her report to Parliament when she was the Legal Ombudsman. In her report, 'The Regulatory Maze' in 2002. She reported that the SCB "was not operating in the public's interest" and that a high percentage of the 42,000 complaints that year in 1996, were not being resolved.

Like most of the population, I was unaware of this, but I now know that my first letter of complaint (and all the letters that followed) would have been immediately copied to my solicitors, Nimble and Anderson who were then in full control of the complaint and probably copied them to Berwins lawyers as well. In my ignorance, three months later, I wrote to the SCB informing them that KK's solicitors had now lodged an Appeal against the High Court judgment. Naturally, I thought that my complaint would be in confidence. In fact, I can now see that the 'Appeal' would have been agreed between both parties of solicitors as a good tactic, entirely for their advantage. It was as a direct result of my complaint to the SCB, in fact, they would not have needed me to tell them!

Having no appreciation of what I was really up against at that time and not realising that there was any collusion between all the solicitors and the complaints agencies involved, I was not concerned when Eversheds asked me to send them my own 1993/4 original file. This contained the original correspondence which referred to the agreement between Nimble and myself upon which the entire defence action with Eversheds was based. I wanted to prove the arrangements, so was happy to let them have it. I didn't think it was necessary to make copies of the documents in it. With the formal complaints agency, the SCB, now being involved, I felt perfectly safe in doing this, after all, they stated that they existed to "regulate solicitors". Importantly, I do have other letters and all the computer discs if I needed them.

Later on, as the complaint developed, I wrote to Eversheds and had to press them for the return of this important file. I was eventually sent the file, but various letters had been removed and it was incomplete. It had obviously been crudely filled up with multiple copies of a few irrelevant documents to replace them.

Eversheds subsequently contradicted themselves when they informed me in writing, that the file, along with other important Law Society files and written evidence, had mysteriously "disappeared" whilst in their care. Such is the level of their corruption and malpractice and this is only one example.

In the meantime, the SCB replied to my letter to tell me that they could not deal with my complaint "until proceedings (the Appeal) are concluded" and that I should defer from making my complaint until it was. They enclosed another form, this time a 'Complaint Referral Form', which cancelled the 'Help Form' which I had previously returned to them.

It all seemed to be very 'professional' at the time and I was innocent of the many far reaching and contrived methods they use to deprive those who complain of fair and just treatment. Many of their devious techniques and methods include very formal and professional looking documents and systems which are devised to create repeated delays and waste very considerable amounts of their clients time.

These would be revealed in due course.

IT WAS NOW 10TH OCTOBER 1996, 5 MONTHS AFTER THE HEARING.

THE APPEAL

Looking back, I had no reason at the time, to believe that Berwins 'Appeal' against the High Court decision was contrived. This is because it could have been beneficial to KK and them all in a number of respects:

i. The SCB did not have to appear to be doing anything to help me and it gave the solicitors more time to put more pressure on me.

ii. The passage of time is always the solicitors friend. The longer everything takes the more frustrated the client becomes and the more opportunities there are for solicitors to make money, charging for time.

iii. I thought that if the appeal proceeded, the long delays in the appeal courts would save KK interest costs if he did, ultimately, have to pay the awards and costs. (At least he seems to have accepted the authority of the court, unlike my solicitors.)

iv. It would enable the solicitors to add yet further costs for me and/or KK.

v. My solicitors were now able to threaten me, saying that if I didn't pay them more money, they would withdraw any further legal support. I had, by then, with great difficulty, managed to pay a sum in excess of £12,000 towards Nimble Thompson's original £25,000 costs estimate.

vi. My solicitors told me that, without their representation, KK could well undermine our victory in court with serious repercussions. I had little choice, but to believe them. I was trapped again.

vii. I knew that KK wanted me to lose my house, so the longer I was in financial difficulty, the better chance he had of achieving his aims. The solicitors would also then benefit by taking whatever money they wanted from the value of our house.

viii. To add to the pressure, I was told that KK's aim was also to force me out of business.

Confronted with all this, my situation was becoming untenable. They knew full well that my bank facilities were already substantially overdrawn, so I certainly couldn't pay them any more money for the appeal or for anything else. I had little choice, but to hold my ground and for the first time, I openly confronted my own solicitors.

I informed Eversheds in writing, that they had been negligent which was confirmed by written evidence in my possession. The result was that the 'Appeal' was dropped within a few days. At the time this seemed once again, to indicate to me that there was collusion with KK's lawyers.

With the benefit of hindsight, they were in fact, covering up their direct link with the legal complaints organisation, the SCB, but the 'appeal' had created some valuable delays for them and put me on the back foot again.

These activities show what despicable people Nimble and Anderson are, as indeed were KK's lawyers for colluding with them. No principles whatsoever.

BY NOW IT WAS FEBRUARY 1997,
10 MONTHS AFTER THE HEARING.

THE SOLICITORS COMPLAINTS BUREAU (SCB) IS REPLACED

During this period I was informed that the SCB was being 'replaced' with a new complaints organisation called the 'Office for the Supervision of Solicitors' (OSS). I was again sent more forms to sign and I found that I was dealing with different people. Naturally, believing the organisation to be new, I wrote and explained the whole story again and they said that the points raised were "interesting" and sent me another leaflet with their new title.

It was not long, however, before I realised that I was, in fact, dealing with the self-same organisation. The OSS were operating from the same address and the Law Society simply changed the personnel around and gave its officials new titles. There were so many employees at Leamington Spa that they were able to make all those people like me, who were already complaining, think that it was a different agency.

My guess is that there had been so many complaints about the SCB that a 'new' agency had been formed to 'improve' the service. What is so remarkable, is that all the people who work at Leamington Spa are so well trained and indoctrinated, (or so well paid?) that they are content to continue to deny justice to the tens of thousands of people who complain. Their bias in support of solicitors is extreme and yet, no matter how evil the solicitors may be, this bias is cleverly concealed and is, by no means, immediately obvious.

It is only when I found out that the Law Society approves all the budgets for payment of the staff there, that one can begin to understand how they have such a high level of control.

The great advantage which these 'legal' organisations have, is that the man in the street cannot conceive that those who are charged with carrying out the law, would undermine it themselves with their own dishonest and devious practices.

The change of name was yet another great opportunity to create, frustrate and delay matters. Once again, for the benefit of the corrupt solicitors, adding substantial time wasting and more costs for all those with complaints.

From the outset, I had also been reporting the events to Ann Abraham, the Legal Services Ombudsman, but I was told that she could do nothing until the legal complaints office had reached their final decision and the Adjudicator had provided his report. It was only later that I discovered that the Adjudicator was also part and parcel of the Leamington Spa organisation and was again controlled by the solicitors being complained about and by the Law Society.

The very organisation which openly supports the interests of solicitors.

So, despite there being a 'new' Complaints agency, The Office for the Supervision of Solicitors (OSS.) I was again, still actually dealing with the same organisation and was still completely in the hands of the devious Law Society.

My correspondence with the OSS continued and letters became longer as they introduced all manner of issues and problems. Their excuses for taking no action were numerous, refined and well practised.

As time passed and I intensified and broadened out my enquiries and investigations, the extent of their control was becoming clear. They said they had "limited powers", and warned me that there were "financial risks" in claiming negligence. The barriers to a fair and reasonable complaints process were now revealing themselves at every turn.

The OSS then advised me to talk to a "competent solicitor", and that "this office cannot deal with negligent solicitors or a failure of duty of care".

This says it all. The OSS and the legal complaints system is a truly dreadful sham.

Completely ignoring the benefits of the High Court Costs Order, they then described what is known as "Taxation" which was said to be the "only way" in which I could establish the reasonableness of the legal 'costs.' I investigated each excuse and it was clear that the Office for the Supervision of Solicitors organisation had no intention of 'Supervising Solicitors'.

This was despite the cover of the OSS booklet boldly stating that it was "Working for excellence and Fairness in Guarding Standards". Its title was clearly a misnomer and was plainly intended to mislead. It is a cruel, costly, unprincipled and undemocratic organisation.

In response to the point above,' Taxation', a little research revealed that once again, that this is another legal device which generally works for the benefit of solicitors and is described later on.

Few people realise just how serious and cunning the entire structure of the 'legal complaints' process can be. Members of the public, like me, set out with the belief that our legal system must be honest and this assumption is taken advantage of by any solicitor who wants to bend the rules for his own advantage. A 'legal' person who is then supported by the Law Society, an organisation whose title is as misleading as those of its satellite agencies.

Ironically, even the hackneyed phrase: "it is the solicitors who always win in the end" also works to their advantage. Any overcharging which may be suspected on a day to day basis, is often accepted, written off and reluctantly dismissed by many people with this phrase.

It must therefore be safe to assume that the tens of thousands of citizens who have gone to the trouble of entering into the formal complaints process, are only the most serious and obvious cases. They must therefore, only be the tip of a truly enormous iceberg.

CHAPTER 32:
THE LEGAL OMBUDSMAN AND PARLIAMENT

It was becoming clear how the SCB and OSS systems are very carefully created and refined to delay progress and ultimately succeed in denying the public a fair complaints service. With levels of obfuscation so extreme, that they are designed to sicken those who complain. Once I had established this fact, I had no choice but to break away from the normal process and ignore 'the rules'. I therefore turned again to Ann Abraham the Legal Ombudsman in December 1997.

I wrote to her describing what I had discovered and the ongoing events in some detail, and asked her if there was any hope of finding legal people with some honour or decency who would not "prey on those British citizens who turn to the law for justice".

After explaining that it was now 18 months since our successful legal action and 4½ years after the debt in 1993, our correspondence continued and I pleaded with her to "give me some hope" and not repeat that it would have to be dealt with later, as previously. I also mentioned going to the European Courts.

IT WAS NOW FEBRUARY 1998, 22 MONTHS AFTER THE HEARING

This time, I received a 5 page report from Ann Abraham which confirmed that she "certainly considers that there may be issues that may require investigation" and that she would like to see the difficulties "speedily resolved", but now, that she also would have to await the outcome of the Appeal proceedings with Eversheds, which had not been withdrawn at that stage. So, it could still only be "dealt with later".

Her terms of reference must have been designed to prevent her interfering.

More delays, but this reply never the less, did make me feel that Ann Abraham was more genuine than the others. I was more hopeful that the Legal Ombudsman would be independent, at the same time, I was concerned to see that she was tied into the established legal systems which could mean that the Law Society and solicitors would still have some control over her.

WIDENING THE SCOPE OF MY ACTIVITIES

I was sure that there had to be some good, honourable and honest people somewhere in the legal system so, in parallel with pressing the complaints organisations and the legal Ombudsman, I began to contact all the legal authorities in Parliament. This included cabinet ministers, my MP and various members of the House of Lords. I also made contact with any and every other organisation which might be able to help, including the courts and the Press.

My question was simple, **"Do The Royal Courts of Justice have any authority or not?"**
I was intensifying my efforts to establish whether or not, an honest British citizen could benefit from the Orders of the High Court.

As time passed, I found that despite my most serious complaints of legal fraud and corruption, many of the Legal Ministers and MP's in both houses of Parliament wouldn't reply to my letters, not even when I pressed them to do so with more letters. Sometimes, one of their staff would write to me to acknowledge a letter, but only to tell me that the person could not intervene.

This negative response and obvious 'cop out' revealed a lack of concern for the man in the street, even one who has been denied the benefits of a High Court judgement. It was yet another clear indication that the Legal fraternity know that they are so safely protected by their intricate and biased complaints regime, that they can simply ignore such important correspondence and any complaints, no matter how serious the allegations.

Most of my letters and reports to Parliament did not mince words, the dishonesty, corruption and the facts were clearly stated and the legal firms and the solicitors involved were named.

By now, I felt that the more people who were aware of what was going on, the safer I was. I had nothing to hide and had plenty of evidence, so the scattergun approach might eventually put me in touch with somebody who could help. I did however, and still do, take the precaution of copying some of the letters to the Police for my own safety.

I am sure that most people who complain eventually tire of the contrived delays and being ignored by the legal authorities, they give up the struggle. The legal complaints systems have been devised for the purpose and have succeeded in doing this for years. In my case the losses were affecting me so badly and the fraud so obvious, that I pressed on regardless. I was now writing hundreds of letters and making appeals to VIP's, to Parliament and even to the Royal Family. I knew the facts and was determined to continue.

One or two notable people did give me some hope and in due course, did take action with very interesting results. I will tell you about these later.

MORE COLLUSION AND DISHONESTY

Whilst all this was going on, my solicitors continued with various tactics which, on the face of it, might have been mutually beneficial, but which, ultimately, were usually found to be for their own advantage. At this time, for example, Eversheds threatened KK's company with a Mareva injunction which succeeded. Like the Judges orders, this action seemed to be a good move since it guaranteed that their costs would be paid by KK and his company. Subsequently, the benefit of this injunction, like the High Court orders, was also ignored because they continued to try to make me liable for all the costs, even though they had no justification. Perhaps it was a case of 'belt and braces' in case they failed to force me to pay them.

I have already explained how my solicitors did all they could to undermine my security and ensure that they could control me and at the same time, maximise their own income. It seems that they knew that I might cause trouble after the hearing, if they weren't able to control me. Looking back to the weeks immediately before the hearing, I can clearly remember another occasion when they were trying to do this.

At one of the last meetings, Anderson asked me if I had dishonestly avoided paying any tax or had done anything illegal. They said they needed to know this in case it came out in court. When I said that I hadn't, they repeated the question more forcefully, but again I said that I had always been honest and had no "skeletons in the cupboard". I can now see that it was only after finding out that they had nothing to use like this to control and intimidate me, that they demanded a valuable security, "in case we didn't win in court" they said. This confirmed that he was aware of Nimble's "punt" and my agreement with him.

As previously explained, I had little choice at this late stage, but to provide it and finally decided to give them a charge on our home, The Old Vicarage. After winning the court action, they had no further right to hold onto it, so I requested that they cancel this formal Charge, but they refused. I repeated the request a number of times explaining that they had no right to it, but they held onto it for over three more years. It was the only lever they had to control me.

With the ongoing recession and not having received the court awards, my bank overdraft remained substantially overdrawn. Royles, my restoration company was desperately short of money for wages etc, so I applied to my building society for a further advance and to increase my small mortgage. The value of the house was sufficiently high that there was plenty of collateral for me to do this. Never the less, the application was refused, along with two more which I made later on during this period, all three were refused.

The building society wrote to inform me on each occasion, that the applications had been blocked by my own Eversheds solicitors. They were using the charge they held on the property to stop me. They did this knowing that I was very short of money and desperately needed the £30,000, which I was asking for, to keep the company running. They were also well aware that this sum was only a fraction of the value of the house and that I could not draw a salary. I was shocked that my own solicitors could continue to be so cruel to their own client.

I was later told that KK wanted his revenge because we had proved in court that his

CHAPTER 32: THE LEGAL OMBUDSMAN AND PARLIAMENT

ROLLS - ROYCE PHANTOM VI STATE CABRIOLET BY FRUA
Chassis Number PRH 4643

Since the concept of the Rolls - Royce Phantom motor car in 1925 many of the finest Coachbuilders in the world have created elegant bodies for this prestigious and versatile chassis. The most ambitious however must be the Phantom VI with the body designed and built by Frua of Italy. Originally intended for state occasions the Frua Phantom VI chassis is extended by two feet with a proportionate increase in height and width to comfortably accommodate the many lavish features of this seven seat fully convertible cabriolet. The hood configurations are: Limousine, State Landaulette, Sedanca de Ville, State Cabriolet and full Convertible. Finest quality hide upholstery and specially woven Wilton carpets compliment the inlaid wood interior which conceals the drinks cabinet vanity unit, television, sound system and numerous other accessories.

Dimensions:

Overall length: 21 feet 1 inch (6.45 m)
Overall width: 6 feet 10 inches (2.04m)
Overall height: 5 feet 9 inches (1.72m)
Weight: 3.49 tons. (3,544kg.)

All enquiries to:
ROBERT JAMES INTERNATIONAL LTD
Bowyer House, Denham Village, Bucks
UB9 5BH England

Tel: (0)1895 832070 Fax: (0)1895 832282

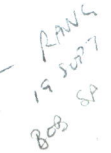

The Frua Rolls Royce for sale by Robert James International Ltd.

affidavit had been dishonest and that his claim had been created in order to avoid paying his bill. I then also learned that he not only wanted me to lose my house, he also wanted to force me to liquidate my business as well. By supporting these evil ambitions, you can see how far my solicitors were prepared to go to ingratiate themselves with their colleagues at Berwins and KK.

The bonus for my solicitors, of course, would be that the Old Vicarage could then be sold, releasing a very substantial seven figure sum from which they all could then draw whatever 'costs' they decided to create and charge.

My solicitors subsequently denied having done this, but as ever, I have written evidence from the Darlington Building Society and letters from me to prove it. Once again, more blatant dishonesty and collusion. It is these extraordinary events, along with even more extreme ones, which I am going to tell you about, which led me to write this book.

LEGAL ADJUDICATORS SUPPORT FOR SOLICITORS

I mentioned earlier, when complaining to the OSS, that Nimble and Anderson seemed also to be collaborating with the Law Society's Adjudicators. One important example and proof of this was revealed when the adjudicator stated, in one of his formal reports, that KK could not pay the awards or the costs "because KK's company had no money" and that "the Rolls Royce was worth very little".

First of all, how could the legal complaints Adjudicator have any knowledge of KK's finances or of his company's financial position or what the value of this unique Rolls Royce motor car would be? Both statements were self evidently untrue and bore no relevance to the situation.

Firstly, he was ignoring the £90,000 bank guarantee to the court and hence, also ignoring the High Court Orders.

Secondly, he was saying that the unused, new and very valuable Rolls Royce was of little value.

Remarkable! Eversheds had already taken £57,000 from the court and I have a document proving that the car was then for sale at the reduced price of £1.2 million, ample monies for all KK's liabilities including our awards and the costs which KK had been ordered to pay by the High Court judge.

Here again is yet more dishonesty and bias in support of the obviously corrupt and dishonest solicitors, this time from a 'Legal' Adjudicator. The following events further confirms this adjudicators collusion with Eversheds and more dishonesty by both parties.

By now, over two years had passed since the hearing and it is my guess that KK realised, correctly, that my determination to have the money awarded by the court was such, that I would continue indefinitely, to press Parliament and the legal authorities for justice. Accordingly, it seems that KK decided to put an end to it by offering to settle. Unlike the solicitors and the Legal Adjudicator, he must have been concerned at the quantity of written evidence building up against them all and probably legal costs as well.

IT IS NOW EARLY IN JULY 1998,
26 MONTHS AFTER THE HEARING.

The next event was when my solicitors transmitted the offer of settlement from KK to me. The offer was stated as being £38,000, this was much less than the £70,000 awarded in court, so I turned it down. It was far too low, especially as it should have also included the £12,000 I paid to Eversheds for costs and the ongoing interest at 8%. This rate was ordered by the Judge, so should have also been included.

Towards the end of August, it came as no surprise to find, and Nimble admitted, that KK's offer had actually been £65,000. Although still below the sums actually due, as soon as I was told this and still being desperate for money, I confirmed acceptance of this settlement sum immediately. Shortly afterwards however, Eversheds informed me that the "period of validity had expired" so the offer was withdrawn. Yet more serious dishonesty, the situation was incredible.

At the time it was, as ever of course, difficult for me to know what was or wasn't true, but later on I received a copy of KK's original offer documents which proved that KK's actual original offer in July was worth £65,000 in total. It was made up of various sums, £27,000 of which, my solicitors had tried to keep for themselves. Yet again, their devious activities, dishonesty and greed had spoiled this good opportunity to put an end to the entire affair! I have the documents on file along with many more to prove the facts.

CHAPTER 33: UNDERSTANDING LEGAL CORRUPTION

Having been brought up to be honest and after a lifetime of confidence and trust in our legal system, I was having great difficulty in believing what was going on. The further I delved into the legal system, the worse it got. I had been greatly impressed by the formal High Court proceedings and the Judges determination to get to the truth. Surrounding this event however, I found that the rest of the legal structure was riddled with corruption and malpractice in one form or another.

Time and again, I was seeing examples of the most unprincipled activities in virtually every direction. Once I realised that both sets of solicitors and the Law Society's complaints agencies were perfectly happy to completely ignore the Court Orders and use me and the KK case, purely as a means to ensure and maximise their incomes, many of the events fell into place. My honest business practices and all my years of worry were of no value, or interest at all, to these people.

With the solicitors agreeing to help each other, they could exploit their 'costs' whenever they wished. I had already seen a most blatant example early on, when my solicitors had readily accepted the obviously loaded £50,000 'costs' charged to us by Berwin's Lawyers for just a few hours work in court in the 'delivery up' affair. I was later told that Eversheds costs in this event were £1,200 and that the costs are usually similar. Furthermore, being common law, the costs involved with this action should not have been charged to me in any event. This example alone, confirmed that they were already grossly loading their costs to an extraordinary degree, especially for Royles. I may be naive, but it was difficult for me to believe that they had no scruples at all.

I saw other evidence of this one day after court, when we visited the 'Benjamin Stillingfleet', the pub across Essex Street from Nerys's chambers. When talking to solicitors there, I learned that lawyers 'costs' can indeed be a movable feast. I simply asked one solicitor how life was treating him, he replied saying that things "weren't too good" and therefore he was having to charge his clients "125% of his time", so much for honesty and fair play, especially at their huge hourly charges in London. If Royles had done this and it had been found in court, heaven knows what the result would have been!

Being now more conversant with the biased and unprincipled legal complaints systems, I realised that solicitors were well aware of the protection afforded to them by the Law Society and all the 'legal' organisations which they control. Solicitors know only too well that, within reason, no matter how high or inflated their charges may be, there is a good chance that they will be beneficial to them. There is no independent authority to control or hinder them, hence their corrupt activities have become so blatant that they are obvious to anybody who takes the trouble to investigate the facts.

When dishonest solicitors operate within the established parameters of the protective systems created by the Law Society, then they don't need to bother to go to extremes to conceal their fraudulent activities. In fact, these systems have been so effective that the sheer number of unresolved complaints which are registered in Parliament is now measured in tens upon tens of thousands of people.

The situation is so bad that even the legal Ombudsmen have felt it necessary to report the facts to parliament.

Solicitors give the impression that their 'costs' are structured and many may operate them that way, but they are a movable feast for those who have few scruples and want to increase their income. They can also be used by them to manipulate the Orders of even the High Court or even effectively reverse the Judgement as they were doing in my case. It is the most serious abuse of our legal system and of democracy itself. They neither deserve, nor are capable of being trusted with Self Regulation.

What is so dreadful is that all this was being carried out by the very people whose duty it is to obey and honour our systems of justice and the Law itself.

TRYING TO MINIMISE THE LEGAL COSTS

At the very beginning, in 1993, in appreciation of what I believed was Nimble Thompson's kind offer to take a "Punt" on him getting his costs from KK, I naturally wanted to do all I could to help him. I thought Nimble's original estimate of the legal costs of £25,000 could be low, so to keep the costs down and because the whole business of going to court was so stressful, I wanted to do all I could to help him finish the business as soon as possible. Although it coincided with my illness and series of operations, I devoted all the time I could to preparing the bundles of evidence, time and job sheets, photographs etc.

Even when I was in Hospital, complete with drips and drains, I was dealing with KK's 308 page affidavit and managed to respond to it with a written, detailed 105 page report. When back at home recuperating, the work also continued for the months which I spent in bed after each operation. After having previously assembled all the documents in the office, I was able to list and number them all and put them into bundles. This was done at home between and after each of the surgical operations, as were the written reports and descriptions of all the 250 photographs. This work was well advanced in 1994.

It then remained for Eversheds to check them, print and duplicate all the information for the court. Not for a moment, did I expect 2½ years to pass before it would come to court. Or that the costs would increase by leaps and bounds before the hearing. There had not been many meetings, perhaps six or seven in all, otherwise little work seemed to be necessary (for my benefit !) during this period.

Now that I know what was going on, the substantial increases are almost certainly the result of the overall plan agreed between both sets of solicitors and lawyers.

Nimbles original 'ballpark' estimate in the autumn 1993 was £25,000

Briefly, for the record, the costs escalated as follows:

Nine months later, I was told Eversheds actual costs were. (This was when I had gathered and organised the evidence)	£39,000
A year later, still 9 months to the trial, Eversheds costs were	£48,000
Along with a final written estimate of	£80,000
KK's 'Delivery Up' hugely inflated costs were said to be	£50,000
Eversheds actual final costs. (700% increase.)	£169,000

LEGAL TAXATION

Formally, any clients who suspects and claims that they have been overcharged by their Solicitors, are told that it doesn't happen but, if in any doubt, they can always have their legal costs 'Taxed'.

It is interesting that they do, in fact, have a formal system when they have already said that it doesn't happen ! To me, by now, it was a foregone conclusion that it would have been devised to benefit solicitors. When it became obvious that I was determined not to accept the costs, I was told that the bill might be reduced if I applied to the court to have them Taxed.

In theory, 'Legal Taxation' is when the solicitor's bills are formally checked for their accuracy and deductions are made, if thought necessary.

Although of course, according to the Judges Orders, I was well aware that I was not liable for the costs anyway, I thought it worth letting them think I would do it, so that I could investigate how this system worked and it enabled me to look into another 'legal' process. The very fact that there was an established process, led me to expect another cunning ploy within the legal complaints system, I was not to be disappointed.

Sure enough, it turned out that this 'service', like many other legal 'services' is a device, a subterfuge. As ever, the client presupposes that Taxation, like the rest of our legal system, must be based upon honesty and will be fair to all who use it. You will by now, not be surprised to hear however, that this is not so. It is not operated by independent adjudicators or accountants, as one would expect, but (and you will have guessed it!) 'Taxation' is carried out by no other, than more solicitors. In this case they are retired and working for the court and of course, they make a charge for this 'service' to those who complain.

Now knowing that corrupt solicitors can substantially load their 'costs' to suit their needs, not necessarily having any bearing on the actual time and costs involved. The taxation officers, being solicitors themselves, are of course familiar with these practices and, as ever, work closely with the solicitor who has been complained about. With such high hourly rates and loaded costs, it will not be difficult to give a reduction of some sort when the occasion demands. This, no doubt, is calculated to make the client believe that his account has now been checked, has been 'taxed' and is now correct.

If the solicitor happens to be honest and his charges are reasonable, inevitably, the reduction will be small, if at all, which would be understandable, If they are loaded then the Taxation official will have more latitude and will, no doubt, agree with the corrupt solicitor what amount should be deducted to silence the complainant. In any event, there will, I imagine, always be ample money remaining for his legal colleagues and himself.

There is, of course, one more catch and an important one. Once a solicitor's bill has been 'taxed', it is in effect, 'concreted in' and cannot again be challenged and the client then has no choice but to pay the bill. End of story.

As ever, when the legal complaints official recommended to me that I should have the bills Taxed, the implication was that they were being perfectly decent and trying to help and be fair to me. The scheme normally must work so well that he was quite surprised when I subsequently refused taxation. Why would anybody turn down an opportunity to have their bill reduced, it didn't make sense?

As ever, the legal schemes are created using psychology to appear to be helpful to the clients when, in fact, the benefits are principally to the legal profession. They were not used to people who had familiarised themselves with their sly and devious practices and who would not fall into one of the many traps set for clients. Traps which abound in the Legal complaints system.

Uncertain whether the official really knew that I understood how the 'Taxation' scheme operated, and spreading the word, I thought it worth letting him know that some members of the general public were not going to be taken in by it. I explained that I knew how it worked in the solicitors favour, not the complainants and it also guaranteed that the solicitors are paid, no matter how much they may have charged.

I quoted the example of KK's Lawyers charges of £50,000 for a few hours in court and that It was blatantly obvious that the costs had been hugely loaded. Adding that whilst a reduction of even £5,000 by Taxation might look generous, in fact it would be almost irrelevant and would ensure that the solicitor would then be guaranteed to benefit by his obscenely loaded costs of in excess of £43,000 for his few hours of work. A grossly excessive and dishonest overcharge. I concluded by confirming to the official that the High Court Orders were clear and that I was not liable for the costs anyway.

There was no comment from the official.

ANALYSIS OF THE COMPLAINTS SYSTEMS

To me, the solicitors behaviour was incredible. I could not believe that a High Court Judgement could simply be ignored. It was only when I delved deeper into the legal complaints organisations that the full extent of their corruption and legal malpractice revealed itself to me. It was the subsequent discovery that the Law Society, the Legal Executive and Authorities in Parliament and the organisations which they control, are guilty of the most serious malpractice and deep rooted maladministration. It is this which has encouraged me to write this book.

The facts need to be publicised, as do the events surrounding my Advanced Amphibious Vehicles project, which are covered in the last section of the book.

Records in Parliament are likely to show that there are some hundreds of thousands of people in this country who have been and continue to be denied a fair and reasonable hearing when they have complained about legal matters. The abuse of power is so serious and widespread that even the Press are not free to print the facts and nobody feels able to state the truth without fear of litigation or worse.

I appeal to you, to read on and find out what else has been happening behind closed 'legal' doors in this marvellous country of ours.

SELF REGULATION AND THE UNDENIABLE EVIDENCE

The Law Society itself, is demonstrating that honesty and fair play are of secondary importance when the income or reputation of solicitors may be jeopardised. As you are seeing, there is a raft of schemes and measures which have been incorporated into virtually every aspect of the legal complaints system which is controlled by the Legal Executive in Parliament and the Law Society, to protect their interests in any event which they choose.

It is very clear that the abuse of solicitors clients, the law and the legal system has continued for a great many years and is, without question, only possible because of 'Self regulation'. Self evidently, the complaints of tens of thousands of citizens reported to Parliament by the Legal Ombudsmen, who's complaints have not been resolved, is proof of this. From what I have seen for myself, I can confirm that the Legal Profession are not to be trusted with such an honour.

THE FACTS

When I started down the long road seeking the awards made to us in the High Court in 1996, I discovered that there were 42,000 complaints registered with the Ombudsman and Parliament for that year alone most of which have not been resolved. I had no idea why there were so many and how such a weight of numbers and a scandal on this scale could be kept from the general public.

Talking to various journalists and people in the press, I began to realise that they are tightly controlled by solicitors and the Law Society, who will sue them or threaten to, at the first sign of any adverse publicity. At one stage, I even tried to place small adverts in the Times and the Telegraph saying;- " If you are dissatisfied with your solicitor, please contact this Box Number". Neither would accept nor publish the advertisement.

SO MUCH FOR OUR FREE PRESS

After our victory in court in 1996 and as years passed, the more deeply I delved into the activities of each of the Complaints Agencies, first the SCB, then the OSS and currently, the Legal Complaints Service, the LCS, the more schemes I discovered which prevented the complaints from being resolved. These cunningly and cleverly constructed schemes and the extraordinary measures which have been incorporated to protect even the most corrupt solicitors, have become so efficient, and the sheer number of complaints is so excessive, that I felt that I should do whatever I could to expose this truly dreadful state of affairs.

For a great many years, British citizens like me, will have been deprived of justice and the possibility of even further abuse has existed whenever a person complained to the Law Society and, or its Complaints agencies.

You may be wondering why such serious matters have been allowed to persist for a great many years and why nobody else has tried to do something about it.

I believe that it is because the honourable individuals involved with the Law, dare not 'break ranks' with their many colleagues and friends within it. Many of them are in Parliament and some in positions of great power. It is a vicious circle.

They would be seen to be jeopardising the security and future income of their colleagues as well as those who have been able to excessively enrich themselves by means of the power wielded by their own organisation, the Law Society, their complaints agencies and to some degree, sadly, the Legal Ombudsman. Over whom they obviously have some control.

CHAPTER 34:
THE CHALLENGE

To begin with, as an ordinary man in the street, I knew that it was going to be a most serious challenge to be taking on two senior partners in Eversheds, a large and powerful legal firm. This was especially so, as they were working together with another legal firm in order to protect their own and their colleagues interests. Never the less, with the benefit of a most successful legal action in the High Court and with honesty and written evidence on my side, I thought that if I pressed on with my efforts, I might be able to make Nimble and Anderson pay me the money awarded to us which they took from the court and also make them obey the Judges Orders for our costs and interest benefits.

As the years passed, and as I delved more deeply into it all, the multi-layered complex of systems revealed themselves to me. I came to realise that an individual like me is confronted with a most carefully contrived honeycomb of schemes which are truly formidable.

Being involved with a wide range of challenges in my restoration work, facing all manner of unknown problems, I am used to work which can take thousands of hours to complete. Having been so upset by the unjust treatment and the serious losses suffered as a direct result of the two corrupt solicitors, I was determined and knew that I would need to have a great deal of patience to continue to try to seek justice and the money which we had worked so hard to earn. I had no idea that my efforts would help to influence an Act Parliament and involve so many other important people.

Not surprisingly, it was the desperate need for our award money which initially drove me on and led me to uncover the widespread legal malpractice. It then was the incredibly cunning and sly nature of the 'legal' schemes which encouraged me to continue and finally to write this book to warn British citizens of the dreadful 'legal' practices which are designed specifically to protect solicitors and by doing so, deny most of us who complain, the benefits of Justice.

NOTABLE EVENTS IN 1998 - 1999.
THE ACTION 'HOTS UP'

I continued to press various legal authorities in and out of Parliament and in the legal system during 1998 and into 1999. Despite being a non-legal person, my determined efforts were succeeding in penetrating the interlinked and cunningly devised legal complaints schemes. I was seeing how they would defeat most people and was learning more about the techniques they used.

I broadened the scope of my activities to include the most elevated cabinet ministers and I also intensified my efforts with my MP, Derek Foster. As many as ten to fifteen letters in a day were going out. My comprehensive files were filling up with correspondence from a wide range of individuals at all levels.

I could see that I needed to focus on the people who were most closely involved. The person most directly concerned was Nimble Thompson, so I set about reminding and pressing him and to a lesser degree Anderson, who seemed to have no scruples at all, of the dreadful and unprincipled treatment which was causing me such serious and unjustified problems. In my letters, I began to include regular newspaper cuttings with reports of solicitors who had been struck off for fraud and others who had been jailed and even a Judge who had been found out. Another brave newspaper journalist described how complaints against solicitors had "shot up by 36% last year" an average of 2,586 complaints per month. The facts were coming out at last.

IT WAS NOW JUNE 1999, 37 MONTHS AFTER THE HEARING

Matters came to a head in June when, unexpectedly, Nimble walked into my office in high dudgeon, complaining that he had just returned from a holiday to find that his desk was overloaded with a great many letters from the Lord Chancellor downwards. He threatened me by saying that if I did not stop my activities with Parliament, he would sell our house, the

Old Vicarage, from under us, using the Legal charge which Eversheds still refused to cancel on our house.

I told him that he had no right to hold the Legal Charge on it or to sell our home since it was only provided as security if we lost the case. He actually accepted this statement, which was an important and revealing admission, but then added that it would be too late for me to do anything about it anyway, by the time it was sold.

On hearing this, I asked him to stand up and hold out his hand, which he did. I shook it firmly and literally, fighting fire with fire, I told him that "if you force the sale and I lose my house – I promise that you will lose your house as well, I will burn it down". I agreed with him when he replied by saying that I would go to jail if I did. I then pointed out that I would make sure that nobody was in the house as I didn't want to kill anybody, but that I would bring a BBC film crew and press reporters with me to witness and film the event and that I would explain to them why I was burning his house down. Nimble turned and walked out.

Shortly afterwards, on 2nd July 1999, Eversheds cancelled the charge on the house and Nimble Thompson resigned his senior partnership, terminating his long career with Eversheds in Leeds.

Some time later, we met at a function and he admitted that he didn't become a lawyer to be involved with such activities. I told him that I was still actively pressing on with all concerned because we desperately needed and deserved the money awarded to us which he had taken.

As was now standard practice with all the events as they unfolded, I reported them, in detail, to various people in both houses of Parliament, to the Ombudsman Ann Abraham and many more. The list shown here will give you some idea of the amount and nature of the correspondence up to February 1999.

LIST OF CORRESPONDANCE UP TO 12 FEBRUARY 1999

Her Majesty The Queen.	8 letters
Mark Addison. Crown Prosecution Service.	3 letters
Ann Abraham. Legal Ombudsman.	44 letters
Tony Blair. Prime Minister.	14 letters
Bar Pro-Bono Scheme.	4 letters
Barristers. Various.	16 letters
Mrs Cheri Blair QC.	4 letters
Citizens Advice Bureau.	5 letters
Court Service.	27 letters
Judge Roger Cox.	3 letters
Durham Fraud Squad.	3 letters
Derek Foster MP.	74 letters
William Hague. Leader of the Opposition.	3 letters
Stephen Hughes MEP.	30 letters
Derry Irvine, Lord Chancellor.	13 letters
The Law Society.	16 letters
Lord Mackay.	4 letters
Austin Mitchell MP.	12 letters
John Morris QC MP Attorney General.	3 letters
Office for Supervision of Solicitors.	33 letters
Press Agencies/TV/Media.	17 letters
Mary Robinson. United Nations.	2 letters
Solicitors Complaints Bureau.	4 letters
Solicitors Various.	49 letters
Jack Straw. Home Secretary.	4 letters
Baroness Wilcox.	5 letters
Lord Woolfe.	11 letters

THE EU PARLIAMENT & BRUSSELS

At this time, I also petitioned the EU Parliament with the help of our MEP Stephen Hughes. The document was dated 22nd Feb 1999. It was eighteen months later that I heard that no help could be given. From memory, I was told that there were around 38,000 legal complaints, each month, arriving at the EU in many different languages and they could not begin to deal with such a massive and complicated amount of work.

So much for the European Parliament.

THE END OF THE 20TH CENTURY

During the four year period just described,

following the Hearing in London, I was constantly being advised to take advice from other solicitors. In fact the then Lord Chancellor, Derry Irvine, recommended that I "should Sue Eversheds". This advice was, as ever, a double edged sword and an extraordinary suggestion. Besides not having the money to do it, for me, an ordinary, non-legal man in the street to sue one of the largest legal firms in the UK would be to commit financial suicide, especially after what I had seen.

If I did employ another solicitor, I was informed and afraid that it would take Eversheds 'off the hook', not only ending their liabilities to me, but also it would relieve them of the trouble I was causing them. In any event, such an action would almost certainly, give Eversheds another opportunity to expose me to more massive costs. I would be taken to the cleaners again!

Previously, I had asked a number of solicitors and barristers to help me get the awards, but when they found that I had no money, they lost interest. I then tried to get Pro-Bono support or any other free legal aid, but not surprisingly, found that there was little chance of any free legal help when it was found that I was going to use it to attack other members of their own legal profession. The very people who had defrauded me of my own money in the first place.

I had also approached the Solicitors Disciplinary Tribunal (SDT) for help, but no matter which way I approached them, they would not even speak to me. They protected the corrupt solicitors by enforcing the rule that only solicitors can deal with and report solicitors to the SDT. As ever, the protection organised by the Law Society was total!

In December 1999, I was talking to an old friend of mine, David 'Banty' Harrison who incidentally, lives nearby in Gainford, told me that he had been in a difficult situation with corrupt officials, but had been helped by a Mr Peter Pescod, one of Hay and Kilner's solicitors in Newcastle upon Tyne.

After making no progress in nearly four years, I thought it worth a try, so contacted him. He kindly agreed to do what he could to help me for a nominal sum and I stressed, and he agreed, that he would do it without relieving Eversheds of their responsibility to pay us the amounts due to us according to the awards made to us in the High Court. With the 8% interest ordered by the judge and four more years having passed since the debt, the award money now owing by Eversheds was increasing quite substantially.

It was now the year 2000, four years after the hearing.

In May 2000, Mr Pescod managed to get nearly £33,000 from Eversheds. It seemed that, despite my four years of serious financial difficulty, begging and pleading with Eversheds for them to pay our awards, and not to block my applications to my Building Society, money had still been available from the court all this time.

It transpired that this sum was the balance left of the £90,000 guarantee after Anderson took the £57,000 award immediately following the hearing.

I thanked and paid Mr Pescod £587, which now seemed to be a nominal sum agreed for his work. I said that I was most grateful and that the money was very helpful, but reminded him and emphasised that it was certainly not accepted as being in full and final settlement of the awards and sums due. In fact, at that time, seven years after the debt, it didn't even cover the 8% interest charges which the judge had awarded to us. Interest which I had to keep paying on the necessary loans needed to keep Royles running in the absence of our awards. These interest costs meant that I had to manage without a salary for some of these years. At least, I was able to repay £33,000 of the loans which still amounted to around £100,000 at that time.

CHAPTER 35:
PARLIAMENT & NESTA IN 2000 AD

Earlier in the year, on the 10th January 2000, out of the blue, the Shadow Lord Chancellor, Lord Kingsland telephoned me to say that he had been discussing my case with Lord Irvine and asked me if I could meet him in London. At long last, it seemed that something was happening as a result of all my letters to Parliament.

Ironically, this good news was overshadowed by the problem of being so short of money for so long, that my first thought was, how was I going to afford the train fare to London. Trips of any sort, especially to London, were not even being contemplated at that time. Living in our lovely old house and being involved with such valuable vintage motor cars, many people had no idea how little money we had at home to live on. The men at the workshops thought I was joking when I tried to explain to them that I didn't have a salary. Of course their wages and running the company always came first, minimising the overdraft second. But I was able to maintain a small income each month for Jo-Jo.

You may remember that, starting in 1987, I had formed a separate company, Covelink Marine Ltd, and was designing and developing the first Advanced High Speed Amphibious vehicles. Even after Royles big debt in 1993 I was, with great difficulty, still managing to maintain steady progress with this R&D project. Although working at cost, by utilising one or two of Royles skilled engineers who were subcontracted to Covelink at cost, both companies were managing to survive with the combination of the restoration and the prototype work, but it was very much hand to mouth.

Throughout this period, as well as battling with Eversheds to get our much needed court awards, I was also constantly trying to raise money for the R & D programme. Being a separate company, with different shareholders, the finances were necessarily completely independent of each other but, as ever, any money which I managed to raise went directly into the project. I didn't think it was fair to my friends and colleagues who were investing in it, to pay myself any salary out of this money. It was more important to keep both companies running.

One of many organisations with which I had been discussing the possibility of funding for many months was from the new National Endowment for Science, Technology and the Arts, NESTA. As luck would have it, it had just been announced that the amphibious vehicle R&D project had won NESTA's first and biggest innovation award. By sheer fluke, I had been invited to come to London to receive it.

It turned out that Lord David Putnam, who was the Chairman of NESTA, had taken a close interest in my 'Roylecraft' amphibians as I was to call them. He was most enthusiastic about the potential of our project and the new technology and realised how useful it would be for flood rescue and the Emergency services all around the world.

Not surprisingly, with him being a most successful film director, he had organised the very first NESTA award ceremony to be held at the BAFTA theatre, which is in Piccadilly. I was invited to attend this important event for the presentations on the 16th May 2000. This was an ideal opportunity to combine the trip with a visit to meet Lord Kingsland, so I rang the Shadow Lord Chancellor to say that my wife, Jo-Jo and I would be in London on that day and he kindly invited both of us to the House of Lords after the presentation, to join him for tea and to discuss the legal affair.

What an interesting day this was going to be!

A GOOD START TO THE NEW MILLENIUM

Because the NESTA Awards were presented before we visited the House of Lords, I will interrupt the legal story to briefly describe the award ceremony. The full story of the Roylecraft amphibious vehicle project is told in the last section of this book.

Having approached Jeremy Newton, the future CEO of NESTA, many months before it was properly established, it turned out that my application was to be the very first which they had considered and I had the good luck to have been given an award. NESTA's very first Innovation Award for Technology.

There was quite a crowd when we arrived at the BAFTA theatre on the morning of the 16th May and I was able to meet some of the winners who had some very interesting ideas. During the reception, I was called upstairs into their recording and broadcasting studio where I met Carol Vordeman who was presenting the awards. I was interviewed for a London radio station and then rejoined the guests and we all went into the theatre itself for the ceremony. The auditorium was full and there were a lot of journalists and photographers as well as all the awardees of course.

Carol came onto the stage as the compere and then introduced a series of short films showing the innovative ideas and introducing each of the awardees in turn. Each was announced individually, but time was passing and no mention was made of my project. It was all drawing to a close and I thought that my project was not going to be mentioned after all. I'm afraid that after battling for so many years and failing to get the court awards, I thought that it was going to happen again. Carol finished describing all the awards and finally handed over to David Putnam who, by then, had appeared on the stage.

As the Chairman of NESTA and after summing up the awards, he seemed to be finishing the proceedings when, out of the blue, I was delighted to hear him make a final announcement. He introduced Roylecraft Amphibians saying that this technology was a very important innovative step forward. He was most enthusiastic and emphasised that they could rescue people in floods and other disasters, as well as being a most useful new form of public transport all over the world. This was the finale of the proceedings.

It transpired that our award was £125,000, the largest individual sum of money presented by NESTA for Innovation. Being the chairman and seeing the potential for my machines, David Putnam went on to do all he could to help us make a success of it. In the fullness of time however, because he was most upset that we could not raise the necessary money for production, he resigned his position. His resignation was announced in the press, but a few weeks later, I was pleased to hear that he had resumed his role as Chairman.

The award ceremony certainly had been interesting and I was absolutely thrilled that my work was being recognised. I still laugh every time I tell the story about my 'BAFTA' award! After the ceremony, Jo and I were just walking down from Picadilly towards Westminster to meet the Shadow Lord Chancellor, (talk about 'name dropping'!) when we were stopped by another radio journalist who quickly interviewed me 'live' where we stood, traffic and all. This was for another London radio station. For a change, it certainly was all happening, and all at once!

TEA AT THE LORDS, THE LEGAL STORY CONTINUES

When we reached the Houses of Parliament, we were directed into the entrance hall of the House of Lords, which was quite a thrill in itself. Once inside, I was bursting for a pee so asked the Sergeant at Arms if there was a loo which was convenient. He directed me to a small, well used room, just off the hall which reminded me of the old lavatories at our boarding school. I couldn't help smiling when I read the well worn notice which was fastened to the old and much used varnished door, it said, "Peers only".

Following this, I rejoined Jo-Jo and we were duly received by the Shadow Lord Chancellor, The Lord Kingsland who turned out to be a most charming man. After introducing himself, he asked us if we would firstly like to see around the Palace of Westminster. This was not expected and was a most fascinating experience. Our host was very knowledgeable and he described the various rooms and halls as we passed through them, included the Queens Robing Room, with the large and famous paintings which decorated them.

We were then taken into the House of Lords Chamber itself with its familiar crimson leather benches. We entered by the main door and sat down near to the members in the main chamber itself, only a few feet away from Lord Irvine, who was on his feet and speaking at the time. I felt very honoured to be there.

Walking around the Palace of Westminster with such a knowledgeable and eminent person, was altogether a most interesting experience. Almost everybody we met was somebody we could immediately recognise and it was difficult not to greet them as friends. Many said 'hello' to Lord Kingsland and to be polite, they included us in the greeting, so we simply smiled and returned the compliment. Going into the Lords dining hall, we sat down at a small table for tea. Funnily enough, at the next table, sitting with a friend, was Jeffrey Archer whom we also nodded to.

Before discussing the legal events, the conversation touched on various other topics, by which time, Lord Kingsland had kindly asked us to use his Christian name, Christopher.

It turned out that Christopher knew that I had been to see Lady Stewart-Clark who had invited me to visit her at her family's Gothic Castle near Edinburgh a year or two earlier. This also had been a most interesting trip when, as requested, I had driven up there in my old Lagonda. I told him that I thought that she was a most amusing and lovely lady who entertained me 'right Royally'. He went on to explain that he was a great friend of 'Jack', her son adding, sadly, that her Ladyship had recently died. I was very sorry to hear this and said so. It was a great pity, since I had hoped to meet her again one day, she was such great fun.

As tea was served, we began to discuss the legal problems which I was having. It was clear that Christopher was most concerned about the dreadful treatment which I had received at the hands of Eversheds dishonest solicitors. At the time, I didn't realise that the information which I was giving to him might be so important and helpful to him in the coming years in Parliament.

Following this meeting we continued to correspond for the next eight years, I was regularly reporting all the unscrupulous events, progressively, as they occurred. I also continued to write and press many others in both houses of Parliament, explaining what was happening and trying to make our solicitors obey the Orders of the High Court Judge. I have a remarkable collection of letters from people in Parliament who were kind enough to express their concern. Copies of just a few of the many letters are included in the book, they vary considerably in their tone and reflect the attitude of the writers.

OTHER ACTIVITIES IN THE YEAR 2000 - 2001

The new millennium seemed to be starting well, it was certainly an improvement on the last decade of the 20th century.

The payment of £ 33,000 which Hay and Kilner's solicitors had managed to extract from the court via Eversheds was helpful. Although far from satisfying the sums now due to Royles as a result of the court orders which, with interest, now amounted to sums well into six figures. This sum reduced the loans and the interest costs and encouraged me to push ahead with Royles 'living museum'. This was another project which I hoped would expand the activities of the restoration company and help to generate more turnover to make it more profitable. Rather than go into this subject here, this project is described elsewhere in this book.

At the same time, the £125,000 award from NESTA for the development of the Amphibious Technology, also took some of the pressure off me and I was able to divert my focus of attention away from the legal battle and with this money, concentrate on improving and finishing the amphibious flood rescue vehicle, the Mk IV prototype. By the year 2000, this new technology was coming together very well, but the lack of funding had been a problem. We were now able to make significant progress.

During this period, we were able to finish the 26 foot, MK IV pre-production model and David Putnam requested that we also filmed it during the test. At this time we were entering into a contract with British Waterways to build the first four advanced 'Roylecraft' water-jet propelled tourist buses. This first contract was the important breakthrough we needed for our amphibians and I was happy to be working with a company which did so much good work maintaining and restoring the 2200 miles of rivers and canals in this country.

As a small boy, for two or three years, our family spent the summer holidays by canals and waterways. My father had a cabin boat called 'Gleam' on the river Weaver in Cheshire and a small holiday home beside the river, which we affectionately called 'The hut'. The boat had been laid up during the war and fathers sketch shows it on the little island where it was left

Father's note book sketch of 'Gleam' in the centre.

until being re-launched, painted and put back into service. At this time, the salt barges still operated on the nearby canals and quite large vessels travelled up and down the Weaver to Northwich. During the last year or two of the war, mother would hitch a ride on the petrol barges to do her shopping there.

By the end of the year, after six months of really intensive work in preparation for the waterways contract, I had completed the designs and we had set up a supply chain for all the innovative components to build the first advanced 40 foot amphibious Jet-Buses. The contract was signed in January 2002 and with the positive and excellent support of their technical directors, I was happy to put the fruits of our fifteen years of R&D work into the hands of British Waterways. I was then able to take the first important step towards series production when we opened a small dedicated 'starter factory' in March.

IT IS NOW 2002

We converted and equipped a secluded, modern farm building only a mile away from our Staindrop workshops especially for the purpose. I took on 16 good engineers to build the new, advanced marine buses and we were continuing to make good progress when, only six months later in August, the relatively new Financial Director of the Waterways company, took control away from the helpful technical directors, one of whom resigned. I was then shocked when I realised that the FD was going to force me to close down the new little factory and take all our assets.

To do this, he stopped all payments to us before the sums due, under the contract, were paid and the contract and the Jet-Buses were finished.

Here I was, yet again, seeing the most serious abuse of power. This time, by the director of a large government controlled organisation (Defra) who, knowing our weak financial position, was trying to force us into liquidation. According to the contract, if this happened, he could then take the incomplete Jet-Buses, all the components and the benefits of our fifteen years of successful R&D work including all my patents and IPR. It was fraud, pure and simple.

Once again, I could hardly stand by whilst part of my life's work was going to be taken from me, so didn't close the factory, but inevitably entered into yet another major battle. This time with a company which employs around 2000 people and also has its own in-house legal department. All this, when I couldn't afford a single solicitor and if I did and won, then the chances are that the court orders could well be ignored again, especially as British Waterways also employs a large legal firm who were, yes, you have guessed it, Eversheds of Leeds!

It was bad enough having battled with them for justice for the last four years, but now having to take on a second big organisation, one which was also linked to the them and the government, was going to be a very serious challenge indeed, but one I couldn't ignore.

The full story of the Roylecraft High Speed Amphibians and the events which followed, is told in the last section of this book.

CHAPTER 36:
THE LAW SOCIETY CRITICISED IN PARLIAMENT

The legal affair was brought back into sharp focus when I received a letter on 6th June 2002. This was from the Law Society telling me that they were going to destroy their files on my case unless they heard from me within 28 days.

I immediately wrote back and requested that they must not do so. Completely ignoring my letter and despite my request that the Law Society do not destroy files, showing their true colours, they replied on 18th June confirming that the file would be "closed permanently" anyway and that it would "not be possible to investigate (our) complaints further". They were obviously and bluntly, trying to put an end to my complaint.

This was very serious, but I was still determined that their documents and records should not be destroyed, so I promptly contacted the legal Ombudsman. She wrote to the Law Society on 26th June, requesting that they retain the file because "matters had not been resolved". The result of this was that the Law Society confirmed, in writing on 2nd July 2002, that "the file will be available for the Ombudsman for further investigation….although no further substantive investigation will take place in the meantime".

This last statement was very important, since it meant that, for the time being, I could still focus some of my attention on the new battle developing with the large and powerful waterways organisation and delay the ongoing struggle with the legal fraternity. I didn't want to jeopardise all the legal work which I had done. Each was an awesome task in itself, but even with no Waterways money coming in, I was still determined to try to finish the contract. I now had my work cut out to pay the wages and overheads of two companies. I had to keep Royles Workshops going and the little factory open, so was faced with having to raise £25,000 a week just for the little factory.

After seeing just how badly people like me were being treated and how devious and corrupt the legal complaints system was, it was especially interesting, at this time, to read Ann Abraham's Legal Ombudsman's latest Annual Report laid before Parliament on 8th July 2002 entitled 'The Regulatory Maze'. This document strongly criticised the Law Society and their complaints service for failing in their duty and not "operating in the public interest". This report also described the need to reform the "entire system of legal services regulation". Honesty out in the open at last!

Reading through it, I could not help but feel that the dreadful activities which I had progressively reported to her and to all the people in Parliament, during the previous six years, may have contributed to this report. I also thought that her subsequent transfer away from the Legal Ombudsman's position to that of Parliamentary and Health Ombudsman, not long afterwards, was no coincidence.

She had dared to challenge and criticise the Law Society and members of the Legal Profession which, of course, includes many members of Parliament who, in her new position, would then be able to ensure that she would toe the line. It is also my guess that she also was transferred to a job where she had all the huge number of NHS complaints to deal with, a staff of 400 and a massive workload. Work which would keep her very busy and put an end to her interference and criticisms of the Law Society's activities.

MORE LEGAL CORRUPTION

With the assurance that the legal files would be retained, I spent most of the next two years raising money to keep the factory running. We finished two of the buses and were able to test, film and demonstrate their success. An important step forward. Raising money and maintaining staff morale was increasingly difficult until eventually, with only five men left and increasing debts, I had no choice in October 2004 but to let British Waterways take the buses and patents and appoint administrators for Covelink Marine Ltd, the amphibians R&D company. As with most of this story, thankfully,

CHAPTER 36: THE LAW SOCIETY CRITICISED IN PARLIAMENT

the BBC were there to film the event. I did not give up however, and was still trying to retrieve the assets of my successful amphibious vehicle company, when an article in the Daily Telegraph on August 13th 2005, 'fired me up' to resume my legal activities.

The newspaper reported an interview with David Gray, the CEO and Managing partner of Eversheds in London. The article and a photograph of him, revealed him to be a rather unpleasant and pompous individual. He admitted that, as a lawyer, he enjoys "an argument" but didn't take it seriously, "it's a bit of a game" he is quoted as saying. Although probably a flippant remark, it is very revealing and shows how far from reality he and some solicitors are. They have no idea of the dreadful pain and injustice which he and some of his colleagues are so readily prepared to inflict on others.

He went on to say that his wife is the same, "you don't want to be a supplier to the Gray household" he said, if there is a problem, they argue between themselves as to "who has the fun with the supplier". So much for the personality of David Gray!

I immediately wrote to him, quoting from the leading part of the article. I explained that as he says his firm, Eversheds are "Client focussed " and "straight forward", he would now have the opportunity to prove it by obeying the High Court judges orders and pay me the large sums now long overdue and owing to me. He firstly replied saying that he would look into it and then later, wrote again, saying that there was 'no substance' in my complaints to, or about Eversheds. Referring to the Ombudsman and legal complaints office, he said that the issues "have already been fully discussed".

After further pressure from me, Eversheds said that they had no liability and had no "intention to make any payments". They were still ignoring the court orders and the fact which was blatantly obvious, which was that it was theft of their clients money. The blatant dishonesty and arrogance of his flat denial encouraged me to set about increasing the scope and intensity of my activities in order to have the benefits of our judgement as ordered in the Royal Courts of Justice in 1996, now nine years earlier.

Without going into a lot of detail, I resumed my barrage of letters to Eversheds and to the many people in both houses of Parliament including Lord Kingsland, to the courts, the Ombudsman and to the highest legal authorities in the land. I calculated the interest on the Awards due from Eversheds and sent accounts to them. The Judge had ordered 8% interest, so the sums due were now over £200,000 and I repeatedly pressed David Gray for payment. This continued throughout 2005 and into 2006.

It was not long before the Legal Ombudsman was writing a series of letters to me to apologise for the ongoing delays in getting the files from the Law Society. These apologies continued for some months in the new year, during which time, I expressed my concern to her Legal Advisor about this. Being told yet again that they "are still waiting for the file" on 6th April 2006, now eight months after the Telegraph article, I wrote yet again. This time I said that, in my opinion, David Gray of Eversheds had probably requested that the Law Society "prevent their files being made available" to her.

The answer came three weeks later, not from the Ombudsman, but this time from the Law Society. They informed me in a letter, that the file had been "inadvertently destroyed". They had done this, despite their written assurance to the Ombudsman that the records would be retained and "available" for her.

It is interesting to note that it took the Law Society three or four months before they told us that the files had been destroyed. We can be fairly sure that this time was spent with David Gray discussing their destruction with the Society. Otherwise they could have told the Ombudsman straight away.

In any event, my prediction had been correct. Once again, the Law Society was clearly demonstrating the extraordinary lengths to which it would go in order to protect unscrupulous solicitors. By writing directly to me, I presume that The Law Society wanted me know that the evidence had definitely been destroyed and obviously assumed that it would put an end to the ongoing trouble which I was causing by pressing all and sundry for my awards and justice.

Seeing yet again, how unprincipled this

organisation is, it had the opposite effect. It drove me on, even more intently, to do all I could to keep going and also warn as many people as possible of the activities of this dreadful regime. Many people who could not help me, even those who are involved with formal and government organisations, have urged me to write this book in order to publicise the extremes to which the Legal profession will go, when large legal firms and corrupt solicitors are involved. They know that the press are not free to do it.

SOME CONSOLATION

By now, Ann Abraham was no longer the Legal Ombudsman and I was now dealing with Zahida Manzoor, the 'new' Ombudsman. I was wondering what she would be like and was concerned in case she would be under the thumb of the Law Society. I was given some hope however, when I read in the Telegraph on 18th May 2006, the month after the Law Society had told me that our files had been destroyed, that Ms Manzoor had fined the Law Society £250,000 for failing to meet the complaints handling targets.

This was backed up some months later, when she published and laid before Parliament, her own Legal Ombudsman's annual report for 2006-2007. This comprehensive document, called the 'Cycle of Change', like Ann Abraham's 2002 report, is critical of solicitors and confirms that there are still serious problems with the Law Society controlled legal complaints offices.

It included examples of the devious activities, similar to those which I had reported, but she added the fact that 70% of the complaints from the public, were not resolved. They did not receive the compensation which they are due to. Their only alternative was to enter into another legal action with a solicitor and turn again to the system which was already failing them. Her report further states that many members of the public are not receiving a proper 'Service' from solicitors, in the true meaning of the word. Importantly, she goes on to say that the Law Society still controls the budget for the complaints agencies which protects and promotes solicitors.

Despite this report, I expect that the Law Society and Eversheds as well, would at least feel safe from further trouble from me, now that their files had been destroyed. Actually, this was not the case.

I thought it must be worthwhile for me to explain and stress to the Legal Ombudsman, the important fact that, I still have my original and comprehensive set of files relating to this case. I went on to emphasise the extraordinary length of time involved with my complaint, now ten years, and the truly dreadful tactics employed by my solicitors and the Law Society to avoid their responsibilities.

A STEP IN THE RIGHT DIRECTION

As a result of this, Ms Manzoor recommended to the complaints agency, currently called the Legal Complaints Service, that they should appoint a Local Conciliation Officer an LCO, who would visit me and examine my extensive files with the written evidence which proves what I am saying is true. They did this and the LCO, a local solicitor, was appointed.

So, ten years after the hearing, he visited me on the 8th August 2006. He interviewed me at length and examined my extensive files and saw that there was ample documentary evidence to justify the facts and truth behind my complaints. Later on, I was not at all surprised to hear that some of his investigations had been frustrated when he made enquiries to Eversheds.

They told him, like the Law Society had done, that the files on this case were no longer available and added, that their own files (including one of mine, which they had specifically asked for) were also not available and had "disappeared". Ironically, this news was satisfying for me to hear, because the LCO solicitor was seeing for himself the barriers being created by Eversheds to prevent him establishing the truth. Despite written assurances to the contrary, they were obviously destroying and 'losing' evidence to protect themselves. They then made matters even worse, by refusing to meet the LCO and would not even discuss the case.

As ever, I reported this ongoing and blatant obstruction and elimination of evidence to the Ombudsman and Parliament and to all the legal authorities with whom I was dealing.

CHAPTER 36: THE LAW SOCIETY CRITICISED IN PARLIAMENT

After much work, the LCO produced a detailed report which was provided three months later, in November. This properly researched report recommended that I should receive the "Maximum Compensation". Subsequently, I saw a letter from the Legal Complaints Service which reprimanded him for his report and for recommending that I should be paid compensation.

I have a copy of this revealing document, one which clearly illustrates their determination to deny me justice and how they do not like any independent authority becoming involved, even another solicitor! A clear example of their lack of principles and lack of concern for the public and for justice itself.

'THE WHITEWASH'

I heard no more about it until a few months later, when one of the Law Society's own adjudicators produced their own report and sent me a copy. At first glance, this Law Society 'in house' document, as ever, looked very professional in its presentation, but importantly and typically, the adjudicator had not inspected my comprehensive files of evidence. Not surprisingly, upon closer inspection and reading through it, there was a mix of truths, half truths and frankly, dishonest statements. This biased document was clearly intended to counter and override the properly researched LCO report and reverse its conclusions, with no compensation to be awarded. No surprises here.

As with my solicitors, the adjudicator also, yet again, blatantly ignored the evidence and the truth. It was yet another clear indication of the total confidence and of the power and authority vested in virtually every individual and branch of the Legal complaints organisation.

The adjudicator audaciously focussed upon the "lack of evidence" due to the 'inadvertent' destruction of the Law Society's files and the 'disappearance' of the solicitors files. By saying this, he was not only completely ignoring the existence of my files and all the written, important evidence, incredibly, he was also blatantly ignoring the properly researched LCO report and of course, the High Court Judgement itself.

He went on to discuss all the costs which were not relevant in this case anyway, because the High Court judgement had awarded to us the benefit of them as well as interest. After all this, he found in favour of the corrupt solicitors who had already resigned, due to their fraudulent behaviour and did not recommend any compensation.

It was painfully obvious that it was a 'whitewash', reversing the LCO report. Another shameful event.

It had been created to protect the Eversheds corrupt solicitors and was truly a sly and dreadful piece of work. In fact, some of the statements made were factually incorrect and had obviously been prescribed and influenced by the corrupt solicitors themselves.

When I explained all this to the Ombudsman and how dreadful it was, thankfully, she rejected the adjudicators report and sent it back for "reconsideration".

IT WAS NOW 2007, INTO THE 11TH YEAR SINCE THE HIGH COURT HEARING.

SERIOUS ACTION AT LAST

Because of Lord Kingsland's concern for my treatment after the Judges orders had been ignored and seeing his positive attitude at our meeting at Westminster in May 2000, I made sure that I continued to keep the Shadow Lord Chancellor well informed of my experiences. I provided him with copy letters and regular reports of all the events, as they occurred, in my ongoing efforts to see Justice done.

After eleven years of little progress with the Law Society and its biased and most unsatisfactory complaints agencies, it was Lord Kingsland who gave me hope when, on 19th April 2007, he wrote to tell me that he was processing a Bill through Parliament which was relevant to my problems. This was good news and although he didn't mention it at the time, I hoped that the information which I was sending to him was useful. He told me that the action which he was taking in the House of Lords was "intended to transform the legal complaints system".

In an earlier letter, 14 July 1998, Austin Mitchell MP clearly showed that he had very strong views on the legal fraternity! He had explained to me that he had been involved with

From: The Rt. Hon. The Lord Kingsland QC

House of Lords

19th April 2007

David A. C. Royle Esq.
The Old School
Staindrop
Nr Darlington
Co. Durham
DL2 3NH

Dear David,

Thank you very much indeed for your letter of 20th March, together with its enclosures.

As you are probably aware, the Legal Services Bill currently going through the House of Lords is intended to transform the legal complaints system. It affects a number of professions, but is chiefly relevant to solicitors. When it comes into force, date uncertain, it will replace the current Ombudsman scheme. However, it is likely to be several years before you could turn to it with confidence.

Meanwhile, in my experience the most effective regulator in the current circumstances is the Legal Services Ombudsman. She has recently fined the Law Society a substantial sum of money because of deficiencies in its handling of complaints. I cannot believe that you haven't involved her in your case against Eversheds and I am really puzzled, if matters are as clear cut as you say they are, that she hasn't taken forceful action.

With best wishes.

Yours ever,
Christopher

Letter from Lord Kingsland. 19 April 2007.

FROM AUSTIN MITCHELL MP

HOUSE OF COMMONS
LONDON SW1A 0AA

Our Ref: AM/JB

14 July 1998

David A C Royle
The Old School
Staindrop
Nr Darlington
Co Durham DL2 3NH

Dear Mr Royle

Many thanks for your letter dated 6 July.

I'm enclosing a copy of my Bill. As you'll see it does provide for an independent complaints machinery. This won't go as far as you want, but I think it will be a considerable improvement on the present which is the Mafia policing the Mafia.

I agree with most of what you say and the issue of redress against lawyers is very important. Indeed, you're quite right in saying that we need some kind of organisation such as the Justice 2000 you suggest. I'd certainly support it, though I can't take it on to play a more substantial part because I'm overwhelmed with work and because as I've found with the Legal Reform Bill, once the issue is broached you get deluged with so many cases, most of them well justified cases, but cases on which I can't do anything because I'm not a court of law nor their M.P. It's a major problem that there are so many abuses that we can't set up a machinery to deal with them - we'd certainly be deluged.

Best wishes
Yours sincerely

Austin Mitchell
AUSTIN MITCHELL

Letter from Austin Mitchell MP. 14 July 1998.

a Bill to try to stop the corrupt activities of solicitors. Seemingly, he had failed to succeed with this, presumably because of considerable opposition from the lawyers in Parliament.

Now that the Shadow Lord Chancellor was behind a Bill to create a fair and independent complaints agency, it had a better chance of success. This was not only because of his position, it was because it was being processed by a man who was, himself, a lawyer and one who also had the support of other honourable and important people. Never-the-less, it must have taken enormous courage to face up to all pressure from so many of the legal fraternity in Parliament.

LEGAL SERVICES BILL

Only two days after it was published, my MP Helen Goodman, kindly sent me the House of Commons Research Paper which provided information about 'Bill 108 of 2006-07 dated the 29th May 2007'. Entitled the 'Legal Services Bill', Lord Kingsland's Act was intended to give the British Public an unbiased and fair Complaints Organisation, one which would be independent of the Law Society's corrupting influence.

The document very clearly and repeatedly defines its purpose, as described above, and states that the current system is "flawed" and needs to be reformed. It goes on to say that many of the lawyers "restrictive practices" cannot be justified and that it must "protect and promote" the interests of the public. To me, this was music to my ears, I never expected to see the truth printed in an official parliamentary document.

The document showed that, when it was being processed through Parliament, a number of Legal Authorities in the Lords were doing their best to water down its strength and authority. This is not surprising, since they could see that the removal of the Law Society's biased and unjust control of the complaints systems, meant that the general public's complaints would, for the first time, be properly heard by an independent body and be treated in a fair and just manner.

The 'paper' also tells how, before the Bill was prepared, starting in July 2003, Sir David Clementi, an acknowledged expert on many legal matters, had been appointed by Lord Falconer to carry out a review of the legal services.

Without realising the connexion, I had also been sending frequent reports to Sir David along with those to the Legal Ombudsman and others in Parliament. I wanted as many people as possible to be aware of the problems which I had encountered and the methods employed in the complaints agencies. Methods which denied me and the tens of thousands of others, a fair and honest adjudication.

It so happens that Sir David is a relation of a friend and neighbour of ours, Canon Jack Lee-Warner ('John', to his oldest friends). He was greatly concerned about the dreadful treatment which we had suffered following our successful High Court hearing and as a result, he recommended that I tell Sir David about it.

Interestingly, neither Lord Kingsland nor Sir David, had told me that they were processing a Bill through Parliament. Presumably, they did not want me to know that my reports might be used in their work. I expect that this was so that I would not exaggerate and that my reports and views would remain, as they had been, objective, true and factual.

Looking back, not knowing Lord Kingsland's parliamentary intentions, but having his sympathetic ear, I felt that I had nothing to lose by being quite outspoken and suggesting all kinds of ideas to him in my reports. For example, during my many years of investigations, I had seen how the "Solicitors Complaints Bureau" then became, "The Office for The Supervision of Solicitors" and later still, how this title was changed again and then became "The Legal Complaints Service". I don't know if Lord Kingsland knew this already, but I told him how each time, it was only the name which was changed.

I explained that I thought that this name change would only occur when too many people began to realise that they were being manipulated and denied a fair adjudication. No doubt, the Law Society would say that they were reorganising their complaints office when, in fact, all they did was change the name. By this devious means, I had seen for myself, how the Law Society had misled the public for years. Each change providing more opportunities to waste yet more time of those who were complaining. This being so, I emphasised to

Lord Kingsland that if anything could be done, he should avoid, at all costs, letting the Law Society again simply 're-brand' their existing biased and unsatisfactory complaints agency.

I strongly recommended that there should be an entirely new complaints organisation set up, one which was independent and employed laymen who would be objective and not be biased in favour of solicitors. One with new premises well away from the Law Society's stronghold at Leamington Spa.

My reports explained that the existing staff there, were so indoctrinated and skilled in the art of polite obfuscation that they had been wasting thousands of hours of the valuable time of all those who had complained. Staff who also must have known that the problems of the majority of these tens of thousands of British citizens, would never be resolved, no matter how serious they may be.
A truly evil and immoral organisation.

Like me, those who complained were seriously misled by their documentation. One OSS leaflet for example states in bold print on the front cover that it is;- "WORKING FOR EXCELLENCE AND FAIRNESS IN GUARDING STANDARDS" and talks about "speedily resolving complaints" giving the impression that those who complained were dealing with an honourable organisation. All patently untrue. Later on, however, the leaflet advises the reader to employ yet another solicitor. The plain fact being that their 'Office' does not 'Supervise Solicitors' and the Ombudsmen's reports to Parliament were proof of this.

After three years of battling with the legal Authorities in both Houses of Parliament starting in The Lords 2004, Lord Kingsland's bill became Law in 2007. The new legal complaints organisation was called the Solicitors Regulation Authority (SRA) which I was pleased to see, would benefit from having new offices away from Leamington Spa at Redditch. I hoped, as intended, that the new authority would also have the benefit of more Laymen being involved.

CHAPTER 37:
LEGAL ADJUDICATERS & OMBUDSMEN

On 12 May 2008, the year after the Legal Services Act was passed in Parliament, exactly 12 years after our high court hearing the Law Society controlled adjudicator, Hannen Beith's "Reconsideration Decision" was received. After reading it, I had to report to the Legal Ombudsman that this document was even further from the truth than the previous one. It was even worse in various respects, in particular, it included entirely opposite and conflicting conclusions. It was also obvious that the conclusions had been printed in such a way as to mislead the reader. Viz:

The Adjudicator begins his report with a clear statement, emphasised in heavy print, quote:

"Finding", "I have decided that the services provided by the solicitors in this case were not inadequate"

Repeating again that, "due to the lack of evidence", no compensation was appropriate, This statement is blatantly dishonest since he was well aware of my comprehensive set of files which the LCO solicitor had examined and recommended the "Maximum compensation". Once again, the adjudicator had made no attempt to inspect them.

Five pages later, in tiny print, alone on the back page under his signature, the Adjudicator, Hannen Beith concluded with, quote:

"Reference in this decision to the solicitors service having been found to be inadequate, signifies that the adjudicator has determined that the professional services provided by the solicitors were not of the quality which it was reasonable to expect from solicitors".

The opposite conclusion to his opening, "findings".

The Law Society adjudicator must have finally realised that it was impossible for him to go on ignoring so much evidence against the corrupt solicitors involved who had already resigned, so felt obliged to cover himself by admitting it, albeit in mild terms in barely discernable print.

He could not bring himself to admit that it was fraud as was the case, or that it was theft of their client's money, or that we should receive compensation. By using very small print he obviously hoped that those who read the report wouldn't see it. Just one more example of the underhanded tricks adopted by the Law Society's Adjudicators.

Pointing out this serious contradiction to Zahida Manzoor, the Ombudsman, along with the fact that, yet again, the Adjudicator had omitted to inspect the evidence, and had ignored the LCO Report and the High Court Orders, and other key issues, I emphasised that it was an even worse report in a number of important respects, than the previous one.

Once again, the Ombudsman could hardly be seen to accept such a dreadful document, accordingly, in July, I was informed in writing that she would investigate it and let me have her findings in early September. The result of her investigations actually arrived earlier, in late August.

In a complete turn round and to my astonishment and great disappointment, she now not only supported the dishonest elements in the report and its conflicting conclusions, she also ignored the final paragraph which admitted that the solicitor's services were "inadequate". Incredibly, she now said that the Adjudicators findings were "reasonable" and that she was "justified in closing the File". In doing so, she stated that no compensation was to be paid.

Extraordinary! She was now supporting an even worse document than that which she had already rejected.

This marked change in her attitude was so pronounced that her decision must have been influenced by somebody. I immediately wrote to her pointing out that her findings ignored all the important evidence and the facts in my favour and were not credible and that her decision was "shameful".

Summing up, in reaching her conclusions, I pointed out that she was ignoring the evidence, she was ignoring the LCO solicitors report and she was ignoring the High Court Orders. she was acknowledging that a Judge sitting in the Royal Courts of Justice in the Strand, London, does not have any authority.

Replying to my letter, her operations manager, Gavin Brown, let the cat out of the bag when, leaping to her defence, stated that "the Ombudsman has made great efforts to assist you". This supportive and well meant remark begs the question: Efforts with who, and why was she not free to assist me? (letter below)

3rd Floor
Sunlight House
Quay Street
Manchester M3 3JZ

Tel: 0161 839 7262
Fax: 0161 832 5446
DX 18569 Manchester 7
E-mail: lso@olso.gsi.gov.uk
Website: www.olso.org
Lo-call Number: 0845 6010794

PROTECT - PERSONAL
Mr D A C Royle
The Old Vicarage
The Green
Gainford
Darlington
County Durham
DL2 3DS

Our refs: 10685, 39149 & 41984.kk

5 September 2008

Dear Mr Royle

Your complaint about Eversheds

Thank you for your letter and enclosure received here on 2 September; I have noted the contents of both.

As the points you make have been rehearsed on numerous occasions, nothing would be gained by my seeking yet again to respond to them here. It is, nevertheless to be regretted that you felt the need to conclude your contact with this Office by seeking to cast doubt on the personal integrity of the Ombudsman. It is, perhaps, worth recalling that of the many individuals and public bodies you have approached over the years, none have been able to secure the enforcement of the orders of the High Court as you have sought but I might venture to suggest that the Ombudsman has made great efforts to assist you.

I now consider this matter to be at an end and I propose to close my file.

Yours sincerely

Gavin Brown

Gavin Brown
Operations Manager

Letter from Legal Ombudsman file closed 5 September 2008.

It is clear and very important that, sadly, this Ombudsman is not Independent and is, ultimately, under some ones control.

As the Ombudsman is the final arbiter in any dispute and will not reply to any further correspondence and as this is considered to be the end of the formal complaints process, then the man in the street is denied the benefits of justice at every level, malpractice is widespread.

As a means to emphasise this, I thought the poem shown here might be sufficiently novel, so circulated the "Little man in the street" quite widely.

Because an Ombudsman's decision is final, as well as continuing to press Parliament, I thought a poem might be a unique way of penetrating the defences of the Adjudicators and Ombudsmen. One which might reach some remote 'corners', which a letter wouldn't, so I have been circulating the following:

The Little Man in The Street

Adjudicator Ombudsman, which masters do you serve?
Not the public, that's for sure, have you lost your nerve?
You should be independent, completely in control,
Not a slave to government, that is not your role.

In all my life, I've never seen, such dire adjudication,
Contrived delays for years, not days, extreme prevarication.
Ignore the facts, ignore the truth, keep your masters sweet,
In fact, ignore your duty, to the little man in the street.

If he complains for far too long, will not give up his battles,
Just serve an order for distraint, and take away his chattels.
The job is done, the battle's won, he has nowhere to go,
Except to court, the costly route, and as your masters know,

Once in the dock, the lawyers clock, ticks at a faster pace,
He'll lose his house, his shirt, the lot, win or lose the case.
So back to you, he has no choice, upon you he should rely,
He begs, he pleads, he curses you, but you will not reply.

But, Adjudicator Ombudsman, you'll find you can't relax,
He's under strain, but won't refrain, from spreading all the facts,
TV, the Press and Parliament, he needs to 'go to town',
You betrayed the trust he put in you, you've really let him down.

He may be just a little man, but a man who's straight and true,
You cannot hide the rogues who lied, no matter what you do,
So, accept the truth, regain his trust, you really must not cheat,
the citizens of this country and the little man in the street.

DACR. 2008.

CHAPTER 37: LEGAL ADJUDICATERS & OMBUDSMEN

From: The Rt. Hon. The Lord Kingsland QC

House of Lords

17th June 2008

David Royle Esq.
The Old School
Staindrop
Darlington
County Durham
DL2 3NH

Dear David,

I have been reading with great sympathy the correspondence you have been sending me about your case. Throughout the proceedings of the Legal Services Bill last year I was constantly reminded of innumerable aspects of your experiences at the hands of the Law Society's legal complaints services.

Unfortunately, the basis for any authoritative powers of intervention that I might have had was removed in June 2007, when the Government transferred the Lord Chancellorship to the House of Commons and I ceased to be Shadow Lord Chancellor. At one point, I optimistically believed that the Legal Services Ombudsman would be in a strong position to exercise powerful leverage on your behalf; but it seems from your correspondence that such efforts as have been made have not had the desired effect.

I do apologise for having to write in this way, but I did not want you to be under any illusions about my power to influence events.

With best wishes to you and the family.

Yours,
Christopher

Letter from Lord Kingsland. 17 June 2008.

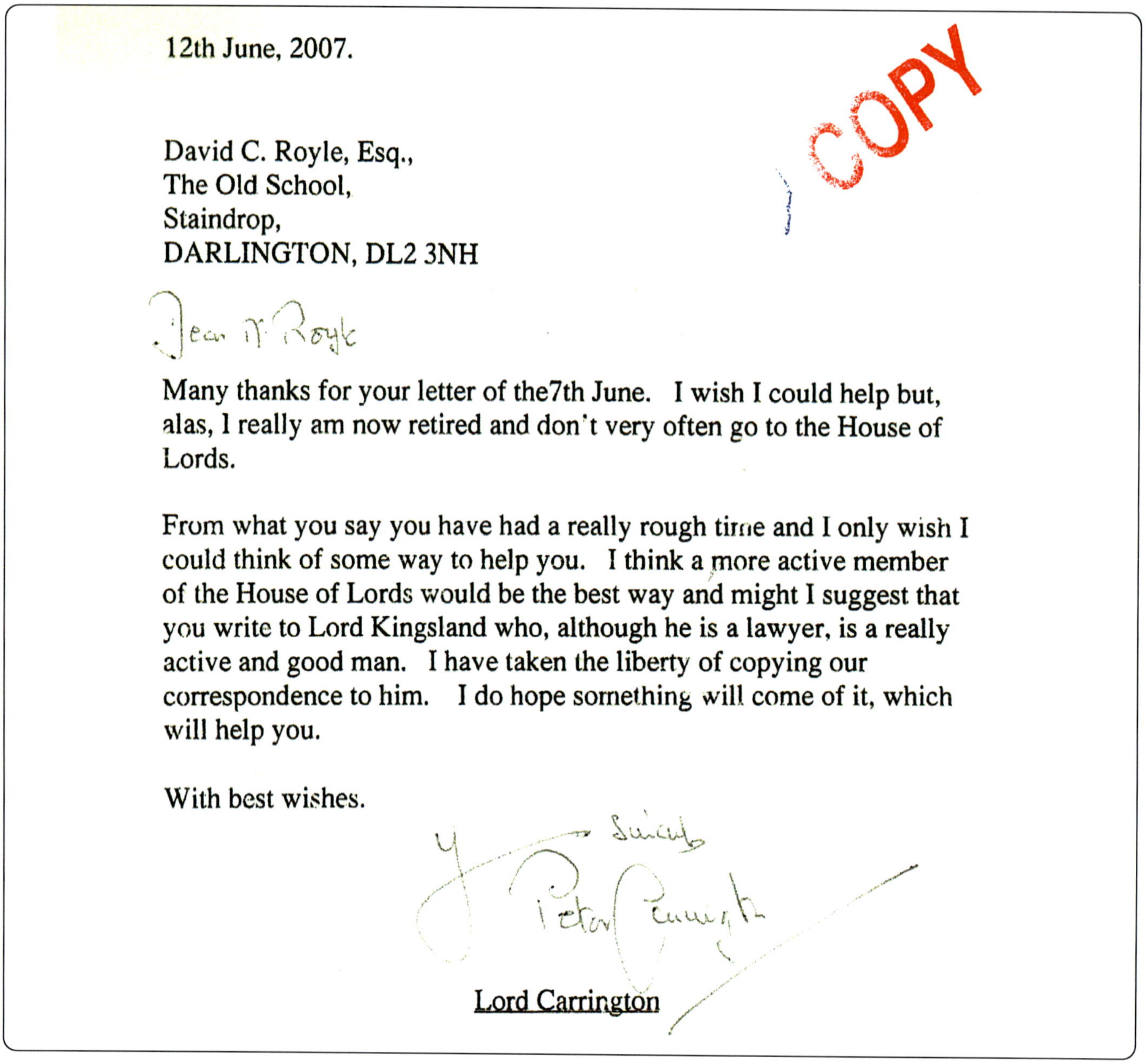

> 12th June, 2007.
>
> David C. Royle, Esq.,
> The Old School,
> Staindrop,
> DARLINGTON, DL2 3NH
>
> *Dear Mr Royle*
>
> Many thanks for your letter of the 7th June. I wish I could help but, alas, I really am now retired and don't very often go to the House of Lords.
>
> From what you say you have had a really rough time and I only wish I could think of some way to help you. I think a more active member of the House of Lords would be the best way and might I suggest that you write to Lord Kingsland who, although he is a lawyer, is a really active and good man. I have taken the liberty of copying our correspondence to him. I do hope something will come of it, which will help you.
>
> With best wishes.
>
> *Yours sincerely,*
> *Peter Carrington*
> Lord Carrington

Letter from Lord Carrington. 12 June 2007.

THE LEGAL SERVICES ACT AGAIN

Barely five weeks after the adjudicators 'reconsideration decision' was received on the 17 June 2008, Lord Kingsland kindly wrote to me again. His letter, which is also shown here, is sympathetic and very revealing. He tells me that soon after the bill was passed, in June 2007, the Government transferred the Lord Chancellorship to the House of Commons meaning that Lord Kingsland ceased to be Shadow Lord Chancellor, so was being denied any further powers. He went on to explain how disappointed he was that the Legal Ombudsman had not been able to help me.

I cannot help, but draw a parallel to the situation with Ann Abraham when she was the Legal Ombudsman. After she had criticised the Law Society's complaints regime in her annual report to Parliament, she also lost her powers to deal with legal matters.

These two incidents alone can be seen as evidence that there are very powerful forces indeed, which are brought to bear upon anybody who dares to support a democratic legal complaints process.

Sadly, the good Lord Kingsland died only twelve months after he wrote to me. He was recognised, by his peers, as one of few honourable legal authorities who would take on all the lawyers in Parliament in order to provide justice to our citizens. He was a most gracious and decent person.

THE NEW SOLICITORS REGULATION AUTHORITY. RECENT UPDATES. 2009 & 2010.

Heeding Lord Kingsland's advice, I thought that I should allow time to pass before contacting the new independent legal complaints organisation, the Solicitors Regulatory Authority, the SRA at Redditch. I was recently prompted to do this after I had been speaking to a legal expert whom I knew. I was just discussing how the new act would be able to help people like me in the future, when he told me that this was not so. He said that the Law Society was back in control of legal complaints against solicitors.

Knowing that the 2007 Act of Parliament set out expressly to create an organisation independent of their control, I thought that this was unlikely, but to check, I immediately rang the SRA saying that I wanted to register a complaint with them. They said that all Legal Complaints against solicitors have first to go via the Legal Complaints Service (LCS) before the SRA can deal with it.

Because the LCS is controlled by the Law Society, it did seem to indicate that the expert was correct, so I then asked to speak to the Chief Executive of the SRA, Anthony Townsend. I was then told, to my horror, that his office is not located at the SRA, Redditch, but at Leamington Spa. The original offices and stronghold of the Law Society and its "flawed" complaints organisations with all its "restrictive practices" which were acknowledged in Parliament and needed to be 'reformed'. thus defeating the very purpose of the Legal Services Act.

My friend was right, all incoming complaints must first go via the Law Society controlled LCS. Lord Kingsland's death has opened the door to those legal people in The Law Society and in the government who will go to any lengths to protect solicitors interests. Once again denying the British Public a fair hearing.

So yet again, as reported by the Legal Ombudsmen in 2002 and 2007, British Citizens with legal complaints, will continue to be vetted and controlled by the very people they are criticising and thus may be denied a fair and honest adjudication.

All the good work done by Lord Kingsland and the Legal Services Act has been undermined and ignored by the unscrupulous Law Society who can continue to deny them justice whenever they please.

It is reminiscent of the evil practices in Eastern Europe before the War.

CHAPTER 38:
LEGAL & GOVERNMENT MALPRACTICE PROVEN

At this juncture, it is important, using my own direct experience as an example, that you compare two properly conducted judgements with six adjudications carried out by legal and government adjudicators and then those carried out by commercial adjudicators.

The first two, which were thorough and detailed investigations, proved that we deserved to be paid for our work and that we were due to awards and compensation.

The six others which follow illustrate, lucidly clearly, what happened when I was judged by Adjudicators and Ombudsmen who represent legal and Government organisations when their own members were at fault.

1. **The Royal Courts of Justice. London.**
Four weeks of detailed examination of the evidence in the High Court by counsel proved, beyond doubt, my personal and my company's honesty and diligence. The Judge found in our favour and ordered that monies must be paid, knowing that ample money was available in court for awards, costs and interest, as ordered. My own solicitors then completely ignored the Judgement and Orders and none of the awards or benefits were given to me after the hearing.

2. **An LCO, Local Conciliation Officer. (Solicitor)** Who also made a detailed examination of my files and the written evidence of the facts, ten years later in November 2006, recommended that the Legal Complaints Adjudicator pay me the "Maximum Compensation".

This report was also ignored by all the 'Legal' Authorities including the Ombudsman and no compensation was paid.

(Note: some very minor sums, each of a few hundred pounds, had been paid piecemeal which were not, in any respect, commensurate with sums under discussion or as awarded.)

When the facts and evidence were properly scrutinised in the two examples above, those sitting in judgement had no difficulty in finding in our favour. Regrettably, both of these important judgements were ignored and undermined by dishonest and devious solicitors and 'legal' organisations. They obviously have no intention of providing a fair and independent service to the public.

To demonstrate this, I list below six other separate occasions when both I and my company have been judged. Initially, all of them were presumed to be independent:

1. **A Legal Complaints Adjudicator.** Who did not examine the written evidence or the High Court Judgement and was dishonest in certain respects. He also ignored the facts and the Local Conciliation Solicitors (LCO) report and recommendations. Incredibly, he found in favour of 'my' dishonest solicitors who had already resigned and no compensation was awarded. When these facts were pointed out to the Ombudsman, she did not accept the report and returned it for reconsideration.

2. **A second Legal Adjudicators** 'reconsideration' report was produced. Again, the written evidence was not examined, the High Court Orders and the LCO report were again ignored and this time the report also included conflicting findings and conclusions. When these facts were again reported to the Ombudsman, she again found the report not to be acceptable.

3. **The Legal Ombudsman.** After twice rejecting the two unsatisfactory Adjudicators reports, she finally reversed her decision and accepted the second report which she had already rejected, saying it was "reasonable". By saying this, she also was ignoring the High Court awards and LCO report. Compensation was not paid for our huge and increasing losses due to interest costs.

4. **The Parliamentary Ombudsman. (Gov't).** Denied the government's responsibility for

encouraging innovation and not providing the promised financial support for new High Value technologies. No compensation was awarded for £4.1 million invested and 20 years work with the amphibious vehicle project.

5. **The Waterways Ombudsman, Hilary Bainbridge (Gov't).**
Despite the waste of a successful multi-million R&D project and the disruption of a contract due to the corrupt activities of a senior British Waterways Director, the Ombudsman still found in favour of this Director who had already resigned. Ordering that no compensation be awarded for our loss of the £4.1million pounds, raised and invested by Covelink Marine Ltd.

6. **The HMRC Adjudicator (Gov't).** Dame Barbara Mills, enforced payment of tax from me personally, on money I raised and all of which was paid out to cover the interest on loans for the R & D company which I had arranged and secured with my property.

After being judged on these eight different occasions, a very clear picture emerges; the legal and government Adjudicators and Ombudsmen will ultimately find in favour of their own officials and organisations, no matter how dishonest and fraudulent.

The little man in the street doesn't have a chance. Honesty, diligence and truth are not respected by those who are supposed to be leading by example.

After fourteen years of intensive investigation into the Legal Complaints and Government Authorities, there is overwhelming evidence to show that even the respective ombudsmen are, ultimately, not independant and free to judge a serious complaint in a fair and reasonable manner. I can only presume that it is their paymasters who are in control and who have the final say.

By protecting those who enrich or advantage themselves by corrupt means, they are undermining the law and democracy in this country.

THE EXCEPTIONS - COMMERCIAL ADJUDICATORS.

There has been two occasions when I have dealt with non-legal and non-government adjudicators. The first was when I made a claim against an insurance company. This time, it was a commercial matter when neither legal nor government officials were involved. The official seems to have been independant and free of control and was able to make an honest evaluation. The evidence was examined and my claim was proved to be legitimate and correct. This time, the adjudicator found in my favour and awarded me fair and proper compensation with interest for the 18 months delay whilst the complaint was resolved.

The second occasion was when a bank failed to carry out instructions. The financial ombudsman examined the evidence, found in my favour and interest and compensation was paid for seven months delay.

In both cases, as in the legal and government adjudications, there was written evidence, but the judgements were based upon the facts and the matters were resolved. The adjudicators were independant, fair and reasonable.

After reading this, you may have noticed, that the Press rarely publicise any criticisms of The Law Society or Legal Government officials. Their own solicitors and legal advisors seem to control them. As ever, the society are super sensitive and will sue at the slightest sign of any criticism. This seems to have happened when Joshua Rozenberg reported matters associated with the passing of the Legal Services Act in the Daily Telegraph. This apparently cost the paper over £35,000 when it was simply a factual report of the Legal Services Act being passed in Parliament.

In my case, the consequences for me, my businesses and my family are so serious that I could not simply 'draw a line under it all'. A phrase which I have heard, time and again, not surprisingly, from lawyers all over the country. After all, it is in there interest to maintain their power. Many people would, no doubt, take this advice after being so frustrated by the lack of progress they were making.

In my case, after losing so much and having nothing to hide, I have not been afraid to go to

AN APPEAL FOR JUSTICE TO HER MAJESTY THE QUEEN. CASE NO 1993 B4538.
Concluded in the Royal courts of Justice the Strand, London
13th May 1996.

May it please your majesty to know that the above successful defence and counterclaim resulted in substantial awards with beneficial costs and interest orders, in favour of David.A,C.Royle, the undersigned, and his company, against a wealthy business man.

The Solicitors handling Royles case for Eversheds of Leeds were:

Peter 'Nimble' Thompson and Simon Anderson.

regrettably

These two solicitors ignored all the orders of the High Court.

FOLLOWING 12 YEARS OF INTENSIVE EFFORTS SEEKING JUSTICE VIA THE NORMAL CHANNELS, VIZ:

The Law Society, The Legal Adjudicators and The Legal Ombudsman, and with approaches and appeals made to the Prime Minister and a number of members of the House of Lords and Ministers in the House of commons, I very much regret to inform your majesty that none have taken any action to ensure that the undersigned enjoys the benefits of the Judges Orders when ample money was in court and available to satisfy them.

The Legal Ombudsman's report was provided 27th August 2008, **twelve years and three months after the complaint was made.**

After witnessing so many years of obfuscation and dishonest legal complaints procedures and adjudications, all controlled by the Law Society and even after the Legal Services Act was passed, which acknowledged this malpractice, the Legal Ombudsman was seemingly obliged to recognise an adjudicators report which she had already and quite rightly, rejected as being unsatisfactory.

Furthermore, despite the thorough investigation of this complaint by an LCO Solicitor who recommended that "Maximum Compensation" should be paid, his report was ignored, as were the **Court Orders.**

Compensation has not been paid or recommended which is, in any respect, commensurate with our losses and interest costs. The sums due were in excess of £331,000 as at 1st April 2008.

These are most serious matters which demand scrutiny. After reporting the facts to:

THE PRIME MINISTER	THE LAW SOCIETY
THE LEGAL OMBUDSMAN	THE LEGAL ADJUDICATORS.
THE ROYAL COURTS OF JUSICE	THE LORD CHANCELLOR
THE ATTORNEY GENERAL	EVERSHEDS SOLICITORS

And others in power, It is clear that they also **will not recognise or implement the Orders of the High Court.**

Seemingly, the Royal Courts of Justice has no Authority and the Law itself is being undermined. I am being denied the benefits of honesty and justice by those who are supporting dishonest and corrupt solicitors.

During this inordinately lengthy period, I have been advised by some to take legal action against Eversheds solicitors.

This is neither practicable or feasible. Having been deprived of the substantial monies due, in excess of £70,000 in 1996, the under-signed has since then, suffered severe financial difficulties. The reluctance of lawyers to act against their colleagues and costs involved in such an action against such a large legal firm would, in any event, be prohibitive. The Law has already failed me and may well do so again.

I would be most grateful if your Royal Highness was able to ensure that our Legal System is not denigrated and that I, as an honest and diligent citizen, receive the awards, benefits and monies due to me as ordered in the Royal Courts of Justice.

I have the Honour to remain, Madam, Your Majesty's most humble and obedient subject.

David.A.C.Royle.

extremes in pressing home my claims, no matter that they involve the highest and most powerful people and organisations in the country. The money was pivotal to the future security of my small companies.

So far, I have not been sued. I believe that this is because I have a great deal of documentary evidence of fraud in the Legal case and many hours of BBC film recording the events and success of the amphibious technology relating to the British Waterways case. I would certainly use every opportunity to publicise these corrupt activities. They are so serious.

So, where can somebody like me go for justice?

My last resort had to be somebody who was not political and is independent of legal or government control. This could only be Her Majesty The Queen. Accordingly, I drafted a Formal Appeal for Justice, which is included here in the book.

This document was sent to Buckingham Palace on 3rd March 2009. As a consequence, I received a note from The Queens private secretary on the 20th March confirming that it had been forwarded to the Minister of Justice, Jack Straw MP.

I had no wish to press Her Majesty, so subsequently wrote to the Minister of Justice myself, requesting a response, but he did not reply. I followed this up with two more letters to him, but had no reply or even an acknowledgement to any of them. This is what I have become accustomed to during the last

BUCKINGHAM PALACE

The Queen has asked the Private Secretary to thank Mr. Royle for his recent letter. Although this is not a matter in which Her Majesty would intervene, the letter has been passed to the Secretary of State for Justice so that this approach to The Queen may be known and consideration given to the points raised in the letter.

Letter from Buckingham Palace. 20 March 2009.

fourteen years, whenever I approach the highest Legal Authorities, The Minister for Justice.

To my knowledge, nothing more has been heard as a result of this document.

CONCLUSIONS

It is my belief that Ombudsmen generally, do try to provide a genuine and honest service to Britain's citizens, especially when commercial firms or large independent service providers are involved. When the complaints concern lawyers and senior officials directly employed in Government agencies however, then, ultimately, the Ombudsmen and the adjudicators are forced to put aside their honourable beliefs and toe the line.

After twelve years of dealings with each of the two Legal Ombudsman, It was with great sorrow that I eventually had no choice, but to accept the fact that, ultimately, they could not be seen to side with me, an ordinary citizen and that they are not 'independent' as is stated in many formal documents. They were not allowed to honour the law, honesty or the evidence.

The other three Ombudsmen representing Government organisations, all women, were also under some one's control. Yet again, their final decisions were seen to be a clear indictment that they had no option, but to support the party associated with the government, disregarding the fact that they had been dishonest, unprincipled and blatantly corrupt.

Each of them completely ignored the indisputable evidence in my favour which proved the facts. Incredibly, they also continued to completely ignore the High Court Judgement, the LCO report and all my files of documents.

In fifty years of business, I have never before witnessed such dishonesty or so many unscrupulous acts. These including the destruction of evidence, threats against my property, blocking me from benefitting from my own assets, biased adjudications, and the theft of our money and assets. All in the face of the highest legal authorities in the land.

THE RESULT - GOOD COMPANIES DESTROYED

What is so regrettable is that this happened to my three small, but very successful and entirely separate companies, with long and honourable records of skilful and diligent work. On each occasion, the unprincipled behaviour was carried out by people who were in elevated positions who abused their power and the privileged information which they had been trusted with, all in order to enrich themselves or their colleagues.

In all cases the result has been the destruction of the companies, the loss of jobs of their employees and the valuable services which they were providing to this country and overseas. In the case of the R&D company, Covelink Marine Ltd, the company which you will read about later in this book, there is the waste of a most valuable new global technology worth hundreds of £millions in exports and the loss of 2,500 potential new jobs. Yes, 2,500 jobs!

ONE IMPORTANT BENEFIT SO FAR

Interestingly, the relatively speedy results achieved by Lord Lofthouse in the miners 'White finger' case, can be attributed to the fact that I had advised him to avoid the Law Society controlled complaints organisations. Avoiding them, he brought the matter directly to the attention of the House of Lords. In a matter of months, the solicitors involved were made to pay back the £millions which they took from the miners. He wrote to thank me for this valuable advice (see letter).

Unusually, the Press were able to report this legal corruption. The difference here being that there were too many people involved for the Law Society, or the government, to keep it quiet and out of the public domain.

LIST OF CORRESPONDENCE 1996 TO 2010

The large number of documents and letters listed here, are a record of the intensive efforts, made over a period of fourteen years by an ordinary man in the street, the author, to draw attention to the malpractices operating in this country's legal institutions to protect even, dishonest solicitors.

The wide range of people listed have been contacted and appeals made to them to put an end to this legal corruption. Systems which I discovered have not only denied me justice, but also tens of thousands of British citizens.

A few of those listed here, have tried to help, but seem to be powerless to do so. Regrettably,

From THE LORD LOFTHOUSE OF PONTEFRACT, F.I.P.D., J.P., K.B.

Telephone:
Home
Facsimile
Pontefract Secretary

LONDON
SW1A 0PW
Telephone: 020 7219 4050
Messages: 020 7219 3000

Please reply to:

11 May 2007

David A C Royle
The Old School
Staindrop
Darlington
DL2 3NH

Dear Mr Royle

Thank you for your letter and enclosure of 2 May 2007 regarding the article in The Times of 26 April 2007 concerning Lawyers double charging for the work involved with the miners compensation.

I can assure you I have noted the contents of your letter, which I find very informative and helpful and I will certainly use the information you have supplied me at every opportunity in my campaign to get justice for the miners.

Thanks for writing to me – Kind regards.

Yours sincerely

The Lord Lofthouse of Pontefract

Letter from Lord Lofthouse of Pontefract. 11 May 2007.

despite this widespread effort, no progress has been made and the government continues to stand back and take no action to protect the general public from corrupt solicitors.

As I write, Parliament has even allowed The Law Society to undermine the principle purpose of Lord Kingsland's Legal Services Act of 2007. Complaints against solicitors are excluded from the Act and the new organisation and, as ever, have to be made to the Law Society controlled Legal Complaints Service at Leamington Spa.

This list clearly illustrates the widespread levels of protection afforded to solicitors which gives them the freedom to continue to defraud the general public whenever it suits them to do so, without fear of retribution.

Also the awareness by the majority of eminent people in and out of Parliament, of the serious legal malpractice and their obvious reluctance to face up to the powerful legal authorities who are bent upon maintaining their control.

LIST OF LETTERS & DOCUMENTS JUNE 1996 TO FEBRUARY 2011

No of Docs.	Person / Organisation
10	HM The Queen
4	Archbishop of Canterbury.
21	The Prime Minister. Tony Blair MP
3	The Prime Minister. Gordon Brown MP
1	The Prime Minister. David Cameron MP
32	Lord Kingsland (Sh Ld Chancellor)
54	Ministry of Justice
39	Lord Irvine (Lord Chancellor Dpt)
7	Lord Falconer. Lord Chancellor Dept
25	Lord Goldsmith, Attorney General
11	Lord Woolfe. Master of the Rolls
8	Solicitor General, Mike O'Brian QC MP
25	Lord Chief Justice
9	Home Secretary, Jack Straw MP
5	Lord Judge. Lord Chief Justice
9	Home affairs Committee
5	Constitutional Affairs Committee.
86	HM Court Service
7	Citizens Advice Bureau
1	Mr Haslett. President
2	Andrew Holroyd. President
20	Legal Services Board
12	Lucy Winskell, President Newcastle Law Society
3	Crown Prosecution Service. Mark Addison
9	Crown Prosecution Service. Chris Enzor
17	Sir David Clementi. Evaluated flaws and failings of legal complaints systems.

Total: 424 documents

LEGAL COMPLAINTS ORGANISATIONS (Law Society)

No of Docs.	Person / Organisation
193	Law Society, Consumer Complaints
100	Law Society and Legal Complaints
2	Solicitors Complaints Bureau
37	Solicitors Disciplinary Tribunal
102	Office for Supervision of Solicitors
36	Legal Complaints Service
37	Legal Complaints Service
3	Legal Services Board
101	Legal Services Ombudsman
67	Legal Services Ombudsman
19	Tabulated Report to Legal Ombudsman
4	British and Irish Ombudsman's Association
19	Solicitors Regulation Authority

Total: 720 documents

JUDGES

No of Docs.	Person / Organisation	
7	Judge Roger Cox (Presiding)	
4	Judge Wilcox	
68	Judge 'A'	Jan 2005 to Oct 2008
54	Judge 'B'	June 2009 to June 2010
2	Judge 'C'	Nov 2008

Total: 135 documents

CHAPTER 38: LEGAL & GOVERNMENT MALPRACTICE PROVEN

HOUSE OF LORDS

No of Docs.	Person / Organisation
5	Baroness Amos
2	Lord Jeffrey Archer
1	Lord Ashcroft
1	Viscount Astor
4	Lord Bingham
5	Lord Carrington
1	Lord Christopher
7	Lord Falconer
1	Lord Henley
1	Lord Heseltine.
3	Lord Digby Jones.
39	Lord Kingsland
38	Lord Lofthouse
9	Lord Mackay
2	Lord Mandelson
20	Lord Mayhew QC DL
1	Lord Patten
4	Lord Phillips
1	Lord Sainsbury
4	Baroness Scotland
2	Baroness Seccomb
1	Baroness Thatcher
1	Lord Truscott
5	Baroness Wilcox

Total: 158 documents.

MEMBERS OF PARLIAMENT

No of Docs.	Person / Organisation
2	Adam Afriyie MP
2	Douglas Alexander MP
1	Vera Baird QC MP
1	Ed Balls MP
5	John Battle MP
5	Hilary Benn MP. Defra.
1	John Bercow MP. Speaker.
2	Vince Cable MP
3	David Cameron MP. Leader of Opposition
4	Kenneth Clarke QC MP. Shadow Secretary of State. BERR
1	Alan Duncan MP
2	Jim Fitzpatrick MP
76	Derek Foster MP
82	Helen Goodman MP and Parliament
29	Helen Goodman MP
1	Nigel Griffiths MP
1	Harriet Harman QC MP
17	William Hague MP
1	Keith Hall MP
1	Keith Hill MP
3	John Hutton MP
1	Alan Johnson MP. Home Secretary.
1	John Mann MP
1	Ian McCartney MP
3	Pat McFadden.
3	Alun Michael MP
1	Ed Milliband MP
23	Austin Mitchell MP
4	George Osborne MP
2	John Penrose MP
3	Mark Prisk MP
2	George Stevenson MP
2	Gareth Thomas MP
1	Keith Vaz MP Nov 1999
10	Ann Widdecombe MP
1	David Willetts MP
2	Gus O'Donell. Cabinet Secretary.

Total: 300 documents.

SOLICITORS AND BARRISTERS

No of Docs.	Person / Organisation
1	Solicitors. Blacket Hart & Pratt
3	Solicitors. Close Thornton
59	Solicitors. Dickinson Dees
75	Solicitors. Dickinson Dees
62	Solicitors. Eversheds / Thompson
107	Solicitors. Eversheds / Thompson (resigned end July 99)
85	Solicitors. Eversheds
78	Solicitors. Eversheds
54	Solicitors. Hay and Kilner
2	Solicitor. Julian Lewis
7	Solicitors. Irwin Mitchell
3	Solicitor. Robert Stirling
31	Solicitor. B.Wake. (LCO Report)
49	Solicitors. Various
16	Barristers. Various
4	Cherie Booth QC
7	Willams QC
19	Bar Pro-Bono Scheme
2	Bar Standards Board

Total: 665 documents.

ORANISATIONS - VARIOUS

No of Docs.	Person / Organisation
9	Business and Enterprise committee and BERR
2	Conservative Headquarters
4	Defra
3	Durham Fraud Squad
8	Durham County Council
2	EU Ombudsman
6	Dr Anne Hicks. Science and Tech Committee in Parliament.
6	HMRC
30	Stephen Hughes MEP.

4	Institute of Directors.
120	Legal Ombudsman
39	Legal Ombudsman
54	Parliamentary Ombudsman
77	Parliamentary Ombudsman
32	Police
65	Press, Agencies, TV, Media
1	UKIC (MGC)
4	United Nations. Mary Robinson.
9	Detailed Reports, widely circulated. E16B, FI 4, Ro3A, 8 PR, OF2, OA9 P. Legal Action Report (LAP) Issue No 1, 24 pages. LAP issue No 2, LAP is No 3. 28 pages.
1	Citizens Report. 5 pages. Widely circulated.

Total: 477 documents.

Total: 2879 documents and letters.

Notes: These numbers include copies of letters and documents sent for reference.

A small percentage refer to the British Waterways affair, but generally the bulk of the BW correspondence is not included.

FINAL AUTHORS NOTE

As a single, man in the street, without power or influence, and having already had threats made against my property by a solicitor because I was reporting the facts to Parliament. I am aware that my personal security may be threatened, for this reason, I have informed the police and a number of influential people that should any serious event occur which affects me, no matter how accidental it may seem, then the possibility of a link to any legal organisation, no matter how remote it may seem, should be the starting point.

CHAPTER 39:
SUMMING UP

I can well understand the need to maintain the public's confidence in the UK's Legal and Government systems, but when legal corruption continues to deny tens of thousands of British citizens the benefits of the Law and Justice, as it is doing, action must be taken to re-establish democracy.

It is deeply regrettable that even previous Lord Chancellors and other elevated legal people, both in and outside Parliament, will take no action to rectify this most serious state of affairs. Why? Because it is entirely for the benefit, usually financial, of their colleagues in the legal profession.

I have no doubt whatsoever, that the legal and parliamentary authorities are acutely aware that many of those fraudulent and corrupt solicitors who have no scruples, are being allowed to continue to practice at huge cost to their clients, and to the country, if my cases are to be taken as an example. My lists of correspondance covering the last 14 years, clearly demonstrate how many formal organisations continue to stand back and will not take action to end it.

Futhermore, by preventing the media from publicising it, they are positively acting to try to keep the general public in ignorance of the legal malpractice.

There are now however, so many people in this country who have been maltreated by solicitors that the level of discontent is increasing. Instead of respect, they are generally treated with disdain. Furthermore, there is a groundswell of awareness by the public, that like me, there is nobody to turn to when legal fraud or corruption does occur. The figures in Parliament prove this.

People now feel that the principal aim of solicitors is not to provide a service to the public, but to use the legal system to maximise their own incomes. The example they are setting is reflected in the sharp practice seen in so many large national organisations these days. In fact, they are helping to undermine not only our democratic processes, but our commercial practices as well. I have seen a marked change and the lowering of standards in so many spheres of business.

One result is that the legal system is now felt to be out of reach to the majority of British citizens. The results of all this is that there are now thousands of people employed in the adjudicator's and ombudsmen's offices to deal with complaints. Despite more people being taken on, they are still failing to cope with the mountainous and ever increasing levels of malpractice now commonplace in so many of our large and formal institutions.

I am sure that there are many good and honest solicitors, but until the Law Society puts its house in order and rids itself of its 'bad apples', they also will suffer as a result of the shadow cast by others in their profession, hence the Formal Appeal to the Prime Minister which follows. Another recent attempt to draw attention to what is a national scandal and another which, to my knowledge, has been ignored.

A recent letter from the Rt. Hon. Kenneth Clarke QC MP. Lord Chancellor and Secretary of State for Justice, initially gave me hope, but as ever, refers me back to those who have already failed. It is my hope that somebody who reads this book, will be in a position to help me and all those thousands like me, to have the benefits accorded to them by the laws of this country.

LEGAL AND CORPORATE CORRUPTION

A FORMAL APPEAL
TO
THE PRIME MINISTER
THE RT HON DAVID CAMERON

TO ENCOURAGE HER MAJESTY'S NEW GOVERNMENT TO ESTABLISH A TRULY INDEPENDENT LEGAL COMPLAINTS AUTHORITY FOR THE BENEFIT OF ALL BRITISH CITIZENS

According to the aims and objectives of the Rt Hon The Lord Kingsland QC when, as Shadow Lord Chancellor, he processed The Legal Services Act through Parliament 2004-2007, in order to establish a democratic legal complaints organisation independent of the Law Society's involvement and control.

It is regrettable that Lord Kingsland's death has enabled members of

The Law Society, once again, to regain control of legal complaints lodged against solicitors and others in the legal profession by members of the public. This has been achieved by introducing the already biased and unsatisfactory Law Society (LS) controlled Legal Complaints Service (LCS) as the first in line, to filter and thus control, all legal complaints before the new Solicitors Regulation Authority/(SRA) can adjudicate. By doing so, the Legal Services Act has been undermined and the independence of its new complaints body, the SRA, is denied.

The Legal Ombudsmen's reports to Parliament in 2002 and 2007 reveal that, as a direct result of LS control, a large percentage of the tens of thousands of British Citizens complaints have not been resolved over the thirteen years of the previous government's control.(eg; 42.000complaints in 1996, 25.000 in 1999)

Recent history clearly shows that the public can be exploited by corrupt and fraudulent Solicitors without fear of retribution, unless their crime is so blatant and obvious that it cannot be concealed. The extreme obfiiscation practised by the last three Law Society controlled complaints organisations, the SCB, the OSS and the LCS, have for many years, deprived the public of a fair and reasonable complaints service entirely for the personal and/or financial benefit of their solicitor members.

In my own case, following a most successful High Court hearing, the Judges Orders were entirely ignored by two dishonest and fraudulent solicitors for their own benefit. They **resigned** from Eversheds when the facts became known.

The second case concerned the Financial Director of a government controlled organisation, British Waterways who, by fraudulent means, took the assets, created over a period of 17 years, of a most successful R&D company, forcing it to be wound up. The FD **resigned** when the facts were reported to Defra

CHAPTER 39: SUMMING UP

In both cases, **the relevant Ombudsmen found in favour of the corrupt individuals who had already resigned.** Evidence exists to show that they also were not independent.

Importantly, despite numerous requests for help, my own MP, Helen Goodman (Labour), will not assist me in this matter, so

I have no representation in Parliament.

With the legal system failing and with the **Legal and Government Ombudsmen** not being free and completely independent (Unlike the 'commercial' Ombudsmen) and also having been deprived of the substantial awards made in the High Court, I have no choice, but to appeal directly to the Government myself. This is the opportunity to prove your election promises.

Directly and indirectly, legal and corporate corruption has caused the loss of two small, honourable and most successful private companies, the loss to their shareholders of £4.5 million and also a new technology creating potential high value exports Worth £550 million per Annum. Documentary evidence can be provided for all the facts.

After a lifetime of dealings with solicitors, Judges and other legal people, I know that there are many good and decent legal people. Following the most detailed examination and successfully proving our honesty in the High Court against a Wealthy and dishonest customer however, the last fourteen years of intensive involvement with the legal complaints organisations, have revealed the most unsatisfactory and devious systems ever seen in fifty years of business.

Having pressed many members of both Houses of Parliament, there can be no doubt that there is concern that this country's legal system is being abused by some solicitors. Lord Kingsland was Well informed of the facts which led to the Legal Services Act in 2007. He was one of few who had the courage to face up to the Law Society and legal powerbase in Parliament to establish a proper and fair complaints regime.

For the good of this country, its citizens and our legal system , I appeal to you to do all you can to re-establish a truly democratic complaints process and provide some means to compensate those who lives have been ruined by fraudulent solicitors and government officials who abuse their power.

Signed,
David.A.C.Royle.

Managing Director of both of the following highly respected companies:

David.A.C.Royle & Co Ltd. (Est 1973) (www. david-royle.co.uk)
Registered with Museum and Galleries Commission and the UKIC.
Wound up with full Order books October 2009.

Covelink Marine Limited. (Est 1988) (cardoxlimited.co.uk)
Created the world's First High Speed Amphibious Rescue Vehicles and Buses.
With a new technology and world-wide IPR. The company was forced into liquidation with Potential Orders worth 55 0 £million in October 2004.

CHAPTER 40:
VEHICLES RESTORED AT ROYLES WORKSHOPS - PART 1

This section lists the hundreds of customers motor cars which have been restored or have had work carried out to them at our workshops in Staindrop.

Each vehicle has its own file and job number and I have retained these files since 1974 when the Railton 10, my first commercial job, was restored for my first customer. The files record all the cars until 2009, by which time we were up to job number 894. The files contain the original detailed worksheets, records and other relevant documents and many of them also include photographs of the work. Where possible, I have included one or two of the photographs with each of the motor cars listed

In those cases where only the job number and owners name appears, this is likely to be so, because the jobs were small and there was little point in taking any pictures of the work.

In most of the jobs listed, I have only included one or two shots. This is due to the need to keep the book to a manageable size. Some of the job files of the comprehensively restored vehicles, can have as many as 200 photographs recording the work. More often it was in the region of 50 to 100 photo's. In total, I have many thousands of photographs, so it would not be practicable to include them all in a book like this.

To give you some idea of the nature and the amount of work involved in a complete restoration, I include 170 photographs of the work to a 1938 Lagonda LG6 Saloon. Job 394. Even this number of photo's does not illustrate the full extent and the amount of work involved in a comprehensive restoration job at Royles. These will show that we check and overhaul every component to ensure that the motor car is mechanically sound and that the chassis and bodywork are in first class condition throughout and is as reliable and well turned out as any vehicle can be which may be 80 or 90 years old, or more.

For those readers who might find them helpful for reference purposes, it may be possible to reproduce sets of the photographs of some of the motor cars shown here as they were being stripped down and rebuilt. In this way, the present owners or people having similar models, can see how their car is constructed and put together.

Please note that the photographs which are used were not intended to be shown in a publication of any sort, a book like this, for example. Their main purpose, was to accompany our monthly reports and copy job sheets which were sent to our customers, progressively, as the work proceeded. They helped to give the owner some idea of the work involved and clarify the nature and details of it. This being so, the background of them is often general workshop conditions, so I hope you will make allowances for this.

ROYLES WORK

I have explained that our work involved the bodywork as well as the mechanical side of vintage motor car restoration work. It is, of course, extremely important that the engineering side of the work is properly carried out and the vehicles put back into first class mechanical condition. There is a huge difference between driving a properly overhauled motor car and one which is badly worn. Although primitive by modern standards, the earliest veteran machines can also be a real pleasure to drive and well worth the cost and trouble of being overhauled. Entirely original, early motor cars are especially valuable, especially the racing cars. These have to be treated with great care and according to their use, balancing mechanical condition with originality and with conservation is the challenge.

Having said this, it is the coachwork of the vehicles we deal with which I found to be most challenging and interesting to me. This was because of the wide variation in style, the quality of the materials and fittings used, as well as the craftsmanship involved in the methods of construction. I much preferred the creative aspect of body restoration work and had a natural aptitude and gift for the specialised nature of it. The satisfaction of doing the work was very considerable and I greatly enjoyed seeing it all coming together. A properly restored motor car is a delight to see and drive.

In the 1950's and 1960's, the owners of vintage and classic cars were generally able to have their engines overhauled by small, local engineering firms and garages up and down the country. These firms employed skilled engineers and some were happy to take on small jobs. They were happy, for example, to deal with cast-on white metal engine bearings and make new parts, like king-pins and bushes, but when it came to bodywork repairs or ash framing, generally speaking, there were very few who were capable of doing it to a high standard. The bodies of vintage cars were originally hand built, therefore time consuming and costly to deal with and there is no simple way of mechanising or speeding up the restoration of them. The result was that this important aspect of overhauling elderly vehicles was not catered for.

THE ROYLE TEAM

When I decided to try to make a living out of restoring vintage motor cars, I was determined to do the work to the highest standards. Whilst I wanted to ensure that the motor cars would be in first class mechanical condition, my enthusiasm for coachwork was such that I decided to specialise in this aspect of the work. I therefore collected together early machinery and equipped the workshops for this specialised work. I would happily overhaul and carry out the mechanical work and often did, but I felt that there would always be more coach work to keep me busy.

This proved to be true and in the fullness of time, I was able to gather together people who had the aptitude and were keen to learn about traditional coach building skills. I was also fortunate in taking on some first class engineers, so together, I was able to provide my customers with the comprehensive service for which we became so well known.

Down the years, our customers recognised the benefits of this and appreciated the range of in house skills provided by Royles highly skilled and dedicated staff and as a result, our work load steadily increased. Our business is markedly different to that of a modern garage, especially nowadays when the work to modern motor cars is controlled by computers. Our work is so specialised that, even today, there are not many companies in this country who provide such a comprehensive restoration service.

Not surprisingly, customers often wonder how I was able to pull together a team of men who are so skilled in traditional, high quality work of this nature, especially in the North East, which is best known for its heavy engineering and not known as a motor vehicle manufacturing centre. (This was long before Nissan came along of course!) As is often the case, it is a combination of factors which I will explain in due course, but in a small company like Royles, every member of the staff carries a lot responsibility. There is no room for any 'weak links' and each man's work must be to the highest standards. Each is a key member of the team who's work is part of an ongoing and complex process, so ultimately, the success of the complete restoration and of the company itself, is reliant upon the skills of every individual employed in it. Quite a challenge when every job is different and when time, cost and safety are so closely linked.

In the years after the war, when the motor industry in the UK was gearing up to produce motor cars again, the practice of using wood for the structural framework had virtually disappeared, but there were still many pre-war hand built vehicles in use which needed repairs. This meant that there were a few people in the motor trade who were still capable of repairing coachwork and bodies built the traditional way. The low value of the cars and the high cost of in-depth repairs inevitably led to a general lowering of standards. My aims were to do the work properly.

As I gradually took on more staff, the underlying problem for me was to establish with them, a regime which had the correct balance between maintaining the best quality of work with the cost. Not surprisingly, some of our customers worried about the costs and the efficiency and when speaking to the men, would emphasise the need to keep costs down. Left to the man at the bench, this constant pressure can easily result in them cutting corners and finally an unsatisfactory job. Without realising it, they could be defeating their purpose in coming to Royles in the first place, which was for a first class job. The result was that I often had the unenviable task of standing between the customer and our staff to ensure that the work was done properly.

When I was able to employ men who were already experienced and skilled in traditional, high class coachwork, it was a pleasure to see them practising his skills. One such person who joined our team early on, was Bill Coe. He joined us in October 1981 and carried out some of our most demanding and complex coachwork restoration work involving the most difficult challenges. He was highly skilled and produced work to the highest standards with wooden framed bodies, usually panelled in aluminium. He was adept at working with wheeling machines and making hand made panels in steel as well as aluminium. To see him planishing a wing was to see traditional coachwork at its best. It was good to have him working with us and it was a sad day for me and Royles when he retired in 1990.

As the years passed, people who possessed his skills were few and far between. There being little or no demand for such people in the modern motor trade, none came along to replace such wonderful craftsmen.

Those who trained as engineers and motor mechanics in the 1960's and later, were naturally familiar with monocoque body construction. This work consisting mainly of replacing damaged panels with new ones. This requires different skills, but in the case of classic cars, the original panels were often no longer available, so once again, there was the need for skilled panel work. Later on, some firms began making panels for some of the post war sports cars for example, but the standard of the panels weren't always up to scratch and special skills and techniques were still needed if the correct body shape was to be maintained and they were to be made to fit properly.

Fortunately, there have always been some men in the modern motor trade who have a keen interest and enthusiasm for vintage and classic cars. They would be employed in modern garages doing mechanical work whilst others attended to the accident repair work and modern body repairs. When they heard about Royles, those men who were interested, came to me to see if they could join us. Their enthusiasm for our specialist work was a good starting point.

After interviewing them and as I gradually took on the new men and slowly built up our workforce, over the years, I was fortunate in being able to work alongside them at the bench, so I could quickly see if they had the right attitude for our sort of specialised work. Their experience with motor engineering and modern bodywork was valuable and I was quickly able to see if they would have the ability and the enthusiasm to develop these skills into traditional coach building techniques.

They were usually skilled at welding, but I was able to advise them and show them how to restore bodywork and, at the same time, conserve and combine some of the original, existing wood framework and then, later, how to build complete bodies. I also explained the variation in the designs and styles of coach building employed as motor bodywork developed during the Edwardian, vintage and post vintage periods.

MY OWN GIFTS AND SKILLS

After the war there were still many apprenticeships in various industries, but there were no academic or existing training facilities which appealed to me and none for the restoration of early vehicles. After my boarding and grammar school education, I wanted to be involved with boats or vintage cars and wrote to Laurent Giles the Yacht designers, but was told that it was an unreliable industry and that there was little chance of any work with them. I also wrote to the British India shipping line and had lantern tests and interviews in London and although accepted, at the age of eighteen, I was older than their normal trainee deck officers, so was advised against it. As previously mentioned, I worked in trainee management at Woolworths for a while, but didn't like the business, so went to work at the factory where I was involved in all manner of jobs.

From my early teenage years, in my spare time, I had been working on boats and my old Avon motor car and found it all to be most interesting, so carried on with them. Vehicle restoration was in its infancy in those days and my practical work clearly showed what facilities were needed to do the work properly. There was a growing number of enthusiasts for old cars, but the driving of them was the fun, not working on them.

Being an impecunious schoolboy, but wanting to enjoy these luxuries, I had no choice, but to build them myself. My enthusiasm was such that I soaked up any information I could find. I acquired and studied drawings of hull designs and books which were about boats and cars.

This, combined with spending all my spare time working on them, I couldn't have wished for a better grounding for what became my future career, it was both theoretical and practical.
I didn't realise that I would finish up spending my life being deeply involved with both forms of transport.

As the years passed, I realised that all the years of study and my gift for practical work with all kinds of materials, combined with my ability for drawing, meant that I was blessed with the natural ability to design and build boats and complete bodies for motor cars. When I started my business and was restoring my customers vehicles, it was good that I had already spent twenty years doing the work myself. I was confident that I could tackle any of the jobs which might come along, but being self taught with no formal qualifications, could occasionally be a problem when first instructing the men. Especially those who did have the benefit of academic qualifications.

The "proof of the pudding" as they say, usually solved the problem. On one occasion, one of the men said that the job which I had asked him to do "couldn't be done". After he had gone home, I made the component and left it on the bench for him to find the following morning. He settled down after that.

It was good to be able to work with the men and see them picking up the techniques of working with wood and the various traditional wheeling, swaging and other antique machines which I had acquired down the years. I was able to advise and show them what I wanted them to do and how I wanted it done as they worked with me to build and restore the cars coming through. At the same time, I was able to benefit from their experience with the more modern and the classic motor cars which came in as the years passed.

Importantly, I was able to instil into them the need to maintain the high standards I wanted to achieve. This was not only in the methods of restoration and conservation, but also in the standards and type of finish of all the different components.

Their enthusiasm was heartening and they enjoyed the interesting cars which came into us. The standards were high and they produced excellent results. Achieving the correct balance between high quality work and commercial viability was always a problem however. Sometimes it was the customers themselves, who couldn't appreciate the time which traditional hand work takes and which is necessary to achieve the high standards which they expected.

Some were concerned that we were not working quickly enough, fortunately some of our customers had tackled various jobs on their own cars, so had a very good idea of the nature of the problems faced when working on vehicles which can be 60, 70 or more years old. They were able to appreciate what was being done and the time it takes when done properly. These customers would bring more work to us and knew that our charges were fair and reasonable.

As time passed and the men's skills developed, it was good to see them also producing work which, in some cases, they themselves, didn't realize they were capable of doing until they came to Staindrop and were given the guidance and the opportunity. Later on, they became so proficient at building complete bodies for example, that I only had to provide them with the line drawings, because they knew what the wooden or steel framework should consist of.

The VMCR team, Judith and the dirty dozen.

As you will see, some of the team whom you may have met, if you have visited us, are visible in the photographs which are shown in this book. One or two of them were camera shy, whilst others were happy to be included in the photographs taken whilst the work was in progress. Because of this, I didn't take many photo's of the staff together as a group, but I have found one which is shown here, which was probably taken in 1981.

IN THE OFFICE

Being one of the first firms to be set up and be equipped specifically for Vehicle restoration, we had no preconceived ideas of billing or paperwork systems. Obviously normal garage practice was unsuited to our work, so Roger and I discussed what we needed and we established systems which worked well. Over the years, it seems that these have been adopted by other restoration people around the country who are involved with this specialised work.

Roger had been employed by Glaxo in their offices at nearby Barnard Castle and whilst he worked with me in the workshop to begin with, his knowledge of book keeping and previous experience was obviously beneficial, so he naturally took over the paperwork. I much preferred the actual restoration side of the business, so I continued to work with the customers and the at the bench with the men, where I was able to oversee the work and ensure that the quality was maintained and the jobs were flowing smoothly through the workshops.

As time passed, the workload continued to increase and with more staff and more customers coming to us, there was the need for more clerical work and management. Roger had introduced computers but, as previously mentioned, it was not long before we needed the help of a clerical assistant and secretary. Judith was the first girl to come to help us and became a valuable member of the team. She left us in 1981 to get married, soon afterwards, we were again fortunate when Irene joined us and also was a key member of staff and a great help to me until the end of the decade. This is when she left to have her baby.

Taking over from Irene was Val who continued with the good work until Julie joined us and then Janet who also proved to be very helpful. We have been very fortunate in having such good people to help us in the office, not least of whom was Edna who not only helped around the workshops, but was also very popular with our visitors and me, because there was always a good supply of coffee and tea. Later on, in 2001, Shelly came to us, but had the misfortune to be in the office at Staindrop during the period when the British Waterways troubles developed and when the legal problems were also dragging on. It was not a happy time for us or for her and sadly, she was with us for less than two years. Finally, it was Irene who came back to us when her daughter Kate, was old enough to look after herself. Irene was still with us when I left to start writing this book at home, in fact she was one of few who could read my dreadful writing so typed out some of the early hand written chapters.

As most of the men in the 'Royle' team appear in some of the photographs and if you have visited us, you will have met our more attractive members of Royles staff, so I thought that they also should be included. You have already seen Judith and Irene earlier on, I don't have photo's of all our excellent secretaries, but I have now found pictures of Julie and Janet. Because they are usually the result of a quick 'snap' shot, I will probably get into trouble when they see them, but that will be just another case of 'situation normal' with these bossy, but splendid secretaries!

THE MOTOR CARS

The wide range of vehicles which came to us was a constant source of interest and kept us all on our toes. Every single car had its own character and no matter whether it was a high quality machine or more of an 'everyday' type of motor car of the 1930's, for example, they were a pleasure to work on. It was impossible to predict what was going to come in next, or in what condition it might be in.

One of the added benefits of our work was being able to road test and check for ourselves, that the work which had been done, was up to standard. This presented us with the opportunity to drive the most remarkable range of vehicles built from the beginning of the 1900's right through to those of the latter half of the 20th

Julie.

Janet

century. Veteran, Edwardian, Vintage, Pre and Post war Classic cars. The first tests were carried out by the engineers and craftsmen who had worked on them, I would then often take over with a clip board looking for any faults which might have been missed or not checked. In this way, I was able to save having to charge our customers for the men's time.

Depending on the design and performance of the vehicle, this could involve driving a few miles on the local moorland roads, especially if it was a small or early design, or further afield if it was a large and more powerful car. One of my test runs was over to the lake district and back. This then included long uphill climbs, some dual carriageways (in more recent years), short steep hills and narrow roads with different road surfaces. It was vital to keep an eye on the gauges to ensure that the temperature, oil pressure and road speed were kept within the normal range.

Nowadays, people have forgotten that all motor cars had to be 'run in' which were built before the war and for quite a few years afterwards. It was well into the seventies before improvements in design, lubrication, filters and metallurgical developments were made, that engines could stand up to the treatment they get today. I have, therefore, always been most careful to keep the engine revs within sensible limits and run the engines up to temperature before driving very far.

I would often find that minor adjustments would be needed as body rattles and minor faults developed as the coachwork and doors settled in due to the road movement. I would sometimes drive the cars home a few times to see how frequent starting from cold, and then stopping after a short run of 7 miles might reveal any other minor faults. It was a most interesting aspect of our work and could be enjoyable.

As previously mentioned, I took many thousands of photographs which record the work carried out to most of our customers motor cars. Sadly, it is not even possible to include a selection of them for each car, which is a great shame as the work involved to most of them is so interesting. This is because the Royle book is likely to be a much larger volume than I expected, it could well extend to over 700 pages. Had there been room, they would also have given some indication of the the amount of work which was involved with each vehicle. Never the less, I wanted to show as many of 'our' cars as possible, so I have included at least one, two or three shots of each vehicle in the next chapter.

INTRODUCTION TO PART 1

Because this chapter includes and lists all the motor cars which we have worked on in Royle's Workshops at Staindrop, it is not possible to include all the photographic records of each one. These would fill a number of volumes, so I have selected a handsome pre-war 1938 Lagonda saloon to give you some idea of what is involved when a complete restoration is undertaken.

In order to give some idea of what goes into a complete restoration, I begin the next chapter with 170 photographs recording the major elements of work carried out to just one of 'our' many wonderful cars, a pre-war 4½ litre Lagonda Saloon. Interspersed amongst the hundreds which follow, I have also included a few with a small selection of photos. These were chosen at random to emphasise the nature of our work. Sometimes the pictures can be confusing, so I have added a brief description to explain what they show.

PART 1 - AN EXAMPLE OF A VEHICLE RESTORED AT ROYLE'S WORKSHOPS.

A photographic record of a comprehensive restoration.

THE 1938 LAGONDA LG6 4.5 LITRE SALOON. JOB 394

This Lagonda illustrates the nature and refinement of bodywork which was still being built in the traditional manner when mass production methods had already been firmly established long before the war. With an Ash timber frame, panelled in aluminium, it was a costly method of construction, but it resulted in a stylish, shapely and light weight body which could be built in relatively small numbers to suit Lagonda's customers.

This motor car has been in one family's ownership from new and judging from the strong tow bar fitted to its robust chassis and the fact that the original 4.5 litre engine had been replaced with a diesel engine, showed that it had worked very hard during its lifetime. Never the less, this handsome vehicle responded well to its complete overhaul and is, once again, as new and being enjoyed by the family.

The photographs are generally in chronological order and I have purposely kept the descriptions brief, avoiding too much specialised or technical information. My aim is for you, the reader, to be able to focus on the interesting story and not be bogged down with lengthy detailed descriptions of all the components. It is important for you to understand that many of the wonderful machines listed in the next chapter, which we restored, have gone through a similar, detailed and lengthy process. This is what is needed for a first class job.

This book is not intended to be a treatise on the many technical and specialised aspects involved in the overhaul and restoration of vintage and classic motor cars. Others have covered the subject, but if there was the demand for me to write such a book, then I could look into the possibility of doing it. After the negative elements which I have included in this one however, if I was ever encouraged to consider writing a book again, I would much prefer to tackle a more light hearted approach to the subject.

1938 LAGONDA LG6 SALOON *continued*

JOB 394

The Lagonda as delivered to the workshops. This motor car has the longer chassis and has worked hard during its lifetime. A Gardiner diesel engine has been installed and replaced the original Meadows 4.5 litre unit which were fitted by Lagonda during this period. The strong tow bar, fitted behind the back bumper, bears witness to the heavy work done and gives an indication of the strength and quality of the engineering incorporated into these pre-war motor cars.

1938 LAGONDA LG6 SALOON *continued*

JOB 394

Before and during the period when the motor car is dismantled, a series of photographs are taken to record the condition and details of construction. These are just a few of the many reference shots. They can be very useful as the restoration work proceeds and during reassembly. These show the rear of the body with wiring and original Bakelite junction boxes. The boot lid and the bonnet have been removed along with the diesel engine.

Various external fittings, lamps, bumpers, filler caps and other parts are carefully stripped off as are the rear wings. I am tempted to use the term 'mudguards' but will only use this term when discussing smaller, non streamlined 'covers' for the road wheels.

The panels have also been removed from the scuttle revealing the wooden framework, the condition of which is now clearly visible.

CHAPTER 40 : VEHICLES RESTORED AT ROYLES WORKSHOPS - PART 1

1938 LAGONDA LG6 SALOON *continued*

JOB 394

Whilst we set about locating an original Lagonda engine, the remaining mechanical components are left in place whilst the bodywork is examined and the extent of damage through wet and dry rot and woodworm is determined and the way forward planned. In this case, body struts have been fitted which, when combined with the rear structure and door pillars help to maintain the body shape whilst the scuttle frames are attended to.

The rotten scuttle timbers and windscreen support frames can now be renewed with the help of temporary support struts. Some of these front timbers have disintegrated with just sufficient wood remaining to act as patterns to enable new ones to be made. New bottom rails and forward bulkhead frames are made and fitted. Note the original centre door pillar upon which the doors are hung is a metal casting, not wood.

1938 LAGONDA LG6 SALOON *continued*

JOB 394

The new body frames are made out of seasoned Ash timber and fitted up. Ash has been used to construct horse drawn vehicle bodies for centuries, and motor bodies in the early years of the 20th century. It is light in weight and is flexible and can survive for long periods of time in the right conditions. As the years passed, the public demanded more comfort and luxury and the wooden frames became encased in panels, preventing the timber from 'breathing'. The result can be seen in a saloon body like this.

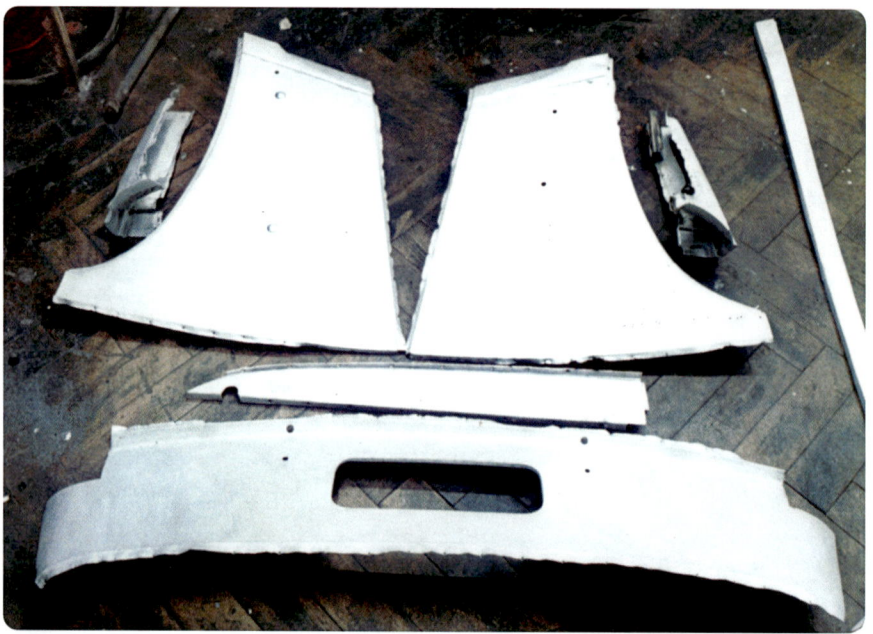

After removal, the scuttle box, top and side panels have been bead blasted to remove corrosion and can be used to check the fit of the new frames as also can the door. The double curvature of most surfaces combined with the complicated rebates as seen in the front cross member, have to be exactly reproduced so that, in this case, the windscreen wiper motor and the associated drive mechanisms can be accommodated. The skill of the craftsman is key when frames are being hand made out of solid balks and planks of timber.

1938 LAGONDA LG6 SALOON *continued*

JOB 394

The top windscreen support frames are made after the roof and rear quarter panels have been removed, these are cut through to facilitate this. New side rails can be now be made to tie the front frames to the back of the body. The original outer panels are used to check that the new scuttle frame assembly is exactly the same as the original.

1938 LAGONDA LG6 SALOON *continued*

JOB 394

With the rear body frame exposed, the timbers are marked according to condition. Some are sound, so only the rotten ones are replaced with new wood. Once again, the curvature and dimensions of them all is critical if all the associated parts are to fit properly. Most of the beautiful Lagonda bodies were designed by Frank Feeley and it is essential that the flowing lines are exactly reproduced.

CHAPTER 40 : VEHICLES RESTORED AT ROYLES WORKSHOPS - PART 1

1938 LAGONDA LG6 SALOON *continued*

JOB 394

Not surprisingly, the rocker frames below the doors needed to be replaced as did some of the door frames once the outer skin had been removed. As well as woodworm and wet and dry rot down the years, sometimes frames suffer as a result of physical damage. Doors and boot lids can also be strained and the hinges forced which causes splitting of the wood for example. This is not surprising when they have been opened and closed and probably slammed, for 50 years!

After repairing the frame, the door skin is bead blasted, new metal welded in as necessary and the original skin then refitted after the wood has been treated and painted to protect it.

251

1938 LAGONDA LG6 SALOON *continued*

JOB 394

Here we can see the entire body frame has been treated with 'Cuprinol' wood preservative and then painted black to further protect it. Painting the framework black was common practice before the war. This was in order to protect the wood and make a professional job. Inside doors for example, the framework may be visible when the windows are down, so a black interior is preferable when there is any chance of the framework showing.

1938 LAGONDA LG6 SALOON *continued*

JOB 394

The boot lid and sliding sunshine roof are stripped down, new frames made and painted, the mechanisms overhauled and the unit reassembled.

1938 LAGONDA LG6 SALOON *continued*

JOB 394

The outer aluminium panelling of the body can now be attended to. All the panelling is cleaned, bead blasted and inspected. Areas which are weak through corrosion, physical damage or metal fatigue, are cut out, new metal beaten and rolled into shape and then seam welded into place.

Here, one of the bottom edges of a rear door has been cut off and new, pre-shaped metal is welded in prior to it being trimmed and then will be worked over the frame, crimped and nailed on to it.

Similarly, the roof panel and scuttle mouldings are restored to the original shape. The sunshine roof and scuttle vent have drains for rainwater and washing, here the scuttle drain is fitted prior to the panelling being refitted.

1938 LAGONDA LG6 SALOON *continued*

JOB 394

The front and side roof panels are beaten and wheeled into shape and welded in place. The rear inner wheel arches are replaced with new shaped steel panels as original and pre fitted to the new timbers of the body frame, removed, primed and painted and then fixed into place.

1938 LAGONDA LG6 SALOON *continued*

JOB 394

The rear quarter panels are refitted after blast cleaning and new metal welded in where necessary. Here we see Steve skinning the new, rear timber wheel arches with new aluminium panelling, the scuttle mouldings and panels been welded together and refitted after checking alignment with the bonnet temporarily refitted for the purpose.

CHAPTER 40 : VEHICLES RESTORED AT ROYLES WORKSHOPS - PART 1

1938 LAGONDA LG6 SALOON *continued*

JOB 394

The front scuttle top vent mechanism and main support castings, along with the spare wheel support bracket, are blast cleaned, overhauled and repaired and the boot lid skin refitted and mounted onto the overhauled bodywork. Bronze castings have been made from patterns exactly the same as the original radiator and twin petrol filler caps. These had been made of 'mazac', an alloy of magnesium and zinc. This metal deteriorates badly over time, losing its strength and the chromed surface blisters, which is unsightly.

These filler caps incorporate an adjustable, eccentric pivot pin and a lever which applies a downward pressure on the cap when it is moved over it and locates with a small, sprung, centre plunger. These are a costly, but important feature of many Lagonda's so we also supplied some to other club members.

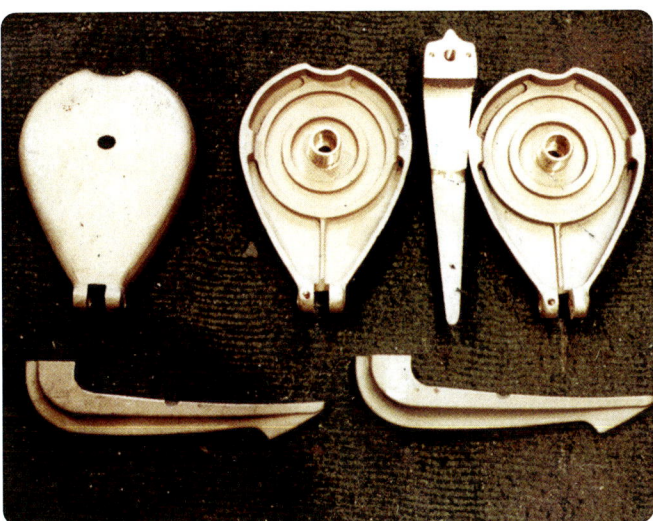

1938 LAGONDA LG6 SALOON *continued*

JOB 394

The wings and running boards have been stripped and blast cleaned and the faults and weaknesses have been revealed. An early reference shot shows a steel front wing mounting and support bracket in situ as delivered and also after removal, on the bench next to a new one being fabricated. The bracket has virtually disintegrated and the wing itself has suffered badly as a result of the electro-chemical reaction between the two dissimilar metals.

Held up to the light, the holes and perforations in the wing can clearly be seen. The metal in this area is very weak and substantial replacement sections are needed to re-establish the structural integrity of the wing. The corrosion to the bottom of the spare wheel well in the wing is far more obvious.

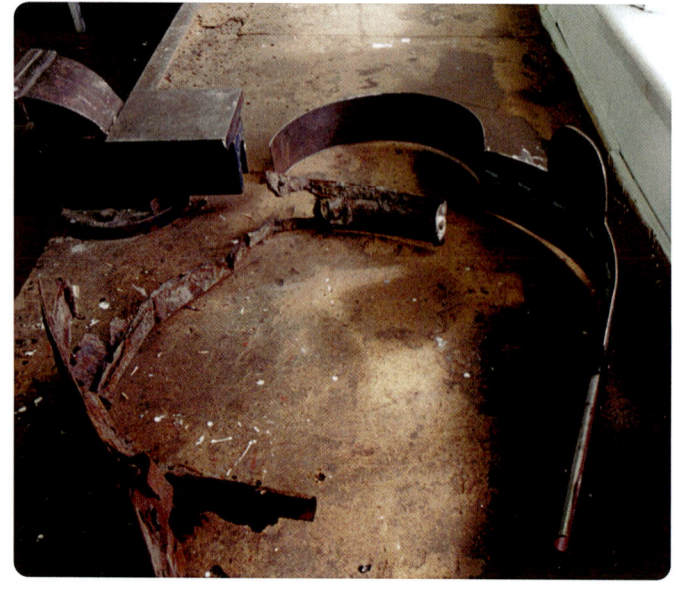

1938 LAGONDA LG6 SALOON *continued*

JOB 394

After the corroded area has been cut out, new metal has been shaped and seam welded into place. The matt surface of the original bead blasted wing contrasts with smooth, shiny new metal. All the wings and external parts were in a similar condition, but I have only included a few of the photographs here to show the condition of some of them. Parts of the back wings had suffered badly, these were in need of substantial repair and the running boards had to be replaced completely.

These photographs should be compared to those taken when the Lagonda was first delivered to Royles workshops. Before the bodywork had been disturbed, the general condition of the car seemed to be reasonably sound.

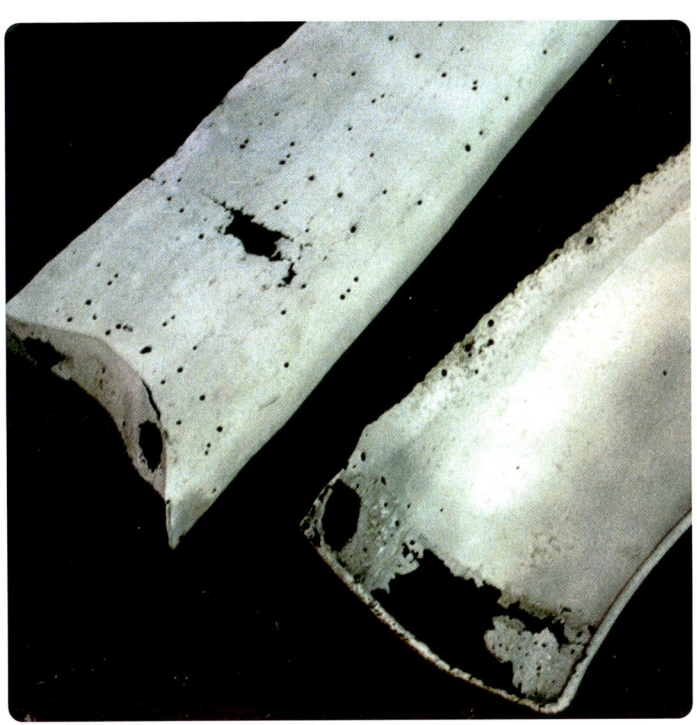

1938 LAGONDA LG6 SALOON *continued*   JOB 394

As has been the case with all of the bodywork, the paint on both surfaces of the bonnet is being stripped off so that it can be examined. The bonnet handles and locks were also removed and checked. The handles were of mazac so patterns were made and new handles cast in bronze to replace them. The restored wings and the running boards are fitted to the body to check for correct fit. New stone guards are made to fit inside the wings to protect them.

CHAPTER 40 : VEHICLES RESTORED AT ROYLES WORKSHOPS - PART 1

1938 LAGONDA LG6 SALOON *continued*

JOB 394

The front apron is renewed as are the inner front valences. The principal components of the bodywork are assembled to check them all in situ.

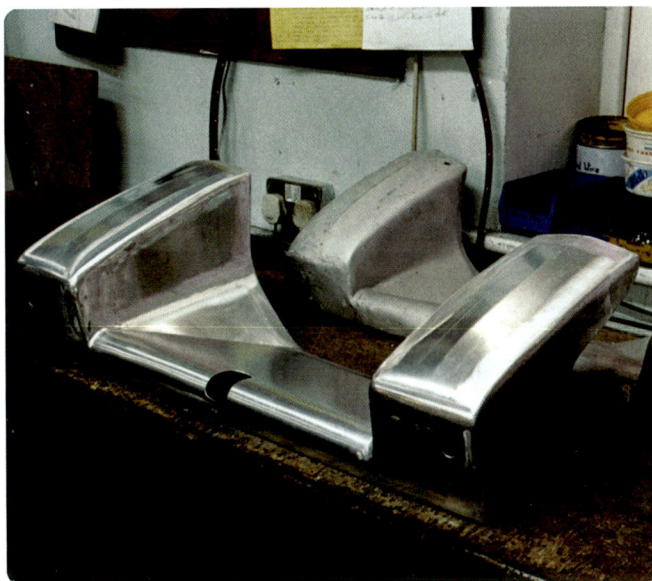

261

1938 LAGONDA LG6 SALOON *continued*

JOB 394

An early reference shot shows the condition of the rear panels below the boot lid. The badly rusted hinged part supports the back lit, illuminated number plate unit. After blast cleaning, this unit can be seen to be badly rusted and perforated right through in some places. It is primed and lying on one of the new running boards. The hinged panel permits a folding luggage grid, which is fastened to the chassis, to be extended out from behind the panel when needed.

CHAPTER 40 : VEHICLES RESTORED AT ROYLES WORKSHOPS - PART 1

1938 LAGONDA LG6 SALOON *continued*

JOB 394

Making a new fuel tank. The original tank was badly corroded so the brass fittings, pipes and mountings have been removed and cleaned in readiness to be used again on the new tank. The original filler necks had to be replaced so new ones have been made up and machined using stainless steel.

263

1938 LAGONDA LG6 SALOON *continued*

JOB 394

The finished rear panels have been fitted to the body to check the fit. New rear chassis extension brackets have been made along with a new set of running board support brackets.

At this point, all the external parts of the bodywork, the wings, running boards etc, are removed from the main body. Having been restored and regaining its strength, this can now be removed from the chassis and placed on a body trolley for the painting process to begin. The un-restored chassis is now exposed and the complete overhaul of the mechanical parts can begin.

CHAPTER 40 : VEHICLES RESTORED AT ROYLES WORKSHOPS - PART 1

1938 LAGONDA LG6 SALOON *continued*

JOB 394

OVERHAULING THE MECHANICAL AND ANCILLORY EQUIPMENT

The wheels have been refitted to check body clearances and also to move the chassis out of the coachwork department and into the central workshop. The chassis of the later pre-war Lagonda's is largely the work of W.O.Bentley who joined them in 1935. These photographs are a few of the reference shots taken before the chassis work commenced and show the condition and some of the features of the designs. The anti-roll bar above the back axle is noticeable as is the independent front suspension.

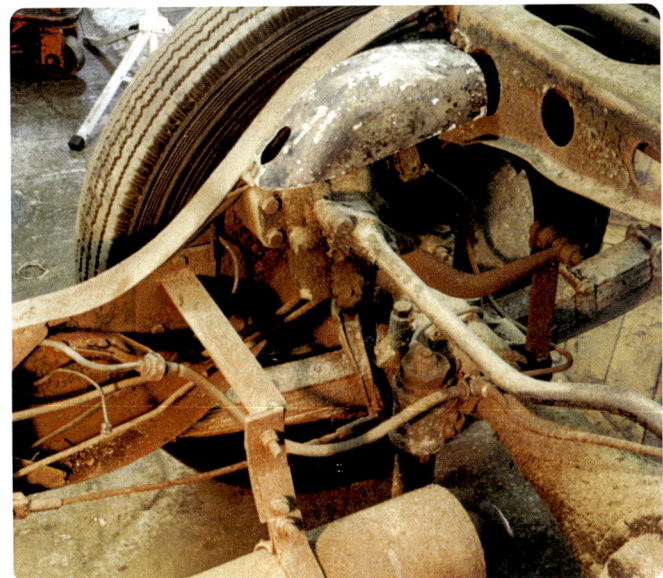

1938 LAGONDA LG6 SALOON *continued*

JOB 394

The chassis cruciform has been cut away to allow the Gardiner diesel engine to be fitted. As is often the case with chassis and suspension components which have remained undisturbed for 50 years, it was necessary to heat up some of the nuts and bolts to enable them to be removed without damage. The judicious use of a welding torch is very helpful in these circumstances. After removal, the parts are washed off in readiness for them to be inspected.

1938 LAGONDA LG6 SALOON *continued*

JOB 394

Once stripped, the chassis was found to be in sound condition with no signs of damage, except where the cruciform had been cut away. A new steel section of the same gauge was formed and welded into place. The chassis itself was then ready to be shot blasted.

All the mechanical parts are now stripped down to their basic components and each is carefully cleaned and inspected. They are checked for wear and crack tested where there is any risk of damage. The work of overhauling all the parts now begins. New bronze and white metal bushes are made and the necessary machine work, grinding and refitting until the correct tolerances once again prevail. Only a few of the parts are shown here.

1938 LAGONDA LG6 SALOON *continued*

JOB 394

The back axle is stripped down and the parts soaked in solvent and then washed off. The brakes are stripped down when two of the cast alloy brake back plates were damaged so new ones were cast and machined. Whilst the front suspension was being overhauled, the back axle half shafts and differential crown wheel and pinion are checked and new bearings fitted and the rear axle re–assembled.

1938 LAGONDA LG6 SALOON *continued*

JOB 394

There are many small mechanical components in a motor car, they all have been in use for 50 years, in this case, and some are inaccessible, so have not been serviced in all that time. There are too many to photograph individually, but I have included some of them to give you an idea of what is involved in a comprehensive restoration.

Here we see the components of the windscreen wiper mechanisms after being stripped down. These fit into the rebated, curved wooden frame above the dashboard, seen earlier. There are two small gearboxes and a transverse drive shaft or cable. The gears and the bearings wear, so need to be carefully checked and overhauled as necessary.

There are also various locks and catches for doors, boot lid, bonnet, tool box, spare wheel case and other panels already described. All need to be stripped and overhauled if they are again to give reliable service. The wear to the door hinges must be attended to if they are to open and close satisfactorily. Here we see the original barrel hinges with the body numbers. Each is drilled to mount and fit each door individually, so must be refitted in the same location. The pins are removed and the hinges reamed out. The new pins are made fractionally oversize to suit the new internal bore. They are then re-chrome plated as new.

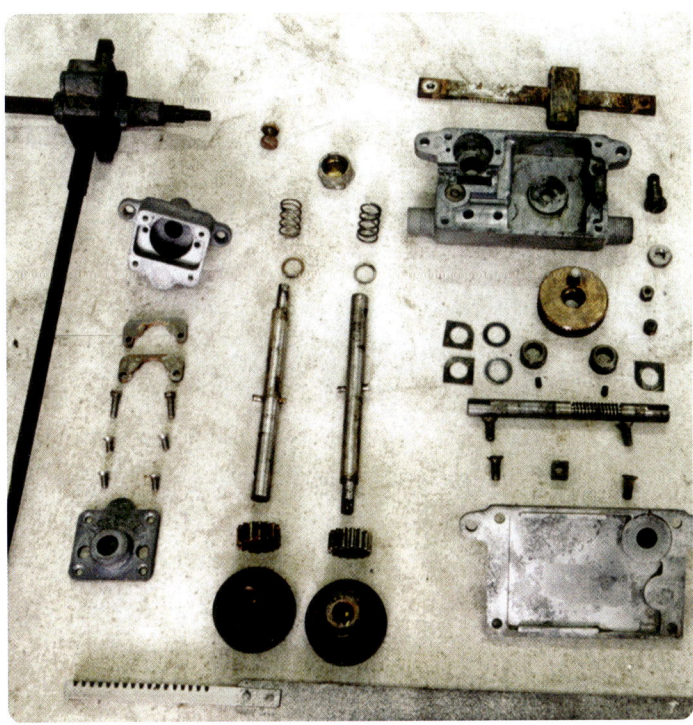

1938 LAGONDA LG6 SALOON *continued* JOB 394

These Lagonda's are fitted with a central lubrication facility and the 'Jackall' central jacking system to enable the owner to jack up the car and change a wheel with a punctured tyre more easily. Both have small bore copper pipes clipped all around the chassis to facilitate lubrication and operation of the jacks respectively. Here we see the cylinders and some of the components of the hydraulic jacks. The nickel silver pump handle used to pressurise the jacking system is mounted on the unit with thumb screws which select the jacks to be operated. The lubrication system is operated by a foot pedal mounted on the forward bulkhead in the car.

New Brake linings have been riveted in place and the large brake drums have been skimmed to ensure efficient braking. The assorted components on the bench and in boxes include the head lamps, door locks, window frames and deflectors, the oil reservoir and the seat runners. These are being cleaned ready for checking, as are the stainless steel bumper bars which need to be trued up. The special bolts for them have been re-machined.

1938 LAGONDA LG6 SALOON *continued*

JOB 394

The radiator shell has been removed from the frame and core, the grills and thermostat levers have been stripped down for overhaul. The wheels have been blast cleaned and re-spoked and are in the paint booth for priming and undercoats. Only the inside of the rim is to be painted in top coats at this stage. The paint on the rolled rims of these wheels is susceptible to damage when fitting the tyres, so the top coats are applied afterwards.

This Lagonda is fitted with 'Ace' Wheel discs, so the back plates are attended to and painted and the discs themselves are to be rechromed and then painted to leave the raised swages showing.

1938 LAGONDA LG6 SALOON *continued*

JOB 394

The dashboard and the internal cappings for the doors and window surrounds and coachbuilders door plates, were put together after removal from the car. They can now be examined and restored. The dashboard veneers were lifting so are carefully removed and new burr walnut veneers cut and applied. New mahogany finishers are shaped and formed to replace those damaged by wet rot and ingress of water. The rear window surround is also replaced. These are fitted after the headlining has been made, tacked and glued into place.

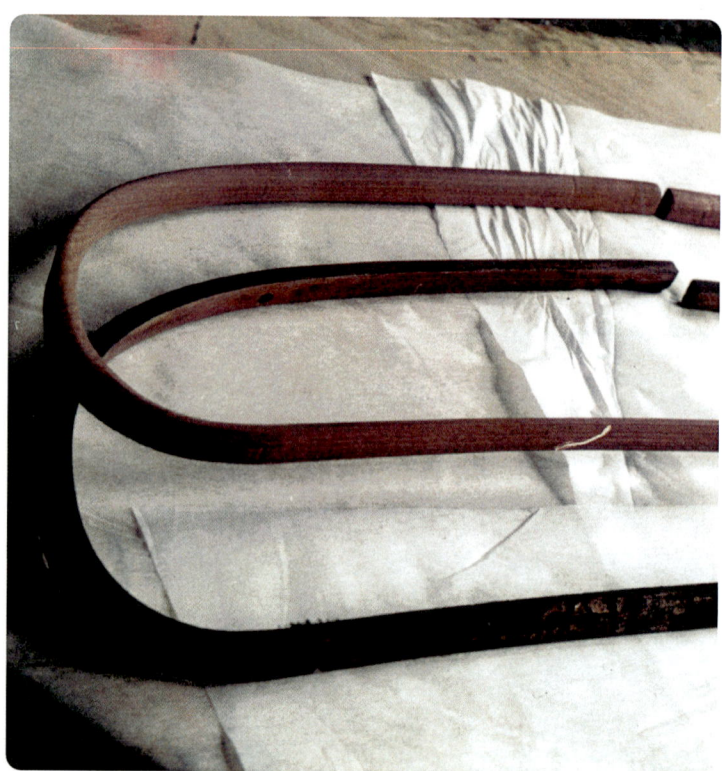

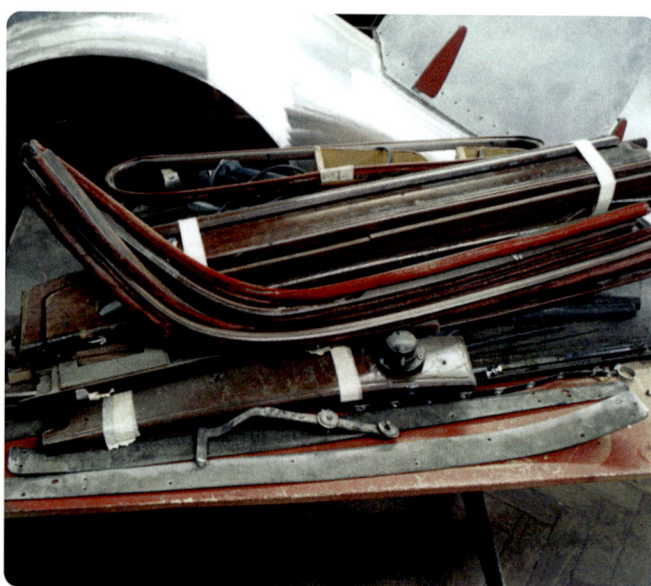

1938 LAGONDA LG6 SALOON *continued*

JOB 394

The gearbox is stripped down. All the components were cleaned and examined. The casing and housings, the selectors and helical gears were all found to be in good condition. As the unit was stripped down, we took the precaution of replacing all the bearings. After reassembly, Don can be seen refitting the gearbox back into the finished chassis. This is the beginning of the reassembly process of the Lagonda.

After repairs to the cruciform, shot blasting, priming and painting, the rust pits are still visible where it has penetrated the surface of the chassis. The damage is so slight, structurally, that the chassis needs no further work. Had the car been prepared for concours display, these imperfections would have been filled in the painting process. The owner wishes to enjoy driving and using the car however, so there was no need to add extra cost for this kind of work.

1938 LAGONDA LG6 SALOON *continued*

JOB 394

A correct 4.5 litre Lagonda engine has been acquired to replace the non-original diesel engine. This is partially stripped down and is firstly steam cleaned to remove the majority of the accumulated dirt, oil and deposits. The components are then thoroughly washed off with solvents in our cleaning tank, after which careful inspection takes place including crack testing.

1938 LAGONDA LG6 SALOON *continued*

JOB 394

The engine block has been re-bored and the camshaft and crank shaft journals ground and new white metal bearings cast on to the bearings. New pistons and gudgeon pins are fitted. These overhauled components reassembled to the block with new timing wheels and new inverted tooth chains. The rotating engine bed is most beneficial for this work. New valve guides are fitted and the valves themselves are ground in and fitted to the cylinder head with new valve springs.

1938 LAGONDA LG6 SALOON *continued*

JOB 394

The clutch has been overhauled and the flywheel ring gear. The main bearings and oil pump are also refitted after overhaul and the block and head painted the original pale Lagonda green colour. The cylinder head is lowered onto the block.

All the ancillary equipment has also been stripped and overhauled including the water pump, fan bearings, dynamo, starter motor and oil filter. The cast alloy water transfer ports and pipes suffer from corrosion, so new castings were made and machined. The twin Scintilla Magneto's have been stripped and overhauled and the air intake also stripped and checked, these last two items can be seen here.

1938 LAGONDA LG6 SALOON *continued*

JOB 394

A temporary radiator and fuel tank are connected up to the built up, completely overhauled engine, so that it can be run up to temperature and tested on its bed for some hours, before being refitted to the chassis.

The rebuilt back axle has been refitted to the chassis with new road (leaf) springs and new hydraulic brake pipes are clipped into place after the hubs, back plates and brake shoes have been reassembled and the drums fitted.

Refitting the many small bore pipes around the chassis begins. The reference shots are especially useful for this job as there are so many of them for the central lubrication and 'Jackall' systems.

1938 LAGONDA LG6 SALOON *continued*

JOB 394

After overhaul and painting, the front suspension has been reassembled onto the chassis and the engine lowered into place. Being separate units, the engine is connected to the gearbox via a traditional fabric joint and drive shaft.

The bulkhead, front hubs, brakes and part finished wheels are fitted along with the radiator. Repairs to the shell and slats have been made in readiness for re-chromium plating.

The wing support brackets and bonnet have also been fitted to check clearances and in readiness for the final check of the entire bodywork prior to all the paintwork being done.

1938 LAGONDA LG6 SALOON *continued*

JOB 394

The main body section has been fitted to the chassis and the tyres fitted to the wheels. The overhauled front wings, apron and inner valances (barely visible), are fitted and the wheel clearances can now be checked. The doors and running boards have now been fitted and the neat and even gaps between all the panels show what a good job has been made of all the bodywork restoration. Similarly, the rear panels fit very neatly and the newly cast and fettled twin bronze petrol filler caps and pipes have been fitted and aligned.

The body has now been painted and is protected with bubble pack. The front and rear wings and other panels are now being prepared and stopped up in the paint shop. In the meantime the steering box has been overhauled, the column re-chromed and the control levers reassembled.

The fuel pumps, petrol supply lines fitted along with the polished air intake and other ancillary equipment. The engine bay is virtually complete and what a handsome sight it is!

1938 LAGONDA LG6 SALOON *continued*

JOB 394

The work in the machine shop continues with new securing rings being made for the Ace wheel discs. The last of the newly cast filler caps has been fettled and dressed off and after checking, they are taken apart and all the parts polished and chromium plated.

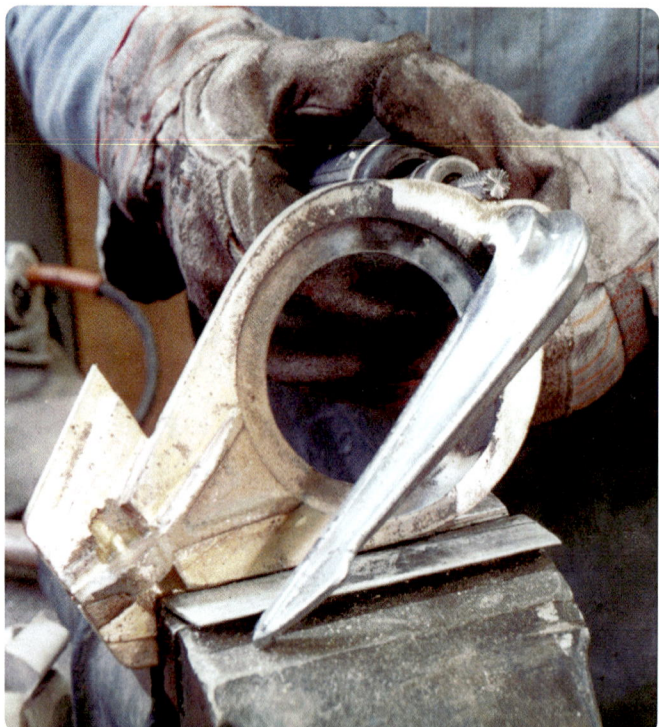

1938 LAGONDA LG6 SALOON *continued*

JOB 394

The dash board instruments have been overhauled and are fitted onto the dash board which has now been re-veneered and lacquered to a high finish. A new wiring loom has been made up and is connected and clipped into place. At the same time the electrical control boxes, junction and fuse boxes have been cleaned and checked.

The horns have also been stripped down, adjusted and tested and the necessary parts re-chromed and new mounting brackets made. The brass side window frames have also been carefully checked and re-chrome plated in readiness for refitting to the doors. The impressive Lucas headlamp shells have been restored and rechromed, the reflectors silver plated and they await the correct glasses to be fitted. Over the years, I have collected such rare items together and these can now be very difficult to find.

In our upstairs stores, I have an extensive collection of new and unused pre-war parts gathered together over the last 55 years. If they can be obtained and have to be bought specially, they can be costly. It has long been my policy to provide these items to good customers at little or no cost, when they are involved with a comprehensive restoration. Such was the case with these large R100 headlamp glasses which we had and which were still in their original boxes.

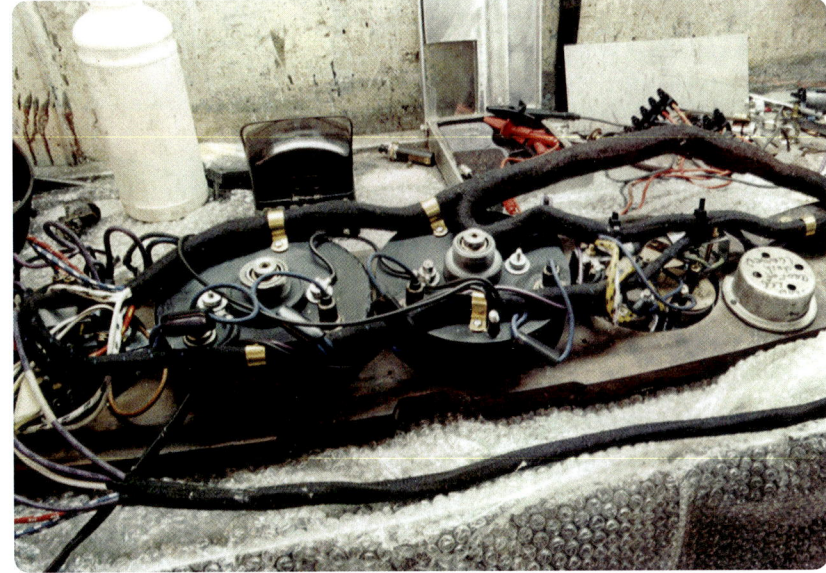

1938 LAGONDA LG6 SALOON *continued*

JOB 394

The interior trim is started. Our customer selected cream hide with dark blue piping for this job.

The original leather interior had been replaced years ago with modern red vinyl material when it was a 'work horse'. The new leather upholstery is made up with sewn pleats over the calico linings which are then hand stuffed with cotton wool wadding as original, as can be seen in this rather poor photograph.

The front seats are fitted with picnic tables and the owner wanted to have a modern CD player fitted discreetly into the glove box so this was done. The rear foot wells and transmission tunnel unit was sound, so was blast cleaned, primed and painted. The plywood floor boards were renewed using the original fittings.

1938 LAGONDA LG6 SALOON *continued*

JOB 394

Once checked, all the removable elements of the body, were removed for painting. Due to all the surfaces of the metal panels, both inside and out, having been stripped of paint, it is essential that they are properly protected. The metal is thoroughly cleaned and carefully prepared before acid etch priming. Each panel and wing is painted separately with particular attention to the edges.

Here you can see all the parts being rubbed down between coats in the preparation shop. The shot of the single front wing in front of the main body section, has already been primed and painted and finished on the underside. The under-coats have been applied on the outside surfaces and a mist coat has been sprayed on. This fine coating assists Jim in the paint shop, to see the slightest surface imperfections before the top coats are applied.

Once satisfied that the body components are up to standard, they are mounted on frames in the paint booth, which is also a bake oven. As can be seen with two of the doors and the radiator suspended in the background, the paint can be sprayed onto all the surfaces of the panel. A finished front wing shows the high standard achieved.

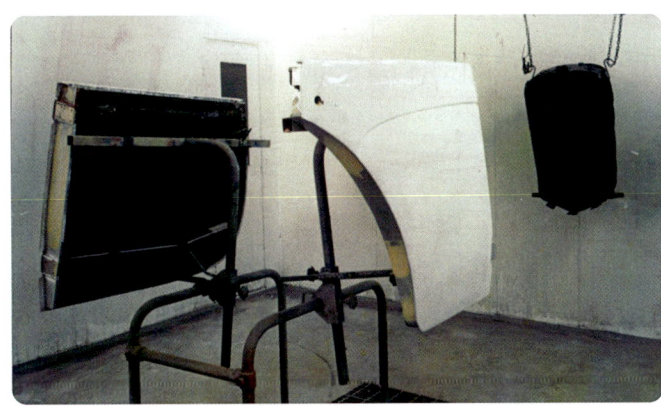

1938 LAGONDA LG6 SALOON *continued*

JOB 394

The running boards and front valences are now finished as are the doors which have been hung onto the centre door pillar.

Fortunately, we had a correct, period back lit number plate unit in our stores to replace the badly corroded one which came off the car. This was in good condition and so was painted white and we were able to make up the correct numbers, saving the owner the costly repair of these complicated components. The robust luggage grid was in sound condition so was painted after blast cleaning.

The doors, rear wings, boot and rear panels are fitted to the body and it is then transferred into the trim shop before the front wings, bonnet and radiator are fitted.

CHAPTER 40 : VEHICLES RESTORED AT ROYLES WORKSHOPS - PART 1

1938 LAGONDA LG6 SALOON *continued*

JOB 394

The Lagonda is now ready for the interior to be trimmed. The carpets are cut and fitted and the edges bound with leather. The one seen here is for the boot. The headlining is to be made in cream leather and is seamed, piped and fitted. The armrests are upholstered and fitted along and the interior lights wired in.

The mahogany finishers can then be screwed to the frame. The patterns for the pleated rear upholstery can be seen. The chromed side window frames with new laminated safety glasses, are fitted into the doors. The dash board has been fitted and is just visible though the front nearside window. The door cappings have been lacquered and can now be fitted along with the finishers.

1938 LAGONDA LG6 SALOON *continued*

The boot is trimmed out and the CD player and twin loudspeakers are fitted unobtrusively to the underside of the rear window shelf. The interior is nearing completion, the front seats and an interior panel are yet to be fitted.

Looking into the car, the rear upholstery has been built in, the window lifting mechanisms have been overhauled and fitted along with the new stylish interior door panels which copy the original patterns. The door handles, the window winders and ash trays have also been fitted along with the restored door cappings and all the mahogany finishers.

The restored dash board with the overhauled original instruments looks splendid and who would think that a CD player was hidden in the glove box!

Looking down onto the car, the restored radiator, Head and side lamps, horns, windscreen, spare wheel and tool box covers and the sunshine roof have all been fitted. An efficient heater has also been neatly built in and the pipes carrying the hot water can be seen running along the nearside of the engine.

CHAPTER 40 : VEHICLES RESTORED AT ROYLES WORKSHOPS - PART 1

1938 LAGONDA LG6 SALOON *continued*

JOB 394

The Lagonda is now finished, the bonnet and bumper bars have been fitted and it has been road tested. The last job is final inspection in the paint shop where any stone chips and marks can be attended to and the car to be wax polished before its owner drives it away. These photographs show what a handsome motor car the LG6 model is.

VEHICLES RESTORED AT ROYLES WORKSHOPS - PART 2

In this chapter all of the vehicles which have been restored or worked upon in Royle's workshops are included. They cover a period of over 40 years and are shown alphabetically under the name of the original manufacturers, commencing with AC.

Due to the many thousands of photographs on file, we have had to limit the number of images to 3 or 4 photographs only for the majority of jobs. To give an idea of the actual amount and quality of the work carried out to many of the cars, interspersed amongst them, we have included some with a few more photographs and a brief description of the work. At the end of this section we have also included a list of the remaining jobs and those for which we have no photographic record.

Looking through the following pages there will be many motor cars which will be of interest to you. Some of them may be familiar and if we carried out any work for you, you might well see your own car shown here. Alternatively, it may be that you have bought one of them after it left us. It would not be practicable to comment upon them all, even though they all are interesting and most of them are familiar to me.

The term 'owner' is used along with the job number in the titles above each of the vehicles shown here. Whilst this will generally be correct, in some cases, it may be an agent acting on behalf of the vehicles owner.

If you would like to order additional images on file for any of the jobs as indicated, please email sales@theroylebook.com

A.C.

JOB: 187 | TYPE: A.C. Cobra 4.7 1964 | OWNER: Mr. K. Schellenberg | IMAGES: 19

JOB: 261 | TYPE: A.C. Aceca 1956 | REFERENCE: Royle Hepworth | IMAGES: 3

A.C.

JOB: 284 | TYPE: A.C. Aceca Bristol 1959 | REFERENCE: Royle Hepworth | IMAGES: 12

JOB: 576 | TYPE: A.C. Aceca | OWNER: Mr. W. Goyder | IMAGES: 110

A.C.

JOB: 873 | TYPE: A.C. Ace Bristol | REFERENCE: Mr. A. Fletcher | IMAGES: 1

ALFA ROMEO

JOB: 47 | TYPE: Alfa Romeo Sprint 1960 | OWNER: Mr. M. Evans | IMAGES: 5

JOB: 631 | TYPE: Alfa Romeo 6C 2500 1949 | OWNER: Mr. D. Brown | IMAGES: 1

CHAPTER 40 : VEHICLES RESTORED AT ROYLES WORKSHOPS - PART 2

ALFA ROMEO

JOB: 643 | TYPE: Alfa Romeo | OWNER: Mr. D. Evans | IMAGES: 50

JOB: 703 | TYPE: Alfa Romeo 8C 2.3 1932 | OWNER: Mr. A. Keller | IMAGES: 13

ALLARD

JOB: 269 | TYPE: Allard Palm Beach 1954 | OWNER: Mr. D. Peddie | IMAGES: 6

JOB: 356 | TYPE: Allard K2 | OWNER: Mr. Haley | IMAGES: 44

ALVIS

JOB: 132 | TYPE: Alvis TA 21 | OWNER: Mr. Whittaker | IMAGES: 4

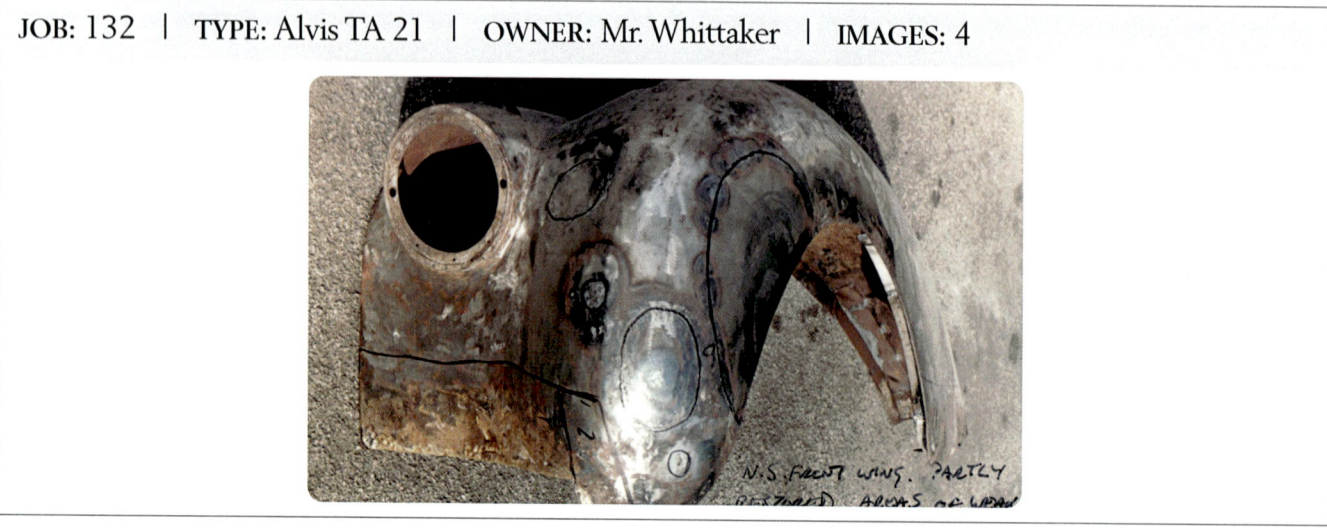

CHAPTER 40 : VEHICLES RESTORED AT ROYLES WORKSHOPS - PART 2

ALVIS

JOB: 52 | TYPE: Alvis Speed 20 | OWNER: J. Whitton | IMAGES: 21

JOB: 161 | TYPE: Alvis TA 14 | OWNER: Mr. Rudd | IMAGES: 18

ALVIS

JOB: 202 | TYPE: Alvis 12/70 Tourer 1939 | OWNER: R. L. Martin | IMAGES: 21

ALVIS

JOB: 202 | TYPE: Alvis 12/70 Tourer 1939 *continued...*

ALVIS

JOB: 208 | TYPE: Alvis 12/50 | OWNER: Rev. Leaming | IMAGES: 8

JOB: 230 | TYPE: Alvis TC 21/100 Grey Lady | OWNER: Mr. Bowden | IMAGES: 128

JOB: 236 | TYPE: Alvis TD 21 | OWNER: Mr. South | IMAGES: 93

CHAPTER 40 : VEHICLES RESTORED AT ROYLES WORKSHOPS - PART 2

ALVIS

JOB: 238 | TYPE: Alvis 12/70 Tourer | OWNER: Dr. A. Mellis | IMAGES: 8

JOB: 249 | TYPE: Alvis 12/50 Tourer | OWNER: Mr. J. Morgan | IMAGES: 108

ALVIS

JOB: 363　|　TYPE: Alvis 12/50 Fabric Saloon　|　OWNER: Rev. Leaming　|　IMAGES: 8

JOB: 370　|　TYPE: Alvis 12/70 Tourer　|　OWNER: Mr. R. Martin　|　IMAGES: 47

JOB: 372　|　TYPE: Alvis 12/70 4 Seat Tourer　|　OWNER: Dr. Mellis　|　IMAGES: 1

CHAPTER 40 : VEHICLES RESTORED AT ROYLES WORKSHOPS - PART 2

ALVIS

JOB: 386 | TYPE: Alvis 1929 | OWNER: Mr. A. Marsh | IMAGES: 118

JOB: 396 | TYPE: Alvis TB 14 circa 1950 | REFERENCE: Royle Cars | IMAGES: 1

JOB: 405 | TYPE: Alvis Silver Eagle | OWNER: Mr. A. Wynn-Williams | IMAGES: 1

ALVIS

JOB: 411 | TYPE: Alvis | OWNER: Mr. S. Fisher | IMAGES: 3

JOB: 420 | TYPE: Alvis TA 14 Tickford 1949 | OWNER: Mr. P. Summers | IMAGES: 72

JOB: 425 | TYPE: Alvis Speed 20 | OWNER: Mr. D. Proffitt | IMAGES: 104

ALVIS

JOB: 482 | TYPE: Alvis FWD | OWNER: Mr. D. Rudkin | IMAGES: 168

JOB: 530 | TYPE: Alvis FWD 2 Seater | OWNER: Mr. J. Robson | IMAGES: 3

JOB: 567 | TYPE: Alvis TD 21 Saloon | OWNER: Mr. J. Ascough | IMAGES: 7

ALVIS

JOB: 591 | TYPE: Alvis SP20 VDP FHC Coupe | OWNER: Mr. J. Betterton | IMAGES: 25

JOB: 611 | TYPE: Alvis 12/70 Tourer | OWNER: Mr. V. Shaw | IMAGES: 1

JOB: 624 | TYPE: Alvis Firebird DHC | OWNER: Mr. A. Marsh | IMAGES: 64

CHAPTER 40 : VEHICLES RESTORED AT ROYLES WORKSHOPS - PART 2

ALVIS

JOB: 690　|　TYPE: Alvis 12/50 Tourer 1959　|　OWNER: Mr. J. Millman　|　IMAGES: 5

JOB: 837　|　TYPE: Alvis 1966　|　OWNER: Mr. S. Lloyd　|　IMAGES: 1

AMILCAR

JOB: 183　|　TYPE: Amilcar　|　OWNER: B. Dearden-Briggs　|　IMAGES: 13

ARGYLL

JOB: 175　|　TYPE: Argyll (prototype)　|　OWNER: Mr. B. Henderson　|　IMAGES: 2

JOB: 854　|　TYPE: Argyll 1910　|　OWNER: Mr. D. Smith　|　IMAGES: 8

ARMSTRONG SIDDELEY

JOB: 177　|　TYPE: Armstrong Siddeley　|　OWNER: Mr. P. Ward　|　IMAGES: 7

CHAPTER 40 : VEHICLES RESTORED AT ROYLES WORKSHOPS - PART 2

ARMSTRONG SIDDELEY

JOB: 449 | TYPE: Armstrong Siddeley | OWNER: H. Carter | IMAGES: 1

ARMSTRONG WHITWORTH

JOB: 275 | TYPE: 1911 Armstrong Whitworth | OWNER: Newcastle Science Museum | IMAGES: 120

Having been in the hands of the science museum at Newcastle upon Tyne since 1930, I believe, this was in exceptionally original and fine condition. It is a well engineered Edwardian motor car and was a delight to work on and drive. Some of the features which are memorable are the flywheel which incorporated fan blades to assist in cooling the engine, its overall originality, the 'letterbox' slot in the windscreen to help visability, the correct linoleum floor coverings and the original paintwork colours and features discovered under a later coat of paint.

1911 Armstrong Whitworth, restored for the Museum of Science and Engineering, Newcastle upon Tyne.

ARMSTRONG WHITWORTH

| JOB: 511 | TYPE: Replica Armstrong Whitworth | OWNER: Beamish Open Air Museum | IMAGES: 128 |

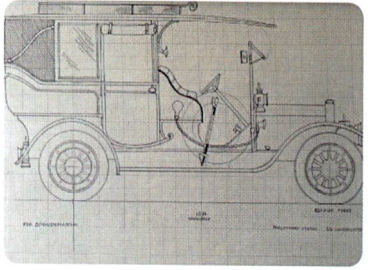
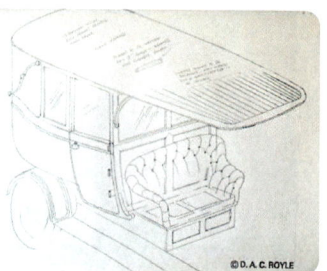

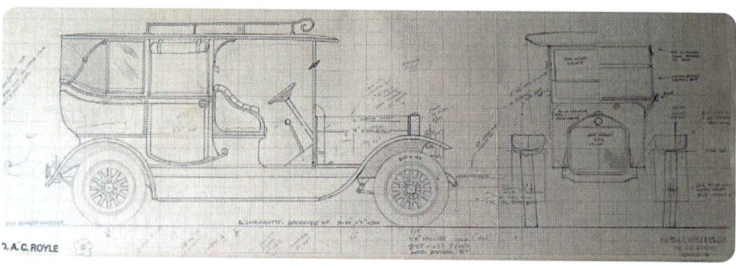

ARMSTRONG WHITWORTH

JOB: 511 | TYPE: Replica Armstrong Whitworth *continued...*

ARMSTRONG WHITWORTH

JOB: 511 | TYPE: Replica Armstrong Whitworth *continued…*

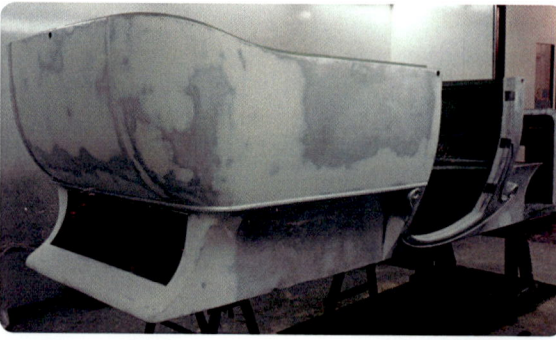

ARMSTRONG WHITWORTH

JOB: 511 | **TYPE:** Replica Armstrong Whitworth *continued...*

Lord Mantagu being driven in the 'Royle' limousine on the occasion of the official opening of the Edwardian Motor Garage at Beamish on 18 May 1994.

ASTON MARTIN

JOB: 10 | TYPE: Aston Martin DB4 | OWNER: Mr. R. Wilson | IMAGES: 3

JOB: 69 | TYPE: Aston Martin DB4 | OWNER: Mr. R. Wilson | IMAGES: 2

JOB: 150 | TYPE: Aston Martin DBX Vantage | OWNER: Mr. Thomas | IMAGES: 6

ASTON MARTIN

| JOB: 172 | TYPE: Aston Martin DB6 | OWNER: Mr. J. Snaith | IMAGES: 18 |

| JOB: 200 | TYPE: Aston Martin DB2/4 1953 | OWNER: Mr. J. Slight | IMAGES: 22 |

ASTON MARTIN

| JOB: 212 | TYPE: Aston Martin DB4 | OWNER: Mr. R. Wilson | IMAGES: 13 |

| JOB: 220 | TYPE: Aston Martin V8 | OWNER: Mr. Best | IMAGES: 9 |

| JOB: 252 | TYPE: Aston Martin 2 Litre 1938 | OWNER: Mr. A. P. Samson | IMAGES: 79 |

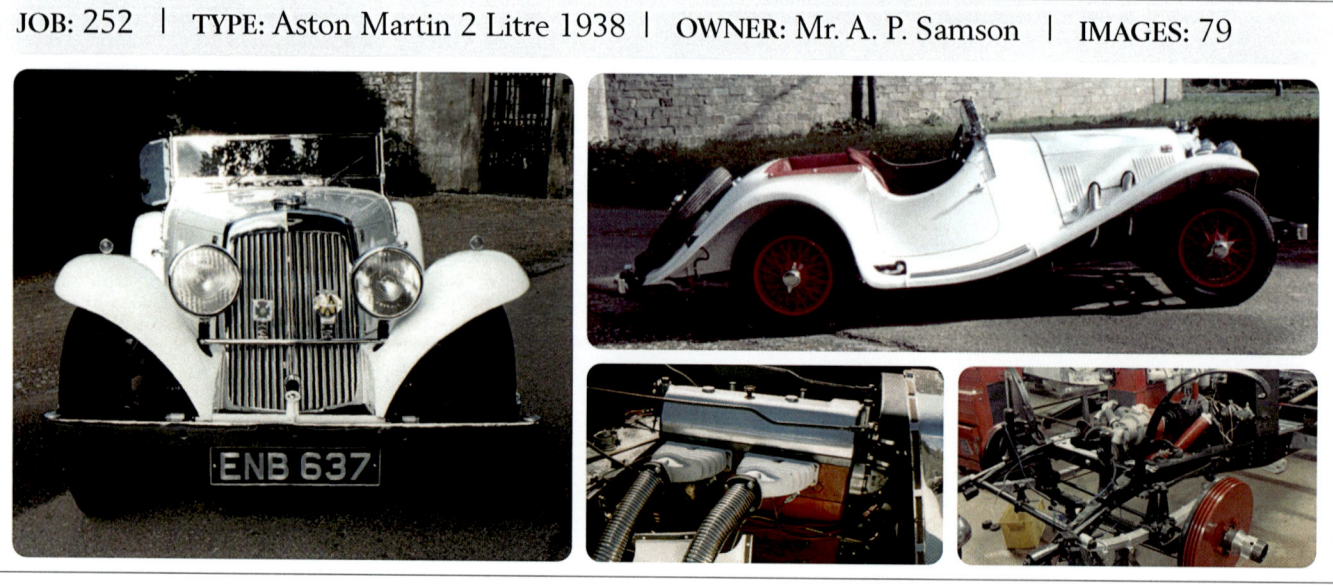

CHAPTER 40 : VEHICLES RESTORED AT ROYLES WORKSHOPS - PART 2

ASTON MARTIN

JOB: 267 | TYPE: Aston Martin DB4 1958 | OWNER: Mr. Stanger | IMAGES: 2

JOB: 270 | TYPE: Aston Martin DB2/4 DHC 1954 | OWNER: Mr. Blackwell | IMAGES: 45

JOB: 289 | TYPE: Aston Martin DB5 | OWNER: Mr. Allison | IMAGES: 9

ASTON MARTIN

JOB: 303　|　TYPE: Aston Martin DB5 1965　|　OWNER: Mr. Lobley　|　IMAGES: 89

JOB: 324　|　TYPE: Aston Martin DB1 1948　|　OWNER: Duke of Hamilton　|　IMAGES: 5

JOB: 336　|　TYPE: Aston Martin DB2/4　|　OWNER: Mr. S. Blackwell　|　IMAGES: 1

CHAPTER 40 : VEHICLES RESTORED AT ROYLES WORKSHOPS - PART 2

ASTON MARTIN

JOB: 368 | TYPE: Aston Martin DB2/4 | OWNER: Mr. J. Slight | IMAGES: 3

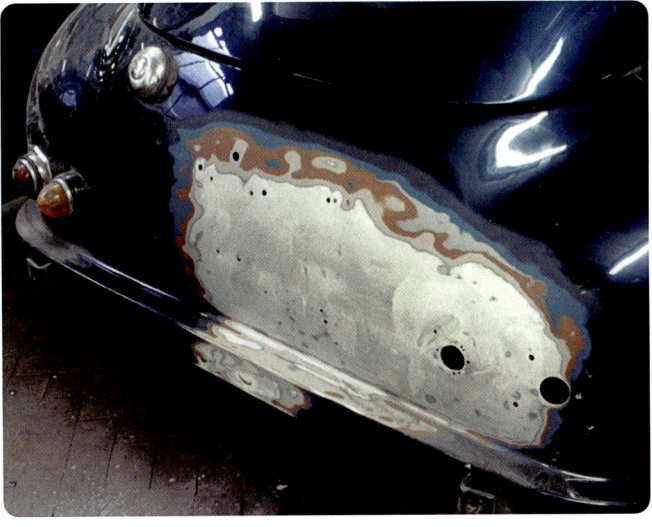

JOB: 522 | TYPE: Aston Martin DB6 MK2 | OWNER: Mr. G. Guest | IMAGES: 12

JOB: 525 | TYPE: Aston Martin DB4 | OWNER: Mr. R. Wilson | IMAGES: 3

ASTON MARTIN

| JOB: 398 | TYPE: Aston Martin DB5 Sports | OWNER: Mr. E. Carter | IMAGES: 122 |

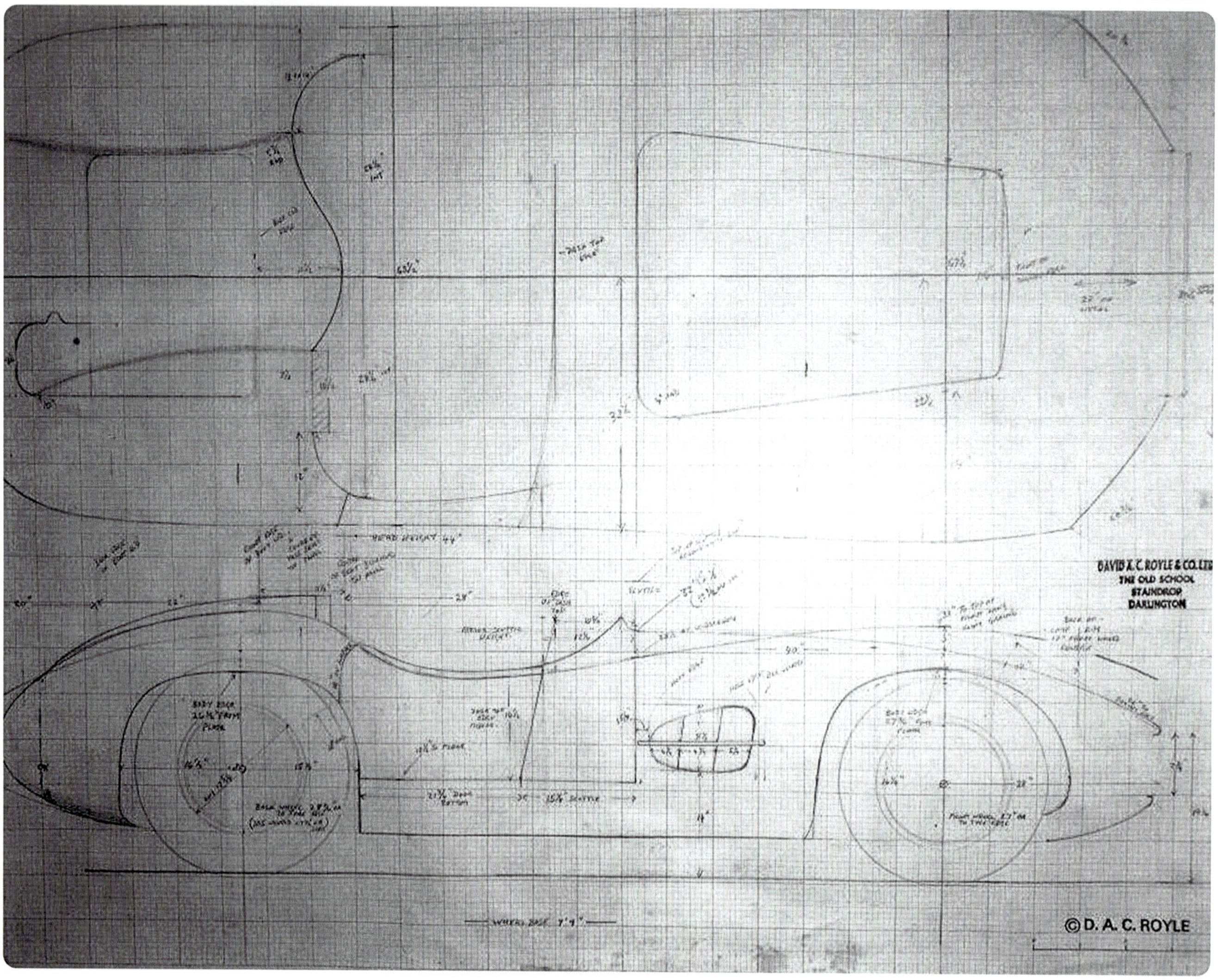

CHAPTER 40 : VEHICLES RESTORED AT ROYLES WORKSHOPS - PART 2

ASTON MARTIN

JOB: 398 | TYPE: Aston Martin DB5 Sports *continued...*

ASTON MARTIN

JOB: 398 | TYPE: Aston Martin DB5 Sports *continued...*

ASTON MARTIN

JOB: 398 | TYPE: Aston Martin DB5 Sports *continued...*

1965 Aston Martin 'BD5 Sports', rebuilt as a grand touring car to resemble a DBR 2 Racing car, using the original mechanical components.

ASTON MARTIN

JOB: 398 | TYPE: Aston Martin DB5 Sports *continued...*

A DBR2 Lookalike

In a recent issue of *The Automobile* magazine a picture of what looked like an Aston Martin DBR2 caught the eye of the Editor. It appeared under the name of Royle and Co Ltd, a vintage motor car restoration business from Staindrop near Darlington in County Durham. A letter enquiring for more details brought photographs and this most interesting reply from the proprietor David Royle:

"A customer of ours brought a DB5 saloon to us which had a most ugly modified body. The original idea was to rebuild it in the style of an Aston Martin DB3/S, but after checking dimensions, it was decided that the DBR2 was a more suitable proposition and of course, the DB5 engine is very close to the original DBR2 unit.

The existing bodywork was removed and the DB5 totally stripped down, all the Aston Martin components being retained. One of the original DBR2 cars was photographed and measured by me and the 'new' car was built to the same overall dimensions.

After completion, there was quite a lot of road testing and setting up of the suspension to give the desired ride, height and comfort. The car is very comfortable to drive, with firm but forgiving suspension; the steering is light and the brakes superb. It is, however, advisable to wear goggles.

To avoid the replica label, a plaque is fitted to the dashboard stating it is an "Aston Martin DB5 Sports", which it truly is; for a one-off special this has turned out to be a very pleasing car.

These two views of the "Aston Martin DB5 Sports" show what a fine job David Royle has done for Edward and Heather Carter. A jolly nice special!

Attached is the fact sheet on the car, giving more details of the work.

AMOC Secretary James Whyman and a few other club officials saw the car in September and the Registrar, Neil Murray, has a few details and photographs for the next Register (when it should appear under 'Specials—Ed.).

The car is owned by AMOC Members Edward and Heather Carter who plan to show the car around the various AMOC meetings this summer."

The single plug head was correct for a DBR2 in 1957. Only the S.U.'s give it away.

ASTON MARTIN DB5 SPORTS

The aim of the project was to produce a one-off car that looked like the sports racing Aston Martin DBR2.

The basis for the car was a 1965 Aston Martin DB5, Chassis No DB5/2082 R. As the 'new' car could not be raced against original sports racing cars of the era, it was decided to make a potent but 'road-usable' sports car, not a competitive machine—it even has the DB5 Heater.

All the work was carried out to a very high standard by David Royle & Co of Staindrop, Co Durham.

One of the two existing DBR2s was inspected, photographed and measured by David Royle before the project was started. The new car has the dimensions and the overall style of the DBR2 but is not a replica. All the original DB5 mechanical parts were used where possible.

The original bodywork was removed. The DB5 chassis was shortened to match the wheel-base of the DBR2 and was strengthened with square steel tubing. Standard front suspension was retained but the rear suspension incorporated DB6 radius arms and adjustable shock absorbers with the DB5 rear axle. New springs, with different ratings to allow for the lighter car, were fitted during road testing. The wire wheels are 15", 72 spoke fitted with Avon Radial 225/70 VR15 tyres.

The twin camshaft 4 litre engine number 400-1298 was overhauled, a new clutch fitted and the assembly balanced. The engine was moved back about 16" and lowered about 5". To achieve minimum ground clearance of 4", the depth of the sump was halved but extended to the front of the engine to retain the original oil capacity.

A substantial steel sump guard was made and fitted. Triple SU carburettors were retained and 'Vantage' camshafts fitted. The ZF 5 speed gearbox is further back in the chassis so the propshaft was shortened and the gear lever bent forward.

A special stainless steel exhaust system was designed and fitted so that it comes out below the passenger door as with the DBR2. A silencer was incorporated but it still retains the typical Aston sound.

The body was built using the 'superleggera' system of rolled aluminium over thin steel tubing. Aircraft anti-corrosion DTD 900/448 jointing compound was applied between all steel to aluminium joints.

The front and rear body sections are easily removable for access. The scuttle area is also removable for access to wiring and instruments.

The use of steel tubing plus stronger 16 gauge aluminium has made the body panels quite robust, unlike the competition cars. The car is painted British Racing Green using modern twin pack paint. The windscreen and headlight covers are made of perspex.

Five beautifully copied spring loaded clips were hand-made to hold down bonnet, boot lid and petrol covers. A full-sized spare wheel is located in the boot.

Although the instruments are all from the DB5, the cockpit does resemble the DBR2. The simple interior is trimmed with black leather and with green leather seats.

With a weight of 23cwt, the new car is substantially lighter than the DB5 but not as light as the DBR2 which is 18cwt approximately.

AM MAGAZINE SPRING 1990

Aston Martin Quarterly Magazine - Spring 1990.

CHAPTER 40 : VEHICLES RESTORED AT ROYLES WORKSHOPS - PART 2

ASTON MARTIN

JOB: 619 | TYPE: Aston Martin Racing Car | OWNER: Yorkshire Car Collection | IMAGES: 5

JOB: 769 | TYPE: Aston Martin DB6 Convertible | OWNER: Mr. T. Zymelka | IMAGES: 37

JOB: 778 | TYPE: Aston Martin Ulster | OWNER: Mr. C. Bennett | IMAGES: 44

AUSTIN

JOB: 3　|　TYPE: Austin Healey 12/4 1926　|　OWNER: Mr. J. Denton　|　IMAGES: 7

JOB: 11　|　TYPE: Austin 10 Lichfield 1935　|　OWNER: Mr. E. Dobinson　|　IMAGES: 1

JOB: 31　|　TYPE: Austin Princess 1955　|　OWNER: Mr. Battye　|　IMAGES: 4

AUSTIN

| JOB: 34 | TYPE: Austin 12/6 1934/35 | OWNER: Mr. D. Hogg | IMAGES: 15 |

| JOB: 81 | TYPE: Austin Healey 16/6 Saloon 1928 | OWNER: Mr. Kerin | IMAGES: 4 |

| JOB: 110 | TYPE: Austin 12/4 | OWNER: Mr. Kerin | IMAGES: 3 |

AUSTIN

JOB: 122 | TYPE: Austin 7 Nippy | OWNER: Mr. Oliver | IMAGES: 1

JOB: 196 | TYPE: Austin 7 Chummy | REFERENCE: Royle Hepworth | IMAGES: 4

JOB: 205 | TYPE: Austin Eton 1935/36 | OWNER: Mr. I. Grinton-Smith | IMAGES: 23

AUSTIN

JOB: 228 | TYPE: 1911 Austin 15 | OWNER: Mr. McKenna | IMAGES: 8

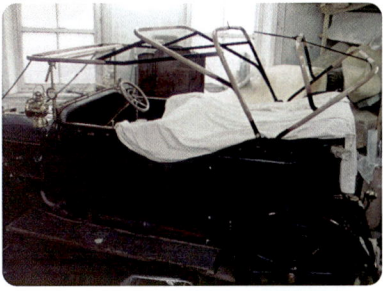

JOB: 244 | TYPE: Austin 20 1925 | OWNER: Mr. Bidwell Topham | IMAGES: 47

JOB: 262 | TYPE: Austin Princess | OWNER: Mr. Shepherd | IMAGES: 3

AUSTIN

JOB: 294 | TYPE: Austin Burnham Saloon | OWNER: Mr. J. Campbell | IMAGES: 7

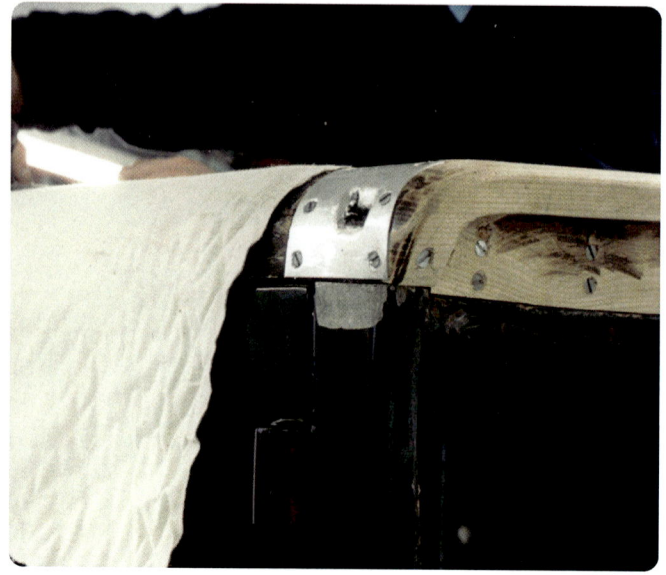

JOB: 308 | TYPE: Austin 7 2 seater 1930 | OWNER: Mr. Bailey | IMAGES: 3

JOB: 339 | TYPE: Austin 10 Sherbourne | OWNER: Mr. Barnett | IMAGES: 6

AUSTIN

JOB: 378 | TYPE: Austin 7 Box Saloon 1933 | REFERENCE: Royle Cars | IMAGES: 1

JOB: 409 | TYPE: Austin 1931 | OWNER: Mr. J. Campbell | IMAGES: 9

JOB: 440 | TYPE: Austin 7 Tourer | OWNER: Mr. P. Lockhart | IMAGES: 49

AUSTIN

| JOB: 453 | TYPE: Austin 10.4 | REFERENCE: Royle Cars | IMAGES: 4 |

| JOB: 478 | TYPE: Austin 20HP | REFERENCE: Royle Cars | IMAGES: 6 |

CHAPTER 40 : VEHICLES RESTORED AT ROYLES WORKSHOPS - PART 2

AUSTIN

JOB: 568 | TYPE: Austin 10 Saloon 1934 | OWNER: Mr. P. Robinson | IMAGES: 24

AUSTIN

JOB: 578 | TYPE: Austin Saloon 1938 | OWNER: Mr. V. Shaw | IMAGES: 1

JOB: 582 | TYPE: Austin 7 Bantam (USA) | OWNER: Mr. C. Oliver | IMAGES: 49

JOB: 665 | TYPE: Austin Heavy 12/4 Tourer | OWNER: Mr. J. Cave | IMAGES: 1

AUSTIN

JOB: 673 | TYPE: Austin Ant 4WD | OWNER: Duke of Hamilton | IMAGES: 19

JOB: 695 | TYPE: Austin 12/4 1926 | OWNER: Mr. R. Duwe | IMAGES: 160

The vehicle is completely stripped down to the bare chassis and a photographic record, as normal, was made progressively as the work proceeded. In this case 160 photographs were taken. A small selection are shown here. It was beneficial to find that, whilst this Austin was built in 1926, it is naturally showing its age after 85 years, but it is a most original example and the ideal basis for restoration.

AUSTIN

JOB: 695　｜　TYPE: Austin 12/4 1926 *continued...*

The bodywork is tackled first, the sound original frames are retained and new timber frames made to replace weak or damages ones. The outer steel panelling is examined and rusty areas are cut away and new metal is beaten and rolled into shape and then seam welded into place without distortion. The result is a sound and strong body once more. The timbers and inside panels are then treated and painted to protect and help preserve them.

The complete engine is removed and mounted onto a rotating engine bed. It is then completely stripped down, thoroughly cleaned, examined and measured. The cylinder block is rebored and the surfaces of the head and block machined and new pistons, bearings, valves and guides fitted, along with a new clutch plates.

AUSTIN

JOB: 695 | TYPE: Austin 12/4 1926 *continued...*

Here we can see some of the components stripped down, the starter motor, its bendix and the commutator, brushes and mounting. The fan, various mountings, the starter dog and housing, the timing wheels, all cleaned and where appropriate, polished.

After overhaul, the engine is reassembled. The crankshaft has been ground and new main and big end bearings cast and fitted, the clutch has had new plates riveted into place and reassembled. The camshaft has also been ground and refitted with new bearings, along with the valve gear. The water pump, timing gear and magneto have been overhauled and refitted and timed and the entire engine reassembled ready for testing on its engine bed, before being remounted onto the chassis.

AUSTIN

JOB: 695 | **TYPE:** Austin 12/4 1926 *continued...*

After removal from the chassis, the Rear axle has been stripped down, blast cleaned, examined and new bearings fitted and the crown wheel, the pinion and half shafts overhauled as necessary. Neil is seen here reassembling the unit after the casing has been painted.

The Front axle has also been removed from the chassis. Like the rear axle, after being stripped down and blast cleaned, all the components are washed off and checked. The leaf springs are overhauled along with the shackle pins and bushes. The brakes shoes are renewed and riveted into place and reassembled onto the back plates which have been re-bushed and painted. The wheel bearings, King pins and bushes have been renewed and the track rod end springs, cups and ball joints overhauled. The axle has been painted before assembly and all grease nipples cleaned and checked.

AUSTIN

JOB: 695 | **TYPE:** Austin 12/4 1926 *continued...*

All four doors have been shot blasted and new wooden frames made and fitted as necessary. The four mudguards have also been shot blasted and new steel repair panels have been panel beaten, wheeled up and then seam welded into place wherever necessary. Sometimes a completely new mudguard has to be made as can be seen here. This will precisely copy the details of the original one.

After overhaul, the bonnet panels, the doors, the mudguards and the running boards are assembled to the main bodywork to check the fit. It is important that this pre-assembly is carried out, as every part has been disturbed and re-worked. Once this has been done and any necessary adjustments made, the main sections of the bodywork can be painted. Here it can be seen outside the fully filtered Paint booth and Bake oven at Royles.

AUSTIN

JOB: 695 | TYPE: Austin 12/4 1926 *continued...*

In 1925 and 1926, the change over from Nickel Silver plating of the many fittings and brightwork used on Vintage motor cars was changing to Chromium Plating. This 1926 Austin retains its period silver finish, but like most manufacturers, was planning to change to chromium plating.

It is worth mentioning here that the work involved keeping Nickel Silver brightly polished is considerable. A shower of rain or just a few drops of water when topping up the radiator, was sufficient to bring out the metal polish and apply a little elbow grease! At this time, many of the soldiers in the 1914-1918 world war had driven trucks and other motorised vehicles, so increasing numbers of people were taking an interest in motor cars for the first time. People who couldn't afford to employ chauffeurs who had traditionally polished the brightwork, so the pressure was on the manufacturers to change to chromium plating which needed little attention to stay bright. The many small components which are shown here are only those fitted to the bodywork, there are quite a lot more fittings around the car, a big job.

CHAPTER 40 : VEHICLES RESTORED AT ROYLES WORKSHOPS - PART 2

AUSTIN

JOB: 695 | **TYPE:** Austin 12/4 1926 *continued...*

These show the Austin Dash board when it came to us. The long term effect of the elements on nickel silver are clearly seen on the bezels of these original instruments. The great benefit of working on vintage motor cars is the quality of the materials used. After stripping them down and re-plating the brass, which they are made of, the result is well worth the effort and cost. When the Austin is being assembled, the benefit of Nickel Silver can be seen. It is a softer and much more attractive finish than chrome and gives pleasure to both the restorers and the owners of these early vehicles.

This photograph of a small area of the car reveals the high standard of finish and details of the fittings. Even the running board step, the Austin door plate, the seat adjuster, the leather piping on the carpet edges and the braiding on the edge of the leather front seat are redolent of a luxury motor car rather than an Austin. The door mirror on the carpet is waiting to be screwed into place.

337

AUSTIN

JOB: 695 | **TYPE:** Austin 12/4 1926 *continued...*

The first shows that the waterproof fabric roof covering has been fitted. This is padded with wadding and covers the laths which can be seen in an earlier photograph. The guttering has yet to be fitted.

The second picture shows the dash board and the many hardwood door, window and interior cappings after being stripped, rubbed down ready to be varnished. There are 54 pieces altogether, each one of which is neatly fitted as finishers all around the interior of the car.

The third picture shows the finishers in place, with the deep buttoned leather upholstery in the process of being fitted. The overall effect and rich colours combine to give this Austin a sense of luxury.

These show the finished car. The Nickel Silver radiator, lamps and fittings setting off the functional shape of the bodywork of these solid reliable vintage motor cars.

CHAPTER 40 : VEHICLES RESTORED AT ROYLES WORKSHOPS - PART 2

AUSTIN

JOB: 705 | TYPE: Austin A40 Farina | OWNER: Mr. R. Calvert | IMAGES: 22

JOB: 714 | TYPE: Austin 20HP Limousine | OWNER: Mr. K. Ritchings | IMAGES: 6

AUSTIN

JOB: 717 | TYPE: Austin Seven Saloon | OWNER: Mr. A. Birkbeck | IMAGES: 24

JOB: 763 | TYPE: Austin 1911 | OWNER: Mr. N. Corner | IMAGES: 7

JOB: 846 | TYPE: Austin 7 Tourer | OWNER: Mr. C. Oliver | IMAGES: 5

CHAPTER 40 : VEHICLES RESTORED AT ROYLES WORKSHOPS - PART 2

AUSTIN

JOB: 755 | TYPE: Austin 16-6 1930 | OWNER: Mr. Collins | IMAGES: 3

AUSTIN HEALEY

JOB: 95 | TYPE: Austin Healey 3000 | OWNER: Mr. Shaw | IMAGES: 12

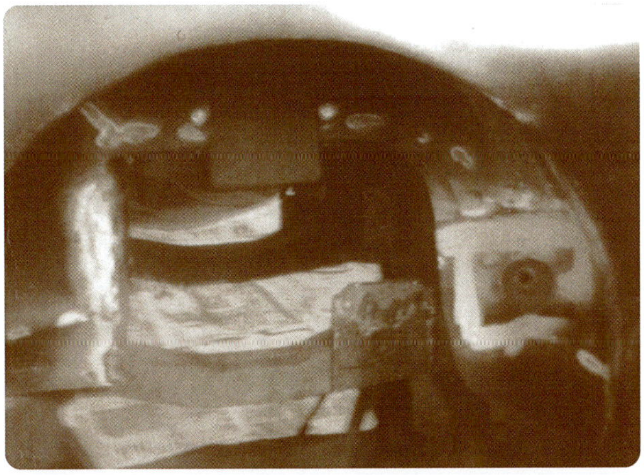

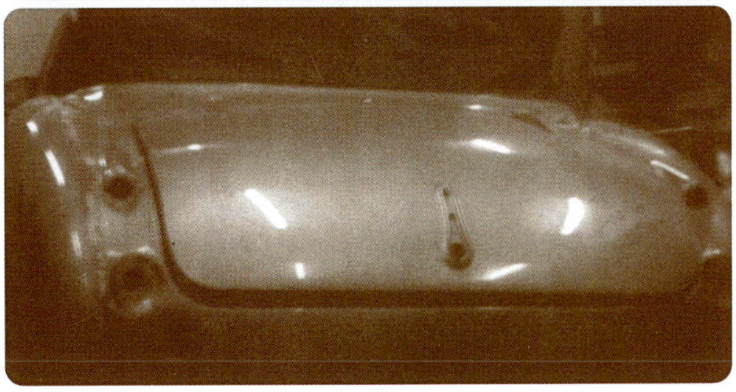

AUSTIN HEALEY

JOB: 213 | TYPE: Austin Healey Sprite MK1 | OWNER: Mr. Newlyn | IMAGES: 1

JOB: 479 | TYPE: Austin Healey 100/6 | OWNER: Mr. D. Phillips | IMAGES: 2

CHAPTER 40 : VEHICLES RESTORED AT ROYLES WORKSHOPS - PART 2

AUSTIN HEALEY

| JOB: 225 | TYPE: Austin Healey 3000 | OWNER: Mr. Grimwade | IMAGES: 34 |

343

BEARDMORE

| JOB: 515 | TYPE: Beardmore Taxi | REFERENCE: Royle Cars | IMAGES: 1 |

BEDFORD

| JOB: 637 | TYPE: Bedford Truck | OWNER: Mr. G. Atkinson | IMAGES: 86 |

BELSIZE

| JOB: 389 | TYPE: Belsize 1919-21 | REFERENCE: Royle Cars | IMAGES: 3 |

BENTLEY

| JOB: 22 | TYPE: Bentley 4.25 Litre | OWNER: Mr. P. Connon | IMAGES: 10 |

| JOB: 78 | TYPE: Bentley 4 Litre 1931 | OWNER: Squadron Leader Balean | IMAGES: 1 |

BENTLEY

| JOB: 129 | TYPE: Bentley Mallalieu 1947 | OWNER: Mr. I. Pitkethley | IMAGES: 1 |

| JOB: 133 | TYPE: Bentley 3.5 Litre | OWNER: Mr. Hamer Boot | IMAGES: 60 |

CHAPTER 40 : VEHICLES RESTORED AT ROYLES WORKSHOPS - PART 2

BENTLEY

JOB: 136　|　TYPE: Bentley R Type　|　OWNER: Mr. Hauxwell　|　IMAGES: 32

JOB: 158　|　TYPE: Bentley S3 Continental　|　OWNER: Mrs. M. Fattorini　|　IMAGES: 29

JOB: 221　|　TYPE: Bentley S2　|　REFERENCE: Royle Hepworth　|　IMAGES: 1

BENTLEY

| JOB: 153 | TYPE: Bentley 3 Litre VDP | OWNER: Mr. H. Salisbury | IMAGES: 116 |

1925 Bentley 3 litre by Vanden Plas, restored for Mr Harold.H.Salisbury.

This substantially original example of a vintage 3 litre Bentley had been stored for many years in a garage on a private estate in North Yorkshire. The entrance was so overgrown that small trees and shrubs had to be cleared away in order to be able to load it on a trailer to take it to Staindrop. This fine, original motor car was stripped down and was found to be in generally sound condition. The leather trim was faithfully reproduced and the bodywork needed some minor repairs to the ash frame. Some small areas of the aluminium panelling had to be renewed by shaping and seam welding new metal into place.

A windscreen of the correct pattern was made to replace the non-original unit which had been fitted. Unusually, this Bentley had its original set of side screens which was a bonus. When restored, they revealed the interesting appearance of these attractive vintage touring cars when fitted up for bad weather. Various aspects of the mechanical components needed attention and these were overhauled and attended to as instructed.

BENTLEY

JOB: 153 | TYPE: Bentley 3 Litre VDP *continued...*

BENTLEY

JOB: 153 | TYPE: Bentley 3 Litre VDP *continued...*

CHAPTER 40 : VEHICLES RESTORED AT ROYLES WORKSHOPS - PART 2

BENTLEY

JOB: 153 | TYPE: Bentley 3 Litre VDP *continued...*

BENTLEY

| JOB: 271 | TYPE: Bentley 4.5 Litre Sports Saloon 1937 | REFERENCE: Royle Hepworth | IMAGES: 1 |

| JOB: 306 | TYPE: Bentley Mk V1 R Special | OWNER: Mr. J. Ambler | IMAGES: 4 |

| JOB: 317 | TYPE: Bentley | OWNER: Mr. J. Ambler | IMAGES: 3 |

CHAPTER 40 : VEHICLES RESTORED AT ROYLES WORKSHOPS - PART 2

BENTLEY

JOB: 319 | TYPE: Bentley 3.5 DHC | OWNER: Mr. Darbyshire | IMAGES: 4

JOB: 327 | TYPE: Bentley 6.5 | OWNER: Mr. Bidwell Topham | IMAGES: 36

JOB: 332 | TYPE: Bentley 6.5 | OWNER: Mr. D. A. C. Royle & Mr. R. B. B. Ropner | IMAGES: 67

BENTLEY

JOB: 353 | TYPE: Bentley S2 | OWNER: Mr. J. Doggart | IMAGES: 12

JOB: 361 | TYPE: Bentley Mk VI | OWNER: Mr. B. Skrentney | IMAGES: 46

JOB: 376 | TYPE: Bentley 3 DHC | OWNER: Mr. P. Thompson | IMAGES: 6

CHAPTER 40 : VEHICLES RESTORED AT ROYLES WORKSHOPS - PART 2

BENTLEY

JOB: 406 | TYPE: Bentley Barnato | OWNER: Mr. K. Schellenberg | IMAGES: 24

JOB: 438 | TYPE: Bentley 1953 | OWNER: Mr. D. Fothergill | IMAGES: 47

JOB: 442 | TYPE: Bentley 4.5 litre Tourer | OWNER: Mr. B. Henderson | IMAGES: 1

355

ROYLE. FROM VINTAGE TO CLASSIC TO AMPHIBIAN.

BENTLEY

JOB: 451 | TYPE: Bentley 3 Litre Tourer | REFERENCE: Royle Cars | IMAGES: 1

JOB: 452 | TYPE: Bentley Mk II DHC | OWNER: Mr. Bidwell Topham | IMAGES: 2

JOB: 466 | TYPE: Bentley 1935 | OWNER: Mr. C. Lunt | IMAGES: 2

CHAPTER 40 : VEHICLES RESTORED AT ROYLES WORKSHOPS - PART 2

BENTLEY

JOB: 494 | TYPE: Bentley S3 | OWNER: Mr. P. Thompson | IMAGES: 170

JOB: 538 | TYPE: Bentley R Type Continental | OWNER: Mr. A. Fletcher | IMAGES: 23

JOB: 596 | TYPE: Bentley Turbo | OWNER: Mr. A. Davison | IMAGES: 25

BENTLEY

JOB: 628 | TYPE: Bentley Continental 1957 | OWNER: Mr. P. Noble | IMAGES: 2

JOB: 653 | TYPE: Bentley Continental | OWNER: Mr. J. Martin | IMAGES: 5

JOB: 663 | TYPE: Bentley Barker Body DHC | OWNER: Mr. J. Martin | IMAGES: 10

BENTLEY

JOB: 669 | TYPE: Bentley Saloon | OWNER: Mr. D. Badby | IMAGES: 1

JOB: 674 | TYPE: Bentley 4.25 Litre DHC | OWNER: Mr. D. Beatty | IMAGES: 1

JOB: 677 | TYPE: Bentley 3/4 0.5 Sports | OWNER: Mr. S. Laycock | IMAGES: 27

BENTLEY

| JOB: 684 | TYPE: H. J. Mulliner Bentley Mk VI DHC | OWNER: Mr. D. Beatty | IMAGES: 36 |

| JOB: 704 | TYPE: Bentley Drophead Continental | OWNER: Mr. J. Martin | IMAGES: 15 |

| JOB: 747 | TYPE: Bentley Derby Hooper DHC | OWNER: Mr. B. Davies | IMAGES: 15 |

BENTLEY

JOB: 758 | TYPE: Bentley 4.5Litre Windscreen | OWNER: Mr. D. Hodgson | IMAGES: 1

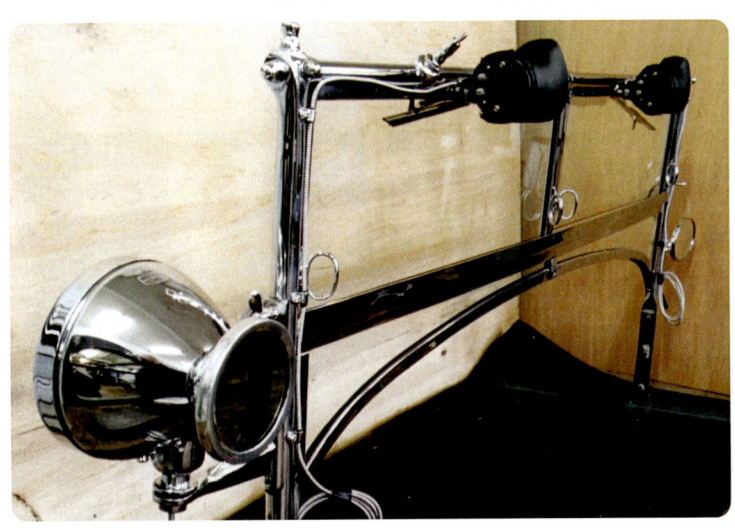

JOB: 859 | TYPE: Bentley Mk VI Sports | OWNER: Mr. A. Lax | IMAGES: 4

JOB: 848 | TYPE: Bentley 3/4 0.5 | OWNER: Mr. Marshall Bailey | IMAGES: 5

BIANCHI

| JOB: 9 | TYPE: Bianchi 1926 | OWNER: The Dobinson Family | IMAGES: 2 |

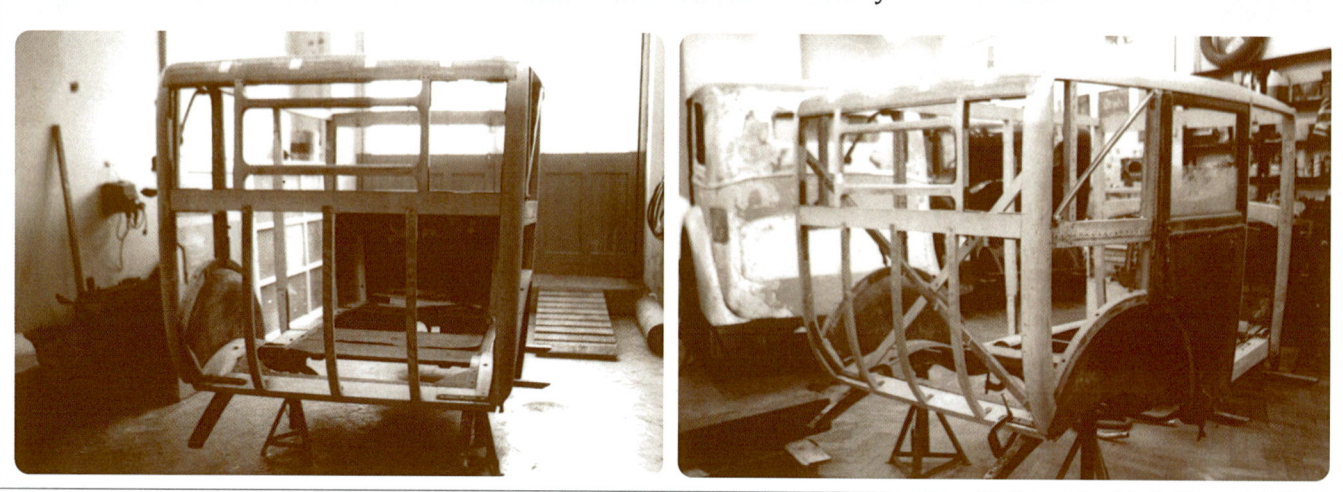

BMW

| JOB: 168 | TYPE: BMW 3.0 CSL | OWNER: Mr. Milbourne | IMAGES: 59 |

A winning pair at Harewood House. Job 168, 1973 BMW 3.0 CSL, and Job 189, 1976 BMW 2002. Both Motor cars restored for Mr Michael Milbourne.

CHAPTER 40 : VEHICLES RESTORED AT ROYLES WORKSHOPS - PART 2

BMW

JOB: 168 | TYPE: BMW 3.0 CSL *continued...*

BMW

JOB: 250　|　TYPE: BMW 2002 1975　|　OWNER: Mr. Milbourne　|　IMAGES: 13

JOB: 283　|　TYPE: BMW 326 1937　|　OWNER: Mr. Pollard　|　IMAGES: 109

BOATS

JOB: 727　|　TYPE: Broom Capricorn　|　OWNER: Mr. D. A. C. Royle　|　IMAGES: 4

CHAPTER 40 : VEHICLES RESTORED AT ROYLES WORKSHOPS - PART 2

BOATS

JOB: 737 | TYPE: Delta Racing Boat | OWNER: Mr. F. Purvis | IMAGES: 11

BOWSER PETROL PUMP

JOB: 462 | TYPE: Bowser Petrol Pump | OWNER: Mr. C. Hough | IMAGES: 4

BRISTOL

JOB: 45 | TYPE: Bristol 403 | OWNER: F. Murray | IMAGES: 3

BRISTOL

| JOB: 309 | TYPE: Bristol 406 1958 | OWNER: Mr. Spencer | IMAGES: 42 |

| JOB: 407 | TYPE: Bristol 400 DHC | OWNER: Mr. J. Howden Richards | IMAGES: 13 |

| JOB: 424 | TYPE: Bristol 405 DHC | OWNER: Mr. R. Peacock | IMAGES: 19 |

BRISTOL

JOB: 460　|　TYPE: Bristol 400 1949　|　OWNER: Dr. J. Issacs　|　IMAGES: 90

JOB: 580　|　TYPE: Bristol 400 Saloon　|　OWNER: Mr. J. Charlton　|　IMAGES: 49

JOB: 616　|　TYPE: Bristol 400 Saloon　|　OWNER: Mr. I. Thomson　|　IMAGES: 10

BROUGH

| JOB: 726 | TYPE: Brough Superior | OWNER: Mr. F. Jenkins | IMAGES: 26 |

BSA

| JOB: 288 | TYPE: BSA Bantam Motorcycle | OWNER: Mr. Park | IMAGES: 3 |

| JOB: 445 | TYPE: BSA Scout 4 Wheel Tourer | REFERENCE: Royle Cars | IMAGES: 5 |

BUGATTI

| JOB: 155 | TYPE: Bugatti Halford | OWNER: Mr. W. Park | IMAGES: 145 |

The Type 35 Bugatti Special. Fitted with a Halford Engine by Lord Ridley for the owner, Mr W. Park.

BUGATTI

JOB: 155 | TYPE: Bugatti Halford *continued...*

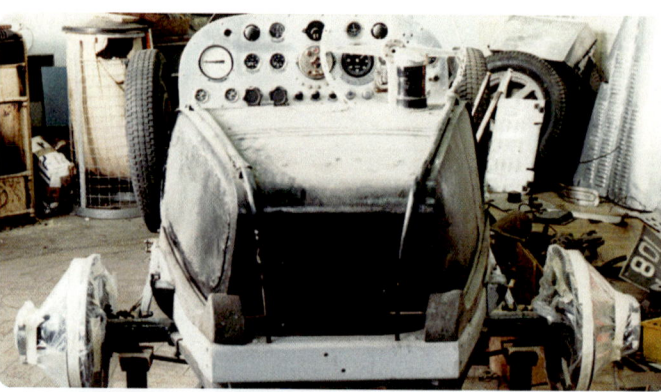

JOB: 155 | TYPE: Bugatti Halford *continued...*

CHAPTER 40 : VEHICLES RESTORED AT ROYLES WORKSHOPS - PART 2

BUGATTI

JOB: 155 | TYPE: Bugatti Halford *continued...*

BUGATTI

JOB: 155 | TYPE: Bugatti Halford *continued...*

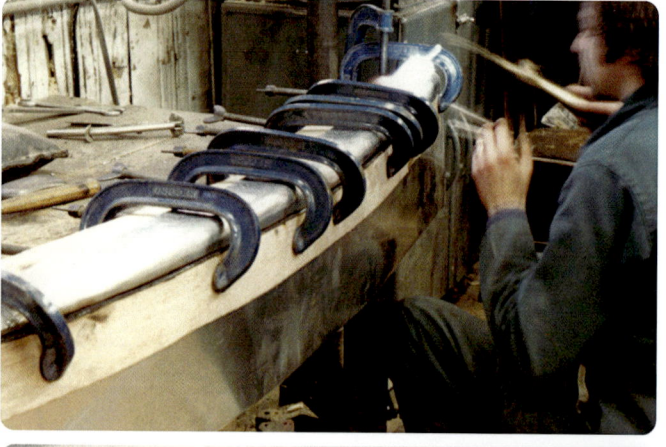

BUGATTI

JOB: 155 | TYPE: Bugatti Halford *continued...*

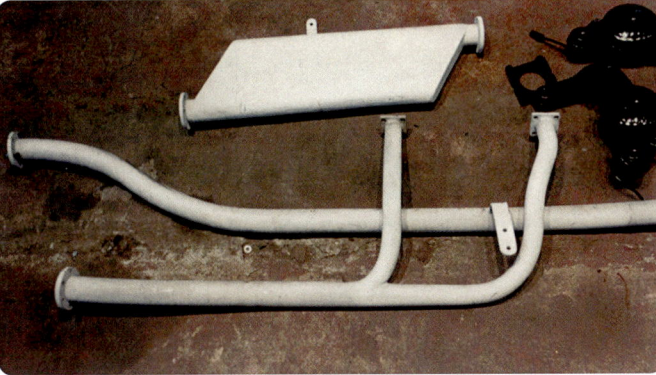

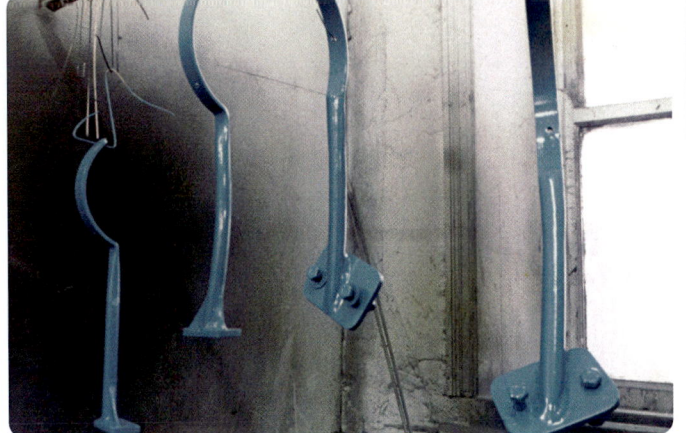

BUGATTI

JOB: 155 | TYPE: Bugatti Halford *continued...*

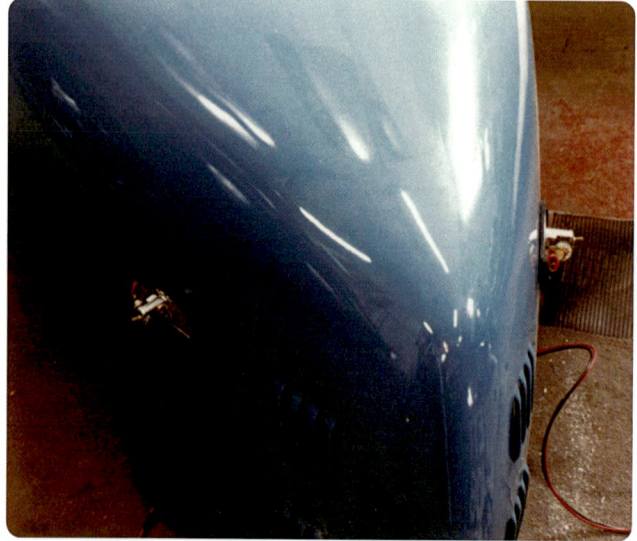

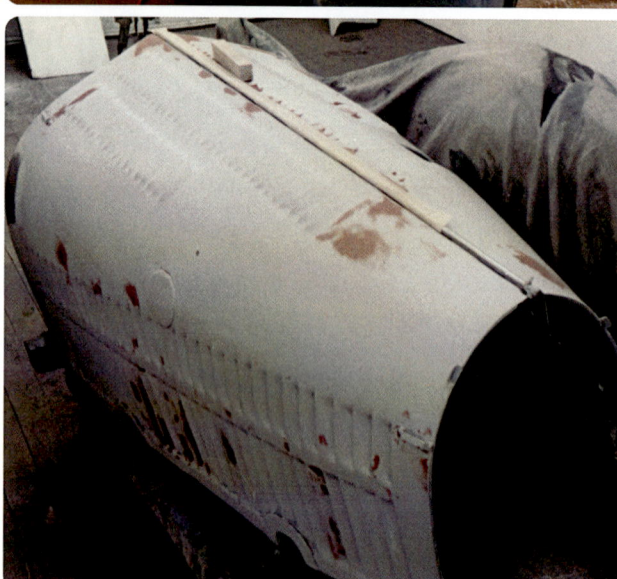

BUGATTI

JOB: 155 | TYPE: Bugatti Halford *continued...*

375

BUGATTI

JOB: 155 | TYPE: Bugatti Halford *continued...*

BUGATTI

JOB: 155 | TYPE: Bugatti Halford *continued...*

ROYLE. FROM VINTAGE TO CLASSIC TO AMPHIBIAN.

BUGATTI

JOB: 155 | TYPE: Bugatti Halford *continued...*

BUGATTI

JOB: 155 | TYPE: Bugatti Halford *continued...*

BUGATTI

JOB: 253 | TYPE: Bugatti Type 23 | OWNER: Mr. D. Fielding | IMAGES: 26

CADILLAC

JOB: 785 | TYPE: Cadillac 1966 | OWNER: Mr. D. Emerey | IMAGES: 3

CHEVROLET

JOB: 377 | TYPE: Chevrolet | OWNER: R. Greetham | IMAGES: 27

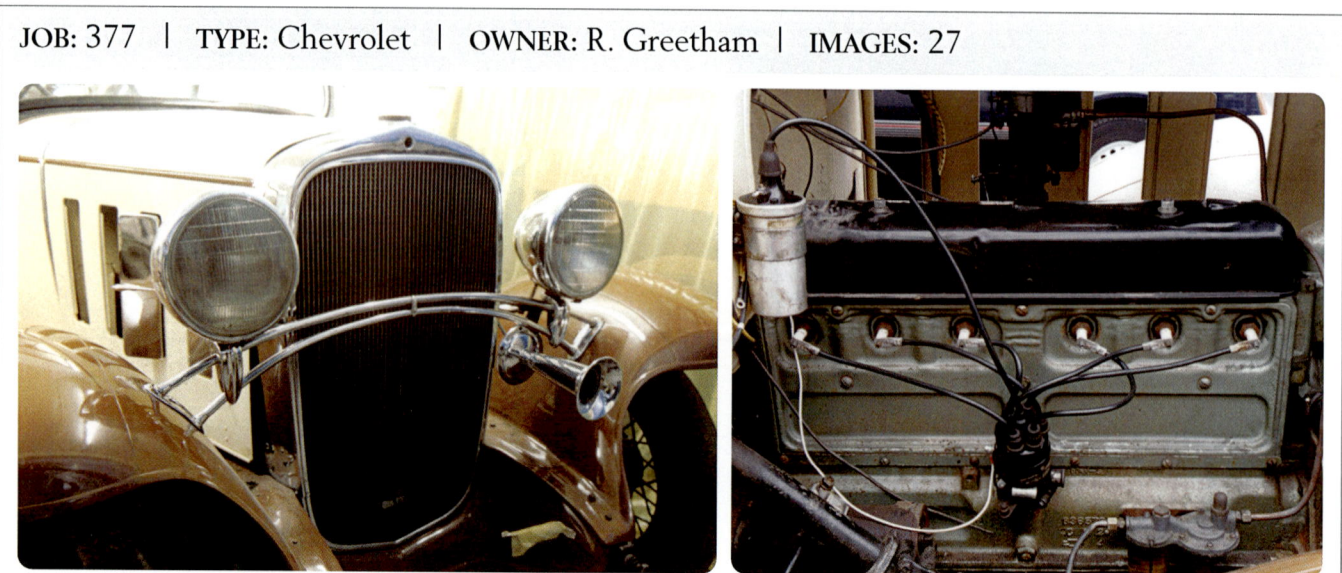

CHENARD WALCKER

JOB: 232 | TYPE: Chenard Walcker | OWNER: J. Hallam | IMAGES: 7

CHRYSLER

JOB: 604 | TYPE: Chrysler Richmond 6 Sedan | OWNER: Mr. Garland | IMAGES: 6

CITROEN

JOB: 518 | TYPE: Citroen Light 15 Saloon | OWNER: Mr. I. Bartlett | IMAGES: 80

JOB: 564 | TYPE: Citroen 'Cloverleaf' | OWNER: Mr. G. Hadfield | IMAGES: 45

JOB: 710 | TYPE: Citroen 1921 2 Seater | OWNER: Mr. G. Hadfield | IMAGES: 9

CITROEN

| JOB: 801 | TYPE: Citroen 'H' Van | OWNER: Mr. D. Mitchell | IMAGES: 16 |

CROSSLEY

| JOB: 495 | TYPE: Crossley 2 litre Tourer | OWNER: Lt. Col. S.C.E. Weld | IMAGES: 1 |

| JOB: 823 | TYPE: Crossley | OWNER: Lt. Col. S.C.E. Weld | IMAGES: 1 |

DAIMLER

| JOB: 167 | TYPE: Daimler ST8 1938 | OWNER: Mr. J. Turbitt | IMAGES: 2 |

| JOB: 178 | TYPE: Daimler Consort | OWNER: Mr. Hawdon | IMAGES: 4 |

CHAPTER 40 : VEHICLES RESTORED AT ROYLES WORKSHOPS - PART 2

DAIMLER

JOB: 239 | TYPE: Daimler Sovereign 1974 | OWNER: Mr. D. Hogg | IMAGES: 18

JOB: 285 | TYPE: Daimler Sovereign 4.2 1974 | OWNER: Mr. D. Royle | IMAGES: 5

JOB: 342 | TYPE: Daimler Empress | OWNER: H. A. M. van Asten | IMAGES: 95

DAIMLER

| JOB: 459 | TYPE: Daimler Light 15 | REFERENCE: Royle Cars | IMAGES: 1 |

| JOB: 512 | TYPE: Daimler Straight 8 | REFERENCE: Royle Cars | IMAGES: 2 |

| JOB: 632 | TYPE: Daimler | OWNER: J. Inge Markhus | IMAGES: 34 |

DAIMLER

JOB: 640 | TYPE: Daimler Majestic Major | OWNER: Mr. J. Bidwell-Topham | IMAGES: 1

JOB: 685 | TYPE: Daimler Barker Special | OWNER: Mr. K. Boardall | IMAGES: 100

JOB: 691 | TYPE: Daimler V8 Saloon | OWNER: Mr. C. Laws | IMAGES: 14

DARRACQ

| JOB: 134 | TYPE: Darracq 1907 | OWNER: Mr. K. Barley | IMAGES: 2 |

DELAGE

| JOB: 286 | TYPE: Delage D8 15N | OWNER: Prince Rainier III of Monaco | IMAGES: 12 |

DELAGE

JOB: 151 | TYPE: Delage DMS | OWNER: Mr. Peddie | IMAGES: 175

1927 Delage DMS Sports Tourer restored for Mr Donald Peddie in Scotland.

DELAGE

JOB: 151 | TYPE: Delage DMS *continued...*

DELAGE

JOB: 151 | TYPE: Delage DMS *continued...*

DELAGE

JOB: 151 | TYPE: Delage DMS *continued...*

CHAPTER 40 : VEHICLES RESTORED AT ROYLES WORKSHOPS - PART 2

DELAGE

JOB: 151 | TYPE: Delage DMS *continued...*

DELAGE

JOB: 151 | **TYPE:** Delage DMS *continued...*

DELAGE

JOB: 151 | **TYPE:** Delage DMS *continued...*

DELAGE

JOB: 151 | TYPE: Delage DMS *continued...*

CHAPTER 40 : VEHICLES RESTORED AT ROYLES WORKSHOPS - PART 2

DELAGE

JOB: 151 | TYPE: Delage DMS *continued...*

DELAGE

JOB: 151 | TYPE: Delage DMS *continued...*

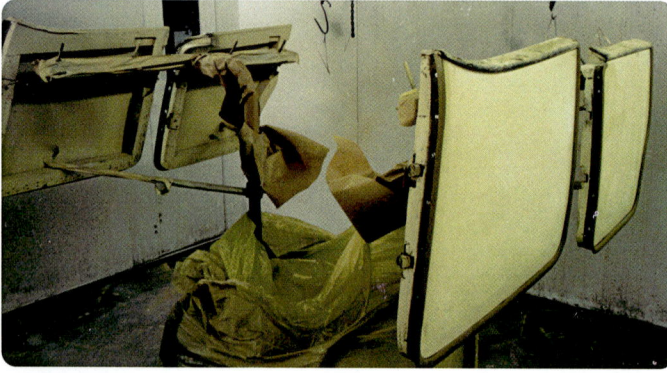

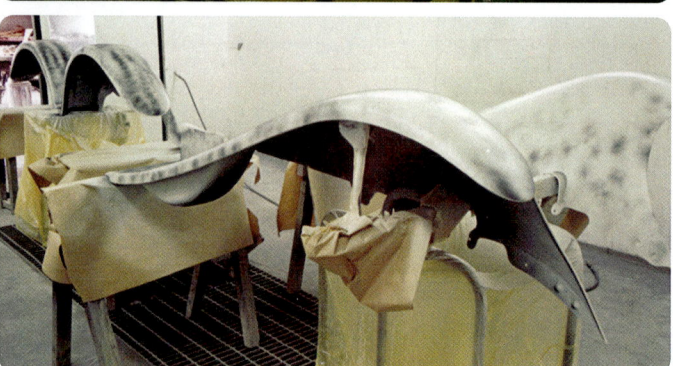

JOB: 151 | TYPE: Delage DMS *continued...*

CHAPTER 40 : VEHICLES RESTORED AT ROYLES WORKSHOPS - PART 2

DELAGE

JOB: 151 | TYPE: Delage DMS *continued...*

JOB: 151 | TYPE: Delage DMS *continued...*

ROYLE. FROM VINTAGE TO CLASSIC TO AMPHIBIAN.

DELAGE

JOB: 151 | TYPE: Delage DMS *continued...*

DELAGE

JOB: 322 | TYPE: Delage D1 | OWNER: Mr. S. J. Fisher | IMAGES: 8

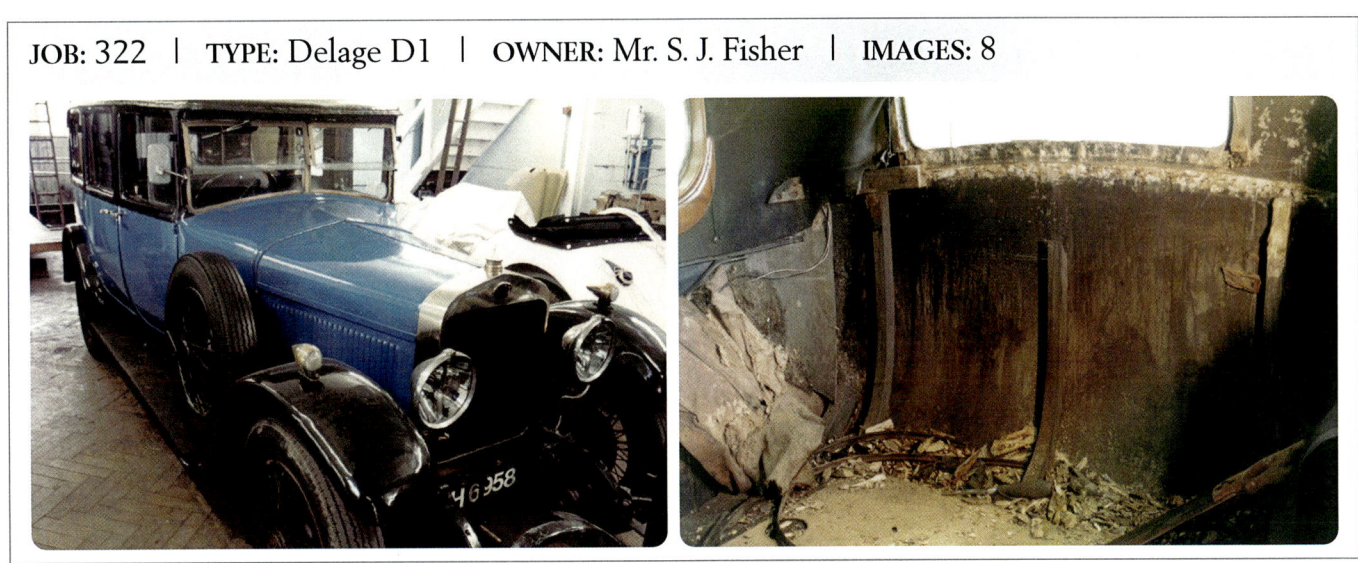

JOB: 713 | TYPE: Delage D8 | OWNER: Mr. W. Esch | IMAGES: 66

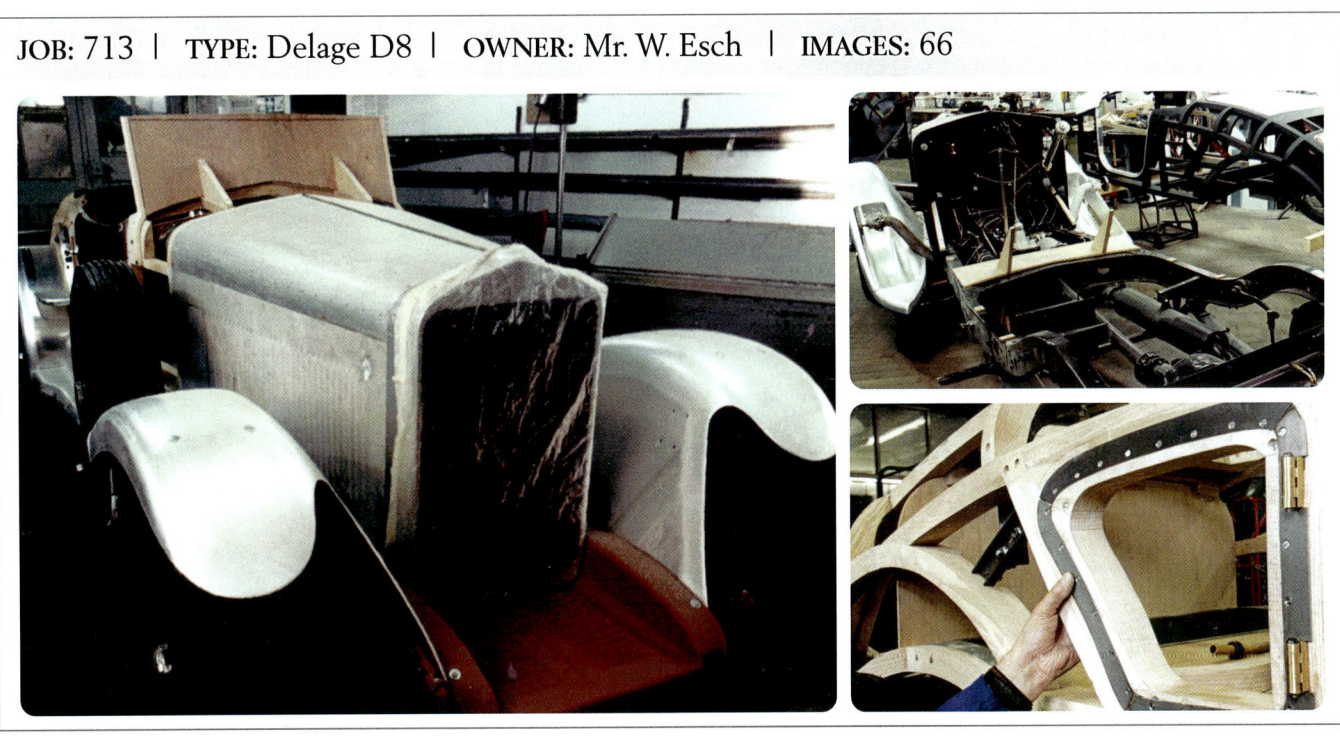

JOB: 683 | TYPE: Delage D6 22HP | OWNER: W. Esch | IMAGES: 79

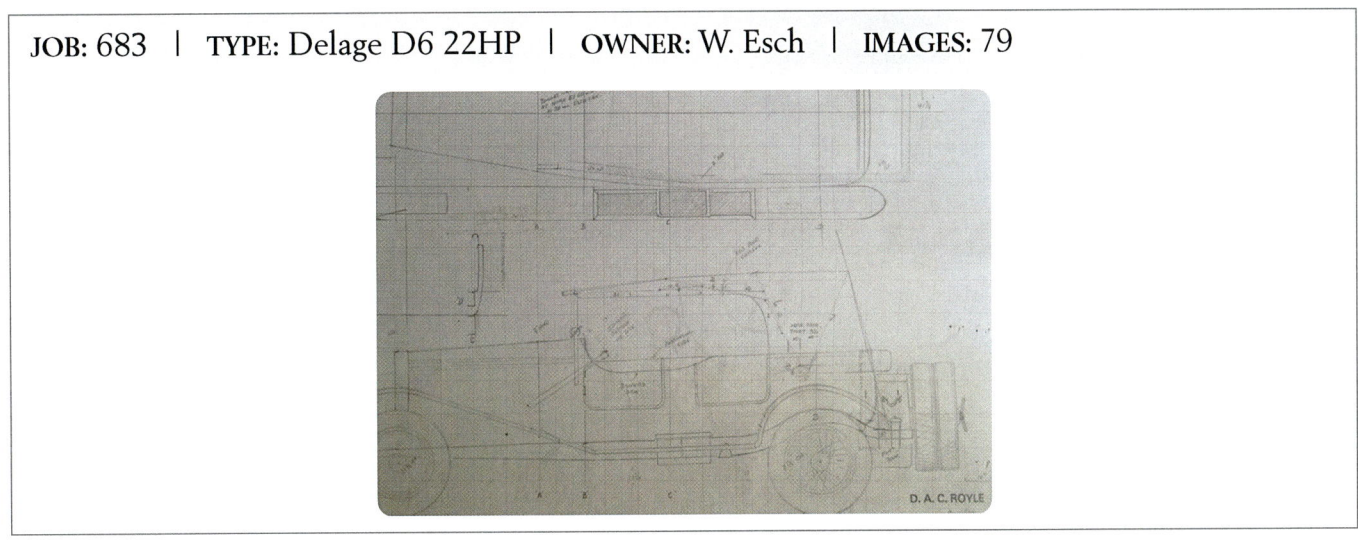

DENNIS

| JOB: 772 | TYPE: Dennis 1926 Charabanc | OWNER: Mr. Harrison | IMAGES: 4 |

ESSEX

| JOB: 621 | TYPE: Essex Super Six Saloon | OWNER: Mr. G. Briggs | IMAGES: 7 |

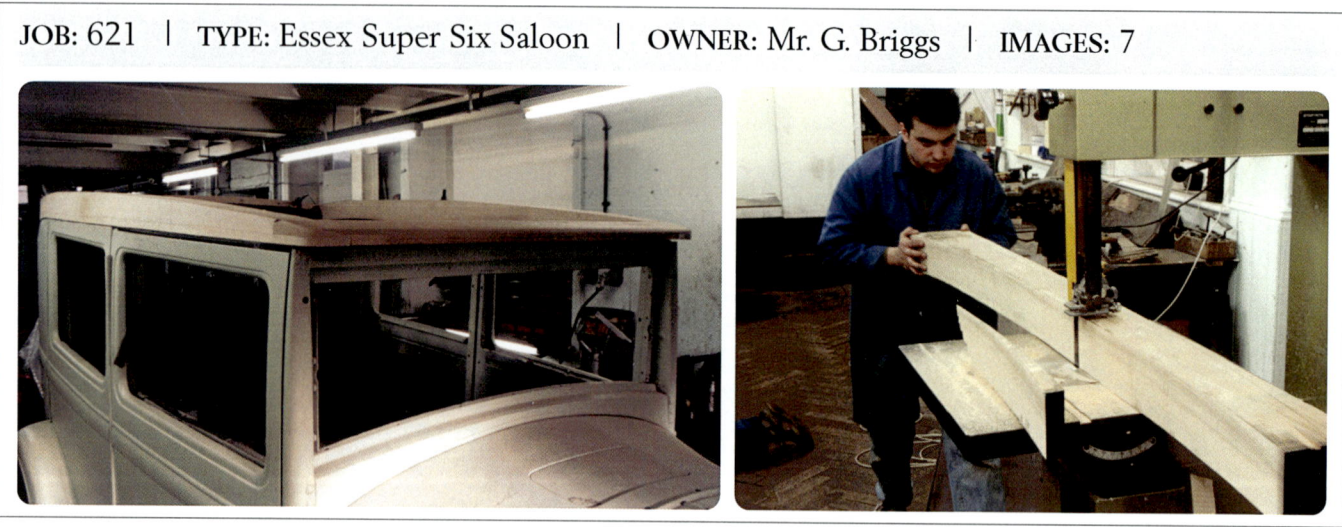

FERRARI

| JOB: 579 | TYPE: Ferrari 250 GT Lusso | OWNER: Mr. A. Fletcher | IMAGES: 36 |

CHAPTER 40 : VEHICLES RESTORED AT ROYLES WORKSHOPS - PART 2

FERRARI

JOB: 590 | TYPE: Ferrari 308 GT4 | OWNER: Mr. W. E. M. Harrison | IMAGES: 50

JOB: 642 | TYPE: Ferrari GT 250 SWB Berlinetta | OWNER: Lord Mexborough | IMAGES: 7

JOB: 827 | TYPE: Ferrari Daytona | OWNER: Mr. Litchfield | IMAGES: ?

403

FIAT

| JOB: 19 | TYPE: Fiat Topolino | OWNER: Mr. M. Williamson | IMAGES: 2 |

| JOB: 192 | TYPE: Fiat 501 Saloon | REFERENCE: Royle Hepworth | IMAGES: 7 |

| JOB: 204 | TYPE: Fiat Dino 1972 | OWNER: Mr. W. Townsend | IMAGES: 1 |

FIAT

JOB: 292 | TYPE: Fiat 514 Van 1929 | OWNER: Mr. D. Hoyle | IMAGES: 1

JOB: 343 | TYPE: Fiat 850 Coupe 1970 | OWNER: Mr. Muir | IMAGES: 15

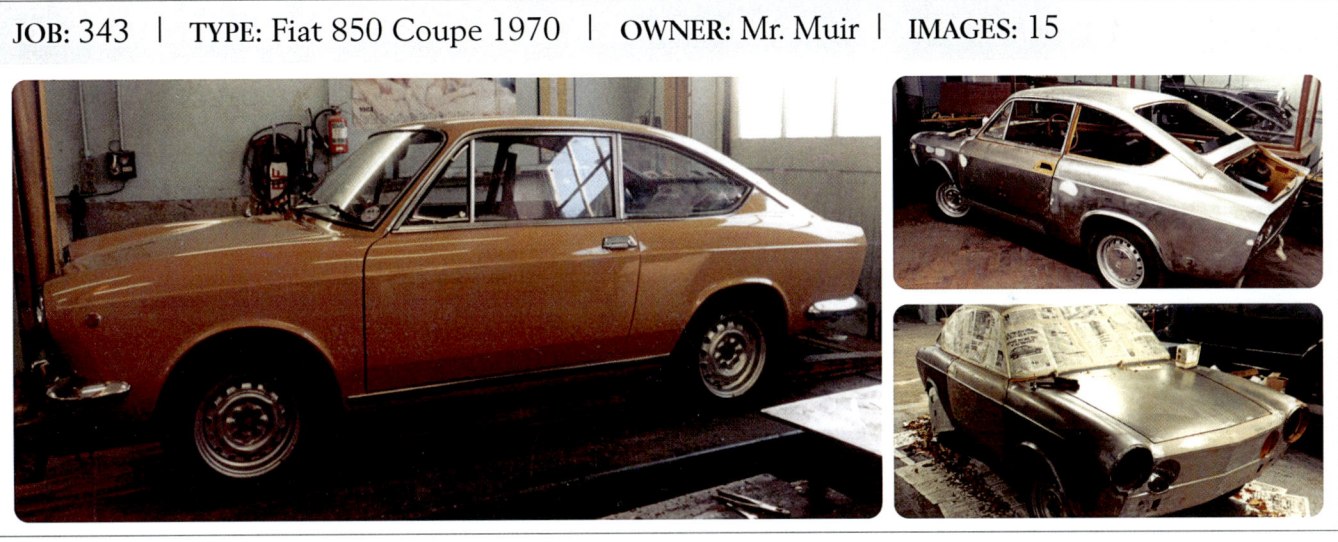

FORD

JOB: 113 | TYPE: Ford Prefect | OWNER: N. Richmond | IMAGES: 2

FORD

JOB: 130　|　TYPE: Ford Anglia 1962　|　OWNER: Mr. Rayner　|　IMAGES: 1

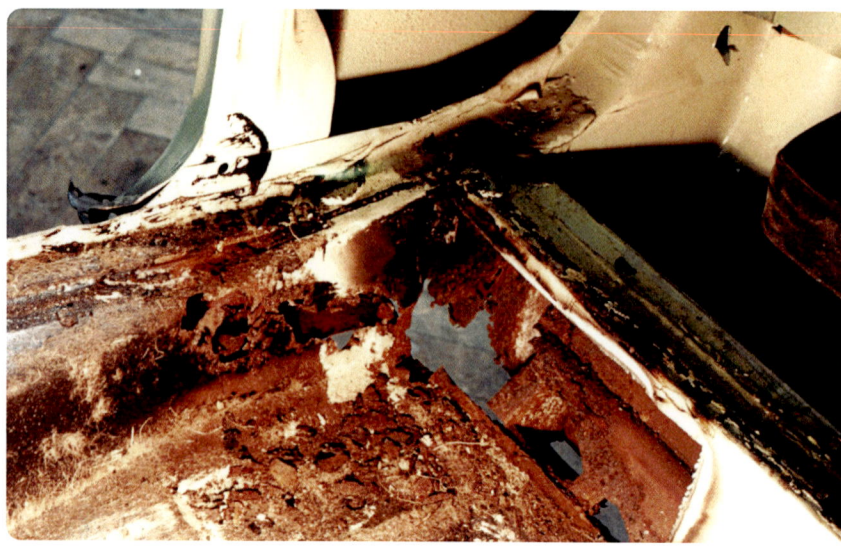

JOB: 207　|　TYPE: Ford Anglia　|　OWNER: Mr. D. A. Ward　|　IMAGES: 8

JOB: 554　|　TYPE: Ford Model A Saloon　|　OWNER: Mr. V. Shaw　|　IMAGES: 8

FORD

| JOB: 650 | TYPE: Ford Lotus Cortina | OWNER: Mr. D. Wright | IMAGES: 16 |

| JOB: 659 | TYPE: Ford (Cologne) Capri | OWNER: Mr. M. Webster | IMAGES: 6 |

| JOB: 712 | TYPE: Ford Lotus Cortina | OWNER: Mr. J. Marvin | IMAGES: 14 |

ROYLE. FROM VINTAGE TO CLASSIC TO AMPHIBIAN.

FORD

JOB: 723 | TYPE: Ford Capri 3000 GT | OWNER: Mr. M. Webster | IMAGES: 10

FRANKLYN

JOB: 701 | TYPE: Franklyn | OWNER: Mr. E. Stanniforth | IMAGES: 22

FRAZER NASH

JOB: 320 | TYPE: Frazer Nash Targa Florio | OWNER: Duke of Hamilton | IMAGES: 7

GILBURN

| JOB: 617 | TYPE: Gilburn Invader Saloon Mk 3 | OWNER: Mr. D. Peddie | IMAGES: 1 |

| JOB: 809 | TYPE: Gilburn Invader Mk 3 | OWNER: Mr. R. Clarke | IMAGES: 1 |

HEALEY

| JOB: 83 | TYPE: Healey Silverstone | OWNER: Dr. J. Keatley | IMAGES: 1 |

HEALEY

| JOB: 279 | TYPE: Healey Silverstone | OWNER: Mr. Peter Hepworth | IMAGES: 16 |

HILLMAN

| JOB: 102 | TYPE: Hillman | OWNER: Mr. G. Rowley | IMAGES: 1 |

| JOB: 304 | TYPE: Hillman Aero Minx | OWNER: Mr. Pawsey | IMAGES: 2 |

CHAPTER 40 : VEHICLES RESTORED AT ROYLES WORKSHOPS - PART 2

HORSE DRAWN

JOB: 169 | TYPE: Cart (Horse Drawn) | OWNER: A. Six-Smith | IMAGES: 8

JOB: 360 | TYPE: Horse Drawn Carriage | OWNER: A. Todd | IMAGES: 2

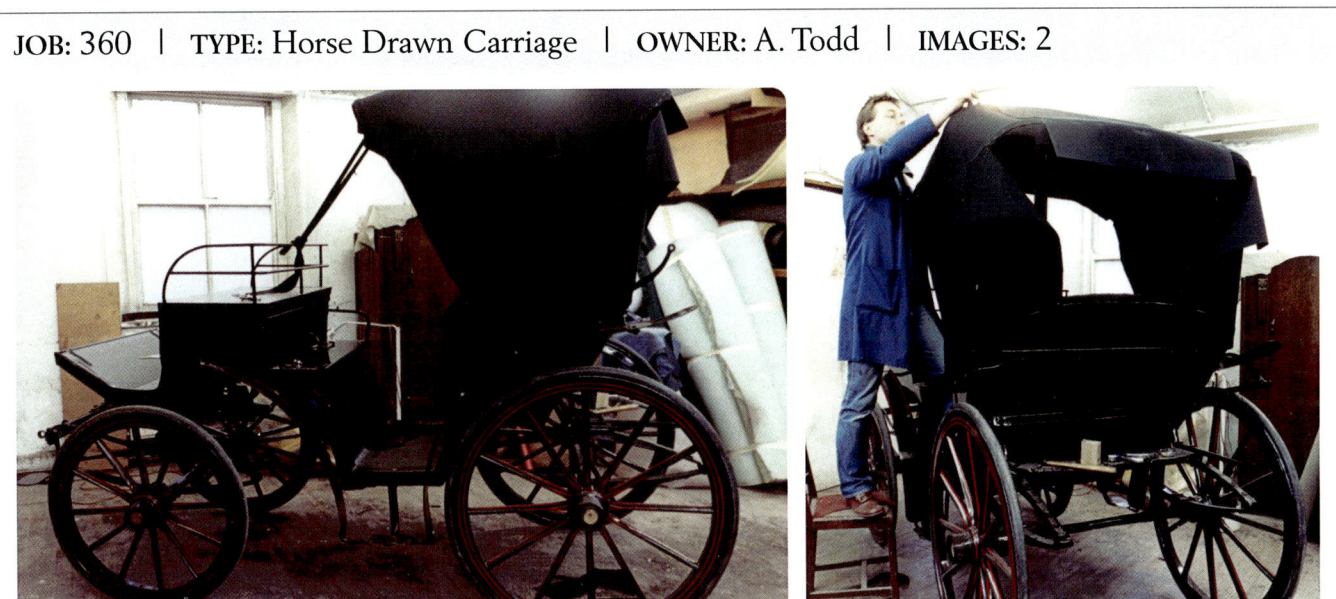

JOB: 793 | TYPE: Horse Drawn | OWNER: Mr. K. Mounsey | IMAGES: 30

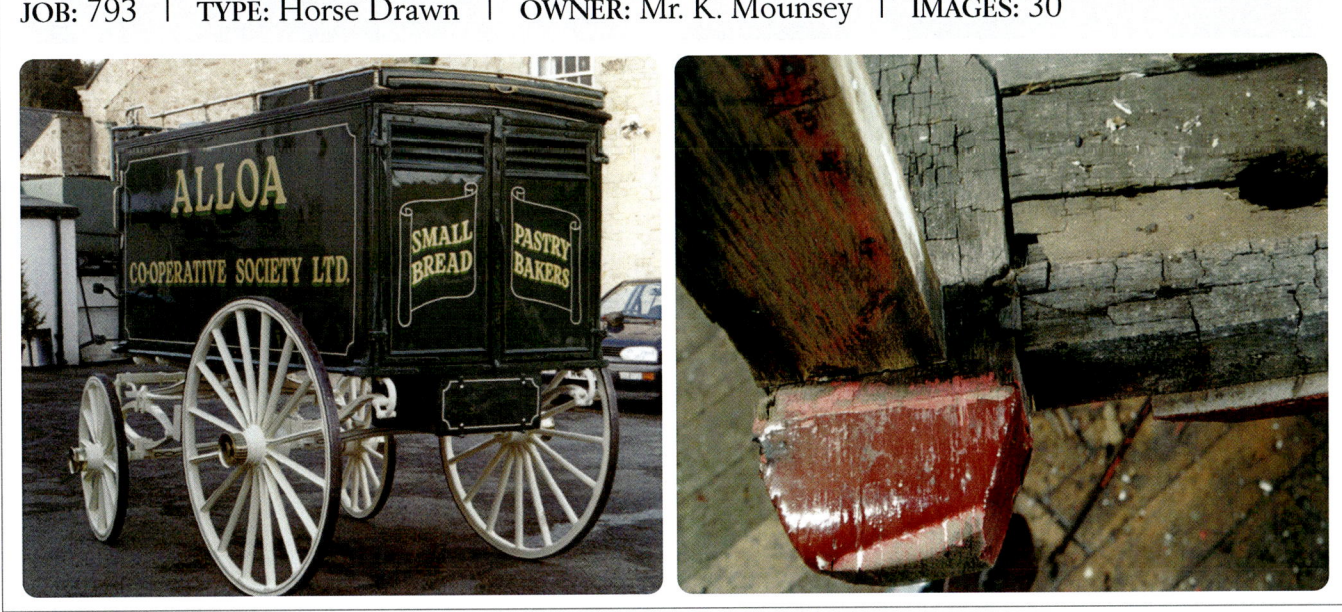

HORSE DRAWN

| JOB: 709 | TYPE: Horse Drawn Coach | OWNER: Harrogate Museum | IMAGES: 92 |

19th Century Park Drag Coach, conserved for the Harogate Galleries Museum.

One of the most interesting horse drawn vehicles to come to us. This was to be conserved rather than restored. Every effort was made to establish the correct balance between the retention and improvement of the sound, original paint finish, the upholstery which remained and yet to make the coach pleasing to the eye for visitors to the Harrogate Galleries. The wooden frame and the coach work generally was found to be in remarkably sound condition. We had the correct woollen cloth to replace the lost seat cushions and the final result was most pleasing.

CHAPTER 40 : VEHICLES RESTORED AT ROYLES WORKSHOPS - PART 2

HOTCHKISS

JOB: 312 | TYPE: Hotchkiss Saloon | OWNER: Sir Charles Ferguson | IMAGES: 49

HRG

JOB: 100 | TYPE: HRG 1500 1949 | OWNER: D. Bate | IMAGES: 2

JOB: 188 | TYPE: HRG 1500 | REFERENCE: Royle Hepworth | IMAGES: 1

HUDSON

| JOB: 224 | TYPE: Hudson Straight 8 | OWNER: Mr. W. Emmerson | IMAGES: 26 |

| JOB: 607 | TYPE: Hudson Straight 8 | OWNER: Mr. D. Mason | IMAGES: 1 |

HUMBER

| JOB: 97 | TYPE: Humber Tourer | OWNER: Mr. B. Henderon | IMAGES: 2 |

HUMBER

JOB: 181 | TYPE: Humber Tourer | OWNER: Mr. Scollen | IMAGES: 25

JOB: 191 | TYPE: Humber 9/20 Saloon | REFERENCE: Royle Hepworth | IMAGES: 2

JOB: 759 | TYPE: Humber Pullman Mk III | OWNER: Mr. C. Wray | IMAGES: 10

CHAPTER 40 : VEHICLES RESTORED AT ROYLES WORKSHOPS - PART 2

HUMBER

JOB: 760　|　TYPE: Humber　|　OWNER: Chatsworth House Trust　|　IMAGES: 24

JOB: 858　|　TYPE: Humber 1944 Staff Car　|　OWNER: Mr. Balfour　|　IMAGES: 17

INVICTA

JOB: 464　|　TYPE: Invicta　|　OWNER: Dr. J. Robson　|　IMAGES: 111

JAGUAR

JOB: 30 | TYPE: Jaguar E Type | OWNER: Mr. E. Robinson | IMAGES: 1

JOB: 88 | TYPE: Jaguar XK 150 S | OWNER: Mr. C. Seymour | IMAGES: 2

JOB: 128 | TYPE: Jaguar 420G 1967 | OWNER: Mr. T. Gray | IMAGES: 3

CHAPTER 40 : VEHICLES RESTORED AT ROYLES WORKSHOPS - PART 2

JAGUAR

JOB: 154　|　TYPE: Jaguar 2.4 Mk II Saloon　|　OWNER: Mr. L. Alvis　|　IMAGES: 23

JOB: 185　|　TYPE: Jaguar E Type 1970　|　OWNER: Mr. Balfour　|　IMAGES: 17

JOB: 197　|　TYPE: Jaguar XK 150　|　REFERENCE: Royle Hepworth　|　IMAGES: 1

419

JAGUAR

JOB: 214 | TYPE: Jaguar XK 120 | OWNER: Mr. G. Woods | IMAGES: 38

JOB: 245 | TYPE: Jaguar Mk II | OWNER: Mr. P. Gascoigne | IMAGES: 12

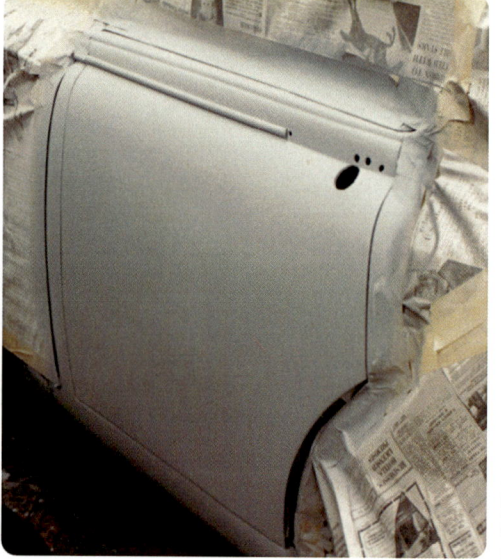

JOB: 256 | TYPE: Jaguar E Type V12 2=2 | OWNER: Mr. Clark | IMAGES: 4

CHAPTER 40 : VEHICLES RESTORED AT ROYLES WORKSHOPS - PART 2

JAGUAR

JOB: 258 | TYPE: Jaguar E Type | OWNER: Mr. C. Traill | IMAGES: 18

JOB: 264 | TYPE: Jaguar XK 140 Special | OWNER: Mr. T. Spier | IMAGES: 45

JOB: 274 | TYPE: Jaguar XK 150 | OWNER: Herr W. Arndt | IMAGES: 1

421

JAGUAR

JOB: 277 | TYPE: Jaguar XK 150 DHC | OWNER: Mr. Milburn | IMAGES: 3

JOB: 278 | TYPE: Jaguar V12 E Type 1973 | OWNER: Mr. M. J. Underwood | IMAGES: 4

JOB: 313 | TYPE: Jaguar E Type 1965 | OWNER: Mr. K. Robson | IMAGES: 4

JAGUAR

JOB: 301 | TYPE: Jaguar E Type Roadster 1963 | OWNER: S. Whitehead | IMAGES: 47

1963 Jaguar E Type Roadster Series 1. Rebodied and restored for Mr. S. Whitehead. As with many Royle restorations, this motor car went on to win many national awards and trophies.

JAGUAR

JOB: 301 | TYPE: Jaguar E Type Roadster 1963 *continued...*

CHAPTER 40 : VEHICLES RESTORED AT ROYLES WORKSHOPS - PART 2

JAGUAR

JOB: 314 | TYPE: Jaguar XK 140 Roadster | OWNER: Mr. F. N. Moller | IMAGES: 12

JOB: 321 | TYPE: Jaguar 2.5 Litre | OWNER: Mr. P. Zissler | IMAGES: 28

JOB: 325 | TYPE: Jaguar V12 E LHD 1974 | REFERENCE: Royle Hepworth | IMAGES: 1

JAGUAR

| JOB: 391 | TYPE: Jaguar Rixon Bucknall | OWNER: Mr. T. Speir | IMAGES: 14 |

| JOB: 393 | TYPE: Jaguar V12 E Type Roadster | OWNER: Mr. Boothroyd | IMAGES: 28 |

| JOB: 415 | TYPE: Jaguar XK 120 FHC | OWNER: Mr. M. Stephenson | IMAGES: 1 |

JAGUAR

JOB: 416 | TYPE: Jaguar XK 120 | OWNER: Mr. J. Pattus | IMAGES: 119

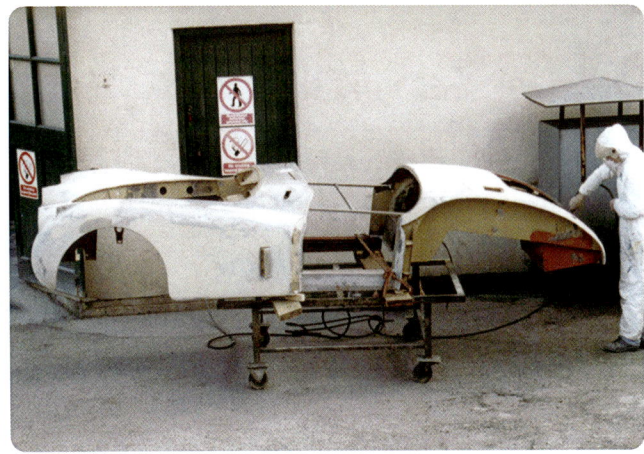

JOB: 430 | TYPE: Jaguar XK 150 DHC | OWNER: N. Efthymiadis | IMAGES: 4

JOB: 472 | TYPE: Jaguar XK 150 'S' DHC | OWNER: Mr. A. Wynn-Williams | IMAGES: 137

JAGUAR

JOB: 480 | TYPE: Jaguar XK 120 1952 | OWNER: Mr. E. Dixon Barker | IMAGES: 125

JOB: 489 | TYPE: Jaguar XK 150 'S' DHC | OWNER: R. B. B. Ropner | IMAGES: 12

JOB: 519 | TYPE: Jaguar XK 140 Roadster | OWNER: Mr. G. Todd | IMAGES: 75

CHAPTER 40 : VEHICLES RESTORED AT ROYLES WORKSHOPS - PART 2

JAGUAR

JOB: 552 | TYPE: Jaguar V12 Type FHC | OWNER: Mr. R. Chapman | IMAGES: 45

JOB: 556 | TYPE: Jaguar 420 Saloon | OWNER: Mr. A. Fletcher | IMAGES: 34

JOB: 581 | TYPE: Jaguar Mk II Saloon 2.4 | OWNER: Mr. T. Pollard | IMAGES: 43

JAGUAR

JOB: 702 | TYPE: Jaguar E Type Roadster | OWNER: Mr. J. Martin | IMAGES: 13

JOB: 718 | TYPE: Jaguar XK 150 FHC | OWNER: Mr. F. Jenkins | IMAGES: 4

JOB: 761 | TYPE: Jaguar XK 120 Roadster 1952 | OWNER: Mr. P. Gibson | IMAGES: 3

CHAPTER 40 : VEHICLES RESTORED AT ROYLES WORKSHOPS - PART 2

JAGUAR

JOB: 784　|　TYPE: Jaguar 1962　|　OWNER: Mr. M. Cassidy　|　IMAGES: 49

JOB: 721　|　TYPE: Jaguar Mk II Saloon　|　OWNER: Mr. M. Reed　|　IMAGES: 5

JOB: 724　|　TYPE: Jaguar XJ6　|　OWNER: Mr. M. Robinson　|　IMAGES: 1

JAGUAR

JOB: 746 | TYPE: Jaguar XK 120 FHC | OWNER: Mr. A. Wynn-Williams | IMAGES: 3

JOB: 751 | TYPE: Jaguar Mk II 2.4 Litre (Inspector Morse Car) | OWNER: Mr. J. Potts | IMAGES: 44

JOB: 753 | TYPE: Jaguar XJS 3.6 Litre 1986 | OWNER: Mr. S. Kennedy | IMAGES: 6

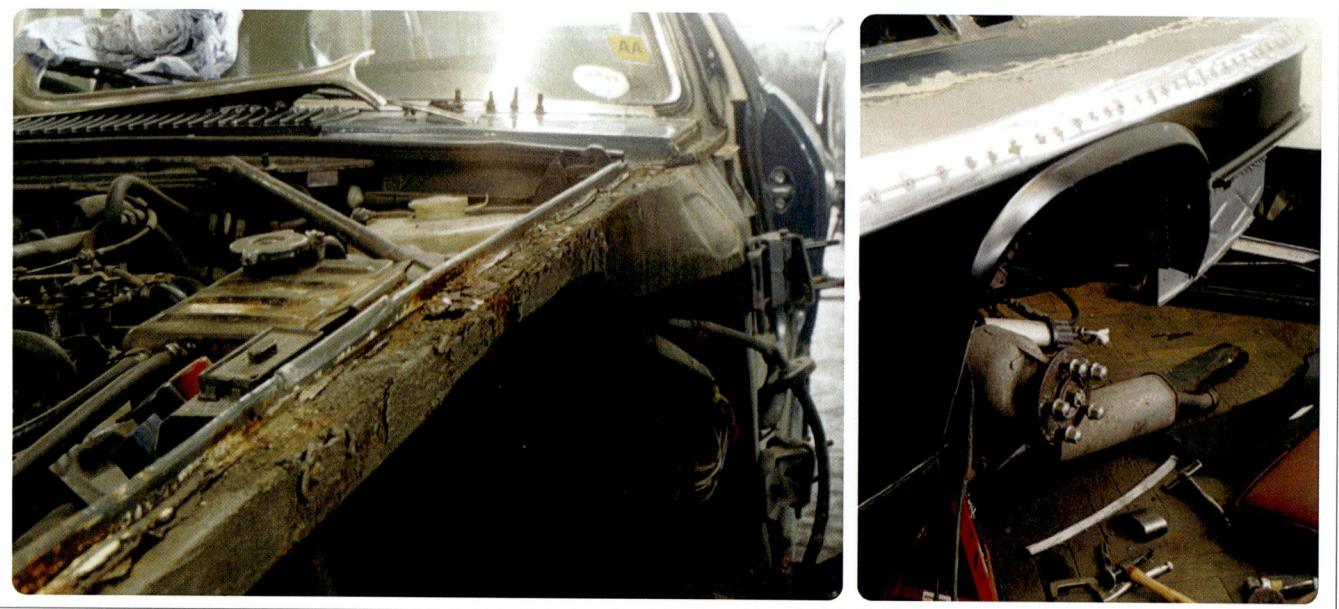

JEEP

JOB: 622 | TYPE: Ford Jeep 1944 | OWNER: Mr. N. Stanley | IMAGES: 35

JOB: 894 | TYPE: Willys Jeep | OWNER: Mr. G. Taylor | IMAGES: 5

JENSEN

JOB: 14 | TYPE: Jensen 541R | OWNER: R. B. Swan | IMAGES: 3

JENSEN

JOB: 272 | TYPE: Jensen CV8 | OWNER: Mr. D. Smith | IMAGES: 18

JOB: 341 | TYPE: Jensen Interceptor DHC | OWNER: Mr. R. Durham | IMAGES: 8

KIT CARS

JOB: 574 | TYPE: A.C. Kit Car Cobra | OWNER: Mr. J. Wood | IMAGES: 2

KIT CARS

JOB: 600 | TYPE: Teal Bugatti Type 59 | OWNER: D. Huntley | IMAGES: 24

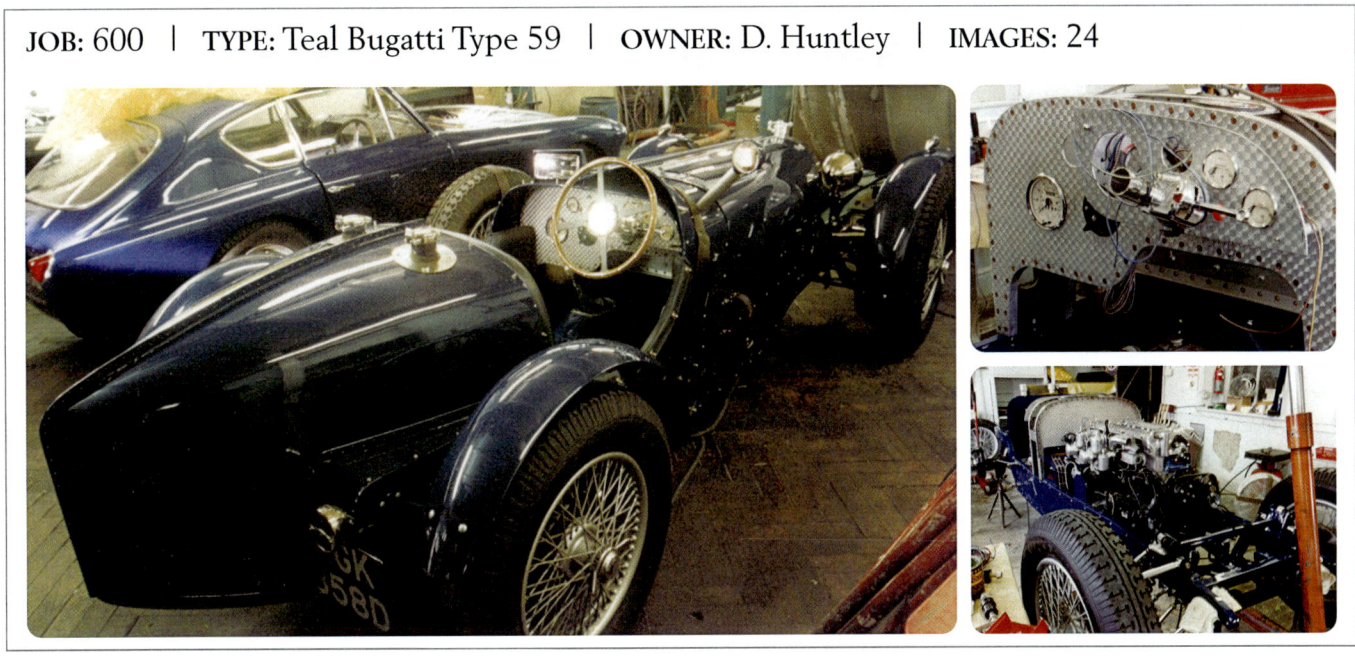

JOB: 629 | TYPE: Royale Sabre Kit Car | OWNER: Mr. Gibson | IMAGES: 5

JOB: 633 | TYPE: Triumph Spitfire Kit Car 1980 | OWNER: Mr. J. Dyson | IMAGES: 4

KIT CARS

JOB: 647 | TYPE: Lomax Kit Car | OWNER: S. Whitehead | IMAGES: 5

JOB: 668 | TYPE: Royale Drophead | OWNER: Mr. D. Lanzkron | IMAGES: 39

KOUGAR

JOB: 186 | TYPE: Kougar Special | OWNER: Mr. A. Wynn-Williams | IMAGES: 2

LAGONDA

JOB: 73　|　TYPE: Lagonda M45　|　OWNER: Mr. A. Brown　|　IMAGES: 17

JOB: 114　|　TYPE: Lagonda 3.5 Litre 1935　|　OWNER: Mr. J. Harris　|　IMAGES: 4

JOB: 120　|　TYPE: Lagonda M45 1939　|　OWNER: Mr. I. Pitkethly for BP Oil Ltd　|　IMAGES: 5

JOB: 138　|　TYPE: Lagonda LG45　|　OWNER: Mr. N. Shaw　|　IMAGES: 90

LAGONDA

| JOB: 119 | TYPE: Lagonda LG6 Saloon | OWNER: Mr. H. Eugster | IMAGES: 150 |

1939 Lagonda LG6 Saloon restored for Mr. Hans Eugster in Switzerland. It seems that this Lagonda was used when testing the 1939 V12 Le Mans racing car at Brooklands and is visible in the background on page 337 of 'Lagonda, ' The History of the Marque' by Arnold Davey & Anthony May.

LAGONDA

JOB: 119 | TYPE: Lagonda LG6 Saloon *continued...*

LAGONDA

JOB: 119 | **TYPE:** Lagonda LG6 Saloon *continued...*

LAGONDA

JOB: 241 | TYPE: Lagonda M45 | OWNER: Mr. J. Bidwell Topham | IMAGES: 18

JOB: 273 | TYPE: Lagonda M45 1934 | OWNER: Mr. J. Bidwell Topham | IMAGES: 30

JOB: 293 | TYPE: Lagonda LG45 | REFERENCE: Royle Hepworth | IMAGES: 5

LAGONDA

JOB: 316 | TYPE: Lagonda LG45 1934 | OWNER: Mr. W. Shaw | IMAGES: 6

JOB: 364 | TYPE: Lagonda LG45 1937 | OWNER: Mr. N. Dodds | IMAGES: 20

JOB: 375 | TYPE: Lagonda Rapier | OWNER: Mr. J. Castle | IMAGES: 78

LAGONDA

JOB: 385 | TYPE: Lagonda V12 Saloon | OWNER: Mr. D. Cooper | IMAGES: 66

JOB: 394 | TYPE: Lagonda LG6 Saloon | OWNER: Mr. N. Shaw | IMAGES: 260

JOB: 412 | TYPE: Lagonda | OWNER: Mr. J. Coles | IMAGES: 159

LAGONDA

JOB: 448　|　TYPE: Lagonda 3 Litre Tourer　|　OWNER: Mr. W. Shaw　|　IMAGES: 33

JOB: 454　|　TYPE: Lagonda LG45 DHC　|　OWNER: Mr. B. Watson　|　IMAGES: 173

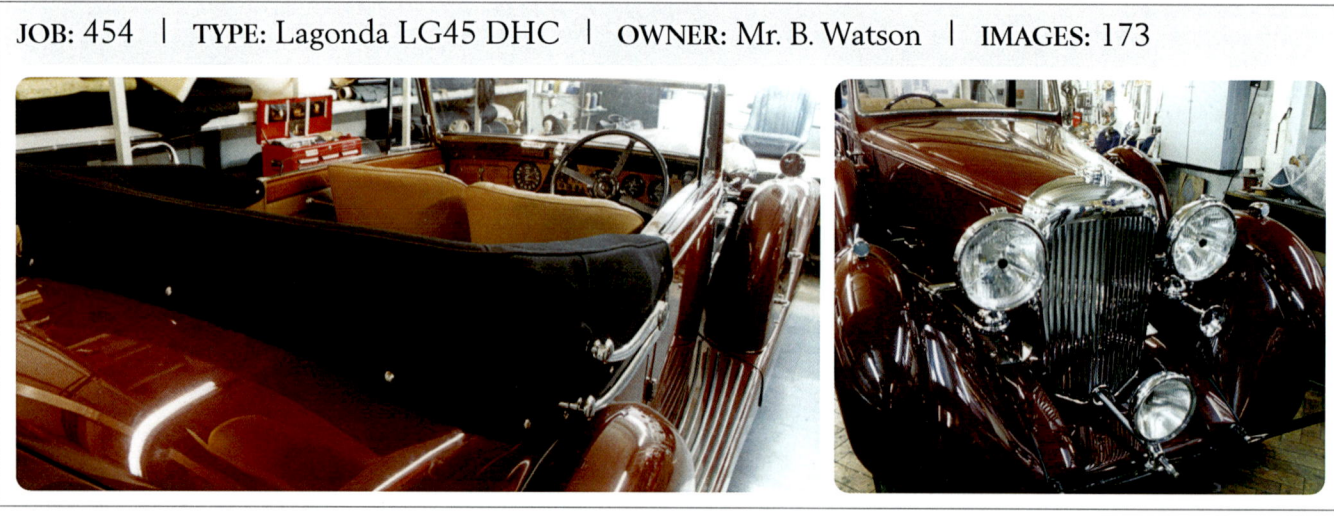

JOB: 463　|　TYPE: Lagonda M45 Saloon　|　OWNER: The Hon. Mark Balfour　|　IMAGES: 101

LAGONDA

JOB: 499 | TYPE: Lagonda Rapide | OWNER: Mr. H. Schofield | IMAGES: 22

JOB: 500 | TYPE: Lagonda LG6 Saloon | OWNER: Mr. J. Longridge | IMAGES: 3

JOB: 502 | TYPE: Lagonda 2 Litre | OWNER: Mr. R. Martin | IMAGES: 10

LAGONDA

JOB: 505 | **TYPE:** Lagonda M45 DHC by Freestone & Webb | **OWNER:** Mr. N. Jubert | **IMAGES:** 47

JOB: 510 | **TYPE:** Lagonda LG45 Saloon | **OWNER:** Mr. A. P. Walby | **IMAGES:** 19

JOB: 630 | **TYPE:** Lagonda M45 | **OWNER:** Mr. D. Todd | **IMAGES:** 74

CHAPTER 40 : VEHICLES RESTORED AT ROYLES WORKSHOPS - PART 2

LAGONDA

JOB: 636 | TYPE: Lagonda 3 Litre 1930 | OWNER: Mr. A. Hitch | IMAGES: 85

JOB: 670 | TYPE: Lagonda 2 Litre | OWNER: Mr. C. Lunt | IMAGES: 26

JOB: 671 | TYPE: Lagonda V12 Rapide | OWNER: Mr. R. Proctor | IMAGES: 90

LAGONDA

JOB: 708 | TYPE: Lagonda 1933 | OWNER: Mr. Alastair Gunn | IMAGES: 70

LAMBORGHINI

JOB: 594 | TYPE: Lamborghini Muira 1968 | OWNER: Mr. M. Kent | IMAGES: 1

LANCHESTER

JOB: 422 | TYPE: Lanchester 15/8 1932 | OWNER: Mr. De Courcey Bailey | IMAGES: 15

LEA FRANCIS

JOB: 43 | TYPE: Lea Francis | OWNER: Mr. M. D. Mudd | IMAGES: 1

JOB: 248 | TYPE: Lea Francis 14 Saloon | OWNER: Mr. P. A. Watson | IMAGES: 1

JOB: 465 | TYPE: Lea Francis | OWNER: Mr. R. Blacklock | IMAGES: 2

LEYLAND

| JOB: 315 | TYPE: Leyland Cub Fire Engine | OWNER: Newcastle Science Museum | IMAGES: 4 |

LOCOMOTIVE

| JOB: 707 | TYPE: Locomotive 1901 Steam Car | OWNER: Dr. David West | IMAGES: 9 |

LOLA

| JOB: 414 | TYPE: Lola | OWNER: Duke of Hamilton | IMAGES: 34 |

CHAPTER 40 : VEHICLES RESTORED AT ROYLES WORKSHOPS - PART 2

LORRAINE DIETRICH

JOB: 603 | TYPE: Lorraine Dietrich | OWNER: Mr. Tim Hallam | IMAGES: 77

1925 Lorraine Dietrich with specially built body, fabric covered with refined features to meet the owners specification and reflecting the continental designs of the peroid.

LORRAINE DIETRICH

JOB: 603 | TYPE: Lorraine Dietrich *continued...*

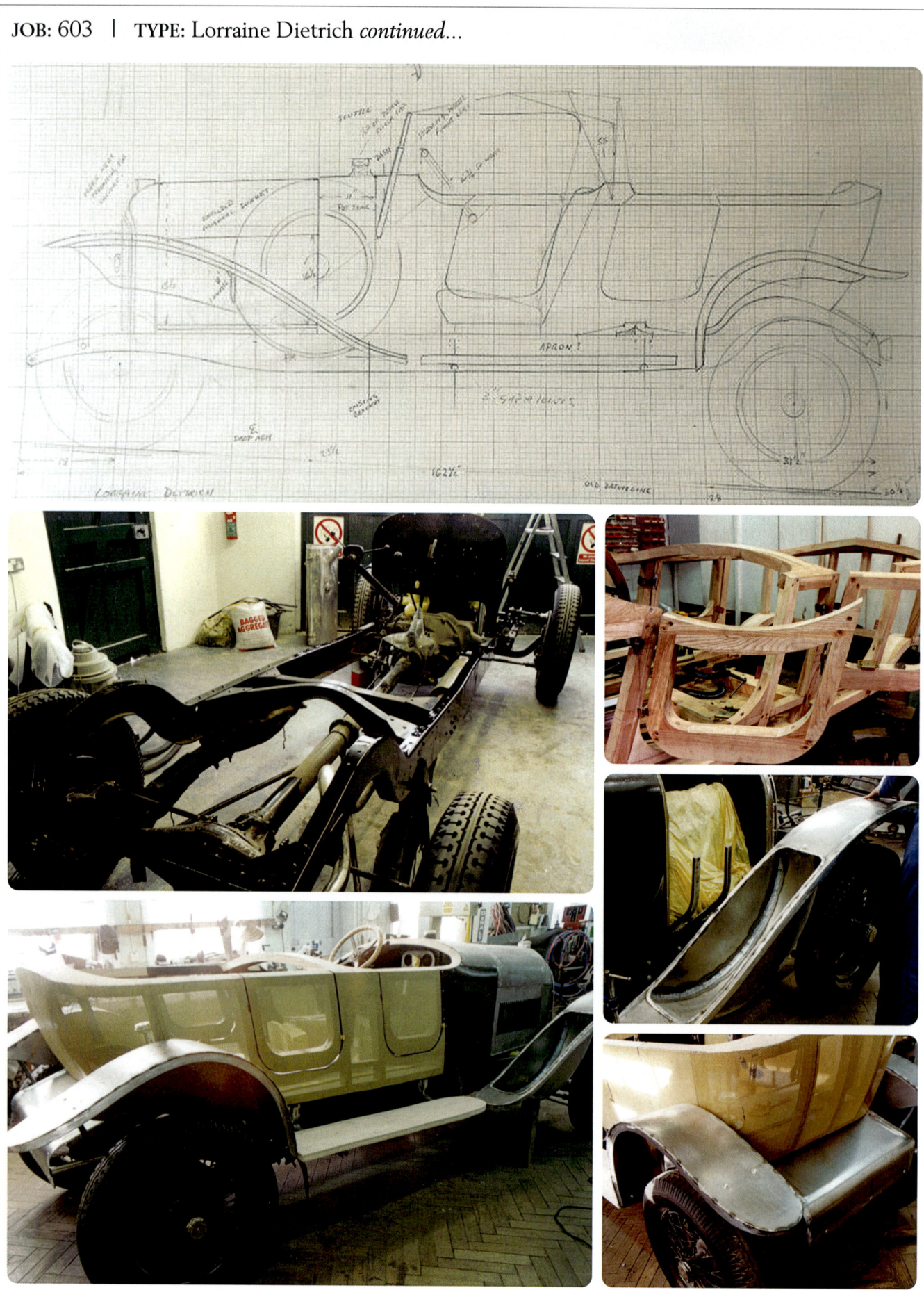

CHAPTER 40 : VEHICLES RESTORED AT ROYLES WORKSHOPS - PART 2

MARCOS

JOB: 318 | TYPE: Marcos 1600 1968 | REFERENCE: Royle Hepworth | IMAGES: 1

MERCEDES BENZ

JOB: 103 | TYPE: Mercedes Benz | OWNER: Mr. A. Clingley | IMAGES: 4

JOB: 730 | TYPE: Mercedes Benz 1972 | OWNER: Mr. M. Childs | IMAGES: 2

MINERVA

JOB: 254 | TYPE: Minerva 1925 | REFERENCE: Royle Hepworth | IMAGES: 80

1926 Minerva Limousine with Sleeve valve Knight engine, restored for Dr. D. Riddle in Texas, USA. This handsome and most original motor car was in service for many years with the Laphroaig Whisky Distillery on the Isle of Islay in Scotland.

CHAPTER 40 : VEHICLES RESTORED AT ROYLES WORKSHOPS - PART 2

MINERVA

JOB: 254 | TYPE: Minerva 1925 *continued...*

JOB: 254 | TYPE: Minerva 1925 *continued...*

MINERVA

JOB: 280　|　TYPE: Minerva 1925　|　OWNER: Dr. D. Riddle　|　IMAGES: 6

MG

JOB: 2　|　TYPE: MG Magnette 1935　|　OWNER: Mr. N. Hart　|　IMAGES: 90

1934 MG NA Type Magnette Brooklands racing car"

This motor car was raced in 1934 and 1935 and then re-built for the well known pre-war driver, Wilkie Wilkinson, as an offset single seater in 1936 for racing at Brooklands. After the war, the MG was racing again at the first Goodwood meeting and continued to compete at various meetings. Subsequently, over 25 years later, this well known racing car was discovered in County Durham by Norman Hart of Durham. The single seater body had gone and an unfinished two seater fibreglass body had been partly fitted. Seeing the large air cooled brakes and other racing modifications, Mr Hart recognised that it was likely to have an interesting history, so he bought the car. He set about researching its history and brought this interesting MG to Staindrop where the research continued with a little help from the author.

MG

JOB: 2 | TYPE: MG Magnette 1935 *continued...*

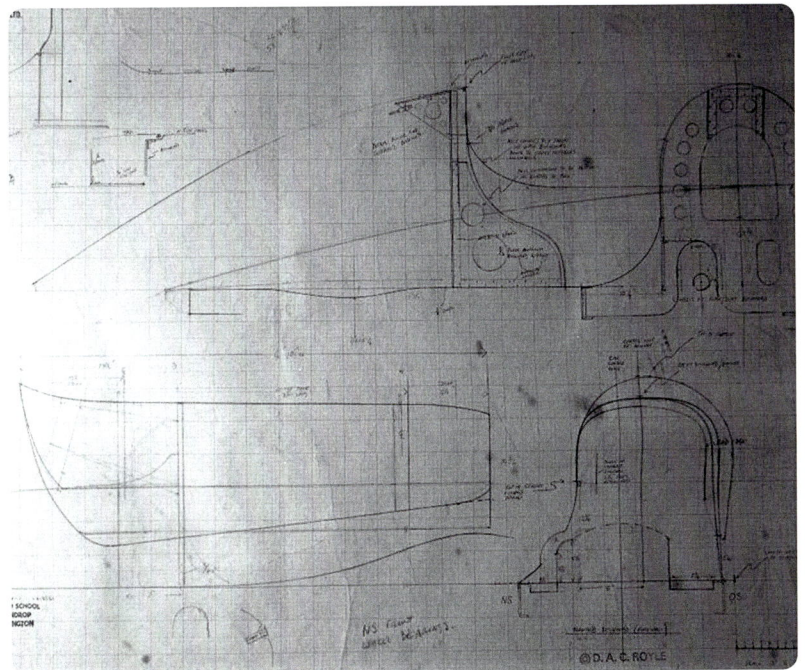

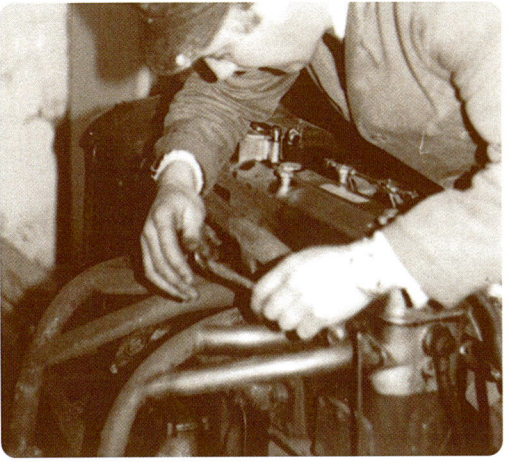

Fortunately, a number of good photographs and some early film, taken when it was racing at Brooklands, had been found. These enabled the author to make drawings of a single seater body. The car had always been raced with two different sizes of wheels, 18" and 19", to facilitate an easy variation of gearing. Once the position of these had been established in the photographs, I had exact datum points for the dimensions of the body, so the drawings could be made very much to the original size and the location of the various features would be correct as had been built in 1936.

It was a fascinating project and work began on a complete restoration in September 1980. All the original components were retained. The offset, light weight, single seater body was built, new straight through exhaust system made as original. Remarkably, the original set of six Amal Carburettors on their original manifold, turned up in Luxembourg and were fitted. The work was finished in September 1981 and the following year, Mr Hart attended the 75th Anniversary of the Brooklands Reunion, when its former racing driver, Wilkie Wilkinson, drove it once again round part of the old track."

MG

JOB: 2 | TYPE: MG Magnette 1935 *continued...*

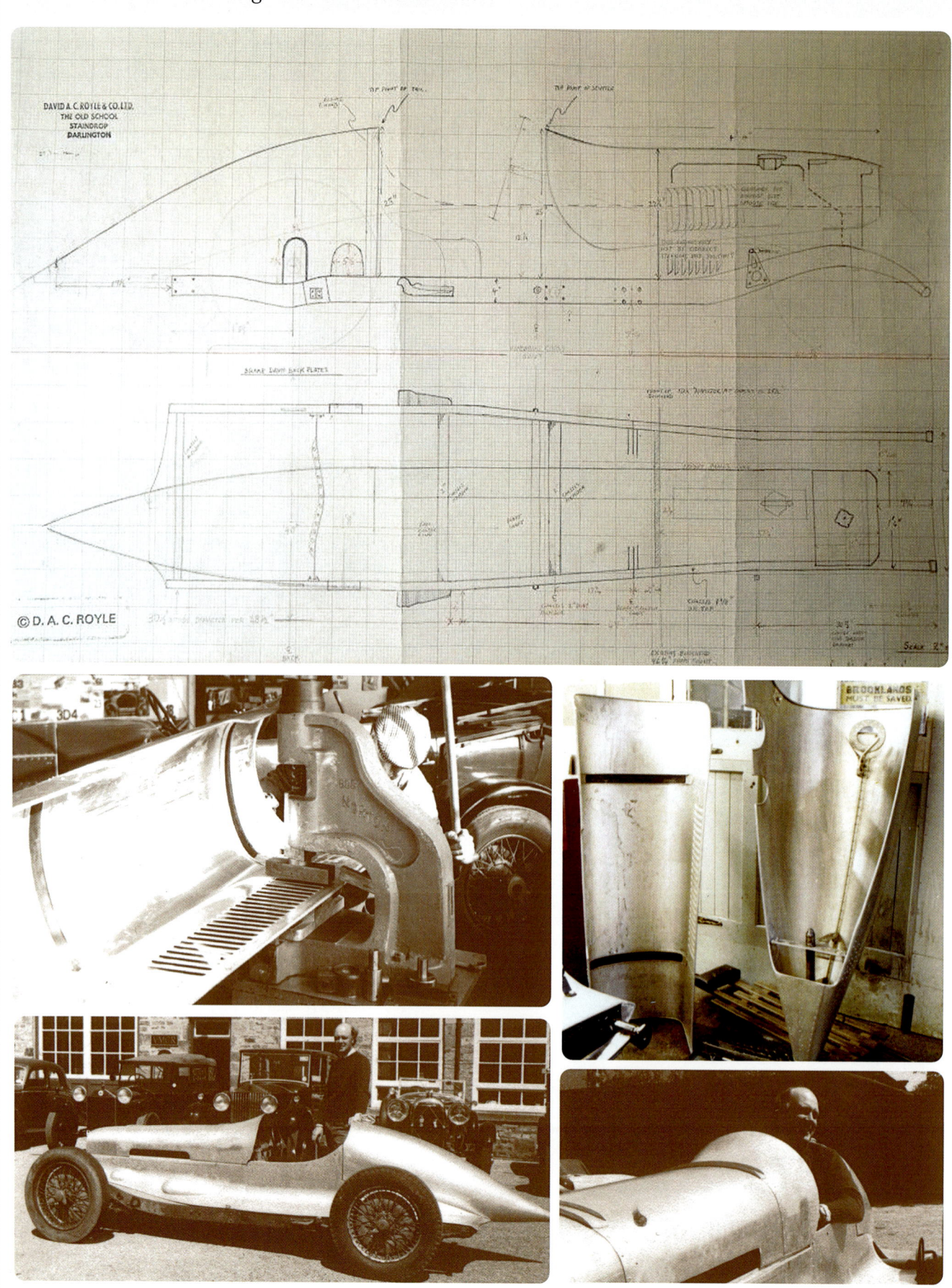

JOB: 2 | TYPE: MG Magnette 1935 *continued...*

MG

JOB: 2 | TYPE: MG Magnette 1935 *continued...*

MG

JOB: 2 | TYPE: MG Magnette 1935 *continued...*

JOB: 33 | TYPE: MG TD 1951 | OWNER: Mr. H. Le Blond | IMAGES: 2

CHAPTER 40 : VEHICLES RESTORED AT ROYLES WORKSHOPS - PART 2

MG

JOB: 93 | TYPE: MG SA Saloon | OWNER: Mr. S. Tozer | IMAGES: 1

JOB: 146 | TYPE: MG TA 1938 | OWNER: Mr. Adamson | IMAGES: 4

JOB: 147 | TYPE: MGB GT 1973 | OWNER: Mr. Greencare | IMAGES: 23

 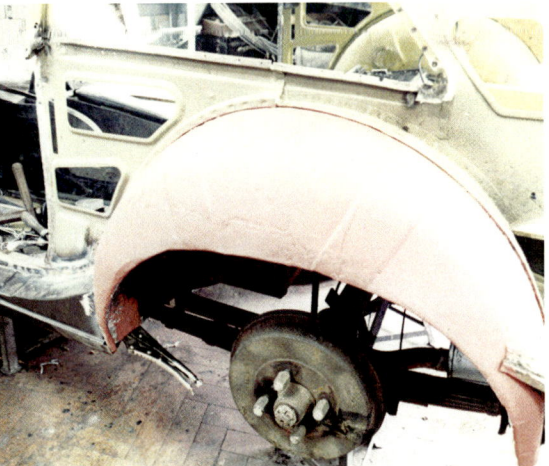

MG

| JOB: 157 | TYPE: MG TD | OWNER: Mr. R. Bradley | IMAGES: 1 |

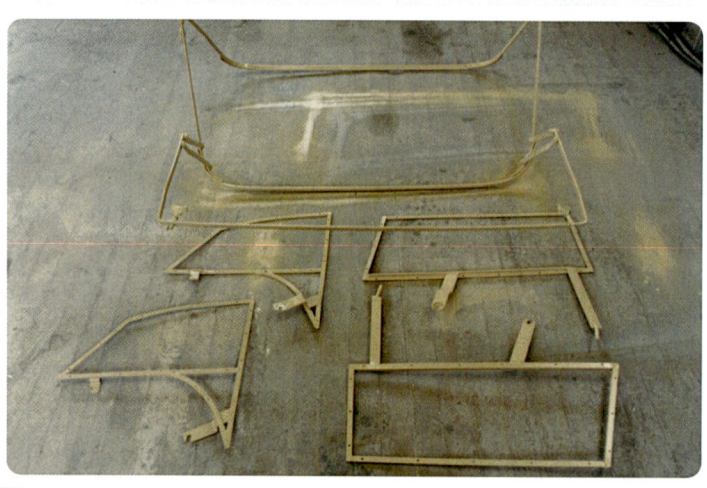

| JOB: 209 | TYPE: MG SA Saloon | OWNER: Mr. Hafner | IMAGES: 3 |

| JOB: 216 | TYPE: MG TF 1954 | OWNER: S. Goldstone | IMAGES: 1 |

MG

JOB: 259 | TYPE: MG PA 1934 | OWNER: Mr. R. Macgillivray | IMAGES: 4

JOB: 392 | TYPE: MG VA Saloon | OWNER: Royle Cars | IMAGES: 2

JOB: 417 | TYPE: MG SA Saloon | REFERENCE: Royle Hepworth | IMAGES: 1

MG

JOB: 477 | TYPE: MG M Type | REFERENCE: Royle Cars | IMAGES: 2

JOB: 546 | TYPE: MG C-GT | OWNER: Mr. M. Dixon | IMAGES: 4

JOB: 654 | TYPE: MG TC | OWNER: Mr. P. Stoelk | IMAGES: 3

MG

| JOB: 661 | TYPE: MGB | OWNER: Mr. E. Nichols | IMAGES: 90 |

| JOB: 699 | TYPE: MG Speed Record Car | OWNER: Heritage Motor Centre | IMAGES: 30 |

| JOB: 767 | TYPE: MG YB Saloon 1952 | OWNER: Mr. R. Whittaker | IMAGES: 20 |

MG

JOB: 781 | TYPE: MG TA Sports | OWNER: Ms. B. Law | IMAGES: 8

MORGAN

JOB: 125 | TYPE: Morgan 4/4 1937 | OWNER: Mr. D. Peddie | IMAGES: 3

JOB: 217 | TYPE: Morgan 4/4 | OWNER: Mrs. P. Fawcett | IMAGES: 7

CHAPTER 40 : VEHICLES RESTORED AT ROYLES WORKSHOPS - PART 2

MORGAN

JOB: 804 | TYPE: Morgan Aero Super Sports | OWNER: Mr. N. Taylor | IMAGES: 8

MORRIS

JOB: 4 | TYPE: Morris 8 1938 | OWNER: Mr. S. Hughes | IMAGES: 12

JOB: 7 | TYPE: Morris Cowley 1930 | OWNER: Mr. M. D. Mudd | IMAGES: 2

467

MORRIS

JOB: 36 | TYPE: Morris Minor Saloon | OWNER: Mr. R. Brown | IMAGES: 2

JOB: 61 | TYPE: Morris 10.4, 1935 | OWNER: Mr. S. Waldron | IMAGES: 1

JOB: 141 | TYPE: Morris Oxford Tourer | OWNER: Mr. T. Southern | IMAGES: 2

MORRIS

JOB: 156 | TYPE: Morris Commercial 1926 | OWNER: Mr. E. Ferguson | IMAGES: 1

JOB: 227 | TYPE: Morris 10.4 DHC 1935 | OWNER: Mr. S. Waldron | IMAGES: 1

JOB: 240 | TYPE: Morris Cowley Bullnose Van | OWNER: Mr. Stark | IMAGES: 8

MORRIS

JOB: 268 | TYPE: Morris Minor 2 Door | OWNER: K. Stoves | IMAGES: 10

JOB: 335 | TYPE: Morris Major Saloon 1931 | OWNER: Mr. J. Humble | IMAGES: 37

JOB: 351 | TYPE: Morris 8 Tourer 1936 | OWNER: Mr. S. Lloyd | IMAGES: 8

CHAPTER 40 : VEHICLES RESTORED AT ROYLES WORKSHOPS - PART 2

MORRIS

JOB: 434　|　TYPE: Morris Cowley Tourer　|　REFERENCE: Royle Cars　|　IMAGES: 2

JOB: 508　|　TYPE: Morris Commercial　|　OWNER: Mr. P. Taplin　|　IMAGES: 33

JOB: 526　|　TYPE: Morris Bullnose Coupe　|　REFERENCE: Royle Cars　|　IMAGES: 7

MORRIS

JOB: 553 | TYPE: Morris 10/4 FHC | OWNER: Dr. Bertolis | IMAGES: 3

JOB: 618 | TYPE: Morris Oxford Bullnose 1924 | OWNER: Mr. J. Bidwell-Topham | IMAGES: 14

JOB: 635 | TYPE: Morris 1000 Van 1971 | OWNER: Mr. I. Marshall | IMAGES: 15

MORRIS

JOB: 682　|　TYPE: Morris Charabanc　|　OWNER: Mr. E. N. Ritchie　|　IMAGES: 5

JOB: 757　|　TYPE: Morris Bullnose Cowley 1926　|　OWNER: Mr. S. White　|　IMAGES: 7

JOB: 807　|　TYPE: Morris Minor SV 1932/34　|　OWNER: Mr. D. Macro　|　IMAGES: 4

MOTORCYCLES

| JOB: 46 | TYPE: Motor CY Parts/Zenith | OWNER: The Cart House Ltd | IMAGES: 2 |

| JOB: 234 | TYPE: Triumph 350 Speed Trim M Cycle | OWNER: Lord David Dundas | IMAGES: 13 |

NAPIER

| JOB: 354 | TYPE: Napier 1913 | OWNER: Mr. S. Fisher | IMAGES: 189 |

OLDSMOBILE

JOB: 756 | TYPE: Oldsmobile | OWNER: Mr. M. Garland | IMAGES: 3

OSCA

JOB: 853 | TYPE: Osca Maserati | OWNER: Sir Stirling Moss | IMAGES: 5

PARTS

JOB: 163 | TYPE: Landrover Mk I Bulkhead | OWNER: Mr. A. E. Ellis | IMAGES: 2

JOB: 246 | TYPE: Pseudo American Car Front | IMAGES: 10

CHAPTER 40 : VEHICLES RESTORED AT ROYLES WORKSHOPS - PART 2

PERAMBULATORS

JOB: 536 | TYPE: Marmet 1950 Perambulator | OWNER: Mrs. Gordon-Duff-Pennington

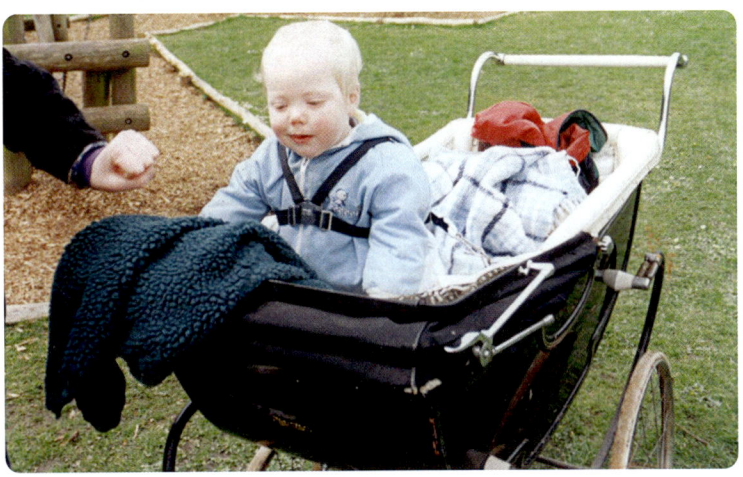

JOB: 537 | TYPE: Victorian Dolls Pram | OWNER: Mrs. L. Juckes | IMAGES: 3

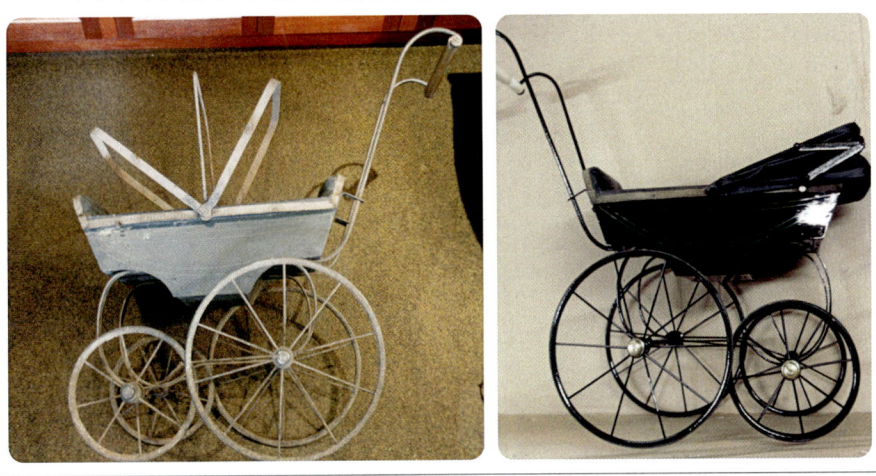

PEUGEOT

JOB: 432 | TYPE: Peugeot Torpedo 1913 | REFERENCE: Royle Cars | IMAGES: 5

PROGRESS

JOB: 437 | TYPE: Progress 1901 | OWNER: Mr. J. Spicer | IMAGES: 9

PROTOTYPES

JOB: 589 | TYPE: Flagpole Test Rig | OWNER: Harrison Steeplejacks | IMAGES: 1

CHAPTER 40 : VEHICLES RESTORED AT ROYLES WORKSHOPS - PART 2

RAILTON

JOB: 1 | TYPE: Baby Railton 10HP 1938 | OWNER: Mr. K. Barley | IMAGES: 27

JOB: 340 | TYPE: Railton Shooting Brake 1935 | OWNER: G. E. Sykes & Sons | IMAGES: 66

RANGE ROVER

JOB: 484 | TYPE: Range Rover Convertible | OWNER: Mr. R. Durham | IMAGES: 2

479

RANGE ROVER

JOB: 623 | TYPE: Range Rover | OWNER: Mr. P. Westgarth | IMAGES: 3

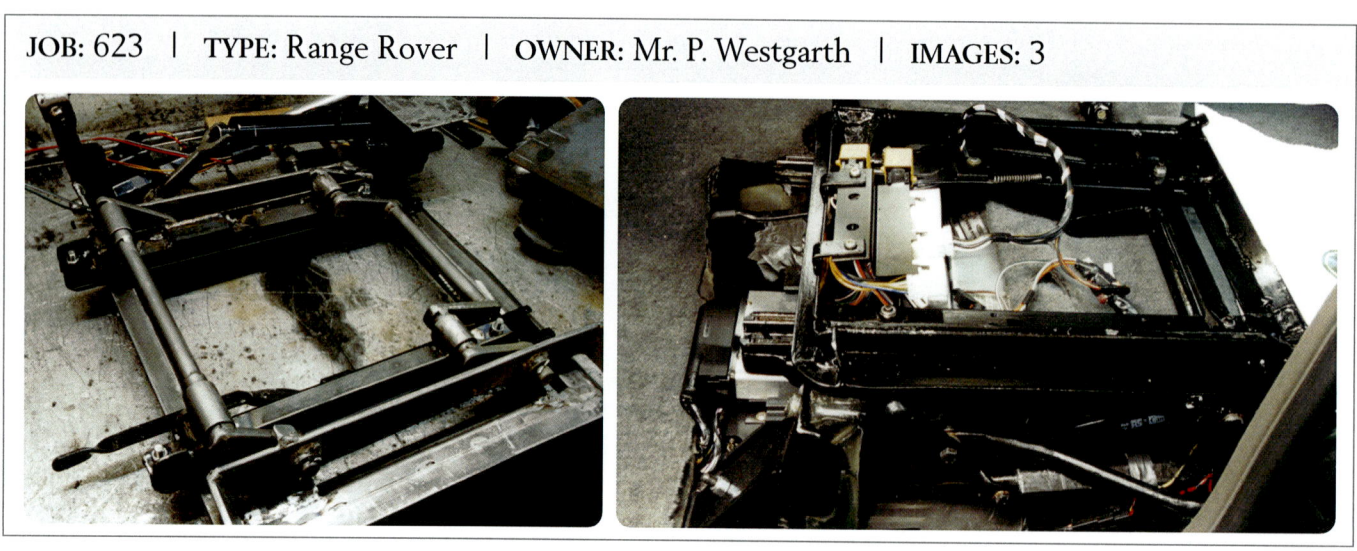

RELIANT

JOB: 597 | TYPE: Reliant Scimitar | OWNER: Mr. L. Powton | IMAGES: 1

RENAULT

JOB: 404 | TYPE: Riley Renault Tourer | REFERENCE: Royle Cars | IMAGES: 3

CHAPTER 40 : VEHICLES RESTORED AT ROYLES WORKSHOPS - PART 2

RILEY

JOB: 137 | TYPE: Riley RMB | OWNER: Mr. S. J. Carey | IMAGES: 25

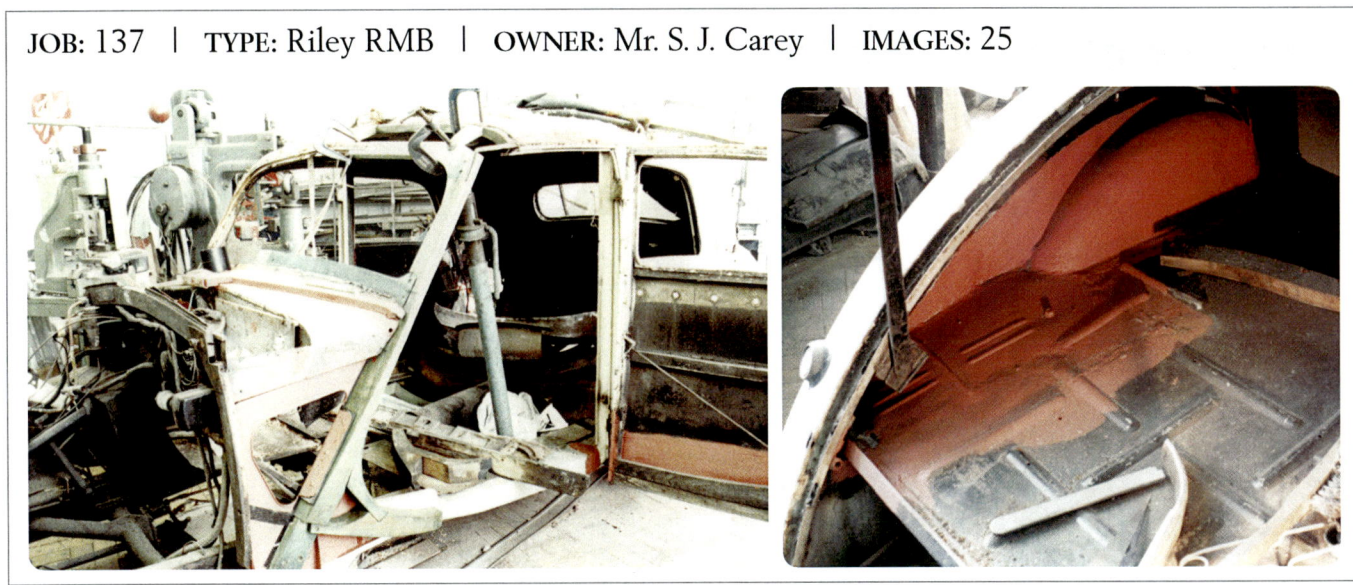

RILEY

JOB: 6 | TYPE: Riley 9 Special | OWNER: Mr. J. Slight | IMAGES: 6

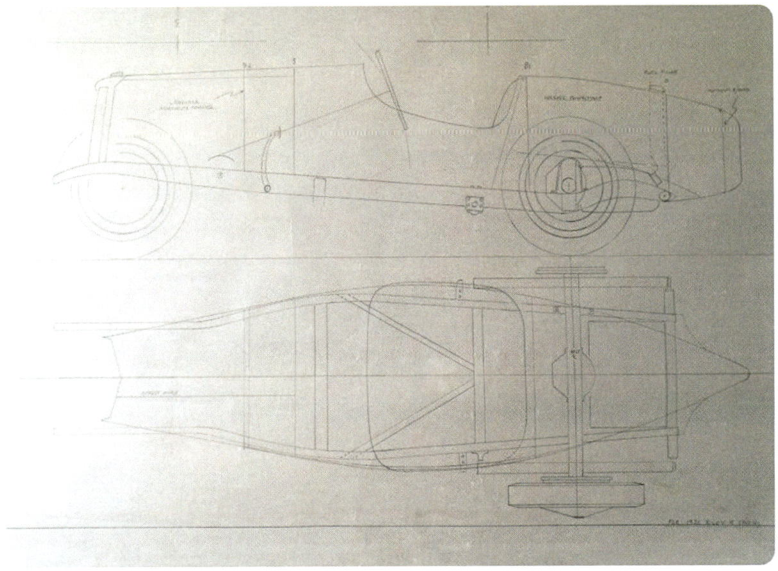

RILEY

| JOB: 176 | TYPE: Riley Special Petrol Tanks | OWNER: Mr. M. Kyle | IMAGES: 1 |

| JOB: 242 | TYPE: Riley Lynx | OWNER: Mr. J. Doggart | IMAGES: 4 |

| JOB: 330 | TYPE: Riley 1.5 Mk III | OWNER: Mr. G. Anderson | IMAGES: 11 |

CHAPTER 40 : VEHICLES RESTORED AT ROYLES WORKSHOPS - PART 2

RILEY

JOB: 331 | TYPE: Riley 9 Biaritz 1930 | OWNER: Mr. C. Hough | IMAGES: 102

JOB: 334 | TYPE: Riley Falcon 12/4 1936 | OWNER: Mr. D. Perkins | IMAGES: 10

JOB: 390 | TYPE: Riley Lynx | REFERENCE: Royle Cars | IMAGES: 2

RILEY

JOB: 429 | TYPE: Riley Lynx Tourer | OWNER: Mr. D. Mason | IMAGES: 31

JOB: 473 | TYPE: Riley 9 Biarritz 1931 | OWNER: Mr. N. White | IMAGES: 51

JOB: 491 | TYPE: Riley Imp | OWNER: Mr. A. Wynn Williams | IMAGES: 3

RILEY

JOB: 493 | TYPE: Riley Sprite | REFERENCE: Royle Cars | IMAGES: 8

JOB: 572 | TYPE: Riley 11HP Sidevalve 1922 | OWNER: Mr. J. Millman | IMAGES: 6

JOB: 672 | TYPE: Riley Roadster | OWNER: Mr. G. Sangster | IMAGES: 58

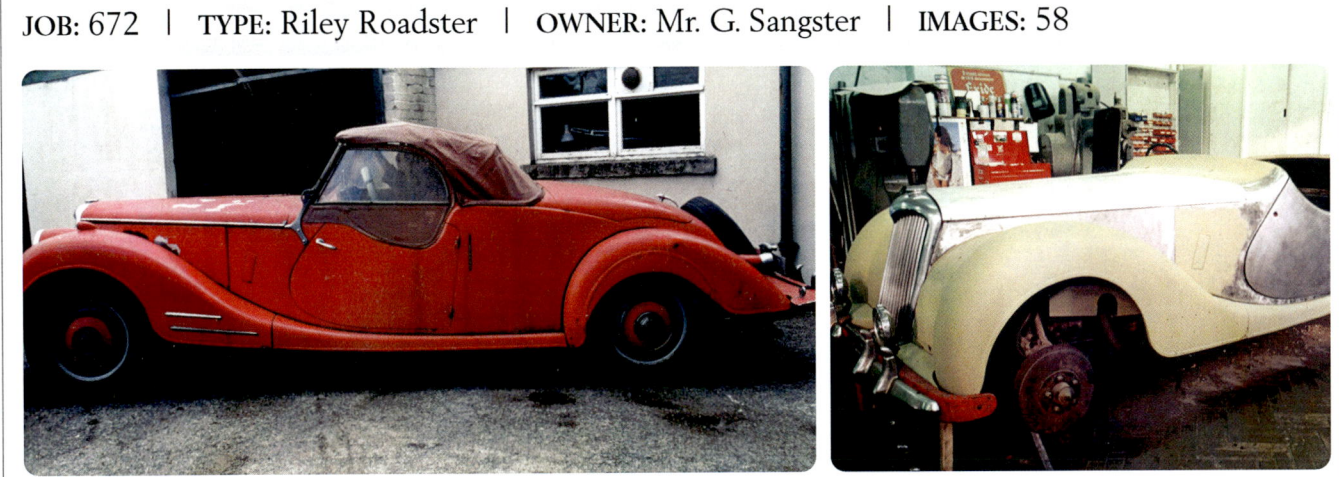

RILEY

JOB: 693 | TYPE: Riley Alpine 14/6 1932 | OWNER: Mr. J. Hawes | IMAGES: 6

JOB: 719 | TYPE: Riley 9 Single Seater 1930 | OWNER: Mr. G. Holmes | IMAGES: 12

JOB: 775 | TYPE: Riley RMC Roadster | OWNER: Dr. J. Chadwick | IMAGES: 10

CHAPTER 40 : VEHICLES RESTORED AT ROYLES WORKSHOPS - PART 2

RILEY

JOB: 806 | TYPE: Riley RMD Cabriolet | OWNER: Dr. J. Chadwick | IMAGES: 3

JOB: 820 | TYPE: Riley 9HP | OWNER: Mr. I. McCarroll | IMAGES: 3

ROLLS ROYCE

JOB: 20 | TYPE: 1935 Rolls Royce 20/25 | OWNER: F. Wake | IMAGES: 2

ROLLS ROYCE

JOB: 21 | **TYPE:** 1930 Rolls Royce 20/25 | **OWNER:** Mr. M. Mudd | **IMAGES:** 3

JOB: 35 | **TYPE:** Rolls Royce Phantom II | **OWNER:** Dr. J. Keatley | **IMAGES:** 10

JOB: 92 | **TYPE:** 1938 Rolls Royce 25/30 | **OWNER:** Mr. J. B. Cable | **IMAGES:** 1

CHAPTER 40 : VEHICLES RESTORED AT ROYLES WORKSHOPS - PART 2

ROLLS ROYCE

JOB: 118 | TYPE: Rolls Royce 1976 Silver Shadow | OWNER: Mr. P. High | IMAGES: 1

JOB: 166 | TYPE: 1938 Rolls Royce 25/30 | OWNER: Mr. J. I. McC. Salvesen | IMAGES: 20

ROLLS ROYCE

| JOB: 218 | TYPE: 1934 Rolls Royce 20/25 | OWNER: Sir D. Chapman | IMAGES: 6 |

| JOB: 235 | TYPE: Rolls Royce 20/25 | OWNER: Mr. S. Weightman | IMAGES: 17 |

| JOB: 344 | TYPE: 1927 Rolls Royce 20HP | REFERENCE: Royle Cars | IMAGES: 2 |

ROLLS ROYCE

| JOB: 237 | TYPE: 1947 Rolls Royce | OWNER: Woodall Nicholson Ltd. | IMAGES: 201 |

1947 Rolls Royce Silver Wraith by Hoopers, restored for Woodall Nicholson Ltd for Dr. Donald Riddle of Texas, USA.

ROYLE. FROM VINTAGE TO CLASSIC TO AMPHIBIAN.

ROLLS ROYCE

JOB: 237 | TYPE: 1947 Rolls Royce *continued...*

ROLLS ROYCE

JOB: 237 | TYPE: 1947 Rolls Royce *continued...*

ROLLS ROYCE

JOB: 298 | TYPE: Rolls Royce Phantom III | OWNER: Mr. R. B. B. Ropner | IMAGES: 146

1939 Rolls Royce Phantom III, V12, Restored with special touring coachwork designed and built for Mr R.B.B.(Bruce) Ropner.

This imposing motor car was shipped to the USA in 1939, returning to the UK in 1988 with 21.000 miles recorded. I designed the bodywork and we rebuilt it for fast, long distance travel. An additional fuel tank was built into this powerful Rolls Royce which then had a capacity to hold 80 gallons. The twin fuel gauges on the dashboard bear witness to this.

ROLLS ROYCE

JOB: 298 | TYPE: Rolls Royce Phantom III *continued...*

© D. A. C. ROYLE

ROLLS ROYCE

JOB: 298 | TYPE: Rolls Royce Phantom III *continued...*

ROLLS ROYCE

JOB: 298 | TYPE: Rolls Royce Phantom III *continued...*

JOB: 348 | TYPE: Rolls Royce 20/25 | OWNER: Ollerton Engineering | IMAGES: 19

JOB: 369 | TYPE: Rolls Royce Silver Shadow | OWNER: Mr. L. Coates | IMAGES: 25

ROLLS ROYCE

JOB: 441 | TYPE: Rolls Royce | OWNER: Mr. K. Kjellqvist | IMAGES: 25

JOB: 444 | TYPE: Rolls Royce Camargue 1980 | OWNER: Mr. M. Bradbrook | IMAGES: 5

JOB: 471 | TYPE: Rolls Royce Frua PVI | OWNER: Mr. K. Kjellqvist | IMAGES: 34

CHAPTER 40 : VEHICLES RESTORED AT ROYLES WORKSHOPS - PART 2

ROLLS ROYCE

JOB: 470 | TYPE: Rolls Royce Phantom V | OWNER: Mr. K. Kjellqvist | IMAGES: 250

1960 Rolls Royce Phantom V Limousine by James Young converted to a Cabriolet for Mr K.Kjellqvist.

ROLLS ROYCE

JOB: 485 | TYPE: Rolls Royce | OWNER: Mr. K. Kjellqvist | IMAGES: 11

JOB: 490 | TYPE: Rolls Royce | OWNER: Mr. Mr. H. Armstrong | IMAGES: 1

JOB: 506 | TYPE: Rolls Royce 20/25 Sedanca | OWNER: Mr. L. Riches | IMAGES: 88

CHAPTER 40 : VEHICLES RESTORED AT ROYLES WORKSHOPS - PART 2

ROLLS ROYCE

JOB: 509 | TYPE: Rolls Royce Wraith | OWNER: Mr. B. Lockwood Goose | IMAGES: 4

JOB: 539 | TYPE: Rolls Royce Phantom II | OWNER: Mr. T. Leonard | IMAGES: 117

Rolls Royce Phantom II restored with special boat tail body built for Mr Terry Leonard of Monaco.

The Owner discovered an old and unusual tapering body frame which was used as the basis for the design. When constructing the body, we also incorporated a dicky seat in this stylish golfer's coupe. After this restoration was complete, the owner toured extensively in Europe.

ROLLS ROYCE

JOB: 539 | TYPE: Rolls Royce Phantom II *continued...*

ROLLS ROYCE

JOB: 539 | TYPE: Rolls Royce Phantom II *continued...*

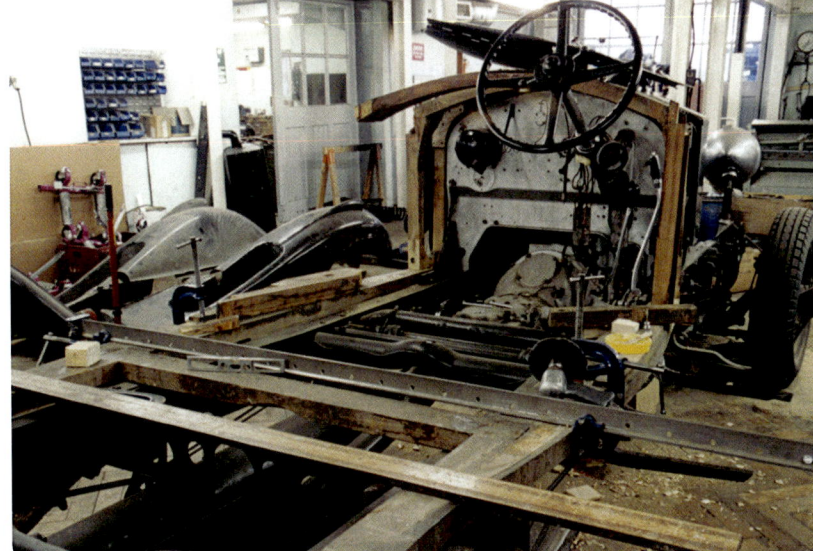

ROLLS ROYCE

JOB: 539　|　TYPE: Rolls Royce Phantom II *continued...*

CHAPTER 40 : VEHICLES RESTORED AT ROYLES WORKSHOPS - PART 2

ROLLS ROYCE

JOB: 539 | TYPE: Rolls Royce Phantom II *continued...*

JOB: 539 | TYPE: Rolls Royce Phantom II *continued...*

ROLLS ROYCE

JOB: 541 | TYPE: Rolls Royce 20HP | OWNER: Mr. T. C. R. Scott | IMAGES: 1

JOB: 586 | TYPE: Rolls Royce | OWNER: Mr. R. Hall | IMAGES: 1

JOB: 601 | TYPE: Rolls Royce P11 Limousine | OWNER: Duke of Hamilton | IMAGES: 5

CHAPTER 40 : VEHICLES RESTORED AT ROYLES WORKSHOPS - PART 2

ROLLS ROYCE

JOB: 609 | TYPE: Rolls Royce Corniche | OWNER: Mr. R. Forster | IMAGES: 10

JOB: 648 | TYPE: 1955 Rolls Royce Silver Dawn | OWNER: Mr. D. Moss | IMAGES: 7

JOB: 741 | TYPE: 1956 Rolls Royce Silver Cloud I | OWNER: Mr. R. Sloan | IMAGES: 26

507

ROLLS ROYCE

| JOB: 799 | TYPE: Rolls Royce Phantom II | OWNER: Mr. C. Scharrrighuisen | IMAGES: 80 |

CHAPTER 40 : VEHICLES RESTORED AT ROYLES WORKSHOPS - PART 2

ROLLS ROYCE

JOB: 799 | TYPE: Rolls Royce Phantom II *continued...*

JOB: 830 | TYPE: Rolls Royce | OWNER: Mr. G. Thomson | IMAGES: 4

ROVER

JOB: 124 | TYPE: Rover 110 1964 | OWNER: Mr. A. C. Day | IMAGES: 5

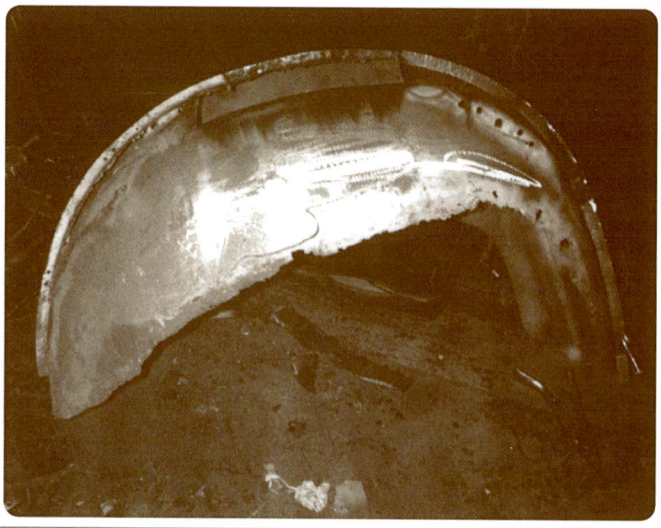

JOB: 182 | TYPE: Rover 3 Litre 1961 | OWNER: Mr. C. English | IMAGES: 2

JOB: 211 | TYPE: Rover Tickford DHC 1938/39 | OWNER: Mr. A. Hetherington | IMAGES: 1

ROVER

JOB: 233 | TYPE: Rover 10 1936 | OWNER: Mr. G. Oxley | IMAGES: 13

JOB: 276 | TYPE: Rover 100 1959 | OWNER: Mr. D. Walton | IMAGES: 18

JOB: 295 | TYPE: Rover 3.5 1968 | OWNER: Mr. L. Coates | IMAGES: 37

ROVER

JOB: 542 | TYPE: Rover '12 Tourer' 1936 | OWNER: D. Moseley | IMAGES: 7

JOB: 639 | TYPE: Rover 100 Saloon | OWNER: Mrs. G. Kennerley | IMAGES: 98

This motor car has been in the same family from new and was completely stripped down for a comprehensive restoration. The bodywork had suffered through corrosion, as is the case with most vehicles of this period which are used on roads which are salted during the winter.

These Rovers have a robust chassis however, and were built to a high standard with their well finished interiors and leather upholstery, not surprisingly, they enjoyed great popularity with businessmen and professional people. With their 2.6 litre six cylinder engines, they were capable of reaching speeds approaching 100 mph.

After a comprehensive restoration, these photographs show why the Rover P4 100 models were so popular and why they are still considered by many, to represent traditional, quality motoring of over half a century ago. This Rover will, once again, now give many years of reliable motoring and pleasure to the family.

CHAPTER 40 : VEHICLES RESTORED AT ROYLES WORKSHOPS - PART 2

ROVER

JOB: 639 | TYPE: Rover 100 Saloon *continued...*

JOB: 666 | TYPE: Rover SDI | OWNER: Mr. A. Hitch | IMAGES: 6

ROVER

JOB: 798　|　TYPE: Rover SDI VDP V8　|　OWNER: Mr. P. Johnson　|　IMAGES: 9

SINGER

JOB: 111　|　TYPE: Singer 9LM 2 Seater 1937　|　OWNER: Mr. D. Connor　|　IMAGES: 4

JOB: 540　|　TYPE: Singer　|　REFERENCE: Royle Cars　|　IMAGES: 3

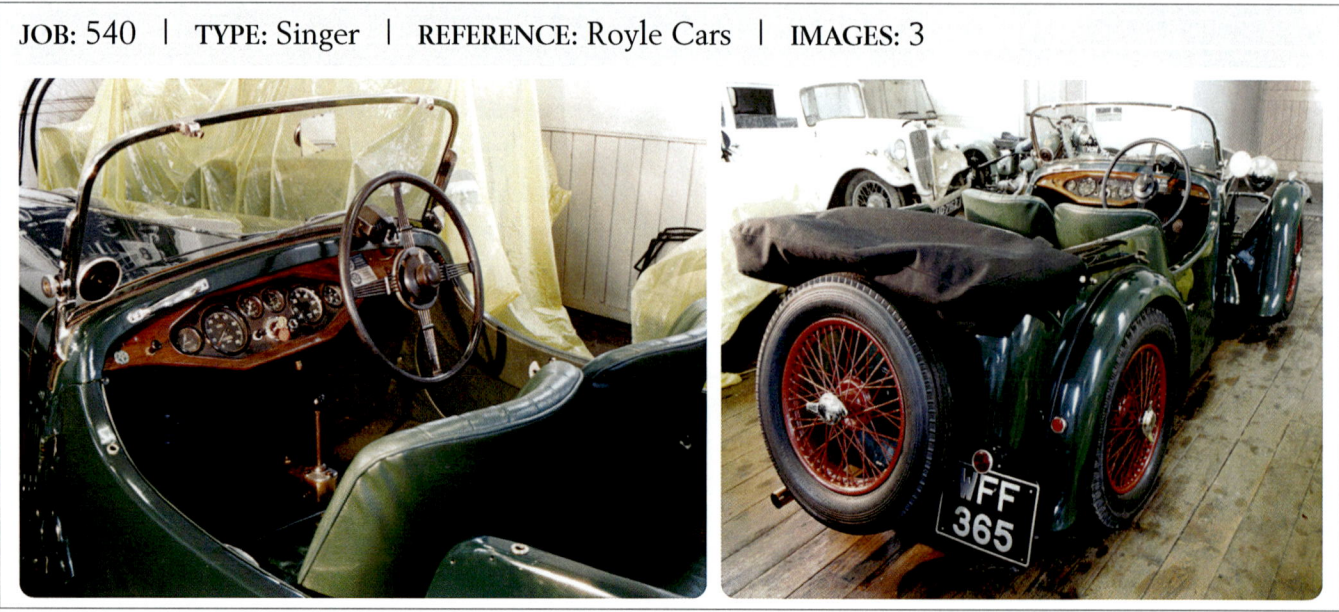

CHAPTER 40 : VEHICLES RESTORED AT ROYLES WORKSHOPS - PART 2

SINGER

JOB: 584　|　TYPE: Singer 9 Le Mans　|　OWNER: Mr. J. Gustavsson　|　IMAGES: 2

SPECIALS

JOB: 722　|　TYPE: Outdoor Canopies　|　OWNER: Mr. M. Stephenson　|　IMAGES: 14

SPECIALS

| JOB: 359 | TYPE: Copy of the 1899 'La Jamais Contente' | OWNER: D. Lambert | IMAGES: 117 |

This was a complete reconstruction of the first (electrically powered) motor car to achieve a speed of over 100 Kilometers per hour in 1899. Most of the features were faithfully reproduced, including the chassis, the body, the wrought iron suspension mountings, lever steering and the road wheels. The exception being a single electric DC motor mounted in the chassis driving through a differential. This replaced two electric motors which had been mounted directly onto the rear wheels, but which kept burning out at the time. Using ten 12 Volt batteries, the owner of 'our' car proceeded to break three current land Speed Records with it in 1988.

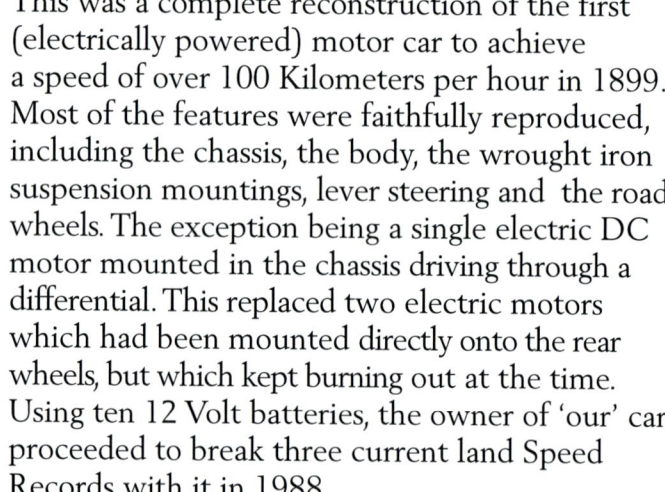

SPECIALS

| JOB: 733 | TYPE: 11 Cast Iron Table Bases | OWNER: Nina N. Campbell | IMAGES: 2 |

| JOB: 800 | TYPE: Bus / Charabanc | OWNER: Beamish - project cancelled | IMAGES: 4 |

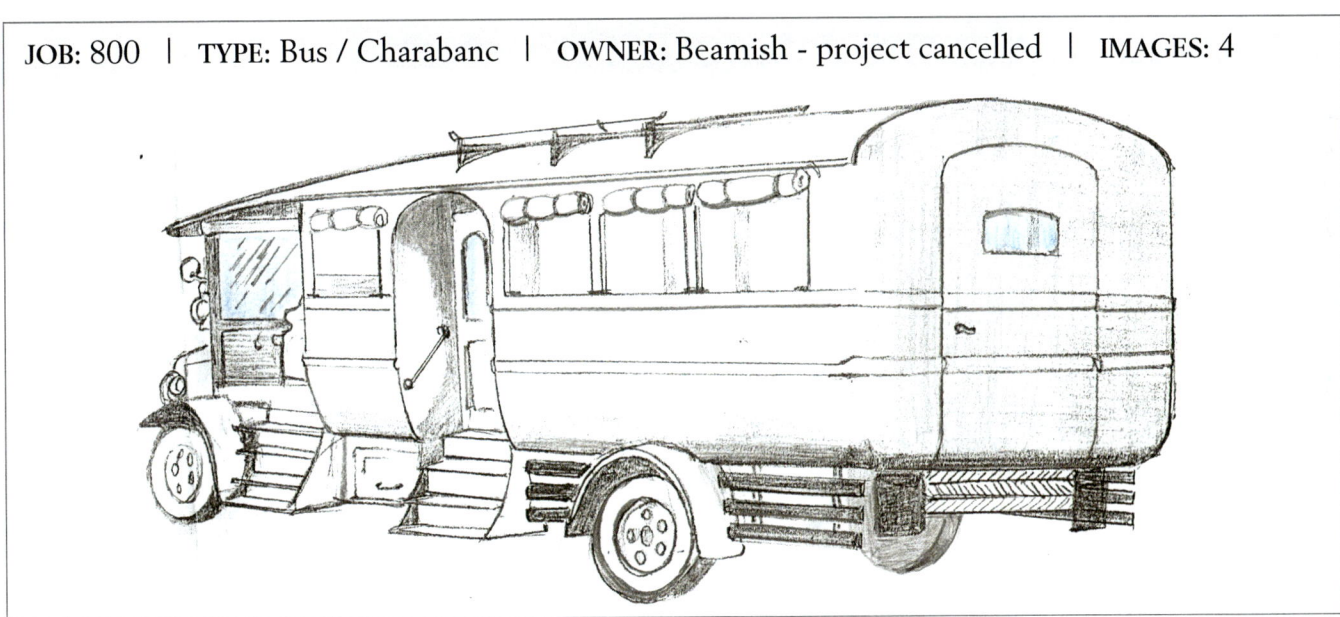

STANDARD

| JOB: 716 | TYPE: Standard Atlas Corvette | OWNER: Mr. A. Bell | IMAGES: 15 |

STANDARD

JOB: 744 | TYPE: Standard Flying 8 1939 | OWNER: Mrs. Pattison | IMAGES: 4

STANLEY

JOB: 850 | TYPE: 1914 Stanley Steam Car | OWNER: Mr. P. Turvey | IMAGES: 2

STAR

JOB: 374 | TYPE: 1928 Star Eclipse 18/50 Tourer | OWNER: Mr. D. Hall | IMAGES: 191

CHAPTER 40 : VEHICLES RESTORED AT ROYLES WORKSHOPS - PART 2

STEAM LOCO

JOB: 16 | TYPE: 7¼ Gauge Royal Scot Steam Loco | OWNER: Mr. T. Booth | IMAGES: 4

STUDEBAKER

JOB: 82 | TYPE: 1915 Studebaker | OWNER: Mr. S. Skilbeck | IMAGES: 2

JOB: 700 | TYPE: 1913 Studebaker A35 Tourer | OWNER: Mr. G. Macfarlane | IMAGES: 12

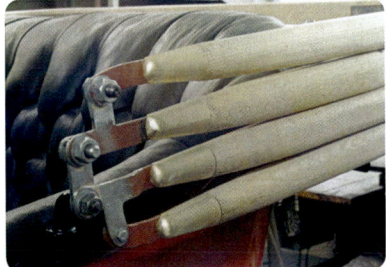

STUDEBAKER

JOB: 811　|　TYPE: 1956 Studebaker President　|　OWNER: G. Macfarlane　|　IMAGES: 28

SUNBEAM

JOB: 226　|　TYPE: Sunbeam 20.9 1929　|　OWNER: Mr. T. C. R. Scott　|　IMAGES: 86

SUNBEAM

JOB: 226 | **TYPE:** Sunbeam 20.9 1929 *continued...*

SUNBEAM

JOB: 226 | TYPE: Sunbeam 20.9 1929 *continued...*

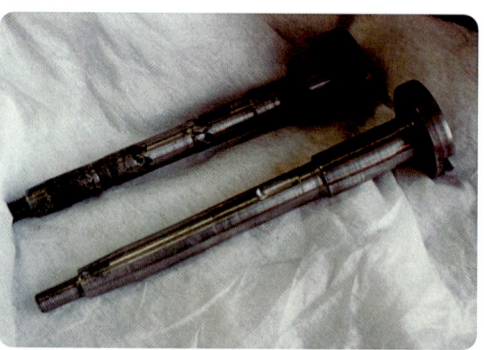

SUNBEAM

JOB: 226 | TYPE: Sunbeam 20.9 1929 *continued...*

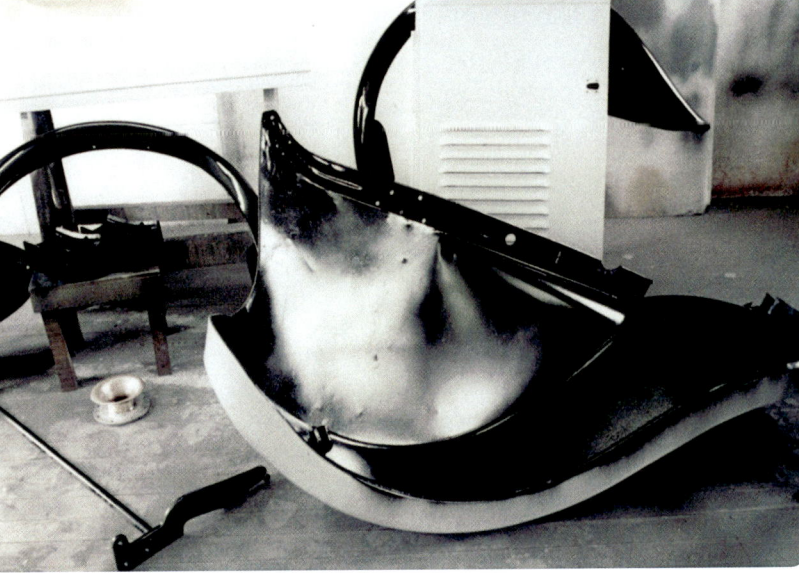

SUNBEAM

JOB: 226　|　TYPE: Sunbeam 20.9 1929 *continued...*

SUNBEAM

JOB: 226 | **TYPE:** Sunbeam 20.9 1929 *continued...*

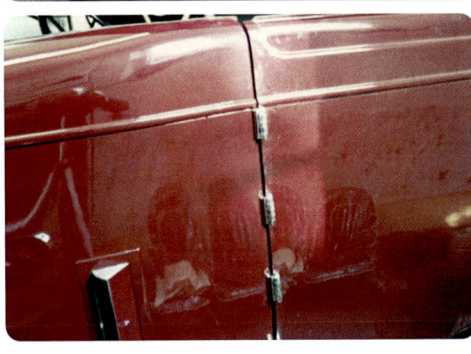

SUNBEAM

JOB: 226 | TYPE: Sunbeam 20.9 1929 *continued...*

CHAPTER 40 : VEHICLES RESTORED AT ROYLES WORKSHOPS - PART 2

SUNBEAM

JOB: 226 | TYPE: Sunbeam 20.9 1929 *continued...*

1929 Sunbeam 20.9 Drop Head Coupe', restored for Mr Terry C.R.Scott.

SUNBEAM

JOB: 290　|　TYPE: 1920 24HP Sunbeam　|　OWNER: Mr. J. Bidwell-Topham　|　IMAGES: 45

JOB: 457　|　TYPE: Sunbeam 1929　|　OWNER: Mr. T. C. R. Scott　|　IMAGES: 8

JOB: 549　|　TYPE: Sunbeam 3 Litre Tourer　|　OWNER: Mr. P. Wignall　|　IMAGES: 1

SUNBEAM

JOB: 592 | TYPE: Sunbeam 1932 | OWNER: Mr. A. Pickles | IMAGES: 65

JOB: 644 | TYPE: Sunbeam 1929 16.9 HP | OWNER: Mr. G. Harper | IMAGES: 60

SUNBEAM TALBOT

JOB: 475 | TYPE: Sunbeam Talbot | OWNER: Mr. R. B. B. Ropner | IMAGES: 10

SWIFT

| JOB: 260 | TYPE: Swift 3 Litre 1914 | OWNER: Mr. J. Bidwell-Topham | IMAGES: 28 |

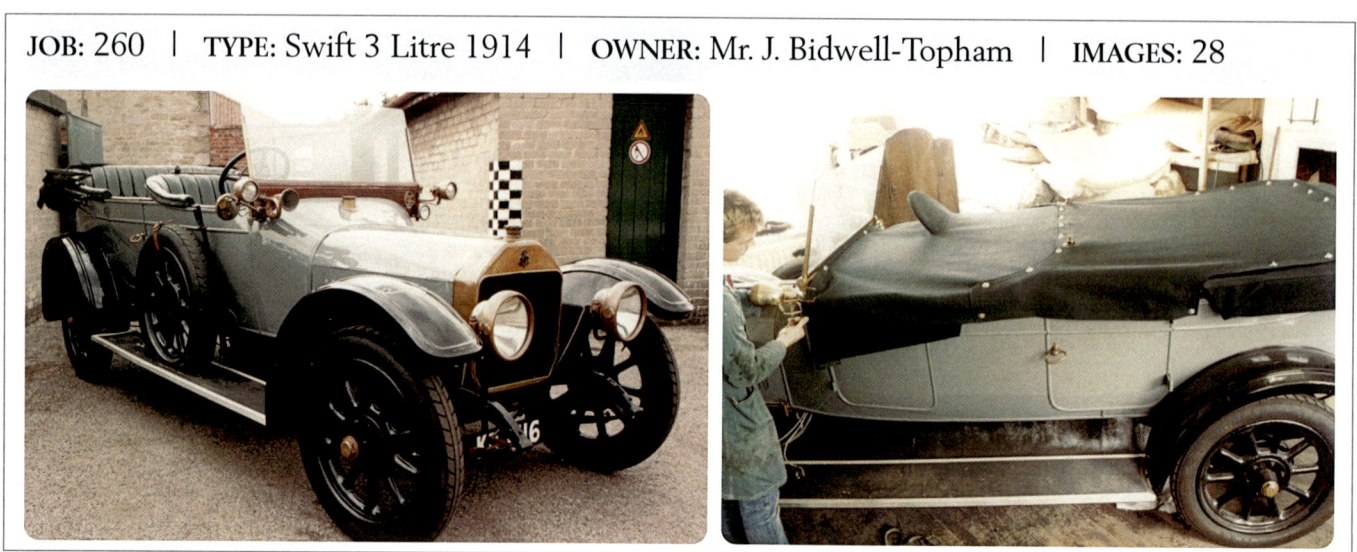

TALBOT

| JOB: 206 | TYPE: Talbot 90 | OWNER: Mr. J. Young | IMAGES: 5 |

| JOB: 610 | TYPE: Talbot 10 HP DHC | OWNER: Mr. F. Custerson | IMAGES: 70 |

TALBOT

JOB: 878 | TYPE: Talbot 20/60 | OWNER: Mr. A. Gibbs | IMAGES: 16

TRIUMPH

JOB: 162 | TYPE: Triumph Roadster 1949 | OWNER: Mr. M. Marr | IMAGES: 4

JOB: 203 | TYPE: Triumph Herald Coupe | OWNER: Mr. G. Rodgers | IMAGES: 4

JOB: 323 | TYPE: Triumph Roadster 1947 | OWNER: Mr. W. Tiley | IMAGES: 20

CHAPTER 40 : VEHICLES RESTORED AT ROYLES WORKSHOPS - PART 2

TRIUMPH

JOB: 382 | TYPE: Triumph Roadster | OWNER: Mr. Charge | IMAGES: 2

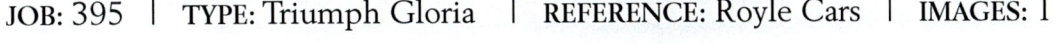

JOB: 395 | TYPE: Triumph Gloria | REFERENCE: Royle Cars | IMAGES: 1

JOB: 467 | TYPE: Triumph Dolomite 1938 | OWNER: Mrs. J. Patterson | IMAGES: 69

TRIUMPH

JOB: 532 | TYPE: Triumph Roadster 2000 | OWNER: Mr. M. Taylor | IMAGES: 12

JOB: 615 | TYPE: Triumph Spitfire | OWNER: Mr. E. Blomfield Smith | IMAGES: 3

JOB: 634 | TYPE: Triumph Spifire 1980 | OWNER: Mr. F. White | IMAGES: 4

CHAPTER 40 : VEHICLES RESTORED AT ROYLES WORKSHOPS - PART 2

TRIUMPH

JOB: 657　|　TYPE: Triumph Vitesse　|　OWNER: Mr. S. Fry　|　IMAGES: 3

JOB: 715　|　TYPE: Triumph Monte Carlo　|　OWNER: Mr. D. Atkins　|　IMAGES: 20

JOB: 791　|　TYPE: Triumph TR7　|　OWNER: Mr. C. Taylor　|　IMAGES: 7

535

TRIUMPH

JOB: 792 | TYPE: Triumph Roadster | OWNER: Mr. G. Prebble | IMAGES: 3

JOB: 794 | TYPE: Triumph TR3A | OWNER: Mr. S. Wildridge | IMAGES: 1

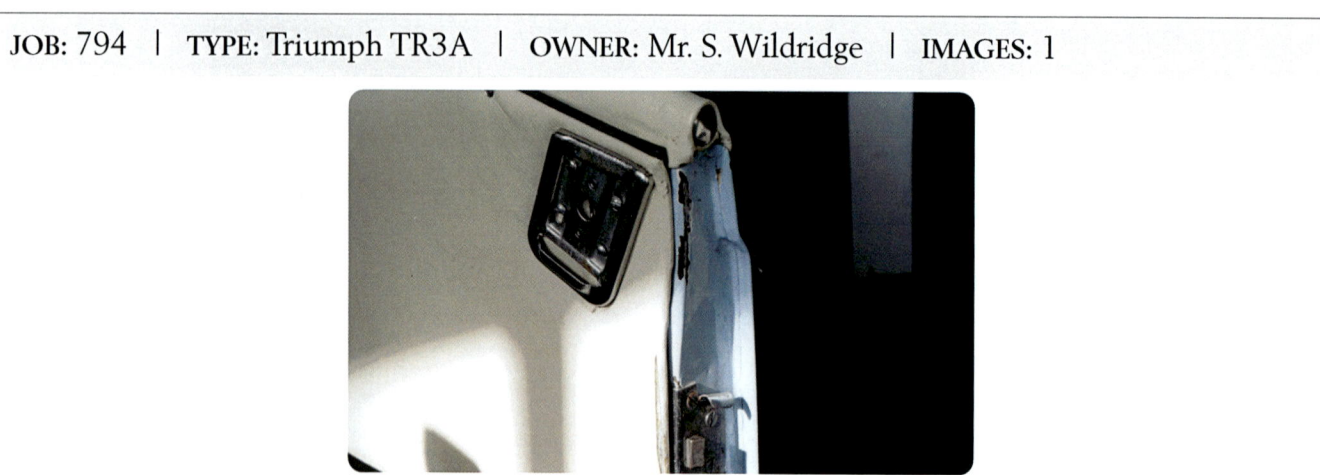

TROJAN

JOB: 199 | TYPE: Trojan 1925 | REFERENCE: Royle Hepworth | IMAGES: 4

CHAPTER 40 : VEHICLES RESTORED AT ROYLES WORKSHOPS - PART 2

ULTIMA

JOB: 655 | TYPE: Ultima Sports GT Kit Car | OWNER: Mr. K. Pickering | IMAGES: 8

VAUXHALL

JOB: 476 | TYPE: Vauxhall 10 Coupe 1938 | OWNER: Mr. G. Woodgate | IMAGES: 1

JOB: 551 | TYPE: Vauxhall 20/60 Tourer | REFERENCE: Royle Cars | IMAGES: 4

VAUXHALL

| JOB: 562 | TYPE: Vauxhall Royale Coue 1981 | OWNER: Mr. P. Smyth | IMAGES: 22 |

VOLKSWAGON

| JOB: 23 | TYPE: Volkswagon Kubelwagen | OWNER: Mr. B. Chapman | IMAGES: 2 |

| JOB: 468 | TYPE: Volkswagon Karman Ghia | OWNER: Mr. L. Storey | IMAGES: 7 |

WOLSELEY

JOB: 49 | TYPE: Wolseley Hornet Special | OWNER: Mr. A. White | IMAGES: 2

JOB: 99 | TYPE: Wolseley 25 DHC | OWNER: Mr. J. Stocks | IMAGES: 8

JOB: 123 | TYPE: Wolseley 10 1923 | OWNER: Mr Morgan | IMAGES: 2

WOLSELEY

| JOB: 215 | TYPE: Wolseley 16/20 1919 | OWNER: Mr. Worth | IMAGES: 2 |

| JOB: 337 | TYPE: Wolseley Hornet 1932 | OWNER: T. V. Smith | IMAGES: 157 |

1932 Wolseley Hornet Fixed Head Coupe' Restored for Mr Terry Smith of Saudi Arabia.

This pleasing Wolseley Coupe' was known as the "Occasional Four" and was built to a high standard with a fine leather interior and a good performance, 5000 rpm being available from its 1270 cc overhead camshaft engine.

This interesting motor car was stripped down to the bare chassis and a comprehensive restoration undertaken. As with most of the vehicles restored by Royle's, the full photographic record would need to be studied to fully appreciate all the work done. The selection here, however, will provide some indication of the nature and extent of it

They show the vehicle being stripped down, the Chassis and wheels after shot blasting and priming and the rear axle being cleaned in readiness for checking and overhaul. Other photographs show the front axle and various components along with the front and rear mudguards and other panels after repair, blast cleaning and priming.

WOLSELEY

JOB: 337 | TYPE: Wolseley Hornet 1932 *continued...*

The engine and ancillaries have been stripped and overhauled and after running on the test bed, are refitted to the chassis after painting. The axles, the fuel and brake pipes and the stainless steel exhaust system have also been reassembled and refitted. In the meantime, the bodywork, doors mudguards and all the parts which make up the body have been painted after all the necessary repairs and restoration work.

When the body has been mounted back onto the chassis, the fabric roof is padded and recovered and head linings fitted into the interior. The cappings and dash board are finished after being stripped and lacquered. The door panels and the unique double leather door pockets have been faithfully reproduced and fitted along with the carpets, seats, wiring, lamps and the entire car assembled.

This fine compact Wolseley Hornet Coupe' is now ready for road testing and tuning before being returned to its owner. This fine example of British engineering was sold with a two year guarantee in 1932.

In 2009, this motor car returned to Royle's Staindrop workshops. It was still in excellent condition, looking every bit as good as it did when it left us, eighteen years after its restoration. This was a credit to Mr Smith, who had obviously taken great care of this exceptional Wolseley Coupe'.

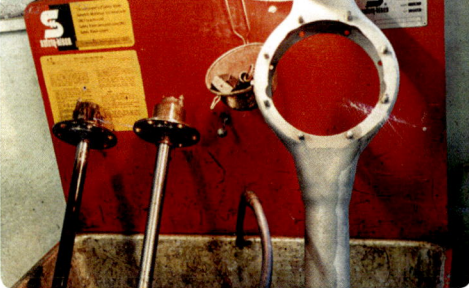

WOLSELEY

JOB: 337 | TYPE: Wolseley Hornet 1932 *continued...*

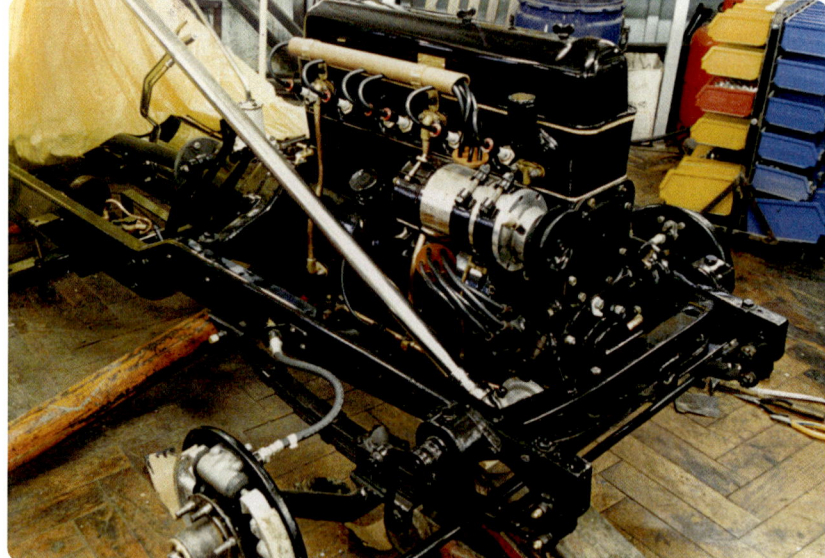

CHAPTER 40 : VEHICLES RESTORED AT ROYLES WORKSHOPS - PART 2

WOLSELEY

JOB: 365 | TYPE: Wolseley 12/48 1937 | OWNER: Mr. G. Telford | IMAGES: 49

JOB: 400 | TYPE: Wolseley Hornet Special | OWNER: Mr. Rasche | IMAGES: 4

JOB: 435 | TYPE: Wolseley Hornet Special | REFERENCE: Royle Cars | IMAGES: 3

WOLSELEY

JOB: 450 | TYPE: Wolseley 1933 | OWNER: Rev. Canon Senior | IMAGES: 2

JOB: 558 | TYPE: Wolseley 9 Saloon | OWNER: Mr. S. Clemenson | IMAGES: 1

JOB: 565 | TYPE: Wolseley 1938 | OWNER: Mr. M. Mills | IMAGES: 7

WOLSELEY

JOB: 880 | TYPE: Wolseley Hornet Special | OWNER: Mr. B. Lawrence | IMAGES: 8

JOB FILES WITHOUT PHOTOGRAPHIC RECORDS

These lists include a number of smaller jobs and over the years, some vehicles were brought in for work more than once, sometimes by subsequent owners. In these cases, depending upon the amount of work done, the vehicle may appear more than once in chapter 40 with different job numbers.

ALFA ROMEO

| JOB: 676 | TYPE: Alfa Romeo | OWNER: J. Bentley |

ALVIS

JOB: 39	TYPE: Alvis 1948	OWNER: J. Feguson
JOB: 56	TYPE: Alvis TA14	OWNER: A. Ainsworth
JOB: 87	TYPE: Alvis TD21	OWNER: B. Johnson
JOB: 131	TYPE: Alvis Silver Eagle 1929	OWNER: Mr. Holt
JOB: 190	TYPE: Alvis 12/40 4 Seat 1924	REFERENCE: Royle Hepworth
JOB: 243	TYPE: Alvis Parts	OWNER: Dr. J. Robson
JOB: 307	TYPE: Alvis Steering Box	OWNER: R. Pettnam
JOB: 367	TYPE: Alvis TD21	REFERENCE: Royle Cars
JOB: 461	TYPE: Alvis Speed 25 Saloon	REFERENCE: Royle Cars
JOB: 516	TYPE: Alvis Silver Eagle Saloon	OWNER: R. Pettman
JOB: 569	TYPE: Alvis Speed 20 Tourer	OWNER: D. Clark
JOB: 593	TYPE: Alvis 12/70 Tourer	REFERENCE: Royle Cars
JOB: 611	TYPE: Alvis 12/70 Tourer	OWNER: V. Shaw
JOB: 765	TYPE: Alvis	OWNER: T. Chaytor Norris
JOB: 776	TYPE: Alvis DHC TC 21/100	OWNER: Mr. Blow
JOB: 782	TYPE: Alvis 1966	OWNER: M. Bridge

ALVIS continued...

JOB: 783	TYPE: Alvis SP20	OWNER: Gledhill Assessors
JOB: 795	TYPE: Alvis	OWNER: G. Wrapson
JOB: 835	TYPE: Alvis TA14 1948	OWNER: R. Stansfield
JOB: 877	TYPE: Alvis 12/50 Tourer	OWNER: J. Millman
JOB: 890	TYPE: Alvis SPD 20 Charlesworth Saloon	OWNER: J. Brown

ARMSTRONG SIDDELEY

JOB: 347	TYPE: Armstrong Siddeley	OWNER: P. Ward
JOB: 656	TYPE: Armstrong Siddeley	OWNER: D. Potter

ARROL-JOHNSTON

JOB: 872	TYPE: Arrol-Johnston	OWNER: M. Hardy

ASTON MARTIN

JOB: 75	TYPE: Aston Martin DB5 Bumpers	OWNER: Mr. Moore
JOB: 311	TYPE: Aston Martin Wire Wheels	OWNER: R. Wilson
JOB: 469	TYPE: Aston Martin DB6	OWNER: J. Wilson
JOB: 679	TYPE: Aston Martin V8	OWNER: R. Harris

ATKINSON

JOB: 90	TYPE: Atkinson Commercial	OWNER: J. Monk

AUDI

JOB: 866	TYPE: Audi A8	OWNER: J. Clapcott
JOB: 867	TYPE: Audi	OWNER: J. Clapcott

AUSTIN

JOB: 15	TYPE: Austin 7 Special	OWNER: C. Booth
JOB: 89	TYPE: Austin 7	OWNER: Mr. Brownless
JOB: 104	TYPE: Austin 7 Wheels	OWNER: Mr. Mc Garr
JOB: 112	TYPE: Austin 7 Saloon	OWNER: Mr. Summerfield
JOB: 139	TYPE: Austin Big 7	OWNER: Mr. Richardson
JOB: 257	TYPE: Austin A40 1966	OWNER: Mr. Calvert
JOB: 345	TYPE: Austin 10	OWNER: Mr. P. Taggart
JOB: 373	TYPE: Austin 10 Saloon	OWNER: Mr. Taggart
JOB: 403	TYPE: Austin 16	OWNER: P. Taggart
JOB: 488	TYPE: Austin 7	REFERENCE: Royle Cars
JOB: 492	TYPE: Austin	OWNER: Bidwell Topham

AUSTIN continued...

JOB: 498	TYPE: Austin Big 7	OWNER: Mrs. Crisp
JOB: 566	TYPE: Austin A35 Saloon	OWNER: F. Tallentire
JOB: 577	TYPE: Austin Big 7 Saloon	OWNER: Mr. Oliphant
JOB: 646	TYPE: Austin Trio	OWNER: B. Lee
JOB: 660	TYPE: Austin 7 Saloon	OWNER: J. Walton
JOB: 662	TYPE: Austin Princess 2200	OWNER: I. Irving
JOB: 725	TYPE: Austin 10 1934	OWNER: Mr. Vipond
JOB: 789	TYPE: Austin 7 Ruby Saloon	OWNER: D. Swain
JOB: 808	TYPE: Austin 7 Arrow	OWNER: C. Oliver
JOB: 825	TYPE: Austin 10/4 1933	OWNER: D. Brown
JOB: 852	TYPE: Austin Commercial	OWNER: J. Miller
JOB: 882	TYPE: Austin 7 Special	OWNER: C. Oliver
JOB: 898	TYPE: Austin Mini 1970	OWNER: T. Burman

AUSTIN HEALEY

JOB: 32	TYPE: Austin Healey 3000	OWNER: R. Reeves
JOB: 105	TYPE: Austin Healey 3000	OWNER: A. Doggart
JOB: 575	TYPE: Austin Healey Sprite	OWNER: G. Amery
JOB: 812	TYPE: Austin Healey	OWNER: S. Brown

BARNARD

JOB: 326	TYPE: Barnard Formula 6 Go Kart	REFERENCE: Royle Hepworth

BEDFORD

JOB: 352	TYPE: Bedford 1960	OWNER: R. Stirk

BENTLEY

JOB: 57	TYPE: Bentley R	OWNER: P. Harper
JOB: 101	TYPE: Bentley 3.5 Litre	OWNER: P. J. Mc Call
JOB: 219	TYPE: Bentley 3.5 Litre	OWNER: M. Grigsby
JOB: 222	TYPE: Bentley 3.5 Litre	OWNER: M. Grigsby
JOB: 300	TYPE: Bentley	OWNER: J. Ambler
JOB: 305	TYPE: Bentley 3.5 Litre	OWNER: Mr. E. Darbyshire
JOB: 333	TYPE: Bentley 4.5 Litre	OWNER: Mr. Cook
JOB: 380	TYPE: Bentley 6.5 Litre	OWNER: Bidwell Topham
JOB: 383	TYPE: Bentley	OWNER: Mr. Hudson
JOB: 433	TYPE: Bentley 3 Litre Tourer	REFERENCE: Royle Cars
JOB: 521	TYPE: Bentley	OWNER: Mr. R. Henderson

BENTLEY continued...

JOB: 602	TYPE: Bentley 3 Litre	OWNER: J. Watson
JOB: 734	TYPE: Bentley 'R'	OWNER: J. Shaw
JOB: 736	TYPE: Bentley 1991	OWNER: S. Best
JOB: 745	TYPE: Bentley Corniche Convertible	OWNER: J. Mayhew
JOB: 797	TYPE: Bentley	OWNER: G. Hampton
JOB: 805	TYPE: Bentley 3 Litre Tourer	OWNER: Prof. T. Anderson
JOB: 826	TYPE: Bentley 3/4 1/2	OWNER: K. Schellenberg
JOB: 847	TYPE: Bentley 3 Litre	OWNER: K. Schellenberg
JOB: 857	TYPE: Bentley S2 DHC	OWNER: W. Rankin

BMW

JOB: 63	TYPE: BMW Coupe	OWNER: J. Davison
JOB: 189	TYPE: BMW 2002	OWNER: Mr. Milbourne

BOATS

JOB: 399	TYPE: Boat Projects	OWNER: CML
JOB: 520	TYPE: Wheel Boat	OWNER: CML
JOB: 534	TYPE: Boat Project	OWNER: CML
JOB: 686	TYPE: Albatross Speedboat	OWNER: J. Lauder
JOB: 735	TYPE: Boat Project	OWNER: CML

BRISTOL

JOB: 329	TYPE: Bristol 400 DHC	OWNER: Mr. J. Howden-Richards
JOB: 605	TYPE: Bristol 411	OWNER: A. Bettess
JOB: 612	TYPE: Bristol 400 DHC	OWNER: R. Peacock
JOB: 818	TYPE: Bristol	OWNER: Sir Hugh Blackett
JOB: 839	TYPE: Bristol 400	OWNER: Sir Hugh Blackett

BUGATTI

JOB: 355	TYPE: Bugatti 35	OWNER: Mr. Park

BUICK

JOB: 126	TYPE: Buick 1930 (bonnet)	
JOB: 514	TYPE: Buick Van	REFERENCE: Royle Cars

CADILLAC

JOB: 771	TYPE: Cadillac 1949	OWNER: Mr. D. Lindsay

CITROEN
JOB: 638	TYPE: Citroen DS Pallas 1973	OWNER: I. Potts
JOB: 651	TYPE: Citroen 1925	OWNER: G. Hadfield
JOB: 689	TYPE: Citroen 2CV Special	OWNER: J. Craven

COMMER
JOB: 728	TYPE: Commer 1972	OWNER: N. Crampton

CROSSLEY
JOB: 843	TYPE: Crossley 14HP	OWNER: Mr. Summer
JOB: 884	TYPE: Crossley Tourer	OWNER: Mr. S. Weld

DAIMLER
JOB: 456	TYPE: Daimler	REFERENCE: Royle Cars
JOB: 528	TYPE: Daimler Straight 8	REFERENCE: Royle Cars
JOB: 550	TYPE: Daimler Saloon	Work not done
JOB: 557	TYPE: Daimler Straight 8 V26	OWNER: Mr. Fothergill
JOB: 620	TYPE: Daimler V26 1934	OWNER: D. Fothergill
JOB: 814	TYPE: Daimler V8 Saloon	OWNER: A. Mc Guigan
JOB: 862	TYPE: Daimler Barker Sports	OWNER: A. Duma

DE DION BOUTON
JOB: 547	TYPE: De Bion Bouton 1904	OWNER: Mr. Jowsey

DELAGE
JOB: 297	TYPE: Delage 14HP 1927	REFERENCE: Royle Hepworth
JOB: 350	TYPE: Delage D8	OWNER: J. Reisner
JOB: 474	TYPE: Delage D8S	OWNER: Mr. R. Brown
JOB: 764	TYPE: Delage Delahyde	OWNER: J. Reisner
JOB: 863	TYPE: Delage 1926	OWNER: M. Hardy

FERRARI
JOB: 159	TYPE: Ferrari Dino	OWNER: I. Calder
JOB: 266	TYPE: Ferrari	OWNER: Mr. D. Parkinson

FIAT
JOB: 749	TYPE: Fiat 850 Sport Coupe	OWNER: Mr. Muir

FORD

JOB: 135	TYPE: Ford Consul Mk I	OWNER: D. Hogg
JOB: 179	TYPE: Ford Capri 3000	OWNER: R. Crossland
JOB: 513	TYPE: Ford Model T 4 Seat	OWNER: Beamish Museum
JOB: 688	TYPE: Ford Escort	OWNER: N. Arnold
JOB: 696	TYPE: Ford Cortina Mk III	OWNER: Mr. N. Ferguson
JOB: 787	TYPE: Ford Y Tourer	OWNER: D. Grace
JOB: 869	TYPE: Ford Ranger	OWNER: J. Clapcott
JOB: 875	TYPE: Ford Fiesta Van	OWNER: DACR Company Vehicle

FRAZER NASH

JOB: 223	TYPE: Frazer Nash 1937	OWNER: Mr. Ford
JOB: 652	TYPE: Frazer Nash 1933	OWNER: R. Brittain
JOB: 838	TYPE: Frazer Nash	OWNER: R. Matthews

GILBURN

JOB: 871	TYPE: Gilburn Genie	OWNER: R. Clarke

GMC

JOB: 263	TYPE: GMC Truck	OWNER: Mr. Richardson

HANSA

JOB: 697	TYPE: Hansa 1935	OWNER: M. Denzler

HILLMAN

JOB: 195	TYPE: Hillman 14 1930	REFERENCE: Royle Hepworth
JOB: 501	TYPE: Hillman Tourer	OWNER: Mr. Newbold

HONDA

JOB: 583	TYPE: Honda Quad Bike	OWNER: B. Ropner

HUDSON

JOB: 524	TYPE: Hudson Sedan	REFERENCE: Royle Cars

HUMBER

JOB: 42	TYPE: Humber Pullman	OWNER: Mechtool Engineering
JOB: 421	TYPE: Humber World War II Staff Car	OWNER: T. Payne

CHAPTER 40 : VEHICLES RESTORED AT ROYLES WORKSHOPS - PART 2

INVICTA
- **JOB:** 142   **TYPE:** Invicta   **OWNER:** Mr. R. Henderson
- **JOB:** 483   **TYPE:** Invicta 1929   **OWNER:** Mr. R. Henderson

JAGUAR
- **JOB:** 54   **TYPE:** Jaguar E-Type   **OWNER:** M. Colescott
- **JOB:** 64   **TYPE:** Jaguar E-Type
- **JOB:** 76   **TYPE:** Jaguar E-Type Chrome Work   **OWNER:** Mr. Patrick
- **JOB:** 127   **TYPE:** Jaguar E-Type 1968   **OWNER:** M. Milburn
- **JOB:** 149   **TYPE:** Jaguar XJ12 Saloon   **OWNER:** Mr. A. Stephenson
- **JOB:** 194   **TYPE:** Jaguar XK150S 1960   **REFERENCE:** Royle Hepworth
- **JOB:** 282   **TYPE:** Jaguar E-Type V12 1972   **REFERENCE:** Royle Hepworth
- **JOB:** 299   **TYPE:** Jaguar XK140 FHC   **OWNER:** Mr. Pinkney
- **JOB:** 338   **TYPE:** Jaguar V12E 2+2   **REFERENCE:** Royle Hepworth
- **JOB:** 358   **TYPE:** Jaguar V12E 2+2   **REFERENCE:** Royle Cars
- **JOB:** 379   **TYPE:** Jaguar XJ12   **REFERENCE:** Royle Cars
- **JOB:** 408   **TYPE:** Jaguar XK150 DHC   **REFERENCE:** Royle Cars
- **JOB:** 418   **TYPE:** Jaguar   **REFERENCE:** Royle Cars
- **JOB:** 431   **TYPE:** Jaguar V12E 2+2   **OWNER:** Mr. Storey
- **JOB:** 447   **TYPE:** Jaguar Mk II Saloon 2.4   **OWNER:** D. Barnes
- **JOB:** 535   **TYPE:** Jaguar XK150 FHC   **OWNER:** G. Todd
- **JOB:** 545   **TYPE:** Jaguar XJS Convertible   **OWNER:** Mr. Blacklock
- **JOB:** 598   **TYPE:** Jaguar XJ6 Series II   **OWNER:** Mr. Middleton
- **JOB:** 739   **TYPE:** Jaguar XJ6 Coupe   **OWNER:** Mr. Wakefield
- **JOB:** 743   **TYPE:** Jaguar V12 E-Type FHC   **OWNER:** P. Gosling
- **JOB:** 762   **TYPE:** Jaguar XK140 FHC   **OWNER:** Mr. P. Townley
- **JOB:** 768   **TYPE:** Jaguar XK120 Roadster   **OWNER:** T. Hamnett
- **JOB:** 770   **TYPE:** Jaguar 420G   **OWNER:** M. Foster
- **JOB:** 815   **TYPE:** Jaguar XK - Parts   **OWNER:** R. Gaunt
- **JOB:** 865   **TYPE:** Jaguar SJR 1994   **OWNER:** J. Clapcott
- **JOB:** 883   **TYPE:** Jaguar E-Type 1961   **OWNER:** J. Barnes

JEEP
- **JOB:** 876   **TYPE:** Jeep Cherokee   **OWNER:** J. Royle

JENSON
- **JOB:** 86   **TYPE:** Jenson Sedan   **OWNER:** E. Coulson
- **JOB:** 247   **TYPE:** Jenson Interceptor DHC   **OWNER:** B. Durham
- **JOB:** 504   **TYPE:** Jenson DHC   **OWNER:** E. Coulson

JOWETT

JOB: 559	TYPE: Jowett Long Four Tourer	OWNER: S. Clemenson
JOB: 832	TYPE: Jowett Javelin	OWNER: A. Drury

KIT CARS

JOB: 517	TYPE: Kit Car Ferrari Detona	OWNER: A. Cox
JOB: 560	TYPE: Magenta Kit Car	OWNER: D. Muncaster
JOB: 625	TYPE: Jaguar Kit Car	OWNER: Mr. Gray
JOB: 649	TYPE: Lamporghini Replica Kit Car	OWNER: G. Hanley
JOB: 667	TYPE: Teal Kit Car	OWNER: Mr. P. E. Searle
JOB: 687	TYPE: Evolution Kit Car	OWNER: J. Knight
JOB: 692	TYPE: Kit Car D Type Replica	OWNER: Mr. M. Norton
JOB: 711	TYPE: Pilgrim Bull Do Kit Car	OWNER: J. Sheppard
JOB: 720	TYPE: Lomax Kit Car	OWNER: D. Poulton
JOB: 729	TYPE: Cobra Kit Car	OWNER: S. Robinson
JOB: 750	TYPE: Pilgrim Sumo (Cobra) Kit Car	
JOB: 774	TYPE: Convin (Porsche) Kit Car	OWNER: Mr. D. Laidler
JOB: 788	TYPE: Kit Car	OWNER: A. Leblond

LAGONDA

JOB: 5	TYPE: Lagonda 16/80 1933	OWNER: R. Clayton
JOB: 96	TYPE: Lagonda Wings	OWNER: J. Wright
JOB: 140	TYPE: Lagonda 2 LT 1929	OWNER: Mr. Wiggins
JOB: 144	TYPE: Lagonda Body	OWNER: M. Williams
JOB: 174	TYPE: Lagonda 2 Litre	OWNER: Mr. Swan
JOB: 180	TYPE: Lagonda Parts	OWNER: Hon. J. Skeffington
JOB: 193	TYPE: Lagonda M35 1934	REFERENCE: Royle Hepworth
JOB: 349	TYPE: Lagonda 2 Litre	OWNER: K. Dobinson
JOB: 446	TYPE: Lagonda	OWNER: I. Harris
JOB: 529	TYPE: Lagonda Rapide	OWNER: C. Peerless
JOB: 543	TYPE: Lagonda 3 Litre Tourer	REFERENCE: Royle Cars
JOB: 573	TYPE: Lagonda 3 Litre Tourer	OWNER: A. W. Williams
JOB: 585	TYPE: Lagonda M45 Tourer	OWNER: L. G. Itskowitz
JOB: 606	TYPE: Lagonda Supercharged 2 Litre	OWNER: R. Brittain
JOB: 742	TYPE: Lagonda 1935	OWNER: K. Boardall
JOB: 802	TYPE: Lagonda LG45 Saloon	OWNER: Mr. Proud
JOB: 840	TYPE: Lagonda 2 Litre	OWNER: H. Kaye

LANCIA

JOB: 834	TYPE: Lancia 1965	OWNER: C. Shore

CHAPTER 40 : VEHICLES RESTORED AT ROYLES WORKSHOPS - PART 2

LANCHESTER
- JOB: 184   TYPE: Lanchester   OWNER: K. Gray

LEA FRANCIS
- JOB: 613   TYPE: Lea Francis Ace of Spades   OWNER: W. Wilson
- JOB: 841   TYPE: Lea Francis 1939   OWNER: J. Delaney

LOTUS
- JOB: 68   TYPE: Lotus 47   OWNER: Mr. Griffiths
- JOB: 121   TYPE: Lotus Elan 1970   OWNER: R. Ellis
- JOB: 587   TYPE: Lotus Esprit Turbo   OWNER: R. Bowden
- JOB: 754   TYPE: Lotus Elan 2+2   OWNER: Mr. Humphreys

MARCOS
- JOB: 357   TYPE: Marcos 1600   OWNER: Duke of Hamilton

MASERATI
- JOB: 28   TYPE: Maserati   OWNER: E. Dobinson
- JOB: 53   TYPE: Maserati 250F   OWNER: N. Corner
- JOB: 74   TYPE: Maserati 350   OWNER: Mr. Waugh

MAZDA
- JOB: 870   TYPE: Mazda Pick Up   OWNER: J. Clapcott
- JOB: 879   TYPE: Mazda Pick Up   OWNER: J. Clapcott

MERCEDES BENZ
- JOB: 145   TYPE: Mercedes Benz 1961   OWNER: Mr. Brittain
- JOB: 287   TYPE: Mercedes Benz 230SL   OWNER: K. Heimer
- JOB: 366   TYPE: Mercedes Benz   OWNER: J. Ogden
- JOB: 752   TYPE: Mercedes Benz   OWNER: D. Carruthers
- JOB: 819   TYPE: Mercedes Benz   OWNER: A. Gray

MG
- JOB: 18   TYPE: MG J2 1933   OWNER: M. D. Marshall
- JOB: 25   TYPE: MG TC 1949   OWNER: Mr Teasdale
- JOB: 62   TYPE: MG TF   OWNER: D. Jewitt
- JOB: 84   TYPE: MG PB   OWNER: E. D. Keighley
- JOB: 116   TYPE: MG NA Magnette 1934   OWNER: J. Morton
- JOB: 152   TYPE: MGB Roadster   OWNER: Mr. Conway

MG continued...

JOB: 255	TYPE: MGYB	OWNER: R. Harmer
JOB: 296	TYPE: MGY Saloon	OWNER: K. Walker
JOB: 427	TYPE: MG TF	REFERENCE: Royle Cars
JOB: 443	TYPE: MG TD	REFERENCE: Royle Cars
JOB: 481	TYPE: MG TC	OWNER: A. Wynn Williams
JOB: 503	TYPE: MG TC Sports	REFERENCE: Royle Cars
JOB: 523	TYPE: MG B Roadster	REFERENCE: Royle Cars
JOB: 570	TYPE: MG PA 4 Seater Sports	OWNER: B. Johnson
JOB: 829	TYPE: MG BGT	OWNER: Gary
JOB: 845	TYPE: MGB V8	OWNER: J. Macallister
JOB: 861	TYPE: MG	OWNER: P. Cryer
JOB: 874	TYPE: MGB GT 1966	OWNER: R. Jones
JOB: 893	TYPE: MGB Roadster	OWNER: E. Dyer

MITSUBISHI

JOB: 833	TYPE: Mitsubishi	OWNER: Mitsubishi L2000

MORGAN

JOB: 85	TYPE: Morgan 4+4	OWNER: J. S. Tucker
JOB: 115	TYPE: Morgan 4/4 1937	OWNER: Mr. White
JOB: 164	TYPE: Morgan 4/4	OWNER: Kirklevington C. C. Garage
JOB: 732	TYPE: Morgan +4	OWNER: D. Gibson
JOB: 821	TYPE: Morgan 4/4	OWNER: Mr. Tough

MORRIS

JOB: 12	TYPE: Morris 10 Saloon 1936	OWNER: J. Edgell
JOB: 24	TYPE: Morris Isis 1932	OWNER: D. C. Clark
JOB: 50	TYPE: Morris 8	OWNER: S. Woodall
JOB: 55	TYPE: Morris Minor Mcevoy Special	OWNER: B. Rasche
JOB: 65	TYPE: Morris 8 Saloon	OWNER: B. Grover
JOB: 79	TYPE: Morris	OWNER: Mr. Leach
JOB: 108	TYPE: Morris 10/4	OWNER: Mr. Leach
JOB: 143	TYPE: Morris Minor	OWNER: T. Dron
JOB: 171	TYPE: Morris Oxford 1925	OWNER: Mr. Clark
JOB: 291	TYPE: Morris 6 Cylinder Head 1950	OWNER: A. Wharrior
JOB: 423	TYPE: Morris Bullnose Oxford	REFERENCE: Royle Cars
JOB: 439	TYPE: Morris 1934	OWNER: D. Scott
JOB: 531	TYPE: Morris Minor 1000 Saloon	OWNER: P. Brown

MORRIS continued...

JOB: 641	TYPE: Morris Oxford Bullnose	OWNER: M. Allan
JOB: 738	TYPE: Morris 8 Seater 11 Saloon	OWNER: Mr. S. Santa Maria
JOB: 779	TYPE: Morris 1937	OWNER: D. Bond
JOB: 822	TYPE: Morris 10/6 Special	OWNER: Mr. W. Dick
JOB: 864	TYPE: Morris Minor	OWNER: J. Clapcott

MOTORCYCLES

JOB: 44	TYPE: Matchless	OWNER: Mr. Rishworth
JOB: 51	TYPE: Scott Chassis Frame	OWNER: T. Darbyshire
JOB: 487	TYPE: Velocette Motorcycle	OWNER: A. Leighgoe
JOB: 496	TYPE: Sunbeam Motorcycle	

NISSAN

JOB: 748	TYPE: Nissan Sunny Coupe	OWNER: C. Hamilton

OLDSMOBILE

JOB: 891	TYPE: Curved Dash Oldsmobile 1903	OWNER: K. Clarke

PANTHER

JOB: 831	TYPE: Panther Kallista	OWNER: J. White
JOB: 842	TYPE: Panther Kallista	OWNER: C. Westwood

PARTS

JOB: 67	TYPE: Cast Iron Lamp Heater	OWNER: Mr. Blyth
JOB: 80	TYPE: Motorcycle Sidecar	OWNER: G. Robinson
JOB: 165	TYPE: MG Wheels	OWNER: K. Reeks
JOB: 170	TYPE: Motorcycle Magneto	OWNER: B. Knots
JOB: 201	TYPE: Motorcycle Petrol Tank	OWNER: T. Turnbull
JOB: 210	TYPE: MG Windscreen	OWNER: G. Mackeith
JOB: 231	TYPE: Steel Window Surrounds	OWNER: P. Taggart
JOB: 251	TYPE: Riley 1948	OWNER: D. Thurston
JOB: 328	TYPE: 2 Cylinder Air Compressor Motor	
JOB: 362	TYPE: Chromework	OWNER: Mr. Bidwell Topham
JOB: 401	TYPE: Car Trunk	OWNER: T. Scott
JOB: 410	TYPE: Lourvres	
JOB: 436	TYPE: Aircraft P51 Panels	OWNER: N. Robinson
JOB: 533	TYPE: Various Bentley Parts	OWNER: Mr. Bidwell Topham
JOB: 548	TYPE: Bentley Parts	OWNER: K. Schellenberg

PARTS continued...
JOB: 664	TYPE: Deemster (radiator)	OWNER: G. Hadfield
JOB: 777	TYPE: Lorry	OWNER: Mr. Breward
JOB: 824	TYPE: Sundry Car Parts	OWNER: M. Neil
JOB: 855	TYPE: Boss Mustang	OWNER: K. Mcananey

PERAMBULATORS
JOB: 486	TYPE: Pram	OWNER: B. Ropner
JOB: 780	TYPE: Marmet Pram 1963	OWNER: Mrs. Cadwallander
JOB: 803	TYPE: Perambulator 1930	OWNER: Mrs. V. Pettifer
JOB: 810	TYPE: Pram	OWNER: S. Vaux

PEUGEOT
JOB: 790	TYPE: Peugeot 205	OWNER: H. Carter

PORSCHE
JOB: 160	TYPE: Porsche	OWNER: Mr. Bewick
JOB: 229	TYPE: Porsche 911 Targa	OWNER: Mr. Plumb
JOB: 455	TYPE: Porsche	OWNER: G. Ratcliff
JOB: 645	TYPE: Porsche 1969	OWNER: D. Wilson
JOB: 658	TYPE: Porsche 911 Cabriolet	OWNER: R. Mair

PROTOTYPES
JOB: 41	TYPE: V8 Project	OWNER: J. & D. Dobson

RAILTON
JOB: 413	TYPE: Railton 10	REFERENCE: Royle Cars

RANGE ROVER
JOB: 786	TYPE: Range Rover	OWNER: Mrs. Shaw

RELIANT
JOB: 588	TYPE: Reliant Sabre	OWNER: P. Wilson

RENAULT
JOB: 731	TYPE: Renault 1909	

REO
JOB: 851	TYPE: Reo 1929	OWNER: Mr. J. Bowman

RILEY

JOB: 17	TYPE: Riley Kestrel	OWNER: R. Reeves
JOB: 38	TYPE: Riley RM	OWNER: Miss Barnes
JOB: 48	TYPE: Riley 9 Lynx 1933	OWNER: P. Ward
JOB: 58	TYPE: Riley	OWNER: A. Cook
JOB: 70	TYPE: Riley Lynx Tourer	OWNER: Mr Hall
JOB: 71	TYPE: Riley 9 Secial	OWNER: J. Mark
JOB: 98	TYPE: Riley 9 Wheels (6)	OWNER: Mr. White
JOB: 109	TYPE: Riley RME 1.5 Litre	OWNER: Mr. Keating
JOB: 198	TYPE: Riley 15/6 Adelphi 1938	REFERENCE: Royle Hepworth
JOB: 384	TYPE: Riley 12/4 Falcon Saloon	REFERENCE: Royle Cars
JOB: 507	TYPE: Riley Falcon 1937	OWNER: J. Mattheson
JOB: 555	TYPE: Riley Kestrel 12/4	OWNER: J. Lorimer
JOB: 849	TYPE: Riley RMB	OWNER: Dr. J. Chadwick
JOB: 860	TYPE: Riley Chatsworth 1927	OWNER: A. Haywood

ROLLS ROYCE

JOB: 59	TYPE: Rolls Royce	OWNER: J. Davison
JOB: 265	TYPE: Rolls Royce 20HP 1924	OWNER: Scotts of Avonmouth
JOB: 388	TYPE: Rolls Royce 25/30	OWNER: P. Kitching
JOB: 397	TYPE: Rolls Royce	REFERENCE: Royle Cars
JOB: 426	TYPE: Rolls Royce	REFERENCE: Royle Cars
JOB: 428	TYPE: Rolls Royce Silver Shadow	OWNER: G. Booth
JOB: 497	TYPE: Rolls Royce Wraith	OWNER: K. Gray
JOB: 595	TYPE: Rolls Royce 1957	OWNER: D. Towler
JOB: 599	TYPE: Rolls Royce Tourer	OWNER: S. McWilliams
JOB: 816	TYPE: Rolls Royce Shadow II 1977	OWNER: Mr. Prime
JOB: 817	TYPE: Rolls Royce Silver Spirit 1981	OWNER: J. Harvey
JOB: 856	TYPE: Rolls Royce 1978	OWNER: Mr. Stokes
JOB: 887	TYPE: Rolls Royce 20/25	OWNER: Mr. T. C. R. Scott

SAAB

JOB: 895	TYPE: Saab 900 1990	OWNER: Mr. A. Hearn

SCAMMEL

JOB: 60	TYPE: Scammel	OWNER: C. Smith

SINGER

JOB: 13	TYPE: Singer 4 AB Roadster	OWNER: I. Wintrip
JOB: 29	TYPE: Singer 4A Roadster	OWNER: Mr. Davidson
JOB: 37	TYPE: Singer Bantam	OWNER: J. Citrone
JOB: 173	TYPE: Singer Bantam 1935	OWNER: J. Citrone
JOB: 310	TYPE: Singer 9	OWNER: G. Austin
JOB: 346	TYPE: Singer 1933	OWNER: T. Gray
JOB: 419	TYPE: Singer II Saloon	REFERENCE: Royle Cars
JOB: 527	TYPE: Singer - work not done	
JOB: 561	TYPE: Singer 9 Sports	OWNER: C. Sellars

SPECIALS

JOB: 544	TYPE: Norris Special	OWNER: Mr. Stirling
JOB: 614	TYPE: One-off Sledge	OWNER: B. Ropner
JOB: 681	TYPE: Batten Special (Ford V8)	OWNER: N. Bennett
JOB: 706	TYPE: 'Replica' Chitty-Chitty Bang-Bang'	OWNER: G. Grant
JOB: 766	TYPE: Triking 3 Wheeler	OWNER: S. Thompson

STANDARD

JOB: 281	TYPE: Standard Warwick	OWNER: M. C. Henderson

STUTZ

JOB: 40	TYPE: Stutz	OWNER: H. Garnett
JOB: 836	TYPE: Stutz 1929	OWNER: M. Blousefield

SUNBEAM

JOB: 571	TYPE: Sunbeam Rapier	OWNER: Mr. Bidwell Topham
JOB: 868	TYPE: Sunbeam Rapier	OWNER: J. Clapcott
JOB: 881	TYPE: Sunbeam Rapier 1964	OWNER: S. Cartudhe

SWALLOW

JOB: 72	TYPE: Swallow Sidecar	OWNER: G. Wright

SWIFT

JOB: 302	TYPE: Swift 4 Seater Tourer	OWNER: Mr. D. Hedgley

TALBOT

JOB: 91	TYPE: Talbot DHC 1923	OWNER: Mr. Paris
JOB: 458	TYPE: Talbot Coupe	REFERENCE: Royle Cars
JOB: 675	TYPE: Talbot 90 Sports Racing	OWNER: Mr. O Brien

TRIUMPH

JOB: 77	TYPE: Triumph Roadster	OWNER: R. Curtis
JOB: 148	TYPE: Triumph Roadster 2000	OWNER: Mr. Dale
JOB: 381	TYPE: Triumph TR4	REFERENCE: Royle Cars
JOB: 402	TYPE: Triumph Spitfire	OWNER: D. Taylor
JOB: 608	TYPE: Triumph 13/60	OWNER: D. Herdman
JOB: 678	TYPE: Triumph TR6	OWNER: Lt. B. Macmaster
JOB: 844	TYPE: Triumph TR4A	OWNER: Mr. Ashton
JOB: 885	TYPE: Triumph Acclaim	OWNER: H. Williams

VOLKSWAGON

JOB: 387	TYPE: Formula VW	OWNER: S. Robinson

WOLSELEY

JOB: 8	TYPE: Wolseley Stellite 9.5 HP 1914	OWNER: S. Skilbeck
JOB: 27	TYPE: Wolseley	OWNER: Mr. White
JOB: 371	TYPE: Wolseley Saloon	REFERENCE: Royle Cars
JOB: 698	TYPE: Wolseley Hornet Special	OWNER: R. Johnson

CHAPTER 41:
THE START OF COVELINK

In August 1987 the family was on another of their many pilgrimages to St Mawes in Cornwall. This time for the regatta's of the Falmouth-Fowey fortnight. It was my third trip down to the boat that year.

We were greatly enjoying living on board 'Meriva', our 43ft sloop which was designed by Holman and Pye and built in 1967. She was of traditional carvel construction built of mahogany with pitch pine below the water line, had beautiful lines and her sleek coach roof and counter stern set off the overall design to perfection. She was the boat of my boyhood dreams. In the cabins, the mahogany planking was varnished and with her 12 foot beam, she was roomy and spacious.

This was our third year living aboard Meriva, having bought her in July 1985. Our two boys, Jeremy and Nicholas, were now in the senior school at Barnard Castle, but were still happy to put up with their parents for the summer holidays! They shared the forward cabin up in the bows which was snug and each had their own drawers for their clothes with a convenient warm hanging cupboard in the spacious 'Heads', so that they could dry towels, wetsuits etc. The heads were separated from their cabin by a sliding door. When I say spacious, I mean compared to many sailing boats. It was big enough to swing a cat and had a lagged hot water cylinder, a hand basin, a shower with a smart teak grating and a Baby Blake lavatory which I had previously stripped down, overhauled and re-chrome plated. This loo was a sight to Behold and a delight for any real 'Vintage' man to operate, but the ladies sometimes were confused by all the knobs and handles!

Moving further aft, the saloon was reached through another sliding door, this cabin had four bunks which were most comfortable due to them having rubber webbing supports for the bedding. There were brown vynal covered mattresses with buttoned backs and an off centre, removable table which converted into a double bed if required. Up two steps through another sliding door was the Galley which also accommodated the generous chart table, under which was a fridge. The galley was, by now, equipped with a new gas stove in gimbals, astern of which was access to a further bunk neatly running under the Port cockpit seat for those on night watch duties.

Up two more steps via two small mahogany doors and into the cockpit which had a handsome wooden wheel and a generator in the lazarette below the aft deck. I had this fitted, so that we always had power for the batteries and the bonus was that Jo-Jo could dry her hair with an electric hairdryer. Not having been brought up to sail, I did all I could to make her feel at home and she had the galley equipped with all her requirements. Having Jo-Jo on board was a boon for us all, she made the boat into a proper holiday home and could cater for any eventuality.

Looking at my diary for the 31st August 1987, for example, this was the day of the Bacardi Rum Race.

We had Terry Stephenson on board who was a keen racing man and he encouraged me to enter 'Meriva''. I didn't often race the boat because my aim was to enjoy the relaxation of sailing, not to have the hassle of it all, but I thought it might be interesting for a change, so off we went.

After a good start in a fresh breeze, I was delighted when we finished first over the line. After applying our handicap, we were further down the fleet. Not surprisingly, with our long waterline length, we should have been somewhere near the front. It was a most enjoyable day and it showed that Jo-Jo was able to cope and had sufficient cups, plates and food to accommodate twenty-two people for tea! Like the racing, it was not an everyday occurrence, which is why it was mentioned in my diary.

After twenty five years of sailing at St Mawes, at that time, we have many good friends there and it is like a home from home. We were however, one of very few who lived on board at our mooring in the Percuil River. At night, the river is wonderfully quiet and the wild life is literally on your 'door step', or you can listen to it walking around on the cabin roof! It is a pleasure to be on board.

CHAPTER 41: THE START OF COVELINK

Many of our friends have houses in St Mawes which their families have owned for many years, some dating back to before the war.

In the early years, before I had Meriva, when I was still a bachelor and also later with Jo-Jo and the boys, we were often invited to stay with the Wilson family and then later, with the Whittons. I would be their crew for the racing, whilst Jo-Jo would take the children down to play on one of the many nearby beaches in the lovely, quiet and sandy coves. It was a good arrangement, but when I had finished the restoration work to my first keelboat, a 26ft Camper and Nicholson stoop called 'Ladybird of Rhu', we were then able to live on board on our mooring with the children.

Meriva at rest and speed.

'Ladybird' was a solidly built GRP cabin boat which I bought from my old friend James Ferrier who was, by then, the Sales Director of Camper and Nicholson, the famous and long established yacht builders of Gosport in Hampshire. 'Ladybird' had been rather neglected and had been laid up ashore in their yard for some years, and was in need of a good refit. The interior was lined with teak which had gone black with age and neglect, but like the rest of the boat, was actually of top quality and I was confident, that it would be eminently restorable.

A good friend 'Dicky' Newhouse, who was always good fun and lived near to us here in the North East, was just completing the conversion of an old railway station at a quiet place called Sexhow. After we had talked about all sorts of names for the house, I was delighted when he took up my suggestion to call it 'The Sleepers', Sexhow, it sounded just right somehow! Anyway, Dicky was a keen sailor, so we agreed to share ownership of the boat and as he wanted to help me with the work, he suggested that we put the boat near his house. The Sleepers' still retained the old raised and stone flagged platform and this turned out to be an ideal height to enable us to walk on and off the boat when we were working on it, she had a deep keel.

Refitting Ladybird with Dicky.

We had the boat transported North by road and straight away, we set about refitting and refurbishing 'Ladybird'. We renewed the rigging and overhauled the original engine. This can be an awkward job, but it came out without too much trouble. The teak interior panelling was hard work, but responded well to being rubbed down and when teak oiled, the rich colour reappeared, as it did with all the internal and exterior varnish work. It goes without saying that I couldn't resist the temptation to restore and rebuild the Baby Blake. I made some smart special brass hinges to fit the new varnished seat and cover which I made out of a solid block of Honduras Mahogany. Although I say it myself, the result was superb, a proper Royle throne!

Altogether the work took four years, during which time Dicky unfortunately, had to relinquish his share in the boat due to unforeseen circumstances. When the work was complete, the boat was once again transported by road, this time all the way to St Mawes onto a mooring which I had bought from a local fisherman through John Castle, the new owner of the Old Freshwater Boatyard. John, as it turned out, was also a keen Lagonda enthusiast and had one of the fast little Rapier models, for which I was to design and Royles built, a sporty two seater body (job 375). We became good friends as the years passed.

Of course, it was not always 'spanking' sailing, sunshine and teacakes on the Cornish coast. There were days when the westerly gales came in from the Atlantic and although we were fortunately on our strong sheltered mooring, the long fetch across the Carrick 'roads' would create waves which, at night, certainly would send you to sleep or otherwise! One memorable night was when hurricane 'Charlie' arrived from America.

By this time, thankfully we had bought 'Meriva'. Being nearly fourteen tons displacement, she was longer, heavier and a more stable boat then 'Ladybird'. She would still move in the swell and of course the wind does shriek in the high rigging on these occasions. We had some Scottish friends, David and Judy Reid from Edinburgh, staying on board. They had their son Robbie with them who was, of course, great pals with our boys. It was around 1 a.m. when I finally decided to turn in after checking the rigging, the mooring and making sure the sails were properly furled and lashed, I went below, changed and naturally visited the heads.

Grasping hold of the main Baby Blake pumping handle, I was surprised to find it was absolutely solid, it would not move up or down. I won't go into the mechanical details, but marine lavatories have their operational limitations and can cope with a blockage. The problem is that if this occurs, usually with too much loo paper, the harder one tries to pump it out, the more the build up of pressure. Nothing will break because they are very strongly made and knowing that our Royle boys and Jo-Jo know these limitations, I could only conclude by the sheer rigidity of the handle, that it had to be the work of a strong, young Scots lad called Robby Reid!

It was clear that his concerted efforts trying to flush the loo, he had created a lot of pressure in the main cylinder, In this case, a very high pressure! There was no alternative, but to get the tools out and tackle the problem there and then, so that it would be working in time for the assembled 'crew' in the morning. Having just showered and feeling fresh and clean, I took the precaution of putting on my bad weather 'oilies' again, plus a pair of deck boots.

Stripping down this particular component entailed serious shipboard risk. I was in no doubt of the likely result when a cylinder full of 'waste' under high pressure is released to the atmosphere. Gingerly, I undid the holding down bolts and as the top casting of the cylinder came loose, the pressure was released. There was a horizontal 'woosh' and the small cabin turned brown and the lower part of me with it. My situation could aptly be described as being dire!

Not wanting to spread the 'stuff' on the other cabin floors, I had no choice, but to slide open the main cabin door and call quietly to Jo-Jo to wake her. I wanted her to fill up a few buckets of sea water to swill down the walls and interior of the Heads to wash it all out. With wind shrieking in the rigging, sleep was not easy and like the Trojan that she is, she got up and putting on her silk dressing gown, switched on

Up the mast.

the cross tree deck lights, opened the cabin doors and climbed up the steps into the cockpit. She soon found the bucket and holding onto the end of the long rope attached to it, she threw it over the side to fill it with water.

As I peered out of my shitty little cabin - there was a sight to behold! Jo-Jo's bucket was horizontal, like a wind sock, on the end of its rope and Jo-Jo's silken gown was flying out behind her like the 'flying lady' mascot on a Rolls-Royce radiator. All this of course, in a boat which was heaving in the swell in a gale of wind - what a girl!

To cut a long story short, she managed to fill the bucket a few times with the help of the long boat hook and I was able to wash the heads cabin down. Fortunately the large teak grating set into the floor, had an extraction pump, so all the contents could be pumped overboard to feed the fish - it was now 3am and so to bed.

With all the noise of the gale in the rigging and the general movement of the boat, our guests were blissfully unaware of the drama as it unfolded, that was until I told them about it in the morning. They thought it was hilarious. "The pleasures of sailing" they said as they happily pumped out the now, fully operational, blessed Baby Blake.

FIRST THOUGHTS OF AMPHIBIANS

I used to manage to spend five weeks living on the boat each season with fitting out in the spring and two fortnights in the summer with Jo-Jo and the Boys on their holidays. The pleasure of being on the water with all the boats moored around you and with friends sailing by, combined with the beauty of the Percuil River and all the sea birds in the area, made for a wonderful environment. There is also something about the contrast in sailing or going shopping in the dinghy and then motoring fast in the speedboat. Whatever the activity, the complete change from living at home and working on and driving ancient, vintage and modern motor cars, couldn't be greater. Each in its own way, being a most enjoyable experience and wonderfully interesting.

I am afraid that all this has echoes of the 'silver spoon' upbringing, actually this is not really the case. The environment which I grew up in and the skills and gifts which I inherited from father and mother, combined with the freedom to do the work which most interested me, resulted in my hobbies becoming my lifelong 'professional' activities, a great luxury in life.

To return to boating, when crossing from the boat to the shore, whether it was to St Mawes or to Falmouth or journeying up river to Truro, the only real problem, which always arises, is when we needed to then leave the boat and travel on the road inland for any reason. The first consideration is coping with the rise and fall of tides 15ft and more in Cornwall (especially during spring tides) it is then a problem of where to leave the dinghy. It often means dragging it up and down a beach or throwing out an anchor and land line. It didn't bother me particularly, but it was a problem if Jo-Jo was on her own, so it started me thinking about a boat which had wheels. A boat which could be driven out of the water and then along the nearest road.

Lying in my bunk at night, the idea grew and I started to sketch some of the ways in which it could be done. Looking back now at my many files and shelves full of documents, drawings, patents and correspondence, I can see that the work intensified during 1987. As ever, to begin with, I would jot down any ideas on the back of large envelopes when no other paper was handy. The ideas developed and as I investigated the history and researched the amphibious transport vehicle designs and the market, it became clear that here was a great opportunity to innovate and create a properly designed and technically advanced dual purpose form of transport.

Starting with my brother John, by now a colonel in the British army, he outlined the military situation. It became clear that virtually all amphibians were built by adapting and converting existing motor vehicles of various types. In the civilian world, an ordinary motor car

Brother John.

1942 DUKW.

would be made watertight for example and then some sort of drive made for a propeller. Other larger amphibians were based upon a truck or bus chassis. The most famous being the World War Two DUKW's. This American amphibious vehicle was based upon a six-wheeled General Motors 2 ton truck chassis. It was developed in great haste in 1942, its beginnings were fraught with opposition by many of the military top brass in Washington.

As it turned out, in the fullness of time, I would find that little had changed. Nobody would see more clearly than me, the enormous difficulties involved with 'selling' a project of this unusual nature to those in control of funding for new projects. However, the pressures were such during wartime, that eventually it was four yachtsmen who persuaded the authorities that they would be a useful form of transport and they set to and designed the DUKW in just six weeks. One of these was Rod Stephens the well known yacht designer of Sparkman and Stephens of New York, another was P. C. Puttnam who was involved with other new vehicles.

Jumping ahead for a moment, by pure coincidence, I was given a lot of support by Lord David Puttnam (a relation?) who was the Chairman of the National Endowment of Science, Technology and the Arts (Nesta) in London. His enthusiasm for this project was such that, later on, after I had won their first and biggest award for innovation, he resigned his chairmanship of Nesta. This, I understand, was because the Nesta organisation would not provide any more money to help put our advanced 'Roylecraft' amphibious vehicles into production. His enthusiasm shines through in a film made about my project by the BBC at the time, in 2000, the new Millennium.

To return to the DUKW's, two other yachtsmen were apparently involved, Messrs Puleston and Warner, both experienced and technically knowledgeable men. Their success and that of the DUKW's is reflected in the 21,000 units that were built from 1942 onwards during the war and proved their worth

Four examples of tourist amphibians based upon 1942 DUKW's

in many important wartime invasions, landing on beaches in Europe, the Pacific and other theatres of war. The amphibians had proved that they could provide facilities which no other machines could do.

My reserch revealed that both before and after the war, various motor cars were made to float and did work and drive, but as with the DUKW's, the maximum speed in water usually was slow, around 9mph maximum. None of the motor car types could travel at planing speeds on water nor were they seaworthy.

Various attempts to build motorised amphibious vehicles and boats have been made since the beginning of the 20th century. There was an early attempt to fit wheels to a boat for example, this is shown in the period photograph shown here from the 'Motor' magazine, 18 June 1907.

'Motor' 18/06/07

Before the war, Ferdinand Porsche experimented with an amphibious motor car, and after the war, quite a number of 'Amphicars' were built, also in Germany, using a Triumph Herald engine. On the road these would cruise at up to 65mph, but on water their performance was poor with a maximum speed of up to 10 mph. The 'Dutton Mariner' was another motor car

The 'Dutton Mariner'.

type. This was a rebuilt Ford with a GRP body. Again, it floated and worked, but was not fast and once again, like the others, it was not seaworthy.

Hobbycar. (France) exhibited 1993 Geneva Motorshow. Mouland Daily Mail 28/11/94.

There have been a number of other civilian vehicles which have been built which floated on water. The Nagisa from Japan, theRenault Racoon from France. The Argocat were built in

The eight-wheel-drive Argo.

Canada and these have been successfully used for various purposes including overland transport for shooting and transporting deer in Scotland for example. These were small, lightweight, chain driven vehicles with six and eight wheels, they had minimal suspension,

The 'Amphicar'.

so were fitted with floatation tyres. Built with an open, moulded plastic tub body, their light weight and all terrain capability satisfied a need and quite a number were sold. Their maximum speed on land was around 20mph, but only 2 mph on water. This was because they relied upon the friction of the rotating road wheels to move them through the water.

Creating an efficient, cost effective amphibian was a challenge which was obviously going to be difficult to meet, especially if high speeds on water were to be achieved.

A military version of a small multi-wheeled machine which floated, has been built in the UK, called the 'Supacat'. This is in production

The 'Supacat'.

at the time of writing and is a more robust, slightly larger machine which is enjoying repeat orders by the MOD. Involved in the design and production of these and a great enthusiast for 'All Terrain' machines and motor cars of all kinds, is the Duke of Hamilton. I have spent a great deal of time and had much fun with him over the years, not only testing some of his All-Terrain Vehicles, but also with many of his interesting collection of motor cars. He is a most unassuming man and his experiences as an aircraft flight test pilot and depth of knowledge, not only of engineering, for which he is highly qualified, but also of Scotland's history, furniture and architecture, is a privilege to enjoy.

The above examples are just a few of the many motor vehicles made to float, but will give you some idea of the range of amphibians which have been built over the years. There are too many military and civilian versions to list here, but the important feature common to most of them is the reliance, principally, upon existing automotive technology. Normal motor vehicles are not designed for immersion in water, especially salt sea water. Aspects of their construction can suffer serious problems if they are ever driven into water of any depth. When any such vehicle is converted for amphibious use, the inevitable result is that their performance suffers in most respects, especially from electro-chemical reaction with salt water and at sea.

After 50 years of working with motor cars and boats of every description, it has always been clear to me that modifying and converting any vehicle which is not designed for the purpose, is bound to be unsatisfactory. This couldn't be better illustrated by the poor performance of most existing amphibious vehicles, they are slow and generally unsafe in a seaway.

REVERSING PREVIOUS PRACTICE.

Since the war, especially in recent years, the performance and refinement of motor vehicles and virtually all other modes of transport, have improved enormously. Even in 1987, it was very clear to me that the same could not be said of amphibious transport.

History shows that It may have been the quickest and most economical method of building an amphibious vehicle, but it was obviously unsatisfactory in many respects. With this in mind, I had to consider reversing all previous practice. Instead of starting with a motor vehicle designed for use on land and modifying it, I realised that I had to start with a boat shaped hull which was designed for use on water and then design most of the mechanical automotive components from scratch, specifically, to meet the requirements of an amphibious machine. One which could drive on the road and would be efficient in both environments.

It was going to be necessary to start completely afresh with a clean sheet of paper.

Not only would it be based upon just any sort of boat hull, it would need to be a hydro-dynamically efficient shape and be designed to travel at speed on water as well as on the road. It would have to incorporate features which would provide stability and safety in both environments. Able to navigate at sea as well as being able to drive safely and efficiently on the road at normal motorway cruising speeds.

All the automotive components and design features would need to take into consideration the important problems associated with electrochemical reactions, weight, displacement, balance, trim and performance, both in the water and on the road. Importantly, I wanted my amphibians, for the first time, to be properly designed to integrate and maximise the benefits of both marine and automotive technologies. Also very important, was that I had to carefully consider the requirements of both sets of transport regulations and these are very extensive and detailed. Fortunately, after a lifetime spent with such a wide range of vehicles and boats, I am familiar with some of these and the important principals behind them.

Meeting people with years of experience designing and racing powerboats and high speed rescue craft, I was aware that a hull with a deep 'Vee' configuration, combines seaworthiness with high-speed facility for smaller craft. If I was going to succeed, it was clear to me that I had to adopt the deep 'Vee' design principle and must design the road-going transmission, the steering and other automotive components, to operate properly in hulls with this underwater shape. From the outset, doing this was going to be one of the many challenges I faced and would be important to the future success of any seaworthy high speed amphibian. A challenge not previously tackled.

This particular issue can best be explained as follows:

With virtually all of the converted motor vehicles relying upon their original principle automotive designs and their existing components and mechanics, the underwater shape of the hulls have to be flat or, at best, have a shallow 'V' shape to the underside of the body. Shapes which are not conducive to comfortable and safe higher speeds in water unless it is calm. This limitation exists because of the design of the components and the road-going suspension. For example, this is designed for a vehicle with a low profile on the road and only permits a few inches of vertical movement up and down. It follows that a marine vehicle with a deep 'Vee' underwater shape cannot be used with normal vehicle components. Put simply, it would be dragging its hull along the ground when driven on land.

This problem can only be solved by entirely redesigning the suspension and the power transmission to allow for a lot more ground clearance for when driving on the road. This alone, involves major engineering design changes to the accepted practice of suspension design. There has to be a very considerable amount of movement created which in turn, leads to the problem of the wheels dangling more deeply when the machine is driven and used in water. This is true whether the vehicle has independent suspension, or if the vehicle has axles. In the latter case, accommodating them creates additional problems. In either case, the additional drag created would further and even more seriously, jeopardise the performance and speed of the amphibian in water.

The solution to this problem is to make the wheels retract, not by just a few inches, but by as much as a metre if necessary. For larger vehicles this introduces more design problems, especially with the steering mechanisms and the power train.

It is clear that there are also a number of other important issues and problems which would have to be resolved if a properly designed amphibians were to be created. A very serious one being electrolysis, which is when different metals are immersed in water, especially salt water. The results of which can be catastrophic if not carefully considered, one not normally associated with existing road going motor vehicles.

Careful study revealed that the full extent and nature of the requirements for efficient, safe, fast and reliable amphibians are such, that nobody it seems, has ever been prepared to tackle them or to go to the expense of doing it properly. The result is that we have seen a century of amphibians which have been unsatisfactory in many respects, especially when they are performing the important service of operating in water. In this environment, as we have seen in the examples described above, they have been slow, unstable, unreliable and not very safe or seaworthy.

Starting with retractable wheels, my research naturally focussed upon the most commonly seen machines with retractable wheels; Aircraft. These also need to reduce drag, so that they are efficient and can achieve greater speeds through the air. In an aircraft, the benefits are that many spaces exist where retractable wheels can safely be stowed away when not in use. There is an ample amount of space in the wings, the fuselage and the tail-plane. In the case of amphibians for civilian use, which are to be driven on the public highway, the overall width and size of the vehicles themselves is strictly limited. In commercially viable and practicable amphibians, internal space is needed for passengers or goods and equipment and is, therefore, at a premium, so the wheels and mechanisms need to be compact and be retracted into the smallest space possible.

Unlike an aeroplane, which uses the power of its propellers or jet engines to move it along the tarmac, the wheels of an amphibian, as well as being retractable, also need to be power driven to drive the vehicle along the road. The transmission system therefore also needs to be very compact as well as also being retractable. There is another important factor when designing and planning to build amphibians for commercial and general service use on the public highway. This is that a road vehicle is restricted to a maximum width of 2.5 metres, just over 8 feet. This limitation doesn't of course, apply to aeroplanes where there is no limit to the width or size generally, so their stability is much enhanced by their wide and long footprint.

So, analysing and comparing aircraft suspension and steering with that of motor vehicles, both existing technologies incorporate features which have been developed and refined, over the last century, to meet the specific needs of each entirely different mode of transport operating in different operational environments. There are some features which can be beneficial to an amphibian, but a fresh start was most certainly needed.

CONCLUSIONS

From the forgoing, you can see that my research revealed that there were a number of significant reasons for the complete lack of any worthwhile progress with amphibious transport during the whole of the last century.

The low cost solutions to creating an amphibian had resulted, down the years, in a series of unsatisfactory, primitive and ungainly machines, none of which satisfied the needs of modern day, dual purpose transport. With there being no existing academic or design institutions set up specifically for this form of transport and with little specialised knowledge of this undeveloped and neglected technology, the vehicles which were built were seen by many as a joke.

Starting from scratch, I also found that nobody had carried out any serious market research and that there was no appreciation of the untapped global market potential for amphibious vehicles. Few realised that the only solution for those who were determined to benefit from this form of transport had no choice, but to turn to the DUKW's. I found that these sixty year old wartime vehicles were being pressed into service all around the world. There was virtually nothing else available which had a service record.

The net result of this widespread apathy became clear as my work progressed. No large, established manufacturing concern would give any consideration to amphibians and very little funding was available from the normal sources. After twelve years of good progress however, with my innovative new technology working well and the development rapidly gaining ground, the situation changed. Some people began to see the benefits of properly designed machines. This was fine, but its success led to very different problems, but I am jumping ahead.

Cartoon by Gordon Westwood.

CHAPTER 42:
UNIQUE & VALUABLE EXPERIENCE

Looking back to the early 1950's when, as a boy, I first began to use my hands, I discovered the great satisfaction of creating and making things. I also found that I had a natural aptitude to draw and found that I could paint portraits, animals and a wide range of subjects. I was also able to design anything which I wanted to make. I could also produce working drawings which were good enough for others to work from. Gifts which I had inherited from my parents.

Earlier in this book, I tell the story about building my 12ft sailing boat in 1954 as a 14 year old boy and how I overhauled my first old motor car in 1957/58. By that time, I was 17 years old and able to legally drive on the road and I was already learning a great deal from my direct, practical experience and gaining confidence in my own abilities.

As a teenager, although living on my basic pocket money of £1 a week, I was fully able to appreciate the pleasures of having my own boat and motor car and having built them myself, knew them inside out, which was most comforting. Without realising it, I was in fact, preparing for what was to be my future career.

Going back over the last fifty odd years, I have enjoyed being able to deal with a wide range of materials and have learned many skills. Working first as a boy, typically, building up my own bicycles and then building boats. The first was built of wood, and I then later on, worked with Glass Reinforced Plastic and aluminium. These included both motor and sailing boats of sizes eventually up to and over 40ft in length.

At the same time, from an early age, becoming involved with the fascinating world of vintage motor cars when wooden framed coachwork was commonplace and when the mechanics were relatively straight forward engineering. I had a good grounding and practical experience with a wide range of wood, metals and modern plastics in both the automotive and marine worlds. I also saw all manner of production and manufacturing techniques when I visited many of the factories during the seven years I was working on the Aycliffe Industrial Estate in the late 1950's and 1960's.

The early chapters explain how, after school, I also had the benefit of 14 years of hands on commercial and management experience in various small and large organisations Following this, I was ready to start my motor vehicle restoration business in 1973 and moved to create Royles workshops in Staindrop.

Now, after having spent 55 years stripping and rebuilding literally hundreds of very different types and makes of motor vehicles and then having test driven most of them, I have been privileged to see, study and understand the benefits and drawbacks of the widest range of mechanical designs imaginable, seeing which mechanisms succeeded and which failed in service.

With these vehicles having been created and built throughout the whole of the last century and with having worked hands-on, at the bench, I could see how suspension systems, steering, and mechanical designs had evolved from the very beginning of motorised transport and was able to compare their performance on the road. Even visiting the actual work shop where Karl Benz and Gottlieb Daimler built their first motor car in Stuttgart in 1885.

So, with my involvement with sailing and motor boats and building and working on them as well sailing and driving them, I was seeing how both marine and automotive transport has developed during this long period of time. I also had some links with aircraft, my father was an amateur pilot after the war so, as a boy, I can remember being taken flying in an Auster Autocrat, a Miles Magister Trainer and other light aircraft. Although never having worked on aircraft, there has always been an interest and I have seen how they are put together and seen some aircraft restoration work as well.

All this experience has been most valuable, especially when some of our customers at Staindrop wanted me to design and build one-off motor cars for them, some of which are discussed earlier in this book. It goes without saying that, with this wealth of practical experience working with many skilled men, I was well equipped for the problems associated with designing and creating technically advanced machines which would successfully combine both forms of transport, i.e. modern amphibians.

By 1988, I had identified the important problems and features which would have to be incorporated in the designs which I was to tackle if they were to be practicable and successful. Importantly, after working with so many different types of vehicles, as mentioned, I also had a working knowledge of the Ministry of Transport Regulations which applied to both private and public transport. I was also aware of the nature

The Renault Racoon.

The Isuzu Nagisa.

of these, which was very helpful and important when designing these advanced machines.

My early sketches and drawings reveal a very open mind. The drawings show that I was working my way through every possible method and technique by which a boat could have wheels which would operate safely on the road and incorporate efficient steering and suspension mechanisms and yet retract into the hull.

One of many knowledgeable and interesting people whom I had the pleasure of meeting, early on, was Don Shead, the racing power boat designer, whose designs and record with deep 'Vee' racing boat hull designs was second to none. He was also a designer of luxury Motor Yachts which was most interesting. He had been thinking along similar lines to myself, as far as amphibians were concerned, so he came all the way up to Staindrop in County Durham from his design centre in Fareham in Hampshire to see me. It turned out that he also had a love of powerful sports and other specialist motor cars, so we had much in common.

During our discussions, he drew some sketches, but when it came to retractable wheels with steering systems, his ketch deteriorated into a frustrated fast scribble. His problem was that of designing road wheels which would retract by up to a metre to cope with a deep 'Vee' hull, ones which would steer correctly and at the same time be able to 'brake' and satisfy the Ministry of Transport (MOT) regulations for safety and have engineering integrity. It was a tricky problem, but one which had to be resolved if high speed amphibians were ever to be built.

Looking back at previous patent records, down the years, there have been various unsuccessful attempts to overcome this problem. It was obviously one which was a major stumbling block and fundamental to the success of the project. It was one upon which I focussed my attention for some months. The question of MOT regulations and safety were, as always, foremost in my mind. There are no specific regulations for Amphibious vehicles, so both sets of road and marine 'Construction and Use' regulations for a wide range of types, needed to be studied, some being in conflict with one another. The challenges were numerous.

It was becoming clear that many of the problems associated with properly uniting marine and automotive technologies had not been understood, never mind not having been satisfactorily resolved. In fact, it seemed and it is still true today, that most people and engineers do not have a real grasp of the range of technical issues involved in creating a successful amphibian. Indeed, throughout the many years of my involvement, very few people seem to have any real appreciation of the importance of the technology which I have created.

Most people, as ever, resort to automotive principles as the basis for their ideas and whilst this is understandable, to really get to grips with the answers, there is the necessity to think 'outside the box' and study the issues intensively in order to create and satisfy the requirements necessary for a safe and carefully considered, properly designed marine vehicle.

By summer of 1988 and after much deep thought, I had worked out the principles of an overall design and also developed some practical and safe ideas for the retractable wheels and the methods of locking them for safe use in both environments. I was now confident that I could create technical, new mechanisms which would result in viable and practicable high-speed amphibious craft. I now needed to find an existing hull which would be a satisfactory basis to build in and test all the innovative mechanisms and my new ideas.

CHOOSING THE HULL FOR THE FIRST PROTOTYPE

Looking at the wide range of high-speed hulls and boats that were available on the market in 1988, I decided upon the 'Broom Capricorn' built by a Company in Norfolk. These are an 18ft boat with a deep Vee hull designed by Jack Broom who had designed the fast motor torpedo boats used during the war. The hulls were strongly built of GRP and with their longitudinal internal stiffeners, they were ideal to build in all the equipment and be used as a test 'rig' for the first high speed amphibious prototype.

Joining me in the venture was Bruce Ropner, a friend who was not only involved with shipping, but also with motor racing and exciting cars. We had built a special V12 Rolls Royce Phantom III for him with sporting open coachwork and also working together, Royles had built a replica Le Mans 6 Litre sports vintage Bentley. He had confidence in my designs and the skills in our workshops, so we agreed that I would buy the Broom and then we would share the initial costs involved with the labour and facilities to build it into our first High Speed Proto-type, probably the first of its kind in the world! Exiting stuff!

Before taking delivery of the 'Broom Capricorn' speedboat in 1988, we specified that it would be fitted with twin 60HP Mariner outboard motors. Most of these boats have a single inboard engine, in other respects it was to be fitted out as their normal complete boat. There were two main reasons for having twin outboard engines. The first was so that we had the maximum space, inboard, to accommodate the retractable wheels and the mechanisms which operated them. The second was so that, at sea, there was the added safety of having a second engine in case there were any problems with either one of them. We also had plenty of power and a good 'grip' on the water, without making the commonly made mistake of having too much power for the hull.

I tested it first in Norfolk with Alan Broom, the son of the designer. It was quite a thrill listening to the twin 60hp engines as the boat quickly accelerated on the smooth water of the Broads. The sound reminded me of a twin engined light aircraft. Later, when testing it in St Mawes in various weather conditions, including gales, it proved to be a first class sea boat for its size. Comparing it with other similar sized boats, the hull behaved wonderfully well in coastal waters, especially when, in bad weather, other similar size speed boats had to turn for home.

The first boat proved to be so useful, that we didn't make it into an amphibian, but kept it in St Mawes and used it as a fast tender to 'Meriva'. We could be in Falmouth or any of the beaches, pubs and restaurants around the Carrick roads and Falmouth bay, in a few minutes and it was good fun for skiing and the boys enjoyed it of course. It was rather flashy with its raised aerofoil and coloured lines, but when I bought it, I thought that this would be good for marketing purposes, as well as being suitable for the first prototype for the amphibious project. As the Vintage Motor business was in a 'boom' period in the late 1980's, I could afford to buy another Broom Capricorn, this time, specifically for the amphibious project.

It is worth mentioning that the vintage and classic car market was so buoyant at this time that Royle's were employing 19 staff and making good profits. As well as the restoration work, our motor car sales department was also doing well under the control of our Sales Director, Piers Leigh.

Always needing storage space, I had bought the old Methodist Chapel in a quiet corner just off the village green and there were usually upwards of a dozen interesting vintage, sports and the odd racing car stored here. Piers was able to use this building as his 'showroom'. Although it had no showroom windows, this didn't matter, because the sales business was always by appointment.

During this period, the workshops were also busier than ever, we not only had 15 to 20 vehicles in the workshops, which was normal, but in order to maintain an efficient workflow for all the staff, we also had a further 30 or so vehicles being stored in safe, dry buildings nearby at Headlam, at Winston and in Streatlam Park.

Streatlam is an interesting place formerly belonging to the Bowes family, now owned by Capt. Nigel Pease, who has kindly allowed me to store our motor cars there for many years. It is an ideal secluded spot which, with its private long drive, is a good spot of some quiet road testing and makes an excellent place to photograph our cars. You may be interested to know that John Bowes was part of the Bowes-Lyons family and lived at Streetlam and is responsible for building the renowned Bowes Museum at Barnard Castle.

Bowes Museum houses a wonderful collection of furniture and other artefacts which John and his French wife, Josephine, collected and eventually put on display in this most impressive building, at the end of the 19th century. Built as a French Chateau and being situated in the beautiful Tees Valley, it is a remarkable structure and makes for a surprising and impressive sight. It continues to be most popular, attracting many visitors. Not surprisingly, the Queen Mother was the Patron of this marvellous museum until she died.

Returning to the amphibious story, with the Broom Capricorn speedboat being so good for its size, not only did I buy an identical complete boat, again with twin 60 hp outboards as the basis for the first prototype, I also ordered a hull and deck mouldings for delivery to the Staindrop workshops to be used for a second and what would be a more developed pre-production version . This is when we were going to develop these into the first proper, high speed marine amphibians, initially for leisure purposes.

There was a lot of special one-off work to be done, work which our work-shops in Staindrop are ideally equipped to carry out. Our team of men have a wide range of skills and having been employed to work on some of the finest cars in the world, they are capable of all manner of specialist engineering, coach building and finishing jobs. The work being done is to the highest standards and includes welding, metalwork of every description, machining, woodwork, trimming, paintwork, shot blasting and many more processes. With our wide range of machinery and equipment in the various workshops, we were able to tackle every aspect of this exciting and interesting project 'in house'.

One of our staff, Allan Barkley, can be irascible at times, but as well as being a skilled motor engineer, he is also knowledgeable about other forms of engineering work, both electrical and mechanical and was also interested in motorboats, having owned one or two himself. He enjoyed development work and was keen to be involved with the many aspects of the practical work involved in building the prototypes. Whilst most of the machining work was carried out by him, other members of the Royle team also became involved as the project developed, as and when their special skills were needed.

To describe all the work involved with this first prototype and with all the other prototypes which I subsequently went on to design, would be a big job. The purpose of this book is not to give detailed technical report of the innovative designs. This may be done later, my initial aim and hope is that the story will be sufficiently interesting for a none technical person to enjoy reading about it and to have some understanding of the work involved in a project of this nature. I will however, mention a few jobs and some of the problems which we had to tackle to give you an insight into the unusual nature of the work involved.

PROGRESS AND INNOVATION

After months of careful study, I was pleased that I had been able to resolve, in principle, the problems associated with designing safe, long reach, retractable steering and suspension mechanisms. When this was done, I then asked Allan to make the various component parts from my drawings in readiness to install them into the Broom hull itself. There can be little doubt that this was the first time something like this has been done and it was good to see them taking shape in metal.

Whilst not built as a road vehicle, as previously mentioned, the Broom hull did have features which I thought would be beneficial. It's sturdily built GRP hull with two parallel stiffeners running either side of the central 'V' keel, which I had noted at the Broom works in Norfolk, proved not only to be useful to mount the inboard engine and other ancillary equipment, they also provided a base upon which the necessary internal supports and 'boxes' for the retractable suspension units could be attached. These are the parts which Allan was then making in our machine shop.

In order to retract the wheels into the hull space, keeping the overall width of the 'vehicle' to a minimum to meet DTLR regulations and maintaining a neat appearance, I incorporated 'wheel boxes'. These were strong plywood boxes, without bottoms, which were bonded onto the hull to make them strong and watertight. We then cut apertures through the hull underneath them so that the wheels could be retracted and withdrawn into the boxes which were later fitted with sliding and hinged flaps. These flaps were carefully designed to close under the wheels in order to maintain the planing surfaces of the hull. I specifically, did not want these flaps to be watertight since, when in use, any seals intended to make them watertight, would inevitably be contaminated with sand, weed, grit or other flotsam, making them ineffective.

The idea was that when the boat was not moving, water could enter the wheel boxes around the edges of the flaps and joints and fill up to the outside water level. As soon as the boat moved and accelerated, the plan was that the self draining vents and tubes which were incorporated in the design, would exhaust all

First prototype - with the 'full' dashboard.

the entrained water in the boxes without the need to have mechanical pumps. We fitted inspection 'windows' and installed small spot lamps inside the wheel boxes, so that we could see how well the system worked in practice.

I was also giving serious thought to various cooling systems for our inboard 10 hp engine which would be used purely to drive the road wheels on this first experimental machine. Engine cooling has always been a problem with amphibians with them not having the benefit of the rammed air effect which is so beneficial for cooling normal motor road vehicles. We also installed various hydraulic rams and the safety locks for the retractable wheel mechanisms. Allan also made and fitted a stainless steel fuel tank which supplied all three engines.

The dashboard was very 'full' with separate switches and controls for all the special components and with gauges for each of the three engines.eg, three rev counters, three Oil pressure gauges, etc. The inboard engine had its own gear lever and a foot throttle next to the brake pedal on the floor. There also were two hand throttle and gear lever controls for the twin 60hp Outboard motors, there were water and land speedometers, two steering wheels, one for driving on the road and one for navigating on water. With all these controls, we would also be able to adjust and test the effects of varying the amount of wheel retraction and movement and the flaps with the switches which were mounted on the dashboard.

Some of the mechanisms in the prototpe leisure version.

Whilst Allan was busy with all this, a smart, brass windscreen was being made which would be Chromium plated and have proper wind screen wipers and windscreen washers. This also would improve the overall appearance of the Broom, the original screen being made of plastic, had no wipers. Two headlamps in cowlings were also going to be made and fitted under the foredeck where the efficient, flared bow would give us the necessary room for them. These also to have their own warning lights and switches.

There was a lot of work involved and as it proceeded and each of the parts was made and tested, the result was very pleasing. If modifications were necessary, it was simple to do them with all the facilities being so close to hand. At times, other members of staff were brought in to help with various jobs, and additionally, we took on one or two part time people as well.

Before it was finished, but as soon as the Broom prototype was drivable, we were keen to test it and see how it felt when driven on the road. The new suspension and retractable rear wheels had been fitted into the wheel boxes along with the hydraulic pump to power the rams. The retractable twin front wheels and road steering was also operational. The fuel tank was fitted as was the 10 hp inboard engine. This was now running and we wanted to see if our experimental rear mounted radiator would cool it.

Prototpe leisure version.

The boat didn't have any wheel flaps or a windscreen at this time, neither had the powerful 60hp twin Mariner outboard motors been fitted. We clamped my old Mercury 5 hp outboard motor onto the transom, so we could at least manoeuvre it in water see how it floated in its incomplete state.

Bruce offered to let us use his estate roads at Camp Hill for this first road test, so we drove the boat onto our normal motor car road trailer in our yard using our special ramp to accommodate the twin front wheels when driving on to it. Always conscious of keeping our work out of public view, once on the trailer with the padded and shaped support blocks in place, which we had made for the purpose, we hydraulically lowered the boat down using the rams which operated its own retractable suspension. In this way, at a quick glance, it looked like any normal boat in transit.

Once at Camp Hill, we parked out of sight behind Bruce's splendid house, I climbed over the side and onto the driving seat, started the inboard engine and operated the hydraulic rams. The boat lifted itself off the padded blocks and releasing the hand brake, reversed off the trailer down the ramp. Allan and Bruce climbed aboard and easing it into first gear, we set off to drive past the house. We had only gone a short distance when there was a loud 'bang' and Bruce shot off his temporary seat.

The boat had only one proper seat for the driver, so he had been sitting on one of the rear

wheel boxes where a hydraulic pipe union had come apart. He had received a generous dose of high pressure hydraulic fluid, but he took it like the gentleman he is and other than a rather wet bottom, he was okay! It was then a question of, back to the workshops for the minor improvement of a better pipe connexion.

Unfinished prototpe leisure version. First test on water.

After further discussion, for the next driving test, we decided also to incorporate a simple water test to see how it floated. This time Bruce arranged for us to use the small lake and private roads on Sir John Ropner's estate near Bedale. Although quite a small lake, it was private and amply big enough for the floatation tests.

This time everything went well and we drove around the lovely parklands as well as on the roads. The soft 'floatation' tyres gave a comfortable ride and the steering was positive. With the roads being narrow and some having a grass ridge in the centre which tended to make the twin front wheels bounce about a bit, I only took it up to 50mph, but it performed well. After having satisfied myself, naturally Allan, Bruce and his son Robert, who was also involved, had a go. We were all very pleased with this very first road test.

We then drove gently into the lake to see how it floated. Without the twin, large outboard motors, which had not been fitted at this stage, the trim was not expected to be correct, especially as the bows had been cut away for the twin front wheels. This combined with the weight of the forward mounted engine, fuel tank and the front steering mechanism, not surprisingly, made the boat float bows down. We started the little Mercury outboard motor and manoeuvred around the lake.

Even with this early test of an incomplete machine, I was seeing for myself how the various elements affected the general trim and performance of this very first, potentially, high speed amphibious boat. I could see that the project was shaping up very well. Allan took some video of these early tests which are now included in the films made later by Les Coates and his BBC team.

By the spring of 1990 the outboard motors, the wheel box flaps and all the wiring and other jobs were finished and plans were made to carry out the first proper trials, speed and performance tests. Obviously the Lake District would be an ideal venue with its wide expanses of water and as luck would have it, we had the opportunity for the ideal place to do it.

An old friend Gavin Knox, had previously introduced me to his friend John Nayler who was most interested when I told him about the project. As luck would have it, it turned out that he was the Commodore of the Windermere Motor Boat Racing Club and he invited us to use their facilities for the all important forthcoming tests. A marvelous slice of luck!

Having sailed on this beautiful lake and with it being early in the season and mid week, I knew that the club would not be busy, so it would be ideal for our purposes. I applied to the Lakeland authorities for a licence number, which is normal practice on Windermere and was amused to find that I was given a red one, when they are normally black. This was 9084, a Trade Licence which made us feel quite 'special'!

CHAPTER 43:
FIRST TEST OF MKI PROTOTYPE

On Tuesday 12th June 1990, Allan and I towed the MK I, as it came to be called, over to Lake Windermere behind my Daimler which was ideal for me. I had colitis at the time and appreciated the comfort it provided. As

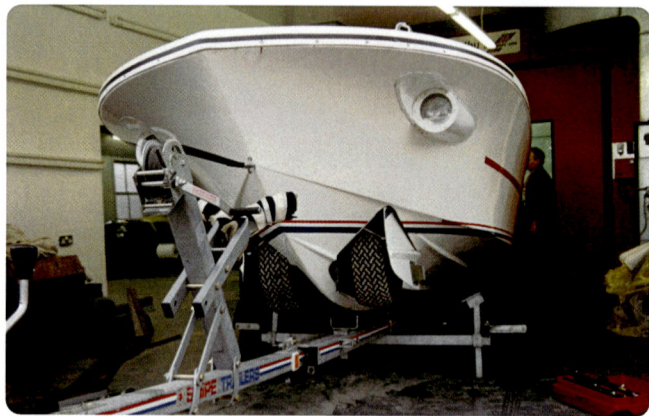

Prototpe leisure version getting ready to go.

before, we used our motor car trailer with a cover over the boat. Arriving at the splendid club house, which is a wonderful example of Lutyens work. We were received very hospitably by Chris Gabbot, the steward and our host at the club house, where we were to stay for the night.

He directed us to take the boat and trailer down the sloping drive to the tree lined boat park close to the lake. Nearby is the boat house with jetties either side of it, each with its adjoining ramps for launching. Altogether, the facilities and conditions were ideal, so we were greatly looking forward to these first proper tests.

Everything was quiet on the lake and with nobody about on the jetties, we couldn't resist starting straight away to get ready for driving it into the water. We were just taking the cover off the MK I when another car drove down with a boat behind it, just what we didn't want at that time! When the MK I boat is on the trailer, or when in the water, it looks reasonably normal, but when driving in or out of the water, 'all is revealed'!

I really was trying to keep the project out of the public eye at this stage. With no other such development going on at that time, it was vitally important to keep it all confidential. This was so that we had the ongoing benefit of lots of time for development. With very limited funding available to me, plenty of time was a key factor.

Standing in front of the boat, we said a friendly "hello" as the two men turned round and reversed and parked near the ramp which, fortunately, was furthest away from us at the other side of the boathouse. They saw our boat on the trailer, but didn't notice that it was special. They, like us were keen to get onto the lake.

Whilst they were untying the ropes ready to launch their boat, masked to a degree by the trees, we put down the ramp, I climbed in and started the inboard engine and using the hydraulic rams, the boat lifted itself up onto its wheels and drove off the trailer without being noticed. By this time, the two men were ready and reversing their boat and trailer down the ramp to launch it. In the two or three minutes it took for them to do this, they were out of sight behind the boathouse, so we quickly drove from the boat park to the nearest ramp and drove straight into the water and tied up against the adjoining jetty. This took about one minute.

Allan and I were sitting in the boat ready to start the outboard motors when from the other side of the boathouse, the two men drove past us to park their empty trailer. The expressions on their faces were a picture! Only a few minutes ago, we had been uncovering the boat in the car park on the trailer facing the wrong way and yet there we were, in the boat, on the lake and ready to go. They knew that they had wasted no time launching their boat. They had not seen us, or our car, or the trailer, or any manoeuvring, launching or re-parking.
They couldn't hide their surprise, how could we have done it so quickly? This was to be the first of some amusing incidents with our first experimental advanced amphibian.

SPEED TESTS. LAKE WINDERMERE. 1990.

In the water next to the jetty, I saw that our boat was sitting slightly lower in the water than is normally the case with these boats. This reminded me of the extra weight which the wheels and other amphibious equipment had added. The trim was fine however which was pleasing since I was concerned to maintain this important aspect of the project.

We started the twin 60hp Outboard Mariner

First prototype by the boathouse at Lake Windermere.

Engines. Being the same as those fitted to the first Broom, and having already used identical engines for two seasons down in St Mawes, I was quite familiar with them. They are smooth and powerful, but use quite a lot of petrol, hence the large fuel tank in the bow of the MK I. We then retracted the wheels and closed the flaps on the front wheel box and the sliding doors which we were experimenting with on the back boxes. Because we were going to see how the boat performed on water, we didn't need to keep the inboard engine running, so switched it off.

Looking at the fully finished dash board, for the first time as the driver, its many switches and controls needed some getting used to. They would be simplified for the final production models, as we were planning to use only one engine for supplying power for both land and water propulsion and the safety locks and flaps would work automatically. As it was, I had wanted to have control of every aspect of this experimental boat and wanted to test the effect and relationship of each component to others on board, as we operated and adjusted the various mechanisms on the water.

The weather was ideal for this first test of a finished prototype. The lake was calm which was ideal for our purposes. Allan untied the painter, climbed in and we set out from the club jetties and down the lake letting the engines gradually warm up and the oil circulate. These engines were brand new and I wanted to ensure that we ran them up gently. Being a great believer in minimising thermal shocks due to rapid changes in temperature, I gradually increased the speed of the engines. At the same time watching the gauges and getting a feel for the boat. Damage is often caused to engines by high revs when cold.

With all the additional weight of the automotive equipment, extra inboard engine etc, and with the loss of some buoyancy due to the water entrained in the wheel boxes, the MK I felt different to the normal Broom boat which I was using in Cornwall. It was good to be able to compare them.

I gripped the two outboard control levers and pushing them forward like the throttles in a twin engine aircraft, we speeded up and the bows lifted, I could see that the acceleration was not as good as the normal Broom, the weight was obviously affecting the performance. We soon reached the 'hump' however, this is the point when the hull changes from having the characteristics of a displacement hull and the boat lifts itself out on to the top of the water and hydroplanes on the surface.

There seemed to be a slight hesitation and then the boat levelled out and there was a noticeable increase in speed, we were over the hump and the speed was climbing and with plenty of throttle, we were soon exceeding 30 knots. Marvellous! We were aboard what is probably the first ever, High Water speed Amphibious marine vehicle and we were both thrilled that the design principles worked first time.

We slowed down and accelerated and repeated the process a few times, noting the way in which it handled. We then carried out some sharp turns and other manoeuvres and found that it banked as normal and handled very well for a heavier than normal 18 foot boat. Not surprisingly, there was a larger wake than usual, this was due to the 'V' hull being slightly deeper in the water than normal.

During these first tests, both Allan and I could sense that, as we accelerated, there was a variation in the trim in that the boat would heal slightly from one side to the other. I slowed down again and stopped in the middle of the lake and asked Allan to take the steering wheels to drive the boat. I wanted to see what was happening inside the wheel boxes.

Looking through the small inspection windows into the dark interior of the wheel boxes, I could see under the entrained water that, there were glimpses of daylight around the edges of the wheel box flaps. This was no surprise as we were standing still and intentionally, did not have the wheel flaps made a watertight fit. Then, in order to see what was happening inside the boxes, I switched on the internal inspection lights, fitted for the purpose. I could then see that the wheels were properly retracted with the water, as expected, lapping around the lower part of the tyres, on our waterline.

I asked Allan to engage the outboard motors and to gradually increase the speed. As the boat moved slowly forwards I could see that there was nothing dramatic happening, simply a turbulence in the entrained water, rather like a washing machine in slow motion. Then, as the speed of the boat further increased, the turbulence in the boxes also increased until, as we were approaching the 'hump', I was thrilled to see the water rapidly disappear leaving only a fine spray inside the boxes as we went onto the plane. An estimated 30 gallons of water was gone from each box in a few seconds. I was thrilled to see the self draining systems working so well. The principal that the surface pressure would help to keep the flaps closed when planning, also worked very well.

Slowing down again, as we motored along, I could see that the slight variation in the alternating healing of the boat was due to the variation in the fit of the rear sliding doors. The rate at which the entrained water was being expelled from each of the rear wheel boxes varied and it was this that was causing the movement. It was clear that we would need to refine and develop this innovative aspect of the designs. I also thought that we would be able to improve the the Wheel Boxes themselves. The important fact was that the principal was perfectly practicable and they worked well with little effect on performance. We knew that we could incorporate them whenever we needed to on future high speed amphibious vehicles.

With the launch of the MK I having been a very hurried affair, other than noting the important fact that the bows lifted OK as we entered the water from the steep concrete ramp, we needed to see how it performed when driving in and out on different surfaces. I remembered that there was a gravel beach which sloped up to an open field at the head of the lake so, if all was quiet there, it might be a good place for our first test driving out on a gravel beach. Also it was a few miles away, so it would give us a good run up to the lake to continue our 'driving tests'.

We cruised right up to the head of the lake at various speeds to where I had seen water skiers on previous trips to Windermere in the summer. Fortunately, no skiers were there and there was no sign of anybody else about. This was, as expected, probably with it being midweek and early in the season. Heading for the beach, I throttled back the outboard motors and we started the inboard engine and with Allans help, operated the switches which released the safety locks, opened the wheel flaps and sliding doors and lowered the wheels which were then locked down.

Engaging bottom gear for the road wheels and holding both steering wheels, with the outboards still driving, but semi tilted with their own rams, we drove on to the gravel beach. As soon as we felt the wheels taking the weight of the boat and driving, we quickly switched off both outboard motors and fully tilted them to prevent damage to the propellers, also, without cooling water, their internal impellors can be damaged very easily. The soft 'floatation' tyres had good treads and gripped well and we easily drove up the beach, over an earth step and up and onto the field. We were pleased with this very first drive out, but again realised that the number of operations involved when transferring from water to land were problematical. The learning curve with all our controls was steep!

We had brought a packed lunch in the boat, so we drove across the field to a nearby high stone wall where we could park out of sight of the road. This looked a good spot to have a bite to eat our and compare notes. We had only been stopped a few minutes when I had to rapidly 'disembark' and run to a quiet spot behind some trees, my Colitus was an ever present problem. Taking the camera with me, I stopped on the way back to take a photo of the boat parked in the field which also showed the

Windermere Park Rangers approaching.

tracks on the beach where we came ashore. By coincidence, upon close inspection later on, I saw that the photo included two men hurriedly walking across the field towards the boat. They were partly masked by the trees when I took it and it was only when I was in the open that I realised that they were there.

I climbed back into the boat which the two men were now leaning on. Allan had started the picnic, so I joined him and tucked into our sandwiches and coffee. One of them informed us that they were Lakeland Wardens and told us that "this field is private" and that "you can't leave your boat here". I explained that I had seen water skiers using it in the past and thought it would be OK. They said that skiers were only "allowed to use the beach, not the field" and firmly repeated their demands, adding that one of us must go to "get the car now and tow the boat away", adding that they would not leave until we had done so.

Realising that they hadn't noticed the wheels, or possibly thinking that we were already sitting on a trailer, I couldn't resist the temptation to 'milk' the situation and have some fun. I said "look, we haven't been here long, we only want to finish our picnic and then we'll go". Becoming more authoritative, the man repeated his demands "no, will you please get your car, now, and take the boat away".

I said that we didn't have a car. The situation then got better than we could have wished for. This was when the man's colleague turned to him and said, "just a minute, there isn't a gate into this field". I couldn't resist this opportunity by saying to the first man, "I told you that we didn't have a car" followed by, "don't be unreasonable, can't you see that we would like to finish our picnic, if you don't mind".

Ignoring this remark, he then asked, "well, how did you get here then?", "we drove here of course", I replied with mock indignation, tucking into another sandwich.

After a slight pause, "alright then, well why don't you drive away". By now the warden was becoming exasperated by this 'clever dick' speed boat owner visiting the Lake District. Not wanting to antagonise him too much, I shrugged my shoulders and we made a great performance of packing up our unfinished picnic, and putting away our flask and cups with the two men still leaning on the side of the boat watching us.

Allan and I had a mock argument about who should drive, but by now, we could see that the two wardens were certain that we were 'taking the micky', so I started the inboard engine and as the boat moved forward. The men's expressions changed from contempt to absolute amazement. Nearly losing their balance when their support moved away from them, one of them looked underneath and said in a loud voice, " Christ, it's got wheels". "NO, NO DON'T GO" they shouted after us. I stopped the boat and couldn't resist the retort, shouting back, "FOR HEAVEN'S SAKE, WILL YOU MAKE YOUR MIND UP, DO YOU WANT US TO GO OR STAY?"

They rapidly caught up with us and a stream of questions followed." Where did we get it from?, how many were there?" etc, we explained that this was the first of many and they were visually shocked, "this spells the end of the lake district" they said dejectedly.

I began to feel sorry that I had led them on, but they were so unpleasant that they deserved it. I put the boat back into gear and we drove off down the field, across the beach and into the lake, smiling rather wickedly as we did so. Another amusing event and we had only been on board for an hour or two!

Having entered the water, we were just lowering the outboards, starting them up and retracting our wheels, when we noticed a skier in the water just ahead of us. He and his companion must have arrived whilst we were talking to the Lakeland Wardens. The driver of the speed boat was slowly heading away taking up the slack in the ski-rope when the man in the water saw us. He shouted to the driver and releasing his grip with one hand on the tow bar, pointed frantically towards us. He had seen us drive into the water and wanted his friend to see our boat. Thinking the shout meant that the line must be tight, the speed boat driver shot off at full throttle leaving the skier still in the water watching us slowly drive past him and then speeding off into the distance.

After this, we thought we would look for another place to test driving out of the water. Trying to find a more secluded place, we came across a sandy beach on the opposite shore to Bowness near the island. This beach had woodlands running down to it with a grassy track leading to the lake, with nobody about, this looked ideal. We slowed down, started the inboard engine, released the wheel locks and lowered the wheels, repeating the same complicated procedures as before. Once again, we drove up the sandy beach without any difficulty. Both of these beaches were only gentle slopes of around ten degrees, but with only two wheel drive, combined with the thrust from the outboards, we had no difficulty coming out on these soft surfaces.

Driving into the wood and finding space to turn round between the trees, we came across a man wearing a faded, peaked yachting hat who was having a pee against a tree. Upon seeing our boat driving towards him, without stopping what he was doing, he swung round, spraying the woodlands as he did so! His face broke into a huge grin and he literally, began to dance a jig, shouting to us that he had "waited all his life for a boat like this".

He stopped dancing and put 'himself' away and came over to us in great excitement. He explained that he owned the boatyard at Bowness and that boats like ours would make life so much easier for him at his workshops. He added that winter storage was also a serious problem for him, but with wheels, the boats could be stored in any convenient buildings away from the lake. We told him what we were doing and he said he would 'watch this space' for developments. He wished us good luck as we said cheerio and drove out of the wood and back into the lake, leaving him with a broad grin on his face and rather damp trousers.

We drove back to the club house and moored alongside the boathouse jetty. A few minutes later, a Lakeland Police Launch pulled in and tied up on the other side of the jetty. Climbing out of his boat, the policeman looked down into ours and said in a broad Lancashire accent, "by gum lads, you've got some gubbins in there".

It was pointless trying to deny the facts, the boat was full of equipment, so we told him about the project and what we were doing. He was clearly very interested and said that he would "love to have one of these high speed amphibious machines, "I could chase the silly beggars all over the lake and even into the pubs, they wouldn't get away from me" he said with a grin. After our friendly chat, he climbed back into his launch and returned to his patrols of the lake.

By now it was getting late, there was nobody about, so we put the wheels down and drove out of the water and up the steep concrete ramp without any trouble and parked it in the boat park. It was between our car and trailer and another boat with a cover on. After checking that all was in order, with the wheels still down, we covered the MK I with the sheet when it looked as if it might also be an ordinary boat sitting on a trailer.

What a day we'd had! Although rather weary after such a long day, we were thrilled with the first days tests. The very first prototype had worked every bit as well as we could have wished. We agreed that we had learned a lot from our experiences and that there was plenty

First prototype planing at over 30 knots.

to discuss. We walked up the hill to the lovely club house and spent a most enjoyable evening. Being the only people staying that night, we had the place to ourselves and were able to recount and evaluate the days exploits over a good supper. As with the first test at the Ropners, Allan kindly offered again to take some video of these trials. We knew that a record of the event would be helpful, so we decided to do this the following morning, if nobody was about.

Fortunately, as luck would have it, there was no activity and no visitors down by the lake so we drove out of the boat park into the lake very slowly to see how well the bows floated on entry. Being a streamlined speedboat, the hull has a fine bow which meant that there is limited buoyancy. An important feature of Booms designs however, is that the hull has flared bows under the fore deck which not only deflect spray, but also help to lift the bows before they begin to submerge. It was clear that this aspect must be carefully considered when I was designing the proper hulls for production.

Rather than turning round and driving back out of the water straight away, we thought that we should take some film in case people arrived, Firstly, Allan filmed inside the boat as we motored along and then I dropped him off at the jetty. He walked along to a good vantage point with his Video camera and being above the lake, he had a good view of the boat. He filmed the boat as I drove it round at different speeds and when the boat was planing. After this Allan jumped back in the boat and we put the wheels down and proceeded to drive in and out of the water. We experimented with different speeds, but because it needed two of us to operate the many controls, we did not film the boat going in or coming out which is a great pity, because it would have been such a useful reference.

The lessons learnt from these tests were very useful and whilst I was delighted that the innovative principles had worked so well, I could see how I could make various improvements to the designs.

With this book not being intended as a technical report, I don't intend to go into detail, there is too much to tell, but some of the features and new ideas are included later in the book.

CHAPTER 44:
CHANGE OF DIRECTION

Having started the project in 1987, by now, in the late spring of 1990, I had spent three years researching the market and with the onset of the recession, I could see that the luxury market was not going to be very active for some time to come. It was also clear that the high costs involved with building an amphibious boat of only 18ft in length would not be viable when in production. This is because it would have to incorporate so much additional, costly machinery and equipment that it would, almost certainly, be too expensive to sell even in limited production numbers.

Twelve years later, this was proved by New Zealander, Alan Gibbs whose 'Aquada' motor car type of amphibian failed to sell in any quantity, mainly because of its high price of £150,000.

The picture which was emerging was that we should aim at the emergency services, Flood Rescue, Commercial Transport and the Public Service vehicle markets. Technically, this did not worry me unduly, in fact, there were a number of benefits to be creating larger versions. They would be more seaworthy and I would have more room in these bigger machines to install all the equipment. They would open up new markets which would create the need for a wide range of vehicles. Beneficially, these amphibians would certainly be commercially viable.

It was clear however, that I would have to raise much more money than we could provide, or had planned for. Fortunately, my restoration workshops were still busy and I would be able to carry on having the help of our men there. The 1990 recession caused a rapid reduction in the value of Vintage and Classic motor cars which resulted in the closure of quite a number of the better known specialist sales and restoration firms around the country. Royles were fortunate in having some wonderfully supportive customers who kept bringing their motor cars to us and having also become involved in the amphibious project, I was able to keep the workshops busy.

Regrettably, I was eventually forced to close down my sales company, Royle Cars Ltd. This company was run entirely separately from the workshops business in an old Methodist Chapel in the village. The Chapel was sold in 1996 to pay off that company's overdraft and our total staff of nineteen at the workshops was reduced down to twelve. The story of how this happened is described elsewhere in this book.

People often say that this project must have been a drain on Royles which made life difficult for me. The fact is that I was sure, in 1987, that the continuing increase in the value of specialist cars was unsustainable. This is why I had been so keen to broaden the base of our activities, firstly with the childrens cars and then the 'Living Museum' project and then developing the amphibious vehicles. A global market which was untapped. After over thirty years of being closely involved and enjoying working upon vintage cars, and having built up such a good reputation, I was determined to keep everything going until the market recovered. I imagined that it might take a year or two, which is why I had kept Royle Cars running until 1996, even though sales had virtually disappeared during 1990.

I was prepared to put money into the restoration company if it was creating new and potentially valuable vehicles for future business, but to pay the staff without sufficient work to keep them all busy, would not have been worth the risk. As it was, there was obviously also a risk building amphibians, but I was increasingly confident that the potential market was big and would be profitable and the government was pushing hard for small firms to innovate and create high value technologies. In fact, we had already received a grant of £30,000 from the Dti and were applying for more.

Although the first prototype had already cost nearly £100,000, the tests with the MKI had shown that we were certainly on the right track. I now knew that, in principal, the tricky and quite serious engineering problems which a high speed hull presented for amphibious transport, could be overcome with the new mechanisms which we were creating.

Knowing that the new designs worked and were valuable and unique, I was aware of the importance of protecting my designs. I did this by registering the intellectual property rights (IPR) and was already building up a portfolio of international Patents, with more ongoing applications in process. To save cost, I was doing the drawings and specifications for these myself and was seeing them being successfully processed around the world. As the designs progressed, I made sure that they could be scaled up to suit larger vehicles. This is important, not only to maintain the IPR, but also to be cost effective when in production with a range of vehicles.

The IPR costs would eventually amount to over £200,000. It is an expensive and time consuming system which is unsatisfactory in various important respects. The fact is that the system can work against those who are subsequently, not able to protect their inventions, or their interests, against wealthy companies or individuals. This applies especially to people like me who create very high value products without having the financial backing on the same scale.

The fact is that the protection which a patent affords, is only as strong as the money which the inventor has to defend it in court.

FICKLE FUNDING

In the past, it seems that all the builders of amphibians were more concerned about getting into production as quickly and as cheaply as possible, rather than trying to solve the technical problems and create properly designed machines. This was driven either by the urgent military needs, as in the wartime DUKW's in 1942, or in peacetime, it was the desire to minimise R&D costs for a fast profit.

After all the years of work with complex vehicle challenges at Staindrop, I knew how demanding a big project like this might be. Importantly, I also knew that I had the determination to see it through. At the start, I did not think that money would be a problem, this was when I was expecting it to be perhaps a 3 or 4 year project. We were making good profits at Staindrop and there were signs that I would have good support for it. I was seeing tens of £millions being invested in new industries in the North and the government was pushing for new 'high value export technologies'. I had already had the benefit of grant aid, so I believed that we had a good chance of further funding.

In the fullness of time, I was to find that when it comes to innovation with an unfamiliar technology, like amphibians, a form of transport which very few people understand, the city's main concern is not to bother to analyse it, they simply are looking to make a 'fast buck'. There is no concern, whatsoever, for its long term profitability or for the benefits to society or of its intrinsic value.

Funding for our work was, later, to become a very serious problem.

Those venture capital organisations which do have the money to invest, put fast profits first and the result of this continues to be seen all around the world, especially with amphibious transport vehicles. This is the principal reason why there has been no progress with this technology throughout the whole of the last century.

Even as I write, existing road vehicles continue to be converted in order to create amphibians at minimum cost. The net result is, as ever, that they will not perform properly on water. They do float, but structurally and hydro-dynamically, their performance is far from satisfactory. Their value is mainly as a gimmick rather than as a serious form of transport. It is this notable lack of progress which spurred me on, the market is wide open with no real competition anywhere in the world.

The recurring floods and the suffering of thousands of people around the world, will benefit hugely from our technology. Converted vehicles are not at all satisfactory for the emergency services. The only alternative are helicopters, each of them costing many millions of pounds.

At times, I am criticised for taking so long with this project when others are already in production with their converted road vehicles, when they started years after me. This judgement ignores the fundamental issue which is, as ever, that there is a very real need and I want to create a worthwhile, well designed, efficient, fast and safe forms of transport. The very limited amount of money available is of course, a difficulty, but we were making good steady progress.

I have no desire to make a 'fast buck' at the expense of creating really worthwhile machines. Done properly, this project and Roylecraft technology will make very handsome profits in both the medium and long term for its investors. Our advanced technology and the machines which it spawns, will prove to be capable of providing many valuable services in many countries around the world for a great many years. I do not want to create yet more unsatisfactory vehicles by modifying normal unsuitable road vehicles.

The high standards and refinement of all other forms of transport today, emphasises the primitive nature of the existing amphibians. Despite this, very few people take the trouble to try to understand or appreciate what the benefits of properly designed vehicles or should I say, 'craft' could be. The opportunities and the services which our fast and efficient amphibians could provide, are very considerable indeed; Relieving congested roads, rescue in ongoing serious flooding and the use of empty waterways are just a few examples of the uses, with tourism and public transport also high on the list. The lack of proper reasearch and market knowledge are the principal reasons why there has been no progress with this technology throughout the whole of the last century.

It was this notable lack of progress which spurred me on, the market is wide open with no real competition anywhere in the world.

THE MK II PROTOTYPE/TEST RIG

Having now proved with the MK I, that my ideas were feasible and the principles worked well and that our specially made mechanisms were overcoming the technical problems, I now wanted to develop and refine the various ideas which I was creating. The MK I was a great success and I could see that it was the first of a new generation of high speed amphibians which would be safe and seaworthy and it proved that this new technology was not only feasible, but it could also result in smart and visually pleasing vehicles. No longer should amphibians be treated as a joke!

The MK II was not intended to be a marketable vehicle however, it was to be a test bed, pure and simple, it's appearance not being important:

I needed to test a water jet and other ideas to improve and simplify the operation of the wheel retraction mechanisms and the safety locks. At the same time, I wanted to keep the cost of doing so to a minimum. Rather than strip down, rebuild and modify the successful MK 1, I thought it better to leave it complete and in one piece and to experiment with a smaller and different shaped hull which we would build economically, ourselves, in our workshops in Staindrop.

I designed the MK II, which we named the "Sea Elf", as a simple, light weight hull constructed of aluminium sheet side panels rolled over a simple tubular frame running around the outer edge of the sloping decks to hold the shape. We also fabricated an alloy sub frame with tubular alloy supports for the mechanical components with an aluminium transom and two bulkheads. The forward one was made strong enough to mount the sliding, lockable front suspension and steering mechanism. Dick fabricated the hull whilst Allan attended to the mechanical aspects involved.

With outboard motors having some serious

Mark II protype. 1991 - 1992.

drawbacks for amphibians, we bought an Italian Castoldi water jet and a second hand Fiat 500cc Motor car for the engine and gearbox. In the machine shop, using these, Allan made most of the special mechanical and transmission components and instead of using floatation tyres as on the MK I, this time, we were going to test different, new retraction mechanisms which incorporated stainless steel chains, as well as hydraulic rams and dampers to operate the small road wheels.

A stainless steel, pillar mounted, double front wheel steering arrangement was made again to suit the MK II, similar to the MK I. The principal of this important innovative mechanism proved to have worked extremely well and variations based upon this steering design would be used on most, if not all, future Roylecraft amphibians.

Whilst the twin front wheel arrangement had benefits for small craft and other specific applications, I had already decided that a conventional four wheel layout would be incorporated in most of the larger production vehicles. They would improve stability when driving onto land and be more acceptable to the future buyers who would, no doubt, be sceptical about such new and innovative forms of transport also having unusual wheel layouts.

Mark II protype. 1991 - 1992.

When testing the MK II one day, one of our party said it was like the 'Reliant Robin of the amphibious world". It was meant as a joke, but from a marketing point of view, it was a remark not to be ignored!

In the fullness of time, it transpired that it was not the potential buyers who had any concerns, it was the institutional and corporate investors. To this day, I am seeing a steady flow of serious buyers from all over the world who are coming to me to buy hundreds of millions of pounds worth of my Roylecraft amphibians.

MK II TESTS

We tested this little MK II machine for the first time in August 1992 on Ellerton lake which

Mark II protype. 1991 - 1992.

belongs to an old farming friend, John Thompson. It was private and secluded and not too far away from Staindrop and we learned much from the series of tests which followed. As well as the Fiat engine, we tested a Kawasaki high revving motor cycle engine. To save costs, we did not fit flaps or doors to the hull, since hull shape and speed were not key factors of the tests with this vehicle. As ever, the work was very interesting and we were happy to devote whatever time was necessary to develop the various important aspects of the technology.

The advantages of a water-jet were seen and the type of retractable suspension mechanisms fitted to the MK II also worked well. It was clear that the various designs and locking mechanisms which we tested with different drives and power systems had various benefits, and as ever, we learned a lot from this 'test bed'. This little amphibian was also filmed and can be seen in the 25 minute DVD, "AMPHIBIAN" filmed and edited by my BBC friends during tests. Altogether, this low cost, second prototype test bed, had proved its worth and I was already planning to move the project into the next phase.

The MK III would be much more of a practicable proposition. It would not be another test rig, but more the forerunner of a proper commercial, private and emergency services production vehicle. It would be designed to look the part and be potentially, more of a pre-production machine.

CHAPTER 45:
THE MK III PROTOTYPE

COMBINING REGULATIONS AND NEW TECHNOLOGY

When I realised the very real benefits of amphibious transport in today's world and discovered that there was no legislation for this form of transport, I knew that I would have to design the machines to meet the most extensive and demanding sets of regulations for any new vehicle. This was because they would have to meet the detailed regulations for both road going and marine transport.

A challenge, yes, especially those which are for public transport, but I was not put off by these since, after being involved with them for over 30 years, I was familiar with the general thrust and purpose of them. Safety being one which I was especially interested in myself. My designs and ideas were very much in parallel with the regulations of the Ministry of Transport, so our aims were fundamentally, the same. This resulted in a good working relationship with the people in the MCA and the DTLR who were most helpful.

I realised that the commonly accepted practice of converting road vehicles to make them float, was not only the easiest, cheapest and quickest method of creating an amphibian, the other advantage was that it also opened the door to certification. With the 'slave' vehicle already licensed for road use, one set of regulations had already been complied with. It is not difficult to see why everybody was converting existing vehicles, it not only minimised the technical challenges and the cost, it already satisfied the DTLR legislation.

I have already explained that my research showed that modifying road vehicles was, in many respects, a most unsatisfactory method of building such a specialised and important form of transport. So, having set out to completely reverse this practice by making a boat drive on the road, I knew that I was confronted with a 'raft' of fascinating challenges. Accordingly, from the start in 1987, when I was putting hundreds of ideas and possible solutions down on paper, I was able to consider the wide range of aspects involved, all at the same time, both technical and regulatory, which was a great advantage.

THE MK III

After testing the MK I and MK II prototypes, I now had the tremendous advantage of having had, not only the benefit of some practical trials, I was also learning more about the market and the implications and the need for the many types and sizes of amphibians. Instead of amphibians of 18 to 20 feet in length, we were now looking at creating vehicles from 20 feet to 40 ft long (7 to12 Metres). Whilst I still had more new and improved mechanisms to test, I could see that the world wide applications for modern amphibious transport, would result in a wider range of design criteria.

When designing the MK III, rather than it being purely another prototype or test bed, I wanted it to be much nearer to being a pre-production machine. It would be one version of the type which could be used for Flood rescue and a range of commercial purposes. For these applications, the Ministry of Transport regulations are much less stringent than for public transport, for example.

ROYLECRAFT STANDARDISED TECHNOLOGY

With the market research having clearly indicated to me that we had to build larger vehicles if the project was to be commercially viable, we knew that the costs of the project were going to be much higher than was originally expected. To minimise these, I could now see that it was going to be even more important, wherever possible, to standardise the various new innovative mechanical designs which we were testing.

Previously, each of the existing amphibians that had been built by others, were different in design and in the automotive components they used to build them with. From the start, I was hoping to create our new technology with mechanisms which were designed in such a way as to be able to be scaled up or down in size. As we were now looking at building a wider range of vehicles, the advantage of not having to redesign the mechanisms for each one was more obvious. When tests were complete and the best mechanisms established, the specialised components would then be made to suit the desired size and weight of each vehicle required by simply scaling them up or down.

As a result of this policy, the potential increase in costs were not as daunting as it may sound. They were related mainly to the size of each vehicle, not to a complete redesign for each different amphibian. Any cost increases were principally for more powerful engines, larger hulls and / or more equipment. Costs which would be recovered by the higher selling prices with similar or greater levels of profit according to the use and equipment required in the vehicle.

INVESTMENTS

I have already mentioned the ongoing government publicity encouraging SME's to innovate and create new high value technologies, and how I had benefitted from some grants. Now, with higher costs, although not originally part of the overall financial plan, I had to intensify my efforts with the government and also try to raise money by selling more equity in the R&D company, Covelink Marine Ltd.

To help and encourage private sector investors, I had registered the company under the Government inspired Business Expansion Scheme. (BES) This ran until 31 December 1993, after which it was replaced by the Enterprise Investment Scheme (EIS). Both of these were tax beneficial schemes for investors which were very helpful for me and resulted in a growing list of shareholders investing in the project. I had maintained regular reports of our progress to interested parties from the outset and these were now also sent out to the new investors.

Although the prototype work helped to cover the workshop overheads and maintain the skilled staff at Royle's workshops, I made sure that any of Royle's work, which was paid for by shareholders investments, was being charged out at discounted rates. With Royles rates already being lower than those of any similar operations, this meant that the work was being done, virtually, at cost. I knew that it couldn't be done more economically, or to the same high standards by anybody else, but I was naturally concerned that Covelink's shareholders did not think that they were making profits for Royles or providing any income for me, which they certainly weren't. This question did arise occasionally, which was most upsetting, especially as Royle's were running at a loss and I was not drawing a salary from either company for most of the years.

Even with the 1990 recession continuing to adversely affect the Vintage motor car world in 1993 and long afterwards, our workshops continued to support the amphibious project with work often being done at no cost at all to Covelink or its shareholders. I continued to minimise costs in every possible way, as already mentioned, by not taking any salary or perks from Covelink for 16 out of the 17 years of its existence. The only exception was much later on during our first and only contract, and then only for 12 months or so.

Being extremely grateful to those who invested in the project and conscious that they had faith in me, altogether working 7 days a week for years, I personally put in around 35,000 hours of work without payment. Along with the very substantial amount of uncharged work done by Royle's down the years, I did in fact, also sell personal assets and in one way or another, invested very substantial sums myself. These finally amounting to around 2.6 £million.

Ironically, some of Royles men accused me of jeopardising their jobs with this project. Had it not existed, this money would not have been invested and some would inevitably have been made redundant or worse like most other restoration firms, I might have had to close the company down in the early years of the 1990 recession.

Whilst the affects of the recession were bad enough, matters were made even more difficult for me in 1993, when the owner of the Frua Rolls Royce Phantom Six, left Royles with debts of £73,000. The story is told earlier in the book, but briefly, we had spent over three years working on this exotic and most luxuriously equipped motor car and exhibited it at the Geneva Show in March 1993 for him. In spite of these financial difficulties and my deteriorating health due to Colitus, I still managed, with the help of friends and our private investors, to maintain progress.

Starting in 1989, I had been suffering from Ulcerative Colitis for four years. On 25 August 1993 I visited Dr Silk in Harley Street, after examining me, he told me that, if I was to survive, it was necessary to operate and remove my Colon urgently. He also explained that this would be followed by a series of in depth operations to have my 'innards' rebuilt after removal of this defective 'component'. The surgeon, Mr Menzies-Gow, did a brilliant job however, and I am still here to prove it, 17 years later! Once again, the story of this is told elsewhere in this book.

As a result of each of these operations, I lost about four stones in weight and was to spend quite a lot of time recuperating in bed after each of them. Lying in our comfortable old bed and in our light and airy bedroom in Gainford, Jo-Jo spoilt me with lots of good food and I had plenty of time to carefully consider the problems associated with my amphibious project. I was also able to design many of the components for the pre-production models whilst I was in bed and also prepare the paperwork which was necessary for the High Court legal action to have Royles £73,000 bill paid for the £2 million Rolls Royce.

REGULATIONS AND CERTIFICATION

I have briefly mentioned how useful it was that I did have a broad working knowledge of the range of transport regulations and of how they are applied. This was as a result of a lifetime spent working on and driving hundreds of unusual and different makes and types of vehicles dating back to the beginning of the 20th century. It proved to be particularly beneficial when, some years later, on 17 April 2002, I attended a meeting in London which was arranged by the then Minister of Transport, John Spellar MP ,who was helping us to arrange certification for the new Roylecraft Jet-Buses. These had been ordered by British waterways for the new and impressive Falkirk Wheel project in Scotland.

On this occasion, there were representatives from both the Maritime Coastguard Agency (MCA) and the Dep't of Road Transport, (DTLR). I was with Alan Priest representing my company Covelink Marine Ltd, along with George Ballinger, Scotland's Chief Engineer, and Jamie Corser from British Waterways.

We were all gathered around a large table at the DTLR at 76 Marsham Street with Ian Bidmead in the chair. Knowing that there are no specific regulations for amphibious vehicles, I discussed and highlighted some of the many regulations which I was confident of meeting and also gave one or two examples of those which were in conflict with one another and which it would not be sensible, safe, or practicable to meet. There was an audible sigh of relief when they all realised that I did have a reasonable working knowledge of both sets of the regulations.
I think they thought that this aspect of the new Roylecraft vehicles was going to be a long, uphill struggle for them.

Early on in the project, I had attended a meeting in Bristol when I was received by a small team of five people who sat facing me across the table. After I explained to them what I was doing and how I was doing it, the response was very cool, to put it mildly. I was told, normally, that the people who were sitting in my chair were the 'top brass' from Vauxhall Motors, Ford or other large motor manufacturers and who was I, especially when I was fitting retractable wheels to boats? They were all getting on in years and were rather pompous and doubted, very much, that I would ever be able to build innovative vehicles such as I was describing to them. Not a good start!

A few years later, I visited the same offices, but this time, the response was not at all negative. The old boys had gone and this time, the younger team I met, couldn't have been more helpful. They were excited by the project and in most respects, were able to give me lots of good advice.

On another occasion, when I was talking to people in Swansea, I asked to speak to a person who was familiar with all the regulations for public transport vehicles, I was told that nobody knew them all, there were so many! This did not deter me however, because being familiar with many of them and the systems and the fact that they were well documented, it was mainly a question of confidence and common sense and that you have to work with the departments, not against them. The regulations would have to be met, but I found that once they knew that you had a reasonable knowledge of them and knew what you were talking about, they were most helpful. This is how and why we made such good progress.

THE MK III

I decided that the MKIII hull would need to be robust and strongly built of marine aluminium if it was to be used for commercial and general purposes, such as flood rescue, work boats etc. For this hull, I wanted it to be fabricated by experienced boat builders. Being aluminium, once in our workshops, we could then easily weld parts to it and cut and modify it as required. An overall length which I thought would not be too costly and be manageable for most drivers on the road and yet carry a reasonable load would be 22ft long (6.77m) x 8ft (2.5m) wide. This hull would also cope with moderate seas and waves of the size generated by average winds in estuaries and be suitable for inland lakes, rivers etc.

Considerable time was spent planning for different sea conditions, wind speeds etc, but there is little point in discussing these here.

As with the MK II hull, I again restricted the design to single curvature panels. This minimises the cost of the prototype without adversely affecting the performance at sea or on the road. When in production the intention was, to 'sweeten' the design by introducing a few double curvature panels. I was sometimes criticised for the simplicity and plain lines of my machines, but there would be plenty of opportunity to improve them when there was money available to do it. The important aspect was to prove that they worked.

Having previously spoken to the north eastern boat designer, Dalton Linklater and knowing that the boatyard he was involved with at Alnmouth in Northumberland, had built commercial craft in aluminium to his designs, I visited Dalton at the yard and discussed my ideas and requirements with him. He very kindly took me out to sea in a water-jet powered craft which they had just built for the MOD and he demonstrated the characteristics of navigating with water jets, which are quite different, in some respects, to normal propellers.

Subsequently, he drew out the lines of a workmanlike hull which we had discussed. The plans met my criteria for this Special Marine Vehicle (SMV) as I called it at that time, and they were specifically designed to accommodate the suspension and wheel flaps which I had planned and designed to fit to this pre-production model. Soon afterwards, he was able to give me a price for the hull and I was able to instruct the yard to build it for me. He recommended that I use Hamilton Water-jets which they had found to be most satisfactory, so we agreed that they could fit a suitable unit for the engine which we were going to use and for a hull of this size, as part of their work.

WORKING ON THE MK III

I collected the hull for the MK III from Marshall Branson on 24 June 1992 and towed it to Staindrop on a new trailer, bought for the purpose, with my trusty, if rather opulent looking, Daimler Jaguar 3.6. Although only 18 months old when this fine motor was bought for me by Royle Cars Ltd in 1990, it was a good bargian because it's value had dropped by over 60%. The Vintage and classic car market was booming in the late 1980's and Piers was doing well running this company at the time. With me being unwell with Colitis, and with my second Daimler Jaguar showing its age, Piers thought that it would give me more up to date, comfortable transport, so organised it for me. This excellent motor car was to give me reliable and wonderful service for 19 years.

Without telling me, he had parked it in my garage at home, where my existing Daimler normally stood. Being the same dark blue colour, he and Jo-Jo laughed when, having just walked past it, for a few moments, I didn't realise that it was a 'new' car.

Back to the MK III, once in our workshops, we could see that Dalton's men had made a first class job of the hull. It was low cost, with it's single curvature panels, yet strongly built of marine aluminium. The design included features which I had insisted upon to facilitate its use as an amphibious craft. Inexplicably, Dalton had added some additional curved box-like ribs to either side of the Bow. I don't know what his thoughts on these were, but they had not been discussed and were not a good idea to my mind. They were not long enough to add any lift and they would, in my view, restrict the flow of water from the bow and cause additional drag. They also did not help the appearance, making the bow look rather bluff. I really couldn't see the purpose of them, but I left them in place until after the first water test, just to make sure that they didn't perform some useful service.

Mark III as delivered on the trailer.

Whilst the little forward cabin was practicable enough, when actually seen in the metal, for the first time, it was very upright and was really too commercial looking for our purposes. With funding being a constant issue, I was, as ever, aiming to use this prototype for marketing as well as for testing and development purposes, so decided to improve its appearance..

With the cabin being just a bare shell and bolted on to the foredeck frame, it was easily removed, so I drew out a slightly more streamlined design. This incorporated a more raked windscreen and a slightly lower roof line with lower cabin top which Dick fabricated in the workshops. Also, to improve the overall appearance, instead of having a semi-circular top and bottom to the cabin door, we made a rectangular one with radiussed corners and modified the existing aperture to suit. At the same time, we fitted a small window for a rear view. Dick then also fitted aluminium framed sliding side windows and two wind-screen glasses made to suit the 'V' shape, all out of laminated safety glass. The roof panels were then lined with sound deadening foam and a head lining which would make the interior quieter and look more professional.

With great enthusiasm, Allan also set about making all the specially designed components and equipment including the improved retractable suspension mechanisms, drive units and the unique steering parts. Generally speaking, the hull was extremely well built and the main structure was ideal as the basis for the new and innovative components which Allan was fabricating and making in the machine shop.

Being well aware that there was a need for various mountings and how the tolerances in 'one off' structures can vary when built without jigs, I did not attempt to have the boatyard make or fit any of the mountings for the mechanical parts. This work is best done by us as the work proceeds and as the components were being made and fitted. This ensures control and a proper fit.

The hull, as delivered, incorporated the wheel 'boxes' with open bottoms for the wheels which were more conventionally located on this hull, one at each corner. This was unlike the twin front wheel arrangement which I had experimented with on the MK1 and MK11 hulls. These had worked well, especially with the deep 'V' hull, but would only be used for specific applications. The wheel apertures on the MK III were modified to make them look more presentable.

For the first series of tests with this new hull, although we would certainly be fitting a marine diesel engine for subsequent tests and when in production, once again, I decided to begin by fitting a conventional motor car petrol engine. This was for the following reasons:

Firstly, it was cost effective, we could buy a new engine with matched automatic gearbox and differential, for much less than the cost of a marine diesel engine alone. Also, I did want to experiment and test the characteristics of an automotive unit with water-jet propulsion in water. We now had a hamilton jet and wanted to see how it performed with an automatic gear box and with a non-marine engine. One which had an RPM range suitable for water jets, but one which I knew, would only just be powerful enough for a hull of this size and weight.

Secondly, with this being our own hull design with a more conventional wheel layout, I was focussing my attention upon the 'feel' and performance of the important innovative steering design and also wanted to test the chosen retractable wheel mechanisms and their safety locking systems. It would be most beneficial

CHAPTER 45: THE MK III PROTOTYPE

to see how the performance of the hull on the road compared to that when it was afloat.

When a completely new and innovative vehicle is built, especially one which is dual purpose and combines two very different technologies, it is important to have some firm 'yardsticks' for comparison. With there being so many new and untested mechanisms, we needed to focus on specific areas rather than be confronted with a wide range of variables, all interacting with each other. Marine engines and their gearboxes are different, in a number of respects, to automotive ones.

Discussing various alternatives power units for our tests with Allan and with him being familiar with Ford components, we decided upon the readily available Granada petrol engine, automatic gearbox, and transmission. These standard components were readily available and by dealing with the commercial Original Equipment (OE) supplier, we would minimise our costs and at the same time, we could compare the performance of the MK III to a normal road going, mid range family saloon with which we were familiar.

Although the MK III amphibian was heavier than the Ford Granada motor car, we knew it would give us enough power for driving this 22ft vehicle on the road, but at less than 140BHP, it was ideal for our water tests because we knew that it was only going to have marginally enough power for planing on water. This was especially relevant, since water-jet propulsion is 10% less efficient, in certain respects, than propellers, but are good for higher speeds.
In this respect we could see the effect of testing with and without flaps being fitted and carry out other experiments with added buoyancy, different impellers etc. These would clearly show which would improve the efficiency and performance of the MK III. Fitting a more powerful engine would be relatively simple, but it would not be helpful at this early stage.

Although petrol engines have a higher power to weight ratio than diesel engines which would be beneficial in some respects, they are, in fact, far from ideal for properly designed marine amphibious vehicles. With these vehicles necessarily incorporating a sealed watertight hull, the petrol fumes gather in the bilges and being highly explosive, for reasons of safety alone, we would certainly be using diesel engines, not petrol, when in production with Roylecraft amphibians.

Another important reason at this time for not starting with a diesel engine in our prototype, was that a number of engine manufacturers were developing light weight marine and automotive diesel engines which would run at higher revs than most of the existing traditional diesel engines. With water-jets now becoming more popular, the new engines would be ideal for our purposes. At less than half the weight and capable of revving up to well over 4000 RPM, nearly double that of the traditional commercial diesel engines, they would be likely to suit our amphibians

Whilst the existing diesel engines were excellent units, they were heavy and slow revving, ideal for use on a wide range of commercial vehicles and boats with propellers. They are very reliable and do give many years of service for the right application, but not really suitable for our light weight, high speed water- jet propelled machines. As mentioned, these traditional diesel engines were also expensive. We were able to buy the Ford engine, gearbox, diff etc for less than half the cost of a good quality Cummins diesel unit alone, for example.

With great enthusiasm and with the new hull now in the workshops, we were able to set about making all the specially designed stainless steel mechanical components and other unique equipment including the new retractable suspension mechanisms, drive units and the unique steering parts. Allan was also able to 'crack on' fabricating and making all the new various mountings for the components in the machine shop.

By fabricating the mountings ourselves, we were able to make any necessary allowances for the slight variations in the measurements which are bound to exist with a hull which has been hand built. I did not attempt to have the boatyard fabricate or fit any of the mountings for the mechanical parts. This work is best done by us as the work proceeds and as the components were being made and fitted. This ensures control and a proper fit.

With it being designed and built expressly to my own requirements and specification, it was a delight to have a structure which was fit for purpose.

CHAPTER 46:
GOOD PROGRESS

After having spent much of the summer in 1993 fitting up the MK III, We were itching to see how it performed on water, just as a hull. The Ford engine had been installed along with Allan's specially built intermediary PTO gearbox and the conventional Ford automatic box. These were connected up with drive shafts made to suit the Hamilton water-jet and drive the wheels. The steering mechanism had also been made and fitted along with the wiring, dashboard and the necessary instruments.

By now, after all this work was done, it was January 1994 and it fell neatly between my second and third operations in hospital, so we took the MKIII to John Thompson's Ellerton Lake near Scorton,, now my favourite test lake. This was not just because it was near to hand, but also because John had built a most convenient 'convenience' next to the lake which was ideal for me with colitis, visits to the loo being necessary every half hour or so.

Being stitched up my front, I couldn't do much 'pulling and pushing' but I was able to drive the prototype and fortunately made notes during the tests. I have retained these reports which vary from neatly written ones on lined A4 notepaper, or on whatever I could find to write on, like the back of large envelopes for example! They include weather conditions and other relevant and detailed technical information.
I include here, a few tidied up 'snippets' to give you a 'feel' for the tests.

THE FIRST MK III HULL TEST.
18 JANUARY 1994.

With the wheels and suspension not yet having been installed, we launched it conventionally, like an ordinary boat on its trailer, behind a small flat bed truck. As mentioned, for its first ever test, we left Daltons front curved 'boxes' in place and had left the wheel apertures open without flaps. With a slight breeze and overcast sky, the lake was calm and we started slowly with this new 2.9 litre engine and were checking the cooling which was by conventional air cooled heat exchanger/radiator with a fan. I was aware that cooling the engines of existing amphibians was a long standing problem and I was expecting to focus upon resolving this particular aspect.

As we applied more power from this relatively small Ford engine, we could see that the performance, as far as speed was concerned, was slow and disappointing, the power was not being transferred into the water efficiently. We were pleased with the general 'feel' of the hull however, and its directional stability and Manoeverability were good.

Mark III prototype testing.

Although it was a preliminary trial of an incomplete machine, It was seen to be a most stable working platform and the small cabin was practicable and worked well. The open space aft of the cabin with its flat floor and high side decks made for a safe and useful working and loading area. Altogether, the hull had all the makings of a good basis for development and we were confident that it would become an excellent general purpose and flood rescue amphibious machine. These tests lasted for four hours.

Back in the workshops, various improvements were made to the MK III. We fitted a folding step to the rear platform over the Hamilton Water-jet to improve access. We also fitted temporary flaps to the rear wheel Boxes, changed the jet impeller ratio due to excessive cavitation, fitted a battery box, rear view mirrors and a higher engine header tank for increased coolant capacity.

SECOND TEST.
31 JANUARY 1994.

With these few modifications we returned to the lake a fortnight later. On this occasion it was blowing a gale of wind, force 6 to 7 and even with such a short fetch, there were short choppy waves. Never the less, we could immediately see an improvement in the performance, but still not as much as we hoped for, so we tied the MK III to a tree on the shore of the lake and then ran the jet at different speeds to check again for any cavitation. This was now OK, but the engine revs were still high compared to hull speed, so the problem was in either the transmission or/and the hull.

We continued with the tests to see what was causing the problem, when heading into the wind and waves, we were kicking up quite a lot of spray. The hull was designed for sea conditions, so the weather itself wasn't a problem, it was just that we preferred to have similar conditions for each test so that direct comparisons could be made. We pressed on, but the water-Jet drive shaft eventually snapped. To minimise costs we had not machined any splines on the shaft. The load was being taken entirely on the welding, which on this occasion, had failed. Such is the price one pays for cutting costs, but it was a prototype and we already had the information which we needed. Being in mid lake when it happened, we drifted down wind onto the lee shore where the trees and bank made it quite a job to drag it back round to the ramp into the wind.

Once we had retrieved the MK III, we took it back to the workshops again for more work!

This time, we removed the curved boxes from either side of the bow, which were not helping and adjusted the Jet bucket and the clutch. We also adjusted the set of the control levers and fitted front wheel flaps, returning to Ellerton the following day.

THIRD TEST.
1 FEBRUARY 1994

When we got there, we found that this time, the weather was bright and clear with a slight breeze. When testing began, we could see that everything seemed to be coming together very well. The performance was very much

Mark III prototype testing.

improved, we were now planing and not surprisingly, especially going downwind, the performance really was exciting and speeds of over 33mph was seen, we had achieved our aim. I was delighted that we had seen this speed with our relatively small engine. It had just enough power, but we needed more for production. This is what I needed to know.

With water-jet propulsion and the hard chine, deep 'v' with two 'flats' hull design, (no, not some sort of two-story housing unit!) more elegantly known as a 'Cathedral Hull', I was keen to see how it behaved when turning quickly at speed. A normal propeller driven, deep 'v' hull speed boat, for example, will bank into turns. In this case, with water-jet propulsion and the new hull design when at full speed, I was fascinated to see it turn absolutely flat. The chine built up a mound of water on the outside of the hull which limited the amount of side-slip and with the benefit of a low centre of gravity, the turn was made quickly and efficiently.

Mark III prototype testing. 90° turn.

Not surprisingly, we were all delighted with the third trial of this entirely new hull. We carried on with various tests, pressing it to the limit until the temperature of the engine crept up

Hose blown off. Overheating. Planing at speed.

and eventually blew off one of the hoses in a cloud of steam. We returned to the workshops again with ideas for the future. The photographs show the high speed turns and the results of overheating the engine.

From the outset, as already mentioned, I was well aware that most amphibians suffer from problems associated cooling the engine, the gearbox and ancillary equipment. This stems from the fact that when all the automotive and marine machinery is encased in a watertight hull, the heat which is generated cannot be easily dissipated. Normal motor vehicles have the benefit of the 'rammed air' effect through a front mounted radiator or heat exchanger. Cool air is also circulating around the engine and transmission and underneath the bodywork of road vehicles where it can escape. Proper marine amphibians cannot easily benefit from any of these features.

Radiators and heat exchangers are fragile and if mounted outside the hull of an amphibian are in an exposed position, they can easily be damaged and also are likely to clog up with flotsam and jetsam especially if mounted near the water level. This was found to be the case by the firm which operates the wartime DUKW's on the Thames in London. Obviously, raw water cooling is available for amphibians as it is with boats when afloat, but when the amphibian is travelling on the road, then this facility is obviously not available to them.

Whilst the results of these first tests were most heartening, it was clear that the performance could be much improved by refining various aspects of the equipment, much of which was of a temporary nature and we still had the suspension and retractable wheels to fit. During 1994, work was continuing with Allan making various components for the suspension at Royle's workshops, I was also organising sub-contractors to make some of the parts which we were not equipped to do. Whilst this was being done, we continued to experiment with various ideas for cooling the engine and to improve the hull performance. This included experiments with ducted air and buoyancy tanks.

FURTHER TESTING

More tests were carried out at Ellerton lake during 1994 to see how the modifications affected the performance. In early December, my notes begin by saying that the conditions were damp with drizzle and that there was 15kph of wind. This was important because we were measuring the speed of the air as it passed down the ducts and trunking from the intake which we were able to test in various positions above and around the cabin.

We were measuring the air speed of the 'rammed air' effect as it travelled down the ducting to the heat exchanger. The air speed rapidly reduced as it did so and was seen to be most unsatisfactory, so It was clear that we needed to create an entirely new and simple system which would overcome the long standing cooling problem once and for all. I set about researching various types of automotive transport and came up with a solution which would give us full control of the cooling, whether the Roylecraft were operating in cold or high ambient temperatures. This was important as most of our vehicles would be in service in widely varying climates all around the world.

By the end of the year it was clear that our tests had been most useful and that we could make some real advances and improvements. Due to our very limited funding for a project on this scale, we would need to continue to utilise the existing hull, but make significant changes including the internal layout, extending its overall length and incorporating better cooling. We would also now fit a suitable diesel engine with more power to drive a larger water-jet, but still with an eye to economy in service.

CHAPTER 46: GOOD PROGRESS

Prototypes show that speed on land and water can be achieved

CRACKING THE CAR/BOAT CONUNDRUM

'OVERLOAD PROTECTION'
TWIFLEX
AIR START CLUTCH

Can save thousands by protecting expensive transmission equipment.

A must for vessels frequently subjected to propeller fouling.

The Twiflex Air Start Clutch combines the advantages of an automatic centrifugal clutch with additional features.

- Engagement at any speed.
- Disengagement at any speed.
- Overload protection by immediate disengagement on heavy overload therefore protecting the clutch and the rest of the transmission equipment.

For more details contact:

The Green, Twickenham,
Middlesex, England. TW2 5AQ.
Tel: 0181 894 1161.
Fax: 0181 894 6056.

The Mk III prototype makes planing speed in trials

Covelink Marine of Darlington, UK, has developed an amphibious vehicle which offers good performance on both land and water.

Covelink is an engineering company which makes specialist vehicles and had seen that the usual car/boat configuration produced a vehicle which was neither particularly good on land or water.

In 1989 the company started developing its version and has now got prototypes which can achieve 70 mph (112km) on land and 30mph (48km) on water and carry a decent payload.

The aluminium hull/body is about 9m long with a beam of 2.5m-about the maximum that can be driven on normal roads- and power comes from a Cummins 250bhp diesel driving a water jet through an Allison gearbox, Covelink transfer box, CWP and final drive by HV chains.

That is the relatively easy bit. The real problem was to design and build a suspension system that could retract for in water operation and yet offer superior performance on the road.

Three prototypes have been produced to test various aspects of the design and the result is a planing hull which can, according to the makers, stay stable in condition of wind force 6-7.

the fourth prototype is a final test bed to allow the engine. gearbox and suspension to be tested under road conditions in a hull similar to the one envisaged for production.

Covelink director David Royle sees a commercial future for the car/boat with its ability to move very quickly in either medium and to move quickly on either medium with bodies such as customs and excise and river patrols.

Well it almost looks like a car-but with a design speed of 70 mph it deserves a bit of attention. Note the retractable front wheel. Road type approval dictates much of the design

Workboat International. February 1996.

FUNDING, PATENTS & SUB-CONTRACT WORK

In the office, there was a never ending need for funding, not only for all the ongoing engineering work downstairs in the workshops, but also for the growing international Patent Portfolio. Once entered into, the amount of work for me doing drawings, writing specifications and the registration and ongoing demands for world-wide protection was considerable. From memory, altogether, sums of the order of £207,000 was spent on Patents, design rights, agents and other associated costs. I was using various monies from my own resources and from selling equity to cover the ongoing costs.

Without going through the many shelves full of files in my office today, you would find it difficult to believe the intensity of work which has been done over the last 22 years to raise money. Without exaggeration, there must be over 6000 letters to and from every conceivable organisation which might have been able to help with funding for the R&D work and to start Production. These include the Banks, Venture Capital firms, Large Industries, Civilian and Military organisations, private investors, UK Government Organisations, EU schemes, etc, etc. Space permitting, I will include a list of them in the appendix. A book could be written on this aspect of the project alone, I had some remarkable and very interesting experiences with the organisations and with the many people involved.

In recent years, some people have said that 'I bit off more than I could chew', so I would like to explain in more detail how this project developed and why the costs increased.

You will remember that in 1987 when I started, the plan was to design and build the first properly designed, fast amphibians which would probably be 20 to 23 feet long, be sea worthy, safe and be suitable for leisure use. At this time, the luxury market was buoyant and expanding. The original project plan which Bruce Ropner and I had envisaged at that time, was that we would invest equal amounts to build and test a prototype which would incorporate my new ideas. Bruce and I had worked together on one or two interesting motor car projects and he was confident of my capabilities and the skills of the men in the Royles workshop.

The government were advertising widely to encourage innovation and the creation of new technologies, especially high value ones, so I knew we might benefit from the grants on offer. The Vintage and specialist motor car market was very buoyant at the time, so the workshops would also be able to support some of the costs of the work, along with some funds from Royle Cars Ltd, my Vintage Car Sales business.

Whilst it is impossible to estimate R&D costs for a project of this nature, I thought that the cost of building a prototype would not be dissimilar to that of restoring a middle of the range Vintage motor car, £60,000 to £80,000. This estimate took into account the fact that we would be using all new components and not having to spend time restoring old machinery.

It became clear, from our market research and with the start of the recession in February/March 1990, that the technology which was being created by us, really was breaking new ground.

Editorials Winter 1995. 'Subsea Diving Magazine'. Articles were now appearing in various UK and European publications including 'Technisch Weekblad" the Dutch technical journal, 'Dagbladet' in Norway and other more distant overseas magazines.

It could be the basis of a very substantial new transport industry, not just for the leisure market. There was obviously a real need for machines which would be suitable for and capable of performing a wide range of services in many different spheres of activity around the world; Flood rescue, Transport buses, tourism, workboats, etc. This change of direction however, entailed building amphibious vehicles which would be much bigger and more costly than we initially had planned for.

Bruce and I both agreed that it was now even more important that our marine amphibians

COVELINK MARINE LTD.

PRESENT

THE WORLD'S FIRST LIGHTWEIGHT HIGH SPEED AMPHIBIOUS VEHICLE

BACKGROUND

Since the turn of the century many amphibious vehicles have been built but, until now, there has never been a road-going vehicle which could perform so safely and efficiently on water.

After seven years of intensive R&D, Covelink Marine Ltd. has developed a revolutionary and entirely new vehicle. The benefit of retractable wheels & suspension and many other innovative features can be clearly seen to provide this HSAV with an outstanding performance, unique in the history of amphibious vehicles.

DEVELOPMENT

The programme of development has been supported by David C. Royle & Co. Ltd., the long established specialist motor vehicle company whose highly skilled staff and well equipped workshops have been able to produce the necessary prototypes at comparatively low cost.

Having proved the concept, the company now seeks additional funding to help carry the project forward into production. Additional notes are available for those who may like to be involved with this exciting and potentially highly profitable venture.

MARKETING

Directors and shareholders involved with marketing are impressed by the International potential of these new high speed amphibious vehicles. There are four major sectors in the market place, commercial, military, leisure & para-military, each being divided up into a number of applications, as described overleaf.

INVESTMENT/PARTICIPATION

Persons wishing to be involved with the future development of the company, whether it be in buying shares and/or taking a more active role in the day to day operation, should contact David Royle as below.

Covelink Marine Ltd. The Old School, Staindrop, Near Darlington, Co. Durham DL2 3NH.
Telephone: 01833 660995   Fax: 01833 660834

Mark III prototype 'flyer'

satisfy the necessary criteria for road going transport on the public highway. This is a key requirement if efficient modern amphibious transport is to be practical and commercially viable. Unlike virtually all existing military amphibious vehicles which are too wide for the public highway, our machines would open up new and viable global markets. The net result was that we were now looking at designing and creating amphibians which would be up to around 40ft long (12m).

We were satisfied that our first 6m, 18ft, High Water Speed prototype, subsequently known as the 'MK I', had still been the best and most economic way forward. It had proved that the concept worked, but we needed to consider how we could raise more money for what was now becoming a major project. We were moving into vehicles/craft which would normally be designed and built by large industrial firms. I was still confident that my designs would satisfy the requirements and with our skilled workforce and comprehensively equipped workshops, we could deal with prototypes of a larger size up to 30 feet.

Bruce and I set about talking to potential investors in both the Private and Public sectors. It was clear that if we could raise sufficient money, the investors would see a wonderful return. This aspect led to us printing a 'flyer' to test the response of the market as we had done with the MK I prototype. There was a never ending demand for Business Plans of all sizes, help for which was provided by various people. Often, this work also added to the costs. I had assistance from people in Durham University, government agencies, our own accountants and other specialists.

The tax beneficial 'Business Expansion Scheme '(BES) encouraged investment by individuals in the private sector, but this scheme had come to an end in 1993. We were following up all the leads, but by February 1994, the details of its replacement, the 'Enterprise Investment Scheme' (EIS) had still not been published, which didn't help at the time.

CHAPTER 47:
THE MARK IV PROTOTYPE

By the end of 1994 I could see that the general principles of the 22 foot MK III design were good and it would be a viable and useful vehicle to build in production. Whether for slow or high speed operations, it was obviously going to satisfy the need for a wide range of private and public services. The lessons learnt from our tests were as ever, most valuable, so I was keen to move forward onto a longer vehicle to meet the demands of the untapped markets.

Now that we had tested three quite different prototypes, each with different hulls and new mechanisms, I was confident that the new ideas, incorporated into each one of them, were practicable and would be used for the correct application. Rather than focus upon any particular prototype and develop and refine it at this stage and at substantial additional cost, it was more important to continue our market research and, at the same time, be able to move on and test a larger machine at relatively low cost. I didn't want to spend a lot of money on the wrong type of vehicle.

I was learning more and more about the potential markets as we progressed, I wanted to be sure that, when we started production, it was with amphibians which incorporated the best technology and which would be the most viable and profitable in manufacture. There was no real competition, only the wartime DUKW's, which are now over 65 years old, and the unsatisfactory converted motor cars and trucks. This was important, because it meant that we had time to properly develop the designs.

SIZE AND TYPE OF CRAFT CRITICAL FOR VIABILITY

It was clear that there are many factors to take into consideration when looking ahead to production and to satisfy the potential markets, but the cost of all the components would be less important and more easily covered in larger machines. The buyers would, in any event, expect the cost of larger vehicles to be more than small ones. A parallel can be drawn when comparing a Rolls Royce motor car with a lower cost vehicle. There are, or were, necessarily more components and of higher quality in these costly vehicles, which is why they never produced a small Rolls Royce. The overall cost of manufacture would not be much different, but it would be much more difficult to sell a small, expensive, luxury car.

The amount of equipment necessary to achieve efficient amphibious transport is, not surprisingly, going to be more than you would find in any normal boat or in any existing motor vehicle. The cost of an amphibian is therefore generally, going to be higher than the equivalent size of motor vehicle or boat. As mentioned, an example of this was produced in recent years and predictably was too costly to sell in any quantity.

THE 'GIBBS AQUADA'

This motor car type of amphibian appeared in 2002. This was 15 years after my first high speed machine had been built and tested at speeds in excess of 30 knots on Lake Windermere. The Gibbs 'Aquada' three seater amphibious sport car is a good illustration of what I describe above.

Multi-millionaire New Zealander, Alan Gibbs had thought about the possibilities of amphibious transport and set about producing an amphibious vehicle without fully understanding the market, the technology, or the viability of what he was having built.

It transpired that Mr Gibbs had started off on the right track by having had built an amphibious boat in New Zealand. He described it to me as a "complete failure". When he visited me on 5 November 1996 to discuss his ideas and to see where he was going wrong. In the hope that he might help me with funding and in confidence, I advised him and gave him the benefit of some of my experience and research.

He told me that he wanted me to design and build a special high speed amphibian for use at his beach house in New Zealand and gave me very specific instructions regarding ground pressure etc. I subsequently made a start on the drawings, answering his questions as we went along, as to what was involved and why I was incorporating particular features. Instead of continuing with this project however, a few weeks later, he seemed to have an abrupt change of heart. He cancelled the project and told me that he did not "want to waste any more money on amphibians". He said that he was going to buy a boat and trailer.

I subsequently heard that, shortly after our meeting, he had bought a patent for retracting normal motor vehicle suspension. It seems that he intended to be the first to manufacture his ideas for a high speed amphibious motor vehicle. Having confirmed to him at our meeting, that there was a demand and having seen my enthusiasm, instead of joining me, he obviously now felt sufficiently confident about the technology to do it himself. He had ample money available and was keen to be the first person to produce modern, fast, planing amphibians.

It seems that in his rush however, he failed to understand the full implications of what he was doing. He spent very considerable sums of money, reported in the press as being up to £60 million, to build his own small planing amphibious motor car, the 'Gibbs Aquada'. To do this, instead of continuing with a boat, he followed the well worn and unsatisfactory principal of making a floating motor car.

With the benefit of having retractable wheels and other aspects, which I had briefly discussed with him, like dispensing with the need for front wheel drive on some vehicles for example, his motor car did plane and was neatly finished. It was annoying for me however, that he claimed that his vehicle was the 'first high speed amphibian' when in fact we had achieved planning speeds twelve years earlier and with a more seaworthy and safe machine. He was perfectly happy to adopt some of my principles without any reference to me or acknowledgement of my work.

As his team were primarily from the motor car world, Jaguar I gather, instead of a boat, his amphibian was essentially a normal looking motor car. It was well presented and drove in and out of calm water perfectly well and planed at a good speed in similar conditions, but the vehicle had not been properly thought through. One of the drawbacks to it's use in this country is that most sheltered and calm inland waterways have six and eight knot speed limits, so travelling on water at planing speeds is illegal. On the other hand, it was not really capable of being used safely in rough water either, especially at sea.

It was also seriously flawed in a number of other important respects. For example, they had fitted a petrol engine which, as mentioned, do have a good power to weight ratio, but are far from ideal for amphibious vehicles. This is because, unlike a motor car, which has bodywork which is open to the atmosphere below the engine, the petrol tank, its petrol pumps and supply pipes, which allows any fumes or leaks to be dissipated, an amphibious vehicle has a watertight hull. This means that petrol and any other flammable liquids and gases are encased. The fumes can't escape and gather inside the body and with this, goes all the attendant and very real risks of explosion.

Another limitation is the retractable wheel mechanisms. These were based upon normal automotive suspension which is unsatisfactory in that it is specific to this small size and type of vehicle. Their movement being so limited that they could not be used in a sea worthy, deep 'V' high speed hull. The result is that the 'Aquada' has a shallow 'V' hull, a shape which slams badly in the smallest of waves, or any sort of rough water.

The overall design therefore, has very limited applications and would be difficult if not impossible to be incorporated satisfactorily in any larger seaworthy amphibians for public transport, the emergency services or other commercial use.

Despite having signed our confidentiality agreement and knowing that some of my innovative principles were incorporated in the Aquada, it also upset me greatly to see him wasting so much of his money.

In his rush to be first into the market place, Mr Gibbs had not grasped the fundamental principal that a motor car shaped amphibian will not travel on water as efficiently and safely as it does on the road, whereas a boat shaped one will! To put it simply, not many people would choose to leave a sheltered harbour and drive into a choppy sea in a motor car, especially with strong winds. Richard Branson did manage to cross the channel in one, but he had carefully chosen a calm day and apparently had two safety rescue boats travelling alongside and of course, Mr Branson does not like to miss an opportunity which attracts publicity for him.

Too late did Mr Gibbs discover that he had made these fundamental and very costly mistakes. Firstly, as described above, the cost of building the amphibious car in relation to its size and usefulness, became apparent when he tried to sell them for £150.000 each.
Not surprisingly, they were perceived as being overpriced for a small sports car. It certainly could plane on water, but it was one which had extremely limited markets and applications.
It seems that he subsequently halved the price, but eventually must have admitted defeat and closed his factory sometime around 2008.

Seven years after our meeting in 1996, and the year after the 'Aquada' had been launched in the press in 2003, he contacted me once again to arrange another meeting. This time he wanted to "swap visits" as he put it. Presumably, he was already beginning to see the error of his ways. After being 'once bitten' by him however, not surprisingly, I was now 'twice shy'. He had completely ignored our confidentiality agreement and not accepted a previous written proposal from me. He had also misled me when he told me that he was not going any further with amphibians.

He knows that I am knowledgeable and enthusiastic and was keen to help him, 'was' being the operative word. He obviously thought that he could use me and my knowledge whenever he wished, but he had shown his true colours. After having suffered huge losses through dealing with millionaires in my restoration business, I had little doubt that any meetings would have been entirely for Mr Gibbs own benefit and unlikely to help me in any respect. He had probably forgotten how he had treated me after the first time we met and I knew that I couldn't trust him, so certainly didn't want another meeting.

It is a great shame that he wanted all the benefits for himself. Some sort of Joint Venture would have saved him literally, tens of £millions and many years work. Together, we could have developed a new and huge transport industry. Instead of which, the Gibbs Aquada had failed commercially and the 'Roylecraft' technology, with all the benefits it incorporates, has suffered years of financial difficulty. We could have been in production within a couple of years and with the orders which I have in hand, we could have been satisfying the huge global demand with a business turning over £500 million per annum, or more. A wonderful opportunity wasted.

Reading through this book, you will see that the most powerful and wealthy people, especially those who have made the money themselves, are usually extremely ambitious and seem to have few scruples. This is why they usually 'win' when dealing with people who are open and straight forward. In this case, sadly, as Mr Gibbs found out for himself, there is a lot more to amphibians than meets the eye. As indeed would a number of others in the future.

RETURNING TO THE ROYLECRAFT STORY

As well as it being boat shaped for sea-kindliness and safety, the length of a marine hull is a key consideration. As mentioned, it is an important consideration for practical reasons and sea worthiness as well as for the commercial viability of the machine. It also affects the level of comfort when fast transportation over water is the target. The next logical step for me therefore, was to build and test a longer hull.

Rather than build another similar design of amphibian from scratch, with the beam being fixed, it was going to be more economic to increase the length by extending the hull of the MK III and then compare the performance. We have all the facilities and skills in house to work with aluminium, so it was something which could be done efficiently and quickly in Royle's workshops. I decided that the existing hull would therefore, be extended to make it 25 feet long and it would then be referred to as the MK IV.

The MK III was properly supported along its length and then literally, cut in half just behind the cabin where the line of the deck was straight and the new metal could be welded in without spoiling the appearance. The cut was made in 'steps' like a 'boiler-makers joint' to retain the strength and integrity of the hull. Other changes were made and new, improved suspension mechanisms were being made and fitted which were different to the previous prototypes. In this way we were able to test and

Mark III hull extended.

Our improved transfer gearbox.

compare the performance of various methods of drive and retraction.

Having cut and lengthened the hull, we also replaced the small experimental intermediary gearbox which Allan had previously made to fit between the Ford engine and automatic gearbox. This was very neat and compact and did work, but was unsatisfactory in a number of respects. With the extended hull, we needed to design and relocate a new gearbox in order to satisfy a different and improved layout. The most cost effective way of doing this was for Allan to fabricate one using square cut gears which would give us the ratios we required and act as a transfer box. We also incorporated an electric clutch for the water-jet.

Although we decided to fabricate the gearbox out of flat steel plate and knew that it was going to be heavier than we would use in production, it was cost effective and satisfactory as an experimental unit. Although not as refined as a modern gearbox, we would be able to test the main principles of the drive, the gear ratios and overall layout without going to the expense of alloy castings etc. This time we mounted it well forward, just behind the cabin, in order to give better alignment and weight distribution. Heavy duty batteries were mounted behind the cabin in their own box and used to counterbalance the weight of the off centre engine

As mentioned previously, the development and advantages of water-jet propulsion were becoming apparent for high speed marine applications, so diesel engine manufacturers were developing high revving, light weight, cast alloy engines to meet the growing demand in the marine industry. In parallel, automotive diesel engines were also being refined and developed, so I could see that, by the time we were ready for production, there was likely to be a range of engines which could be ideal for our purposes. With this being the case, time was on our side and whilst we were experimenting with the prototypes, I was able to continue to explore and investigate the diesel engine market.

MK IV. MAKING SUSPENSION, STEERING AND OTHER MECHANISMS

As mentioned, we had made and tested different new mechanisms for the retractable wheels and for the steering on each of the prototypes. Whilst all the different designs worked, the tests had revealed the benefits and drawbacks of each of the innovative techniques used and we had also experimented with hydraulic and electric power for retraction. From the beginning, I realised that mechanical transmission would be the principle method of actually driving the vehicles themselves, when on the road. Other methods to drive the wheels may be used, but only when specific applications were subsequently being considered.

Reports to shareholders show that 1995 was especially difficult for us. This was due to the need for more funding. To maintain progress and to pay the staff working on the prototypes I had no option, but to continue to sell my personal assets and I was also continuing to press shareholders and all other possible sources. Sadly, it was not long before I had no choice but to make two of my men redundant. From then on, progress was frustrated by lack of funding, but by selling more of my assets, we were able to continue to make the components and make slow, but steady progress.

Unfortunately, prior to this, one of our most helpful and enthusiastic investors thought that we should be fitting a more powerful diesel engine straight away. He and his family were concerned that the overall costs were steadily increasing without seeming to be getting any nearer to production. They thought that this was as a result of being constrained by the shortage of funding, or it might have been that they thought that I was simply creating work to keep the workshops busy. In any event they wanted me to start production ASAP to earn some money.

On the face of it, this concern was perfectly understandable, because it can be difficult for those not closely involved with the development process, to understand why it all seems to take so long. In our case, funding was indeed a continual problem, but the shortage of money did in fact ensure that we spent the absolute minimum, so was a good form of control. I was also determined that we would not fall into the same trap and end up with another unsatisfactory machine like all those which had been built in the past. After all, there were no salaries or management costs and so our costs were a fraction of those normally associated with the creation of such large and complex vehicles.

Despite explaining all this and still believing that we would progress more quickly, he insisted that we fit a large commercial diesel engine, a Cummins 250BHP unit which he and his family would pay for. With help from our chairman, Sir Alex Smith, we tried to explain to him that this engine was unsuitable, it would not speed up our progress and would be a waste of our potential resources. Whilst it would have plenty of power, it was slow revving and being of cast iron, weighed nearly ¾ of a tonne, so was very heavy and it was in conflict with our plans for the road and water jet transmission and the special gearboxes and would upset the overall balance and the planned engine installation and it would not really be suitable or helpful at this time. He was obviously under a lot of pressure from his family who were also investing quite substantial amounts of money. They had successfully used one of these engines on their farm machinery, so they insisted that I bought one.

I was left with no choice, but to order a marine version of these reliable units, so it was supplied with keel cooling equipment. Whilst fitting it into the hull, I again brought in the Water-jet manufacturers, but as previously, they confirmed that it simply was not suitable for our application and for the refined marine vehicles which we were creating. There was no point in even running it, so sadly, we had to remove the engine and refit the Ford Granada petrol engine into its original engine box at the stern. This was most upsetting since our investor was keen to help.

For anybody to fully understand the situation, they had to have an intimate knowledge of the designs and the many aspects involved when overcoming the problems associated with building the world's first ever, properly designed, efficient, high water speed commercial amphibians. The answer was not a slow revving, heavy engine. Even though it was diesel and turbocharged, it was not the correct type of unit for this highly specialised installation. To have developed this vehicle using this unsuitable engine, would have been a serious retrograde step. The hull and every component in our vehicles are interrelated and have a bearing upon the nature and design of all the other components, especially when weight has to be minimised.

Whilst water speed was a key factor, it would have been easy to have fitted a very powerful unit. As an old motorboat racing friend down in Cornwall, John Sanders, once said to me, "you can make a brick plane if you fit a big enough engine"! But we weren't planning to build bricks. We were aiming at a much more refined product, one that would satisfy the needs of the future operators. We already knew that we had an efficient, fast amphibious hull and safe operational retractable wheels and suspension. We were working towards having the correct, efficient engine, transmission and the right equipment to maximise the speed and loads it could carry. There are far too many aspects to list here which determine what is, or is not satisfactory. Every single component has to be scrutinised and assessed if the final result is to be successful.

The problem for somebody in my position, is that few people in this country understand the value of my experience, or of the knowledge acquired by me during half a century of practical work. After spending many years of both my leisure time and business life, working at the bench and on vehicles of every description and then test driving them, as well as working on slow and high speed boats and sailing them on inland and coastal waters, I do have an unusual breadth and intimate knowledge of both forms of transport. With the benefit of all this and now, after eight years spent studying the subject of amphibious vehicles and designing, building and testing them, by 1995, I was very well aware of what is needed to make this new, highly specialised technology, a viable proposition.

Very few people have had the privilege of my experience and with this project being of such an unusual nature, combining as it does, both automotive and marine technologies and with amphibians having such a poor record with much adverse publicity having been given to a number of previous amateurish attempts, it was vital that our amphibians are treated with respect and are recognised as serious, advanced forms of transport.

When ploughing my own furrow and tackling the many issues involved, some enthusiastic and well meaning people, not surprisingly, have questioned my decisions and knowledge and have reached conclusions without really understanding the ramifications associated with the complex and intricate nature of the technology. The case of the Cummins Diesel engine is an example of this, but some were less obvious.

This lack of specialised knowledge is a problem which has held back the development of advanced amphibians for most of the last century. It is an unknown technology with no academic or professional institutions or appropriate qualifications to give it any credence. Even during the second world war, there were serious objections raised against those who could see the value of these machines and went on to build them.

Because of the unique problems involved in this work, especially when confidentiality is an ever present issue, I am still reluctant to describe, in detail, what they are, or explain how I overcame them. This may seem very selfish, but as you read on, you will discover why I have had to be very careful. The net result is that very few people understand the technology and do not fully appreciate how I was able to create the first modern, refined, economic, fast and efficient machines in the world. I apologise if this sounds as if I am bragging, but those who know that I have achieved technical success, like Alan Gibbs, have tried to do it themselves and I believe, may still be trying to follow in my footsteps.

CHAPTER 48:
JET ENGINES & SUPERCHARGED SUPPORT

It was in October 1991, that Sir Alex Smith first contacted me after he had heard about my innovative engineering work. He was very interested and soon became closely involved with the High Speed Amphibious Vehicle project. It transpired that he was the Chief Scientist for Rolls Royce Aero and had been knighted for his services to industry. He also was responsible, as the first Director of the Manchester Polytechnic, for it becoming "the largest and most successful of the Polytechnics" (Ref, Sunday Times)

This small, stocky Scotsman was at the very peak of advanced jet engine development and had been involved with other very important technologies. He was extremely supportive of me and of my work and his professionalism and experience was a boon and I couldn't have wished for a better man to help me and our little R&D firm. Added to all this, was that he was very good company, had a good sense of humour and his stories were fascinating. I was delighted to have his help.

It was not long before I invited him to be Chairman of Covelink. "What will my salary be David?" he asked and I replied, hesitantly, that it would be the same as mine –Nil, "I thought so", he said and promptly accepted the position. His nature was such that he would quite happily demean his own incredible achievements.
He was obviously immensely proud of his Knighthood, but his sense of humour came out when he told me about the day he had gone to Buckingham Palace to be presented. "There were only two of us " he said, "just me and Charlie Chaplin" - "two comedians" !

Along with helping to develop the first Nuclear Submarines and Radar, Alex was also responsible for the RB 2II Jet Aero Engine. He told me that Lord Hives, the MD and later the Chairman of Rolls Royce, called him into his office one day and said, quite perfunctorily, "Smith, you did well making a Nuclear Submarine, now I want you to build me a really powerful Jet engine". Equally briefly, Alex said that he simply replied by saying "certainly sir", turned round and closed the door behind him.

It is strange how separate events can connect, it turned out that Sir Alex had worked at Rolls Royce Aero's with another old friend of mine, Geoffrey Wilde. Geoffrey had visited me at Staindrop some years earlier, he was the Chief Engineer at Rolls Royce in Derby and with Sir

Rolls Royce RB211 Nacelle.

Alex, had designed the triple shaft RB 2II jet engine. Alex confided in me that it really should have been Geoffrey who was knighted, because it was his idea to build a triple shaft jet engine, unheard of at the time.

I remember the day in 1979, when I spent a wonderful day at the RR factory in Derby. This was when Geoffrey invited me to visit him. He took me into restricted areas where, after jet engines had been tested to destruction, the parts were laid out and then carefully analysed. He also took me into the test house which has a vertical exhaust the size of a cooling tower.

Standing inside this concrete block house, below a huge RB 2II jet engine which was suspended just above us on its test 'bed', was a most impressive sight. The shiny cowlings and blades of this powerful engine contrasted sharply with the pitch black, soot covered concrete walls. The build up of carbon no doubt, being the result of all the engine testing. Geoffrey then took me round into the adjoining control room where his team of white coated engineers were facing a wall of screens, dials and controls. Very James Bond!

He sat me down between them and then, standing behind me, instructed them to start the engine and run it up. He was holding my shoulder as he did so and as the gauges recorded the revs steadily increasing- 5000, 8000, 12000RPM and the speed and resonance inside the room continued to build up, his grip tightened as he called out the ever increasing thousands of pounds of thrust. Very exciting to be there, especially to be with the man himself and to see him still so thrilled by his own magnificent and powerful creation.

Geoffrey's earlier work was also extremely interesting, he had been closely involved with the most important wartime development of the power output of piston engines. He played the leading role in supercharging the Rolls Royce Merlin Aero Engines. He was the man behind the variable and two-stage superchargers which dramatically increased the power output and which were fitted to the Spitfire and other fast warplanes.

After the war, he went on to develop various jet engines and also led the team supercharging the 1.5 litre BRM racing car. He confided in me that the V I6 cylinder BRM engine was overly complex for its capacity, so to improve its power output was going to be a serious and costly challenge. Some years later, when the project was shelved, he told me that he had been instructed to destroy all the equipment. After all the work involved, he admitted that couldn't face the idea of scrapping the remaining new and unused BRM supercharger which he still had, so he instructed his engineer to put it out of sight at the back of the bench. It remained there until he retired when he took it home. He was a brilliant engineer and a most interesting and charming man.

Returning to Sir Alex and the Roylecraft story, he was very enthusiastic about our project and was a wonderful and supportive chap. He would often stay with us at Gainford and I spent many enjoyable hours in his company and we went on many interesting trips and to many meetings together. His wife, Lady Jennifer, was a lovely

The BRM supercharger.

and lively person who would also occasionally come to stay with us.

Alex was especially 'at home' when in the 'chair' at a meeting. One occasion comes to mind, when the directors of Mayflower, at that time, the largest bus and coach-building group in the country, attended a meeting at home in our dining room at the Old Vicarage. Sitting round our dining table in our tall, oak dining chairs discussing the possibility of some sort of linkage or Joint Venture, they became rather 'cocky' about their company's size and wealth compared to our tiny SME company. This was when Sir Alex, small in stature though he may be, put them all in their place beautifully. Slowly turning and looking around our spacious and elegant Regency dining room, Sir Alex paused and then slowly said "yes, but we struggle on".

It was only a year or so later, that Mayflower went into liquidation. If we had joined them, we would probably have been closed down with them.

Jumping ahead in this story, Alex continued to actively help and support us in every possible way throughout the 1990's and into the new Millennium. There were many visits to London for meetings with Venture Capital firms, with Nesta and with other funding organisations. We also travelled to various offices and exhibitions up and down the country. His support for me was 100% and he would not accept any criticism of me, the technology or of my achievements. He had evaluated my innovative engineering designs and had no doubts about their value. His complimentary reports boosted my morale whenever it was at a low ebb.

His involvement and confidence most certainly helped us with all the applications for grants and with raising money from private investors.

With his extraordinary achievements, both technical and academic and with his history at Rolls Royce, it was easy for him to open doors to any board room in the country. Once inside however, he began to see how small innovative companies like ours, were treated. On a number of occasions, we would walk out of a meeting and he could barely contain himself. He was furious as he began to realise why so many new ideas failed to have the support they deserved. In our case he knew how good the engineering was and that there was a clear need for Roylecraft in so many areas of the emergency services and for transport generally.

With his help, during 2001/ 2002 we had been making really good progress and he was delighted to see our small starter factory being set up near Staindrop. At last, we were seeing some real daylight. He wrote to me on the 4th June 2002, to apologise, saying that he was unable to visit us for a meeting a few days later as expected. This was due to him having his Pacemaker replaced. He had been very fit, but was now 80 years old and wrote to say that he might have to be on Oxygen for quite some time.

Sadly, Alex's health began to deteriorate during November 2002 and the next three months saw him gradually becoming very ill. As he was now bedridden, Jennifer asked me to drive over to visit him at their home in Cheshire. When I arrived, she took me into the sitting room and explained how she wanted me to reassure him that our project was making excellent progress.

In fact, our situation at that time was very serious indeed. During the last three months, we had suffered badly as a direct result of the most extraordinary and corrupt activities which I had ever seen. People whom we trusted were, by fraudulent means, contriving circumstances in order to deprive us of all the benefits of our fifteen years of work. The result was that I had sixteen staff and no income to run our little starter factory. Matters were very serious indeed.

So, as I climbed the stairs to his bedroom, I had to bolster up my thoughts and with great difficulty, tried to adopt a most positive stance in preparation for telling him that we were now sure of our success. Lying in bed, reliant upon his oxygen bottle, for the first time I saw him looking very frail. His arms were outside the bedclothes, so I held his hand to give him some comfort. It was difficult for me to remain controlled, but I think that I managed to sound positive as I assured him that all our work was going to lead to the resounding success which we all had worked so hard to achieve.

His condition deteriorated and he died not long afterwards on the 27th February 2003. It was a great privilege to have known him and we shared many happy times together during the last twelve years of his interesting and productive life. His book entitled "Lock up the swings on Sundays" is a most entertaining read and covers all sorts of remarkable events, before and after the war, I can recommend it.

ANOTHER ALEX AND BIG STUFF

Also involved during this period was another 'Alex', this time Alex Marsh, a director of Babcocks, the large company which had taken over and were developing the Royal Dockyards at Rosyth on the Clyde, for industrial use. He visited Royle's workshops when we were working on his 1929 vintage Alvis Silver Eagle tourer, a vehicle which he much enjoyed driving and in which he covered many miles, including a trip to the Arctic Circle.

Before the war, this motor car had belonged to Henry Williamson, the man who is famous for his book, 'Tarka The Otter'. Strangely, I think that it was also one of very few 'Royles' cars which had my initials 'DR ', on the number plate, Job Number 386.

Seeing the work going on with our Amphibious Prototypes, Alex could see the market potential and was keen that Babcocks be involved. I went up to Rosyth a few times and was intrigued to see the Nuclear submarines moored in the basin and very impressed by the scale of their facilities and by the Aluminium fabrication work which was a feature of the high speed water-jet ferries which they were building. On one visit, the Ark Royal was being refitted. Some of their work was on a smaller scale however, so there was an obvious synergy between us.

Discussions continued for two years or so, but finally, the decision was reached that they couldn't be seen to be building Amphibious Craft which their own design team hadn't created. This was a great shame, since it would have created additional employment on the site which was being developed as an industrial estate. Many people were being made redundant due to the Dockyard being run down at that time.

It was through Alex Marsh that I met one of his co-Directors of Babcocks, Richard Fletcher and later also Richard's wife, Dr Ann Fletcher, who had been the Project Manager for the Harrier Jump-Jet vertical take-off aircraft. Both Alex and Richard became directors of my company, Covelink Marine Ltd. As our work progressed, I continued to meet many interesting and supportive people who helped with the Project in one way or another. They are mentioned as the story progresses. As ever, I am getting ahead of myself again.

CHAPTER 49:
1996. ANOTHER EVENTFUL YEAR

1996 was, as ever, a most difficult, frustrating and busy year for me. Both Royles and the Covelink R&D company were very short of money. I had arranged for a stand at the Inventions Exhibition held at the Barbican in London on 7th March in yet another attempt to publicise 'Roylecraft' to attract funding for the amphibious project. I was also involved with Babcocks at Rosyth in Scotland. I had two legal cases to deal with and was also planning to establish a new and exciting 'Living Museum' at nearby Greta Bridge on the A66 with new restoration workshops being the core attraction.

There was much publicity to create tourism and everybody who visited Royles loved to see all the work going on and all the wonderful cars and this was another excellent project which would have considerably improved Royles profitability. A great deal of effort was being put in for this marvellous opportunity. The story is told later on in this chapter.

Whilst Allan was making the suspension units and doing other work to the MK IV as well as some restoration work to help maintain cash flow, I was dealing with all these other matters. As they do occur at this juncture in the amphibious story, I will interrupt the 'flow' and tell you about them.

THE BARBICAN INVENTORS EXHIBITION

The exhibition at the Barbican proved to be very interesting and I very much appreciated the help of an old friend Anthoy Todd, better known as 'Toddy', who spent the whole six days on Covelink's stand without any payment. Our amphibians did attract a lot of interest. The visitors were from all over the world, including some from South East Asia. They represented a wide range of interests; fish farming, flood rescue, tourism and public transport, to mention just a few. We followed up the enquiries in the coming weeks and months and we did attract some new investors from the London area.

Adjoining our stand was one manned by Tim Smit, the man who regenerated the Heligan Gardens in Cornwall and went on to create the even better known and most successful Eden project. He is an amusing chap and Jo-Jo and I subsequently visited him in Cornwall where he kindly showed us all round each of the projects when they were in their early stages. Most enjoyable and very interesting!

Just along from our stand was Trevor Baylis, he also was a very entertaining and interesting character and had invented the Baygen Wind Up Radios which don't need batteries. On the back wall of his stand, was a framed letter which had been sent to him by a highly qualified engineer. This document announced, with technical reasons, why his radio's would not work because the energy required could not be supplied by a clockwork spring. Below it, was one of his radio's loudly playing with its clockwork spring fully operational. I had to smile!

THE END OF THE CAR SALES COMPANY

With the onset of the 1990 recession, the telephone in the Royles Cars Ltd sales company office stopped ringing and the market virtually disappeared up here in the north east of England. Although I had not originally planned to buy and sell vintage motor cars, this separate, small company had been a valuable adjunct to the restoration business and had brought in much needed additional turnover and profit. Believing that the recession would not last too long, Piers Leigh, our Sales Director, stayed with us and we did all we could to maintain the company.

One of the few motor cars which Piers sold in 1992, was a 1934 Lagonda 3.5 litre open tourer. This, I believe, is the actual car which appeared

Still from 'Doctor in the House'.

in the popular series of doctor films, from memory, 'Doctor in the House'. The car was seen in the middle of a 'fight' between some students who were throwing bags of flour and soot at each other. The film starred that most popular of actors, Kenneth More. An actor I always greatly admired and with whom I much enjoyed spending the day at the Steam Train Cavalcade at Shildon near here. This was when the Timothy Hackworth Railway Museum was first opened in August 1975. He told me that his father had been involved with the railways on the Channel Islands, so he had always been interested.

Kenny, as he was affectionately known, was the guest of John Hunter and his family, who were

Kenneth More, DACR and Jeremy as a small, shy boy!

great friends of ours. He would only come to the event on condition that he would be incognito. This was achieved and we all had a most enjoyable day watching the parade of steam engines. I found him to be a most charming man and every bit the sort of person one would wish him to be.

Back to the 1934 Lagonda, the car was in very original condition and was complete with its original leather upholstery and all the correct fittings. It drove well for a car which was unrestored and nearly sixty years old. Piers sold it to a solicitor who lived near Birmingham and he drove it the 150 miles home and later, told Piers that it had run very well. A long run like this, is good test for an old car.

A few months later, apparently, there was a water leak from the cylinder head gasket. Instead of just fitting a new gasket which would, in all probability, have corrected the leak without too much trouble and expense, the mechanic he had employed, reported that the engine was worn and recommended a complete engine overhaul. Being nearly sixty years old at the time and not having been restored, the engine was bound to be worn, but as it had been running well, I can only presume that the mechanic was looking for work because of the ongoing recession.

The result of this was that the new owner, being a solicitor, sued Royle Cars Ltd for the cost of overhauling the engine. The condition of the Lagonda had been accurately stated in the advertisement as being an "original, un-restored" car. It was one which we had sold on commission for the previous owner. I could not see how we could possibly be liable or held responsible for sixty years of wear to an engine of an un-restored, pre-war motor car. One which was precisely as described and one which we had not built, owned, restored or carried out any work to.

As ever, with legal matters, arguments ensued and the years passed before the case was eventually heard at a court in Birmingham in the week beginning the 4th March 1996, by which time, quite a number of solicitors and counsel were involved, including Eversheds of Leeds, who were acting for us.

Because I had already booked the stand at the Barbican in London for the inventors exhibition the same week, I needed to focus my attention on something positive rather than spend time fighting the claim against Royle Cars Ltd. A claim which was so obviously ill founded, that I knew that my solicitors, who were already going to be in court, would be unlikely to need me to be there as well.

On the second day of the action, Eversheds rang me in London to tell me that "the charges against Royle Cars Ltd had been dropped". This came as no surprise, but the previous owner was then judged to be responsible for the engines worn condition. This was because the Judge apparently said, that the Lagonda had not been "properly serviced" by the previous owner, so he should pay for it to be overhauled. In fact, not surprisingly, the Lagonda had many owners in its 62 years of use, so it was hardly fair to blame the last owner for its worn condition.

Sadly, I could only conclude that the judge had little or no knowledge of vintage and pre-war cars or their values. He was treating this 62 year old car as if it was a modern, second hand vehicle. By doing this, it is clear that the judges sympathy lay with the buyer, a solicitor whom he, no doubt, would believe had been taken advantage of by some 'unscrupulous second hand car dealers'. He would also expect that the benefits of the action should lie with his legal colleagues who would be paid for their legal work associated with the action. Work which the Lagonda's new solicitor owner had entirely created himself, and who would then also have the benefit of a freshly overhauled engine.

It was obviously intended to be a 'win-win' situation for the legal profession, because the Judge made the previous owner liable for one third of the legal costs of £65,000 and despite having had the charges dropped against us, Royle Cars Ltd were ordered to be liable for the balance of around £44,000, two-thirds of it. Apparently, our barrister stood up to object, saying that we had 'no case to answer", but was promptly told to 'sit down', by the Judge.

It is worth noting that, if the Lagonda engine had been overhauled, (serviced!) then this important fact would have been mentioned in the advertisement and the price would have been higher. If the whole car had been properly and fully restored, then the price would have been double the sum the solicitor paid for it. In either case, if Royles restoration company had overhauled the engine or restored the car, then there would have been no difficulty, because our work is guaranteed and we would have corrected any problem, as has always been our custom on the rare occasions that a fault has developed with one of 'our' cars.

It then became clear that neither the Judge nor the solicitor buyer, really knew about the Royle businesses at Staindrop. When examining the documents later on, I found that the claim against us wrongly stated that Royle Cars Ltd, the company which sold the car, "specialised in the restoration and resale of vintage and classic cars". The most rudimentary research at Companies House or even looking at our letterheads, would have shown that this statement was demonstrably untrue and that there were two separate companies in Staindrop, each involved with very different operations.

It is my belief that the judge would not only think that we were some sort of back street, second hand car dealers, buying, 'tarting up', and then selling them, but also think that we had made plenty of money from our 'sharp' dealings. He was entirely wrong on both counts.

After having visited Royles, no doubt the solicitor and hence probably the judge as well, mistakenly believed that it was Royle Cars Ltd which employed a number of people in their well equipped workshops, offices and showroom and that they would, like solicitors, make a lot of money and be easily capable of paying costs in the order of £44,000. The final outcome however, was very different to both the solicitors and the Judges expectations.

In fact, Royle Cars Ltd had no valuable assets and none of the workshop facilities. The few assets which were in the chapel showroom happened to belong to me personally and to the restoration company, David.A.C.Royle & Co Ltd. A different company which was not directly involved with this car.

Too late, did they discover that Royle Cars Ltd was purely the sales company which had been virtually dormant for six years since 1990. It was overdrawn at the Bank and had no assets, nor did it own any motor cars. Furthermore, by 1996, when it came to court, because the recession had continued to seriously affect us, Piers had left the company so, by then, it had no employees, no offices and no assets. Royle Cars Ltd could not possibly pay the £44,000 costs as ordered. Some months later, I heard that the previous owner of the Lagonda also could not pay anything towards his share of the legal costs. I expect that this was why he sold the car in the first place.

Royle Cars were refused permission to appeal the Judges decision, because incredibly, I was told that the legal argument was that Royle Cars were "not a party to the action"! The legal fraternity were having it both ways. As nobody could pay his self-inflicted legal costs, the solicitor, then set about petitioning for a Winding Up Order for Royle Cars Ltd and suing the previous owner for Bankruptcy.

When we remember whose original, ill-conceived, ill informed and ill-judged claim this was, the one which led to the legal action in the first place and to four years of aggravation for all concerned, I thought that for him to then try to destroy those whom he had wrongly challenged in the first place, was vindictive in the extreme and most disturbing.

You will remember that at the time, I was already deeply embroiled in the Frua Rolls Royce case with Eversheds and the events in Birmingham reinforced my worries about the handling of the case which was due to be heard only a few weeks later, in April, in the High Court in London. You will remember that it was Royle Cars Ltd which exhibited the Frua Rolls Royce at the Geneva Motor Show and it is interesting to note that an element of the awards made in the High Court were to be paid to Royle Cars Ltd. It was therefore partly due to the fact that my own solicitors had already ignored the judges orders and taken their own clients award money, for their own purposes, that there was none to pay the Birmingham solicitors. Too many solicitors had their snouts in empty nose bags.

To finish the story, subsequently the order to 'wind up' Royle Cars Ltd was processed in the High Court and I rang the surprised Official Receiver the minute I was informed. He said that people normally waited until the court rang him, but when invited, he came straight over to Staindrop to discuss it. I told him what had happened and he saw for himself the nature of our business. After checking the facts he said that, unusually, he was happy for the High Court Order to be rescinded. I thanked him, but asked if this would again make me liable for all the unwarranted legal costs, he confirmed that it would, so I said that I would prefer to close down the company.

He could see that I had no desire whatsoever to pay people who abuse the legal system and honest citizens and then expect the innocent party to pay them for doing it. The net result was that I sold the Chapel showroom to repay Royle Cars Ltd's bank overdraft. Actually, I did not have to do this, since it was my own personal property and the company did not have a charge on it. But such is my view of life, I arranged the facility, so felt honour bound to repay it.

That was the end of Royle Cars Ltd. Although I did not know it then, it was not to be the only company I would lose as a result of the misuse of power and serious malpractice.

1996. THE 'LIVING MUSEUM' STORY

This story begins in the autumn of the same year, 1996, so it is included here. Being quite a big and worthwhile project, the work necessary to plan it all and to try to raise the money to carry it out, takes some years. Because this and a number of my other projects, cover fairly long periods of time, I will tell the complete story here rather than having to interrupt the amphibious story as we go along.

With not having received the substantial awards due to us after winning the important hearing in the High Court, I had to consider other ways of regenerating Royles restoration business.

The Amphibious project was progressing, but the shortage of funding meant that it was taking much longer than we would have wished. I thought that it might well take another three or four years to come to fruition. I therefore needed to do something which would help the restoration business to generate additional income streams and profit at the same time, provide some good publicity for our work.

You may recall that, previously, to broaden the base of our activities, we had designed and built over thirty half scale Austin Seven children's motor cars. They worked well and could be driven by children and even adults, but being of high quality, the cost was such that most of the production ended up in museums and as collector's items. They would not generate sufficient additional turnover to keep the company running, so I was again looking at ways to improve the business.

We had been members of the Museum and Galleries Commission for some years and were now also registered with the UK Institute for Conservation (UKIC). As a result of this, I had worked with a number of museums and had presented Papers on the subject of Professional Restoration work to various bodies. These included universities, the National Motor Museum at Beaulieu and to an international gathering of museum operators at the

The author speaking at the World Forum for Museums in Germany.

World Forum for Museums held in Stuttgart, Germany.

With our good reputation and being closely related to our core restoration business, it occurred to me that I should look into the idea of developing and creating a 'Living Museum' in Teesdale. The government were pushing hard to improve tourism facilities in the North and already being familiar with the problems of viability and operational methods employed with various museums, it seemed that to combine restoration work with a visitor centre, could be beneficial in a number of ways.

I began by noting down and sketching various ideas as to how it might work, this was in the Autumn of 1996. The idea was to take advantage of the fact that all those who visited our workshops in Staindrop, were fascinated by the wide variety of activities and the constantly changing range of up to twenty different and interesting vintage and classic motor cars which we were working on.

As with all my work, I began by studying the feasibility of it. The benefits of having a fully operational and successful business at the heart of the museum was the key to its potential success. There already were a number of new museums which had failed commercially. This was mainly due to the seasonal nature of tourism in the UK and the fact that once visited, the display remained virtually the same, so there was not much point in going again. In any case, in the wintertime the overheads continued, but the visitor numbers fell away considerably.

The benefits of incorporating a busy and viable restoration firm which is fully staffed throughout the whole year into a museum designed for the purpose, were obvious and would be key to its viability. Especially beneficial would be the constantly changing array of motor cars and vehicles of every description for the visitors to look at. Repeated visits would be worthwhile and would be a unique feature.

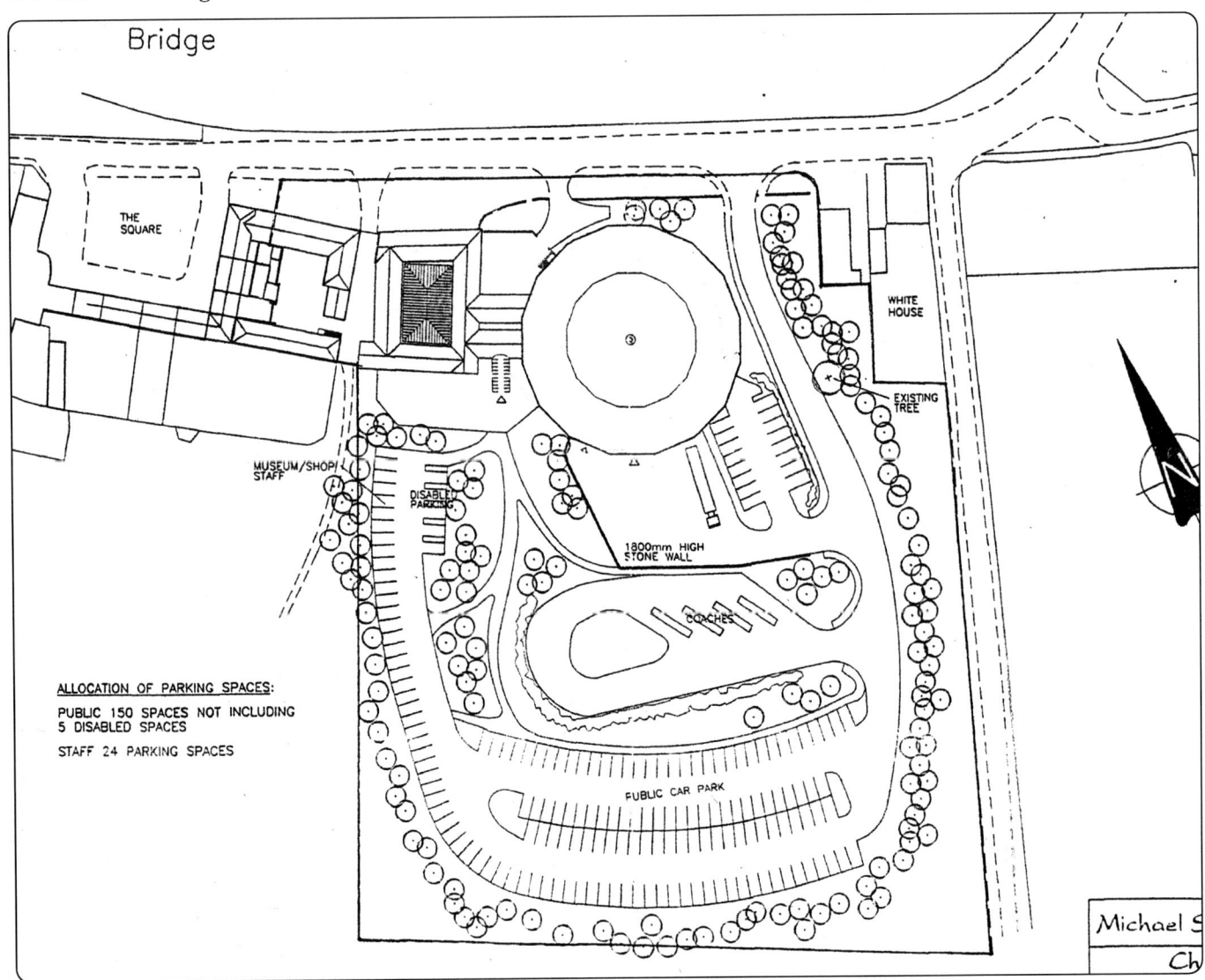

Living Museum site plan.

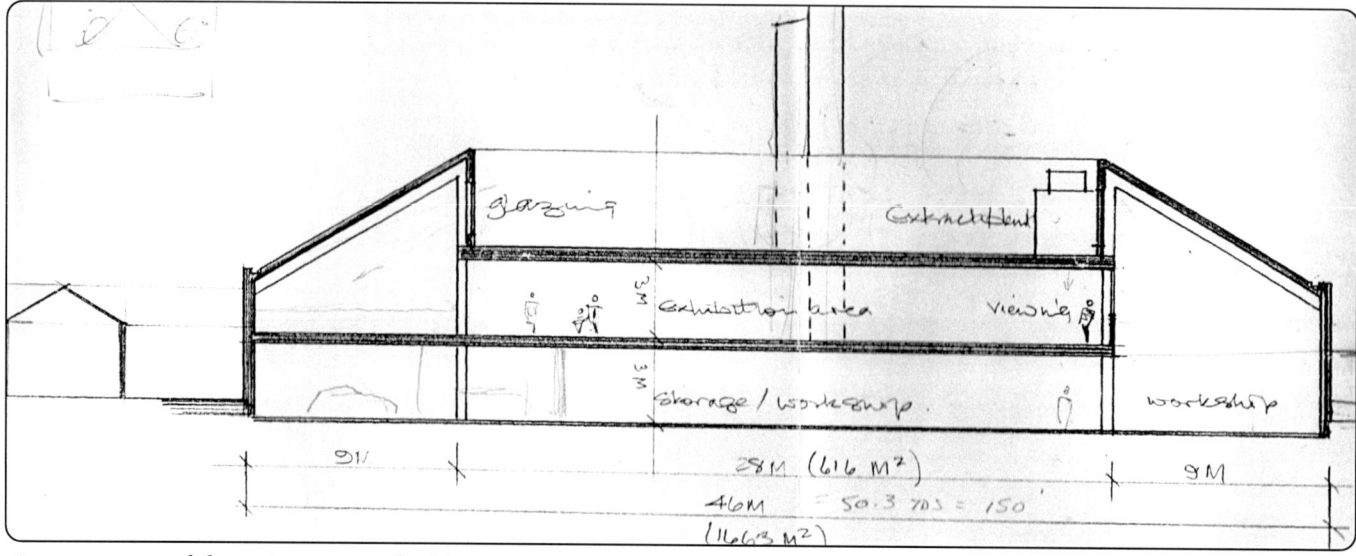

A cross section of the main museum building.

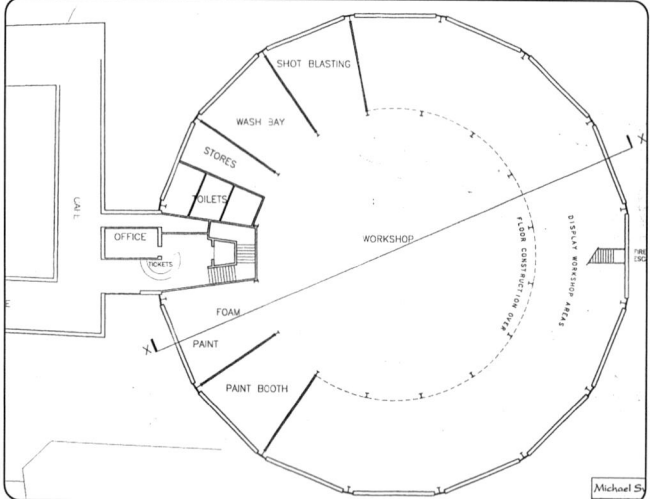

Plan view of the circular 'Living' Museum.

Additionally, I planned to incorporate a range of novel attractions, ones which would appeal to both sexes and to children. Instead of the quiet and studious nature of many museums, I planned to have music and a lot of small mini film exhibition 'studios'. These would have a specific car or exhibit which would be placed in a soundproof, dark room with perhaps 20 seats and a screen. There would be a 5 minute film show incorporating the exhibit. For example it might be one of the Beatles cars with their music blasting out, or perhaps a wartime Jeep with a noisy battle going on behind it, or the engine of a record braking car or boat with the film of the event and racing engine noises, the list goes on.

There would also be shops with low cost ladies and children's clothes, a gallery for local artists, a cafe with simple foods, etc etc. The name which was adopted for the visitor centre was the Motor Heritage Centre.

The central location of our workshops in Staindrop village had been beneficial for our work in many ways, but as the business grew in the 1980's we were, from then onwards, always short of space. When discussing the museum project with the planners, the idea was well received, but they quite rightly, said that we would not be able to do it at the Old School, there simply wasn't enough room and parking space.

Casting around to find a suitable site, an old friend, Peter Gilbertson who lives at Greta Bridge, suggested that we use and develop the farm buildings which are near the Morrit Arms Hotel and the beautiful River Greta and are next to the A66 Trans-Pennine dual carriageway. This was an excellent site, so plans were drawn up by my old friend and creative architect, Michael Swinney in Darlington, to incorporate these.

The plans included a round central building which had circular overhead viewing galleries looking down on wedge shaped workshops. These being rather like the slices of a cake with the central space beneath the upper floor being used as storage space for vehicles which are in the process of being restored. The existing farm buildings being used for the ancillary activities. It was all very impressive and would work well.

A great deal of planning and other work ensued over the next three years. There were various feasibility studies, applications for Listed Building Consent and change of use of the farm Buildings. We also needed to have Planning permission for the new buildings and there were a great many meetings with the various councils and planning departments. The overall feeling was very positive and I was given a lot of

CHAPTER 49: 1996. ANOTHER EVENTFUL YEAR

CLASSIC CAR EXPERT WELL ON THE ROAD TO REALISING VINTAGE DREAM

■ Motoring masterpiece: Classic car restorer David Royle and a classic 4.5 litre Bentley/Neg No. 99/3/603C   Picture: MIKE URWIN

A £1.5m WORKING museum featuring classic car restoration and believed to be the first of its kind in Europe, is planned for the North-East.

David Royle, who has been restoring classic cars for 42 years, hopes to build the museum next to the A66 trans-Pennine trunk road at Greta Bridge, near Barnard Castle, County Durham.

The project will include transferring Mr Royle's existing car restoration workshop from its base in the Old School House, Staindrop, near Barnard Castle, to the new site while providing viewing areas, a shop and a cafe.

Mr Royle, from Darlington, said yesterday that he had been working on the project for two years and has now applied to Teesdale District Council for planning permission.

"The idea is to build a high quality living museum," he explained. "It will be unique in Europe – there is no other museum like it."

A new, circular building with a central viewing area offering views of the various workshops is planned for a former farmyard at Greta Bridge.

Listed farm buildings will also be renovated.

"We need more space," said Mr Royle. "We've been in Staindrop for 25 years and have restored about 700 vintage and classic cars."

He hopes to use the planned museum's location on the A66 to encourage visitors travelling east and west to view cars being restored and to also direct them to Barnard Castle and the villages of Teesdale.

"Every customer says how wonderful the workshops are and say it's a shame that the public can't see what goes on behind the scenes," said Mr Royle.

Twelve people work at the Staindrop workshops but the proposed expansion could see that figure double.

FRI MARCH 26/99

Northern Echo Living Museum Editorial. 26/03/99.

help by the many people involved.

I studied the various books which are considered to be essential reading for the establishment and operation of museums and also had meetings with those who have the expertise and great practical knowledge of running them. Especially helpful were John Gall and Michael Ware. John was the leading light at the Beamish Open Air Museum for whom we had built an impressive and fully operational 'Edwardian' Armstrong Whitworth limousine. This was used to transport their visitors around their wonderful site. I also had detailed discussions with my old friend Michael Ware, the Curator of The National Motor Museum at Beaulieu.

Both of these museums are most successful with visitor numbers in the region of 350,000 to 450,000 per annum. I also planned to link up with The Bowes Museum whose visitor numbers are understandably lower due to its specialised nature, but being so close, there would be mutual benefits.

After careful consultation, TMS in Edinburgh, were selected to carry out the feasibility study. I selected this company from a number of others, because I gathered that some southern firms were overly optimistic in their predictions of visitor numbers. In my experience they are more down to earth and realistic in Scotland.

With the planned site being next to the A66 road which runs East-West across from industrial Teesside to the Lake District and the West coast, The feasibility study showed that the traffic numbers are high, being 476,000 vehicles a year which were estimated to result in around

70,000 visitors p/a to our visitor attraction.

As with any worthwhile project, I wanted to create a first class operation, not some amateurish, badly planned affair. Accordingly, I needed to raise substantial sums of money, in the region of two million pounds. After many meetings and with the help and support of a number of organisations and local people including Derek Foster our MP, Durham and Teesdale Councils and the Enterprise Agency and others, various applications were made. These were to my bank, Business Links, the Heritage Lottery fund (HLF) and to the EU for an ERDF grant. Some monies were made available and received towards the cost of the feasibility studies and £ 30.000 was to be available for the project from the ERDF, but I was relying upon the HLF for the bulk of monies needed.

They seemed to be the most likely organisation to provide the necessary money and so, starting in January 1997, we put in a huge amount of work to support our applications, With it being necessary for HLF grant aid only to be given to charitable organisations, I set about separating the visitors areas from the commercial restoration work. The Charitable company was called the Teesdale Motor Industry Skills Preservation Society.

The amount of work done during the four years of dealings with the HLF was very considerable. The turning point was when one of their officials, the 'team leader', travelled up from London and visited me on 30th April 1998 ostensibly to evaluate our proposals. After initial discussions in the office, I then showed this lady around the workshops, but it soon became apparent that she had little knowledge or interest in what we were actually doing, or of the range of skills she saw being demonstrated in the many aspects of our work.

The truth came out later in the day, when two other HLF people, both men, called in at the workshops to collect the lady and drive her back to London . These two men had also travelled North and had been over to Hartlepool to discuss HLF support for the ongoing work to the 'Trimcomalee', the Historic square rigged ship currently being restored in the dry dock. Interested to see what we were doing, they asked me if they also could be shown around the workshops whilst they were there, which I was pleased to do.

Part way round, they turned to the 'team leader' lady and enthusiastically said what a wonderful project this would be for the HLF. I couldn't help hearing and seeing the result. This is when she responded by digging the nearest man in the ribs and hissed at him, saying that they were "not supporting this application".

Time after time, I have seen and suffered as a direct consequence of people making important judgements with far reaching effects about matters which they don't understand and which are obviously of no interest to them. They seem to have no knowledge of the subjects involved or of the markets. In particular, not suprisingly, it has often been women who are sitting in judgement. You won't need me to tell you that the 'fair sex' are not the section of the community who normally enthuse about vintage cars, engineering or restoration work. This includes a number of ladies in Parliament, it was happening again!

So, her visit was a sham, she was not really evaluating it, she or the 'powers that be', had already decided against it. Without any proper evaluation or detailed knowledge of our company, they had turned this unique opportunity down. My guess is that we were again considered to be some sort of 'second hand car dealers' who were jumping on to the HLF bandwagon.

Shortly afterwards, writing to London to explain how important the visitor centre was to us and to this region, they sent more application forms for other grants programmes. Our proposals seemed to fit in so well with their criteria for support and after so much work had already been done, I pressed on with the HLF for another two years. After all, it really was a marvellous chance to create a good and profitable tourist attraction.

Finally, in April of 2001, I realised that the whole exercise had been a massive waste of time and the correspondence ended. This was yet another example and proof that the North East really is the graveyard of industry.

AND A FEW YEARS LATER

There is a foot note to this particular story

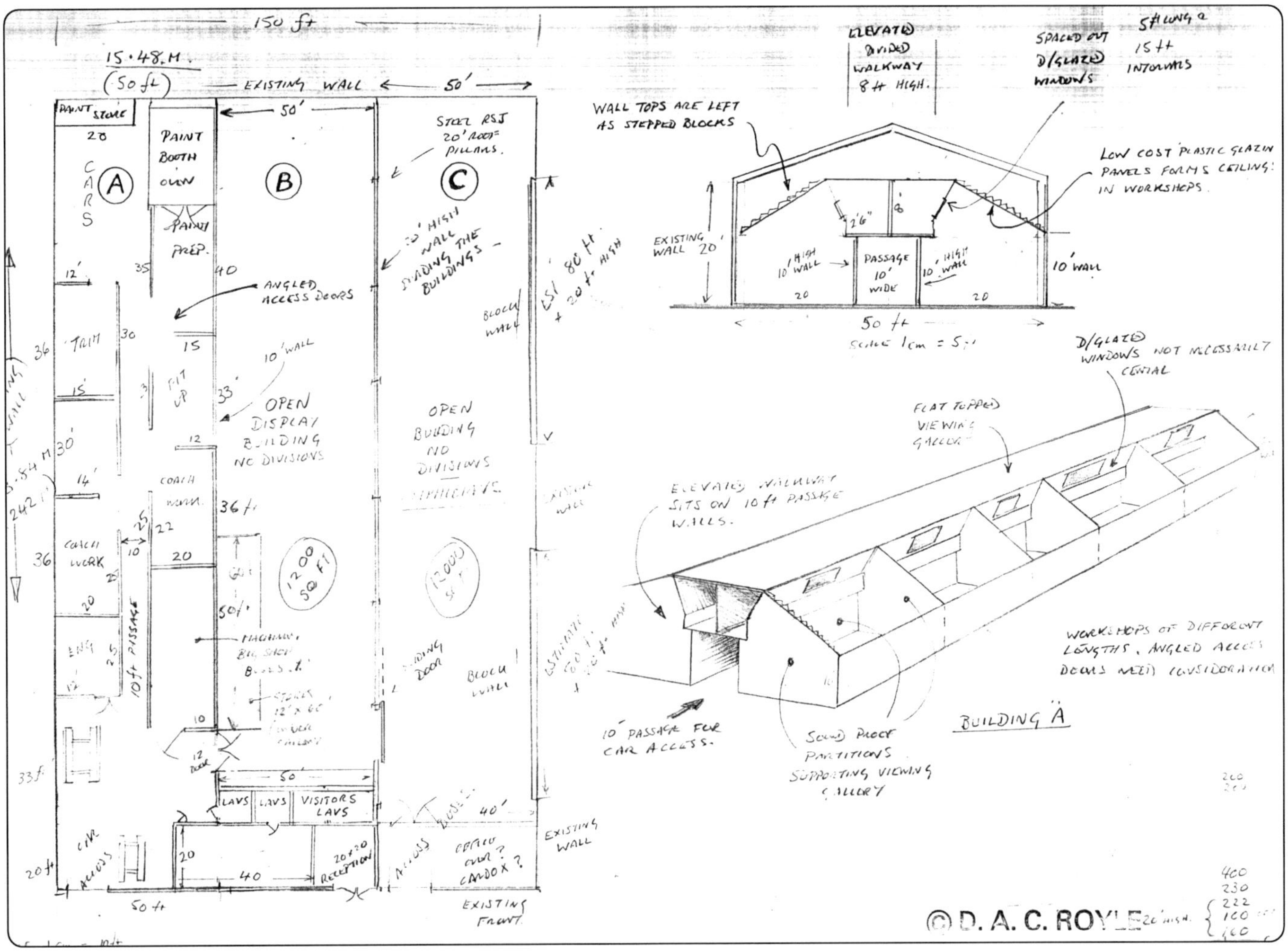

CHAPTER 49: 1996. ANOTHER EVENTFUL YEAR

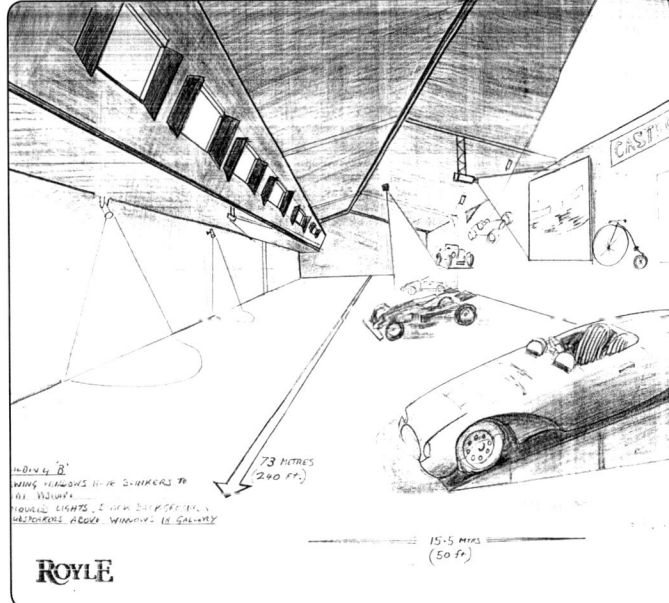

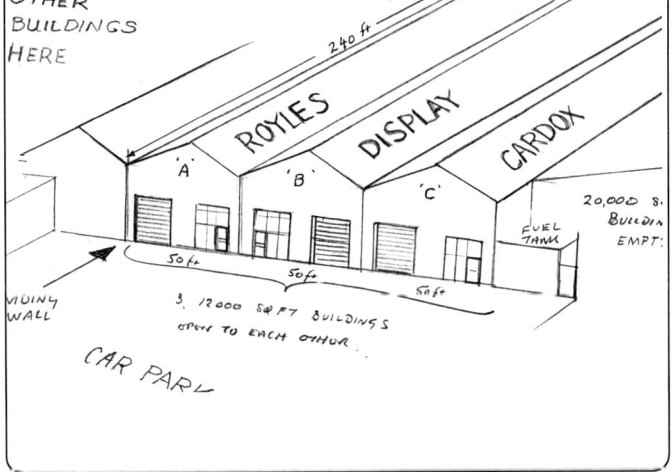

My excellent old Daimler outside a range of factory Buildings at Aycliffe Industrial Estate. These sketches show how they would have been used to house the Restoration workshops with the Living Museum display and with the Cardox Roylecraft production facility adjoining them.

when, more recently in 2008, I discovered that the HLF had now established an office in Newcastle upon Tyne. With it being near to hand and with my activities being known about in the North East, I thought it worth having another try. This time, I explained that I had been considering another plan, and that we could reduce the costs by not having a purpose built museum and visitor centre. Instead we could use one of the many empty industrial buildings in this area.

Taking some of the documentation with me, I was able to visit their offices in person, this time to describe the plan and work done. Although the staff were, once again all women, this time, they did seem to see what a good potential there was with our proposals and were enthusiastic. Not long after the meeting however, it seems that, from memory, their HLF funding of £6 million was being substantially reduced by £4.5 million to finance the Olympics in London. There would not be enough left, to support their existing applications, let alone support a project like ours.

No wonder there are hundreds of empty buildings here in the North East, I have lists and lists of them. Buildings of all sizes, many of which could have been used for our Living Museum, for new technologies, for new business and for many other useful and creative developments. In my experience alone, the sheer waste of good opportunities to protect existing businesses and generate new jobs is truly dreadful in this region. Some government officials have quietly admitted to me that if I had been operating almost anywhere else in the country, but the north east, I would have succeeded with my projects.

The amount of good, creative and imaginative work which has been wasted is most depressing. Looking back at the many files relating to this project going back to 1996 remind me of the detailed planning and many meetings attended during this five year period and the hundreds of hours of work done and the time and money that was spent on what would have been a really successful venture. It is no wonder that there is so much money swilling around in the south, the money rarely reaches this far north.

CHAPTER 50:
RESUMPTION OF MK IV STORY

Ongoing in 1996 and 1997 was the very considerable effort being put in to raise funding via the private investors and Venture Capital organisations. Efforts which are clearly shown by the huge number of documents on file and the rows of files which fill the shelves in my office. I needed the money not only for the Living Museum project, but also for the ever increasing Patent portfolio, the cost of materials and the labour cost of making the components. There was also the overheads, including insurance, storage and the loan interest on borrowings.

With the help of Sir Alex we were seeing some interest from the Venture firms and I was also discussing possible linkages and Joint Ventures with firms like Babcocks in Scotland, Vickers and various other organisations in America and the Middle East. There was also the possibility of a link with a PLC which was on Offex and the Highland Council were also showing interest in 1997. During this year, even with all the interest in the project, we had not seen any money coming in from outside sources.

Sir Alex and I had shown the MK I speedboat prototype to people, but they couldn't translate the technology into flood rescue and public transport vehicles. We had to have a commercial looking machine. Therefore the stumbling block was a typical 'catch 22' situation. We needed to raise money to finish the MK IV to demonstrate the technology, but couldn't raise any money because we hadn't got a demonstration unit which they could understand.

Without any salaries to pay and by keeping costs to the bare minimum, Royles managed to keep it all going and pay all the associated costs and we had been steadily progressing with the work involved making all the special components. These were the many special innovative parts, including the suspension and steering parts as well as the retraction and locking mechanisms. Being mainly of stainless steel, the metal is hard to work and with all the parts being 'one offs', it takes quite a lot of time to machine them. Reluctantly, Allan accepted lower wages than the other men, in order to keep his job and maintain progress. It was not a happy situation, but was appreciated.

NESTA

Whilst all this was going on, I was as ever, continuing with efforts to raise money from every possible source in 1998 and 1999. I was hopeful that we might well be able to benefit from a new government organisation which was being set up in London. This was to become The National Endowment for Science, Technology and the Arts, Nesta.

Earlier on in the book, when I was talking about the dreadful legal affair and our visit to the House of Lords in 2000, I mentioned the Nesta award ceremony which was held at BAFTA's premises in Piccadilly. This was when we won their first and biggest award for innovation at that time. The events which led to us winning this award were as a result of a letter which I had written to Anne Widdecombe MP, to see if she could help me in any way.

Miss Widdecombe always seemed to talk a lot of sense and it was after I had contacted her that I first heard about this new organisation in April 1998. She was very helpful and recommended that I write to John Battle MP who was the Minister of State for Science, Energy and Industry at the time. He in turn, put me in touch with Jeremy Newton who was in the process of setting up this new organisation which was to promote and provide seed-corn funding for innovation and new ideas. At this time, Mr Newton had just moved from Piccadilly to an office at 2-4 Cockspur Street, behind the Bank of England, which I thought must be a good sign!

It was very early days for Nesta and in the coming months, I was able to visit Mr Newton and discuss the problems and weaknesses of the existing funding organisations which failed to support so many new ideas coming along. After telling him that I had already spent eleven intensive years applying to every possible source of money for R&D, and having, at that stage, raised and invested around £1.5 million, he realised that my experience and knowledge

ROYLE. FROM VINTAGE TO CLASSIC TO AMPHIBIAN.

New craft could help in flood rescues and take victims straight to hospital
Award will help get boat onto land – at 70mph

BY SHEILA DIXON

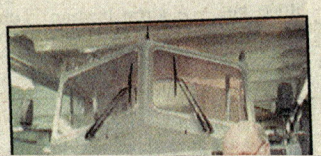

A VINTAGE car restorer has been awarded £125,000 from a national fund set up to nurture British creativity and innovation, to enable him to develop a boat which can be driven on dry land.

Mr David Royle is a self-taught craftsman who has rebuilt and re[...] 700 cars in the last [...] been just that: cars which sail. But Mr Royle approached the concept from the opposite angle, creating a boat which could be used at 70mph on the road.

The grant, which was announced at a ceremony in London on Tues[...] nies involved in pipeline maintenance, while a 30ft craft called Dragonfly, which can carry up to 18 passengers, goes into pre-production.

The possibilities of use are almost limitless feels Mr Royle, with the potential to take part in flood rescues, lifeboat duties which can take [...] o hospi- e activi-

irman of ould fill nent and do that it dventure nistakes. es to cre- museum n hold for art of his

£125,000 for inventor of swimming car

A DURHAM inventor has received a £125,000 Government grant to develop a car that thinks it is a boat.

David Royle, head of Covelink Marine Ltd, will receive his National Endowment for Science, Technology and the Arts award at a ceremony in London today.

He is well-known in the Durham area for his business restoring vintage cars, but over the last 12 years has been working to develop a different type of vehicle.

Mr Royle, 60, said: "The problem is that being a luxury trade, we are affected by the market place. After the 1990 recession, we suffered until two years ago.

"My other love is boats so it seemed like a good thing to look into the amphibious world."

The result is an amphibious motor vehicle.

It is a multi-purpose cross between a van, minibus and lorry and is capable of carrying equipment and luggage but small enough to be of practical use.

The enduring popularity of the DUKW, the amphibious landing vehicle used by troops for the D-Day landings in the Second World War, gave Mr Royle the idea.

With his award Mr Royle can now complete, demonstrate and develop his finished prototype – the 25ft long Mark 4 – into a production model.

Car that thinks it's a boat: David Royle, of Covelink Marine Ltd, with his Roylecraft vehicle.

The Newcastle Journal, Business. 16/5/00 and D&S 19/5/00.

could be useful to him. This was because I could explain the problems from the inventors point of view.

This was an unusual opportunity and I was able to emphasise the importance of them having experienced specialists who could properly analyse and evaluate the projects which would be put in front of them. I explained how many of the venture capital firms and banks, which I had approached, relied upon their 'financial experts' to evaluate projects. People who had little or no specialised knowledge and who were really in no position to make a decision about any technical project which they didn't understand.

As an example, I told him about my project, which was an unfamiliar technology, so when it came to funding, I was turned down time after time. This was despite the fact that by creating a properly designed, new form of transport and was opening up untapped global markets with huge export potential, they would turn it down in complete ignorance of the technology and its open markets.

Various meetings took place and I was asked to answer many questions in their lengthy consultation documents. I was pleased to have the opportunity to help and influence a new funding organisation which seemed to really want to help fund and create new products. Although there were unexpected delays during the formation of Nesta in 1999, they eventually moved into their 'new' offices at 110 Upper Thames Street and we did have the benefit of their funding.

This new government organisation was to have the interest on a sum of two million pounds invested to support and encourage those who are prepared to take risks with new innovative ideas.

Although the award of £125,000 was formally announced at the ceremony in 2000, we were already benefitting from it and Allan was again paid the full rate. It was a great help towards the cost of the final modifications necessary to complete the MK IV prototype.

Whilst these costs were estimated to be around £300,000, with the award, we were able to attract more funding from other sources to complete the work. I should mention here that Sir Alex Smith's involvement strengthened our appeals for funding in general and the application to Nesta in particular.

During 1999 and in early 2000, we made good progress and were able to afford to complete the work to the MK IV. We had rearranged the layout of the mechanical transmission and had completed the retractable wheel assemblies with their safety locking mechanisms and also the new steering mechanisms. When the chosen suspension assemblies were complete and had been tested in the workshop on test rigs, they were then fitted into the hull. We found that more room around the front wheel arches was

The MK IV at Staindrop prior to water testing.

A retracted front wheel and the flarred wheel arches.

needed to permit full lock on the steering, so flared wheel arches were fabricated and then welded in place. This was because I particularly wanted a good steering lock for both environments. An important facility which I had intentionally allowed for in the mechanical designs and which they were easily capable of providing.

Our award was especially important because it was sufficient to buy the new, light weight, high revving Yanmar diesel engine which I now knew would meet our needs. Testing had also shown that we needed to install a larger capacity Water Jet, so we were now also able to buy the correct unit to suit the 25 foot hull and new engine. We made excellent progress and completed all the work to the developed MK IV.

With the larger water-jet and the high revving diesel engine the tests proved that 25 feet was indeed a most useful size, it would readily come onto the plane and was the basis for a really good, general purpose vehicle, especially suitable for the emergency services, flood recue, and other commercial and private transportation. We had also fitted improved lever controls for the various mechanisms with large warning lights to keep the driver informed of the wheel positions and locking mechanisms. I knew that these would be helpful and yes, I was not allowed to forget the time I had tried to drive out of the water when the wheels were still retracted !

The dashboard and controls.

Further tests were carried out at Ellerton lake again and we found that the MK 1V, handled extremely well and the unique steering mechanism worked equally well when driving on the road as it did on water. We found that we needed to improve the brakes and we also experimented with various ratings of road springs. On water, we tested front and rear

Water testing. Working on the water jet.

wheel flaps comparing the performance, with and without them, we were also again testing various water evacuation systems from the wheel boxes. I was pleased that the techniques we were using ensured that these would self bail and not need any form of powered extraction pumps. The less there is to go wrong, the better, especially when at sea.

The longer hull was, as expected, even more stable and the first tests showed that the machine generally, worked extremely well. The MK IV

Water testing. Planing at speed.

would, once again, obviously be a viable amphibian. The tests showed that the entirely new, innovative and previously untested transmission and the different retractable suspension mechanisms also worked well, but as expected, would need to be refined for production.

Whilst we were most pleased with the operation of it all, the weight was increasing and it was now over four tonnes. There was room for weight reduction when the money was available to build the production models. As mentioned, for example, our own gearbox was very heavy being fabricated out of steel plate. It was a low cost method of testing the gear ratio's and for assessing its location and was fine for the needs of a prototype. Similarly, the overall appearance of the MK IV was acceptable for a prototype. We had installed the equipment where it was needed to test the operation of it, but to minimise costs, we had not spent time tidying it all up. Having satisfied ourselves that it worked well, we now knew that we could considerably improve the overall appearance and finish for when they went on the market.

It was clear that the demand for general purpose vehicles like this, would be considerable, so in readiness, I drew out plans for the first proper production version of it.

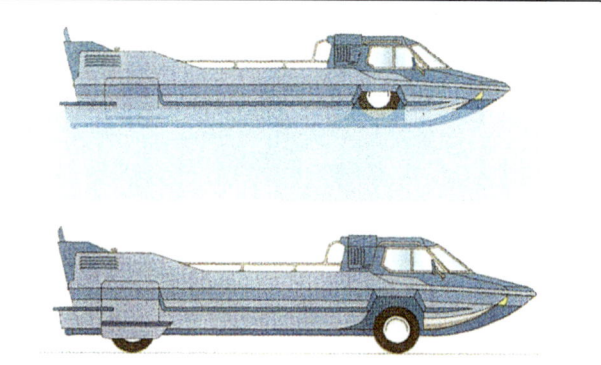

Over Land and Sea

The ability to keep your feet dry when going ashore as a charter guest in your Gucci loafers must be a priority. The handfuls of shopping that need to be carried from the local high street shops to the tender in the port, if anchored offshore, can be a pain for crew members. We may have found a solution for both scenarios.

Known as the Royle Craft, this series of prototype amphibious vessels can operate at speeds of 30knots on water and up to 70mph on land. The difference to similar amphibious projects that we have seen in the yacht market, is that the designer of this craft has used his knowledge to create a design that has a hydrodynamically efficient hull and fully retractable wheels not disimilar to those you see on an aircraft.

The first prototypes incorporate an innovative suspension system made largely of stainless steel, special gearbox and drive systems with hulls in marine alloys and GRP. They range from 22' to 38', with four seat runabout configurations to 30 seat water taxi style layout, all of which would suit today's large yacht market.

After twelve years of development, the prototypes have been thoroughly tested - all the company needs now is a client to show sufficient interest to go to a full manufacturing stage. The interesting factor with this product is the fact that the market is not only limited to large yacht tenders that can drive ashore to the door of the casino, it has huge potential in harbour patrol, water borne police, river authorities and other commercial applications. Perhaps this is one of those interesting technical innovations and ventures that could spark the birth of a new multi-million dollar business.

Covelink Marine Ltd
Tel: +44 (0) 1833 660995
Fax: +44 (0) 1833 660834
e-mail:
enquiries@david-royle.co.uk

The Yacht Report Magazine. May 2001.

CHAPTER 50: RESUMPTION OF MK IV STORY

These would be very similar in most respects, but they would be smart, well finished and eminently more saleable. For the purposes of identification they would, initially, be known as the Mark Five. I would have dearly liked to have started selling the MK IV to generate some income, but as it stood, it was a prototype and could not possibly be sold on the open market. The fact that we had progressed this far with so little money, was in fact, a major achievement.

The MK V would be 30ft long, have an 8'2" beam (9.14 x 2.5m) be faster and more powerful. It would provide accommodation for six persons in the small cabin rather than three, as in the MK IV and it would satisfy the need for increased carrying capacity and cope with rougher weather conditions. There was no need to build a prototype, since I was now confident that it would perform even better than the MK IV for those who wanted a bigger vehicle.

It was at this time that we were contacted by the North West Development Agency who had been approached by Mitsubishi in Japan in connexion with our amphibious development work. This was excellent news, but was to create a step change in our plans.

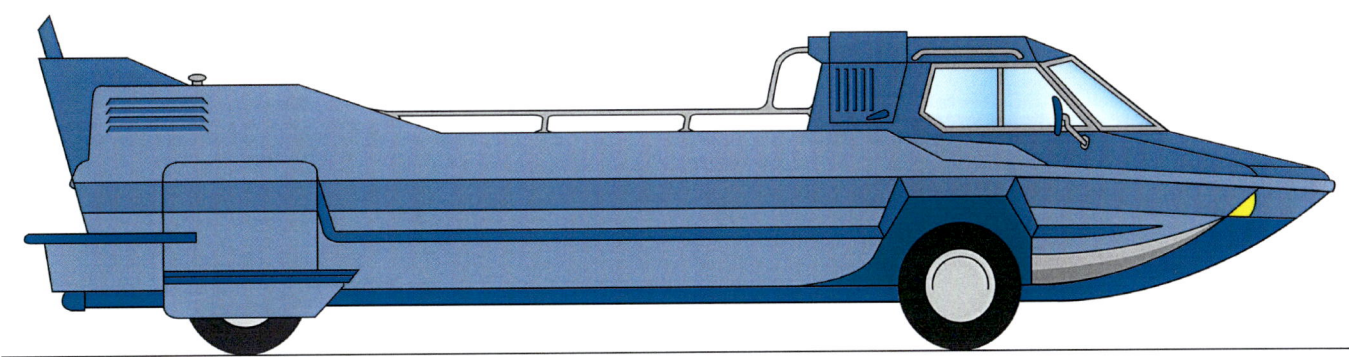

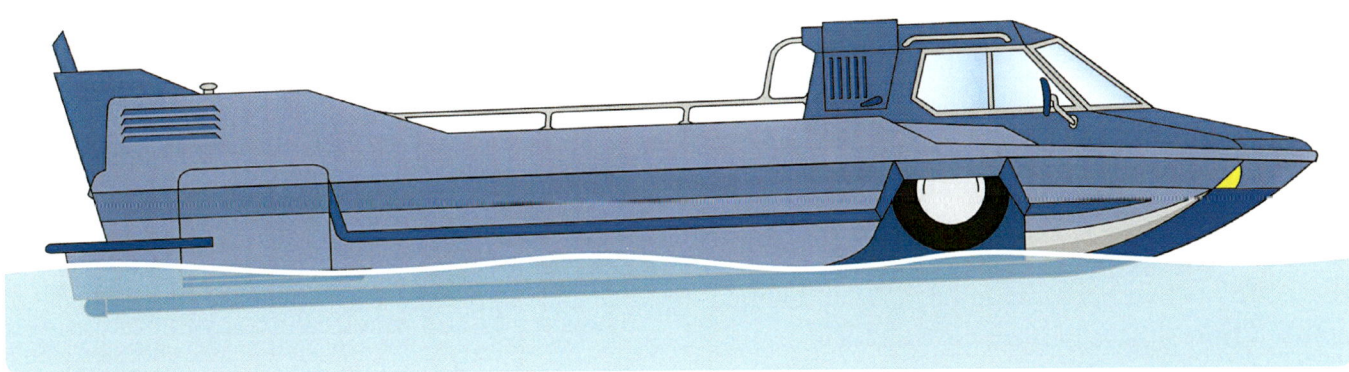

The Mk V Roylecraft.

CHAPTER 51:
DESIGN METHODS & PHILOSOPHY

At this point in the story I should explain the methods which I employ to design and turn new ideas into working vehicles. These differ considerably from those practised by large organisations in established industries with specialist teams of people involved.

The benefits of having one principal designer with his own small team of skilled engineers and craftsmen, working in well equipped workshops, are numerous. There is no unnecessary paperwork, reports etc, and the responsibility lies with one man, me. Any changes and new ideas are instantly actioned and progressed, no time wasting delays.

Beneficially, the project attracted some very experienced and knowledgeable people. Individuals who were at the very forefront of this country's most important and advanced technologies. Whilst none had been involved with amphibious vehicle development, their experience in their own specialist fields was of value and introduced aspects which were relevant. One such person was Dr Anne Fletcher, she, like Sir Alex Smith had been working at the leading edge of aerospace technology and was always helpful.

TECHNIQUES DIFFERENT

She is a jolly and attractive person and her experience and knowledge often gave me food for thought. I was cheered up by the fact that she was one who really did appreciate that the project costs had been extremely low and was amazed that we could have designed and developed such innovative machines, on this scale, with so little money. Anne kept in regular contact by e-mail and later on, her husband Richard, would help with business plans and with overseas contacts. Anne was also kept busy creating a database of all the incoming enquiries from around the world, quite a big job.

I always welcomed Anne's advice and help and on one occasion, when we had been discussing details of the designs, she explained to me that my methods of design were very different from those of the aero industry. I wasn't surprised, since amphibians have no design history, other than being converted motor vehicles of one sort or another. This is discussed early on in the first chapter of this section of the book. None had been specifically designed for their dual purpose function.

Aircraft are quite different, they have benefitted from their 100 year history of progressive development and refinement. Their high speeds and efficiency, encouraged huge investment over the years and this resulted in them, not surprisingly, becoming the most successful and popular rapid form of global transport.

In contrast, there had been virtually no serious development of amphibians throughout the whole of the last century. The wartime DUKW was the only vehicle of any size to have been built in quantity, and this was a General Motors 6 wheel truck converted to make it float. Other amphibians of any size were also heavy military machines which were very costly and not designed for civilian use. The smaller ones were generally for leisure activities or purely for fun and were built by converting motor cars to make the bodywork watertight. A number of them are shown at the beginning of this part of the book. None had really tackled the problems associated with creating modern, efficient amphibious machines which could travel quickly over water.

There were no academical institutions, there was no technical data and no specialists in the subject, it was wide open for development with serious study and practical experimentation.

The essential difference with aircraft, Anne explained, was that all new aircraft designs were entirely created on Computers with teams of people working with computer-aided facilities. They had a bank of technical data which has been gathered, developed and refined over the last 100 years as airspeeds increased and the size and range of aeroplanes was developed and improved. There had also been improvements in the engines which had been specially designed and built for aircraft. With amphibians, there was no such bank of knowledge, data or engines built especially for them.

To me, it was the challenge of starting afresh and having the complete freedom and importantly, the time to do the work, which appealed to me. I was confident that my years of practical experience and the knowledge gained after working with so many land and waterborne forms of transport, could be used to great advantage. It was exciting to know that I would be the one who would be creating and refining the new design principles. I also had the gift to be able to design and draw it all on graph paper. Traditional though my methods may be, it was the only way that a completely new form of amphibian would be created. With the added benefit of having all the practical skills and equipment to build prototypes, working with my team in the workshop, I knew that it was the ideal opportunity to create something new and worthwhile.

I wouldn't have considered, for a moment, tackling improvements to the refined designs of modern high speed aircraft or attempting to improve on the design of modern motor cars. Vehicles which have also benefitted from more than a century of refinement and in more recent years, computer aided facilities. I have had neither the experience nor the specialised knowledge to consider such work.

To my knowledge, nobody had ever taken a blank sheet of paper and set about properly combining two very different technologies from scratch. It was not a case of refining existing amphibious technology or working with an existing bank of known criteria and data, there wasn't any. It was a unique opportunity to tackle design problems which had remained since the beginning of motorised transport. This, combined with the benefits of an untapped market, was a challenge for which I was ideally suited and one which, if successful, would be the foundation of a new and very profitable export industry.

I was setting out to establish the ground rules and create the framework for a completely new technology. I needed to resolve technical problems, ones which would result in safe, fast and seaworthy machines on water and be designed, from the ground up, to combine the best features of both marine and automotive types of transport for which existing automotive components were not suitable. This meant a lot of original thought and ideas which are best jotted down on paper in the first instance, which I would then develop into scale drawings. So it was best done by somebody like me, a single individual rather than a committee, with complete freedom to think 'outside the box' as they say these days, but with the benefit of knowing what is in it!

When Sir Alex first came to see me he was delighted to see some of my early drawings. He used to be upset that none of his Rolls Royce team would reveal where they started for fear of looking foolish. It was important that he knew what their thought processes had been which led to the final designs, even if the ideas were scrapped.

Anne was interested to see me still drawing on graph paper with a pencil. It sounded very primitive in comparison to aircraft design, but I did have the comfort of knowing that it is a method still favoured and still used in certain industries. In Vickers for example, they start with drawing boards which I saw in their design offices. Essentially, this method relied upon the knowledge, skill and artistry of the designer.

I had heard this from two entirely different experts. The first was the chief designer for Farina in Italy and the second from the Chief Engineer of Vickers on Tyneside where the Challenger Tanks are built, as mentioned above. One great advantage being that the designs are not restricted by predetermined limitations and the existing criteria already on the Autocad systems. As the designer, Anne was also interested to see that I had the complete freedom not only to design and create new and innovative mechanisms, but I also had the facilities to then make the parts and build the complete prototype amphibians themselves and then test them.

With the new parts being made in metal and tested within a few days and weeks of being drawn, Anne could see that it was a quick and efficient method and the figures proved that it was a most economic way of working. The technology was, of course, different to aircraft, but some of the principles were similar in that they had to operate in two completely different environments. Aeroplanes on land and in the air, amphibians on land and in water. Like aircraft, I had retractable wheels and weight was an important factor. The mechanisms in them there were not really comparable however, due to a number of different factors discussed elsewhere.

2005 REPORT ON NEW TECHNOLOGY

ROYLECRAFT - WHAT IS DIFFERENT IN DESIGN?   16 November 2005 Report

Since the beginning of the 20th century, virtually all amphibious transport has been built using an existing automotive chassis or road vehicle. Most were for military applications. Being essentially a road going assembly their performance on land was satisfactory, but their speed through the water was slow, rarely over 9mph. The chassis or vehicle was made to float by making the bodywork watertight or by fitting an outer skin around the chassis as in the wartime Dukw when a GM truck 6 wheel chassis was utilized.

In 1986, David Royle decided to begin by making a high-speed boat drive on the road. This showed that it is possible to travel quickly, safely and efficiently over water and also on the road.

An entirely new kind of amphibious vehicle has been created, one which will plane on water at speeds of over 30 knots and travel on the road at motorway cruising speeds, thus offering effective total journey times.

FUNDAMENTAL DESIGN OPPORTUNITY

Having unsurpassed experience building, rebuilding and designing motor vehicles and boats with over 900 different machines having passed through his workshops, David was in the unique position of being able to integrate the two very different technologies, from the very beginning of the project.

This radical design approach achieves:

- Planing speeds on water.
- Normal road cruising speeds.
- Smooth transfer from water to road.
- Minimum driver controls for easy operation.
- Shallow draught but good ground clearance.
- Long life in fresh and salt water.

The cornerstones of the designs at every stage have been:

- Marine principles without impairing road performance.
- Many safety features incorporated.
- Advanced technology for compliance with regulations.
- Fully integrated marine and vehicle technologies.

ROYLECRAFT DESIGN SOLUTIONS

Systematic design developments have been resulted in:

- Hydrodynamically efficient hulls for speed.
- High lift retractable wheels to minimize drag
- Shallow draught for canals.
- Low profile hull designs for low canal and river bridges.
- Low maintenance.
- Marine servicing techniques.
- Double safety locked wheel retraction technology.
- Automatic dual ratio steering.
- Constant dry brake system.
- Efficient dual motive power cooling system.
- Rapid entrained water evacuation.
- Engine characteristics to satisfy marine and road drive.
- Safe marine propulsion - no propellers.
- All round crew access to hull when afloat.
- Water jet intake jetsam clearance system.

- Minimized electro chemical reactions.

Further design features which have been incorporated are:

- Road going and marine design principles harmonised.
- Stability optimised by weight distribution.
- Weight to strength issues balanced .
- Buoyancy maximized.
- High material specification.
- Automotive elements designed and manufactured for marine conditions.
- No reliance upon standard unsuitable automotive componentry.

RESULTING DESIGN PHILOSOPHY

- The creation of components and mechanisms to satisfy the needs of both a marine vessel and a road vehicle.

- Their place within the entire vehicle.

- The integration and harmony of all the design solutions which together will satisfy the needs of the amphibian.

WATERBORNE PERFORMANCE

The design of the hull/body shape is hydrodynamically efficient but also provides directional stability and combines rigidity and the necessary structural needs for point loads. The balance between lift and wave penetration, buoyancy where required, minimum weight and the proper provision for the automotive elements has been struck in order to give all round good road going and water borne performance.

Normal automotive axles are not suited to amphibious operations. Being designed for use on land, both front and rear automotive axles are designed and built without any consideration for water borne performance or total immersion in salt or fresh water. Their shape, purpose and design features disregard the following important aspects for marine use:

- Water pressure
- Electrochemical reaction
- Shaft seals
- Hydrodynamics
- Suspension methodology
- Installation
- Integration into marine hull
- Brake system immersion
- Retraction
- Fixed dimensions

So transmission and suspension systems specifically to be fit for purpose have been designed.

ROAD GOING PERFORMANCE

A safe, strong and well engineered mechanism permits the front road wheels to steer on the road and yet be able to retract substantially when in water and remain permanently linked to the steering mechanism at all times to ensure that the Ackerman angles remain constant. The mechanism incorporates a suspension/damper system and is safely locked in the roadgoing position to avoid any risk of collapse or accidental retraction when on the road. The wheels have safety locks also when retracted so that in rough water there is no risk of coming loose. Furthermore the mechanism are of materials which resist salt-water corrosion and electro chemical reaction with associated components. At the same time they are designed for minimum servicing and have lubrication seals which are specifically designed to operate in salt water.

All this was achieved through an entirely new mechanism which incorporated components not seen in nny previous steering system on boats, motor vehicles or aircraft. The design solutions in this assembly then also satisfied the needs of the vehicle as a whole, by being linked by levers which are not only well above the water level, which is particularly beneficial when the amphibian is navigating in water, but advantageously are inside the vehicle itself. They are therefore safe from damage, corrosion, dragging weed, and causing drag which reduces speed in the water.

There are added benefits in that the locking system is such that the greater the load, the more firmly locked the mechanism becomes and this happens automatically. Most of the assembly is of marine quality stainless steel and benefits from minimum servicing requirements.

There is independent suspension all round and importantly, the transmission, suspension and steering systems do not incorporate any reciprocating parts where the watertight hull is penetrated near or below the waterline. This is an important safety feature and unique to our designs.

Brakes are mounted directly on the stub axles and so are immersed whilst entering and leaving the water prior to retraction. There are also inboard brakes which are permanently dry and therefore efficient at all times.

The process of driving in and out of the water and up a ramp onto the road can be achieved smoothly and efficiently. As our amphibians are designed to be functional, they can do this without the need for intensive driver training. Normal driving skills are all that is required. The gearing, drive train mechanism and water jet are combined in such a way as to make the transition a smooth and straightforward operation.

INTEGRATED DRIVE. SUSPENSION AND STEERING

The rear wheel drive and suspension is encased in stainless steel housings which are sealed against ingress of water. The suspension is safety locked and the drive operates in an oil bath. Low maintenance being a key feature. Drag is minimized by high lift wheel retraction. When two rear wheels are fitted at each side in tandem, there are different spring ratings front to back, this achieves various benefits and copes with varying loads, DTLR regulations and vehicle performance

Specially designed transmission and gearboxes have resulted in new lightweight units and drive systems which incorporate multi-drive, backwash, hydraulic and mechanical drives, automatic and selected gears. The aim and result being easily driven vehicles wilh a minimum of manually operated driver controls. With these amphibians being capable of being operated in salt water, the electrical and electronic componentry has also been minimized. This helps to ensure reliability in long-term service.

Not only are the steering systems for water and land in constant mesh, they also are integrated to give a correct different gearing for both environments by means of the unique compensator. This mechanism permits the high-geared steering ideal for navigation in water and at the same time provides low geared steering for driving on the road. Importantly, it also incorporates a safety mechanism whereby the road going steering mechanism will still operate, even in the unlikely event that underwater damage was sustained to the navigational steering mechanism or its efficiency was impaired in any way. The steering mechanisms themselves are mounted inboard and well protected from the external environment. Once again low maintenance is a feature of the system.

ENGINE COOLING

Engine cooling has been a common problem with most previous amphibians. Being enclosed within a watertight hull, the normal road vehicle radiator cannot be exposed to the beneficial rammed air-cooling effect. This important benefit is therefore lost when traveling at speed on land or in water.

This is when the engine is working its hardest. Once again particular attention has been given to this significant problem. The wide variation in operational environments and in ambient air and water temperatures, creates the need for an efficient and infinitely variable dual purpose cooling system.

Being capable of high cruising speeds on the road and in water, the amphibians engine is working its hardest when planing. As with most boats, raw water cooling is the most efficient system and Roylecraft benefit from water cooled marine heat exchangers. For road work an efficient and infinitely variable air heat exchanger/cooling fan system is also incorporated which can also cope with high ambient temperatures. The operation of both these systems has been designed to be automatic and yet they operate together or independently without any manual or complex control systems according to the conditions.

ANCILLARIES

There are a number of ancillaries which also satisfy the needs of functionality and road and marine regulations (MCA and DTLR). One example of these is the sealed headlamps which are designed to operate in air and underwater and consequently are unaffected by rapid changes in temperature. There is also a retractable underrun bar mounted at the stern, the back of the amphibians. This protects the water jet on the road as well as meeting the DTLR road regulations. The windscreen is laminated safety glass with heating elements incorporated to counter misting up. The access steps are of marine alloys and stainless steel and are folding to act as wheelchair ramps for jetty access or if required, for pedestrian access when in service on the road.

HULL DESIGN

The body/hull of these amphibians also is designed specifically to satisfy both the uses; as a road going vehicle and a marine vessel, in this case with high speed planing ability. The overall dimensions satisfy the operational requirements for road transport (DTLR) at the same time they meet the needs of the MCA. The principles of automotive monocoque bodies and marine boat hulls are combined with facilities to allow the fitting and retraction of the road wheels and the mounting of the unique suspension units along with special unique transmission drive assemblies.

With the judicious use of additional planing surfaces combined with water jet propulsion, buoyancy and correct weight distribution and the efficient evacuation of entrained water, high speeds are available when required.

The design or our amphibians permits operations in shallow waters, the draught is 0.5 metre (20 inches) ideal for canals. The low profile afloat, 2 metres (80 inches) of the main structure is suitable for low bridges. Whilst windage is minimized, the fitting of bow thrusters when required are helpful when navigating on exposed narrow canals or rivers at slow speeds.

CERTIFICATION DESIGNED IN

In the design process, the requirements for MCA and DTLR certification have been carefully considered. Many regulations can be met for both road vehicles and shipping. There is however no specific legislation for amphibians. This is advantageous since the UK government recognizes the benefits and technical advances which we have made and is therefore prepared, and is working with us, to create a framework in which our new machines will be certificated and licensed for use.

Thoroughgoing and rigorous design has given us the lead in advanced, high-speed transport for use on water and on road.

End of report on 'Roylecraft' high water speed amphibious technology.

CHAPTER 52:
PATENTS & IPR

From the time when I was a boy at school, I saw my father's various Patent applications and Specifications in his desk. So from an early age, I realised that protecting new ideas and inventions was important. Although he died in 1947, I still have his handsome desk and they are still in the drawers. In fact I made my own first application for a patent when I was in my late teens and another one in my early twenties. It is extremely interesting to tackle unsolved problems and very rewarding when a solution is found, especially when practical tests show that it works!

When embarking on the High Speed Amphibious Vehicle Project in 1987, I was aware that the challenges involved could well result in some new ideas and innovative designs and mechanisms. As with everything I do, I wanted to make a good job of it and was well aware that Automotive and Marine technologies are so fundamentally different, that I was bound to encounter a wide range of complex issues when combining them together, properly, for the first time.

With all previous attempts having followed the same, low cost, relatively simple, but unsatisfactory method of converting existing road vehicles and with no serious up to date development work having been done, it was a wonderful opportunity to be able to start with a clean sheet of paper and have the time to study, in depth, the problems associated when creating a substantially new form of transport.

After spending and enjoying over forty years of being closely involved with boats and motor cars, not just sailing and driving them, but stripping, rebuilding and designing them, I felt confident that I would be able to do a decent job of it. Being acutely aware of the high potential costs involved and the dangers of people copying them, I decided to speak to Eversheds solicitors in Leeds whom I knew had some good people. They produced a Confidentiality Agreement for me to use whenever I was discussing my ideas with anybody. I did this and as a result, I now have a great many of these signed documents on file, dating from the very beginning of the project.

As the design work progressed, I soon could see that I would indeed, need the protection of Patents and have the benefit of Design Rights to protect the Intellectual Property (IPR), so early on, I appointed Sue Behrens who lived locally to be my Patent Agent. Due to family commitments, later on, she passed me on to Urquhart, Dykes and Lord in the mid 1990's and finally I was working with Harrison Goddard Foot until 2004 when British Waterways took all the IPR. By this time I had spent around £207.000 on International Patents covering 39 countries. This was in spite of being highly selective when deciding for reasons of economy, which of my new ideas should or should not be patented.

In this case, because Roylecraft were being designed to meet a global need, each new patent needed to cover 39 countries. These being the leading industrial nations which I had identified, some of which are covered by international treatise. This process is a huge job in itself, especially when, to save money, I was also doing most of the drawings and writing out the specifications myself. In fact, when Sir Alex Smith first saw all my files and shelves full of Patent documentation, he was visibly shocked and told me that they had a whole department at Rolls Royce who were responsible for the IPR. The lists overleaf will give you some idea of the number of patents.

THE PATENT TREADMILL

Looking back, it seems to be a sensible requirement for the Dti to insist on this protection for the inventors and their innovative ideas. They want to ensure that their grants and support is not wasted. In a large and complex project like mine however, where many components are involved, registering patents sets in motion a most serious ongoing financial liability for any innovator who has limited funding. It is a treadmill which, once begun, creates a never ending demand for money. This went on for 17 years in my case.

Money is needed, not only to apply for patents,

it opens the door to ongoing annual costs which are necessary to maintain every patent, or the protection is lost. When the IPR is registered in many countries of the world, these costs are a dreadful liability for the applicant who, in my case also did not want to let his investors down.

In fact, I was aware of these costs and did minimise them by carefully selecting what should, or should not be patented. I also knew that no matter how strong a patent or the IPR is, if the inventor doesn't have the money to protect them in a court of law, then any wealthy individual or Large company can still take advantage of them. This is especially so for many inventors who often stretch their resources to the limit to develop their ideas. I was such a person. These are just one of the many problems which face the individual or small company which innovates.

Throughout the project and here in the book, I have stressed the difficulty of raising funding. With all the other, more obvious, financial problems being in the forefront, the constant drain with IPR is often forgotten. Also rarely discussed or appreciated is the important fact that I have solved many serious, technical challenges. I think this is because very few people know what problems existed.

I hate having to blow my own trumpet, but it has taken me tens of thousands of hours of study in order to overcome the historic problems. Additionally, there has also been the 17 years of work put in by my small 'team' in the workshops making all the components. Whilst they did have the benefit of being paid for it, they worked with a will and with great enthusiasm helping me to overcome them.

I should also mention the support which we have had from so many people who, like me, have worked without payment. This has helped me to achieve our technical success at extremely low cost and in the face of real financial and physical difficulties.

Despite the dreadful problems to come, which you will soon read about, I believe that our technology, at the time of writing, still leads the world in this specialised and useful form of transport.

PATENTS & APPLICATIONS

COUNTRY	APPLICATION No.	DATE	PRIORITY	TITLE
Australia	35423/89	28.04.89	04,05,88	Amphibious Craft
Australia	452/89	28.04.89	04.05.88	Amphibious Craft
Australia	458/89	28.04.89	04.05.88	Retractable Wheels
Australia	35532/89	28.04.89	04.05.88	Retractable Wheels
Austria	89304373.7	28.04.89	04.05.88	Amphibious Craft
Austria	89304372.9	28.04.89	04.05,88	Retractable Wheels
Belgium	89304373.7	28.04.89	04.05.88	Amphibious Craft
Belgium	89304372.9	28.04.89	04.05.88	Retractable Wheels
Canada	598539	03.05.89	04.05.88	Amphibious Craft
Canada	598533	03.05.89	04.05.88	Retractable Wheels
Denmark	452/89	28.04.89	04.05.88	Amphibious Craft
Denmark	89304373.7	28.04.89	04.05.88	Amphibious Craft
Denmark	2620/90	31.10.90	04.05.88	Amphibious Craft
Denmark	2621/90	31.10.90	04.05.88	Retractable Wheels
Denmark	458/89	28.04.89	04.05.88	Retractable Wheels
Denmark	89304372.9	28.04.89	04,05,88	Retractable Wheels
E.P.C	89304373.7	28.04.89	04.05.88	Amphibious Craft
E.P.C	89304372.9	28.04.89	04.05.88	Retractable Wheels
France	89304373.7	28.04.89	04.05.88	Amphibious Craft
France	89304372.9	28.04.89	04.05.88	Retractable Wheels
Germany	89304373,7	28.04,89	04.. 05,88	Amphibious Craft
Germany	89304372.9	28.04.89	04.05.88	Retractable Wheels
Greece	89304373.7	28.04.89	04.05.88	Amphibious Craft
Greece	89304372.9	28.04.89	04.05.88	Retractable Wheels
Italy	89304373.7	28.04.89	04.05.88	Amphibious Craft
Italy	89304372,9	28.04.89	04,05,88	Retractable Wheels
Japan	1-504934	05.11.90	04.05.88	Amphibious Craft
Japan	1505143	05.11.90	04.05.88	Retractable Wheels
Liechtenstein	89304373.7	28.04.89	04.05.88	Amphibious Craft
Liechtenstein	89304372.9	28.04.89	04.05.88	Retractable Wheels
Luxembourg	89304373,7	28.04.89	04,05,88	Amphibious Craft
Luxembourg	89304372.9	28.04.89	04.05.88	Retractable Wheels
Netherlands	89304373.7	28.04.89	04.05.88	Amphibious Craft
Netherlands	89304372.9	28.04.89	04.05.88	Retractable Wheels
Norway	452/89	28.04.89	04.05.88	Amphibious Craft
Norway	458/89	28,04,89	04,05,88	Retractable Wheels
P.C.T	452/89	28.04.89	04.05.88	Amphibious Craft
P.C.T	458/89	28.04.89	04.05.88	Retractable Wheels
Spain	89304373.7	28.04.89	04.05.88	Amphibious Craft
Spain	89304372.9	28.04.89	04.05.88	Retractable Wheels

CHAPTER 52: PATENTS & IPR

COUNTRY	APPLICATION No.	DATE	PRIORITY	TITLE
Sweden	89304373.7	28.04.89	04.05.88	Amphibious Craft
Netherlands	89304373.7	28.04.89	04.05.88	Amphibious Craft
Netherlands	89304372.9	28.04.89	04.05.88	Retractable Wheels
Norway	452/89	28.04.89	04.05.88	Amphibious Craft
Norway	458/89	28,04,89	04,05,88	Retractable Wheels
P.C.T	452/89	28.04.89	04.05.88	Amphibious Craft
P.C.T	458/89	28.04.89	04.05.88	Retractable Wheels
Spain	89304373.7	28.04.89	04.05.88	Amphibious Craft
Spain	89304372.9	28.04.89	04.05.88	Retractable Wheels
Sweden	89304373.7	28.04.89	04.05.88	Amphibious Craft
Sweden	89304372.9	28.04.89	04.05.88	Retractable Wheels
Switzerland	89304373.7	04.05.88	04.05.88	Amphibious Craft
Switzerland	89304372.9	28.04.89	04.05.88	Retractable Wheels
UK	88104799	04.05.88	-	Amphibious Craft
UK	9009576	27.04.90	-	Amphibious Craft
UK	8909832.1	28.04.89	04.05.88	Amphibious Craft
UK	9012820.8	08.06.90	27.04.90	Amphibious Craft
UK	9202834.9	11.02.92	-	Improvements in Retractable Wheels
UK	9219406.7	14.09.92	11.02.92	Improvements in Retractable Wheels
UK	8909775.2	28.04.89	04.05.88	Retractable Wheels
USA	07/606851	31.10.90	04.05.88	Amphibious Craft
USA	458/89	28.04.89	04.05.88	Retractable Wheels
Norway	170527	PCT 458/89	28.10.92	Retractable Wheels
UK	2218052	8909775.2	22.04.92	Retractable Wheels
UK	2219555	8909832.1	29.04.92	Amphibious Craft
USA	5176098	607359	05.01.93	Retractable Wheels
EPC, I.E.	0341008	89304372.9	13.01.93	Retractable Wheels
Austria	0341008	89304372.9	13.01.93	Retractable Wheels
Belgium	0341008	89304372.9	13.01.93	Retractable Wheels
Denmark	0341008	89304372.9	13.01.93	Retractable Wheels
France	0341008	89304372.9	13.01.93	Retractable Wheels
Germany	0341008	89304372.9	13.01.93	Retractable Wheels
Greece	0341008	89304372.9	13.01.93	Retractable Wheels
Italy	0341008	89304372.9	13.01.93	Retractable Wheels
Liechtenstein	0341008	89304372.9	13.01.93	Retractable Wheels
Luxembourg	0341008	89304372.9	13.01.93	Retractable Wheels
Netherlands	0341008	89304372.9	13.01.93	Retractable Wheels
Spain	0341008	89304372.9	13.01.93	Retractable Wheels
Sweden	0341008	89304372.9	13.01.93	Retractable Wheels
Switzerland	0341008	89304372.9	13.01.93	Retractable Wheels

ROYLE. FROM VINTAGE TO CLASSIC TO AMPHIBIAN.

SECOND SERIES

APPLICANT	COUNTRY	CATCH WORD
Covelink Marine Ltd	AU	Amphibious vehicle
Covelink Marine Ltd	CA	Amphibious vehicle
Covelink Marine Ltd & British Water	GB	Amphibious vehicle
Covelink Marine Ltd	US	Amphibious vehicle
Covelink Marine Ltd	CA	Amphibious bus
Covelink Marine Ltd	GB	Amphibious bus
Covelink Marine Ltd	JP	Amphibious bus
Covelink Marine Ltd	US	Amphibious bus
Covelink Marine Ltd	GB	CML-General
Covelink Marine Ltd & British Water	AU	Vehicle with retractable wheel
Covelink Marine Ltd & British Water	CA	Vehicle with retractable wheel
Covelink Marine Ltd & British Water	CN	Vehicle with retractable wheel
Covelink Marine Ltd & British Water	EP	Vehicle with retractable wheel
Covelink Marine Ltd	GB	Improved front suspension
Covelink Marine Ltd	GB	Improved front suspension
Covelink Marine Ltd & British Water	JP	Vehicle with retractable wheel
Covelink Marine Ltd & British Water	NZ	Vehicle with retractable wheel
Covelink Marine Ltd & British Water	US	Vehicle with retractable wheel
Covelink Marine Ltd	WO	Vehicle with retractable wheel
Covelink Marine Ltd	GB	Spring loaded safety mechanism
Covelink Marine Ltd	GB	Spring loaded safety mechanism
Covelink Marine Ltd	GB	Spring loaded safety mechanism
Covelink Marine Ltd	WO	Spring loaded safety mechanism
Covelink Marine Ltd	GB	Hull structure
Covelink Marine Ltd & British Water	AU	Suspension raising/lowering
Covelink Marine Ltd & British Water	CA	Suspension raising/lowering
Covelink Marine Ltd & British Water	CN	Suspension raising/lowering
Covelink Marine Ltd & British Water	EP	Suspension raising/lowering
Covelink Marine Ltd	GB	Suspension raising/lowering
Covelink Marine Ltd & British Water	JP	Suspension raising/lowering
Covelink Marine Ltd & British Water	NZ	Suspension raising/lowering
David Royle	AU	JetBus
David Royle	CA	JetBus
David Royle	EP	JetBus
David Royle	GB	JetBus
David Royle	JP	JetBus
David Royle	NZ	JetBus
David Royle	US	JetBus
David Royle	AU	Jet Truck
David Royle	CA	Jet Truck
David Royle	EP	Jet Truck
David Royle	GB	Jet Truck
David Royle	JP	Jet Truck
David Royle	NZ	Jet Truck
David Royle	US	Jet Truck

STATUS	NEXT ACTION	DATE
Granted	Renewal	19/10/06
Granted	Renewal	18/01/07
Granted	Renewal	20/04/05
Granted	No further action	
Granted	Renewal	13/12/06
Granted	Renewal	26/05/05
Granted	Renewal	02/05/05
Granted	No further action	
Examination requested	No action	
Lapsed. May be capable of restoration		
Pending	No action	
Response to exam report required		07/06/??
Abandoned		
Abandoned		
Exam request due		29/04/05
Grant pending	No action	
Abandoned		
Expired		
Abandoned		
Abandoned		
Abandoned		
Abandoned		
Abandoned		
Exam request		10/03/05
Restoration required		10/05/05
Issue fee due		17/02/05
Renewal		23/08/05
Abandoned		
No action required		
Lapsed (may be reinstated)		29/01/05
Requested	Renewal	29/04/13
Requested	Renewal	18/10/19
Abandoned		
Requested	Renewal	01/11/12
Requested	Renewal	05/03/14
Requested	Renewal	01/11/09
Requested	Renewal	23/11/14
Requested	Renewal	30/04/13
Requested	Renewal	25/09/06
Opposed - obervations filed		27/05/05
Withdrawn		
Registered	Renewal	16/01/14
Registered	Renewal	02/11/09
Pending	No action required	

CHAPTER 53:
SALES & MANUFACTURING

Whilst the MK IV was still being tested and discussions were getting underway with potential buyers, I was becoming sufficiently confident that we were very near to having a saleable product. I had produced drawings for the MK V, which was a larger and improved version of the MK IV. We had now been working on the various prototypes for thirteen years and I had spent a lot of time talking to all manner of people, buyers, potential partners and potential manufacturers. Being such a high value product, large companies could see the value in them and as there was no direct competition around the world and as they were not price sensitive, good profits could be made.

I had been in discussions with a number of companies during the 1990's, including Vickers and Rolls Royce. I already had contacts at all levels in both of these firms, however it was Babcock and later on, Vosper Thorneycroft (VT), who showed an active interest. Both wanted to be involved and to manufacture my machines, but despite many meetings and visits, ultimately I could make no progress with either of them. Mitsubishi in Japan also started to show interest in 1999 and were keen to become involved, but I will explain about them later on.

In any event, although not seen as being practicable by many, I was confident that we could organise production ourselves, I had some experienced and good management standing by. Never the less, it was clear that funding for it was going to be very difficult if not impossible. The lack of knowledge of our work and of our abilities, combined with the pronounced lack of practical experience by those who controlled funding, was the principal reason for most of our financial difficulties. The focus on academic qualifications in this country has continued to devalue the tremendous advantages of actually and physically handling products and machinery and learning by experience.

People had no comprehension of the problems which we faced on a daily basis and overcame with the hundreds of motor vehicles dealt with when organising a steady flow of all the vehicles through Royles workshops. Vehicles for which parts were virtually impossible to find and every vehicle was different to the next. Each and every one also dated back many years. Compared to this, production of vehicles which were new and all the same was a prospect which we could relish. In the fullness of time we did set up production and proved that we could do it perfectly well and it was done efficiently and economically.

BIG COMPANIES

I have already mentioned one of Babcock's directors, Alex Marsh, who could see the potential of RoyleCraft amphibians, I trusted him and I was happy for them to make their own detailed drawings of the MK III Prototype on Autocad. I was confident that they would honour my IPR, and was optimistic that we could work together, indeed discussions and visits continued for a couple of years, but we made no progress. It seems that the problem was not only the imbalance in size between our two companies, we being a 'Micro' SME, whereas they are a very large global organisation. It seemed that it was not acceptable for them to be seen to be paying for an 'outside' design, when they had their own design team.

With VT, (Vosper Thorneycroft), their directors travelled all the way up from Portsmouth to see me on a number of occasions. They also could see the demand and were well placed to build them, especially for the MOD who they often supplied. As with Babcock, it would have been good to work with them, but when I asked them to pay towards the years of work and costs incurred with the design and development work, no money was on the table. It could well have been for the same reason as just described, they could not be seen to be paying for outside designs.

Each time they came, they asked for the drawings of the MK IV. As ever, I had to be very careful, since once in their possession, it would not have been difficult for them, or any other company for that matter, to make modifications to the drawings and then to say that they were their own designs. So, the drawings remained with me.

CHAPTER 53: SALES & MANUFACTURING

The fact is that these large companies knew we were very small and after working on a project on this scale, they knew that we were bound to be financially stretched. After all, this was why we were keen to do business with them. I don't suppose that they would realise, however, that I could not even afford the frequent trips up and down to Plymouth for meetings, let alone the hotel costs etc. They would be aware that we would be unlikely ever to be in a position to employ legal representation on a scale necessary to face up to these large organisations. This was a constant worry, since I knew that I could never afford to enforce the patents in court when up against such big companies.

History shows, time and again, how inventors and innovators have lost the benefits of their work as soon as they try to sell them or work with large companies. A sad reflection and the reason for many failed projects.

Some of our shareholders thought that I was so determined to remain independent and manufacture the vehicles ourselves, that I was not giving prospective partners a fair chance. Others thought that I was not prepared to share the equity. Neither was, in fact, the case. If we could agree terms with any worthwhile organisation who was prepared to be fair and reasonable, then we would have proceeded. It may have looked as if I was being overly cautious, but I did have the benefit of advice and support, during these discussions, from my co-directors and others who were involved and wanted to help.

It is difficult for those who were not closely involved, to think that I was not taking advantage of the opportunities. After 14 years of financial struggle, both personal and corporate, the truth is that I would have been delighted to have shared the responsibility with an organisation which could have built and sold our machines. The fact is that I was regularly discussing them with Bruce Ropner (Shipping), Richard Fletcher (Aerospace) and Sir Alex Smith, (our Chairman). Similarly, with other helpful and active supporters like Alan Theakston, the International President of the Institute of Chartered Secretaries and Administrators. (ICSA) who, along with others, also was not paid for his support

Another old friend, Alan Priest was also helping me at this time. He had seen the publicity on television and in the press and not working at the time, asked if he could come to work for me. He explained that he had been in charge of Business Development in his old family business which involved Sales and Contracts with large companies. He thought that he would be able to help me with this particular aspect of Covelink Marine's future business. Because my experience had been mainly on a more personal level with Royles Restoration customers, and with my ongoing failure to conclude a deal with the big companies, I could see that he might be able to help me with this.

Alan was also prepared to work without payment to begin with, but being full time, as soon as we had money coming in from a contract, he naturally wanted a salary. All in all, it was good to have his help in the office every day. This was especially so at this time, because of all the additional Covelink work with marketing, financial projections, business plans and the arrangements for production. As ever, I was always very busy with all the different demands on my time including overseeing Royles ongoing restoration work.

We were also involved with Nesta at the time and they needed detailed documentation and records of the use of their award. They also wanted us to have a decent film of us testing the prototypes. This was, I am sure, the well known film director Lord Putnam's idea, he was Chairman of Nesta at the time and it turned out that he was a great supporter of our project. We had some previous BBC film, but it was mainly short clips from local TV news items rather than being more carefully planned and paid for, as was now going to be the case.

FILMING

With the work at Staindrop being connected with so many wonderful and interesting motor cars of all kinds, the TV companies were always happy to film them and I have quite a collection of films which they made including Nick as a boy, driving the prototype half scale Austin 7 Chummy children's car. There is also a film made for the 'Record Breakers' television series when we built a replica of the 1899 French World Speed Record car 'Le Jamais Contente' powered by electric batteries. Our customer, who lived in Liverpool, decided to see if our car would beat the existing land speed record and it did. It broke three current world land speed records for electrically driven motor cars. There was also a good film about our work at Staindrop and various motor cars filmed by the BBC for the popular 'Dales Diary' Series which are good to watch.

With having this long standing link with various members of the BBC and ITV film crews and interviewers, they were only too pleased to take some film of the prototypes. One of the best known cameramen is Les Coates. His reputation is such that he has won national awards for his work and when widescreen TV was introduced, he was nominated to train many of the country's film people in the skills needed to cope with the original and new systems.

He had seen so much of what we were doing and was so impressed with Royles work that we were asked to restore his father's Rover for him. When Nesta wanted to have the MK IV prototype filmed, I immediately contacted Les. He and his film crew went to London especially to film Lord Putnam at Nesta at their lower Thames Street offices. I treasure all these and other films provided by Les and others which I copied from BBC and ITV news items.

CHANGE OF FOCUS FROM PURELY COMMERCIAL TO PUBLIC SERVICE ORGANISATIONS

Having seen how little progress I was making with the big commercial manufacturing companies, I thought it might be preferable to make contact with organisations which would actually use and benefit from operating the amphibians themselves. Accordingly, I shortlisted Customs and Excise, the Royal National Lifeboat Institution (RNLI), and British Waterways (BW), and approached each of them in turn. I hoped that they would appreciate having the benefit of the new technology and not be purely focussed on maximising their profits, possibly at my expense and that of my shareholders.

After speaking to the people at H.M.Customs and Excise in London, I was pleased to see that they could see the potential and usefulness of my amphibians and I seemed to be making steady progress. Sadly, my contact there

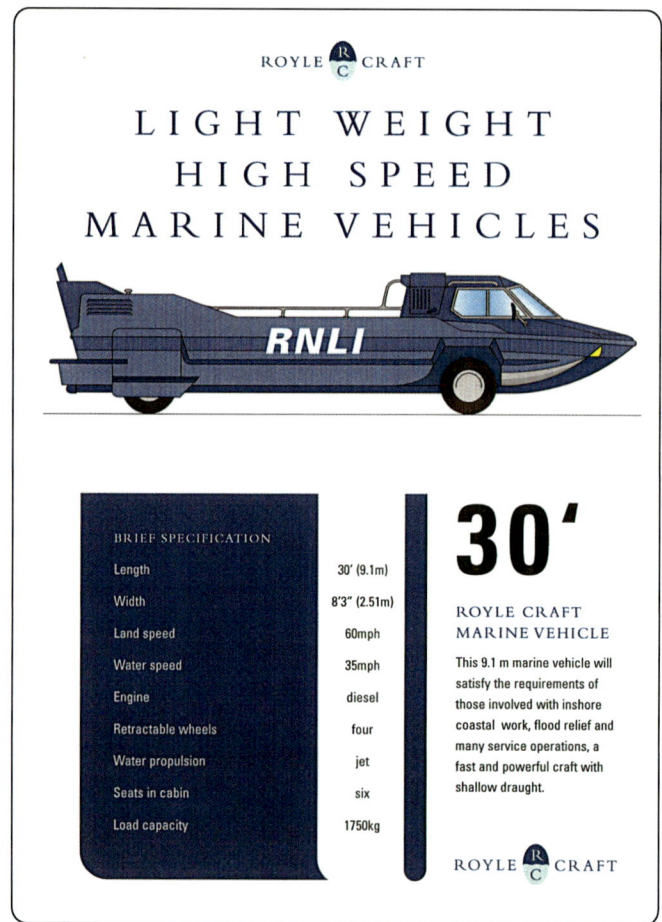

Covelink R.N.L.I. A5 leaflet.

suffered a serious motor accident during our discussions and I could not find anybody else who would take an interest. History was repeating itself, only one or perhaps two people in any organisation having a sufficiently open mind to be able to grasp what was being offered.

I then spoke to the Chief engineer Bob Cripps, the Engineering Manager of the RNLI in Poole. He invited me down to their headquarters with Alan Priest, who was now becoming more involved. We wanted to tell him about the benefits of our new technology. The meeting began with an RNLI film which Bob and his colleague, Andrew Tate, showed to us in a darkened room. It recorded the launching of one of their sea going lifeboats over a pebble beach near Aldebrough on the East Coast of Suffolk. It was a remarkable film:

Mounted on a trailer, with its bows pointing towards the sea, the big lifeboat was being pushed down the beach, from behind, by a tractor with caterpillar tracks. The tractor cab was watertight and the unit headed down the beach straight into the teeth of an onshore gale with breaking seas and surf perhaps ten feet high, or more. As the bows punched into the huge waves, the tractor driver released the locking device and the big lifeboat slid off the trailer into the foaming water. With all the confused water and breaking seas, the driver had launched it too soon. The lifeboat was not floating, but was sitting on the bottom with the waves breaking over it.

A DRAMATIC SCENE

The force of the waves quickly turned the boat sideways, the sea was now crashing along the length of the boat and we next saw the crew bravely clawing their way forward along the side decks towards the bows through all the spume and spray. The Helmsman then engaged drive and we saw the large twin bronze propellers start to spin, churning the foaming water and pebbles as they did so. We were amazed to see the lifeboat turn and drive itself backwards, stern first, into the oncoming waves. It was pivoting on its bows helped by the weight of the crew holding it down. Even with the waves now breaking over the stern and raking along her decks, the big lifeboat floated off, stern first, into the tumultuous sea. A remarkable and brilliant piece of boat handling.

"Well what do you think of that"? said Bob. "A most remarkable display" we replied. "Would your Roylecraft Amphibians be able to do that"? he asked, knowing that few vessels would stand such abuse. "With a water-jet, you certainly couldn't 'walk' on your propellers" I explained, but then added that "we wouldn't have launched there in the first place". I went on to say that with our machines, we would not be restricted to a fixed launch site. We would have driven along the road to a more sheltered spot.

We then showed him our film of the MK IV driving along a road and being launched at speed and then driving out of the water again. Admittedly it was into calm water, but that was the point. Bob and Andrew were obviously impressed and said that they didn't realise how advanced our machines were. This compliment was most pleasing, but strangely, Bob went on to say that our aluminium hulls would not now be acceptable to the RNLI because they were then insisting that new Lifeboats were to be built of modern, advanced composites.

We explained that our craft would eventually be built using both types of construction, but that the cost of moulds was high, so this would happen, but only when sufficient money was available to do it. Discussing this later with a boat designer, he explained how he had seen such a lifeboat damaged and a piece of the hull broken off when it had simply clipped the corner of a jetty wall as it was leaving harbour.

BRITISH WATERWAYS (BW)

Sadly, matters did not proceed further with the RNLI, because meetings with the technical directors of British Waterways (BW) were progressing well and they thought our technology might satisfy their needs for a particular application in Scotland.

I always respected BW for their restoration and maintenance work of this country's canals and rivers. I have had much affection for these waterways ever since my boyhood days in 1945 and just after the war. This was when the family spent many happy holidays at Weaverham in Cheshire with an old motor cruiser and seeing and having trips on the ships and salt barges which ploughed up and down the river and canal there. The biggest ship was called 'Jolly Days' and this looked very impressive when sailing along such a relatively small waterway. I have some of my father's interesting old 9.5mm film of this which is now on DVD and also some early Glass slides of the canals taken by my grandfather at the turn of the 19th century. Some of them have been enlarged and hang on the staircase at home in Gainford.

Our first approaches to BW resulted in conversations with Stewart Sim, the main board Operations Director, with the result that he visited us at Staindrop in May 2001. He had been a director of BW for many years and not surprisingly, was a most respected expert on the operation and technical matters concerning the 2.200 miles of inland waterways in the UK. Not surprisingly, like most knowledgeable people, seeing Roylecraft for the first time, he wanted to find out about our technology and whether or not, it would be suitable for BW's purposes.

Due to the successful tests of the commercial type, the MK IV, I saw it as being especially useful to BW as a general purpose work boat type of amphibian, so was aiming this at BW. We explained the advantages of this craft to

Stewart telling him, for example, how it could cover a number of canals and rivers in one day, driving from one waterway to another on the roads. I remembered seeing workboats moored on canals which were not only exposed to vandalism, but would also waste a lot of time when moving from one location to another along the narrow, speed restricted canals.

With our machines, I told him how a single person could operate it and deal with a number of problems or jobs at different locations and then drive it home afterwards. This would not only be a most efficient form of floating office or mobile workshop, it would also quickly transport the engineer and his equipment to his work and avoid any risk of vandalism. He could see all these advantages and in the fullness of time, Ian White the Regional Director in their Leeds office, proposed that we should supply such machines to BW. I produced some specific designs with small cranes which would meet their needs, but that was two or three years later.

Whilst we were discussing the advantages of our technology and the various applications in our office at Staindrop, Stewart was looking at drawings and photographs of the various prototypes which were hung on bulldog clips along my office wall. He noticed a drawing amongst them which I had produced as a possible idea for a 40ft (12 metre) version of a Roylecraft Amphibious water Jet-bus for Mitsubishi in Japan. Stewart asked about this and I explained that I had produced the design, based upon the successful prototypes, as a possible tourist bus for the Universal Studios development in Japan and for public transport on the city canals in Osaka.

All this clearly interested him and he was pleased to find that my retractable wheel mechanisms and specification would allow our 40ft Jet-Buses to operate in swallow water only 20 inches deep (500 mm). Stewart said that this is ideal for Britain's shallow canals and rivers. It was impossible, he explained, to use existing military amphibians like DUKW's, because their wheels would drag in the mud, he also said that they were too wide for some of the narrow canals. He then went on to explain that they had been considering using amphibious buses for their impressive Falkirk Wheel Project which BW were completing in Scotland at that time, but had not been able to find any amphibians which were satisfactory.

Stewart then described The Falkirk Wheel itself. It was a most exciting and impressive engineering project which was an important element of the £78 million Millennium Link project. BW had incorporated this major innovative construction in the overall plans to lift boats up from the canals which linked Glasgow, the Clyde and the Firth of Forth canal to the Union Canal which was to Edinburgh. Canals and waterways which had been closed to navigation since the 1960's.

Following this meeting, we made good progress with BW and had a positive and helpful response as more and more BW people were becoming involved. It transpired at a technical meeting on 6th July 2001 held at Staindrop with Scotland's Chief Engineer, George Ballinger and Iain Herbert, who were controlling the development contract at Falkirk,

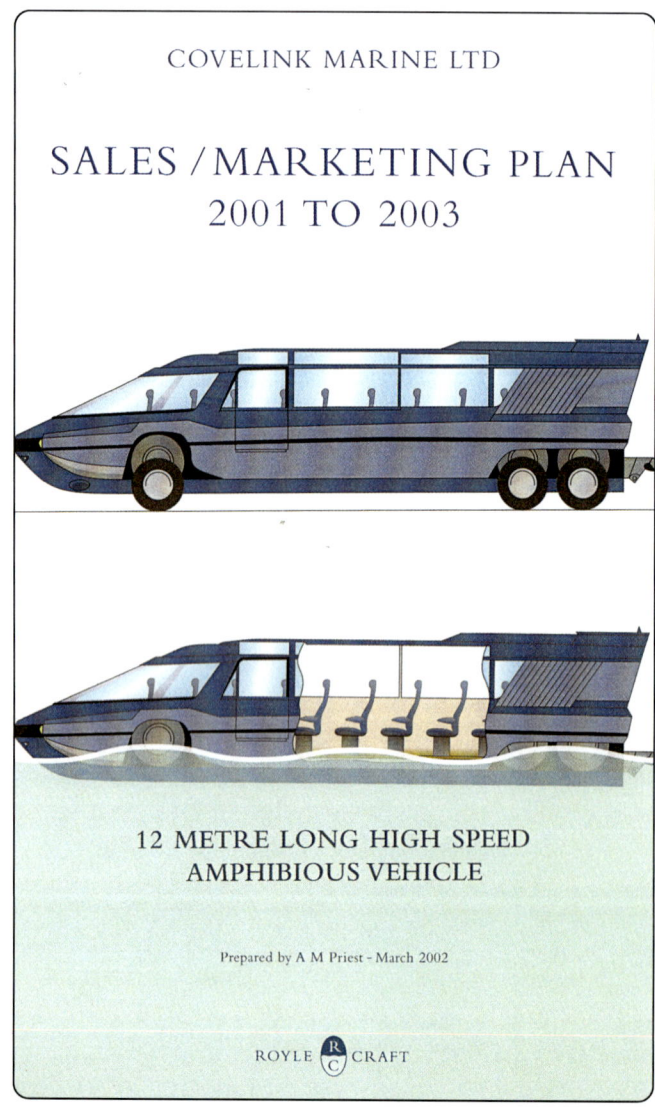

Cover of Covelink Marine Sales/Marketing plan.

that Four Roylecraft Jet-Buses would be required for the visitors. BW were an ideal customer because they would be buying them and operating the amphibians themselves.

When asked if we could produce the four buses in time for the opening in May 2002, even then, it was only ten months later, I said that we would do our best, but certainly couldn't promise. Meeting this deadline was going to be very difficult for many reasons being 40ft long, they were too big to build in our Staindrop workshops, so we had no space or facilities for production, for example.

This potential order was great news, but with it being for Public Transport Buses and not for the general purpose, commercial type of amphibians, which I had hoped to supply them with, it introduced a raft of new issues, not the least of which was certification. I knew that this could be a most involved procedure, one which the MK IV commercial type of craft would have avoided. I thought we would be able to do it, but how long this aspect alone might take, was a serious worry.

Soon after this, Alan Priest, who was with me at the meeting, composed a letter to them on the 11th July, confirming their serious interest and their potential order for Four Amphibious Buses. Worryingly, I noticed, when he asked me to sign it, that he also confirmed that we could deliver the buses in time to meet their programme. Not only that, but at my estimated price of £262,000 each. From memory, I had made no allowance for the time that certification might take or for the time and costs of establishing premises and employing more staff to do it.

To make such assurances about delivery times and costs, at this early stage, seemed to be very risky. Although I had estimated the price, it was for the world's first ever, advanced, amphibious water jet-propelled bus. One which had never been built before and one which incorporated a raft of new mechanisms and new technology. It therefore, at best, could only be a ball-park estimate which I had put together to discuss with them.

In all the years of working on motor vehicles, I had never given a fixed price or date for completion. I discussed all this with Allan but he explained that no large company would place an order when the terms would be so opened ended. If we wanted the order, we would have to give a firm price and delivery date. To be realistic, I was unlikely to have any more information in the near future as to how long they might take to build or what the cost of building them would be, so we had no choice, but to use this estimate.

The contract for four Jet Buses was going to be worth £1.048 million and this set in motion various Cash Flow projections and also Business plans for BW. Alan Sperrin produced the figures for me. He was a business consultant for Durham University and had worked with me for some years. He was very familiar with the Roylecraft project and knew that, in the fullness of time, it was likely to be very profitable, but he was always most conservative when it came to producing turnover and profit forecasts. Because of all the great difficulties I was having with trying to raise money for the project, this cautious approach used to be of concern to me, because I wanted him to spell out the proper potential, but he would never do it.

Alan Priest naturally attended the meetings with me as discussions with BW about the contract progressed, they liked his positive attitude and he came over very well at meetings. When I mentioned that I was still very worried about the costs, time frame and other problems, he explained that we had to be positive if we were going to get the contract. I couldn't argue with this.

My concern was that Alan may not have been fully aware of what was really involved with our technology or the project as a whole. He had only been with me for a short time and had little experience with our specialised transport. Also, I worried that I didn't have the resources of a large business behind me, like he had with his old family business. With him having been primarily concerned with sales and marketing, as far as he was concerned, his aim was to get the order, It was then the job of the production people to meet it.

In Covelink Marine Ltd, I was not only the 'production people' but also the MD and the designer and the one who was taking all the risks!

With most of my work having been difficult, if

not impossible to cost, down the years, I had always given myself some latitude by operating all the jobs on a 'time and materials' basis. Under these extenuating circumstances however, I felt that I had to agree with Alan and confirm the price. After so many years of financial difficulties and failing to make speedy progress, the MK IV had taken five years to come to fruition for example, and after failing to make any progress with the big companies, who admittedly wanted our technology without paying for it, there was nothing for it, but to do my best to honour the letter, which said that we could do it.

Ultimately I would have Alan to help me, if we got the contract, but I was conscious of the fact that it was me who would be doing most of the work and was liable for the consequences. It would mean however, that as well as Alan having the benefit of a salary for the first time since he joined me, I would also have one. In my case, this would be for the first time in the 14 years since I started the project in 1987, so there were other advantages!

BRITISH WATERWAYS PERSONNEL

G.W. Ballinger. Bsc. C.Eng. Msc. Chief Engineer Scotland.

K. Butcher. FCIPS. National Procurement.

J. D. Corser. B.Eng C.Eng MICE.

R. Evans. CEO of British Waterways.

R. E. Jackson. C.Eng. MIMechE.

N. I. Johnson. Solicitor.

W. Schlegal. C. Eng. MICE.

I explained my concerns about the costs and time it might take to Stewart Sim and he said that he fully understood my worries and that there would be additional funding available to him, if we could show that it was needed. He was a good 'company man' as well as being a practical person. It later transpired, when assuring the other senior directors of our abilities, that he was not only happy about our technology, but was also content that we were genuine people to deal with.

Looking ahead, his support was a key factor when, six months later, in January 2002, I signed the extremely lengthy contract which consisted of three 'books'. We were making good progress, but had not yet opened the little 'starter factory', or taken on the staff to build the Water-Jet Buses at that stage and we were then only four months away from the delivery date. Stewart gave me much confidence for the future success of the contract however, and I knew that I could depend upon him to be realistic about the risks and time involved.

Stewart Sim. Operations Director.

Alan Slater. Tees River Manager.

M. Smith. FCCA. Financial Director.

J. M. Stirling. Director. Scotland

P. J. Wear. Business Development

Ian White. C. Eng C.Env. Regional Dir

J. Whitehall. DipM MIMgt. Support.

CHAPTER 54:
THE FIRST CONTRACT

As mentioned, all I had in the summer of 2001 was the outline graphic picture of the Jet-bus hanging on the wall when Stewart Sim first visited us. This had been scanned onto Autocad from my first bus drawing. He didn't ask, and I didn't mention the fact that that I had not designed the details of the structure of the hull, the double retractable rear wheel components or even finally decided upon the actual transmission. Nor had I decided which of the gearbox designs I wanted to use, or which of the suspension locking mechanisms would be best suited to this size of vehicle. I was not especially worried about these or about designing them, as long as the money was available to pay for them, I was confident that we could build them successfully.

All the components would be subcontracted to local engineering firms, our new staff would primarily be concerned with assembly. There was a lot of planning work and decisions to make. When it came to costs, I also had a lot of work to do. Because it all happened so quickly, I did not have the benefit of any quotes for the components or for the hull, nor did I know what the overall cost of assembling and handling a vehicle of this size might be. Whilst I was familiar with the costs associated with all of the hundreds of Vintage and classic motor cars we had restored and rebuilt, I was also well aware of the wide variations in cost which can occur with these. The problem being that there are so many components incorporated in motor vehicles. In this case it was, at least, helpful to know that all the components would be new.

My other concern was that we were going to be building the first advanced 40ft amphibious buses of their type in the world, without us having even built and tested a prototype. To make matters worse, they would be going directly into public service and they were also going to be very much in the public eye.

On the other hand, I had of course, spent fourteen years designing, building and testing the different amphibious prototypes. I had developed my new technology, so I had all the information I needed and was confident that I could do it, if I had sufficient time!
Not wanting to jeopardise losing this first contract, I had only included a small Margin for profit. Despite this, Mark Smith the Financial Director of British Waterways, still thought that they were "expensive".

Throughout the many years of my involvement with motor vehicles, boats and restoration work, I have heard similar remarks made by many people. Usually they were made by those who have little knowledge and do not understand what they are dealing with. In this day and age, there are few people who have any experience or have a real grasp of the skills and time which are involved with practical and creative work on this scale.

This serious lack of knowledge and judgement stems from the focus of attention being upon academic results rather than practical experience. It also stems from a misunderstanding of how the very low cost of virtually all the products we buy nowadays, is as a direct a result of the benefits of efficient mass production. This is especially so, when the products come in from the Low Cost economies in the East. As you read this story, you will see a clear example of how damaging this ignorance can be when those in authority have little knowledge of the technology they control. But I digress.

Although we did not yet have a contract, it seemed that we were going to be given an order to supply the four buses, so I had to be ready to produce drawings for all the innovative and non-standard components and every aspect of this entirely new, water-jet propelled, 40ft amphibian.

To my knowledge, it was the first bus of any kind, ever to be built as a monocoque without a chassis, also to be fitted with retractable wheels and steering mechanisms. It also incorporated new cooling systems and virtually every part of it, except the engine and the jet unit, being unique and innovative. I also knew that I had to obtain the actual costs for all the components and place orders for them and set up a complete supply chain. Along with all this

I had to locate and equip a small factory, employ and induct a team of new engineers and fitters to build the amphibians, the like of which they, nor anyone else, had ever built before.

Quite a challenge with just £11,000 in the bank, money remaining from the Nesta awards!

To do all this work in less than nine months and with no written order at that stage, was going to be risky and difficult, if not impossible. It was now July and even without a contract, I had to start straight away if I was to give the project any chance of success. I swallowed hard, cancelled my summer holidays and got out my drawing board.

THE BW CONTRACT PROCEEDS

I knew that there were no specific Transport Regulations for Amphibious Vehicles, a fact which alone, could well have deterred any large companies from tackling this type of transport. After a lifetime spent dealing with the most unusual and diverse range of vehicles, I was aware however, that our MK IV general purpose type would be the easiest to license for use on the road and in water, which was why I had been 'pushing' BW to take and use this commercial type. If absolutely necessary, we could have 'self certificated' this type of vehicle and risked using it straight away.

When it comes to buses, Public Service Vehicles (PSV), the regulations for normal road going vehicles and for 'normal' sea going ships are so extensive that nobody, even in the DVLA, would admit to knowing them all. After further enquiries, the DTLR and the Maritime Coastguard Agency (MCA) decided that the appropriate legislation for my Roylecraft Amphibious Water Jet-Buses would be that for an M3 Tourist Bus on the road and for a category 5 Passenger Ship when on water and at sea.

I acquired and studied both sets of these detailed and extensive regulations and although I could see that some of them were in direct conflict with each other, I knew that if I incorporated and met as many of them as possible, I was confident that we would be able to certificate the Jet-Buses.

A visit to the Falkirk Wheel was arranged for Friday 20th July 2001 where George Ballinger and Iain Herbert showed Alan and I around the

Falkirk Wheel construction. Myself with Alan Priest.

site and explained what we were looking at. It was very much a case of 'work in progress' with the major engineering components of the Wheel itself still laid around the site and the canals and associated basins still unfinished earth-works with no water in them They particularly wanted me to look at the road bridge above the site. There were two tight bends here which the buses would have to negotiate when driving the visitors over the bridge to or from the wheel. I was able to tell them that it presented no difficulties because I had designed-in a good steering lock and minimised the wheel base and turning circle by ensuring that the tandem rear wheels pivoted on the leading ones.

Later on, a visit was arranged to Falkirk for all my restoration staff, so that they also would know what was involved in this development. This was to foster interest in case any of them would be playing a part in the project.

Looking at drawings and pictures of the finished development, the Wheel was obviously going to be a most remarkable structure. It was

CHAPTER 54: THE FIRST CONTRACT

Falkirk Wheel tour for Royle's staff.

Falkirk Wheel construction.

Falkirk Wheel construction.

Falkirk Wheel tour. Nick with the empty top canal.

Falkirk Wheel Visitor Centre under construction.

the world's first and only Rotating Boatlift. It would lift canal boats in its two gondolas, each of which holds 300 tonnes of water, a hundred and fifteen feet, 35 metres, from a basin linked to the recently restored Forth and Clyde Canals up to the Union Canal. These linked the North Sea and Atlantic coasts and by means of this remarkable new structure, boats could then travel along the Union canal to Edinburgh.

Adjacent to this most impressive and spectacular piece of engineering and the basin which served it, a modernistic visitor centre was being built. Stewart and his supportive team of directors and managers were confident that the Falkirk Wheel would attract a lot of visitors and with our Advanced Jet-buses being the latest technology, they thought that Roylecraft Amphibians would nicely compliment it and be an exciting and efficient method of transporting the visitors on it. Roylecraft would enable them to ride in the gondolas over the wheel and along the canals and return by road. They could experience the wheel at the same time as riding in the most advanced form of Amphibious craft in the world.

They calculated that four of our new Jet buses which, with their unique, quick turn-round facility by using the road as well as the canals, would accommodate sufficient numbers of the expected number of tourists to meet their needs.

MEETING AT HEAD OFFICE

On 22nd October 2001, Stewart arranged a meeting at BW's head office so that he could introduce me and Alan Priest, who's title was now Business Development Manager, to the British Waterways CEO, Robin Evans and to F.D. Mark Smith, an accountant who had fairly recently joined BW as their Financial Director. The meeting was held at BW's attractive Willow Grange offices at Watford. In the central quadrangle which the offices created, was a beautiful pond which virtually filled the space. The purpose of the meeting was to discuss various aspects of the formal contract to supply four Roylecraft tourist buses to BW for the Falkirk Wheel visitor centre.

At the meeting, the impression was that Messrs Evans and Smith were not as confident, or as enthusiastic of us as Stewart was. It seemed that BW had suffered as a result of having placed an order for a ferry or some sort of special boat, with another small firm, the directors of which had let them down badly. Allegedly, its MD had run off with somebody else's wife! With Covelink being another small firm, it was rather simplistic, but it seems that we were being tarred with the same brush. This was despite Stewart having explained and stressed to them that we were a long established and reliable company.

Throughout the entire meeting, we could see that the CEO and FD were very much working together, with Stewart Sim seeming to be rather on his own and not saying very much. They were not showing the same positive attitude, or level of enthusiasm for our project, or for my small company. Later in the meeting, we were joined by Peter Wear who had recently been appointed by Mark Smith, to negotiate the Joint Venture which BW had proposed between Covelink and BW. The impression was that Stewart Sim, as Operations Director of BW for many years, was not 'in' with the 'new boys'.

I was very happy to have a Joint Venture with BW and share the benefits of Roylecraft with this old established and highly respected organisation. They had decided that the contract was going to be conditional upon this JV and requested that Covelink provide them with access to our accounts with an 'open books' arrangement. After having run my restoration company with an open books facility for our customers from the outset in 1973, this was normal practice for me. I had absolutely nothing to hide and it let BW see that we were not overcharging them and that we run an efficient business. It would hopefully, give these two doubting directors more confidence in us. Stewart said that the contract would be conducted on an "informal partnership" arrangement.

Shortly after the Watford meeting, we were asked to give a presentation to a group of the Waterways Regional Directors and managers who controlled various areas of the country's waterways. This meeting was a great success with the assembled managers being really enthusiastic and seeing a range of useful applications, in their regions, for our amphibious craft around the country.

Remembering the negativity of some directors in the large companies which I had previously dealt with, the attitude of the CEO and FD was still slightly worrying. As the weeks and months passed, the enthusiasm and confidence shown by the increasing number of BW people with whom we were coming into contact, was most heartening. We were dealing with many departments, not only in Watford and Scotland, but also at Falkirk, and in the Leeds and other regional offices as well. Too many people to list here, but all were good 'company people' and the overall impression was very good with positive feed-back.

Not surprisingly, the work load was intensifying and we were kept very busy dealing with all the various departments. At the same time, I was progressing well with the designs and there was a genuine appreciation by the MCA and DTLR officials, that I was incorporating the necessary safety and other features to meet the regulations. They could see that I was keen to work with them, only negotiating variations where necessary and then being very much aware of the safety aspects involved. They were most helpful and common sense prevailed whenever both sets of regulations were in conflict with each other.

Whilst the actual designs were mine, the good progress made with the drawings benefitted from the advice and help of some good people, namely Prof Neville Fawcett, the dynamics Director of Newcastle university, Jim Bone, a first class design engineer, Alistair Cameron for high speed hull design, Ken Lovell of Sunderland Ship Design services and other engineers and suppliers who were keen to be involved in what was now obviously going to be a most successful, ongoing and expanding business.

Working full time, seven days a week, I was often doing the design work in bed at weekends where I could work undisturbed and was, as ever, spoiled by Jo-Jo. It was all very exciting,

'Q' gets ready to launch his top secret water bus

By JULIA BREEN

BEHIND metal shutters, in a top-secret location close to Darlington, the future of transport – and possibly a jobs lifeline for the North-East – is taking shape.

David Royle, who models himself on James Bond's Q character, has spent the past 15 years building an invention which could change the face of travel, and bring up to 200 jobs to the region.

As a vintage car restorer, he has drawn on his skills and equipment to design the Roylecraft, a vehicle which can travel on land and water.

Mr Royle, who employs 16 people at the factory, has just secured a contract for four Roylecraft water buses from a secret bidder.

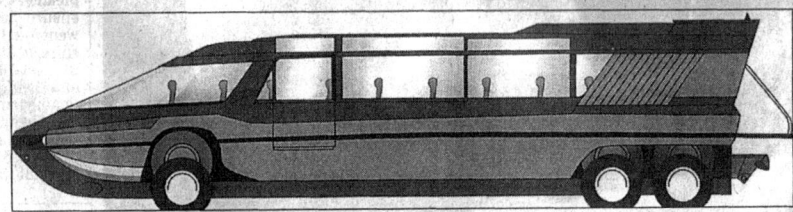

Carrying high hopes: David Royle's water bus which could lead to jobs being created

He said potential orders were coming in worth as much as £100m, which means he may have to employ up to 200 people at the factory.

The amphibious water bus seats up to 32 people and can travel at speeds of up to 70mph on land and 35mph on water.

Interest in the product has come from as far afield as Australia, Japan and Disneyland in America.

Testing has been taking place on a privately-owned lake near Staindrop, County Durham, and the buses will be launched for trials soon.

Mr Royle, whose vintage car business is based at Staindrop, County Durham, said: "Certainly our target is to create 100 jobs but if capital is available, it could be up to 200 jobs within the next five to six years. The world market for it has been estimated at around £300m per year.

"I will stay in the North-East because there is a skilled workforce here and I am hoping to take people on from the former Blue Circle cement works, and GlaxoSmithKline, and the like.

"There is huge potential in this market – the list is endless. So many people have been in touch. The vehicle could be used for flood rescue, the RNLI, oceanography, mobile home boats, island hopping, and so on."

Roylecrafts are the first land and water-based vehicles in the world to incorporate the technology of having retractable wheels, and the ability to travel at motorway speeds.

The vehicles cost from £200,000 to £400,000, depending on the size and specifications, and range from 22ft to the bus at 38ft.

Northern Echo. 01/11/02.

but the need for money was ever present, however, Stewart Sim was doing all he could to assist us.

THE 'STARTER FACTORY'

I wanted to build the buses as near and as convenient to Staindrop as possible, so that, when necessary, we could utilise Royles existing workshop facilities, minimising costs and time. I discovered that a relatively new 4000 sq ft agricultural building happened to be empty and available at Nesbit's Farm only a mile away from our workshops. The planners were very co-operative and were happy for a 'change of use' from agricultural to light industrial purposes. Later on, we also benefitted from some funding which was provided by Glaxo in Barnard Castle. They had recently reduced their workforce and had set up a scheme to assist in the creation of new jobs in Teesdale, which was helpful.

Importantly, the building was away from the main road and I asked Allan Barklay, our 'prototype engineer', to organise the necessary equipment to be installed and he also built a suitable, small office and tea room inside the building. He enjoyed a wide variation in his work and, as ever, I wanted it to be done in such a way as to prevent visitors from seeing the Jet-Buses under construction, so that confidentiality was maintained.

Stewart arranged for a £50,000 payment to be made, in advance of the contract, for machinery and equipment for the little factory. This amount was paid on 27 September 2001. This sum was not shown as being for the factory equipment, but as part of the contract for the Buses. With our open books arrangement, I was not too concerned since all the invoices were copied to BW and we were working in an informal 'partnership', so they knew what this money was used for.

I would like to say again, that the ongoing discussions with Stewart Sim as BW's Operations Director, gave me much comfort. He and other technical directors and managers were familiar with innovative projects of this nature and that after fourteen years of R&D costs, were well aware of our weak financial position and that their support was key to its success. We had frequent meetings with the many people who were involved when every aspect of the project and our technology was discussed in great detail. They had confidence in us and were all keen to make a success of the project.

I told Stewart about the High Court action five years earlier in 1996 and the aftermath. Knowing this and because he was now familiar with us, he had complete confidence in our honesty and that we were continuing to go 'all out' to make a success of the project and of our total reliance upon BW to support us.

Stewart was well aware of the problems which can arise with projects of this sort and confirmed and clarified a previous remark which was that, if there were any delays or additional costs for modifications, development work or whatever, then there was a fund of up to £500,000 available to him for such eventualities. Indeed, he explained that there had been the need for some additional £millions for a shortfall with the development and construction of the wheel itself. By comparison this contract was on a small scale. In any event, Ken Butcher, the National Procurement Manager, kept a tight control of costs and I was confident that our progress and all costs would be covered and correctly recorded.

SPONSORSHIP & FUNDING

Despite Alan Priest having introduced BDN, a local firm who were acting as project managers to help us by certifying the invoices, even with money available, there were still delays in the payment of them. Looking at the files, there are a number of letters from me, appealing for monies to cover the considerable six figure sums for which we were liable as a result of having ordered the new parts as soon as possible. This was to try to meet the deadline of supply. We were constantly pressing for these payments and I couldn't help feeling that the FD, Mark Smith, was not as speedy as he might have been, when authorising them.

Being acutely aware of the short time available to us, I was establishing the supply chain and issuing orders to potential suppliers as soon as I had completed the designs of the various components. Because these were all specially made and using high quality materials, Stainless steel, etc and were costly, it was only because of Royle's excellent reputation in the North that we were able to open the accounts with these new suppliers. As it turned out, most of these orders were placed many months before the contract was actually finished and signed in January 2002. Such was my confidence in Stewart and others in BW with whom we were working.

Whilst all this was going on, I learned that our contract with BW was going to benefit by being sponsored by Barrs who are the firm which make 'Ironbru', the well known soft drink which is so popular in Scotland. This company operates on various BW sites and they were planning to have a children's play area at the Falkirk Wheel. I learnt that they had offered £1 million towards the cost of our amphibians. This was good news, since it meant that BW was not going to be exposed to much of the project costs.

As a result of this sponsorship, we were being asked to do various jobs and make changes to the specification. The additional work included painting the amphibians Blue and Orange, Barrs 'Ironbru' house Colours and then, for reasons of confidentiality, they asked us to disguise them, so they were painted again in a different colour and then repainted yet again in the original colours. This occurred a number of times over the period when we were working on the buses.

Whilst the preparatory work was progressing, we were also being advised by Roy Turner who is a naval architect working with Marel, the enterprise agency at Barrow in Furness. Because Her Majesty The Queen and The Duke of Edinburgh were going to be riding in our machine for the grand Opening of the Falkirk Wheel in May 2002, he was obliged to check and ensure the safety of the Royal Family. I presume this was because such a small company was building the craft in which they would be riding on the opening day

I had designed a set of rear access steps and handrails for the Jet-Buses. These would have avoided the right and left hand drive variation for future export vehicles and the location was similar to those used and acceptable on other amphibians. There was now a new requirement however, this was for there to be access at both sides at the front of the buses. Because of the dual purpose nature of amphibians, these doors had to be specially designed. Being well above ground level, it was necessary to build special folding staircases and incorporate access ramps for wheel chairs These were to enable all passengers, initially the Royal visitors, to board our vehicles, either on land or on water and at either side of the vehicles. These were actually quite a challenge to design and costly to make and fit.

Having already finished the Jet-Bus hull designs, which were a monocoque construction, cutting into the hull in two places, involved changes in the structural design to accommodate them.

A serious change in specification, but one which I was able to overcome. Not surprisingly, they added substantially to the time and costs involved. They were not invoiced for, since everybody knew about them and they were built 'in house'. We needed additional stainless steel and other fittings and materials, but it was mainly the cost of the extra work which added cost.

We also were asked to provide spares for the suspension and other important components. For reasons of simplicity, these were complete suspension and transmission assemblies, rather than individual component parts. These alone, added a six figure sum to the extras which were requested.

We were happy to do whatever was required for BW, but it all added quite measurably to the time taken and to the total costs of the contract. Because of our good working relationship with Stewart and the open books arrangements, we did not produce additional estimates or invoices for all this work. From the start, as we were working in an "informal partnership" arrangement with open books, we did not formally advise them in writing listing all the work, although they did, of course, see all the extra work being done and did have copies of all the invoices for materials, fittings, etc. These additional costs and the £50,000 payment towards setting up the little factory, weren't mentioned later on, but all added considerably to the total.

CHAPTER 55:
STARTING PRODUCTION

THE HULL DESIGNS

By the end of 2001 rapid progress had been made, I had finished the Designs and drawings for the hull of the Roylecraft Jet-Bus and was working closely with Alastair Cameron, whose boat design studio is at Shoreham in Sussex. Alastair is one of the most respected boat designers and is recognised internationally for his successful, high speed, offshore craft. He has designed many boats for Customs and Excise, the RNLI and the like. I was also in regular touch with A & M Fabricators who were building the first two of the four hulls for us on the Isle of Wight.

Camper & Nicholson inspecting hulls.

Roylecraft Jet-Bus hulls taking shape.

I chose to have this element of the work for BW carried out on the South coast because my old friend, James Ferrier, recommended the people down there. James had shared my bachelor cottage in Headlam in the 1960's and, like me, was a most enthusiastic sailing man. He was now the Sales Director of the famous yacht builders, Camper and Nicholsons in Gosport.

James's family had been involved with yacht design and construction from the days when the big 'J' class were being built and raced at the turn of the last century. He has devoted his life and career to boats and knew who could be relied upon to do a first class job of the hulls for our Jet-Buses. He was and still is a keen and active supporter of the project and has always done all he can to help me. During the construction of the hulls, he very kindly arranged for Camper & Nicholson's top people to inspect and report on the welding and quality of work as each of the hulls was built. His file reveals the dedication and trouble he took to ensure that the work was done properly. When I visited A&M to check on progress and to make sure my designs were satisfactory I could see that the work was being done well and the reinforced bows had also been welded into place. This was another request made by BW to protect the hulls from supermarket trolleys, old prams and other metal objects and rubbish

Hull ready to float test.

'Bus' hull float testing.

CHAPTER 55: STARTING PRODUCTION

Jet-Bus shell complete.

thrown into canals. The hulls were float tested before delivery to us and you can see the streamlined and pleasing shape of these new hulls. The first of their kind in the world. To this day James and I are in regular contact and his interest hasn't waned, we have a lot of fun and he is a great friend.

SUSPENSION, TRANSMISSION & STEERING

Building the hulls on the Isle of Wight was, in fact, an exception in that I wanted to create employment here in the North and the North East. Accordingly, I made sure that, whenever possible, we appointed local subcontract engineers to manufacture the major components. These included the suspension units, transmission, gearboxes, steering components and many other parts.

When I was progressing and 'pushing' the sale of the MK IV, I had asked the gearbox manufacturers, Websters, to make some special differentials and rear drive shafts for me. Not surprisingly, after initial successful tests with the MK III, the Ford Granada differential we were using, had eventually failed later on

The MK IV differential.

during tests of the MK IV. It had done its job, so I had some special, stronger diff units and drive shafts made for the MK V. I wanted to incorporate inboard disc brakes from the start, but had to make do without them for the early tests. Now that we were nearer to building production units, I was able to specify them to be incorporated in the differentials.

Although we were obliged to fit normal disc brakes on the wheels themselves to satisfy the DTLR requirements, I also wanted to have inboard brakes as well. These would stay dry and would always provide a safe backup when leaving the water. Although made for the lighter 26ft amphibian, with the deadline for Falkirk and with having already incurred six figure costs for components in advance of payments from BW and of signing the contract itself and having these differentials and drive shafts in stock, I decided to risk using these smaller MK V units for the Jet-Buses.

After I had been repeatedly pressing BW for money to pay for the important, new and costly components, some money eventually did come in. In the meantime a schedule of payments and cash flow forecasts were being prepared to help us. We were working and incurring substantial debts on the basis of verbal agreements and didn't see the actual contract itself for the buses, until the beginning of 2002. I knew that Stewart Sim wouldn't let me down.

The contract was being prepared by Eversheds of Leeds for BW. When we eventually saw it, it was a substantial document which consisted of what amounted to three 'books'. Thankfully, Alan Priest was dealing with this all-embracing contract which was based upon an MF2 contract plus a 'book' of amendments and a third 'book', which provided the Patents and IPR as security for BW. This was because we had no money or any other assets to offer as security.

Because BW is a government organisation, is publicly funded and would be paying substantial sums of money for our amphibians, I could understand that the contract was bound to be in their favour to protect them from any irregularities. The details were examined by the legal firm, Dickinson Dees of Newcastle on Tyne, but to my knowledge, we had little or no input into the contract. Knowing that, in any event, we were entirely in BW's hands and in no way, were we able to afford to pay for legal representation to challenge BW before, during or after the work was done, I signed the contract.

Although the CEO and FD were rather negative I had seen how supportive and enthusiastic Stewart Sim and the technical directors were and by then, we had established a good working relationship with the managers and the BW team. I was quite happy to put my trust in them and as we were already fully committed, I was happy to sign it.

THE 'STARTER FACTORY'

The new little factory at Alwent Hall was finished by February and knowing that there were many unemployed engineers in the North East, I only advertised the new jobs in the Teesdale Mercury which is, very much, a local newspaper with a small circulation. Being involved with so many different aspects of the project and with time being a valuable commodity, I didn't want to be inundated with applicants. I wanted to be able to interview each of them personally.

The overall plan was that we would not be manufacturing any of the main components ourselves, the little 'Starter Factory' was, principally, going to be used to assemble the subcontracted parts. Despite this, after 45 years of involvement with manufacturing and assembly work, I was well aware that we needed to have experienced and skilled engineers rather than fitters. This was partly because the work involved would not be a straight forward assembly job. Building up, for the first time, these completely new types of amphibious vehicle with their many new and innovative mechanisms, would require engineering skills..

In the meantime, the new engineers would be using their own knowledge and experience to help with any mountings or modifications which were necessary. In fact, this proved to be a real morale booster, because the new team were then helping to create these exciting new machines themselves. There was also quite a lot of work to do to the actual hulls. We had to make most of the superstructure including the rear 'engine room', the sliding roof and window units, fit the front GRP cab unit to the first bus and then fit the large curved, sloping, high spec front windscreens to this new unit.

As delivered to our 'Starter Factory', there is still much work to be done.

Whilst the 40ft hulls were welded together on Jigs, it is often the case that when drawings are translated into 'the metal' for the first time and when they are the first of their kind, there is always the likelihood that some alterations and minor modifications would be needed. The hulls were very good and well made and I was very pleased with them, but the work involved later on with the sliding windows and the folding staircases proved to be quite challenging and time consuming.

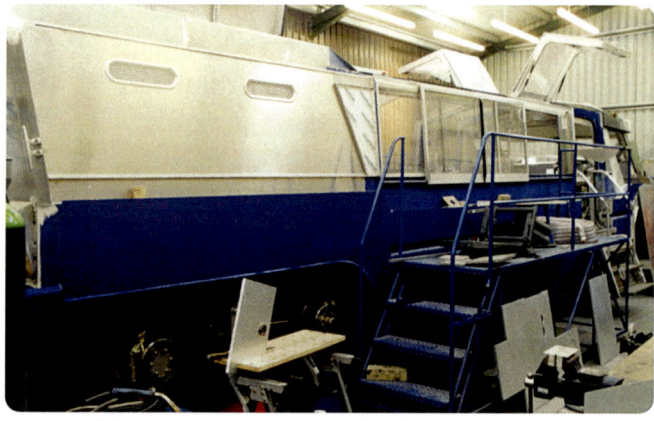

Jet-Bus fabrication work at Nesbit's farm 'Starter Factory'.

There had been no time for me to write out a fully detailed specification and description of the assembly details or of the layout of the components, so I had produced some simple layout drawings and a brief description with which I could induct the new team of men as they were taken on. The plan was that, when we were further advanced, I would then write out and produce a proper handbook with the full specification, operating and servicing procedures.

Taking into consideration the urgency and the space available within the hulls, to begin with, I thought that six men would be the maximum number of men who could work on any one

One of the folding staircases.

Jet-Bus at one time. Nick, my younger son, was an enthusiastic engineer and I was pleased that he was working with me. He had already been employed working on the MK IV and was familiar with my designs and I wanted him to help me to run the factory. He could deal with our subcontractors, chase up supplies and with Allan, our machine shop engineer acting as foreman, they could, between them, oversee and advise on the assembly work and the fitting out of the new Roylecraft Jet-Buses.

Both of them had been employed by Royles, but as this contract was expected to be the start of a continuing manufacturing process, it was agreed that it would be best if they were now taken on and employed by Covelink Marine Ltd. In this way, they were no longer sub-contractors, but full time employees working on, and entirely concerned with the BW contract. After setting up and equipping the convenient little factory, Allan was still also able to utilise the machine shop and all the many and varied facilities at Royle's workshops as well. Between the two companies, we had a wide range of equipment and could use whichever machines were necessary to meet the needs of the Buses.

As soon as I knew when the first of the four hulls was due to arrive from the Isle of Wight, I was able to take on the new members of staff for the new Covelink team. I had already interviewed some of the applicants who had applied for the new jobs in February, so that we would be ready to start work at the factory as soon as the hull had been delivered. I stressed to them how urgently the buses were needed for the contract and they were happy to put in lots of overtime from the outset.

When they joined us, they signed the confidentiality agreement and I inducted them with the drawings and information which I had produced especially for the purpose. When the second hull was delivered, more men were taken on during March. As they became more familiar with the work, we were able to employ three more people in May to further speed up the work. Because of the size of the buses, it became apparent that I could have more than six men working on each vehicle.

The atmosphere at the factory was very good, the new team were enjoying the creative nature of the work and knew that these innovative vehicles presented a great opportunity for the future. Most of the new men soon proved that they were highly skilled and experienced and so I was able to explain how they would, in the fullness of time, probably form the nucleus of a much larger workforce.

With the number of serious, potential buyers coming to us from all over the world, and with the Joint Venture being discussed with BW, I could see that we would need a much larger production facility to satisfy the demand for our machines. The future looked very exciting.

NICK ROYLE

Having mentioned my younger son Nick, I would like to tell you how he came to be involved. He joined me at Staindrop in 1999 and had been working with the men at Royles building the MK IV prototype. He had recently returned from Australia where he had spent a lot of time working with an engineering firm near Perth. With his interests following, in some respects, those of his father, he was essentially a practical man and had acquired a range of useful engineering skills, including welding with sheet aluminium which was especially helpful with our alloy hulls. He was also valuable in the office assisting me with the huge amount of work involved.

As ever, being the 'bosses son', it was assumed by the men that he would have a charmed life and be carried along by his father. He put up with the usual banter, some of it not that pleasant from Allan, but it was not long before people realised that he was no fool, could handle himself and was a valuable member of the staff. He is a conscientious, kind and considerate person who will help anybody he can. I was glad to have him with me.

When the factory opened, he took on the job of procurement, chasing parts and materials and running the office generally. His knowledge of the designs and my requirements for the project at the factory were a great help to me. For reasons which I will explain later, a consultant called Colin McAusland was employed by BW at the factory. Nick learnt a lot from him about forward planning, bar charts and the like, they got on well and I was pleased to see them working together so well. I could see from Nick's office documentation, that he was very organised and did a thoroughly good job of it.

On the practical side, from being a babe in arms, he had grown up throughout his childhood in and out of all kinds of motor cars and then in his teens, spending a lot of time motorcycle trials riding. He enjoyed competing in speed and the tough cross country events, including the arduous 'Scott Trial' and the 'Scottish 7 days' and later on Enduro competitions in the UK and EU. These introduced him to the mechanics involved with motorbikes and not surprisingly, motor vehicles and machinery of all kinds.

Both he and his elder brother, Jeremy, spent many long and happy holidays with us all living on, sailing and driving boats of all kinds in St Mawes in Cornwall, so he was also a most capable man for boat handling. Added to this, he loved working on friend's farms driving tractors and all sorts of agricultural machines. More recently, this breadth of experience included that of handling very large and specialised agricultural machinery when working and manufacturing them in Australia. His knowledge of hydraulics and electrical work was also to prove to be most useful.

All this experience was especially advantageous when we launched the very first, new Roylecraft Amphibious Jet-Bus on the river Tees near Stockton. I was delighted to have Nick there to drive it. Being an entirely new design, 40ft long and packed with innovative controls and many new mechanisms, it needed somebody who had a broad width of experience.

It must be remembered that sitting in the driving seat for the first time, he was immediately confronted with controls for driving on land and water using facilities which, other than in our prototypes, had never previously been incorporated, or used in any boat or road going vehicle before, especially one of this size. Added to this was the fact that there was a BBC film crew and BW representatives with a rescue boat standing by, watching his first ever drive into and out of the water. A cheer went up as he drove back up the ramp after his first test.

Driving it in and out and manoeuvring it on water and driving it on land, he soon proved himself to be very capable Despite having water Jet propulsion, retractable wheels and entirely new controls, he quickly learned how to handle the very first Roylecraft Jet-Bus.

I subsequently had the time and opportunity to drive it myself and I have to say that I was delighted with the 'feel' and its handling. The longer and bigger hull mirrored the cross section of the MK IV and was very stable on water. When I drove it on the road around Croft Motor Racing circuit, I quickly found that it gave the driver a lot of confidence. There were so many unusual features which, when tested, proved to be every bit as good as I could have wished for. The safety features, locking mechanisms, the retractable suspension and unique steering designs which I had developed over the previous 15 years proved themselves to be a great success, although I say it myself.

But, this was in November 2002 so I am ahead of the story again.

CONCENTRATED EFFORTS

According to the contract with British Waterways, the first bus was due to be delivered to Falkirk in March. Our little factory had just opened in February and the assembly of the first hull had just begun in March. The second of the four Hulls had just been delivered and staff were still being taken on in March, so it was abundantly clear to everybody who was closely involved, that we could not possibly meet the deadline.

CHAPTER 55: STARTING PRODUCTION

With the official Royal opening of the Falkirk Wheel fast approaching, in eight to ten weeks time, in late May, It was also clear that the assembly and construction of these completely new, dual purpose machines, was by no means going to be possible in such a short time, let alone be able to test and certificate even one of the buses in the very short intervening period.

It is worth remembering that in July 2001, only nine months before, nothing existed of these machines except an outline drawing on the office wall.

Being forty feet long and eight tonnes in weight and the first of their kind in the world, despite every possible effort having been made, working intensively seven days a week, from July 2001, six months before we even signed the contract in late January 2002, I knew that all the work involved could not possibly have been done more quickly or efficiently. The progress we made was clear evidence of this.

It should also be remembered that I had no salary during this period and was taking big financial risks due to the constant shortage of money. Never the less, by the end of 2001, I had already placed orders worth around £600,000 for components. This was entirely because I wanted to do all I could to express the work in every possible way to please BW and try to meet the deadline dates.

I know that Stewart and the other Technical Directors and managers were well aware of all this which is why they were so supportive. It seems however that there was a weakness in the transfer or acceptance of the information by Stewart Sims co-directors on the main board. Although money was starting to come through the FD, Mark Smith, questioned the costs and seemed to have forgotten that the contract had to be 'front loaded' due to most of the money being needed early on, to pay for the four forty foot hulls and all the costly, high quality, marine components which had to be specially made from scratch.

Naturally, to minimise the production costs for the four buses, I ordered all the parts together in batches of multiples of four of everything and six when it came to wheels, for example. At least, that was in the beginning, before the additional need for spares was considered by BW.

The whole project happened so quickly that spares were only thought about after most of the assemblies had been ordered. Another set of complete assemblies were then immediately ordered, adding a further £150,000 of costs to the contract price as mentioned, working as we were, in great haste in an informal 'partnership' I did not formally notify or invoice BW for any of the increasing number of these additional costs. For the same reason, a margin for profit was not even thought about or added, since I thought that such matters could be dealt with later. There were many more important jobs to be done and my attention was focussed on the vehicles themselves.

Later on, it became clear that the additional work and costs with the folding Staircases and ongoing changes to the specification requested by BW and the MCA, plus the painting and repainting of the hulls requested by Barrs, were conveniently marginalised and ignored by the financial director. We were working flat out at the time, doing whatever we were asked to do in order to meet everybody's requirements as efficiently and quickly as we could. After all, it was the opportunity I had been working towards for fourteen years.

The fact that the factory had just been fitted out and opened in February with new staff continuing to join us in March and April along with the first two hulls and some of the components being delivered at this time, I really did not think it was necessary to formally state the obvious, in writing, that we would not have a bus ready in time for March or for the grand opening in May, as stated in the contract. With the instructions coming from BW and all the regular and ongoing meetings and reports, there was no doubt in my mind, that everybody was well aware of the situation. They knew the risks in time and costs and that we couldn't possibly have done more to meet the terms of the contract.

SABOTAGE

Only a matter of weeks before the work to the Falkirk Wheel was finished and when the Queen and Duke of Edinburgh were due to open it, the Wheel was sabotaged. By some means, the waters in the canal above the Wheel were released and the control room, its computers, electrical controls and mechanisms were flooded by hundreds of tonnes of water cascading down from the top canal. This caused serious difficulties for their engineers and contractors, but remarkably, they did well and managed to overcome them just in time for the opening.

This crisis however, led to a second one, this time for us and our small company, Covelink Marine Ltd. A visit to our factory by Barrs, the sponsors, had been planned prior to the official opening, but with all the commotion, it seems that they had not been informed of the situation and still had the impression that the buses would be ready in time. Perhaps nobody had plucked up the courage to tell them! It was only when the sponsors finally arrived, that they were extremely surprised and very disappointed to find that none of the buses were going to be ready in time.

Not being in direct contact with them at any time, other than having been sent the details of the blue and orange colour scheme by their marketing consultants, I didn't realise that BW had not updated them with progress reports and with the current situation. I was most apologetic to Barrs people and BW when I was criticised for not having finished the buses. It transpired however, that Barrs were not even aware that the factory had only recently been opened and that we were still taking on new members of the staff to build the Jet-Buses.

THE ROYAL OPENING OF THE FALKIRK WHEEL

Her Majesty, The Queen opening the Falkirk Wheel. 24/05/02.

The weather was kind for the Royal opening on 24th May 2002, I was invited along with Alan Priest and there was a good turnout with crowds of people in attendance. Her Majesty the Queen and the Duke of Edinburgh boarded a boat and crossed the now smartly finished basin in front of the Visitor centre, to the central walkway and jetty by the Wheel. This was to have been the point in the proceedings when our Roylecraft Amphibious Jet-Bus would have transported them. It goes without saying that I was bitterly disappointed about this, but knew that I could not have worked harder or any longer hours than I had done during the last ten months. To cap it all, the Director for Scotland, Jim Stirling, whom I had not met before, came up to us and told us how badly we had let him and everybody in BW down.

I already felt dreadful, but now, deep down inside, I was frustrated and extremely angry. Here was a man in a most senior position of a national company with, seemingly, no comprehension whatsoever of what we had achieved in the last nine months, nor of the nature, extent or complexity of the new technology which we were creating and all at extremely low cost. Admittedly, as mentioned, we had signed a contract, but only four months earlier and after so many months with so many meetings and visits by his staff in Scotland and with many other people from BW in Watford, discussing and explaining every aspect involved, he must have known that we couldn't possibly have done more to try to please them.

Compared to BW employing overall, perhaps 2000 people, we were a tiny company with only three employees until three months earlier and were even now, just building up to sixteen staff, often with a slow and limited supply of funds and taking big financial risks.

Once again, it seemed that the BW technical directors and managers, with whom we were working so closely and who understood precisely what the situation was, were being ignored or were not respected by some members of the Main Board. Most of the BW people couldn't do enough to encourage us and help us achieve success, these others seemed to be happy to criticise and to ignore our intensive efforts and our total dedication the project. One which ultimately, would be the basis of a new industry which could export High Value goods worth £500 million a year and generate profits for both our companies.

At that time, I will never forget the astonishment on the face of Dr Ann Fletcher, the lady who was in charge of the Harrier Jump Jet project, when she found out that our entire development programme had only cost, at that stage, around £2.5 million. Alright, so we were not building innovative aircraft like the Harrier Jump-Jet, but she pointed out that even when it had been built and was flying, the development costs alone, were still £8 million. Whereas, I was happy to know that Stewart could get up to £500,000 if it was found to be necessary.

CHAPTER 56:
BW CONTRACT CONTINUES AFTER WHEEL OPENS

The work of building the first two jet-buses continued after The Queen and the Duke of Edinburgh had officially opened the Falkirk Wheel in May 2002. Importantly, it was now clear that the sponsors for the Jet-Buses, Barrs, had not been aware that we had just opened the little Starter factory, or of the amount of work involved for us to build these new vehicles. I was pleased to hear that they thought that a more realistic launch date would be "in the spring of 2003". This gave me more hope.

The benefit of us now having met Barrs People during their visit, was that they were now aware of the facts and could understand why 'their' Jet-Buses could not have been built in time for the Royal Opening.

I couldn't know what was going on in BW's boardroom, but I could see that key information was not being transmitted to those who, in this case, were going to be providing the bulk of the money, £1 million, to pay for the new amphibious buses. It was a relief for me to know that the sponsors were now in the picture and were content to have the buses after we had the time to build and test them.

I was also relieved to see that Scotland's chief engineer, George Ballinger, who was in charge of the Falkirk Wheel development, also refers in his correspondence, to the fact that the contract money alone may not be sufficient to cover any unknown costs and development work once the buses had been finished and tested. This was comforting and supported Stewart Sims earlier remarks when he said that there were monies of up to £500,000 available if they were necessary.

I didn't anticipate that we would need much money for development, as most of the components were now being made to proper production standards rather than as parts made purely to test design principles. There would, of course, be the additional costs for the extra work, spares etc, so there would be some more monies needed for these later on, probably around £250,000, but as yet, these hadn't been costed and were not 'development costs', they were additional items added to the contract.

With the benefit of the ongoing meetings, the BW people were getting to know us well and with the Informal partnership and open books arrangement, they could see that everything was in order and the costs were genuine. They had confidence in us and quite rightly so.

I was relieved that we were able to press on after the Royal event and was thrilled that we were making such good progress with the first two buses coming together so well. I was happy to continue working seven days a week and, following the signature on the contract in late January, I was able to pay a salary to Alan Priest and for the first time, also draw one myself. With the additional men taken on in May, everybody at the little factory continued to put in as much overtime as possible and the atmosphere was very positive.

Mark Smith, the Financial Director of BW however, was still not happy. Some money was coming through, but he continued to question the costs generally, now it was not only the costs of the 'front loading' of the components, he seemed to believe, incredibly, that we should be operating some sort of a 'just in time' system for the supply of parts.

I believe that he had previously worked for Marks and Spencers which, no doubt, has established facilities for bulk buying of low cost items from large, well established suppliers with a draw down facility. Under the circumstances prevailing, he was either being unrealistic and really didn't understand what he was dealing with, or he was trying to undermine our handling of the project and trying to discredit us.

The simple fact was that my years of experience with Royles Restoration work necessitated the supply of small numbers of specially made components. I was therefore, acutely aware of the possible delays in the supply of the unique suspension and steering components from the sub-contractors for the

Jet-Buses. We were trying to meet the BW deadline which was virtually impossible, but doing our utmost to supply as soon as possible anyway.

It would have been pointless asking our new suppliers to provide the parts we needed, one or two at a time. We weren't setting up a production line and needed them all desperately quickly. We had to pay for them all at once anyway, as we had no history or leverage with them.

It was important that our suppliers knew that the future potential for new business was going to be worthwhile and profitable for them, especially with every order being for unique and costly parts. Even an order for four sets (later it was five sets, including for spares) was still at a very low level of batch production, but the reduction in price, even for these few, was never the less substantial, when compared to the cost of one-offs. It was also essential that we obtained very competitive prices, even though we could only hint, but not promise any future business at this stage.

As soon as I had finished the drawings, my main concern was to have the new components made as soon as possible, even though I didn't have the money to pay for them, or the security of a signed contract when I was actually placing the orders. Such was my confidence in the Operations Director Stewart Sim and with everybody else in the BW team with whom we were working. They were dedicated and good 'company men' and they would do all they could to help the progress. Back at Watford, Ken Butcher kept a very close eye on procurement, at the same time keeping a tight rein on costs and the work in hand. With all this backup, there was absolutely no need or reason for the FD to be so doubtful about everything.

It is my view that he had no liking for innovative projects or for people like me, who took risks with new ideas and technologies. I don't think that he or the CEO wanted to have any relationship with a tiny company like ours, one with minimal clerical and management staff. A company which even had difficulty in meeting the ongoing demands of his various departments when asking for written reports, costings and risk assessments.

From the outset, it was obvious that the FD was not enthusiastic about the project. He seemed to have no idea that our costs had been and still were, a fraction of those normally needed, in any similar industry, to produce such advanced, complex and large machines. He also gave us no credit for our previous technical achievements, or having been able to design, open accounts and set up a supply chain, all in six months, to build our entirely new forty foot amphibious craft.

It should be remembered that the 1990 recession had affected the North East for ten years and there were over 240 empty factories in this area. As a result, new companies, especially innovative ones, had to prove themselves to each sub-contract supplier before they would do such costly and specialised work. We had, therefore, initially traded on Royles good name, whose reputation as a reliable and honest company, was most helpful.

SAVINGS AND SUPPLIES.

Whenever I tried to explain to the FD, at meetings, that BW was benefitting from the extremely low R&D costs and that the Jet-Buses were not expensive, there was usually a big intake of breath. Either he was determined to discredit us in any way he could, which seemed likely, or he genuinely had no comprehension of what was involved. For those who are not familiar with R&D and engineering costs, especially in the UK, the following example will give you some idea of the difference between manufacturers and then one-off and five-off specially engineered products, like gearboxes for example.

After fifteen years of research exploring the market and discussing my specific requirements with the various manufacturers of existing units, I knew that the gearboxes would have to be specially made. The big manufacturers like ZF and Allison were keen to help, but they wanted orders for hundreds of them worth tens of thousands of pounds before they would even consider making special boxes. I could see why previous amphibious vehicle builders had used 'off the shelf', unsuitable gearboxes. Even the cost of these standard units was around £12,000 to £14,000 each. These are of course good, tried and tested boxes, but still unsuitable for properly designed amphibians.

Exploring the possibilities for some years, I had been in discussion with Peter Sellers, (yes, a memorable name!), Peter is a design engineer and works with Webster Drives of Bolton. He told me that they were happy to make small numbers of special gearboxes, so we had been exploring the implications and costs associated with what I wanted, he knew that they had to be fit for purpose. I often quoted the old song which had been adopted by Eric Broadley when he was building his Lola racing cars, it was "Whatever Lola wants, Lola gets". It had to be the same with my amphibians, if they were to be a success.

With Allan having built our own experimental gearboxes and drive units in our machine shop, we had tested each of them in the prototypes, and had learnt from these, so when the order from BW came, we knew what was needed, including a reverse drive to the water-jet. I wanted this facility to enable the driver to be able to back-flush it, when flotsam or jetsam restricted the water-jet intake. To do this, Websters suggested a separate hydraulic motor which they could also use as a slow 'creep drive' facility. As gearbox specialists, I relied upon their ideas for this, so was happy to let them incorporate this motor.

The cost of each of these special units, even when made only as a batch of five, was less than the standard ZF and Allison boxes, but there were risks. Although made with light alloy castings and more refined gears than ours, there were elements which were still untried and would need to be tested.

In April- May 2002, the technical Directors were obviously confident about our project and of the future benefits of our technology to BW. As well as supplying the Jet-Buses, we were also in discussions with Ian White, BW's Regional Director in Leeds. Ian was looking into the possibility of us supplying a twelve metre amphibious workboat. He was an experienced engineer, had been working with BW for many years and was well aware of our activities at the little factory. He was obviously confident of our technology and capabilities and I set about designing an amphibian which was to be equipped to carry out various jobs around the canal system.

This workboat was to be similar to our MK IV but even bigger than the planned MK V. Its equipment was to include side mounted small cranes for lifting materials, rubbish and the occasional dead body out of the rivers and canals. Sometimes, large animals would fall into the water and were very difficult to retrieve, so this vehicle would be an all round general purpose machine. I produced some designs and outline drawings for him and was pleased that BW were looking ahead to develop new amphibious craft along with the buses.

As the spring progressed towards summer we were at last, receiving steady payments of around £100,000 each month. This helped us to continue to make good progress at the little factory. Meanwhile, in Scotland, improvements were being planned and made to the ramps and access roads to the canal above the Falkirk Wheel site.

After leaving the gondolas, the plan was that the amphibious Jet-Buses would travel along the high aqueduct canal, through a tunnel and into a basin where the Amphibians could enter or leave the canal and then travel by road to or from the visitor centre. This was via the narrow bridge with tight corners mentioned earlier. They were improving the gradients up to the road bridge and providing a better access into the basin. Despite the FD's negativity, the indications were that the prospects for the entire project with BW were good.

BIG MARKET POTENTIAL

Negotiations were ongoing with Peter Wear about our proposed Joint Venture with BW. By now, BW were finding out for themselves that the market potential of Roylecraft was very good indeed. They had seen a positive response from a number of canal operators around the world, one of them being the director of the Swedish Canal systems whom I also spoke to at the Royal opening, he wanted twenty of our buses for the Gotha Canal, so this alone represented some millions of pounds.

Prior to BW's involvement, during Covelink's R&D period, my research with various organisations, large and small around the world, had re-enforced my confidence in the size of the market. I knew that the demand for our machines was going to make all our investment in time, effort and money, most worth-while and be the foundation of a large new industry. I was more confident that BW could also now see that there was little doubt that Roylecraft Amphibians were going to be a great success. This gave me much hope that our future Joint

Venture with them would be the basis of a whole new industry.

THE AGE OLD PROBLEMS BEGIN

I became increasingly worried during June and July however, that the situation seemed to be developing with BW, one which I had previously seen when discussing JV's with other large commercial organisations. This was when Peter Wear's expectations of BW's share of the equity in the Joint Venture increased to the point when it was completely out of proportion to the investments and costs already involved in the project.

He became more demanding as time passed and it was clear that the age old situation was developing where the big powerful company flexes its muscles and overrides that of the financially weak little innovating company. It was developing into the classic case of 'power corrupts'. It also worried me that Peter Wear was working under Mark Smith, the FD who had little respect for me or the project.

As you know, I had hoped to avoid this dreadful predicament, because BW was a government controlled organisation (Defra) and wouldn't allow unfair or malpractice of any kind to influence dealings of this sort. After all, it was firm Government policy to support SME enterprise. I had seen how helpful and considerate Stewart Sim was being and was confident that the other directors of BW would continue to treat us fairly and respect our small size and all the work and money which we had put in to create these new vehicles. This confidence was backed up by the good working relationship which had developed with so many of the people I was dealing with in BW. This had given me great comfort, not only with Stewart who was, after all, the Operations Director, but also with a number of other directors, executives and engineers.

Despite good progress being made with the buses and the fact that the project costs were well below the contracted sum, even disregarding all the additional work instructed by BW, and that constant diligence on costs was being made by BW, It seemed that there was a tightening of the screws by all concerned. Although many BW personnel had an intimate knowledge of every aspect of our project due to frequent visits and the open books relationship, never the less, during June and July, there was a noticeable change in emphasis. The positive approach and helpful support for Covelink seemed to disappear and was replaced with a negative attitude which quickly became widespread. Everybody seemed to be affected from Watford up to Falkirk. It must have been orchestrated by the main board.

From the outset, Mark Smith had openly shown his dislike for us at our very first meeting with him and the CEO Robin Evans at Watford. Without any knowledge of Roylecraft or its technology, he said that our estimated price of £262,000 was expensive. We could already see that he was against the project, so thought that he 'would say that wouldn't he'. On the other side of the coin, like most people who are not technical or experienced in the cost of high quality, specialised, advanced machines, Smith may have compared the cost to that of a standard bus, truck or possibly even a Canal Long Boat, in BW's case. Vehicles and boats which are not at all comparable and are not as costly.

I argued strongly that the price quoted was, in fact, low for marine vehicles such as those which we were building. Military machines which were not so refined, were three times this price at around £800,000 each. Even Alan Gibbs little Aquada car had cost a total of 60 £million to develop and produce, according to the press in 2002, when it first appeared in London.

After the first meeting with the CEO and FD, the order for our Jet-Buses was confirmed which clearly indicated that Stewart Sim had the authority and that the price was acceptable.

Note: With Roylecraft being the first of their kind in the World, and the most advanced, there are actually, no machines with which the FD was able to compare prices. Later, I found that the occasional one-off, newly built amphibians which are not as advanced or comparable, were costing £350,000 each. These were built out of military components. They were slow and couldn't even drive on the public highway, but were commercially viable. It was this price which I was to settle on as being both realistic and profitable, even when hand built. It is at this price that currently, at the time of writing, I have potential global orders worth around £550 million.

BLATANT ABUSE OF POWER

There was a noticeable increase in BW's demand for Business Plans, analysis and cost projections along with all manner of technical enquiries and a requirement for other detailed information not previously asked for. This was despite Ken Butcher, their National Procurement Manager, being well on top of all costs and already having endless pages of detailed information on file. They also now wanted detailed breakdowns and estimates of potential shortfalls in the contract price, even though their payments to us were still well behind the actual costs.

It soon became clear that they were ignoring and taking no account of all the additional work which we had done to meet BW's requirements and instructions. There were hundreds of hours work to make the structural design changes, the additional doors, folding staircases for the Royal Opening, there was also the £150,000 additional costs for spares, the frequent covering and repainting of the sponsors colour scheme, the reinforced bow and the ongoing MCA and DTLR certification requirements, not to mention the £50,000 which Stewart had helpfully provided to us to help set up the Factory, a sum which the FD was now including as part of the contract price.

With all the good progress we were making, the timing of all this and the upset being caused, didn't make sense. Looking back, with the benefit of hindsight, they were doing it before any of the buses had been finished and tested. We were in a weak, vulnerable position. There was no mention of the Barrs million pound sponsorship, or the £500,000 which Stewart had said would be available if we needed any of it for later development costs.

Whether it was political, personal or simply a means to enable BW to acquire the assets for the JV for much less than they were worth, I will never know, probably all three. One thing for sure, was that the FD was entirely confident that he had the whip hand. With the benefit of the open books and informal partnership arrangements, he knew that we had no money. He also knew that we had substantial financial liabilities to our suppliers, ironically, entirely for BW's own benefit, and with me having, openly put my faith and trust in his company, he knew only too well, that we were entirely reliant upon BW for the future security of the company and our technology.

He had no concern at all for the fact that we had devoted every penny we could raise and spent every available hour creating our technology for fifteen years at the time, and everybody knew that we couldn't have done more to please BW and make a success of the project in every possible respect.

On top of all this, with around £500,000 still due on the contract, Smith now demanded that we raise money from outside sources to make up for any possible theoretical 'shortfall'. Being beholden to BW for everything from the outset, I had no choice, but to continue to be co-operative and helpful, despite being extremely angry and upset.

PILING ON THE PRESSURE

Even more cruel and worrying, not satisfied with our already extremely weak financial position, BW began to focus upon and quote the contract itself and our failure to meet the delivery dates and supply any finished buses for March and May. It had been abundantly clear to all concerned and everybody knew, when the contract was signed only six months earlier, in late January 2002, that it was impossible for us to manufacture, let alone test and certificate even just one of the buses, the **same month we opened the starter factory**, or even supply a Jet-Bus two months later, in May, in time for the opening.

Despite Stewart Sim's ssurances that further monies were available, they had us over a barrel in every possible way and I had trusted them, yet they were still piling on the pressure. Under the circumstances, it was a most dreadful exhibition of contrived, unjust and unnecessary corporate malpractice.

CONTRACT COSTS AND CASH FLOW

Although Payment of monies amounting to around £100,000 were being made to Covelink, approximately monthly, this covered the wages and overheads, but was still not sufficient to cover all the costs incurred entirely on BW's behalf, including those of all the components and the additional extra work which they had instructed.

CHAPTER 56: BW CONTRACT CONTINUES AFTER WHEEL OPENS

The original contract for four Jet Buses at £262,000 each, was worth £1,048 million. To this figure however, must be added the additional costs mentioned above. Conservatively, including these, the total contract value would be around £1.3 million if not more. There was also the £50,000 which BW had provided to help us set up the factory which should have been outside the contract, but was obviously now being included as part of it. The total amounts actually paid by BW so far, came to approximately £800,000 which was well below the sum due and even then, we had been making excellent progress.

Altogether, Instead of the supportive and helpful atmosphere which had prevailed, our position was now being made extremely uncomfortable. There were obvious underlying reasons for this change. All those who had been so helpful and positive, seemed to 'harden up'.

I wrote to Stewart Sim in early July expressing my serious concerns about how I was under pressure to hand over control of Covelink to BW in the Joint Venture. I explained that it would be entirely counter-productive for BW if Peter Wear went all out to maximise BW's equity in the JV for a relatively small sum of money, which was, I believe, £140,000. This entirely unsatisfactory sum of money was a true indication of the power which BW believed they had over me and our little company.

Worse still, BW's idea was that this money would also be used to cover the 'shortfall' in the contract, which of course, didn't really exist anyway, there was no shortfall. I pointed out to Stewart Sim that Covelink's shareholders, quite rightly, insisted upon us retaining at least 51% for the £2.5 million invested at that time and for the 15 years of work. Not to mention all the global Patents which alone had cost in excess of £200,000 with me creating them at no cost to the company.

As with the legal fiasco following Royles successful defence in the High Court, it never ceases to amaze me how these people in positions of power and trust, are not only unprincipled in the extreme, they seem to have no knowledge of psychology. They expect to get away with their obvious malpractice and seem to think that the people like me, whom they are abusing, will simply bow down and let them carry on, indefinitely, exploiting us for their own financial gain.

THE PROJECT IS UNDERMINED

Regrettably, I received no reply to my letter to Stewart Sim, so later on, I wrote to him once more, but again there was no reply. It became clear that Stewart had left the company and Mark Smith had taken direct and complete control of the project.

This was after Stewart had given a great many years of dedicated service to the company. I had seen for myself, that he was conscientious and a true company man. I was never given any reason for the unexpected departure of this senior board director with whom I was working. It looked very much to me that Mark Smith was behind it and had his own personal axe to grind. He did not care (or know?) that BW was losing the key figure who understood innovation and our new technology and would have ensured the success of the contract.

After working with Stewart for over twelve months, he had a firm grasp of the nature of Roylecraft designs and had given me various assurances which might no longer be recognised but which, with his help and guidance, BW would have seen huge benefits from our technology, both operationally and financially. There was mutual trust which I could now see would never exist with somebody like Mark Smith.

It rapidly became clear that here was a man who didn't really know who or what he was taking control of. He had no real knowledge of our technology or of my desire to succeed and was prepared to risk disrupting a cost effective and important contract, for the sake of an ill-conceived and corrupt scheme.

I often wonder what those BW people, with whom I had been working so well, were told to make them change their minds about me and the contract. They were good company people and would obviously follow the company policy, but their attitude towards me and the project had so obviously and completely been changed that, whatever it was, it must have been pretty serious. If any of them should happen to read this book, I would be pleased to hear from them. Because, as in the legal case, I was left very much in the dark.

GOVERNMENT AGENTS GANGING UP

Back to the story. Peter Wear obviously now felt

confident that he couldn't fail to take control of the JV. He knew that he was 'negotiating' from a position of BW's hugely superior power and strength and with the benefit of the CEO, Robin Evans and Mark Smith, the Financial Director, behind him and with the benefit of all our confidential company information, he was in the driving seat.

Due to BW's slow payments and our financially weak situation, I was again trying to raise money, this time, to complete BW's contract. Along with many other government and funding organisations, I asked Nesta for funding. I knew that their chairman, Lord Puttnam, was working hard to help us in any way he could. Later on, I was dealing with Mark White who assured me that Nesta's aim was to continue their support for Covelink and was helpful. He had joined them as the Director of Invention and Innovation.

During the summer of 2002 however, their position had obviously changed. It turned out that the £140,000 which BW was planning to use to take control and the majority shareholding of our company, Covelink, via the Joint Venture, was being provided to them by Nesta. Instead of helping us, one of their own awardees, they were now supporting colleagues in another government organisation. One which was trying to deprive the inventor and his shareholders of most of the benefits of their project for a fraction of the £2.5 million invested, not to mention its very considerable potential worth.

My company's position was now being even further compromised, by BW introducing Nesta into the negotiations on their side. We had lost another source of funding which would actually, have helped BW.

It soon became apparent that the more organisations which I approached for funding, the worse our situation became. This was especially so if they had a link with government. Not surprisingly, each would say they were trying to help us but, as ever, they knew exactly who had the power and where the money lay and it certainly wasn't in my little company. We were lambs to the slaughter.

There could now be little doubt that BW were no longer working with Covelink in any sort 'partnership'. An arrangement which Mark Smith now completely denied had ever existed, despite there being written references to it by BW themselves, in their own correspondence and a certificate. Like the Legal case, the longer it all went on, the more dishonest they had to be to try to cover their backs.

British Waterways Partners Certificate.

BW were now gradually exerting all the forces which any large organisation with 2000 employees can so easily bring to bear on a company with a core management of only three people, 14 shop floor engineers and no money.

It was precisely the scenario which I had tried, so hard, to avoid.

THE COUP DE GRACE

In spite of many proposals and lengthy diplomatic letters which I sent to BW's Directors in order to try save the Project and the JV, the position was finally made clear in August 2002, when we were informed by Mark Smith that **BW would make no further payments to Covelink.**

The total which had been paid at this stage by BW was £900,000 and they were well aware that this was insufficient to cover even the basic cost of the ongoing contract. This was confirmed by their own National Procurement Manager, Ken Butcher, who stated that substantial sums were still due for payment he calculated that £154,000 was still owing under the original contracted sum. This sum did not, of course, include the many additional costs for work and additional components which BW had instructed, but we had not invoiced and therefore, in reality, we would be owed around £400,000 for the actual costs involved with the contract.

Under it's terms, if Covelink became insolvent and failed to supply the buses, then the buses, associated hardware, the drawings, patents and IPR would belong to BW.

CORPORATE MALPRACTICE

It was now obvious that Mark Smith, presumably with Board approval, had conceived a scheme to bankrupt our successful, but very small R&D company. This was being done by starving us of money before any buses had been completed, tested or delivered and when we were exposed to creditors for the parts and materials which were bought for BW. With the 'removal' of Stewart Sim, he had not only removed the man who would have ensured the success of the project, but he also had eliminated the promises of additional financial support which Stewart had assured us would be available, if needed.

Speaking on the Telephone to Mark Smith soon after this was made known and that the funding from Nesta was also not going to be made available to us 'for some time'. He made it clear that, with no income, he confidently expected me to have no choice, but to close down the little factory straight away, liquidate Covelink Marine Ltd and immediately transfer the assets to BW.

Apparently he was already making arrangements to have the buses taken away from our starter factory and delivered down to Newark on Trent where BW had their own boatbuilding and general workshops.

So, only six months after opening the 'starter' factory, with all going well and with their sponsors in place, BW were trying to close it all down. A truly dreadful and malicious plan.

Here was the Financial Director of a large, national government organisation, an accountant with little or no practical experience or knowledge of our amphibious technology, prepared to commit fraud and confidently expecting to get away with it. Mark Smith was obviously ambitious and by bankrupting our R&D company, he would, seemingly, be able to kill five birds with one stone:

- He would be able to grab Covelinks assets for BW;
- Remove Stewart Sim from the board;
- Rid himself of me and presumably;
- Use Barrs sponsorship money to pay BW's own engineers to finish the buses.
- Importantly take all the future multi-million pound business entirely for BW's benefit;

Saving money and scoring points all round. What a clever and cunning scheme it was.

BW's SCHEME DOESN'T GO TO PLAN

Mark Smith and presumably the main board in due course, would obviously be shocked when, during the same telephone call, I told him that I had no intention of closing the little 'starter' factory and giving BW the assets. That was the last thing I was planning to do. I was going to finish the buses for BW and complete the contract, with or without their money.

Being an accountant and steeped in big company practice with a secure income, I imagine that he could not begin to contemplate such a response to what he believed would be his master stroke. He obviously had no conception of the personal dedication and huge input needed to create a new technology on this scale and with only the bare minimum of money. In some respects, my determination to carry on was a repeat of the events following the High Court case.

It is remarkable that here I was again, dealing with a highly paid executive in a large and powerful organisation. One who was unable to comprehend what fifteen years of work means to somebody who has designed, and in this case, has also built and tested the most technically advanced Amphibious vehicles in the World. (Whenever I say this, I feel uncomfortable, but I do believe it to be true.) It is also especially relevant, as in the legal case, when that person has risked most of his own money to achieve success and has not received a salary for most of the time.

People like Mark Smith cannot begin to understand personal commitment on this scale or ever think that I would carry on without BW's money. A very serious challenge, yes, especially now having sixteen staff to pay with no income. Not to mention some of the high quality stainless steel and other costly components still to pay for. Being so near to success, it had to be a risk worth taking. Having already spent 15 years developing our amphibians without any formal or guaranteed source of income, I was no stranger to difficult situations like this. Although now, with a small factory to support, it was certainly going to be a major challenge!

The important fact was that I had retained control of the project and still had my R&D company. I still had a chance, although admittedly, it was a slim one.

I finished the conversation by confirming to the FD that I would do all I could to keep the factory running and complete the BW contract and supply the buses, with or without the help of British Waterways. Mark Smith was silent.

Somebody near to him once confided in me that he thought that Smith was a "cold fish" and it is probably an apt description!

CHAPTER 57:
AUTUMN 2002. HERE WE GO AGAIN

Although there are always stories of fraud and corruption, I thought that much of it was exaggerated and that if I continued to be straight forward and open in my dealings, then I should be OK. I also thought that if I worked to the highest standards and used first class materials and adhered to the basic principle of honesty, then people would value this and be pleased to work with me. By behaving like this, I always felt comfortable and confident should there be any problems.

For many years, this seemed to be the right way forward. There were instances when people took advantage of this, but the extraordinary outcome of our most successful defence after the intensive High Court hearing in London however, and the recent developments with British Waterways, were real eye-openers!

Firstly in 1996, I found it difficult to believe that my friend and solicitor, 'Nimble', would not only go so far as to completely ignore his promise to me, but would also be in Contempt of Court by ignoring the Orders of a High Court Judge and then commit legal fraud. You will remember that this was after the four week hearing and the most thorough examination, when our honesty and diligence were proved beyond any doubt. The Judge awarded us sums worth over £70,000 for the work we had done, including interest and also with the benefit of costs. Many people were astonished, including the legal ombudsman, when the award was taken by our own solicitor, 'Nimble', especially when ample money was available in court and from the Swedish millionaire to pay to pay all the awards, costs and interest, later losing and destroying the files with evidence to prove it (or so he thought!)

You may remember from the earlier chapters, that the millionaire brought the action to try to avoid paying us for our work to one of his Rolls Royce motor cars. We received no money after the hearing. I was told that our award money was used to pay the opposing millionaire's lawyer's costs after he told them that they wouldn't be paid if they lost the case. By doing this, my solicitors reversed the judgement.

Now I was seeing another serious example of corruption. This time by the Financial Director of a government organisation, British Waterways. What was so surprising to me, was the blatant and obvious way in which these people did it. This is a clear indication of their confidence in the amount of power they wield and in the protection afforded to them by their colleagues. It seems to me that, when it comes to large sums of money and business, honesty is of little value.

The factor common to both of the above events and another legal matter described earlier in the book, is that people with power are quite happy and prepared to use it dishonestly.

The earlier case was when my other motor company, Royle Cars Ltd was forced to close down by another solicitor. Once again, the man was using his legal knowledge to take advantage of other innocent parties in spite of the fact that they had no liability to him. Again, he completely misjudged the situation, and still believing that he should be paid for his misguided legal action, then went on to commit malicious acts which resulted in the loss of my sales company and the bankruptcy of another person who, like me, did not have the money to protect himself.

At home, with the BW affair, sleepless nights again became the norm. Fortunately I had recovered after all my medical operations and as ever, Jo-Jo did all she could to support me through these difficult times, but she was naturally worried about it all. With the benefit of the BW contract, we had enjoyed the luxury of me having a salary (£35,000 per anum) for a few months, the first time since Covelink Marine Ltd was established in 1988. Sadly, we were soon back to having to manage again without one. There is no point in drawing a salary when I was continuing to put all the money I had and could raise, into the project.

Although it was now six years since we won our case in the High Court, I was continuing to battle with every legal authority to try to get the money awarded to us. I had managed to recoup nearly £33.000 through the efforts of

Hay and Kilner, solicitors in Newcastle. This sum still remained guaranteed to the court, but being paid seven years after the original debt in 1993 four years after the hearing, it didn't even cover the ongoing interest costs which we also had been awarded by the High Court judge.

The dreadful story of this legal fraud is told elsewhere in this book and I continue to press the legal powers for justice to this day. I am still writing to Parliament, to every legal minister known to me and to every possible authority, including the Royal family and estimate that I have now sent out over 2800 letters! Legal corruption is part of a national scandal on a scale which resulted in losses for the tens of thousands of British citizens who have no independent complaints organisation to turn to. It is known to Parliament, but nobody will do anything about it because it affects our powerful legal institutions.

Royles never fully recovered after this loss and as I write, in 2010, in spite of still having a full order book, I have now been obliged to close down David.A.C.Royle & Co Ltd after 35 years of successful work with, as you will have seen, hundreds of specialist motor cars restored.

COVELINK & ROYLES

Few people realised the very careful market research and planning which lay behind the Amphibious Project. They did not understand how it was my main hope for the future security of both companies or that it has such a huge potential for considerable profits with what I now know to be its potential for 2500 new jobs with an annual turnover of around £500 million exports, and these are conservative figures.

Another problem in 2002 was that three of my good team of men at the restoration workshops left me after many years of service and set up on their own in nearby Barnard Castle.

In 1996 they had been called as witnesses for Royles in the High Court and had seen our eminently successful defence and knew that the Judges Orders had been ignored leaving us with major debts to the banks etc. This worried them as it was seriously affecting the profitability of the workshops and they had already seen Royles Cars Ltd closed down by another misguided solicitor.

Despite all this and the ongoing recession, using my own personal resources, I had managed to maintain their wages and also kept the amphibious project going. This was done by mortgaging the house and borrowing money from friends and elsewhere. The North East always suffers worse and longer than the South when the economy is weak and in recessions.

The men leaving Royles was sparked off by a customer of ours from Luxemburg who wanted me to reduce our costs for him. We had restored his vintage Delage motor car and Dick had built and fitted a special, one off body which I had designed for the man. Altogether it had cost him, from memory, around £70,000, not a high cost for a job like this, in fact lower than some. I explained that we could not charge him at a lower hourly rate despite him offering us five more vehicles which he said he wanted to have restored. I told him that this was because our margin was already less than 10%, which was true. He obviously wouldn't have believed the fact that, as it was, I had not been able to draw a salary from Royles for some years.

Apparently, he had travelled over and met Dick one weekend and offered him the five restoration jobs if he would leave Royles and set up on his own and do the work at a lower cost. So much for trading with the EU! This resulted in Dick having the confidence to create a new business in 2002. It is a free world of course, but I was not at all happy about this, having spent 28 years, working with him and training him to work on vintage cars. Shortly after leaving, he persuaded two more of our long served staff to join him.

After everything else, this was a great disappointment to me. They were all good men and talented and had worked with me for years. I had shown them how to restore and build period coachwork and given them the opportunity to develop these specialised skills. Furthermore, I had maintained their jobs at considerable personal cost during the 1990's recession and I felt badly let down. Subsequently, I gathered that the EU customer did not give them the five cars to restore as promised after all, but they carried on and are still working now, with almost all of Royles staff.

DR FUNDING BUT BW PLOTTING

Returning to the British Waterways story. After the thrill of achieving our first order and having made such marvellous progress in just a few months after the very first meeting, it was now just over six months since signing the contract that the dubious activities intensified. I could hardly believe that I was again, watching a most successful process being undermined by one or two corrupt people. It was incredible that such a hugely valuable and worthwhile development was being put into jeopardy without any good or justifiable reason.

Once again, wealthy and powerful individuals believed that they could make substantial financial gains at our expense. They were content to deprive those who had worked for many years to create a worthwhile new form of transport, by misusing their power over a few devoted people. They would trample on anybody to achieve their aims. It was dreadful.

After 8 years of financial difficulty with the restoration company and at the same time 15 years of financial struggles with no regular source of income to design, build and develop our new amphibious vehicle technology, I was now faced with a much more serious challenge. Instead of the flexibility of having just one or two men to pay for doing Covelink's work, as part of the team in Royles workshops, I now also had a separate, small factory to run and maintain. Not only that, but also the wages of sixteen full time staff to find every week and very costly components to pay for. The target was £25,000 per week. All this with no income, was quite a challenge, I needed money ASAP, so I set about raising this money from wherever I could get it!

I had already cashed my pension fund and sold my 3 litre Lagonda. I had bought this fine, vintage sports touring car when I was 21, spent two years restoring it and had 34 enjoyable years of fun and fast, reliable motoring.

I had also sold my lovely old sailing boat 'Meriva', This was a boat which I had dreamed about from childhood. She was to the designs of Holman and Pye, was 43 feet overall with a counter stern and built by Tucker Brown of fine Mahogany and Pitch pine in 1967. She displaced 13 tonnes and sailed like a dream.

These assets had already gone, so once again, I stopped drawing a salary, as did Alan Priest, I mortgaged our house again, the Old Vicarage. The deeds reminded me of an old, green, pre-war motor car log book, dog-eared with use! This time I also mortgaged the workshops in Staindrop as well.

You may remember that I had previously mortgaged the house to keep Royles going after the legal fiasco, but fortunately I had been able to repay this and another loan a few years later. I say 'fortunately', but this was out of money left to me from my mother's estate. My dear mother, Dorothy, had sadly died in the year 2000 from MRSA which was becoming so prevalent at this time and had occurred after an operation. This was following a fall when she broke her hip in her 90th year.

My mother was always full of fun and was still joking to very near the end. Like the rest of our family, she was independent and a pretty determined person. She had run our lighting business at Aycliffe Industrial Estate after my father died in 1949. In those days it was quite unusual for a lady to be running a factory, small though it was, let alone also becoming Chairman of the Aycliffe Directors Club in 1952-1953. She had been on her own for some years, so we were all very pleased when she sold out in the early 1960's and married an old friend of my fathers, the Reverend Tom Grinham. He was also full of fun and had 'Taken the Cloth' later in life. Mother went to live with him in Cheshire.

In my new and ongoing need for money for the starter factory, I redoubled my efforts making contact with every possible source in both the Private and Public sectors, including all the government funding organisations in the North East. Most of them were used to me pestering them, so it was nothing new. After seeing the difference in Nesta, another government agency, I was on my guard with the local agencies but it was worth risking it - 'any port in a storm'. At one time, before BW came into the picture, they did say that they could provide a seven figure sum, but only if I could raise similar amounts at this level from the private sector.

From the very beginning of the project, in 1987, I had produced regular progress reports every few months and sent them to those who had invested privately and who were supporting me. This included friends and business colleagues. They were, therefore, well aware of the current situation, so I now contacted them all again to see if any would increase their shareholding. Some did, and other friends also introduced me to their colleagues and money began to come in again from new investors.

Not surprisingly, the men at the new little starter factory were concerned about the difficulties which BW were creating, but they knew that I was making very determined efforts to raise money and saw for themselves, the steady stream of visitors and potential investors whom I was showing round. I was worried that they would leave the company as Royles men had done.

SMITH'S PLANS FRUSTRATED

The 'removal' of the Operations Director Stewart Sim, from BW, presumably by Mark Smith was unforgivable and was a most serious blow, the repercussions of which continue to this day. Stewart was a real loss to me and to our valuable project of course. To my knowledge, here was a most experienced and dedicated waterways man who's heart was with BW and who wanted nothing more, than to do his best for this illustrious company.

I believe that he was a key figure in the development of the Falkirk Wheel and for putting together a complex funding package to pay for it, minimising BW's exposure to the costs. After a great many years of service, his being 'pushed out' was, as far as I could see, completely undeserved. It was especially galling when control of our project was taken over by a relatively new director who clearly had little knowledge of canals and engineering in general and our amphibious project in particular.

When dealing with us and Roylecraft, it seemed that Mark Smith really didn't understand who or what he was dealing with. Unlike Stewart Sim who, before proceeding with us, had visited my workshops and carefully evaluated our project and knew exactly what and importantly, who he was dealing with. Mark Smith had, at this stage, only visited the factory once I think and knew very little about us or the new technology, over which he was now taking control.

It was forty years since I had been closely associated with a big company and I was beginning to remember how I had seen a similar situation to this before. A good company man being displaced by a new man, one who 'looked good', but in my opinion, wasn't in the same league, I have seen it again since. I also saw how the positive attitude of so many good people in BW, changed for the worse under Smith's or the board of directors influence.

To begin with, when he suddenly found that his ill-judged scheme to close down Covelink was failing, I imagine that Mark Smith wouldn't know what to do. He obviously couldn't possibly have imagined that I would carry on working to complete the contract without BW's financial support. As a big company director, the thought of a director putting his own money into the company to support it, wouldn't appear on his radar. I imagine that his aim would always be to maximise his income, maximise his expenses and get as much money as possible out of the company. Scoring points wherever he could, as he did so!

After stopping all funding for the contract and with ongoing meetings and much correspondence continuing with various people in the company, it later transpired and the correspondence reveals that, in order to prepare the ground and achieve his aims to grab the assets, Mark Smith had made serious, unfounded and untruthful criticisms about me and our management of the project revealing the nature of the man.

In fact, of course, I had plenty of opportunity to explain to everybody I met in BW that I was mortgaging the house again and the workshops and doing all I could to try raise additional money to complete the contract. This would not, I expect, sit very comfortably with the stories which Mark Smith must have been putting about to support his ongoing attempts to close us down. They would have little choice but to follow the financial director's wishes.

During this period, there is a flurry of activity, Smith is asking for more figures, looking at every possible way in which he could force Covelink to be put into liquidation with a CVA (interestingly, with reports copied to Nesta). Another of Smith's plans which failed.

It was interesting and pleasing to see that our suppliers wanted us to continue trading and were prepared to let me have credit. They had faith in me and seen the potential for future business and they knew that I had devoted all my resources to the project, they did not want to support a formal Creditors Voluntary Arrangement, but I don't think that Smith wanted to hear this.

With my hands already very full, not only with raising money again, but with maintaining progress building the buses, I had no choice, but to continue to be diplomatic and to wait to see what his next move might be. Early on in the Contract, Smith had pressed me to establish an overdraft for Covelink, but I refused to do it because I didn't trust him. My view was that it was up to BW to fund and pay for their buses, not me. I had already poured hundreds of thousands of pounds into the BW project.

After BW's payments ceased and the wages had to be paid every week, I then had no choice, but to arrange a facility at the bank whilst I was raising money to continue the work. Of course, as ever, I had to underwrite it personally. At least at this stage, being in control again and not reliant upon Smith for money, I was more independent and could decide how I would run the overdraft. I was not expecting any money from BW, so knew where I stood.

FAILURE OF GOVERNMENT TO SUPPORT SME'S

The devious activities of BW's board of directors flew in the face of their own government's publicly stated wish to see large companies supporting and working to help little firms develop new high value technologies and products. Instead of this, **here was the governments own company** trying to defraud me and steal our technology! I was also soon to see how Covelink's bank, the RBS, was to show how far it would go, to further the future of new technologies and help the small firms who create them.

History and my own experience clearly showed that big firms mistreating little innovative companies is not unusual and is considered by many, to be normal practice. It is well known that over 90% of innovation fails in Britain and that, as a direct consequence, this country has suffered the loss of many new products and industries for most of the last century. This story very clearly illustrates how and why this can happen. If Covelink had been a large company, the lawyers would have been called in immediately and the problem resolved. In fact, had this been the case, BW wouldn't have tried to close us down or take the assets in the first place.

I don't know what all the various managers, engineers and departments in BW were actually being told or what they thought about the overall situation. They certainly knew that there were only two of us in my office and Nick at the starter factory ordering and chasing up materials, so criticism coming from the Financial Director of such a big company, would hopefully be seen for what it was.

They did know that we were making good progress and that the workmanship and technology was good. They also knew that we had won a number of National Awards for it, but they would also now have seen Stewart Sim being pushed out of BW. With the staff relying upon BW for their income, they would have little choice, but to follow the instructions of the financial director who was now controlling this project. They remained friendly to me, but were constantly having to refer to contractual formalities and toe the FD's line.

Despite this, Smith was now in a difficult position. I was ploughing on regardless of his plans to shut down the factory and Covelink and obviously, I was intent on doing all I could to finish the buses. I continued, politely, to ask BW for financial assistance, at the same time acknowledging that we had not met the delivery terms of the contract, but emphasising the sound reasons why it was impossible to do so from the outset. I was now more independent of BW and of Smith, which also didn't please him.

SMITHS DEVIOUS EFFORTS CONTINUE

Having already appointed a part time 'mentor' (a 'mole'?) for me, paid for by Nesta, Smith was now introducing a second man who would, this time, spend most of his time at the factory and report back what was happening. This man, Colin McAusland, came to us on 29th October 2002. In effect, BW now also had a permanent 'Spy' in the camp. In fact, Colin was a most experienced engineer and seemed to be positive and helpful. Interestingly, Smith, as ever, covers his back by writing a long and detailed letter saying that Colin could not be held responsible for anything in the factory.

Examining the many hundreds of documents in my files and as I write this today and recall these events, I am reminded of just how difficult it was for me to know who genuinely wanted to help us and who was part of BW's corrupt plans.

From the outset I had been very careful to keep my detailed drawings well out of the way, so had not let Colin see any of them. Even this worked against me when I heard from BW that Colin had told them that we didn't have any drawings for the Jet-Buses.

When Harry built our new offices into the roof spaces at Staindrop, I had asked him to make an unused adjoining part of the roof into a document store. Access was by what appeared to be a small cupboard in the office wall. This was very useful for all Royles job records, and where I kept all the drawings, specifications and much of the patent documentation for Covelink.

It may be that BW were being clever, if so, it worked because it would have been virtually impossible to carry out an innovative and complex project of this nature without detailed specifications and working drawings. Feeling that, as ever, I had to prove myself, I showed them to him, hundreds of them, but not in detail. They proved that the project was properly planned and executed, but also that they existed.

BW could see that the first bus was now virtually complete and looking very businesslike. They were also now even more aware of the huge potential of Roylecraft with a number of important large UK and overseas companies showing serious interest in buying our vehicles.

In November 2002, BW people were writing to say that we had not honoured the delivery dates in the contract and had not proceeded with "due diligence". Obviously Smith was doing all he could to reinforce his plans to take all our assets and using every means at his disposal to try to denigrate and undermine our good works. So it was around this time, that Smith arranged for an independent engineers report. No doubt he expected some criticism which would be useful in his ongoing attempts to discredit us and force us to close down.

The man inspected the factory and the buses being worked upon and apparently, concluded his report to BW by saying that our work was good and was being carried out at above average efficiency and at a lower cost than is normal in this industry. After this glowing report, no doubt a great disappointment to Smith, he was still determined to find irregularities, so then arranged for a senior cost clerk from BW's Leeds office to come to Staindrop and examine our books. As ever, I was quite happy for them to do this, since we had an open books arrangement and had nothing whatsoever to hide. Smith must have been very disappointed yet again, because the reports came back that everything was in order. Our books were in order, correct and honest in every respect.

It was a replay, on a different scale, of the attempts by the Swedish millionaire in the big legal case, trying hard to show that we are dishonest, so that he could have taken advantage of us.

Looking back, I am really disgusted to be reminded of the lengths to which some people will go to in order to achieve their disgraceful aims. They really are showing what dreadful and unprincipled people they are, it is they who are dishonest and fraudulent - not me!

MONEY RAISING EFFORTS INTENSIFY

Faced with BW's efforts to undermine me and the good work which we had done, and take this successful project away for their own benefit, my only route to success was to raise as much money as possible to keep going and finish the buses.

In round figures, I needed to introduce funds in excess of the £100,000 a month if I was to catch up with the outstanding debts, continue to pay the wages and pay the sub-contracted electrical and hydraulics engineers who were also working with us on the buses. It goes without saying that this is a tremendous challenge for any individual in a small company. This was made even more difficult because BW insisted that I could not establish a website for the project, nor could we build or sell Jet-Buses to anybody else until the buses for BW had been supplied. As ever, despite their dreadful treatment, I had to accept their dominance and

I complied with their wishes. They would do anything to stop me succeeding.

After having already spent fifteen years raising money for the project from most of my personal resources and contacts, I had already covered most of the 'normal' sources. As soon as I knew that BW had stopped all payments, I was having to act quickly so that I could at least continue to pay the wages each week.

I have already mentioned that I mortgaged our house again and this time, my workshops in Staindrop as well. This immediately brought in £190,000 which, along with additional sums coming in from private investors, gave me a breathing space whilst I set about widening the scope of my efforts. As ever, I continued making contact with every possible source, the Banks, venture capital firms, various institutions, military companies and private parties of high net worth. Anybody whom I thought might have the amount of money necessary for them to be able to invest in this project.

To help me to do all this, we had produced

DACR cartoon. 'How about a little cushion for your head David?' The financial cushion didn't materialise anway!

various forecasts and a funding plan which was circulated to any interested parties, including BW!

Mark Smith was cornered and now had no choice, politically, but to appear helpful. This plan resulted in various relatively small sums of BW money being offered and discussed by Smith, far less than was due under the contract, but he still made sure that he was not committed to paying even the smallest amounts. He did this by saying that any monies were conditional upon and subject to any monies being payable by Nesta whom I knew was already working with Smith to deprive us of the benefits of our project. Those who had originally helped me, had left by now.

Later on, Nesta's attitude hardened and like BW, now made the supply of any further monies to us conditional upon us relinquishing our control of the entire Roylecraft project. This time, control of Covelink was to be handed over to Mark White, the director of Innovation of Nesta, rather than to the directors of British Waterways. A man who had not been with them when they were previously so helpful and a man who did not inspire me with his approach to business or his knowledge of our project. He, like BW, certainly had no rights to it, in spite of his predecessors in Nesta having given us grant aid.

As well as the carefully worded letters when we asked BW for money, we were now presented with a remarkable, long and detailed legal looking contract by Nesta. This was designed to take full control of Covelink and its assets, if funding was to be provided. So now, a second government organisation was out to take over and control the assets of our company.

There was no doubt that they all now knew how valuable Roylecraft technology is. It was also clear that the policy of all concerned was the determination to deprive me and all who had invested, of the benefits which were clearly due to us. They were going to do this in any way they could, despite the fact that none of them had any rights to it and they didn't really understand what they were dealing with.

It was also obvious that both organisations had power and the advantage of full legal services. BW not only had its own legal department, but it also employed the services of all people; Eversheds. The very firm whose two solicitors had defrauded me of the money due from our High Court success. Taking on either one of them, not only meant taking on one or more powerful government organisations, I would also not be able to avoid taking on one of the biggest legal firms in the country. A firm which originally, years before, had helped me, but which I was also already reporting to Parliament

as being corrupt and who had literally stolen their clients money, our court awards. I had clearly seen how the courts were ignored by solicitors when it suited them, so couldn't turn to the legal system for any help anyway. For this reason I needed help from anybody in authority. I had no option but to approach more and more eminent people in both houses of Parliament in order to explain the facts about the incredible treatment being metered out to me by solicitors and by the Directors of British Waterways.
I strongly dislike complaining about anything, but I could hardly believe what was happening

I think that it is safe to assume that they all knew that I was an individual who had no money, so could be manipulated in one way or another. They also presumed that Roylecraft was a relatively simple technology created by this 'little man' who was an inconsequential Vintage Car enthusiast in the North of England. A person whose assets could be taken without too much difficulty and then used for their own advantage.

The fact that Mark Smith had already stopped all payments to us of the money due to us under the contract and had also shown no concern whatever for me or our shareholders, all without any legal response from me, indicated that legal action was unlikely. He therefore obviously felt safe in enlisting support from other government related organisations. Although I could see that it would be foolish to rely on any money which was associated with BW or Nesta, I couldn't predict how far Smith would go with other government agencies, in order to achieve his corrupt aims, so I carried on talking to them all, but I continued to be wary.

CHAPTER 58:
TWO YEARS OF REMARKABLE ACTIVITY

At this point in the story, my efforts to raise money intensified to such a degree that so many people and different organisations became involved, that it would be impractical for me to try to describe, in detail, all the events and activities which were going on.

Looking back through my diaries, reports and shelves full of files for the years 2002, 2003 and 2004, they show that life was extremely hectic dealing with the financial problems, contacting every possible source of funding, coping with BW's ongoing devious activities and also with the ongoing pressure of the work necessary to finish the buses themselves. These alone, would fill a book and probably be very boring!

I want to make this book as readable as possible and at the same time, let you see why it is so important that the salient facts are brought out. The reason behind writing this book in the first place, was that it is the only way in which I am ever going to be able to let people know what I was having to do to keep the companies running and have the benefits properly due to me and those who had invested in Roylecraft, when I was up against such unprincipled and powerful people.

In previous chapters, you have already seen why my interesting motor car restoration business was in such difficulties and I want you to know that, in parallel with this BW affair, I was still pressing all the Legal authorities, including Eversheds, Parliament, and the Legal Ombudsman, to have the benefit of the High Court Orders carried out. The money long overdue to us from this successful action, would have been very helpful, especially to Royles workshops at this difficult time.

THE FIRST JET-BUS TESTS

Despite the serious financial problems and BW's attempt to close us down, we pressed on with the work at the factory and the first Roylecraft Jet-Bus was finished and ready for its first water and driving test on Wednesday 18 December 2002. Nine months after opening the little factory. Their efforts to disrupt the project and prevent progress had failed so far.

Making good progress.

Although I say it myself, I think this was quite an achievement when I hadn't started to design these entirely new and highly innovative 40 foot amphibious buses until August 2001, sixteen months earlier. In this time, I had designed the hull and all the special components, had consulted and had the valuable assistance of a number of academics and the top specialists in the marine and automotive fields, and then had set up a supply chain and manufactured;

THE FIRST WATER JET-BUSES

With the help of Allan, Nick and our team, we had converted and equipped a 4000 square foot starter factory from a bare agricultural building, taken on and inducted 16 new staff and built the first two Jet-Buses, one of which was now ready to be tested. All the components and hulls for the other two were ready to assemble. All from an outline drawing hanging on my

First day of testing on the Tees. 18/12/02. I wonder how many innovative projects on this scale, came out for the very first test with TV news cameras and 'partners' who want it to fail, in attendance!

office wall 16 months earlier. I was sorry that Stewart Sim wasn't there to see it.

We transported the bus from Winston to the river Tees Rowing Club near Stockton on a low loader. We couldn't drive it there on the public highway, because the bus was not tested or certificated by the DTLR.

We had previously visited Alan Slater and the people employed on the River Tees Barrage who, although they were now part of the BW 'empire' had been most helpful. They had arranged for us to use the rowing club's facilities. Being midweek, there was nobody about and there is a good ramp with room to unload the bus. The river is wide here and there are no tides because we are above the Barrage. Although it was December, it was a lovely sunny day and we couldn't have wished for better weather or for a more ideal spot for the very first launch of a Roylecraft Jet-Bus!

Nick was driving the bus and some BW men were in attendance along with a safety boat. Although not there, Mark Smith was probably hoping and praying that it would sink! I was asked by one of BW's men if I was worried about this first ever launch of a Jet-Bus, "Not a bit" I honestly replied. I was perfectly happy and looking forward to seeing it driving into the water. I had also let the BBC know about the tests, so was delighted to see Les Coates and his men there filming the event for the local BBC and ITV news.

From the early trials of the prototypes, the BBC and other TV companies had filmed and followed the progress of Roylecraft and had been most helpful. They, like me, were excited that such an important new development in transport was being created here in the North East and it was, of course visually, a good subject for television. I have copies of a lot of their films and it has appeared on various news items and on the 'Working Lunch' business programmes.

Being an entirely new design, 40 feet long and packed with innovative controls and many new mechanisms, it needed somebody who had a broad width of experience to deal with such a machine.

It must be remembered that sitting in the driving seat for the first time, Nick was immediately confronted with controls for driving on land and water using facilities which, other than in

First time afloat.

The Jet-Bus after it's first test.

our prototypes, had never previously been incorporated, or used in any boat or road going vehicle before, especially one this size. Nick was just the man for the job!

As the bus entered the water, the bows or front of the bus, lifted and floated up beautifully and I was pleased to see that the waterline was exactly where I had calculated that it would be. Nick took it very slowly for this first dip, and after a slow drive around on the river, he headed back for the launching ramp. At the critical moment, he found that it was necessary to quickly operate the transmission drive selector and a cheer went up as he drove it out of the water and up the ramp onto the apron in front of the rowing club.

Driving it in and out and manoeuvering it on water and driving it on land, he soon proved himself to be very capable. Despite having jet propulsion, retractable wheels and entirely new controls, he quickly learned how to handle the very first Roylecraft Jet-Bus.

You may remember that to save money and time, I had previously decided to risk fitting the small drive shafts and differentials to the buses which I had previously had made for our smaller MK IV and MK V Roylecraft workboats. These were designed for vehicles weighing up to 4½ tonnes, not for the buses which weighed over eight tonnes. It was therefore, no surprise that one of these rear road wheel drive shafts failed when trying, later on, to drive the bus out of the mud when it became bogged down in some soft ground on the apron in front of the rowing club.

Not being especially innovative components and easily replaced, it was important that we were able to continue these first trials as there were many important new mechanisms which we wanted to test in operation. So we replaced the broken shaft with another similar spare shaft and it did last for some months which was long enough to continue with the tests on water and driving on the road. The temporary ones had done their job and saved time and delayed the initial costs of manufacturing the proper rear shafts and suitable differentials.

THE PROOF OF THE PUDDING

I subsequently had the time and opportunity to drive it myself and I was delighted with the 'feel' and its handling. The longer and bigger hull mirrored the cross section of the design of

Driving around Croft Racing Circuit.

the MK IV and was very stable on water. When I drove it on the road around Croft Motor Racing circuit, I quickly found it gave the driver a lot of confidence. The Jet-Bus incorporated many unusual features which, when tested, proved to be every bit as good as I could have wished for. The safety features, locking mechanisms, the retractable suspension and unique dual ratio steering designs which I had developed over the previous fifteen years, proved themselves to be a great success, although I say it myself.

The author, Nick Royle and the Jet-Bus during tests.

So the first series of tests proved that the important new features of the overall designs worked very well. The innovative wheel retraction mechanisms, safety locks, the innovative steering mechanisms, the water-jet and the hull design, conclusively proved themselves by the excellent handling of the bus and its performance in both environments, in water and on the road. It was stable and smooth in operation and gave a lot of confidence to all those who had been working on it and building it. Although I am very critical by nature, I was delighted with the results.

It became clear to us that the quick operation of the drive selector lever by Nick when driving out of the water for the first time, was due to the 'Creep Drive Motor'. You will remember that Websters had suggested this feature as an added benefit to their gear box, but unfortunately it wouldn't do the job. I was not at all sure about this hydraulic motor, but they thought it would easily drive the buses up the ramp at slow speed. They are long established and experienced gearbox manufacturers and always had been very helpful and had worked with me for some years at minimum cost, so naturally I had faith in them. The principle behind this variation in the design seemed good, but their calculations must have been at fault, because it was not man enough for the job.

As soon as they heard about it, Websters kindly came over to inspect the gearbox in operation for themselves. The new transfer gear box itself, seemed to be working well and the tests were doing their job, which was to find out if and where there were any weak points. Whilst checking the transmission, we all agreed that the automatic gear change could be improved as it tended to 'snatch' and wasn't as smooth as it could be. I thought that it was mainly due to the operation of the fluid flywheel. I was not too concerned about these issues, since they were entirely new and untried mechanisms and there was bound to be the need for some modifications or adjustments and in this case, they were minor.

Being transmission specialists, I knew that Websters would be able to rectify the problems and improve them. They were not major or costly development problems for a brand new type of vehicle of this size and complexity, so whilst attending to this, we also placed orders with Websters for the heavier duty differentials and drive shafts at the same time. There were no 'heavy duty diffs' which incorporated inboard disc brakes which is why we couldn't use standard 'off the shelf' units and why I had risked using the smaller ones in the first place. It was important that our advanced amphibious vehicles had a set of inboard brakes which were always dry and efficient and were not immersed when the amphibian and its wheels were in water. The brakes on the differentials did this.

It is important to emphasise that when a completely new and complex technology is created, there are always improvements and adjustments to make. This is the development phase and is perfectly normal practice with all new vehicles and boats. It is an important part of all innovation work. In our case, it was especially so, because the project had been carried out at the minimum of cost, so some risks had to be taken with the prototypes.

What was unusual in our case however, is that a completely new technology and innovative vehicle of this sort is rarely tested in the full glare of publicity. Especially on their first ever test run. I did this to prove that our Roylecraft vehicles existed and that we had created them and that they worked. It was worrying for me however, to know that all the results were being relayed to a key figure in BW who was bent upon finding fault, so that he can take it away from its creators and is looking for any excuse to do so.

In the New Year, knowing that we had been testing our first Jet-Bus, BW was asked by Barrs

At Falkirk Wheel February 2003. Irn Bru tests on BBC film.

IrnBru, the Sponsors, to take our Jet-Bus up to the Falkirk Wheel for a demonstration and to see it being tested there. I was not at all happy about this, because the vehicle was still undergoing its very first tests and was not at all ready to be used as a demonstrator. BW knew that the small MK IV transmission drive shafts could easily fail again and I was concerned that Smith could use this as an excuse to poison Barrs confidence in us.

I was determined not to meet Barrs personally, because I was so angry about the contrived financial problems which BW had created and I knew that I would not be able to contain myself. As a result, I ensured that Nick, who would be driving the Jet-Bus, made Barrs well aware of the small drive shafts situation. I didn't want to give Smith the slightest opportunity to say that Roylecraft were a failure. Despite the fact that it was not an innovative feature and was easily rectified.

I had no excuse, but to accept the situation, especially as BW were going to pay the transport costs, so in early February of 2003, the first Jet-Bus went up to the Falkirk Wheel without me. The fact that we had painted and re-painted the bus to their specification, blue and Orange, Barrs corporate colours, impressed and greatly pleased their PR Manager, Edna Cunningham who was in attendance for the tests.

The drive shaft did fail again, but Nick somehow managed to drive the bus into the pool in front of the Visitor Centre. Once in there, Nick was still able to drive the bus around the limited area of the pool breaking the ice, which was an inch thick, as he navigated around this small stretch of water. Edna Cunningham was delighted when she was driven in the bus into one of the gondola's.

They were then lifted high into the air on the wheel and then entered and travelled along the top canal into the tunnel which leads to the pool by the road bridge above the site.

The whole episode was filmed by the BBC and with not having been there, it was interesting for me to be able to see the film of it all. Having been told about the weak drive shaft, Edna was not at all concerned when it snapped and apparently was thrilled about the demonstration. She can be seen happily sitting in the bus in the BBC film of the event with a broad grin on her face.

CHAPTER 59:
BACK TO THE BW FUNDING STORY

In order to keep the factory running as mentioned, I now needed tranches to be in the order of £50,000 to £100,000. This was in the short term and be followed by even more substantial amounts later on. This would be needed to set up a bigger factory to meet the demand which was already becoming apparent from the visitors and potential buyers who were now pressing me from all over the world. The BBC television news items and articles in the press had attracted interest, not only from the UK, but also from overseas.

A business plan created by James Burtenshaw of Vantis Corporate Finance, who is a good man and who had the respect of local government, proposed a minimum figure of £3.2 million for future production. Quite a challenge for me, but a small sum in relation to the huge amount of potential business.

Having already approached many of the financial institutions and Venture Capital firms (VC's) listed in the British Venture Capital Association. I see that I had ticked forty-two firms in their list of members. The many meetings and discussions with them, as well as with other national organisations in both military and civilian spheres of activity, had proved to be fruitless, so I was really up against it. I had no choice but to broaden the scope. Looking at my files and books of visiting cards, reminds me how many and widespread my approaches were. I was again approaching all the VC's, but focussed on the funding organisations in the North, including those who wouldn't help me in the past. I was also talking to people who were connected to funding organisations all over the world.

Remembering all the government publicity aimed at small firms encouraging them to innovate, I increased the pressure on them again and although I had previously spoken to the County Durham Development Company (CDDC), another government agency, on a number of occasions, I tackled them again, literally pleading with them to support me.

Their offices were in County Hall, Durham and although I had been talking to them for years, I had not been able to prise any money out of them. But again, I contacted Greg Johnson who was their Business Services Executive and also Stewart Watkins their CEO. They seemed to be aware of the up to date situation and knew that I was talking to a number of government organisations for funding. Bernard Robinson, their Chairman, was also involved and had his own ideas how funding could be organised.

THE FUNDING PACKAGE

The general consensus was that I needed to put together a funding package, saying that it was no good for me to rely upon piecemeal investments. All this is easily said, but after sixteen years of intense effort, I had failed to find a single institutional investor, let alone a number of them to put a 'package' together. Without these relatively small piecemeal amounts of £10,000 or so coming in, I wouldn't have been able to continue. In the first place, I had the wages of sixteen men to pay every week.

From the very beginning, it was clear to me that those who operate in the formal structures of government, cannot comprehend a situation when money is continually needed and **needed now**. Having regular incomes with their guaranteed salaries, they assume that people like me, enjoy the same benefits and that there is always time to organise funding with a proper scheme, one with all the t's crossed and i's dotted. In fact, we had done this at the start of the project, but the results of our market research involved us in a much bigger and more worthwhile project. This is when we discovered that the governments promises weren't reflected by their actions. Some money was occasionally provided, but it was out of scale with a project of this size and nature and there were always delays which intensified the need.

After working on the project for sixteen years, mainly without a regular cash flow or income for me or the project, I was now in a desperate situation. I had already invested all the money which I had and could raise. The powers 'that be' have no conception of what it is like to run a company with no proper source of income at

Business Link. Managing business growth.

Business Link brochure.

N-E 'must shake off the shackles of the past' article and CDDC ad.

all and when even the legal system is failing and anyway, is out of reach. In my case, as you know, my solicitors had already stolen our court awards, their own clients money, leaving my restoration business burdened with huge debts. Royles workshops situation was already difficult enough before this problem added to it. Our profitability had been marginal and it was for this reason that I had taken a number of calculated risks in order to develop innovative new products and business's.

BW, Nesta and the people I was now approaching again, knew very well that I had failed to get money out of the VC's and yet they and other government departments were still demanding to see private sector money on the table before they could or would help. This might well have been government policy, but the fact was that they had stood back for years, in my case, with valuable global orders coming in, and watched me squirm whilst pressing and begging them for money.

This situation goes against everything they were saying in public and in the media, after all, I was going to great lengths using my own resources to create many hundreds of jobs and tens of millions of pounds in much needed exports, precisely what the country needed. With 240 empty factories here and industry having shrunk by a reported 80% in the UK, I was shocked that the government would ignore such a good opportunity.

Knowing that people like me are on our knees, they had two choices; they could let good projects like this go to the wall rather than helping and they are quite happy to do this.

Alternatively, other government organisations with whom I was already dealing, had shown that they would go to any lengths to take most or all Covelink's assets from me and my shareholders. It didn't seem to matter to them how dishonest or fraudulent their methods were to do it.

Being well aware of this, I was now interested to see what these government people would do, people whom I was again asking for money. As ever, I was keeping a wary eye open for any more devious activities. As it turned out, I was wise to do so.

The irony of this whole extraordinary situation was that it existed entirely as a result of the activities of the FD of a government agency, British Waterways. This was so sad, because, ever since childhood, I have had a deep love of rivers, canals, lakes and the sea and I know that BW have done a marvellous job of maintaining and restoring them. I was delighted to work with them and had been happy to put my faith and the future of my company into the hands of their enthusiastic Operations Director of long standing, Stewart Sim. He understood our project, was in full control of it and was as confident as we were, of making a success of it.

At the risk of repeating myself, not for a moment, did I think that such ridiculous and unnecessary interference by a non- technical director, would see this good man removed. Nor did I ever expect to see all our good work and reputation sullied by undeserved and untruthful criticism and the full force of the BW contract which, instead of a means to create success, was being used to ruin a most worthwhile project.

Despite all the difficulties of achieving it, I never the less, could do no other than agree that the CDDC's suggested funding package was a good idea, but I had serious doubts about the intentions of those whom I was now relying upon to help me put it together.

My aim, initially, was to raise around £750,000. I estimated that this amount should be more than sufficient to cover the £400,000 owed to us by BW on the contract to finish the four Jet-Buses. The balance used to carry out the minor development work and then certificate the Jet-Buses for public transport. A sum less than the £500,000 Stewart Sim said was available. But of course, it would not include the £3.2 million which was then urgently needed to set up a proper factory for production, so was still only a stop gap.

As discussions progressed in 2003, I explained to each of the various parties involved, which included BW, Nesta, the CDDC and others, that I finally had no choice, but to arrange and underwrite the previously mentioned bank over-draft facility. This was for £30,000 and I also told them that I was personally putting in more money, this time, in excess of £190,000 to pay creditors and to keep the factory running. With this £220,000 of my own private sector money, I was asking them what sums of money they could add to it from the public sector.

BW said they would add £212,000 and Nesta £75,000 (both with proviso's). Government office One North East had previously said they were organising an EU de Minimis loan of £250,000 by providing our bank (the RBS) with a 100% government guarantee for this sum. They explained that this had been arranged with great difficulty and also said that there was the possibility of a Smart Award, and the CDDC said they would lend me £50,000, in the interim now knowing that I was desperate.

OUR BANKS SUPPORT FOR OUR PROJECT

As these sums covered the three quarters of a million target, the situation looked promising, but another difficulty arose from a new and quite different quarter. I had previously informed our bank, the Royal Bank of Scotland, that we were being offered a 100% government guarantee for the EU loan of £250,000 (later reduced to £199,000). I told them how important it was

CHAPTER 59: BACK TO THE BW FUNDING STORY

COVELINK MARINE LIMITED MEETING

LOCATION : One NorthEast - Stella House

VENUE : Room FF02 at 10h00am

DATE : Thursday, 24th April 2003

PURPOSE : To review progress on and possibilities for:

    a. Raising Private Sector Finance
    b. Reversion of IPR to Covelink
    c. Provision of Bank Guarantee by One NorthEast

ATTENDING :

For ONE North East
- **Mike Collier** - Chief Executive, ONE (**Chair**)
- **Rick O'Farrell** - Manager, Business Finance Team
- **John Clayton** - Senior Business Finance Executive

For British Waterways
- **Mark Smith** - Finance Director

For Covelink Marine Ltd
- **David Royle** - Director.
- **Alan Theakston** - Company Secretary

For CDDC (County Durham Development Company)
- **Bernard Robinson** - Chairman
- **Stewart Watkins** - Deputy Director
- **Greg Johnson** - Business Development Manager

AGENDA

09h30 – 10h00	Arrival and Refreshments
10h00	Introductions by Chair – Mike Collier
10h15	**Covelink** – Progress overview on Raising Private Sector Finance **British Waterways** – Overview of IPR current and future status **One NorthEast** – Commentary on Bank Guarantee Progress
11h45	End of meeting and light buffet

and that it formed part of a £0.75 million funding package which might fail if we didn't get it.

Yes, you've guessed it, our bank refused to accept the government's 100% guarantee, so would not provide the money!

I could hardly believe that this was how small, innovative firms are treated by their own banks. I later wrote to Benny Higgins the Chief Executive of Retail Banking at the RBS in Edinburgh to repeat my request, but he also turned us down. I subsequently found that HBOS might accept it, but the delay meant that we were now faced with other serious problems.

LOCAL GOVERNMENT MEETING (APRIL 2003)

A meeting was arranged to discuss the provision of funding for Covelink at the governments new One North East offices, Stella House on 24 April 2003. This was the first time I had seen this building, I could immediately see where a large amount of the government funding for small business was really going. It is a large, imposing and very stylish, architect designed building complete with a spacious and modernistic Atrium situated near the river Tyne, west of Newcastle.

Roylecraft Jet-Bus in Barr's colours.

I include here a copy of the notice and agenda of the meeting. Those attending the meeting were the principle parties mentioned above, all government related people including Mark Smith from BW.

As you can see, I had said that I would bring along Alan Theakston who was a most wonderfully helpful and knowledgeable man who had previously agreed to be Covelink's company Secretary, unpaid like the rest of us! He had risen through the ranks of Ropners Shipping Company to be their company secretary and was honoured by becoming the International President of the Institute of Chartered Secretaries and Administrators. (ICSA). His expertise was ideal for this event. He was another generous supporter of mine and to this day, we keep in touch and he remains as helpful as ever.

Some months before this meeting, in October 2002 one of the many individuals of High Net Worth whom I had contacted and who came to inspect the Jet-Buses was Karl Watkin. He had been awarded the North East Businessman of the year in 1991 and an MBE and had a string of successful businesses behind him. Like many people of his ilk, he was known to be very tough to deal with and had apparently upset some people in the city who had warned me to be very careful in any dealings I might have with him.

Like many self-made people, he is an interesting character, but, after showing him the Jet-Buses at the factory, he couldn't resist playing the 'old game' of devaluing the project which interested him, by saying in this instance, that they were "over engineered". Such critical and derogatory remarks were predictable and were no surprise, so I literally dug him in the ribs and said "really?" At which point he smiled and admitted that these impressive vehicles were "fantastic". As is often the case with such people, he hadn't grasped the real benefits of the technology, or that they would satisfy and create new and untapped markets in flood rescue and public transport. He went on to prove this later, when he proudly said he already had an order from the USSR for carrying munitions.

After visting the MOD in Whitehall and spending a lot of time with the Defence Research Agency (DERA) and various Armed Forces Procurement people, the military market is familiar to me and has great potential, but with military budgets being cut, it is not at all the sector of the market for which these first machines were designed or suitable. The design requirements for carrying heavy loads are quite different and it was clear that Karl didn't understand this. He also didn't seem to accept the fact that orders were not what we needed, we already had plenty of those in the pipeline. I was, by now, being pressed to supply many

CHAPTER 59: BACK TO THE BW FUNDING STORY

COVELINK MARINE LIMITED MEETING

LOCATION	:	One NorthEast - Stella House
VENUE	:	Room FF02 at 10h00am
DATE	:	Thursday, 24th April 2003
PURPOSE	:	To review progress on and possibilities for:

        a. Raising Private Sector Finance
        b. Reversion of IPR to Covelink
        c. Provision of Bank Guarantee by One NorthEast

ATTENDING :

For ONE North East
    Mike Collier - Chief Executive, ONE (**Chair**)
    Rick O'Farrell - Manager, Business Finance Team
    John Clayton - Senior Business Finance Executive

For British Waterways
    Mark Smith - Finance Director

For Covelink Marine Ltd
    David Royle - Director.
    Alan Theakston - Company Secretary

For CDDC
(County Durham Development Company)
    Bernard Robinson - Chairman (**Apologies for absence**)
    Stewart Watkins - Deputy Director
    Greg Johnson - Business Development Manager

Minutes of Meeting

Mike Collier, Chief Executive of One NorthEast chaired this mornings meeting and, after 2 hours discussions, the following positions were agreed:

1. **One NorthEast** – We are prepared to sign the Bank Guarantee in respect of a loan of £199,000.00 from the Halifax Bank of Scotland contingent on the receipt of a written Board resolution from Covelink Marine Limited accepting that if, by the 20th May 2003, they have not secured alternative finance to fund the business, Covelink Marine Ltd. will accept an offer of between £1 million and £1.7 million for a 60 % shareholding in Covelink Marine Ltd. from the "Tree of Dreams" investment Consortium headed by Alex Worrall.

2. One NorthEast will fund the placement of a company doctor to join Covelink Marine Limited to give advice on moving the business forward and reporting to One NorthEast on progress on all business related matters including access to funding streams as discussed in point 1 above.

3. The current business plan prepared by Vantis Corporate Finance will need to remove any reference to further monies being injected by British Waterways and acknowledge that a sum of at least £364,000.00 will be required to be set aside for potential purchase of IPR from British Waterways.

4. **British Waterways** - Mark Smith agreed that he would reconstitute the British Waterways stage payment plan immediately given the expectation that One NorthEast sign the Bank Guarantee contingent on the points outlined above. Mark further confirmed that British Waterways would be flexible in negotiating the reversion of IPR to Covelink Marine Limited directly or via a consortium of potential investors.

5. **Covelink Marine Limited** – David Royle and Alan Theakston agreed to call an immediate Board meeting (within the next 48 hours) and pass a resolution accepting, in writing to Mike Collier, Chief Executive, that if, by the 20th May 2003, they have not secured alternative finance to the Tray of Dreams Consortium, they will accept an offer from Alex Worrall and the Tree of Dreams Consortium, for 60% of the shares in the Covelink Marine Limited for between £1 million £1.7 million.

   In addition Covelink Marine Limited welcomed the proposal to send in a company doctor funded by One NorthEast, to give advice on Business Development and report back to One NorthEast on various business progress metrics including access to private sector funding streams.

John Clayton
Business Finance Team

Roylecraft amphibians to Mitsubishi and other interested parties around the world, but not for military use. The military market would be dealt with later.

After the meeting, the second document shown here, was sent to me by Mark Smith. This includes the minutes of the meeting and shows that Bernard Robinson, the Chairman of the County Durham Development Co (CDDC), had sent his apologies for absence. They had already arranged and I had gratefully accepted the £50,000 loan from them in February, which, as ever, I had been obliged to secure personally, but it had helped to keep Covelink running. Bernard's non-attendance was however, very interesting.

Bernard knew and had confidence in Karl Watkin, his colleague Alex Worrall and their associates; "The Tree of Dreams" and seemed keen for them to be involved with the amphibious project. In fact, at a previous meeting at Headlam Hall Hotel, Karl had talked to me about his company having 80% to 90% Covelink for a relatively small sum, and told me that I would be having no further part of the project. These remarks were very revealing. They showed how confident he was of not only being involved, but actually being in full control of our situation. They also revealed an intimate knowledge of our financial difficulties and proved that he had complete confidence in the support which those in local government, whom I was pressing for money, would give him.

Interestingly, Karl had also turned up at a previous funding meeting held at Nesta's offices in Thames Street in London. On this occasion, he was working with them and it was obvious, even then, that he wanted to take control of Covelink.

It was becoming painfully clear to me that he is one of a network of people with access to money, who circulate round the government's seed-corn funding agencies knowing that there are inventors and people like me who are left high and dry after the government grants run out. They know that the VC's and the banks rarely provide funding, so can take advantage of the innovator's poor financial position and know that they can take most of the equity for a fraction of its value. I expect they tell the agencies that they can access the funds, so repeat the hackneyed phrase, 'a small slice of the loaf is better than none at all' (for those who take all the risks and innovate to create new technologies in our case.)

Everybody forgets that there would be no 'loaf' at all if it wasn't for our creative talents and extreme dedication investing all the money we have.

I wrote to Bernard a month before the Stella House meeting, telling him that Karl's offer was typical and as with BW's JV negotiations, I pointed out that the shareholders of Covelink would not consider parting with 80% or 90% of the equity, nor would they be prepared to dispense with me as the designer and principle investor. I also pointed out to him that I had come across others who seek out valuable companies which are financially weak and ripe to be exploited.

History is littered with failed British inventions because of the lack of a fair and equitable system to fund new products. It is shameful and wasteful.

The attitude of those who have no concern for inventors are inevitably people who will tread on anybody to make money and who will take few risks themselves. They argue that 'business is business', forgetting that businessmen rarely invent anything. This is because they won't take the risks or have the dedication and original thought necessary for innovation. The net result is that it is not only the inventor who is the loser, but often it is the country as well.

I suggested to Bernard Robinson that Karl's colleagues could have 15% of Covelink's equity per £million invested and as the current Vantis Walker business plan showed that we needed £3.2 million, Karl could have 33% if he invested £2.2 million in total. Being private sector money, the balance could then come from government, adding that my knowledge was "unique and valuable to the company" and reminded him that we had by then, invested over £3 million ourselves and were still doing so, along with 16 years of work at that stage. Although a fair and equitable suggestion, it was ignored, this is not the way they do business.

THE MEETING

In the minutes of the meeting, shown here, not only do they show that the Chairman of the CDDC did not attend. The reason for which became perfectly clear as it progressed, the minutes at the foot of the page confirm the remarkable fact that if we hadn't raised alternative finance for the business within three or four weeks, then the supply of the government's EU £199,000 funding was conditional on us handing over control and 60% of the equity in Covelink to 'The Tree of Dreams', Karl Watkin and Alex Worral's private consortium. They were well aware, of course, of the extreme difficulty which I had experienced for sixteen years in trying to raise large sums of money. So, as far as they were concerned, it was a fait accompli. So now, there were <u>three government linked organisations</u> which were trying to take over control of the assets of our company. Once in control, heavens knows what they might do. Karl's reputation went before him and, as already mentioned, he had previously made it clear to me that he wanted me out of the way.

My guess as to the reason why Bernard Robinson didn't attend the meeting, was because he realised the serious implications of making the provision of public funding conditional upon control and 60% of the company, being handed over to a local millionaire businessman friend and his colleagues. From the minutes, you can see that the money referred to, was the £199.000 deminimis EU funding from government office One North East.

Alan Theakston was shocked and concerned to find that the minutes were not in accord with the notes which he had also carefully taken during the meeting himself, independently, and wrote to them accordingly. The minutes which they had produced opened the door to us having to accept an offer which could be £700,000, less than the £1.7 million figure actually discussed at the meeting, which we certainly hadn't agreed to. This money would, of course, be going directly into Covelink, not to me or the shareholders, as would all the other monies.

By now, if the money spent by BW on the Roylecraft project is included, along with all the other sums raised and arranged by me from both private and public sectors, the total amount invested was approaching £5 million. They wanted 60% and control of the project for as little as 20% of the costs so far, not to mention the real value. They now demanded our Board of Directors decision within 48 hours.

You may think that I was, perhaps, questioning these opportunities unnecessarily, but the underlying problem I had, disregarding the unrealistic offer and the unfair and dreadful tactics employed, was the thought of spending the rest of my life being controlled and instructed by people who didn't understand the technology. This would have been a nightmare and insufferable after sixteen years work.

In this case, it was as usual, the fast buck they were after. They looked upon the project, not so much as a new and useful form of global transport, but more as a piece of saleable goods. The company and it's assets, IPR etc., being the commodity which they would turn into cash for themselves as soon as possible. Not using the vehicles and technology as the means to create jobs and exports. They may well have done this, but they had absolutely no concern for me, my investors or for the long term transport facilities and benefits which Roylecraft would provide here in the North East and around the world.

MORE OF THE SAME

Also once again, I was obliged to accept yet another mentor. This time not so much a 'mole' as a 'persuader', This time he was an accountant and was referred to in the minutes as a 'company doctor' who was to advise me on how to move the 'business forward'. Obviously this title implies that I was not well, or fit to cope with company matters. This 'doctor' was supposed to persuade me that it was a good deal for us to sign away control and most of the equity in the company for a sum yet to be decided, by them, one which was not equitable. Once again, we were seeing techniques which were as insulting as they were obvious. They wanted to take most of the benefits of Covelink and were using methods reminiscent of a third rate crime novel.

After years of experience, an additional mentor or 'doctor' came as no surprise. I already had two of them in the 'camp' and this made three in all. I already had a BW man in attendance at the factory working for Smith and also Nesta 'mentor' regularly visiting me from London and BW had various others working behind the scenes. In fact they were all helpful at times, this third mentor was a decent fellow and he said that, in his professional opinion as an accountant, he could not possibly advise me to sign an agreement which was so obviously against our interests. It was also heartening to know that the previous inspections carried out by the engineering consultants and BW's clerical staff on Mark Smiths instructions, had found in our favour, BW couldn't manipulate everybody.

Whilst this gave me some hope, the situation was not unlike that of the Legal Battle with Eversheds. When I was involved with people who, on the face of it, were supposed to be advising and helping me, but who were, in fact, in league with those who sought to take advantage of my weak financial position. I really didn't know who I could trust and I had little or no information as to what was going on behind the scenes. I could only see what was happening around me. As with my solicitors in the legal fiasco, I had to judge for myself, what they were up to. Whatever it was, I had no choice, but to appear to be going along with it all, no matter how devious or counterproductive it may have been. It was clear to me however, that there were plenty of people who had their own 'axes to grind'.

This is an awful situation to be in when I had everything to lose and already had serious financial problems at the factory and at Royle's workshops. Not only were those around me secure with good incomes they, of course, knew that I had substantial borrowings and that I had no idea if or when any money would come in. Those who had most to gain and who were behind all the malpractice, obviously had no scruples or concern for me or for anybody but themselves. Strangely enough, knowing this, gave me an inner strength. They wanted something which I had and their methods were so obvious, that ironically, it gave me some comfort.

If nothing else, all this trouble and activity proved beyong doubt, that I had created something, which was worth a great deal of money.

So, here I was, after 16 years of successful innovative work, having to face yet more disgraceful behaviour by officials misusing their power and position. It didn't please Mark Smith, but now knowing how I stood, I had little to lose by reminding him and his co-directors, that this whole extraordinary and unnecessary performance was as a direct result of his unprincipled activities. This was when he cut off the supply of funding for the contract with British Waterways. He would never admit to this of course and simply repeated the terms of the contract.

It was incredible to think that Mark Smith, presumably with the boards support, had dispenced with the services of the Operations Director, Stewart Sim who was helping me to make a real success of the project. Whereas now, under Smith's control, the project was in serious difficulties, it was deprived of its income, was slowing down, progress was extremely difficult and not surprisingly, some of my men were beginning to leave due to concerns about job security.

Mark Smith, had misjudged the entire project, misjudged me, and with little or no practical or technical knowledge, had shown that he could not evaluate the project or the costs. He said that he didn't believe me when I told him that the contract was a bargain for BW and that it was being done economically. Indeed, his own consultants had confirmed to him that everything was in order and that we were more efficient than was typical for our sort of work. But he didn't want to know this, so carried on regardless.

It was becoming clear that he was so intent on depriving me of my work and assets, that he had lost sight of the benefits to BW, to the Falkirk Wheel and of the sponsors million pounds. After all, with this, it was going to cost BW very little at the end of the day. He also did not seem to realise that Covelink's investors were not likely to give it away. The whole process was continuing to deteriorate to a remarkable degree.

THE OUTCOME OF THE MEETING

Following the meeting with the government people, we had a board meeting at short notice as demanded by them and, desperately needing

Smart Awards. 15/10/03 by Hugh Morgan Williams OBE. CBI Chairman.

the EU money, we came to the conclusion that we should sign to accept the offer on the table so that we could at least have the chance of having the £199,000 de minimis 'loan', if a bank could be found that would accept the 100% government guarantee. We decided that we would see how matters progressed after that, but had the comfort of knowing that they couldn't legally enforce an agreement which relied upon the use of public funding as a lever to make us part with 60% of our equity and control our company at an unrealistically low figure. This combined with the fact that it was all in writing on government paper and in their e-mails, was sufficient evidence of malpractice to stop any further pressure. The Tree of Dreams didn't in fact, confirm their offer and most of the people involved with the Stella House meeting moved away soon afterwards, to other jobs I believe.

Covelink did finally get the £199,000 EU money, but it came as no surprise and was entirely predictable when BW and Nesta later announced that they would not, after all, be putting in their £212,000 and £75,000 offered at the Government's Stella House meeting in April. This was also in spite of me having honoured my personal financial commitments and provided, by then, over £230,000. They proved yet again, that they would do anything rather than help us to make a success of the project. Their excuse not to provide their money they said, was due to delays and their time critical proviso's and also, because we had not passed control of Covelink to Karl Watkins colleagues.

This and the minutes of the meeting, once again, openly confirmed again that BW were aware that public funding was being used, inappropriately, to influence and press the directors of Covelink to hand over control of the company to a millionaires private consortium at an unrealistically low price.

Despite all this going on, I was presented with a Smart Award in October of 2003, by the CBI chairman, Hugh Morgan Williams at a ceremony held at Beamish Hall, the handsome building near to the Open Air Museum. His advice to me was familiar, he suggested that I should be prepared to release a lot of the equity to potential investors. I said that we were very happy to do this, but only when there was a fair and equitable deal on the table with people who had the money and whom we could trust.

CHAPTER 60: FACTORY PROGRESS INCREASINGLY DIFFICULT

Time was passing and Nick was having to ring me up from the factory more frequently to see if we could afford to buy the odd sheet of aluminium and other components needed for the Jet-Buses. The rate of progress was slowing which, in turn, meant that the overheads were absorbing a greater percentage of whatever money I could raise. The overall situation was very worrying and I felt very sorry that I had placed Nick in such a dreadful predicament. He knew that I had no salary so he was even using his own wages to pay for things to keep everything going at the factory. He also had the unpleasant job of explaining the problems to the men every day, as well as dealing with the creditors when he was trying to persuade them to supply parts and materials.

The creditors were regularly ringing both of us to ask for money, but their attitude remained helpful and supportive. This was because they knew that we were doing all we could to pay them and were simply trying to create business and industry and they wanted to help us.

Not having a website was a drawback to my funding efforts. This was because I had, as ever, tried to accommodate BW and the sponsors, Barrs, by keeping the project out of the public eye. Now that Mark Smith had shown his true colours and made BW's position painfully clear, I had nothing to lose by having a Covelink website. The results of the website have been remarkable. It brought in and continues to this day, to introduce a steady flow of potential buyers from all over the world. They can see the benefits of Roylecraft technology.

When we were testing, we sometimes had visits from overseas buyers with us to see and test our amphibians for themselves. They can be seen on some of the BBC films. They wanted to buy our Jet-Buses at what had become the established and acceptable price of £350,000 each. I had to explain that despite the serious problems created by BW, we were still tied to them with a contract which forbid us to supply anybody else until their contract had been fulfilled.

The files of potential orders for Roylecraft technology from all over the world worth £550 million.

Altogether, I now have four large lever arch files full of written potential orders worth over £550 million here in my office. These have come in mainly as a result of our website, we have spent no money on advertising Roylecraft. It is remarkable to think that we can create 2500 jobs, and this is a conservative figure, and yet the city, the VC's, the banks and the governmnet stand back and watch me struggling to survive.

We seem to be still leading the world with our technology, others are copying me, but it seems that nobody, to my knowledge, has been able to resolve the problems which I so successfully tackled and overcame more than twenty years ago.

AIM FLOATATION

The discussions with Karl Watkins and Alex Worral continued into the summer of 2003 and it seemed that, once they had taken over control of the company, their plans had been to raise substantial sums of money by floating our company on the AIM unlisted Securities Market. I had been previously told that we were not really in a position to do this, because the project wasn't sufficiently advanced and also due to being tied to our contract with BW.

At the Stella House meeting, BW had agreed to cancel the contract for them, so that they

ROYLE. FROM VINTAGE TO CLASSIC TO AMPHIBIAN.

Water bus could bring 200 jobs to North-East

UP TO 200 jobs could be created in the North-East by an innovative industry.

Covelink Marine, at Staindrop, County Durham, which has designed an amphibious tourist bus, has secured a contract to build the vehicles for use in Scotland.

Managing director, David Royle, who has spent the last 15 years preparing his invention for commercial production, said a business plan had been drawn up to pull together £3.2m to set up a new factory in County Durham by 2004.

It would employ 100 skilled workers, who had been made redundant from firms like Black and Decker, Lefarge Cement Works and Sanyo, and 100 contract workers. Mr Royle has already taken on 15 from Sanyo, Lefarge and Glaxo Smithkline.

The business is involved in a funding programme being supported by One North-East and other commercial parties but, despite good Government support, Mr Royle is still seeking funding from commercial or funding bodies for the project.

The potential market for the amphibious vehicles is estimated at £200m a year, but the company is aiming at 7pc of that.

Mr Royle said: "We will take over an existing factory and it will definitely be in County Durham."

The Japanese are interested in buying 150 of the buses and Covelink is working with the British Embassy in Tokyo to secure the business. The company also has an Australian agent in New South Wales.

Mr Royle, who also runs a vintage car restoration business, said his Roylecraft water bus, which seats up to 32 and can travel up to 70mph on land and 35mph on water, had been undergoing tests on the Tees at Stockton.

Other vehicles range from 22ft to 38ft and have the potential to be used for flood rescue, by HM Customs and Excise, and as ambulances.

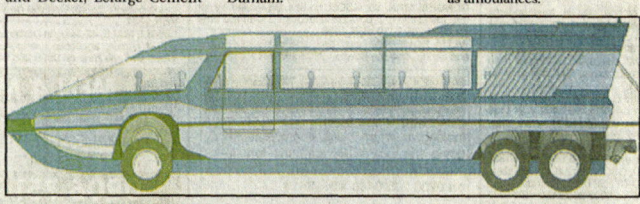

JAPANESE INTEREST: a drawing of David Royle's amphibious bus

Editorials. Darlington & Stockton Times. 09/05/03.

Showing true enterprise!

ABOVE: After the presentations at The Morritt Arms on Thursday night, the winners are photographed with Derek Foster, MP.

AN awards dinner was held on Thursday evening to reward enterprising businesses in Teesdale.

The dinner, hosted by the Teesdale Enterprise Fund at The Morritt Arms, was attended by a number of guests including Derek Foster MP, and Paul Londesborough, GlaxoSmithKline site director.

Since it was set up in March 2002, the fund has helped to create 247 full and part-time jobs. If this rate of take up is carried on throughout the fund's two-year lifespan, then it will have exceeded its target by two or even three times, said chairman of the Fund Management Panel, John Teward.

"This success speaks well of the initiative and enterprise of all forms of business activity in Teesdale, from those venturing into self-employment to those expanding and developing their already established businesses," he said. "This evening we look to celebrate your endeavours and give recognition to achievement in a number of selected categories."

The winner of the *Employer of the Year* category was Anthony Nixon Furniture of Barnard Castle. The award was for setting levels of good practice for improving performance and growing through its people. The business had encouraged excellence in development and training and had created a culture of continuous improvement, making it more competitive in its field. "It is the company's 10th anniversary this month and this recognition means a great deal to us," said Chris Dauber. "Keeping traditional skills alive by investing in youth has always been central to our philosophy although, if we are honest, this has as much to do with self-interest as any crusading zeal! We would like to thank Glaxo and TEA for their support and also all of our skilled and committed staff, without whom we would not exist."

The *Young Entrepreneur Award* was given to Richard Cooke of Comtek. This award is given to a young entrepreneur, who has demonstrated, often against adversity, that they have the stability, integrity and determination to succeed in business.

Covelink Marine Ltd of Staindrop, who design and manufacture new high-speed amphibious vehicles, won an award for the *Most Innovative Business*. This was presented for developing a unique product or service and for showing an enormous amount of patience and overcoming many barriers in achieving their aims.

The *Heritage Award*, for excelling in traditional and craft industries in Teesdale, was presented to Peter Coverdale of P&S Coverdale masonry contractors. This award is given for building upon the traditions of the past to develop a financially viable business with the makings of a stable future.

There were two prizes for the *Business of the Year*. Honeyman Associates and law management consultancy firm, the Ridley Partnership, both won the award, for developing a business with outstanding skill, enthusiasm and professionalism.

Teesside Mercury. 09/04/03.

SOUTH DURHAM BUSINESS FOCUS
Compiled with the assistance of Darlington Business Venture

Business Link Tees Valley – helping and build businesses in Darlington
01642 806666, www.teesbusinesslink.

Award for inventor of amphibious bus

By JULIA BREEN

A BUSINESSMAN who designed an inventive amphibious "tourist bus" has scooped an award.

Staindrop-based David Royle, who also runs a vintage car restoration business, set up Covelink Marine to develop his invention, which he has been working on for the past 15 years.

The Roylecraft is the first land and water-based vehicle in the world to incorporate the technology of having retractable wheels, and the ability to travel at motorway speeds.

Mr Royle was honoured by the Teesdale Enterprise Fund last week, receiving an award as the area's most innovative business.

The award was presented for developing a unique product or service and for overcoming many barriers in achieving his aims. Mr Royle was presented with the award at a dinner hosted by the Enterprise Fund.

Other businesses to receive awards included Anthony Nixon Furniture, of Barnard Castle, Peter Coverdale of P&S Coverdale Masonry contractors, which received a heritage award, and Richard Cooke, of Comtek.

Mr Royle has taken on 15 extra staff and hopes to take on more from the local skilled workforce, following redundancies at the Lafarge cement works, Black and Decker, and Glaxo Smithkline.

He secured a contract last year for four Roylecraft water buses, which seat up to 32 people and can travel at speeds of up to 70mph on land and 40mph on water. Testing has taken place on a privately owned lake near Staindrop and one bus has been launched in a trial on the River Tees.

He believes the smaller craft can be used for flood rescue, the RNLI, oceanography and island-hopping. The vehicles cost between £200,000 and £400,000, depending on size and specifications, and range from 22ft to 38ft.

Pioneering vehicle: David Royle with a part-built model of his Roylecraft land and water operating vehicle

Darlington & South Durham News. 23/04/03.

CHAPTER 60: FACTORY PROGRESS INCREASINGLY DIFFICULT

Is it a boat or a bus? Covelink's amphibious craft shows its versatility during tests in the North-East, before it heads for its new home in Scotland

By MIKE PARKER
Business Editor

Covelink water bus sails through testing times

TESTING is well under way to turn the world's first purpose-built, amphibious bus into a job-making machine.

The pictures above show the passenger vehicle in full testing on land at the Croft motor circuit, near Darlington, and on water at the Tees Barrage.

Covelink Marine Limited has invested £5m in developing the skills needed to build the craft which is bound for a tourist attraction in Scotland.

The deal is the first contract placed with Covelink in its 15-year history – testament to the difficulties caused by trying to develop vehicles suitable for road and water travel.

The craft has to pass stringent tests posed by both the Maritime Coastguard Agency to take to the water and the Department of Transport to use the roads.

Nick Royle, Covelink's project manager, said: "Before we started this contract it was all design and development work.

"We built four prototypes – starting with a speedboat. It has been very hard work.

"There has been a lot of interest in this from all over the world but people want to see them working."

Businesses in Japan have got very excited about the proposition, with the company working in conjunction with the British Embassy in Tokyo to secure a contract for 150 buses.

Covelink operates from a workshop in Staindrop, County Durham. If all goes to plan, the firm intends to set up a factory employing 200 people in the area.

The expansion plans depend largely on its performance when it enters active service.

The vehicle is in the advanced testing phase ahead of being delivered to British Waterways for use at the Falkirk Wheel, between Glasgow and Edinburgh.

The wheel is the world's first and only rotating boat lift which links two canals with water levels 115ft apart.

It replaces a laborious system of 11 locks to transfer boats between the Union Canal and Forth and Clyde canal.

The wheel is the spectacular centrepiece of the £84.5m Millennium Link, the UK's largest canal restoration project. The Covelink craft will enable British Waterways to take visitors on a 40-minute tour around the site.

Twenty five passengers can travel in the six-wheeled bus which is 39ft long and 8.2 ft wide – the legal maximum width for a regular road vehicle.

Falkirk Wheel: The world's first and only rotating boat lift

The rear-wheel drive vehicle is powered by a 240bhp, 3.5-litre Japanese Yanmar engine.

The buses are enormously versatile, with uses ranging from inland water tourist buses for theme parks, to river police vehicles, flood rescue craft, island transport systems, and land to ship ferries.

It can even be used as an amphibious paramedics vehicle.

Mr Royle said: "It has huge advantages. For example, if someone was drowning out at sea you could go out and rescue them, drive straight out of the water and take them to hospital without having to shift them from one vehicle to another."

If successful, Covelink's aspirations to create manufacturing jobs would be an enormous fillip to a county devastated by job losses to cheap labour countries.

Editorials. Northern Echo. 12/08/03.

Tourist bus order sparks hunt for factory and staff

AN innovative industry could create up to 200 jobs in the North-East by next year.

Covelink Marine, in Staindrop, County Durham, which has designed an amphibious tourist bus, has secured a contract to build the vehicles for use in Scotland.

The company's managing director, David Royle, has spent the past 15 years preparing his invention for commercial production. He said a business plan had been drawn up in order to find £3.2m for setting up a factory to make the vehicles in County Durham by next year.

He said the factory will employ 100 skilled workers who

By JULIA BREEN

have been made redundant from companies such as Black and Decker, Lefarge Cement Works and Sanyo, and 100 contract workers.

The business is involved in a funding programme supported by regional development agency One NorthEast and other commercial parties.

However, despite good Government support, Mr Royle is still seeking funding from commercial or funding bodies to undertake the project.

The potential market for the vehicles is estimated at £200m per year, but the company is aiming at seven per cent of this, which would result in an annual turnover of £14m.

Mr Royle said: "We will be taking over an existing factory and it will definitely be in County Durham.

"There are plenty of buildings and, of course, a great availability of skilled workers because of all the recent redundancies in the area.

"We are excited about the potential of benefiting from the skills which are available in the North-East."

He has already taken on 15 workers from Sanyo, Lefarge and GlaxoSmithKline.

The Japanese are interested in buying 150 of the buses and Covelink is working with the British Embassy in Tokyo to secure the business.

The company also has an agent in New South Wales, Australia, to win contracts there.

Mr Royle, who also runs a vintage car restoration business, said his Roylecraft water bus, which can seat up to 32 people and travel at up to 70mph on land and 35mph on water, has been undergoing tests on the River Tees, at Stockton.

Other vehicles range from 22ft to 38ft and have the potential to be used for flood rescue, Customs and Excise, and ambulances.

Order secured: David Royle with one of his amphibious vehicles

Editorials. Northern Echo. 02/05/03.

would be free to float the company when they would expect to see the value of their shares multiply considerably in value (see the minutes). I spoke to one or two of our shareholders who thought it was still certainly worth us giving it a try with or without BW's blessing. Accordingly, in July 2003, I was in touch with the London Stock Exchange who said that we had to appoint nominated advisors and brokers. After doing this, we were advised that if we were able to do it, we could expect between 2.5 to 4 times the total capital invested, in which case, we could expect to see up to £15 million raised. This really would get things moving again!

Amphibious bus company's director makes staff cuts

By JIM McTAGGART

A COMPANY that aims to market a tourist bus that can travel on land and water has had to pay off some of its staff.

David Royle, the managing director of Covelink Marine, at Staindrop, near Barnard Castle, County Durham, said yesterday the move was temporary.

He said five people had left voluntarily and three had been paid off, leaving seven staff. However, he said the future was still bright.

He said: "We are planning to float on the stock exchange in June or July.

"I am confident that we can open a large factory in the region. We will be a multi-million pound company and employ several hundred people.

"I have had to pay wages for the last 18 months without money coming in, and it got to a stage where I had to cut overheads.

"It is regrettable for the staff involved and I realise it is a setback for them, but it is temporary for the firm."

Mr Royle has been working on plans for the amphibious vehicle for 15 years, and it has proved successful in trials.

It has a top speed of 70mph on land and can reach 35mph on water.

Each will cost between £200,000 and £400,000 depending on size.

Mr Royle has received an order from Scotland to supply some of the vehicles once his factory is in production. There has been interest from around the world, mainly from Japan.

Some potential customers want to use it for tourist businesses, while others want it for commercial routes. It could also be used by emergency services.

Mr Royle hopes to find investors to back his plans for a factory, because he believes the potential market for the vehicles is worth £200m a year.

He received an award from Teesdale Enterprise Agency last year for the area's most innovative business.

Mr Royle also owns a vintage car restoration company in Staindrop, which attracts customers from around the world.

'Temporary problem': David Royle with one of his vehicles

Editorials. Northern Echo. 04/02/04.

Floating bus is left high and dry

BY LOUISE BAILLIE & MAXWELL MacLEOD

A FUTURISTIC floating bus project at a Scots tourist attraction is floundering after vital funding ran out.

The buses are designed to DRIVE in and out of the canal at the Falkirk Wheel in Stirlingshire.

But the boffin who invented them claims the project is close to sinking.

David Royle, 64, sighed: "It's so disappointing to get so near and yet so far."

Splash

Bosses at the £17 million Wheel – the hi-tech rotating boat lift which links the Forth and Clyde Canals – are hoping to make a splash with the buses.

Visitors will board the bus as it floats beneath the wheel, before driving out of the canal, along a road behind the wheel, and back into the water at the top. The bus, which has retractable wheels, will then be lowered back to its starting position on the Wheel.

David's company Covelink is building two of the 38ft buses, which were ordered by British Waterways in 2001 and have so far cost £2 MILLION.

But David, from Durham, said: "One bus is completed and has been tested at Falkirk, and the other is nearly finished. But the project has stalled because we've run out of cash."

A British Waterways spokesman said: "We're fully supporting Covelink while they work to resolve their difficulties."

SINKING FEELING: David Royle
HI-TECH ATTRACTION: Falkirk Wheel

Jobs lost as firm fails to attract funds

A COMPANY that came up with the idea of a vehicle that can travel on land and water has had to lay off some members of staff.

But managing director of Covelink Marine, David Royle, which is based at Staindrop, says the move is temporary.

Five people have left of their own volition, and three have been paid off, leaving seven remaining. Mr Royle is confident the future is still bright and plans to float the company on the Stock Exchange in the summer.

His aim is to open a large factory in the region, with the potential for hundreds of manufacturing jobs. Having already spent 16 years trying to open one in the North-East, he is disappointed that he does not seem to get the same element of support given to larger companies coming into the region.

"I have had some support from local government agencies, but it has been difficult for those agencies to find schemes that can provide the funding necessary to start a factory," he said. "It's disappointing when incoming large companies, often from abroad, seem able to access substantial funding in order to set up in the North-East.

"It's regrettable for the staff involved and I realise it's a setback for them, but it is temporary for the firm," he added.

He has been developing the amphibious vehicle for 15 years, and it has proved successful in trials. It has a top speed of 70mph on dry land and 35mph on water and costs from £200,000-£400,000 depending on size.

There has been interest from around the globe, and potential customers have inquired about its use as a tourist vehicle for island hopping or for commercial routes. It could also be used by the emergency services.

Mr Royle hopes he can find the necessary investors to back his factory plans, feeling the market for the vehicles to be worth as much as £200m a year. He received an award from Teesdale Enterprise Agency last year for the area's most innovative business.

(Not entirely true!)

News of the World. 08/02/04.

CHAPTER 60: FACTORY PROGRESS INCREASINGLY DIFFICULT

Floating bus becalmed as costs increase
Inventor struggles to fund final design for vehicle to ferry visitors to the Falkirk Wheel

Inventor plans to float his amphibious bus company

by James Johnston

A STAINDROP company that builds amphibious tourist buses is planning a £10 million stock market flotation.

Covelink Marine, who manufacture the Jet-bus on the outskirts of the village, hope to complete the floatation on the AIM stock exchange in June this year.

Managing director David Royle says that although the move is usually associated with larger businesses, he is confident that it will succeed.

He explained that the money raised would allow the company to build larger premises and increase production to fulfil current orders.

"The AIM stock exchange is for smaller companies and the £10 million will allow us to build bigger workshops to increase production," he said.

Earlier this month (Feb), he was forced to reduce staff numbers at the company - five people left voluntarily and three were paid off - to reduce overheads. For the last 18 months he has been paying wages without money coming in.

But Mr Royle, who also owns a 30-year-old vintage car restoration company in Staindrop, insists that the cuts are only temporary and that he will do all he can to keep the business in Teesdale.

"I'd certainly like to keep it in the area, but it's all down to planning, grants and support."

He has been working on the project for 15 years and the vehicle has proved successful in trials, reaching a top speed of 70mph on land and 35mph on water. The Jet-bus costs £350,000 and the Jet-truck, the second model, £250,000.

"Nobody else in the world is doing this. People need to understand the combination of different technologies that goes into it - it's not just a bathtub on wheels -, I wanted a boat that you drive on land rather than a truck that floats. This is a genuinely innovative idea."

On water: The Jet bus can achieve a nippy 35mph

On land: The Jet bus can reach speeds of 70mph

Editorials. Teessdale Mercury 18/02/04.

To begin with however, we were advised by our brokers that we needed to raise £1.25 million to maintain progress at the factory and prepare for the floatation in spring 2004. It seems that this sum was that which Karl and Alex were aiming to raise. The advisors also stressed the need for a complete management team, demonstration vehicles, certification, and firm Orders. All this was understandable and was in process so, once again, I renewed pressure on all possible sources including all the existing shareholders.

When all came to all, after many more months of work, it became clear that, as ever, we simply could not even raise the immediate sums needed to prepare for the AIM. Although we had an excellent working relationship with MIRA, the MCA and the DTLR people, who were most helpful, the ongoing certification process and testing programme was both a protracted and costly process. As time passed the ongoing shortage of money took its toll. Not satisfied with failing to honour the money due to us under the contract, we were still faced with BW's determination to deprive us of our assets.

BIBBY'S AGREE HEADS OF TERMS

With the help of others, I was still very actively pressing on with funding in 2004 when early in August 2004, Bibby's, the long established and highly respected shipping company in Liverpool began to show interest in Roylecraft. This company was also involved with road transport logistics and had a substantial fleet of wagons and they also provided vehicle Leasing and financial services. An ideal combination to benefit from our technology and project as a whole. They could use and operate our vehicles and also sell them with the benefit of their lease purchase vehicle finance arm. It was an ideal opportunity which would benefit all concerned.

Over the ensuing weeks a whole series of meetings took place with various directors of Bibby's companies carefully evaluating our project and the technology. We explained our situation with BW and by September, we had agreed a detailed Heads of Terms document for a Joint Venture with them. They would inject sums amounting to £3 million and we would have equal equity in the new company to be formed.

At last, we had made contact with an organisation which was seriously interested and prepared to agree to an equitable arrangement. A final round the table meeting was arranged with a number of their executives and agreement reached, subject to final confirmation by their Chairman, Sir Michael Bibby. In a final check following the detailed due diligence work put in by his team, Sir Michael explained that he decided to ring British Waterways.

The phone rang in my office the following morning, it was Sir Michael to tell me that the deal was cancelled. I asked him what had caused his company to have such an abrupt change of heart, especially after so much work had been put in by both sides to establish the facts and put together a detailed Heads of Terms.

He refused to give me an explanation.

There followed a number of phone calls which were made to me, even at home at the weekend. These were from the directors who had been closely involved with the proposed JV. They simply could not understand or explain what had happened and were as surprised as I was. Each one apologised profusely for this inexplicable failure of what promised to be such a successful joint enterprise.

There could be little doubt that Mark Smith and/or other BW directors, had spoiled a marvelous opportunity for Covelink to be properly funded with a good company. It seems that they were determined to support the government officials dubious activities to ensure that Karl Watkins 'Tree of Dreams' group took over control of Covelink. They obviously knew that they were going to benefit from this arrangement, judging from the fact that, in item four of the minutes of the Stella House meeting, BW were going to 'reconstitute' their 'payment plan' and be 'flexible' in the 'reversion of IPR' to Covelink, but not for us.

Following Bibby's sudden 'U' turn and the failure of the JV, I made another attempt to establish the truth and so I wrote once or twice more to Sir Michael and to his brother David, who had visited me previously, to try to find out what BW had told them. I can only presume that it was libellous, otherwise they could have explained the reason. Whatever it was, it stopped the JV with Bibby's dead in its tracks, dreadful.

Yet again, I can only presume that people who had clearly shown themselves to be corrupt were continuing to do all they could to deny me and all those who had helped me, the benefits of 17 years of dedicated and creative work and our ongoing and substantial investments. BW had ruined their own marvellous opportunity and were quite happy to spoil it for us and another organisation which wanted to benefit from our work. Bibby's would have been able to share with us what I now knew to be worth £500 million a year global business and benefit from Roylecraft's excellent technology.

This was the last straw. I realised that it was pointless to press on trying to maintain progress at the factory. When the directors of a big national company will go to any lengths, no matter how unprincipled, to grab the valuable assets of a small, financially weak firm or, failing that, will take whatever steps they wish, to cripple it, then there is no point in continuing.

JET-BUS UPDATE

Now nearing the end of 2004, two years had passed since August 2002, when BW had stopped paying us the balance of the money contracted and due to Covelink. This resulted in a gradual depletion in the number of men working at the factory, but throughout this period, we had still been making steady progress with the Jet-Buses and had been able to film and demonstrate them to potential buyers.

On my part, there was a great deal of time taken up with fund raising and dealing with Mark Smith's ongoing devious and extraordinary activities. Two buses were finished and we were working on the third. I had managed to raise enough money to pay the wages and other ongoing overheads. I had also managed to pay for most of the remaining, costly components including the costs of transport each time we took the Jet-Bus for further trials.

Trevor Chaytor-Norris who runs Croft Racing Circuit, very kindly let us use the race track for road testing and I was delighted to see how well the bus handled. To start with, we would take it gently, but as we saw how stable and positive the innovative retractable wheels and suspension was and how well the entirely new steering mechanisms worked, we speeded up and were driving it like a fast motor car, I was delighted to find that it was so tractable and such a pleasure to drive.

Overall, the testing had proved that the Jet-Buses were most certainly a viable and safe new form of transport. They handled on the road and in water equally well, 95% of the important innovative components had worked precisely as they had been designed to do. The few minor faults were not a serious worry or costly and experienced engineers were surprised that a completely new, dual purpose amphibious vehicle incorporating so many innovative features, was such a great success on it's first and ensuing tests, especially at such minimal costs.

In terms of the visual aspects of the Jet-Buses design, I expected, from the start, that I would improve the external features and shape of the buses as we progressed into proper production. The main features including the sliding roof and side panels, were included because originally, Mitsubishi specified that they wanted an amphibious bus which could be open in the summer for their tourists in Osaka in Japan. The rest of my relatively straight forward external design shape was made for a number of important reasons which include various aspects of the marine and automotive regulations, as well as cost.

All in all, my aim was to achieve the technical breakthrough and incorporate all the new mechanisms. At the same time, I wanted to make it look businesslike, but not be too costly to build in the early stages. In any event, they were good enough to attract orders for hundreds of them coming in from international buyers all over the world. They could see that our machines were technically advanced and they wanted to buy them.

Whilst the faults which we discovered and have mentioned were few and minor in comparison to the overall success of the vehicles, they were, never the less, now being blown out of all proportion and used by Mark Smith and BW in order to criticise and denigrate the project. This again, illustrating their desire to undermine my work and enable them to take our assets at minimum cost. Alternatively, although unlikely, it could be seen as Mark Smith's most serious lack of knowledge about innovative engineering on this scale, especially when the potential development costs were only going to be perhaps £30,000 to £50,000 when even the creation and development cost of ordinary motor cars are measured in tens of millions of pounds.

ADMINISTRATORS FINALLY CALLED IN

In the autumn of 2004, the day finally dawned when we were down to just five men at the factory, the debts were building up and the RBS, our bank, was overdrawn to the limit. Money was still coming in, but only in dribs and drabs and it was not sufficient to pay the wages and make any worthwhile progress with the creditors or the buses. I therefore decided to refuse any further offers for shares. It would not have been fair to the very supportive private investors, who were continuing to have confidence in me, as the money would have been wasted. It was clear that I had no alternative but to call in the Administrators.

Strangely enough, without realising and entirely by coincidence, it was 7 October 2004, my 65th birthday. Any ideas of retirement were far from being in my mind however, after seventeen years of good work, I wasn't ready to give up yet, in spite of the fact that Mark Smith had finally achieved his aim to force Covelink to close down.

As the project was obviously going to be at a

standstill for some time, I took the opportunity to have the gearbox removed. This was not only to modify the creep drive motors, this fault was not so serious that it had prevented our tests and ongoing trials, but prolonged testing had also shown that one of the gearbox bearings was overheating.

As needs must, I had specifically asked Nick to carry out some extended testing to reveal any faults such as this. We needed to ensure future reliability. Again it was not a particularly serious or costly fault, it was partly due to complying with the requirements of the MCA. Although the engine was in a separate compartment, they wanted me to fit a bulkhead between it and the gearboxes which was understandable, but unfortunately, it restricted the air flow over the gearboxes, so the cooling needed to be improved. Also, in an effort to keep the costs to a minimum, Websters had not incorporated an oil pump in the special transfer gearboxes. This is not unusual in such a unit, since the oil can often circulate perfectly well by 'splash feed'. These two factors were the cause of the problem and not difficult to rectify.

Not surprisingly, Websters were one of our creditors and were owed money. Admittedly, there were problems with their gearbox, but they had been very helpful and continued to support the project all the way through and had done their best to keep their costs to the minimum. Never-the-less, the company had recently been taken over and now needed to see, at least, some of the outstanding debt paid off before they were able to rectify the problems and return the gearboxes to us. I could understand this and could not complain as we had insufficient money to pay them.

The administrators whom I had appointed, were Robson Laidler of Jesmond in Newcastle upon Tyne. They were helpful and set about their formal duties and began to establish who owned what and how to raise the money to pay the creditors and sell the assets. Not daunted, I was still extremely busy doing all I could to try to rescue the project.

With the little factory now dead quiet and nothing happening, as previously promised, I transferred Allan back to Royles where he could continue with restoration work in the machine shop and also retained Nick for a short time to help me with the paperwork. With all the remaining staff having gone, I was again confronted with yet another depressing stage in what, I previously had every reason to believe, was going to be a roaring, commercial success.

The administrators then asked me to put together the drawings and the patent information and IPR. After seventeen years of the most intensive and personal application to all the challenges which I had to meet, gathering the huge number of documents, files and drawings was an extremely upsetting task.

They represented tens of thousands of hours work. Designs created in bed, in hospital, in the office and also during the holidays on the boat. All done without any salary, in fact, quite the reverse. I had been ploughing in all the money I could raise from any possible source, many of my treasured posessions having been sold.

The administrators were visibly shocked when they saw box upon box of documents, files and drawings. Once again, like most people, they had no real understanding of the amount of work involved when creating a new and innovate form of transport on this scale.

I also had the unpleasant task of facing the Nesbitt's who owned the farm and the 4,000 foot building which we had fitted out and equipped expressly for the purpose of assembling and developing our new vehicles. We owed him rent and yet he was visibly shocked when I told him that I had sold assets, mortgaged my home and workshops and used my pension fund to pay the wages and pay the rent until I could go on no longer.

Another person who had no idea what I had done to progress this far. In the end the administrators gave him the £60,000 worth of machinery and equipment which we had installed in his building to cover the rent due which, from memory, cost me around £10,000 per annum, so I imagine he would come out of it satisfactorily.

MORE TROUBLE

The next challenge came from the CDDC, this was when I received a demand to appear in court in nearby Bishop Auckland. They were going to enforce repayment of their £50,000 loan plus interest. They were of course, entitled to this money. I had agreed, personally, to guarantee the loan to the company, so I had no defence. I thought that it was worth having my day in court, so attended the hearing.

In preparation and before the hearing, I sent a report to the court judge which explained what had occurred at BW along with one of the BBC films on DVD, which showed our MK IV Prototype and the Jet-Bus undergoing tests. This DVD also included one of the BBC 2 Working Lunch programmes in which I was appealing for money for production to meet all the potential orders coming in.

In the event, on 21st April 2005, the judge was most sympathetic, but confirmed that the money had to be repaid. With the help of John Clapcott, who was working with me at the time, I was able to avoid having to pay the interest charges. This was helpful, because the only way I could repay this company's loan was to further increase my already substantial mortgage on our house in Gainford.

After closing his book, the Judge asked my permission to lend the DVD to the Development Corporation's legal representative, so that they could know what they were failing to support, and then asked the man to return it to me afterwards. He followed this up by saying "how can we get the money for this excellent project?"

So ended my day in court.

CHAPTER 61:
EXTREME FUNDING EFFORTS

Whenever there seemed to be a chance that I would raise the money for production, I had visited local Industrial Estates to see which of the many empty factories would best suit our purposes. There were plenty to choose from, with over 240 of them standing empty at this time and this was before the 2008 recession began!

My experience after eighteen years of really intensive effort, contacting literally hundreds of possible sources of money, showed me, painfully clearly, why there were so many empty factories. Even then, in 2005, this country was suffering record trade deficits year on year. A fact which was rarely mentioned in the press. The whole affair didn't make sense and defied reason. Nobody seemed to want manufacturing or to create profitable jobs or real money, earned from exports.

I had, by now, spent eighteen intensive years speaking to hundreds of sources of funds and was now also taking it up with the most eminent people in the country, desperately trying to draw attention to our extraordinary predicament.

One of the many people I approached early in 2004, was HRH the Duke of Edinburgh. Once he knew about my problems and having seen some of the BBC films about our Roylecraft, His Royal Highness was as surprised as I was, that we couldn't raise the money for production. He went on to suggest possible contacts and tried very hard to help me in any way he could.

In one of the many welcome letters, posted over the years, variously from Buckingham Palace, Balmoral Castle, Holyroodhouse and Windsor he said, in what I visualised as being his usual dulcet tone, "I'm surprised that it has not driven you round the bend". He could see how useful my machines would be in the many floods and for the emergency services around the world. It was always a great morale booster to hear from such an eminent and busy man whose naval experience equipped him to see the benefits of our advanced amphibious craft.

The following year, Prince Philip very kindly helped me with a personal introduction to a half hour documentary which was produced from the BBC films, to show the history and development of Roylecraft.

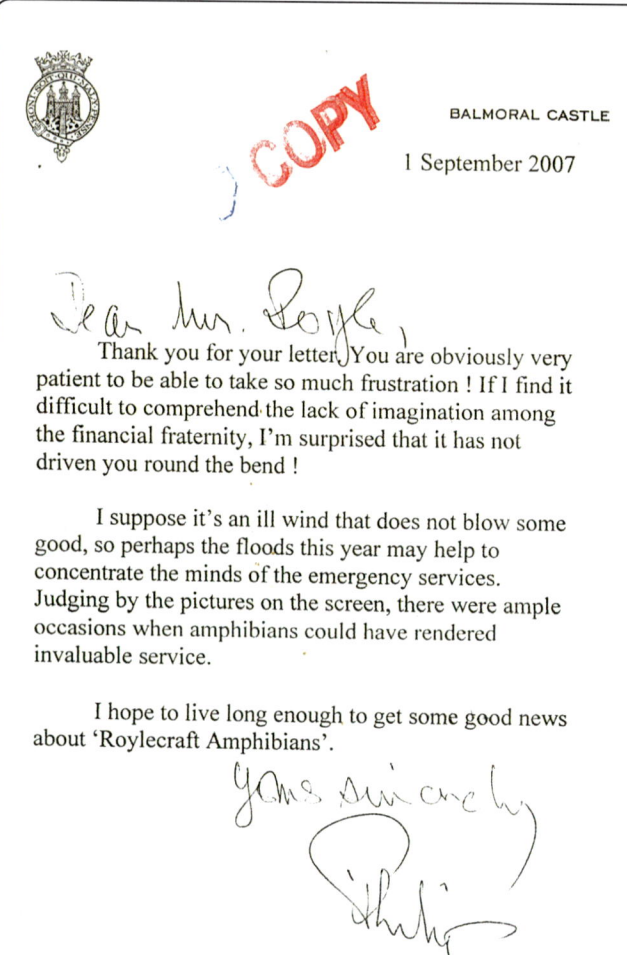

One of many letters from Prince Philip.

Obviously, when writing to Buckingham Palace, I had some fun with my Royle name, all of which Prince Philip took in good faith. We remained in regular contact until the loss of my companies and the project, necessarily curtailed the amount of correspondence. I am most grateful and have been privileged to have been supported by Prince Philip and I would also like to include my thanks to his Private Secretary, Sir Miles Hunt-Davis, who has also been extremely kind and considerate during the last six turbulent years of the project.

Another interesting person with whom I was in touch was Sir Eddie George, the Governor of the Bank of England. Although well above the level of providing funds for projects of any sort, I thought it worth letting him know what was happening to a man in the street who was trying very hard to create business in the UK. He was interested in my problems and wrote to tell me that he had asked the Bank of England's Northern Agent, David Buffham to come to see me.

When Mr Buffham visited me in Staindrop, he was, not surprisingly, most charming and after I had explained to him why I needed to raise money, he explained that he and his colleagues are more involved with policy making, rather than arranging funding, which of course, I realised when I first contacted Sir Eddie. Never the less, he said how surprised he was when I explained what I needed the money for.

He then went on to say that there were no unemployment problems in the north east and couldn't understand why I was working so hard to create exports and jobs. I asked him if he had noticed any empty factories on his journey down from Newcastle. He said he had noticed one or two. "One or two" I replied, showing him a book which listed them, "there are over 240 of them, some of them covering acres of space". He said that they get the figures from the government and they indicated around 2.5% unemployment in this region. "If that is so" I replied, "where have all the thousands of people gone who worked in all the empty factories, have they gone to live in Surbiton?" I couldn't help making this slightly cheeky and unfunny joke to emphasise the point. I could see that Mr Buffham was genuinely surprised to hear this. It was a moot point.

The outcome of the meeting appeared three weeks later in a small article in a right hand column of the Daily Telegraph. This announced that "The Bank of England had appointed a committee of six people to look into the governments figures". At least the facts had reached Sir Eddie's desk, the point had been made, but as ever, not surprisingly, no money arrived!

Not daunted, I continued to make contact with anybody who might be able help. To give you a flavour of the broad scope, these included:

Trevor Baylis (wind up radios), Tim Smit (Eden Project) I had a stand at an inventors fair at the Barbican near to both of these amusing and interesting men. I also wrote to Richard Branson, Terry Disdale (Super yachts), Ray Nagin (Mayor, New Orleans Floods) and in the media, John Humphrys (radio 4) and Jeremy Paxman, Jeremy Clarkson (Top Gear). The buses got a mention saying our machines would be good "to take some of the traffic off the roads". Adam Hart-Davis, Peter Snow, Bob Geldof, Jonathan Porrit, various Dragons Den people (Too much money for their TV show), James Dyson and many, many more. Some were interested but I couldn't now demonstrate one of my machines to them.

ADMINISTRATORS EFFORTS TO SELL THE ASSETS

I helped the administrators to produce an Information Memorandum and then they began to see the problems when prospective buyers for the assets approached them. Although I was not surprised, it was extremely upsetting for me to see nominal sums being offered for everything that I had spent so much time, money and trouble to create. In the hope of picking up a bargain, offers of around £300,000 would come in for what, by then, had cost over £5 million including BW's money. The buyers knew that there were potential orders worth hundreds of millions of pounds, so the 'green eyed god's eyes' were shining brightly.

It was all very well when discussing these rock bottom, nominal offers in the office or on the

Allan in the engine bay of the Jet-Bus.

Another under-floor view of part of the Jet-Bus mechanisms.

telephone, but when the buyers actually inspected the Jet-Buses in the factory, they would see the complexity and innovative mechanisms and then turn to me and ask if I would help them and also transfer some of my Royles men to finish off the work. They offered to pay the wages of course and with the administrators aim being simply to cash the assets and move on, understandably, they were not at all pleased when I explained the position.

Once again they, like most people, had no conception of my eighteen years of work and intensive dedication without any income for most of the time, and the fact that the project was technically, a huge success. On top of this, I explained that I was looking at a loss of over £4 million, £3.1 million of it personally and yet they expected me to write off half my lifes work and still carry on working on it.

I had to tell them that Royles were busy and committed to ongoing restoration contracts with a workforce which was already reduced and that I wasn't going to further jeopardise that company for one which I had just put into administration.

The last thing I wanted for all concerned, was for the new buyers to become another BW, especially if I was to be working with them. As my team had now been disbanded and the ongoing work with the MCA and DTLR disrupted, there was only one way forward. There needed to be sufficient funding not only to finish the Jet-Buses to the necessary high standards and if they wanted to sell them, they would have to then test and certificate them. After this, they would hopefully have enough to take the whole project forward into production, otherwise the huge opportunity which I had spent half my life creating would be wasted.

Naturally the administrators job is selling the assets, but the buyers soon realised that they did not want to be involved in the long term investment needed to finish the development work and then certificate them. It was not the 'fast buck' situation which they were hoping for.

By now, it was very clear and yes, I said that I was talking in millions of pounds, and that I was fed up with short term, quick money making schemes when I was trying to create what was, so obviously, going to be a large and very worthwhile and profitable new industry. I was desperately short of money and extremely angry that I had been so stupid as to believe the governments many calls for innovation, saying that they would "invest heavily in world class science and technology" and give "fast access to all the support you need when you need it" as stated in the DTI and Business Link leaflets.

It was not dissimilar to the Karl Watkin and One North East situation. Although some money might have been made available, there was no way that I would be put in a 'fast buck' situation. I was again surrounded by people who didn't understand what they were dealing with and thought the Jet-Buses could be turned into money fairly easily and quickly. It was demanding enough, to process the project in an efficient and proper manner, but once again, the thought of being under the control and instructed by people who didn't understand the design principles and their purpose and probably wouldn't have all the money to do it, appalled me.

It would be a nightmare situation similar to that which had killed other designers like Frua of Italy. I would rather write off the whole project, than argue with people who didn't understand what they were dealing with and whose only interest is making a fast buck when massive benefits were in the offing. It is precisely this quick profit motive that has contributed to a century of stagnation and which had denied the benefits of fast and efficient amphibious transport around the world.

Even if a buyer was found and the Jet-Buses were finished and sold. The chances are that the buyers would not set up production, but would sell them on to overseas companies who had been pressing me to buy them. Once they had them, they would probably copy and reverse engineer them and the benefits to this country and to those who had invested, including me, would be lost.

I had reached the stage some time ago, when it was clear that we needed far more than just the money to finish the first four Jet-Buses. The original plan and benefit of the JV with BW, was that they would have provided the necessary money to go into production. I was already gearing up our Covelink's team for this and they were good engineers and were perfectly capable of doing it, if BW had not upset the applecart. The market and the orders were there, I wasn't interested in spending half my life doing so much work creating a new technology, just to build 3 or 4 buses.

The only way to benefit from the huge and intensive efforts made, was to start series production. My ongoing research and meetings with a great many people in this country and overseas, confirmed that this project would create employment for well over 2000 people and establish a new and profitable global industry. Grand and ambitious, yes, but perfectly feasible and practicable, especially with the spade work already done and no serious competition. We'd had good people and engineers around us and the basis of an experienced management team already in existence.

I believe that some people thought I had grandiose ideas of sitting at the head of a large boardroom table and controlling the new industry. I have no wish to do this, just as long as I have a skilled, honest and experienced management team who respect me for what I have done and respect my judgement of the technology itself, I would be happy to leave the running of the company to them. I would of course, want to see a proper return on my years of work and investments.

I'm afraid that the administrators thought that I was uncooperative, but throughout my life I have helped people when I can, often against my own interests. On a number of occasions I had finished off customers vintage cars and not charged them for thousands of pounds worth of work. All because the cars were in worse condition than any of us anticipated and they didn't have the money to finish them.

The plain fact is that having designed these new vehicles from scratch without payment, I am only content to be entirely responsible for them and their future technical success when in service around the world, if I am in control and will benefit for all the work which I have done.

Sooner or later, especially with some of them being operated in extreme weather conditions by the emergency services, there are bound to be accidents. If others are in control of the development work and any new designs and if any alterations or changes to the specifications are made, then I would not want to be involved in any respect.

It became clear as the months passed, that the administrators couldn't sell them and might as well let BW take the Jet-Buses since they did have some rights to them even though I had raised substantial sums to pay for some of the work and one or two of the hulls and some of the components. This was after BW had stopped the contract payments. I did retain my original prototypes though.

BW TAKE THE BUSES (JUNE 2005)

Knowing that I had many hours of BBC film showing the various stages of the development of our prototypes, my appeals for funding and other aspects, including appearances on BBC 2 and on the Politics Show, it seems that BW were determined that they would not be filmed when they were taking the jet buses away.

The agreement was that they would collect them on the Wednesday 15 June. Knowing how their minds work, I warned the film crew that they may try to be clever, so asked them, if it

British Waterways loading the Jet-Buses onto their trailer units.

was at all possible, to be ready at a moment's notice. Sure enough BW came on 14 June the day before they were expected. The minute their trucks arrived, I was on the phone, and in no time at all, the crew arrived to film the evil act.

I am sorry to say that I did break down when being interviewed, but thankfully, it was cut out before it was shown, shortly afterwards, on BBC 2 Working Lunch Programme. The project was included in three of their programmes altogether and it brought in a few potential investors, but not the big investor we really needed.

The two finished Jet-Buses were without their gearboxes, so were not running. The incomplete third anf fourth hulls and all the 16 tonnes of components were also taken down to Newark on Trent where BW had a boat building and canal servicing yard. This depot was complete with a large dry dock which is where the Jet-Buses and hulls were stored. (Picture sent to me by Waterways World magazine.) I imagine Mark Smith's intention was that BW's own engineers

Jet-Buses in the dry dock at Newark on Trent.

would finish the work of assembling, testing and putting the buses into service. If this was the plan, I expect he thought that it would save money and BW would also then have the benefit of the one million pound sponsorship from Barrs.

I actually saw them at Newark when Jo-Jo and I called in to see them on 14 July 2005, on our way home coming north from Cornwall. Although we no longer have Meriva, we still go to see our friends there.

BW FACES THE FACTS

It was not long before I heard that, despite having my hundreds of drawings, patents and IPR, British Waterways engineers couldn't make any progress and weren't sufficiently familiar with the new technology to carry on with the work. This was not surprising, not only because the Jet-Buses are very different, in so many respects, to normal marine craft, it is also because the automotive components are very different to those in any previous type of motor vehicle or boat.

Importantly, because I was under so much pressure to design and then assemble, test and complete the buses for BW and with the all the troubles created by Mark Smith, I hadn't had time to produce a detailed, instruction manual for the Jet-Buses. With the gearboxes also having been removed and taken to Websters to have oil pumps fitted and more powerful creep drive motors, BW's men couldn't even drive the Jet-Buses.

Obviously, I was now extremely upset and angry, so they couldn't very well ask me how it all worked, so they contacted the specialists whom I had consulted.

BW could see the names which accompanied mine on some of the drawings which they now had. Not having an Autocad system, I had drawn the designs on graph paper in the traditional manner and when discussing any details with marine architects, engineers or people at the universities for example, each of them would, with my permission and in confidence, reproduce my drawings by scanning them onto their Autocad machines. This meant that their names were also pre-printed on the Autocad drawings. When BW's engineers had contacted each of my consultants, they reported this back to me, saying that they had confirmed to BW's people that the designs were mine, which they were, and that naturally, they couldn't help and that they should speak to me.

This confirmed what I had suspected all along, which was that Mark Smith, like many people, had no real conception of the very specialised and of the advanced nature of the technology incorporated in Roylecraft and that they had underestimated the innovative designs incorporated in my successful work. This was especially true in his case, because he was an accountant and had little or no technical knowledge of what he had taken control of.

Once again, Mark Smith and his co-directors had completely misjudged the whole thing. They probably thought that David Royle was only some sort of vintage car enthusiast and that his creation was bound to be a relatively simple design. If so, how wrong they were!

British Waterways must, by now, have begun to realise what a diabolical mess they had made of the entire project. Soon afterwards, BW closed down their Newark workshops and, like our good team at Covelink's starter factory, I heard that the BW engineers were also made redundant. A really good and valuable project being ruined and more jobs lost through sheer ignorance and what was rapidly becoming obvious, blatant maladministration!

It may be that Mark Smith was trying to prove how clever he was to make savings and take over control of Covelink at no cost to BW, or that Defra were also tightening their belts and limiting the money available to BW, but if the JV had been properly and fairly arranged, BW would, by then, have been starting to make substantial profits from our technology.

MORE FRUSTRATION

Time was passing and it was now a year since I had called in the administrators. BW had made no progress and wanted to clear the Newark workshops so apparently the Jet-Buses were loaded up again and along with the wagon loads of components, they were transported, this time, to a large corrugated iron shed near the canal at Northwich in Cheshire. This is where they were to remain, gathering dust, for the next four years or more.

It is truly difficult to find words to express the extreme frustration which I experienced and still do. Potential buyers from all around the world continued to contact me with orders for our machines. Some of them had visited and tested our Jet-Buses like Mitsubishi from Japan and others from Australia had done and were pressing hard for me to supply them with Jet-Buses. The orders were steadily accumulating and now amounted to hundreds of millions of pounds and yet here we were with no factory, no staff and with the vehicles locked away and doing no good for anybody.

CHAPTER 62:
DESTRUCTIVE DISHONESTY

Probably because the directors of BW were now in an increasingly difficult and untenable position, I discovered to my horror, that they were now telling people that the Roylecraft vehicles "didn't work". After spending three desperate years employing the most devious and fraudulent tactics in order to aquire the assets and IPR relating to my technology, BW now were embarking on the most extraordinary volte-face, one which contradicted all they had been doing. They didn't care that "incredibly irresponsible behaviour for the senior directors of a large national government company," would undermine and irreparably damage the 18 years of successful innovative work and the important benefits of the entire project. This untruthful and destructive new policy was obviously designed to cover their backs.

It was becoming clear how very serious the situation was. They had ruined a wonderful transport opportunity for tourists at the Falkirk Wheel and also one which would have revived the UK's waterways and the canals and river systems around the world. We had created a modern and useful form of dual purpose transport, ideal for public and commercial transport, flood rescue and for the emergency services. It was, unquestionably, the foundation of a new and profitable export industry.

With the failure of the previous independent engineers inspections to find fault and now urgently needing backup to support their extremely damaging and dishonest claims, it seems that Smith and BW even went so far as to pay Colin, BW's 'consultant' who had spent his time at the factory, to confirm in writing that "Roylecraft didn't work". Interestingly, this is the man who can clearly be seen and heard cheering on the BBC film when the Jet-Bus was driven so successhully by Nick on the River Tees during it's first tests - money talks!

This was another example of how BW would stoop to the lowest level to protect their reputation. They had no concern for the fact that there were many hours of BBC film which proved that Roylecraft worked and did so brilliantly well.

Faced with statements like this, people who had not been involved, would tend to believe the Directors of a large organisation like BW rather than believe "David....who? Being the designer of Roylecraft, he would say they were marvellous, wouldn't he!"

It was particularly galling for Colin to be helping to nail down our coffin. He had praised us so often for the success of these machines. He had spent hours with Nick driving in the Jet-Bus on water and on the road and knew precisely how good the designs were. I was absolutely horrified and told him so in no uncertain terms.

Here we were, yet again, seeing dishonest, immoral and unprofessional behaviour, equal only to that of the corrupt solicitors following our success in the High Court Legal case. Again, it was money and the abuse of power, this time, by the directors and associates of British Waterways covering up the fact that they had made a mess of an excellent and important contract.

Worse was yet to come. This was when I learnt that Smith and BW were taking even more drastic steps by allowing the valuable Patents and the world wide IPR to lapse. This was the ultimate insult in their truly destructive and counterproductive activities. The lists of global patents shown earlier in the book, shows how extensive they are. I have never experienced such extremes of wickedness and corruption.

After thousands of hours of innovative design, my Patents reflected and protected this innovative work and are an indication of the importance of our achievements. Especially in the automotive and transport industries, where patents are particularly challenging. This is because there has been over a century of patent applications for every conceivable automotive and marine mechanical device, at least until Roylecraft came along!

The creation of even one new, single, strong and unique patent is quite an achievement. To have a number of them which are 'strong' is a clear indication of their originality and acknowledges the innovative nature of the mechanism. It was not a simple matter, nor especially clever, it was the result of approaching problems from a different angle and then devoting a great deal of time and thought to resolve them.

REPORT TO DEFRA & BW BOARD

Early in 2005, I was told that the Dept for Environment Food and Rural Affairs, Defra, the government body which controls British Waterways, were asking BW for a formal report as to why the contract with our small company, Covelink Marine Ltd, had failed.

Believing that they should hear the truth and my side of the story, I decided to write my own Formal Report. This covered the background to the technology, the awards and the details of how the contract was made and the reason for its failure. In it, I included references to documents and letters as evidence of my statements and sent the finished 17 page report dated 16th February 2005 to Defra in Parliament. I also sent copies of it to the board of BW and to other interested parties.

A copy of the report is included at end of the book, in the appendix, but it might interest you to see the facts which are summed up on the pen-ultimate page of the Report and repeated here:

- BW has had to write off sums approaching £1 million which it spent on the project.
- BW has ongoing costs at the Falkirk Wheel for less suitable, ordinary boats when efficient Jet-Buses could now be in service.
- BW and Barrs (sponsors) have no benefits from the new technology to enhance and provide tourist facilities at Falkirk.
- The probable loss of substantial sponsorship (£1 million) from Barrs.
- The possible waste of a new technology and seventeen years work.
- The possible waste of £3.4 million of private and public sector investment excluding BW's investment.
- The potential loss of a worldwide market worth 500 £million per annum.
- The loss of jobs and industry in the North East.
- The waste of years of support by many people in industry, academic institutions and Parliament.
- The potential Loss of flood rescue vehicles in the UK and around the world.
- The imminent loss of valuable world-wide patents and IPR.

I concluded by saying that this list and the fact that BW specifically excluded reporting any discussions about Covelink from the published minutes of their board meetings, showed that they had something to hide and the reasons which lay behind their decision to close down Covelink and destroy the project, were not democratic, not commercial and would be very damaging to BW if published.

The effects of this report may have been two fold:

An article was published in the Guardian soon afterwards, on 3 April, with the heading, "Government slams British Waterways record". Defra in a "stinging attack "said that BW was not "focussed on its core task" and was 'Not an effective custodian of our waterways.' A copy of the article is shown here.

THE IMPORTANT RESULT IN JUNE 2005

Not long after that, I heard that Mark Smith, the Financial Director had resigned. I wasn't informed by BW about this of course, but after seeing the most contrived, ill judged and wasteful disruption of an excellent project, although too late, he certainly deserved to have lost his directorship. At least the truth was known to Parliament and some justice was seen to be done.

Although displaying a remarkable lack of judgement, I couldn't help feeling that, to a degree, he had been made, as the Americans would say, the 'Fall Guy' to carry all the blame for actions which must have had boardroom support. Because the minutes concerning Covelink, were not published.

So, after suffering three years of repeated denials of any malpractice by Smith and other members of the BW board of directors, when the true facts became known, presumably as a result of my report to Defra in Parliament, Mark Smith finally resigned. I have continued, to this day, to write to the CEO and to the board of directors of BW to demand compensation for me, my shareholders and those who were defrauded of the huge benefits due to them by BW as yet, none have been paid. See recent letter in the appendix.

Government slams British Waterways record

Nick Mathiason
Sunday April 3, 2005

Observer

British Waterways, the custodian of 1,988 miles of canals and nearby land across the UK, has suffered a stinging attack from the the government department responsible for it.

In a carefully worded 51-page report published just before Easter, the Department of the Environment, Food and Rural Affairs has indicated that BW is not focusing on its core task, and highlighted a conflict between its public role and its growing commercial interests in property and marina businesses.

'In the ... consultation, there was a lack of clear understanding about how the public policy objectives sat alongside requirements to act commercially, and how priorities were determined,' the BW policy review stated. It added that the agency needed to engage with its stakeholders and 'must have due regard to the principles of fair competition, the limits of its statutory powers and its core competencies'.

'The state of British Waterways is a deep embarrassment for the Government,' said Norman Baker, the Lib Dem environment spokesman. 'It's clear that BW is not an effective custodian of our waterways. It is a poor man's Railtrack, seeing itself more as a property company.' However, Robin Evans, BW's chief executive, said: 'The report ... is a firm endorsement of our strategy to use our assets commercially to secure the long-term future of the inland waterways.'

Guardian Unlimited © Guardian Newspapers Limited 2005

The Guardian news item. 3 April 2005.

This affair was not dissimilar to the situation with my restoration company, Royles, when my Eversheds solicitors, also resigned. Again, this was when these equally corrupt, highly paid people had, on that occasion, literally stolen money awarded to us in the High Court. Again they resigned when the facts were reported to Parliament, but it left this small, honourable company in financial difficulties for 14 years without adequate compensation.

THE OMBUDSMEN

Because I had seen how easily the orders of even a High Court Judge were ignored when they were completely in our favour and because of my debts and serious financial predicament, I could not possibly afford, and it was certainly not worth the risk of taking legal action against either of these big organisations. Both the lawyers and the government are probably the most powerful organisations in the country and it became clear that no solicitors or barristers would take up my cases, especially Pro- Bono, when they would be setting out to 'do battle' with their own colleagues at their own expense.

I had no choice but to take both of these important cases to the appropriate Ombudsmen.

The full story behind the legal case is told earlier in the book, but briefly, the facts in the High Court event were reported to the Legal Ombudsmen, firstly to Ann Abraham, who was later transferred to become the NHS and Parliamentary Ombudsman, so then it became Zahida Manzoor who was dealing with my case. Her report was finally presented to me **twelve years** after the hearing when the solicitors had ignored the Orders of the High Court and ignored other undeniable written evidence. She tried to help, but was finally forced to find in favour of the Solicitors, despite both of them having already resigned. Sadly, I could only conclude from written evidence that she is not an independent authority, as is stated in the official ombudsman's documentation.

I was now going to find out, in this second case, what the Waterways Ombudsman would do, so I reported the facts to Hiliary Bainbridge, another female ombudsman. Once again, I saw a most protracted and cleverly executed performance demanding time consuming reports and correspondence. Not from the Law Society controlled legal complaints agency, as in the fraudulent legal case, but this time from the waterways Ombudsman herself.

When she was confronted with undeniable written evidence of very serious malpractice and the painfully obvious huge losses and the truly dreadful results of it, she paid little heed to it all. Yes, you've guessed it! she found in favour of British Waterways and Mark Smith, even though, as in the legal case, he also had already resigned.

There can be no doubt, what so ever, that it was another most serious example of a complete whitewash and maladministration, this time, by the waterways ombudsman.

Like the legal case, she was obviously not independent, this time of BW. Not only, once again, was the Ombudsman ignoring the facts in the case and yet again, that the guilty party had already resigned, this time, she also even ignored Defra's critical Parliamentary report and the adverse publicity in the press.

In both of the above, the ombudsmen are representing powerful Parliamentary and legal forces and there can be no shadow of doubt, and the evidence clearly proved, that fraud and corruption were the cause of the problems. Neither of these ombudsmen were independent, as is claimed for all ombudsmen and there can be little doubt that the public are being cheated of a fair adjudication and democratic complaints process.

MORE UNFAIR TREATMENT

On another occasion, when I was taxed on monies which, with great difficulty, I had to find, (£1500 every month) to pay the interest on the loans which I had arranged in order to pay the wages to keep Covelink's little factory running after BW had cut off the supply of money (again with no salary or benefit to me) I also took this up with the HMRC adjudicator, Dame Barbara Mills DCE QC.

Once again the adjudicator was a woman, I really don't understand why they are called "ombudsmen" when most of them are not. I must say, however, that this lady went to considerable trouble when, on 10 September 2008, she wrote to me to explain, in some detail, why I was obliged to pay the tax. It consisted of four pages and clarified the issues. I had told her that the whole business was due to fraud and cirruption in legal and BW offices, so she was being careful not to implicate the tax demand in any way, with these serious matters when, clearly, it was the root of the problem.

Having no salary with which to pay the interest on the company's loans, I had used the rent from the west end of our house which is let along with rent from the workshops. I had previously stopped charging the restoration company rent, because it was still struggling as a result of the ongoing debts after the legal fiasco. These were the only sources of money to pay the interest, except for my state pension, after 2005.

It turned out that the tax demand was a blunt and simple instrument. It was purely because the money was rent payable to me as the owner of the properties. It did not matter that none of it was for my benefit and it was being used entirely for the R&D company. I always thought tax was only charged on income or a benefit and had sent bank statements to show that I didn't receive the money.

Believing that I could not possibly be liable for the tax of £1962.15 on money which was of no benefit to me and not being able to pay it anyway, I fought on for two years. This was when the HMRC threatened to send the bailiffs to take our treasured family furniture away. Hence the lines in my poem, 'The Little Man in The Street'. I wrote this because, once a decision is made, ombudsmen do not reply to any more letters, so I thought this might penetrate their defences. It is included in this book.

By this time, tax offices located, literally, the length and breadth of the country, were dealing with me. It was obviously a 'hot potato', in fact, it was a lady in one of the many offices, actually in Cheshire, who could see how unfair it was, who suggested that I write a book about it.
I hope she sees this!

When all came to all, the demand had increased by £5893.18 to £7855.33 with penalties and interest but, with great relief, I was able to pay it because, by then, I had sold another asset.
I still think that it was an unwarranted demand, coming as it did, on top of the other biased and unfair ombudsmen's and adjudicators decisions against me who are linked to governmnet and 'legal' complaints organisations.

By comparison, I have taken other issues to Ombudsmen who deal with commercial matters which are not related to solicitors or government. On these occasions, they seem to have been free of influence or control by either of these powerful institutions and have conducted their adjudications in a fair and reasonable manner.

CARDOX & THE WORK GOES ON

Now that Covelink's little factory was closed, this good little company wound up and even with the Jet-Buses and components having been taken away, I still thought it worthwhile to try to rescue the project, but my task of raising money was made much more difficult. The Jet-Buses were now sitting in BW's large shed at Northwich, so I was not easily able to show them to potential investors, This meant that any other interested parties would now be in as good a position as I was, to raise money and take them, but I didn't give up.

My other original company, Cardox Ltd, which was formed at the same time as Covelink in 1988, now became the 'vehicle' for my discussions after Covelink was forced to close down. I had set this company up with Bruce Ropner, originally, to hold the Patents, all of which were later transferred to Covelink. Although now dormant, I had maintained it with Companies House in case it might be useful, which now proved to be the case. In fact, it is this company which has been used on our website, www.cardoxlimited.co.uk.

Throughout the previous eighteen years of the project, various people had become involved and helped when they could. There are too many to mention individually, so I have included a list of them along with the investors in the appendix at the back of the book. They could see that it was a most interesting project with great potential. Some stayed with it for years, others came and went. Many were from different backgrounds, with different skills, but they all did what they could to help. Regrettably with such limited funding available, few ever received any payment for their work.

This, of course, did not apply to those who were employed by me full time at the little factory and at Staindrop in the workshops and offices. They were always paid for their employment with me. The latter continued to work on the specialist motor cars and now that the starter factory was closed, I was in the process of taking on more staff to try to make the workshops profitable again, after losing some of the men in 2002.

Along with Alan Theakston, who was always a wonderful help to me whenever I needed him, were Richard Fletcher and his wife, Anne. These two people had helped me whenever they could, but being kept busy with their own work, they were only able to come north occasionally due to them living in Dorset. Richard's position as a director, formerly of British Aerospace and latterly with French Aerospace, EADS, did not allow him much time to play a regular active role, but he would do what he could from a distance. Like a number of people, we were always happy to have them to stay at Gainford when they did visit the North. He was a director of Covelink for many years and was unpaid like the rest of us.

CHAPTER 63:
2005. NEW DEVELOPMENTS

In June 2005, Anne re-established contact with colleagues in Germany who were also aero industry people, Chris Von Kienlin and Dr Werner Ott. They were key members of the Copac Group who operated from Munich and were involved with Mergers and Aquisitions. When they were in the UK, we had meetings at the Institute of Directors in Pall Mall and we passed on some of our contacts to him and his partner. They were well connected and we thought it would be beneficial to have people seeking funds in Europe.

Copac had many international contacts and set out to raise the substantial funding necessary to acquire our assets from BW and establish manufacturing with a development centre here in the UK. Richard and Anne set about creating their own business plans, organising agreements, licensing contracts, equity and fee structures. These were created on the basis that the new funding would be some millions of pounds, sufficient to progress through into production to meet the ever increasing number of potential orders being offered to us. Mainly as a result of the website.

CHINESE CONNEXION

At this time, I was also in touch with another new contact who was also keen to be involved, this was Charles Chan whose offices were in East Kilbride. He had been with the British Army in Ireland and had various businesses in China. He was an interesting man and his Glaswegian-Chinese accent was as unique as it was challenging to listen to and understand. I explained to him that I was aiming to raise £5 million. He had connections with military as well as commercial people around the world as well as in China. I introduced Charles to Richard Fletcher, so they were working together along with all the others mentioned above. They both later travelled over to China when Richard was able to see the situation over there for himself.

Charles was most enthusiastic about amphibious transport and at one meeting held near Birmingham organised by John Claplott, he presented a most comprehensive slide show. He had put this together after researching all the amphibians which he had been able to trace all around the world. It was very interesting and showed that most of them were of a military nature and as usual, with converted motor vehicles being the principle method of construction. The larger civilian ones, were again road going buses and trucks converted to make them float, as ever, following the usual unsatisfactory formula. Most of them were familiar to me, since over the years, I had come across the majority of them before. I was pleased that Charles had found out for himself that there was nothing to compare with our Roylecraft machines.

BW OFFER TO SELL ASSETS BACK TO US

Before Mark Smith resigned from BW, he'd previously had the occasional meeting with Richard Fletcher in London. With Richard also being a 'big company man', the directors of BW were happy to speak to him on the same 'level', and were prepared to discuss the situation. It was at one of these meetings that BW suggested to Richard that we could buy back the assets for a sum of between £350,000 and £450,000 according to the method and rate of payment. This sum was not unreasonable considering that BW had spent over £900,000 towards building the Jet-Buses out of the total cost of around £1.3 million including spares, extra work etc. Most of the balance was put in by me.

Cardox and I would be the buyers. As mentioned when Covelink was closed down, I used Cardox as the 'vehicle' to represent our interests. I renewed my efforts with all my original shareholders who, in spite of Covelink being liquidated, I had assured would have the same level of equity in relation to mine, no matter what company or JV was created or formed, as long as I was in control.

BW had realised that the Jet-Buses were likely to sit in their store indefinitely, so had decided to offer them, the Patents and the IPR back to us. Even with all the widespread effort which we were putting in, and all the people we were speaking to, I still could not raise the necessary money to buy them back. With my six figure borrowings, made to keep the factory going and repay the CDDC, I was in no position to buy them, especially as over and above these debts, the RBS were also demanding repayment of Covelink's overdraft.

MORE PEOPLE JOIN IN WITH THE FUNDING EFFORTS

The total numbers involved trying to raise funding for this project are too numerous to mention individually, it would fill the book just to mention them all. With BW now prepared to sell the assets, and not hold me to the contract, people could again see that I had the chance to put Roylecraft back on the map and I was delighted to have their support. They were quite happy to devote their time to raising money and helping generally, knowing that I wasn't able to pay them to do it. I have already mentioned a few of them, but they all had skills which would be valuable once production was underway.

As well as the list of supporters, I have also included a list of VC's and others who were approached for funding in the appendix. These organisations were all contacted and often, meetings were arranged. The numbers involved will give you some idea of our determination to succeed, especially when you know that, in some cases, discussions continued for 20 years, with local government, for example.

To give you a flavour of the range and activities of just a few of the helpful people involved, both before and after the factory closed down, I will briefly mention some of them here.

Early on, in 1999, we were contacted and have remained in touch with Max Kolesnic a most interesting Russian man who was acting in Japan for Mitsubishi. They could clearly see the benefits of our amphibians and I first drew out the lines of the 40 foot Jet-Bus for them.

Max brought their people over to see, film and test the Jet-Buses on no less than three occasions. They were thrilled with Roylecraft and wanted to buy quite a number of them. I still hear from him occasionally to see if we have been able to start production. Mitsubishi were desperately keen to use our vehicles in Osaka. In fact Alan Priest went to Japan to visit them and our people at the embassy in Tokyo to confirm their interest, but we couldn't supply.

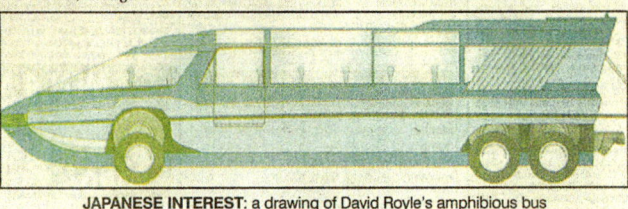

Editorials. 2001.

Another man who was helping us with his overseas connexions was Capt. Peter Wijowski. He was the captain of a super yacht which operated around Australia and he became our agent out there. He picked up some orders for our vehicles, but as ever, we couldn't supply any. He organised a visit from the people who operate amphibians in Sydney Harbour. They came over to join us when we were testing and also wanted to buy our Jet-Buses. Peter was very patient and kept in touch for years and he also tried to raise money for production.

In December 2004, I had the pleasure of meeting Graham and John Gifford when they travelled up from Southampton to see our amphibians. They had made contact previously after they had read about my problems with funding. This was when they had telephoned and urged me not to lose faith.

They told me what a struggle it had been for Sir Christopher Cockerell when he invented the first hovercraft and how he had similar difficulties when he was developing his new technology. It was as a result of Sir Christopher's request to John's father that they had set up the world's first commercial hovercraft operating company in Southampton in 1976. This was when they built their hovercraft more like a boat than an aeroplane.

They were most impressed with our machines and were keen to look into the possibility of working with us in the future. They felt that whenever they couldn't sell Griffon Hovercraft, they were confident in being able to sell Roylecraft amphibians as an alternative. Because they are a relatively small company however, they couldn't provide any funding, but were going to see if they could help in any way.

The feature which appealed to them was not only the ability of our machines to be able to travel quickly over water, but also to be able to drive on the road. Hovercraft are not able to do this, but of course, they can operate over mud, ice and other surfaces which wheels or boats are not capable of doing. They could see a joint sales operation working very well.

Derek Foster, our local MP, was another very active person who was doing what he could to help. Firstly with Royle's Legal problems and also he went to some trouble looking for potential

Three Griffon Hovercraft.

investors in Roylecraft. He introduced Grenville Burn to me who operated a funding organisation which met regularly at the Dorchester Hotel on Hyde Park. I went along to one or two of the meetings there, gave a presentation and met various potential investors. Derek did his best to help until he went into the House of Lords, by which time, I think he had enough! Grenville carried on trying to introduce potential investors until I could go no further. He is a charming man and worked closely with Derek.

Another person who became involved via Derek, was John Clapcott, an accountant from Sutton Coldfield near Birmingham. He had been involved with people in Formula One and with Noble sports racing cars and had helped set up manufacturing them in South Africa. He was always on the look-out for interesting projects and first appeared in March 2005. He soon became a regular visitor to Staindrop and, as he had to drive up from Birmingham each time, he was also invited to stay with us at Gainford to save him the cost of hotel bills. Like all the others, he was not paid for his work and I wanted to do all I could to minimise his costs.

His interest was in both the amphibians and the motor restoration work. He became closely involved with every aspect of both companies activities and obviously enjoyed it. I much appreciated having his help and he worked with me usually for three days each month and I was happy for him to attend many of the meetings. In fact, as mentioned, he arranged some of the meetings in the Birmingham area which was convenient and equidistant from Richard, Les Shore, Glyn Wheeler, myself and Alan Theakston. He became very much a part of the team and came to know most of my contacts during the four years of his involvement.

Mentioning Les Shore reminds me that when Nesta first became involved in 1999, one of the Marel engineers who came to inspect my drawings was Les Shaw. He became a regular visitor and a helpful contact and would have been a key member of the team which would have organised and run production at a big factory, if we could have raised the money.

It was clear that potential investors wanted to see a good management team and Les was a qualified engineer and one who had large scale manufacturing experience. Another man just mentioned, who became involved and was very much at the forefront of industry was Glyn Wheeler. He previously, had been a director of Corus (was British Steel) and was another respected executive with an impressive management record.

CONFIDENCE FADES

Even with my agreement to forgo 60% of the equity for any investors who would introduce in excess of £5 million which Richard or Copac in Munich, might be able to introduce, I was still also trying to raise money mtself and hoping to retain a reasonable level of control of the assets. With Richard and Anne being in the forefront, I was confident that they would look after my interests.

Because Richard had always been involved with very large aircraft projects which would entail hundreds of millions of pounds, this gave me hope that raising the few £millions which we needed, would be well within the realms of possibility for him. I soon became concerned however, when I could see that he was following in my footsteps. I found that he was talking to the same people whom I had already approached on many occassions, including local government. I still hoped that he might pull it off when I hadn't been able to. As the weeks became months, I could see him becoming very frustrated. It wasn't long before he was finding that he was making no real progress and felt that he was wasting his time.

When trying to raise money there are always those VC's who will say they can help, but to do so, they explain that they will need some money up-front first. I had heard this for years, but I had always thought that, in fact, it must be counter productive and take away some of the incentive. The normal and accepted practice in the city being a success fee of 2% to 2.5% of the capital raised when it was a 7 or 8 figure sum. This commission being paid out of the funds raised.

Too late, did I discover that Richard had paid out some hundreds of pounds to one of the funding organisations and no, he didn't get the money we needed, or any money at all, from those concerned. I had previously wondered if

Firm offering to build amphibious coach

A DURHAM vehicle builder is offering to build the World's first amphibious coach which can take roads and rivers in its stride.

Covelink Marine says it's just an order away from turning designs and prototypes into a working, 30-seat vehicle which can drive straight from the road into rivers, lakes and even the sea. For £250,000, it says, an operator could be the first owner of a purpose-built 'amphcoach'.

Managing director David Royle says the idea arrived nine months ago in the form of a phone call from a potential Japanese buyer. Covelink has already built four prototypes in shorter lengths and is now testing a 25-foot vessel.

"The key to our craft is a retractable suspension system, specially designed and built by us," said Mr Royle. "It's more or less all stainless to resist saltwater and, when retracted, reduces drag and allows the vehicle to 'plane'."

The first prototype was capable of 30mph on water and 60mph on land. The vehicles - for which the County Durham firm has registered 40 patents - uses a fan-cooled 300 bhp turbo-charged diesel engine powering water jets, with the drive switchable to the rear axle.

The amphicoach planned would be the legal maximum width of 2.55 metres and almost 12 metres long but, due to the shape of the hull and the bow, would carry around 30 seats.

But total weight of the vehicle is expected to be around six tonnes due to its weight-saving construction.

"It's a very rigid structure, monocoque-style which uses welded aluminium throughout," said Mr Royle.

He said the major hurdle was getting type approval, since the craft may have to adhere to both land and sea regulations.

Mr Royle also said it would be a question of retraining coach drivers to understand the rules at sea, or training experienced skippers to drive a coach.

"We have spent easily seven figures on research, and have had very little in the way of grants from Government," said Mr Royle. "It is quite a challenge to meet the regulations, so we want to find out if there's any interest in the coach or even bus trade in running these vehicles."

● Mr Royle can be contacted at Covelink Marine, The Old School, Staindrop, near Darlington, Co Durham DL2 3NH, tel: 01833 660995, or through *CBW*.

Box-section aluminium build makes Covelink's 'amphicoach' a 12-metre vehicle weighing around six tonnes

Coach and Bus Week. 25/11/99.

I was wrong not to pay when these requests were made. Richard's experience indicated that I was right not to do so. I was sorry that he didn't tell me about it, since I could have warned him. His well meant payment was wasted, because it didn't help us at all.

In the meantime I was continuing to press every possible source in the city and elsewhere. I reminded those who might be able to raise the large seven figure sums now needed, that they would have a good commission and/or a share of the equity if they succeeded. To be fair to our existing shareholders, my aim was to try to persuade serious investors to take shares which were equitable in relation to the sums already invested and to the value of the project. After all, the project had been carried out at a fraction of the cost which would normally be incurred to create new, innovative machines of this size and on the scale of Roylecraft, so the equity was at a very low price anyway.

I was doing all that I could to ensure that those who had invested in the project during the early years, when the risks were at their greatest, retained fair value for their money. As the value of the project would increase with the new money coming in and in the event of a new company being formed, I reminded them that whatever the value of my shareholding in the 'Newco', it would be divided in the same percentage as existed in Covelink before it was wound up. I had 76%, the BES and EIS shareholders had 24%. Any more private investors would pay £8 per share as previously. As we had now invested £4.1 million and BW £900,000 the total amount invested so far, was £5 million.

In fact, as mentioned above, the project had to be worth a great deal more. The R&D would normally have cost perhaps £30 to £40 million (The R&D costs for new motor car is £80 to £100 million). The market was wide open with no serious competition and the potential orders in hand are worth over £500 million.

THE BUYERS WANT ROYLECRAFT

Whilst mentioning potential orders, I would like to clarify the position with these.

From the time when people could see that it was a serious project and that progress was being made in 1992, enquiries and potential buyers started to come to me. The first was Greenpeace who were "very impressed with the work done so far" and could see the benefits for their organisation. There then was interest from Lord St Leven of Marazion, St Michaels Mount and also Viscount Boyd both in Cornwall. Although from private individuals, they also could see the benefits which amphibians would have. I then had a number of people from the Far East including the British High Commission and a number of companies in Singapore.

Without any advertising, enquiries were also coming in from firms like Asarco in Malaysia, Blue Star Marine in Sri Lanka and there was also a UK holiday company in Gambia, West Africa. Others in Madras, India, the emergency services in Syria and a shipping company in San Diego, California. Nearer to home, there was the Port of London Authority, people in the Channel Islands and others in the UK of course. Correspondance continued with most of them, with more and more serious buyers coming to me all the time.

I begged and pleaded with an ever increasing number of potential sources for money in order to prepare and start production during the 1990's, but none of the normal institutional providers were sufficiently interested to offer any funding at all, let alone the substantial sums needed to set up a factory.

The number of buyers continued to increase during the first decade of the new millennium and the enquiries continue to come to this day. They are serious and cover most of the countries of the world. They now fill four lever arch files and are worth hundreds of millions of pounds.

Following the demonstrations to potential buyers and with my continued discussions and meetings with people who were operating amphibious buses around the world, I have established that a viable and realistic selling price is be £350,000 for a Jet-Bus. Now that we had actually built the first Jet-Buses, I knew the costs involved and could see that, even when built in small numbers, that this would produce a realistic 40% gross margin of profit. My original estimated price for BW was £262,000, with the benefit of hindsight, this price was low, but could have shown a small profit if they hadn't spoiled everything! So it was a very fair deal for them.

SOME OF THE HUNDREDS OF POTENTIAL BUYERS AND THEIR REQUIREMENTS

Quotes from a few of the 233 listed potential buyers and interested parties.

AMSTERDAM - SCHIPHOL AIRPORT.
"Thanks a lot for the DVD, it says more than words can say! Regular service from airport to city centre..."
- Ellen Blom. New Business Development, Amsterdam Airport.

BAHAMAS - NASSAU. *"Three Jet Trucks for leisure purposes"* - Andreas Heinel.

SINGAPORE. *"we are very keen and would like to know more."* - Lim Tze Yong.

BANGLADESH ARMY. *"for the purchase of six ...amphibious APC Ambulance ...for UN mission..."*
- SM Nasim ul Nizam. Sales Director.

BRAZIL. *"We have interest to buy your amphibious vehicles... delivery price..."*
- Oscar Vilas Boas. Sudamerica S.A. Florianopolis.

BROOKLYN, NEW YORK USA *"..subway link from Manhattan will be closed ...amphibious bus service..."* - Alun Williams. Co Director, Parkers Box, Brooklyn.

CHILE, PATAGONIA *"we believe that your technology could make... amphibian for military purpose... high rate of sales."* - Partnership/manufacturer - Jorge Sepulveda-Haugen.

CHINA *"I really interested in your designs... these types of amphibious vehicles will really popular in our China... (and) ...all over the world"* ... *"How about Joint Venture to manufacture?"*
- Josh David, Sales Manager. Hubei XinChuFeng Aotomobile Co. China. Part of large Chinese Gov't Dongfeng Corporation.

COLUMBIA, SOUTH AMERICA. *"Universida National de Columbia, mineral exploration."*
- Jorge Ivan Alvarez G. Bogota.

COSTA RICA. *"... amphibious bus... running tours... on beaches of..."*
- Eng. Bernado Escobar.A. San Jose de Costa Rica.

FRANCE - RIVER SEINE PARIS.
"... working with Paris City Council to launch commercial tour on land and water..." - Eduard Troubat.

GERMANY, BREMEN. *"I have stayed in contact... three years... like to ask if very interesting amphibious vehicles still under development."* - Christof Schramm, Elbe Sea Services.

GREEK ISLANDS. *"...looking to purchase two land/water buses as tourist attraction..."*
- Nicole Vorias. New York, USA.

HAWAII - PAKISTAN FLOODS. *"Urgent Roylecraft needed for flood relief Pakistan."*
- 23 August 2010. Telephone call. UKTI.

BUDAPEST, HUNGARY. *"Please contact me about pricing and availability"* - Andrew.G.Szabo.

REYKJAVIK, ICELAND. *"Price of a jet Truck and Jet Bus in $$$."*
- Eybor Smari Heidoarsson. Brekkulaek.

INDIA, WEST COAST. *"... please quote... one truck and one bus to try..."* - Rikhave Shantilal. Shantilal Shipping & Chartering PVT Ltd. Gandhidham.

INDONESIA, JAKARTA. *"we are interested to use and sell."* - 10 Vehicles. Operator/dealership. Goesdianto Go-Roxy Mas.

IRELAND, CO. ANTRIM. *"... please e-mail price list..."* - Kristin McKnight. Carrickfergus.

ISRAEL. *"... very much like your amphibious..."* - Luis Filipe. Mr Erez.

ITALY, VENICE. *"... like to have info re. 12 m Roylecraft JetBus... tours of nearby Venice in chanal... we can organise a meeting"* - Marco Quaglio.

CHAPTER 63: 2005. NEW DEVELOPMENTS.

JAPAN. *"... following recent discussions... serious intention to purchase 1 Jet Bus and 1 Jet Truck..."* (to demonstrate to 16 Japanese State Organisations and bus and rail companies. Visited UK and tested Roylecraft.) - Yasuhiro Suchi, Vice president, Japan Duck Co.Ltd.

JAPAN, OSAKA. *"Mitsubishi Corporation have researched the potential of this vehicle and see a massive market developing... (for) modern up to date designed and built product."*
- Joint Venture. Martin Toomey. North West England Development Agency.

JAPAN, OKAYAMA TRANSPORT BUREAU. *"... have been promoting your vehicles... they very interested in your vehicle... if (production) is started, you will get too busy, which is good."*
- Maxim Kolesnik. Falcon Trading Inc.

MADEIRA, FUNCHAL. *"... very interested in your amphibious."* - Luis Jardim. Portugal.

MALAYSIA, SELANGOR. *"... in tourism industry and in process of purchasing 2 units"* - Carmen Liew.

MALTA. *"... open an amphibious tour business in Malta... planning to purchase one to three vehicles..."*
- Christopher Magro. Isle of Wight.

MENAI STRAITS - WALES. *"... establish a ferry bus service..."* - Franklin Scrase. Bangor Devp't Trust.

MEXICO, CABO SAN LUCAS. *"we reading about your series II Jet Bus... send more info"* - E.Dutko.

NEW ZEALAND. *"... tourist operations on harbours, lakes and rivers..."* - Theo Perry. Wanganui.

NIGERIA, LAGOS. *"... like to confirm if you can supply us some of your product..."*
- Dayo Smith, Mushin, Lagos.

NORTH AFRICA & SUDAN. *"Danfodio Petroleum Services. Part of holding company with Turnover of 350 Million US Dollars... Khartoum Sudan... possibility of representing and marketing Roylecraft Jet Bus & Jet Truck for clients oilfield services... at earliest possible registration."* - M.S. Hyder. Manager Operations.

NORWAY, LOFOTEN - ISLANDS. *"...transporting tourists in Lofoton Islands...1 or possibly 2 vehicles..."* - Jan Nesje. Gravdel, Norway.

PAKISTAN, ISLAMABAD. *"... I need about 20 Bus."* - Badawi Saeed.

POLAND, KOSZALIN. *"... We are deeply interested in purchasing your amphibious vehicles... DVD has proved real its real existence... future co-operation... lake Jamno."*
- Roman Bielecki. President of Management.

PORTUGAL, LISBON. *"my client is really interested in your vehicle... when do you expect to start process with us?"* - Buyer/Operator. Pedro Mendes, Antonio Silva, Carristur.

QATAR. *"We are very much interested to purchase.... dealership in Gulf region"*
- Ravindra Aher. Doha-Qatar.

RIYADH, JORDAN. *"... Parmaei has shown rapid growth in marketing amphibious products... now offices in Jordan, Saudi Arabia, Egypt and Switzerland... add more products..."*
- Sobhi Azmi Al-Shakhsheir. Gen Manager. Parmaei, ICA.

SCOTLAND, FORT WILLIAM. *"... offering water/land tours... JetBus cost... both sea and fresh water lochs..."* - Damian Forster. Inverness Shire.

SINGAPORE. *"we are very keen and would like to know more."* - Lim Tze Yong.

SOUTH AFRICA, JOHANNESBURG. *"Amphibious tour bus for harbour."* - Les Booth. Sandton.

SOUTH KOREA, SEOUL. *"Thank you for your great help and wonderful info..."* - Arnold Hwang, Dongnama Shipping.

SPAIN, BILBAO. *"...USOA company in N.Spain, want to create 'duck tour'... what is best amphibious type..."*, *"Contact David Royle who knows more about these matters than anyone else in the world"* - Nigel Souter. T. Ward Shipping, Edinburgh.

SPAIN, BARCELONA. *"...to implement the first amphibious tour of Barcelona."* - Jorge.

SPAIN, MEDITERRANEAN RIVER *"... Jet Bus... availability, price, guarantee, approval... max speed..."* - Carlos Blazquez.

SYRIA. *"... we would like to establish commercial relationship... fire fighting equipment..."*
- Vasken A. Keshishian. Tartous Ind Zone.

TAIWAN. *"Your design for amphibious bus is very attractive... high intention to work together... for Asia market, Taiwan, China, Japan, Indonesia, etc... long term cooperation with you."* - JV. Tim Hsiao and Woody Chang, CAEngineering Co Ltd., Taiwan.

THAILAND, KRABI. *"Looking for vehicle that can be used year round... waiting time for new one?"*
- Barry. J. Yaxley, Marine Operations Manager.

TURKEY, ISTANBUL *"interested very much in (your) vessel/vehicle... need around seventy vehicles...."* Buyer/Operator. Mesut Baysal.

TURKS AND CAICOS.
"your vehicle... would probably be about right for us..." - Alastair Dods. Caicos tours Ltd.

UAE, DUBAI. *"... I liked very much both Jet-Bus and Jet truck, I would like to buy one or two."*
- Amer Belhabala. Dubai.

UK, LONDON CITY AIRPORT. *"It is with great interest that our Operations Director spotted... the..."* (High speed amphibians for airport rescue) *"... keen to discuss. To be ready this calendar year."*
- Simon Butterworth. Deputy Director, Airside Development mkand Safety Management. London City Airport. Royal Docks.

UK, PORT OF LONDON AUTHORITY. *"... be suitable for use on river Thames... very interested to receive more information and details about these vehicles."* - Robert Bass. Commercial Manager.

UK, LONDON. *"I am looking to start a business... tours of London."* - Rob Branston.

UK, NEWCASTLE UPON TYNE. *"We need to replace the Shields ferry. Three of your amphibious Jet buses would cost the same and would improve the service linking up with the Tyneside Metro Service."*
- Andrew Bairstow. Alan Parks. Nexus.

UK, NORTHUMBERLAND.
"School Bus for Holy Island children." - Paul Johnston. Northumberland county Council. Morpeth.

UK, PLYMOUTH. *"... land fish from small fleet of fishing boats... as alternative to building concrete pier."*
- Nick Jacobs. London.

UK, SCOTLAND, PERTH. *"... Stagecoach UK Bus... availability and cost."* - Adrian Havlin.

USA, NEW YORK. *"Big Apple Ducks... have you made any progress yet... is it available for use in the States... still very interested in your vehicle..."* - Scott Baker. Brooklyn.

USA, HOUSTON, TEXAS. *"we are interested in buying some of the boats... quotation for 10 units."*
- Raymond Littleton. Houston.

USA, SARASOTA, FLORIDA. *"need for transporting people and goods... Intercoastal Waterway..."*
- Steve Ellis. Consultants.

USA, PORTLAND OREGON. *"... amphibious vehicle for fresh water river tours..."* - Charles Lewis.

USA, WILMINGTON, NORTH CAROLINA.
"... like pricing? logistics... delivered to Wilmington..." - Gary McManus.

VIETNAM, HANOI.
"... we do have a budget for just this kind of amphibian... please send some technical and performance data..."
- Shalom Shaphyr. Senior advisor, Science, Technology & Commerce Corp.

WARSAW, POLAND. *"start operation next year... 30 passengers... price..."* - Jurek Stefaek. Warsaw.

WESTERN AUSTRALIA. *"... setting up tour business... high currents... High speed vessel would be best... can I get cost and design details..."* - Allan Gillis. Warnbro. W.Australia.

CHAPTER 63: 2005. NEW DEVELOPMENTS.

USE ORDERS TO FUND PRODUCTION

As with many aspects of this project, people make assumptions and sometimes criticise me, usually with no real knowledge of the subject. When it comes to discussions relating to orders for example, some questioned why I didn't use all the value in the orders to make the business succeed. Why, for example, couldn't I translate all these hugely valuable orders into money using them to secure bank loans or whatever? This seems to be a perfectly reasonable idea and I had, of course, considered it.

In fact, a number of buyers, including Mitsubishi, were keen to help and had also offered to pay 30% of the price per unit, up front. This would have amounted to over five hundred thousand pounds alone, just on their first small 'sample' order for five Jet-Buses.

Unfortunately, there were some very important reasons why it was not possible for me to take the money or accept the orders, these were:

- It is illegal to sell a public transport vehicle which is not certificated. Ours weren't and despite huge effort, I couldn't raise the money to complete the certification process, sadly one which had been going so well.
- We were tied by the BW contract at the time, which forbade us to sell any vehicles before theirs had been supplied.
- The deposits alone would not have been sufficient to re-equip a factory, employ the staff, certificate the buses and set up production to meet the orders.

NB. The first point illustrates very clearly why I tried to sell commercial and general purpose vehicles first. Unlike buses, the MK IV and MK V don't need this certification.

BW DEALINGS

In spite of now having more people trying to raise the necessary money, time was slipping by and the ongoing failure to obtain money from any of the formal institutions was of serious concern. They all seemed to turn it down out of hand without clear explanations of why they did so.

As 2005 progressed, I was also making little progress with BW's board of directors. Relationships were strained, not only because of my report to Defra, which was so critical, but also because I was continuing to press various people in Parliament including Derek Foster my MP, Alun Michael MP, Patricia Hewitt MP and also begging the Prime Minister, Tony Blair, Gordon Brown and anybody else who would listen, for funding to enable me to start production again. There are many files with literally thousands of documents covering the huge effort I made to get funding during the period 1999 to 2009 - see the list in appendix.

In 2005, the BW board were still denigrating Roylecraft technology and its viability. They simply denied the facts, even when they were provided with written evidence that our technology deserved "considerable financial support" from some of the most highly qualified Engineers in the country.

Earlier in the year, in March 2005, Robin Evans the CEO of BW confirmed in writing that he and the board of directors backed Mark Smiths actions 100% which was interesting, especially when two or three months later, they let him take the blame for the complete mess they had made of the contract, when he resigned from BW. Writing to Robin Evans and the board later on, they didn't deny it, so my report to Defra and the bad press which followed, must have 'hit the spot', but they would not try to rescue the project or give me compensation for our huge losses and still haven't done so as I write.

THE ASSETS ARE SOLD

Towards the end of 2006 BW were becoming anxious to clear their storage building in Cheshire, so the price they were asking for our assets was dropping and they had come down to as little as £50,000. The impasse which existed between me and the BW board was overcome when Robin Evans finally asked Ian White to deal with me and the arrangements for disposing of the assets. Ian was the regional Director in their smart Leeds office. He was an experienced director who had worked with Stewart Sim and with me and had seen the benefits of our machines for use on the canals and rivers in many areas of the country.

John Clapcott was also dealing with Ian White and eventually negotiated a final figure of £25,000 for the assets. This included all the Patents, IPR, the drawings and the two complete Jet-Buses, the two bare hulls and the tonnes of components to finish them. So this is what it came down to, 19 years of intensive work, a portfolio of international patents and IPR and five million pounds.

I could have the lot for half of one percent of the costs!

If only BW had done this four years earlier, the outcome could have been very different. I could easily have bought it all back, certificated the Jet-Bus and sold them ten times over. As it was I now had six figure debts for the company, I had not had a salary for some years and was having to find £1500 every month interest to maintain the six figure borrowings (mortgages), so I couldn't possibly buy the assets myself. I suggested that Richard might buy them rather than allow them to be sold to an outside party or be scrapped by BW which was the alternative. We would then be able to maintain control of them and not let anybody else get hold of them. Not having invested any money in the project in previous years, I suggested that Richard might like to have some equity to reflect his £25,000 investment.

OVER A BARREL

Whilst in the process of subsequent discussions, Richard sent an all embracing legal document to me which he asked me to sign. This gave him and Charles Chan complete control of all the assets and the rights to them, including any new designs which I might produce. This worried me and I told him so, but he said that I could trust him and that it was necessary if I didn't want them to be scrapped or be lost elsewhere.

So, once again I was, as the Americans would say, 'between a rock and a hard place'. I knew that BW would happily destroy and scrap the Jet-Buses, because they were incontrovertible proof of the success of Roylecraft technology. On the other hand, to sign a document which not only handed over all control of the assets, but one which could also deny me the benefit of my own specialised knowledge in the future, was a dreadful piece of work.

Of the two choices, and after all the years of working together, I thought that I could trust them, but I was over a barrel. The very fact that they had employed solicitors to draw up such a 'strong' document however, was extremely worrying, but the last thing I wanted was for all my work and IPR to be scrapped and wasted, so with serious concerns, I signed it.

In the event, he and Charles Chan bought them jointly and set about establishing a new company called International Performance Amphibians. I said that I was concerned to ensure that all the previous supporters investments and my huge input would be protected and Richard assured me that he was looking after all our interests.

AL HAKIM AND CHAN

A lot of effort continued to be put into raising money. I was also still battling with parliament and the Legal authorities to have the money paid to us as ordered in the High Court and was still working seven days a week and putting in 9 to 10 hours per day. It had been the norm for years and still is.

Various meetings took Place, one of them, later on in February 2007, was held at the Institute of Directors in Pall Mall where we all met a Gentleman from Dubai, Dr Karim al Hakim who lived in England, but represented an investment group over there. Interestingly, this particular man had approached me directly as a result of the Cardox Ltd. website. As I had still failed to conclude a deal for any large seven figure sum, despite all the intensive years of work, I thought it was better to let Richard and his high powered expert 'funding team' deal with this enthusiastic man.

At the meeting, Dr Hakim offered to pay for my flight and hotel accommodation in Dubai so that I could meet his colleagues. This was a solid opportunity for us, but apparently at a meeting which they had a few days later, Richard and Charles Chan apparently demanded a million pounds up front, before we would go any further. The result was that Dr Hakim immediately lost interest. It is my guess that such a proposal might be acceptable with large, established companies such as those which Richard had worked for in the aero industry. With their unknown new company and with Richard and Charles not having any history, however, investors are unlikely to deposit such amounts, even though there is the possibility of 'escrow' arrangements. I wasn't at all happy about losing this man, since I knew how rarely serious investors came to us with offers like this.

Not long afterwards, Charles kindly arranged a meeting with me in London at the China British Business Centre on 29th March 2007. He was an executive of this organisation. Upon arrival, I found that there were twelve people around the table. They were mainly Chinese and operated various Chinese companies involved with shipping, vehicle manufacture and associated industries. Sitting next to me was a charming man called Cyril Lyn who is an ex Harvard man and was also a professor at Oxford. He spoke excellent English and kindly translated for me when others were speaking in Chinese. I began the meeting with a technical description of our amphibians, this lasted around an hour, after which Charles followed on by explaining the commercial aspects of them.

The meeting was then open for questions and discussion, the outcome was very interesting. As this part of the presentation proceeded mainly in Chinese, Cyril told me that they anticipated a demand for around 7500 vehicles for China alone. With China having been reliant upon water transport for centuries, they could easily see the benefits of Roylecraft technology. This included quite a large number of Military Vehicles as well as those for public transport and commercial use. This number of vehicles at UK production costs, represented a turnover of around £2.6 billion, and these were only for China. With 40% gross profit margin, we are looking at very substantial new and profitable industry.

Built in China the production costs of our machines would, of course be less, but the profit margin could remain, or be higher, since I knew that a price of £350,000 was acceptable and was the going rate for newly built amphibians in some parts of the world. As previously mentioned these were often being assembled from military and automotive components and were large, heavy and slow machines which generally were too big for use on the public highway. In my view, this last point is a serious drawback, because the main benefits of combining water and road- legal transport is lost. Being able to travel quickly and efficiently on the Road as well as in water was the principal reasons for me to start afresh with the innovative Roylecraft designs.

CHAPTER 64:
THE NEW REGIME

FACTORIES & STORAGE

When British Waterways had first started talking of selling the buses back to us, I realised that if we could raise the money to do it, then it would be beneficial if I could rent a suitable factory building large enough to accommodate both Royles restoration workshops and the Roylecraft company. Doing this, I would be able to sell the Old School workshops to repay the debts which were making life very difficult at home for Jo-Jo and me. By now, fortunately, I was drawing the State Pension which was marvellous, it was our first regular income for many years.

After Richard and Charles bought the assets, I continued to visit local industrial estates to see what the costs of renting or even buying one of the many empty ones would be, especially an older one, if it was cheap enough. Although there were already 240 empty factories in this region, and this was before the 2008 recession, I was surprised to find that none of the agents or factory owners would negotiate to provide us with space at a moderate price.

I simply couldn't understand why they would not want to rent them when some had been empty for so many years. Indeed some had grass growing on them! To add to this ridiculous situation, the government were helping developers to build new ones! So there were also quite a number of empty brand new factories as well. I explained that we were happy to pay a commercial price which was commensurate with the age of the buildings.

I eventually discovered the reason for this and why the owners of the factory buildings were happy to let them stand empty. What was happening was that they belonged to investment companies who had been selling them on to new investors every two or three years and making profits each time. With the substantial increase in property values from the late 1990's through to 2008, the value of commercial, as well as private property, was attractive to investors, especially those further south, in London for example, where there had not been the number of factory closures and unemployment as we had in the North East.

Upon each change of ownership, the buyers assumed that the values would be increasing in the north as they had done in the south, so, the prices asked for them had increased sufficiently for the vendor to be able guarantee a reasonable rent to the buyer out of the profit they made when they sold the empty buildings. Consequently, when a new 'start up', like our company, wanted to move in, it was therefore considered to be a risk. The new owners might lose their guaranteed rent, so they didn't want to rent them out and certainly wouldn't negotiate a reasonable rent for us. I saw factories being bought and sold 2 or 3 times in the few years I was looking at them.

It was a most extraordinary and ridiculous situation. We were simply trying to create employment, it was difficult enough to raise money and without the availability of what should have been low cost factories, it was no wonder that manufacturing in this country had reduced by over 80% during the previous ten years.

It was in the summer of 2007 that I became extremely concerned when I discovered that Richard and Charles had uplifted the Jet-Buses and the tonnes of components and special equipment from BW's dry, safe storage building and were content to leave them out in the open, sheeted over, sitting on wagon trailers in a 'secure yard' somewhere. I was very worried about this because they were all valuable components and some were perishable, eg, there were dozens of brand new upholstered seats, electrical equipment, costly large windscreens etc, Together with everything else, it had all cost £5 million. It turned out that they didn't think it worthwhile to even pay for dry storage, let alone factory space.

When I expressed my serious concerns, Richard and Charles assured me that they were OK sheeted down with rubber and car tyres to prevent the sharp corners from tearing the sheets. This gave me little comfort. The fact which was becoming painfully obvious to me, was that they hadn't invested millions of pounds in these assets as I had done. Their risk was only £12,500 each!

To me, the entire project was going from bad to worse. Nobody knows better than me, what happens to vehicles, boats and equipment standing outside, especially when they are in pieces and have already stood unused for four or five years, as in this case. If they are then exposed to further neglect and still not used, sheeted up maybe, but open to dampness and constant changes of temperature, then...?

I didn't go to see them, it would have been too upsetting. I have seen it hundreds of times before with vehicles of every description, engines, hydraulics, electrics, bodywork and upholstery. They all deteriorate and the cost of restoring them to good running condition can be very high indeed. Another additional cost which we could well do without. It was all most depresing.

FROM BAD TO WORSE

There was now a great deal of ongoing correspondence with Richard and Charles. They were asking about technical matters and the design details which I provided for them and we all continued to try to raise funding.

The reason for this renewed interest in the design details was revealed when they informed me that they had agreed a Memorandum of Understanding with a firm which built marine vessels in Shanghai. The people in China obviously needed to know all about our new technology.

After all the years of my concentrated efforts to protect my designs and IPR. I now had no control over the information which was being given to anybody whom they might be able to link up with. As we had all failed to raise the necessary money to create the business here in the UK, I did what I could to help and provided them with detailed explanations of the technology. They were doing their best to launch our vehicles wherever they could and I had seen how there was a great opportunity in China.

Generally speaking though, I was still not at all happy with the way it was all going, especially as I was no longer directly involved with discussions and future plans. Matters got much worse however, when they told me that they had taken a large proportion of the equity, 50 to 60%, in their new company, for themselves. I had expected to retain control of most of this equity, so that it could be used to secure the millions needed for production. We also needed funds to finish the last part of our own ongoing development work and certification here in the UK. But 60% for just £25,000!

My position was very clear when Richard and Charles then told me that they had allotted me 35% of the remaining shares. They were now in total control of 'my' project. Gone was the team spirit and concern for all the investors and supporters, gone was any sense of fair play. Our relationship further deteriorated when, subsequently, my accountant informed me that in reality, I had no equity whatsoever, in their new company, they had 100%. He discovered this when checking with Companies House for our financial year end.

Presumably, they felt that they had the upper hand and that I would have to toe their line if I was to have any benefits for all my years of work and the millions of pounds which I had raised and invested. The fact that they had paid precisely half of one percent of the total costs of the project to buy it, was of little concern to them. They had the hardware, the Patents and the drawings and that was that. If I wasn't going to co-operate, they obviously felt safe with all the assets..

I never cease to be surprised by the fickleness of human nature. When the opportunity is there for big profits, all principles seem to go by the board. In this case, there was a marked change in their attitude. Two people who had been helpful and considerate, were now showing that there was little consideration for my huge investment, nor for the fact that I was in serious financial difficulty as a direct result of creating and paying for the very assets which they were now intending to profit from. All acquired for a tiny fraction of the cost and value.

Without the last £300,000 which I had recently borrowed at a time of extreme difficulty, they would not have the benefit of the two finished Jet-Buses nor of two more 40ft hulls and the complete sets of components necessary to build them with. My money had made this possible. When completed, these four buses are worth £1.4 million and as mentioned there are plenty of people standing by who are keen to buy them. What was Richard doing with these valuable assets? Nothing, after four years gathering dust, they had now left them sitting on wagon trailers in a yard somewhere.

The entire affair had now deteriorated into the dreadful situation which I had feared whenever others had previously tried to take advantage of the project without paying a fair price for it and when they didn't have the money or facilities to complete it. Their financial risk was minimal, so the project was now simply a means to make a profit for them as quickly as possible. It didn't matter that it had taken me over twenty years of work and would have benefitted this country and all those involved, in so many ways.

Like previous potential buyers had done, they offered me payment for any future work which they wanted done, but no piecemeal payments could ever recompense me for half my life's work and for my huge losses, let alone even repay my current debts for the project. This important fact didn't seem to occur to them.

After all the most serious legal and BW upsets, I still find it difficult to express how deeply upsetting the whole affair had become. I could hardly believe that matters could get worse and was sickened to the core by Richard's attitude, not only towards the Roylecraft project, but by his complete lack of any concern for me and Jo-Jo. After having believed that he was a trusted friend, staying at home on countless occasions, it was incredible that he (and Charles Chan) would now just grab everything and have no consideration, what so ever, for us all, for my work or for all our years working together.

I really now began to question my judgement and faith in human nature. After having already encountered such extreme examples of unscrupulous and corrupt behaviour, I would never have believed that matters could get worse, but I was now seeing even more unprincipled and disgraceful activities.
This time, not unlike those in the 'KK' affair in the early 1990's, by people who were considered to be personal friends as well as business colleagues.

As ever, I try to see the best in people and looking back, it may be that some of the problems stemmed from the fact that Richard was then embroiled in what must have been, a most distressing divorce. You may remember how his wife, Ann, who had managed the Harrier Jump-Jet project, although living in Dorset, continued to be very helpful to me via emails. She was compiling the lists of the ever growing number of potential buyers. As a result, I occasionally rang her up to see how her work was progressing. It was during one of these conversations that she explained to me how difficult life had become and how their domestic life was in turmoil. This might have contributed to the change in Richard's attitude

AND THEY STILL EXPECTED MORE!

All this was upsetting enough for all of us, but their expectations really were astonishing when Richard said that they now wanted me to redesign the Jet Buses so that they could be built of GRP and modern composites for the people in Shanghai. The plain fact is that I was not building bathtubs or even ordinary boats. To make such a request revealed that either, they had no comprehension of the specialised and high Tech nature of Roylecraft, or they assumed that I would be so dedicated and yes, foolish, as to waste even more of my life trusting them to look after my interests. Interests for which, they were already showing so little respect.

Whilst on the subject of building Roylecraft machines in GRP and Modern Composites, I should mention that I had carefully considered this method of construction at the outset. In fact, it had been part of my long term plans once we were in production and when we were generating good profits. There are a number of advantages to this method, including lower production costs and the fact that, in build, the dimensions are not open to such variations as when they are fabricated by hand, even on jigs, which is important during assembly.

The ever present assumption seemed to be that I had carried out this project without a great deal of thought and planning when, in fact, there were very good reasons for not building the first machines this way. The additional work and up-front costs involved, when preparing for production with GRP and Composites are very considerable indeed. For example, there is the need to build large and very costly moulds before starting to construct and test the new hulls themselves. It is not a programme of work to be taken on without very careful planning and the availability of very substantial sums of money. This is why I started with aluminium hulls.

In any event, the situation now was very different. The thought of redesigning the machines when I had no control of the project, no staff of my own and when I would be working in China where I didn't even speak the language, was bad enough, but when I would also be controlled by people whom I could no longer trust and who wanted most of the benefits of the project for themselves, meant that it was an entirely unrealistic expectation. Echoes of Frua's problems with the Phantom Six Rolls Royce came to mind, problems which proved to be fatal for him.

Despite the bleak outlook and having been marginalised, I could see that they still had not been able to raise the money for the planned development centre which we had previously agreed would be located here in the north, or for production in the UK. I therefore thought it worthwhile to continue to meet prospective investors, after all, if I could raise the large sums required, I felt that Richard and Charles would be only too pleased to make a quick profit and hand over control to a big investor and the project could then go ahead as planned.

After the BW debacle, when they had separated the inventor from his machine and then didn't know how to complete the Jet-Buses, it was interesting that Richard and Charles still believed that they also could, more or less, dispense with my services. At least, that was until the need for the GRP/Modern Composites designs alerted them to my usefulness. By now, however, our relationship had soured to such a degree that my only hope of regaining any ground was to introduce substantial funding with new investors. People who would, hopefully, recognise my importance in continuing to play an active role in developing the project.

From the time when the project was well advanced and I continued to seek substantial investments, I was surprised to experience such a wide variation in the attitude of the investors to me, as the creator and designer of Roylecraft. Some insisted that they would not proceed without me, whilst others couldn't wait to be rid of me, organisations like BW and latterly,

Nesta, One North East and now Richard and Charles. It may be that my weak financial position combined with having most of the equity was at the root of this and made me an easy target. On the other hand, they may have thought that I was incompetent and hadn't managed the project properly.

Whichever it might be, I am pretty sure that the majority of those who wanted rid of me had completely underestimated the implications of what I had achieved and how I had overcome technical problems which they didn't even know had existed.

Hopefully, I have explained how the changes in our economy and the results of my market research underpinned the decisions reached along the way. This is one of the reasons for writing this book. I may not be the sharpest business man, but I believed that the project would speak for itself and it did, but sometimes to the wrong people!

Over the next few months, an influential friend of mine arranged meetings with three separate parties, each of whom had access to the very substantial funds we needed. They came to Gainford and I was able to show them the films and they knew that we were talking in terms of a minimum of four to five million pounds. They understood this and could clearly see the potential, especially as all of them were involved in the offshore oil business.

When I explained the shareholding situation to them, they were not too happy, but agreed that I should ask what amount of money would be needed to buy the assets. After all, there was plenty of value in them and still the opportunity for a good profit for Richard and his partner. I contacted Richard twice after each of the first two meetings, but he would not quote a figure. Despite this, my friend arranged a third meeting for another investor group. This time, I asked my friend if he would be so kind as to make the call himself. He did this and contacted me later to tell me that they wanted £12 million. Not a bad profit on their investment of £25,000!

At this point I finally gave up trying to raise the money, it was pointless. Once trading, the assets were actually well worth this amount of money, but they were no longer mine and as I now had no facilities or staff and no longer was in control of the project, I had nothing to show for my work.

CHAPTER 65:
THE LAST POINT OF CONTACT

Time passed and then Richard asked me to attend one or two meetings on Tyneside with the management of a small engineering group. Being not too far away, I agreed to go and took Allan with me who had worked for me on the project from the very beginning. The meeting was at a small factory and it turned out that the directors, apparently, had agreed to finish the Jet-Buses for Richard at their own expense, as a gap filling job. The two complete Jet-Buses were parked in their yard and the two hulls and all the components were now in Northumberland, apparently.

Presumably, the engineering firm were going to be given some of the equity in return for their work to refit the gearboxes and after standing for five years, get the Jet-Buses gunning again. I know that Richard wanted to be able to demonstrate the buses, but whether this was part of the overall plan with China, I didn't know, but it was obvious that Richard had not been able to raise the money to do it.

As mentioned, he had knocked on the same doors which I had done, including those of the local government. It was no surprise to me therefore, to hear that he had failed to raise any money at all. He only gave it three or four months, when I had pressed them for nearly twenty years. At least, I did manage to prise around £400,000 out of them over that period of time, but this region was, as ever, proving itself to be the graveyard of industry.

Later, I expressed my ongoing dissatisfaction to Richard. The entire affair had continued to deteriorate with the Jet-Buses going from pillar to post with all and sundry seeing how the vehicles were designed. I also reminded him that I had solved the serious problems which had held back any development work and improvements in amphibious transport for most of the last century. A technology which many people around the world had asked me how I had done it. I have no idea what protection remains with the patents and IPR, or whether Richard and Charles are maintaining them.

Hearing nothing more from Richard for quite some time, I eventually wrote to the people at the factory at the beginning of May of 2009 to ask what was happening to the Jet-Buses, but received no reply. So I do not even know if the Jet-Buses are still in the north. The last time I saw them, they were still standing outside the factory in Tyneside, but I gather that they may have put one of them into running order.

I wrote to Richard and Charles shortly after this, to say how concerned and unhappy I was about the position generally and about the huge imbalance in our relative positions. I said that that I felt badly let down. They replied with an extraordinary letter telling me that I was now working for them and that I should attend a meeting to validate my costs and investment. They questioned various aspects of the project, in particular, they doubted the level of investments made since 1987. Astonishingly, they were trying to devalue my input so that they could argue that they were entitled to a great deal more than 0.5% of the project.

They knew that the Gibbs 'Aquada' amphibious motor car project had cost tens of millions of pounds and yet, they had the audacity to try to devalue all my years of intensive work and a total cost of only £5.1 million, (including BW's costs). Independent experts had confirmed that this is an incredibly low figure to design, build and test a number of prototypes and create new and innovative forms of transport which are up to 40feet long. This being especially relevant when they properly combine two very different technologies and are the very first high speed amphibious vehicles in the world.

In some respects, once again, here were people acting in a similar manner to the corrupt solicitors who, as the years passed after our successful High Court hearing, were losing ground and found themselves to be in an increasingly untenable position. You will remember that they also had ended up grasping at straws as their arguments became more ill-founded and illogical. The solicitors eventually had to destroy all their evidence and the files to try to protect themselves, and then, after threatening me and still failing to frighten me off, they finally resigned as did the Financial Director of BW.

Talking of legal matters, it is relevant that BW had acquired Covelink's assets by fraudulent means so, in law, they would have no right to sell goods which didn't belong to them. This would invalidate Richard and Charles ownership of them.

Returning to the question of the investment and costs incurred to create Roylecraft, under no circumstance was I going to attend a meeting to explain myself. The proof and evidence of the work and costs was undeniable. In fact they themselves, had put a value on it of £12 million to my recent prospective investors, so they knew, full well, what others would think was a realistic cost and what the value of the project might be.

After having been involved for so many years, I was surprised that Richard could possibly begin to question my input and the money invested. For the record, as you would expect, and now will be aware, I have ample proof and can easily show that over five million pounds was raised and invested. It was a combination of private and public sector investments.

The records include details of 35 BES and EIS investors and my own money raised by selling valuable assets, using inherited money and mortgaging my house three times and the workshop buildings at Staindrop once. There are hundreds of documents recording 22 years of my input and also a huge number of worksheets detailing the fifteen years of Royles work. My staff were involved on a continual basis with, at times, up to three men working on each of the various prototypes at once. We also had the money coming in from government grants, a number of national awards and loans from the CDDC and the EU and finally, the money from the British Waterways contract. Some of the figures have been mentioned earlier in the book.

Having read about this already, in the book, you will see that I have become so used to having to prove myself and my honesty, that I cannot stop doing it. As far as Richard and Charles are concerned, it was clear that the relationship had degenerated to such a degree that I wrote a lengthy letter to them in which I emphasised the differences in our approach to life and concluded by saying that as a group, we were going nowhere.

ENOUGH IS ENOUGH

The fact was that I had gone on long enough. Having begun the project in 1987, when I was 47 years old, I was now nearing 70 and I had made up my mind that I needed to be fully recompensed for half my life's work before I would do anything else.

Throughout this period, I had struggled to maintain a fair and equitable share policy to make sure that that all those who had shown such faith in me and had invested their money into the project, would finally enjoy a good return on their shares. I had maintained regular reports from the beginning, which I sent out at regular intervals, not only to the shareholders and directors, but also to those who had supported the project without investing money, like Sir Alex Smith and Richard of course and the others who had helped whenever they could. There is a list of shareholders and supporters in the appendix.

The time had come when all my energies should be redirected to those at home who, without fail, had given me such wonderful support throughout all the ups and downs of the last twenty years. I mean of course, my family. Both of my boys, Jem and Nick and of course, Jo-Jo, the best wife I could wish for. We all had enjoyed the good times and there were plenty of those and when times were difficult, I had done my best to keep as many of the problems to myself. Try as hard as I could, there were occasions I'm afraid, when my frustrations did show.

It is difficult to describe how deeply and personally involved people like me become when creating and controlling such large, costly and complex projects. One occasionally hears phrases like "eating, sleeping and living" a project. I did this for 22 years and by doing so, was able to draw and focus on all the knowledge accumulated over the fifty years of a most productive life. I also had to use every facility available to me to raise money for it, but despite all this, I still lost my project.

CHAPTER 66:
MEANWHILE, BACK AT ROYLES

As a result of the 2008 recession and with the stock market being in such a dire state, people were looking to invest in antiques and any other secure and movable securities. The Vintage and Classic motor car market was therefore strengthening from 2008 onwards and was very active with prices rising at the auctions.

Even with all Royles legal and financial problems, the exciting potential and the demands of the amphibious project had been sufficient to draw my attention away from Royles in 2001. Even after losing some good men in 2002, I still had little time to focus upon this company. I knew that the Roylecraft amphibians would create valuable business and substantial profits which would quickly repay Royles debts and re-establish its security. Roger had been with me for over 27 years and was prepared, with the help of John Clapcott later on, to try to keep it ticking over whilst I strived to make a success of the amphibious project.

As it turned out, and as you have seen, I was also soon fighting to keep Covelink's project alive as well as battling on with the extremely devious and unprincipled legal authorities trying to get the money awarded to us in the High Court.

By 2006, the staff at Royles were becoming increasingly concerned, because they knew that I still had big debts and that I was thinking of selling the business, or the Old School buildings to repay the substantial loans. I stressed to the men that I had no intention of closing down the company. If the latter, the purpose was then to rent a factory which could accommodate Royles or preferably, both companies. The staff had attended the successful High Court hearing as witnesses and knew the situation and I had always kept them informed of events.

I eventually managed to make the time to interview three or four new men for Royles and by the following year, I had taken on three new, good and skilled men, so was hopeful that matters would improve. It turned out that John Clapcott was keen to run Royles company. He enjoyed the workshops and was knowledgeable about business and motor cars, especially racing and high performance ones. Knowing this and now being 68 years old, I decided that I would like to wind down and spend more time at home and possibly write a book about it all.

I was ready to take more of a back seat and had managed to keep sane, but only just, in spite of all the years of extremely serious and disastrous problems. I mentioned earlier that I had the support of some wonderful people. Including the Duke of Edinburgh who realised how difficult life had been for me and he was surprised that I had not been "driven round the bend", as he put it. He had seen the frequent flooding round the world including ;- Mozambique in feb-March 2000, Missisipi 2003, Bangladesh in 2004, 2008, 2009, 2010. Carlisle in the UK in January 2005, and Pakistan in 2010. And he could see how Roylecraft could have provided valuable transport for the emergency services to help those many people who were suffering so badly.

'RETIREMENT' AT HOME

An overall plan was agreed with John and Roger which included that we would have regular meetings at Gainford, John would inject some money and re-energise the company and continue to look into moving Royles to new premises He was also arranging to buy a cottage in the village of Staindrop where he could stay when he was visiting the workshops. It all seemed to be falling into place, so I had a meeting with the staff and handed over control to John and Roger at the beginning of March 2009.

John thought that I should have a computer at home which didn't really appeal to me at all. This was mainly because Irene and Roger had always done whatever was needed, and I wasn't familiar with PC's, but he offered to install one for me, so a 'Windows Vista' duly arrived and he kindly set it up in March-April 2008. I took over what, originally, had been the old coachman's room above what had been the old coach house and stables, but was now Jo-Jo's kitchen. This had been used as the boy's sitting room when they were teenagers.

I transferred my many files and photographs and made it into my 'retreat'. It was conveniently near to all the daily activity going on downstairs, but I was still out of the way and I was soon able to make a start on the book.

I began to gradually pick up some of the PC systems and began by scanning in some of the pages which Irene had previously typed for me from my early hand written drafts. They say that you can't teach an old dog new tricks and how right they are! Sometimes it drives me up the pole.

It was going to be a big job, going through old family documents and company records. Starting with the witchcraft story in 1612, I then started ploughing through literally thousands of letters, business and family records mainly going back to the mid 19th century. There are so many documnets and boxes of records and together are so heavy, that I was worried the floor might collapse. There must be well over 2000 files.

It was not long after leaving the office at Staindrop and after I had settled into my 'new' room at Gainford, that there was a marked change in John's attitude and his behaviour. His trips north became less frequent as the months passed. We had discussed various ideas and had a written agreement which clarified the future plans for Royles company which John was to carry out.

Because I wanted a clean break and did not want to interfere and also wanted to focus my attention on the book, one of the points we had agreed was that we would have regular meetings at Gainford. This was so that John could keep me in the picture with events at Staindrop. These meetings however, became less frequent and I began to be concerned about it. There was a long gap when John did not return my phone calls, so I visited the workshops and found that there were more modern cars parked in the yard than was normally the case. I asked Roger what they were doing there, and he explained that they were John's vehicles and that he had become embroiled in an acrimonious separation from his wife.

At a subsequent meeting I could see that he was a changed man. His professional attitude had gone and he was clearly most embittered about his predicament. I wasn't involved in his domestic affairs, so do not know the details, but the parallel with Richard Fletcher and the Covelink affair couldn't be ignored. Both men seemed to be devoted to their wives and families and I was very surprised and sorry when I heard about their respective situations. With both of them living so far away, I was relieved not to be directly involved.

Whatever the case may be, much of what we had agreed was not carried out and our relationship deteriorated. John didn't inject any money, he failed to keep the regular meetings, cancelled the contract to buy the cottage and made no attempt to relocate Royles Workshops.

I asked Roger how he felt about it all and he said that John was in touch regularly by phone and that the men were busy at the workshops, so he didn't think it necessary for me to move everything back into the office. This was a blessing because it had been a big job to remove 35 years of paperwork from our document store and empty my old office in Staindrop. I was in the middle of sorting through these piles of records and the thought of hearing about John Clapcott's problems after fourteen years of battling with corrupt solicitors and BW,s directors, was more than I was prepared to contemplate. I'd had enough and was pleased that Roger thought that he would be able to cope!

SOLVING THE DEBT PROBLEMS

The interest on the loans to finish the Jet-Buses and on Royles overdraft were making life very difficult, not only for both companies but also at home. Because I had now gone without a salary for most of the last 12 years, I decided to see if I could 'quietly' find a buyer for the Restoration company. To do this, I wrote to a few of friends and customers who might be interested. Because of the recession, the legal and more recent debts and the men leaving, our figures had been poor in recent years. Whilst it didn't help, at least I was able to explain the situation to each of the four prospective buyers who came north to see me.

Each of them turned out to be people who were already working in the restoration business. They were offered the company with or without the Old School premises. You may remember that I had bought The Old School when I started the business as a 'Sole Trader', so the buildings belonged to me personally. Regrettably, none of the buyers went ahead, mainly they said, it was because their businesses were located much further south and overseeing the work up here would be difficult for them. I could understand this, even though the asking price was nominal.

One or two others I spoke to about it, explained that the business was unsalable simply because if they wanted it, they could offer my men more money and take the business that way, without having to pay for it. What a lovely country this is!

At the time, in 2007 and 2008, as you know I was looking into the possibility of renting one of the 240 empty factory buildings in the area. One which would not only be big enough to accommodate both Royles and the Roylecraft Amphibious vehicle project but also could be used to incorporate the low cost version of the Living Museum.

The benefits and economy of having all the skills under one roof were obvious There was plenty of choice and it was a practicable idea but, as ever, it was reliant upon attracting the necessary funding which I was, again, trying hard to raise. With this in mind, I adopted a different approach and wrote to a few people who might be interested in buying the premises only, as an investment

The property market was buoyant and with the workshops being centrally located in the village next to the junior school and near the shops, church etc, it is an ideal site for development. I had meetings with the planners who told me that they would be happy to have a dozen or so houses there.

This time, one of the people who had been helping to point me in the right direction for funding, was interested in buying the property and was also happy to lease the buildings back to me. The sale went ahead so, outwardly, Royles could carry on as before. The rent however, was now at a proper commercial level and was based upon the sum paid. This was more than twice the amount which I had recently charged the company, and then, I only charged rent when it was absolutely necessary. This increase in overhead costs didn't improve matters adding, as it did, to the financial problems which we already had at Staindrop at the time, but never the less, I was greatly relieved that I had found a buyer and was able to sort my finances out.

After so many years of putting the companies first by not drawing a salary, selling assets and securing substantial loans with my personal assets, this time I was determined to use the proceeds from the sale of the property for the security and benefit of the family at home. Even though the old school was my property, I still felt guilty doing this, such is my attitude to maintaining the jobs and the companies.

I used the money to pay off the debts for the Jet Buses. These were the various mortgages, mainly on the house, but also the workshops. As I was now nearly 69 years old, and had cashed my pension fund for Covelink, what was left was invested as pensions for Jo-Jo and me. It was not a huge amount, but it was the first time since 1993 that we were not in debt and underwriting both of the companies loans. It was a great relief to me, especially with the onset of the latest recession in 2008.

MATTERS COME TO A HEAD

Although I was concerned about Royles, I knew that they had plenty of work and I decided to leave it to Roger who still thought he could manage with John helping in the background. The overdraft was often fully utilised, but I knew that if I had increased this facility which, as ever, I personally secured, the account would soon be up to the new limit as had previously happened before when I had done this. They were on the front line and It was vital for them to deal directly with, and improve, the credit control, so it was better if I was out of the way and was able to continue sorting out all the documents and files and writing the book.

The months passed, but matters came to a head in the early summer of 2009 when John informed me that he had arranged for some rough and ready figures to be produced. These showed that Royles owed the HMRC substantial sums of money. The situation was serious and, as is usually the case, this was the result of a number of factors.

Like me, John had not been drawing a salary, as

agreed, but neither had he introduced any money into the company which he said that he would do, so he still had no equity. There were now large sums owed to us by some of our customers. There were those who were questioning the costs of the work. This did happen occasionally, but in one case, we had tried hard to minimise the costs to please our customer by leaving part of the framework of his saloon bodywork unrestored. Although this was against our normal practice, our customer was complaining loudly, so to minimise his costs, we left the panelling and frames untouched on the rear quarters which looked reasonably sound. When the car was back on the road however, this part of the bodywork settled and we then had to do the work which was not done the first time.

This situation is not untypical of the problems associated with restoration work. In this case, we had tried to help our customer who then refused to pay for the additional work which we would have normally done in the first place. It was many weeks of work which he had benefitted from, but he refused to pay and the company's debts increased accordingly. The plain fact was that the credit control, which John was to implement, had failed to materialise and the overdraft was now fully utilised, virtually all the time. This, together with the HMRC debt, placed the company in a very precarious situation.

I intervened and informed the staff verbally and in writing that we were in a weak position and suggested various ideas, including a 10% reduction in pay. Our position wasn't improving, all the books were taken to the company's accountant Nick Upton. After due consideration, he advised me to put the company into Voluntary Liquidation. With great sadness, once again I appointed Insolvency Practitioners and the dreadful performance of winding up this good little company began.

It was no great surprise to my staff when I regrettably, had no option, but to make them all redundant. They knew that I had done all I could to try to maintain their jobs. Roger, for example, had been with me for thirty-five years and others for nearly thirty years. They were highly skilled, dedicated people and needed to be devoted to their work in order to maintain the highest of standards which I always aimed to achieve and which we were well known for.

After 35 years of business, this was indeed a sad end. Royles had built up a wonderful reputation, both nationally and internationally, and whilst it is a difficult business to run, in some respects, it proved to be as interesting as I had hoped it would be. When I first started working on motor cars in 1956, I had no idea that later on, it would become such an important part of my life. We had many marvellous customers, some of whom became firm friends.

I have explained, in previous chapters, that I started the business because I enjoyed the challenge of high quality restoration as well as the work itself and not because I thought it would be very profitable. Although our labour charges were low, our customers were still faced with large ongoing bills due the labour intensive nature of the work, so it was difficult to avoid occasional bad debts. Down the years, I found that it was very difficult to make up for these, because our profit margins were so small.

The worst debt was £73,000 which arose out of the work to the Frua Rolls Royce in 1993, the fifth car of this make for the same owner. The full story is told earlier which explains why we failed to recover this money, despite a most successful court case, when our awards were taken by corrupt solicitors. With the high interest rates in the 1990's and the ongoing liability of this loss, we never fully recovered and with later debts adding more problems, the business was wound up during October/ November 2009.

Finally, an auction of all the machinery and stores was held at the Old School on the 2nd December 2009, when people from all over the country attended. I was having a small surgical operation on my back that day, but had no desire to be at the auction anyway. Like the old school itself, most of the assets had been originally bought by me, personally, in the years before the company was formed. Fortunately these were listed when a formal valuation had been carried out some years earlier in 1996 , so the money raised was easily divided and credited to me and the company respectively. Thankfully, my assets at Staindrop were nearly sufficient to pay off the company's bank overdraft which I personally secured, with the remaining money from the company's assets paying the creditors.

You may wish to know that Roger and three of Royles team have now set up on their own under the name of "Classic Car Workshop Ltd" near Croft Racing Circuit at Cockleberry sawmills.

PERSONAL NOTES

Now that I have finally reached the end of the book, I regret to say that it has taken me so long to write it that as a result, you will have noticed that parts of the earlier chapters are now dated. I hope this is not too confusing, I would still be amending it if I had continually tried to update it! When I started writing, Royles for example, was still in business. I sincerely hope that this passage of time has not deterred you and that you will have had the patience to read most, if not all of it.

Hopefully, you will have found some parts interesting and informative. It has been quite a challenge for me to maintain continuity due to the various and quite different activities which were going on in parallel. Because they are inter-related, I thought they should be included. The description of the hospital operations for example, was relevant to the events surrounding them, so I hope that they didn't detract from the story.

Whilst I didn't set out to make this book auto-biographical, it was when I was trying to maintain some sort of continuity and when looking through my diaries, that the chronological order and other events 'crept in'. It seemed to improve the 'flow' and be the most practicable way of doing it.

I wanted to tell you about the wonderful motor cars which have passed through the workshops. Vehicles which I found to be so interesting and which have also given me so much pleasure when restoring, driving, testing and evaluating them. I was also keen to include the story about the amphibious vehicle project. I found this to be a fascinating challenge and when it turned out to be as extraordinary in the same respects as the Royles affair, I wanted you to know what can happen when an individual creates very valuable products and a new technology without the benefit of having sufficient money to protect them. I may be naive and my open and honest attitude seems to be out of step these days. It may be this which has left me exposed to those who will take advantage of this.

It was whilst putting all this into print, I felt that you should know a little about my background, so included a brief outline of the family history and life during the war, along with some notes about my school days. It seems that some people are surprised to find that I have no qualifications other than half a dozen 'O' levels and can't understand how I am able to do what I have done. This boils down to the fact that practical experience and lots of it, combined with an open mind and plenty of enthusiasm, can be every bit as valuable as academic qualifications, in fact more, in some circumstances.

As a youngster, I was thrilled to find what I was able to do with my hands and with very little money how, by the age of eighteen, I was able to have my own car and a boat as well. These led me on to spending the rest of my life following these interests, a great luxury in this day and age. I consider myself to be very fortunate in having been able to do this. Whilst the work can be very demanding, the satisfaction of creating and enjoying beautifully restored motor cars, boats and also later on, houses, must be one of the most pleasing ways to spend your life.

My interest in motoring and sailing also brought me into contact with some remarkable and interesting people who were a delight to meet. Many have been extremely kind to me and remain friends to this day. Had it not been for the few dreadful people whose remarkable lack of principles and judgement contributed to the loss of my successful small businesses, I think that we all would have been amply rewarded for all the work.

When I say this, I don't just mean financially. It would have been wonderful to see my amphibians in use all around the world, especially wherever there are floods, being used to rescue people and provide efficient transport in emergencies. Also, they would have brought the thousands of miles of little used waterways back into everyday use and linked them to the roads to form a properly integrated transport system.

As the years passed, I was shocked to be repeatedly confronted with levels of malpractice which I wouldn't have believed could exist in a civilised country like ours. I hope that anybody who is likely to be involved with creative work similar to mine, will realise that there are people who, as soon as they see the full potential of an idea, will go to any lengths to try to take it for their own benefit.

To protect themselves, normally, people would take legal action, but after having seen for myself how the legal system had failed me and how solicitors are protected, even when they ignore the highest court in the country and literally steal their clients money, I had no choice but to fight my corner and am still trying to recoup my losses.

The whole affair was so dreadful that I decided that I should do my best to tell the full story about it all in this book. I want to warn people of the dangers of trusting and dealing with people and organisations which, I thought, were bound to be honourable and decent. The sadness is that there are those who will 'trade' on this good faith and the presumptions made by people like me. The events surrounding Roylecraft are as remarkable and worrying as are those of the legal affair.

The waste of this tremendous opportunity is truly depressing.

Writing this book has been a mixture of emotions. Some parts brought back happy memories whilst others reminded me of the long and painful years created by people who have no respect for honesty, or for the efforts of others.

In 2009, I couldn't resist the temptation to send my 'special' Christmas cards to various government officials and others who stood by and watched these good little companies and the jobs they created, be destroyed . I include a copy of it at the end of the chapter. The comments inside varied from being apologies for being so silly for trying to create jobs and exports, to the ultimate sarcasm saying how much relief and happiness the closure of my companies would bring to the many government agencies which I had pestered for over twenty years!

Throughout this book, I have mentioned home life and the family only occassionally. This is because I have been blessed with a wonderful wife and two boys who have given Jo-Jo and me a lot of pleasure and fun. They are both high spirited, but generally didn't cause too much trouble. They have not been 'little angels' of course and each of them did write a car off, for example, but we were very lucky, nobody was hurt. They have enjoyed and developed different interests and have always helped to make our family life run smoothly at home.

During the difficult years, which began in 1993 when KK's debts left us with huge borrowings, Jo-Jo and the boys still maintained a happy atmosphere in Gainford which continues to this day. We managed to survive without a proper income with Jo-Jo's clever use of food and brilliant shopping techniques and by using

The Family. 11/10/09. From left, Jo-Jo, Helen, Claire, David Royle, Nick, Jeremy. Sitting in the chair, Beatrice, Camilla, Jonny and Alfie.

produce from the garden. We ran our cars until they fell apart, Jo-Jo's red Jeep for 14 years, my Daimler for 19 years. It was no hardship, because we enjoyed them and the men at Staindrop kept them running for us.

Here at home, in the last two years, the family have been quite content to leave me working on 'the book'. Glad, no doubt, that I was out of the way and busy in my cluttered room surrounded by files, photo's and piles of documents. I am sorry to have to admit, that I would occassionally go storming downstairs when I couldn't master the PC or when I was reading letters which reminded me of the terrible things which people had done in the later years.

With having plenty of room, the house comes

DACR room for preparing this book. 'Organised chaos'.

alive on a regular basis. This is because we are very fortunate in having both the boys and their families living only a few miles away from us. They can pop in and out and we can easily perform the normal duties of baby-sitting etc. In recent weeks, we have had Nick, Helen and the twins staying whilst the builders are extending and improving Glebe Cottage. The only regular interruption to the writing, being by the grandchildren, Alfie, 'B', Milla and Jonny. This is when they come up the stairs and hang around suspiciously in my room waiting for me to open the bottom drawer of my desk and invite them to have 'sweeties' out of the tin. It is an up to date version of those days, thirty-five years ago when Jeremy, as a little boy, would totter round to the wheelhouse workshop in Headlam for the same little treat out of a tin on my workbench.

As the work to the book is nearly finished, I have been thinking about having it printed. Whilst Jo-Jo and our 'boys', and my brother John, have generally wanted me to write it as a record of family affairs, whenever I discuss it or mention vintage cars or amphibians, the usual response is loud yawns and "must go, have lots to do". A few months ago however, Jeremy expressed surprise when, on a rare visit to 'my room', he discovered that I was going to be spending quite a lot of money to have it published.

After studying marketing and business at Bristol and now having his own design company, he was obviously surprised that I hadn't asked him if he would like to do it for me. Thinking that he would be bored and fed up with his 'old man's' diatribes, I didn't ask him if he wanted to be involved. The net result is quite the reverse, he is now cracking on with it and I am delighted to have the whole thing produced, literally, 'in house', as it were.

To finish these personal notes, and mentioning my brother, John, we were all delighted to hear that it had been announced in the London Gazette, 26 November 2010, that my brother, Colonel John A. N. R. Royle MBE, has been appointed to be Deputy Lord Lieutenant of Northamptonshire. At least one of us is doing quite well!

THE FINAL ANALYSYS

Standing on my soapbox, we all now know that our recent Prime Ministers, Tony Blair and Gordon Brown, gave the greedy bankers a free rein which triggered the recession in 2008. The worst recession in living memory. In the first decade of the 21st century, they have precipitated a catastrophe which was even worse than that which had been predicted by many academics when New Labour first came to power in 1997.

Nobody has seen more clearly than me, how they turned their back on industry and manufacturing which, according to the press, shrank by over 80% during their time in government. The many empty factories which I visited here in the North East were the visual proof of this.

Roylecraft was a big project with huge potential and needed big money, some money was provided but in reality, the government did no more than pay lip service to support SME's and the creation of new technologies. In fact New Labour had relied upon the bankers themselves to produce the 'profits' which would maintain the UK economy. They put all their eggs in one basket and they ended up making Britain a worse 'basket case' than any other countries in Europe.

As an ordinary man in the street, I never ceased to be amazed that people in their position, could have so little common sense and such a lack of experience of commercial practice. Time and again, they showed what an ill advised and misguide group of people they were. Property prices were climbing, imports were cheap and yet Brown kept borrowing money from the

IMF, an organisation which kept advising him against it. They even sold the UK's gold reserves when gold was at its lowest value. "No more Boom and Bust", indeed!

Prior to the 'crunch' in 2008, record Trade Deficits were being seen year on year and yet it was hardly ever mentioned and manufacturing and exports were allowed to continue to shrink. My own personal and bitter experience and the dreadful waste of hundreds of millions of pounds worth of potential business and exports, is the most lucid illustration of an opportunity thrown away by the lack of an efficient system to properly evaluate and support one of this country's innovators. Combined of course, with in-depth corruption and maladministration in many spheres of activity.

After nearly fifty years of working at all levels, with my hands at the bench as well as in management running small companies, a clear pattern has emerged. Each of the Royle businesses which I created, or helped to create as in the case of Royle Hepworth, required funding of amounts which were at a level which one is able to raise from the banks and secure with a house or personal assets. When it came to a really big project, which when in production, could create over two thousand jobs then at that stage, I had no choice, but to rely principally on funds from government and institutional sources. Despite years of publicity encouraging SME's to innovate and promising the vital large scale funding, it was not provided.

We had the benefit of an assortment of financial innovation awards, government grants and loans which, in total, amounted to around £400,000. These helped of course, but were spread over a period of eighteen years. All other funds were provided by me and the private sector. Throughout the development periods, a great deal of work and time went into careful planning and research and preparing detailed and realistic Business Plans. I still have many of these, but they proved to be a waste of time and money. We had no support, whatsoever, from any normal commercial source or venture capital funding organisations.

The net result was that the funds we were able to raise were only sufficient to prolong the development periods but failed to achieve the principal aim, which was to actually establish new businesses, create jobs, tourism and high value export production facilities.

You might well think, and I was certainly worried, that there had to be some very serious underlying reasons for my repeated failure to attract proper funding. My record in business was good, I had helped to run a small factory in the 1960's, had established and run Royles restoration firm and other related businesses, for over 35 years. I had organised and set up a starter factory and built the first Jet-Buses in a matter of months and had an impeccable record with the tax authorities, Companies House and the many organisations with which I had been involved. The ultimate test was the most detailed examination in the High Court which proved, beyond doubt, my honesty and that of the systems we operated.

The businesses which I tried to create precisely fitted the criteria demanded by the government and the funding organisations, but despite intensive and prolonged effort with every possible source, it was impossible to raise the vital money. The result, as you have now seen for yourself, was that I was exposed to anybody who wanted to take advantage of my weak financial position to take all the benefits of my work and ideas for themselves. The events which this book describes, are far reaching and were the most remarkable and extreme which I have ever experienced.

With the waste of so much good work and with the recession now really beginning to 'bite', and the facts about the government's policy emerging, I can see that there was indeed, an underlying reason for the lack of institutional support for new business and industry. According to the press it was government policy, New Labour had written it off.

The loss of Royles and the waste of the marvellous opportunity for the unique 'Living Museum' was a great disappointment to me. Perhaps the biggest shock, however, was the way in which British Waterways treated us, they were our ideal partner in the UK. They are held in high esteem around the world due to this country's long history of operating canals and were ideally suited to develop this new industry and benefit from it. Due to the unique Roylecraft designs, my machines are the only

Commercial amphibians which are capable of being operated on Britain's shallow canals and rivers.

Left to Stewart Sim, BW's Operations Director and those who supported him, there is little doubt that our vehicles would have been in service in 2003 and at relatively low cost. It was astonishing that the opportunity for a million pounds worth of sponsorship from Barrs, which would have covered most of the cost of the Jet-Buses was not utilised.

My theory is that once they realised the size of the market and huge potential of Roylecraft, Mark Smith and some of the other BW directors couldn't bear the thought of me and my little SME shareholders, enjoying the kudos and the huge success which they could see was bound to follow, once the amphibians were in service and on the market. We were very pleased to have a Joint Venture with BW, but when we wouldn't part with the lion share of the equity for a fraction of its cost, let alone its full value, that is when they thought they would take it from us, anyway.

It is my guess that as Covelink was such a small company with no money or power, the other directors felt that they could easily manipulate me and the project. All they had to do, they thought, was to criticise the work, starve us of money, bankrupt us, take all the assets and let their own men finish the work. They would also, it seems, be able to remove Stewart Sim from the company and take all the credit themselves for having finished these new Jet-Buses. Once they were in service, BW would then also have all the financial benefits of the world markets for themselves.

In theory, it was a 'clever' scheme, after all, they had Covelink's 'open books' and were working 'in partnership', so knew every aspect of our business and our critically weak financial position. They also had 'spies' in the camp and a contract which was bullet proof. They seemed to have had everything in their favour.

After they had played their dirty tricks and finally did succeed in getting the assets, it must have come as a dreadful shock when they discovered that they didn't have the knowledge or the necessary skills or information to deal with them. How could this "little vintage car enthusiast" possibly create a machine which they couldn't deal with. After all they were directors of a large, national company with 2000 employees. They couldn't be seen to be wrong, so they then displayed what truly unprincipled people they are.

Rather than admit their mistake and to cover their backs, they then decided to discredit and 'kill off' the entire project by denigrating the technology and telling people that "it didn't work". Shameful in the extreme.

It can only be a guess of course and I couldn't know for certain, but I had the impression that the tremendous success of the Falkirk Wheel (350,000 visitors a year) and the restoration of the Clyde and Forth canals and the publicity surrounding them were a feather in Stewart Sim's cap. There might well have been some boardroom jealousy and as it developed, it seemed that this project was going to be yet another success for BW's Operations Director, Stewart Sim.

The BW directors may have had good reason for their terrible behaviour, some sort of government cuts for example, but if this was the case, why did Stewart go ahead with us in the first place and why did Defra publish such harsh criticisms of BW in the press when the contract was spoiled and why did Smith resign?

The great sadness is that, once in service at Falkirk and then in production, the substantial profits would have been most beneficial, not only to BW and Covelink but also to the whole country as well. We are talking, quite realistically, of an annual turnover of around £500 million with a gross margin of 40% of this sum. It would have made a measurable difference to BW's profitability and with the sales being 95% exports, this project alone, would have helped to reduce this country's record trade deficits which were increasing, year on year, at this time.

Looking back, their 'cunning plan' failed on a number of counts:

Firstly, the early consultant's reports didn't criticise us as they had hoped, completely the opposite in fact. They, quite rightly, praised us for our efficiency and economy.

Secondly, when I wouldn't close the little

factory when they cut off the money supply, they couldn't understand what real determination is and forgot that I had already managed for 15 years without any proper source of income.

Thirdly, BW's engineers couldn't finish the Jet-Buses. The directors had underestimated my abilities and the nature and complexity of the designs.

Finally, despite ,or because of my determination to try to see it through, they couldn't understand that I didn't have any money left when they eventually offered the assets back to me. They didn't realise that by then, I had exhausted every possible source of funding and was unable raise any money to buy the assets back.

When all came to all, Defra and the government recognised that BW had misjudged so many aspects of the entire business. My report, the resignation of Mark Smith and critical Guardian news article, all within a few weeks cannot have been a coincidence. My guess is that Smith was a scapegoat, although he did seem to be at the root of the project.

The net result was that the whole project ended up gathering dust in a shed when tens of millions of pounds worth of orders were pouring into my office.

My report to Defra must have been a huge embarrassment to BW, they lost the benefits of a worthwhile new form of transport, they also lost Stewart Sim who was a forward looking, experienced and technically knowledgeable man. One who understood innovative technology and human nature and would certainly have gone on to help us make a complete success of it.

They destroyed my successful company, Covelink Marine Ltd, and indirectly contributed to the demise of Royles restoration workshops, which had supported the project for many years. The people I employed lost their jobs in both my companies and their own engineers were also put out of work at Newark on Trent.

I can think of no better way to summarise the reasons behind the failure of my companies and the waste of great opportunities than to include copies of two letters dated 27 November 2010. The first, to Eversheds, is similar to a great many sent out over the last fourteen years. The second, to British Waterways, reflects many of those written to the directors during the last six years. Occassionally they will reply denying the statements made, but the written evidence proves the facts, and they know it.

UNFINISHED BUSINESS

Having read this book, you will now know why Britain's 2000 miles of canals and rivers remain little used and then mainly for leisure purposes, when they could once again become a valuable transport facility. With this network, our unique advanced marine vehicles could have been used to relieve congestion in city centres and for many other commercial purposes.

Importantly, our Roylecraft technology would also have been especially valuable to rescue and provide relief to those thousands of people who are suffering in the ever increasing number of flood disasters around the world. The great number of enquiries and documents on file here are clear evidence of this.

The global demand is for thousands of vehicles which will create many jobs and a new and high value export business. Despite applying to literally hundreds of sources of Venture Capital for over 20 years, (The list is in the appendix), I know that it is virtually impossible for me to raise the millions of pounds necessary to establish a satisfactory level of production. You now know what happened.

If you believe that you can help me to be properly compensated along with all those who have invested in this project, or know somebody who will, then l would be pleased to hear from you. We have been let down very badly, despite the most extreme efforts which we made to succeed.

The extraordinary events in the legal case are another example of the damage caused to business and jobs in this country by corruption. This time by dishonest solicitors who know that they are so secure in the protection afforded by the legal fraternity, that they can blatantly ride roughshod over the law and even ignore the orders of the Royal Courts of Justice, if it benefits them. If you know of any means to ensure that the orders of the High Court judge are carried out, and the sums due to me are paid, then l will be pleased to hear from you.

AUTHORS NOTE

N.B. When writing this book, I have had to make certain assumptions, this is not only because I have been excluded from information circulating within the legal fraternity and within British Waterways offices but also because there has been so much dishonesty, it was sometimes, difficult to know if what I was being told, was true or not. Whenever possible, I have used my own documentary evidence and that which is recorded on film, mainly BBC and ITV and on the word of those who do seem to be reliable. I have made every effort to describe the events correctly and apologise if there are any glaring errors. My intentions have been to truthfully describe the events correctly as they occurred.

Throughout this book I have referred to the considerable amount of written evidence in my possession. Evidence which proves that much of what I say is true.

After seeing how some important legal documents have been "inadvertently destroyed" by the Law Society whilst other evidence "disappeared" when requested by Eversheds solicitors and placed in their care, I wish to confirm the following:

Without wishing to sound too dramatic, I feel that I should confirm that not only have copies of my documentary evidence now been provided to other parties, I also have made further copies of the relevant files and removed them from these premises and taken both sets to different locations away from family and close friends, to places of safekeeping.

The legal and corporate matters included in this book are very serious and it is important that the evidence is protected.

Christmas card sent to government officials, BW and others who helped destroy the businesses and projects.

27th November 2010

THE OLD VICARAGE.
GAINFORD.
DARLINGTON.
Co DURHAM.
DL2 3DS

The CEO and Board of Directors.

British Waterways.,

64 Clarendon Road,

Watford.   Herts   WD 17 1DA

Dear Mr Evans,

I regret to see that you and the members of your board, continue to remain silent about the fact that your board of directors have, by fraudulent means, deprived me and my shareholders of the benefits of our £4.1 Million investment in what, I believe, is still the most advanced amphibious vehicle technology in the world. One which would have breathed life into our wonderful rivers and canal systems and provided valuable services for flood rescue and the emergency services all over the world.

The very fact that you have not replied to my last letter dated 26th August 2010, confirms that you are confident that you can ignore and trample on anybody you please, without fear of retribution.

I wish to confirm that, until Defra or your board makes good our huge losses, I will continue to do all I can to broadcast the facts about the corrupt methods you employed to destroy our small, industrious and creative company. Worse still, how you have gone on to denigrate the technology when you found that you didn't have the knowledge to deal with it. Truly dreadful.

The losses to me and my shareholders pale into insignificance however, when compared to the losses in exports which our technology would now have been earning for this country and for both our companies ;- conservatively around half a Billion pounds GBP, per Annum. Yes, £500.000.000 and this is only 1500 vehicles per annum. Buyers who tested and inspected our machines, continue to come to me from all over the world, the global market is relatively untapped

I presume that you are behind the small, untruthful and damaging article in September's edition of 'Waterways World' which says that "British Technology was not up to the challenge"... of providing amphibians such as are now in use at Rotterdam. In fact, our technology was and almost certainly still is, way ahead of the vehicles being used. They appear to follow the same unsatisfactory method of construction being, yet again, road vehicles converted to make them float. Amphibians which in any event, you know perfectly well, are not capable of operating on many of our waterways.

In fact, as you know, we were asked to supply a great many 'Roylecraft' for service in Holland, but couldn't do it because you destroyed us.

If your board of directors had the courage to be honest with yourselves, you are now seeing a crisp example of the results of the misguided and extremely damaging attitude to innovation and to those who create it, which pervades the boardrooms of many large companies in this country, including yours.

After losing over 80% of its manufacturing industries in the last decade, this country is virtually bankrupt and desperately needs new, high value innovative products. This is exactly what we had spent 18 years to create and were happily sharing and working with your company to produce. Machines which, without a shadow of doubt, were the roots of a whole new transport industry. A form of transport which had been neglected for over half a century and one which you all have so successfully destroyed.

As ever, I will copy this letter to some of the leading scientists, designers, engineers and academics who worked with me and to other interested parties, in the hope that they will do all they can, in future, to put a stop to the waste of this country's new technologies and future industries.

Yours sincerely,

David.A.C.Royle.

CHAPTER 66: MEANWHILE, BACK AT ROYLES

27th November 2010

THE OLD VICARAGE.
GAINFORD.
DARLINGTON.
Co DURHAM.
DL2 3DS

Brian Hughes Esq. Chief Executive.

Eversheds Solicitors.

1 Wood Street,

London.   EC2V 7WS   Case No 1993 B 4538.

Dear Mr Hughes,

I regret to inform you that, despite ongoing efforts on my part, your organisation continues to ignore the Orders of the Royal Courts of Justice in the Strand, London. This occurred after a most successful defence and counterclaim against a millionaire in the High Court. This resulted in awards to us amounting to over £70.000 at that time, with the benefit of Costs and Interest. (at 8%). The sums now long overdue and owing, amount to in excess of £500.000. The precise figure can be calculated when your firm pays it to me.

The Eversheds solicitors, representing me and my company, blatantly ignored the Judges Orders in their entirety and we received no money at all, following the hearing. The principal award, I understand, was used for the benefit of the losing party's solicitors, who were not going to be paid by their dishonest millionaire client if they lost the case. Our own Eversheds solicitors have effectively reversed the judgement against the interests of their own client.

Incredibly, your firm has denied responsibility for their corrupt activities and for the serious damage, both financial and personal, which the undersigned has suffered as a direct result of the theft of their own clients money.

It is this which prompted my detailed and ongoing investigations into the legal complaints systems. These reveal that I am only one of tens of thousands of British Citizens whom the Law Society is denying a fair adjudication process.

They control the legal complaints organisations for the benefit of solicitors, whether they be honest or otherwise.

The information which I gleaned was reported to Parliament and the two senior Eversheds solicitors involved resigned, but to this day, the awards remain unpaid and no compensation has been provided. I urge you to obey the law and make proper payments to me according to the Judges orders, plus damages in recompense for my substantial losses and the trouble caused.

The facts were also reported to the Legal Ombudsmen, Ann Abraham and subsequently Zahida Manzoor who's reports to Parliament in 2002 and 2007, confirmed my findings. These in turn led to the Legal Services Bill being processed from 2004 to 2007 by Lord Kingsland, the shadow Lord Chancellor.

Regrettably, the purpose of this long overdue legislation has now been undermined in order that the Law Society can, once again, protect fraudulent solicitors when it chooses to do so, without fear of retribution. The abuse of people like me continues.

I also continue to actively press every possible authority including Her Majesty The Queen, the new government and eminent legal authorities in Parliament. Please do not tell me that I am 'out of time', the Legal Ombudsman took 12 years trying to dispense justice, but was finally overridden. This matter is so serious, that I will continue broadcasting the facts until justice is done.

There is a great deal of correspondence and I have a recent lengthy personal letter from the current Lord Chancellor and Secretary of State for Justice, the Rt Hon Kenneth Clarke QC MP., in which he tells me that "it is extremely important that the integrity of solicitors is maintained" and that "unprofessional conduct by solicitors undermines that integrity". I will continue to maintain contact with him and will copy this letter to him and to the Chief of Police, as has been my custom for my own safety. The corrupt solicitors threatened me if I did not stop reporting the Facts to Parliament.

Yours sincerely,

David.A.C.Royle.

APPENDIX

**LIST OF ACTIVE SUPPORTERS INVOLVED WITH THE PROJECT
THIS LIST INCLUDES THE SHAREHOLDERS**

(Qualifications are included when known, apologies for any which have been omitted.)

HRH Duke of Edinburgh.
Duke of Hamilton. MA. MIMechE.
D. Andjel.
H. M. & B. Andjel.
M. Andrew.
J. Atkinson - Business Link.
Capt. A. Cashmore.
A. Bairstow. W. Baker-Baker. FSI
J. R. Barker. LLB. ACI. Arb. MCMI.
F. Barter.
C. J. Bentley.
M. Beresford. BEng.
B. Bevan. C. Eng MIMechE.
R. Blacklock.
P. Bland.
J. Bone. BSc. C. Eng. MIMechE.
G. Bonner
G. P. Brown.
M. Brown. MBA. C. Eng. B.Tech (Hons)
V. E. Brown.
G. Burn.
J. H. Burtonshaw. FCA. BA (Hons)
A. Cameron.
C. Chan. MBCS. M.I.E.
T. Chaytor-Norris.
M. Clarke.
N. Clark.
J. P. Clapcott. BA FCA.
L. Coates.
T. W. Coburn. BSc (Hons) C. Eng MRINA
P. Cocker. ONE.
A. Coultas.
R. M. Cripps. BSc (Hons) C. Eng FRINA
C. Daniels.
T. R. Drake.
A. Earl.
V. Emmerson.
A. Farrington.
Prof. N. Fawcett. PhD C. Eng. FIMechE
J. R. Featherstone.
A. Fletcher.
R. W. Fletcher.
N. Fox. MBE MIQA.
S. D. Freeman.

P. Frost.
G. Gifford.
D. Goddard.
R. Gordon-Head.
C. Green.
R. V. M. Hall.
W. E. M. Harrison.
G. Harvey.
D. G. Humphreys. FCIB FCIBS
J. A. Isaacs
G. Johnson.
Digby Jones.
J. Just.
E. J. Keighley.
F. W. Keighley.
D. Keighley.
P. B. Kent & Co. Ltd.
C. Von Kienlin.
L. Knight.
Maxim Koiesnik.
D. Lanzcron.
C. Lin. BSc. (MIT). MRP (Harvard) MA
M. Lloyd.
N. J. Lobley.
K. Lovell. FRINA C.Eng
C. Lunt.
D. W. G. Miller. DLC C. Eng. MIMechE
J. R. Mitchell.
K. Mitchell.
D. Moss.
M. M. Needler.
J. Newton. CEO NESTA
A. T. Noble.
J. Osborn.
A. Parks.
R. Parsonage.
Lord D. Putnam
K. J. Steel.
R. B. B. Ropner.
S. Ross.
D. A. C. Royle.
J. E. Royle.
N. E. W. Royle
J. C. N. Royle.
Col. J. A. N. R. Royle MBE DL

T. Sales.
M. Sessions-Hodge
R. Sidery.
Sir A. Smith.
A. D. Sperrin.
N. Speechley.
J. Stirling.
L. Shore.
J. Sillwood.
D. Smythe.
J. G. Stirling.
R. Swan. OBE
A. J. Tate. BSc (Hons)
A. P. Theakston FCIS ICSA President
A. Thurlbeck.
G. T. Todd.

W. Tyrens.
N. Upton.
S. Watkins.
P&P. Weegram - S. Taylor.
M. H. Weightman
Prof. P. L. Weightman
G. Wheeler.
Capt. P. Wijowski
I. Williams - ONE.
A. Winton.
S. Wood. British Embassy, Tokyo
H. D. Woodcock. MBA FICS.
A. Wright.
A. Wynn-Williams.
Suchi Yasuhiro.
Ohga Yoshiyuki.

LIST OF MP's APPROACHED 1995

Rt Hon. Michael Allison. MP.
Robert Banks MP.
Michael Bates. MP.
Jack Cunningham. MP.
David Curry. MP.
Tim Devlin. MP.
Rt. Hon. Derek Foster. MP.
Michael Heseltine. MP.
Peter Luff. MP.
John Major. PM.
Sir Marcus Fox. MBE. MP.
Dr Keith Hampson. MP.
Michael Jack. MP.

Robert. B. Jones. MP.
Timothy Kirkhope. MP.
Richard Page. MP.
James Paice. MP.
Elizabeth Peacock. JP. MP.
Mrs Marion Roe. MP.
Alan Milburn. MP.
Emma Nicholson. MP.
Michael Stephen. MP.
John Townend. FCA. MP.
Neville Trotter. FCA. JP. MP.
Tim Yeo. MP.

POTENTIAL VENTURE CAPITAL PEOPLE & FUNDING ORGANISATIONS APPROACHED. 1987 TO 2008.

3i PLC.
Abel Venture Managers Ltd.
Abtrust Fund Managers Ltd.
Adams & Associates. Croydon.
Alan Patricof Associates.
Allied Dunbar.
Allied Marine Services. Essex.
Alvis Plc.
Apax Partners and Co Ltd.
Armitage McGovern Group.
Ashquorn Ltd.
Australian High Commission.
Axa. D. Pinckney.
Baker Tilley.

Bank of England. London.
Bank of Scotland.
Barclays Bank.
Baring Capital Investors Ltd.
Baring Venture Partners Ltd.
Baronsmead PLC.
Base International.
BBC London and Newcastle.
Beer & Partners. Cheshire.
Beeson Gregory.
Beijing Four Dimensions Ind. Group
Bell Lawrie White & Co Edinburgh.
Berlin Capital Fund.
Beta Technology Group.

APPENDIX

Bibby Line Ltd.
C. Blyth.
R.C. N. Branson.
Brewin Dolphin Sec. Leeds.
Bridges Community Ventures.
British Coal Enterprise Ltd.
British Aerospace. Farnborough.
British Linen Bank Ltd.
British Coal Enterprise.
British Steel (Industry) Ltd.
British Technology Group.
British Venture Capital Assoc.
Brown Shipley Venture Managers.
Business & Enterprise. North East.
Business Links. Co Durham.
Business Links Liverpool.
BWD Rensburg Ltd.
BZW Private Equity Ltd.
Cambridge Venture Management.
Candover Investments PLC.
Capital Access. Manchester.
Capital Exchange.
Capital For Companies Ltd.
Capital Partners International PLC
Carlisle City Council.
Cavendish Management.
CBI London.
CCL Finance. York.
CDT Enterprise.
Channel Services Ltd.
China- Biz.biz.
Choice International Ltd.
ClNVen Ltd.
City Cruises Plc.
Cleaver & Co.
Close Brothers.
Clydesdale Bank Equity Ltd.
Compass Investment Bank Ltd.
Co-operative Bank.
County Durham Development Co.
County Durham TEC.
Cummins Engine Co.
CVC Capital Partners Ltd.
Daimond Capital. Chicago.
Darlington Borough Council.
Darlington Business Venture.
Darlington Chamber of Trade.
Defence Procurement Agency. Bristol
DERA.
Design Council.
Dyson. James,
Durham University.
Durham County Council.

Emka Productions. Nick Mason.
Entrust. Newcastle on Tyne.
Eureka Secretariat. Brussels.
E.U. Coal & Steel Community.
E.U. Commission. S. Hughes. MEP
E.U. Commission. Neil Kinnock.
E.U. Commission. R Verrue. D.Gen.
E.U. Venture Consort Assoc.
Express Engineering.
Federation of Small Businesses.
Fletcher International Sportsboats Ltd.
Ford Motor Company.
Foreign & Colonial Ventures Ltd.
Future Start. Commercial Venture Fund.
Gartmore Investment Management.
Garwood Financial. London.
German Embassy. C. Lindemann. FA.
Gerrard.
Global Quality Solutions. E.Kilbride.
Glover Webb Ltd.
Government office. One North East.
Grant Thornton.
Greater Manchester Innovation Centre
Green Flag. Ernest Smith.
Greenpeace. London.
Grenwich Millennium Trust.
Griffon Hovercraft.
Grosvenor Estate.
Haines Watts Corp. Finance.
V. E. Hartley Booth
Hartlepool Enterprise Zone.
Hartnell Scientific investments Ltd.
Haynes Motor Museum.
Hill Murray Ltd.
Hill Samuel Investment Services.
Hilling Wall.
R.Holland.
HSBC Bank.
IFG Capital. London.
Jasper Capital. London.
JCB.
John East & Partners Ltd.
Impex Southern Ltd.
Indiana Dep't of Com. Indianapolis.
Inventorlink. London.
Isis UK Ltd.
Itochu Corporation Japan.
Janarden Batt Org.
K. C. Commercial Finance.
LINC.
Lloyds Bank.
London Stock Exchange.
Lombard. Newcastle on Tyne.

Lombard Feltham.
Lord Vestey.
Lowermant. London.
Mackenzie Partnership. Harrogate.
Mayflower Buses.
Nadlan. PLC. Oldham.
Management Projects Group.
Manchester Innovation Centre.
Marshall Hatchick. London.
Manufacturing Advisory Service.
Michelin Tyre Plc.
Midland Bank.
Midland Enterprise Fund.
Ministry of Defence. London.
J. P. Metcalf Associates.
ML Laboratories Plc.
Mountloy Research Centre.
Base International.
BBC London and Newcastle.
ML Laboratories Plc.
M&R Brokers, Jersey.
MTI Managers Ltd.
NAP Associates.
National Physical Laboratory.
National Westminster Bank.
NatWest Ventures.
N. Star. Ltd. New Ventures.
Northern Development Company.
Northern Enterprise Ltd. Newcastle.
Northern Venture Managers Ltd.
Northumbrian Trust Ltd.
New Millennium Experience. 1997.
Newcastle University.
Noble & Co Edinburgh.
Numerica. Corp Finance. London.
John Ogden Properties.
Pathfinder Team Consulting. UK/USA.
Pall Mall Capital. London.
Alan Patricoff Assoc. London.
PERA. Melton Mowbray.
Peter Black Holdings Plc.
Platarg Engineering Ltd.
Port of London Authority.
Prelude Technology Investments.
Preston Rabl.
Price Waterhouse Coopers. Leeds.
Prodrive. D. Richards.
Professional & Comm. Southampton.
Richard Branson.
Rolls Royce.
Rover Group Ltd.
R. Rowland-Hill.
Rowlands Consultants Ltd.

Royal Bank of Scotland. Darlington.
RTC North Ltd. S. Too-Chung. EUPM
Rural Development Commission.
P. de Savary.
Scottish Enterprise. Borders.
Scottish Environmental Protection Agency.
SCS. Henley on Thames.
Shannon Development.
Shildon & Sedgefield Devpt Agency
Singer & Friedlander Ltd.
Sir Donald Gosling. NCP.
The Skern Group. Aberdeen.
Slingsby Aviation. Kirbymoorside.
Small Business Service. Newcastle.
Sports Mondial Plc, London.
Stancliffe & Co. Middlesbrough.
Stronach Investments Ltd.
Sumitomo Japan.
J. Sutton.
Swordfish International Ltd.
Tees Valley Development Co.
Teesside Development Corporation.
Teesdale Enterprise Agency.
A. Teufl. Vienna.
The Titan Group.
Thompson, Clive & Partners.
Toyota Motor Corporation.
Trade Exchange PLC.
Trade Partners. Brit Embassy. Tokyo.
Transort for London. Competition.
Trevorrow & Associates Ltd.
Trinity Holdings Plc.
Tyne & Wear Development Co Ltd.
Tyneside Training and Enterprise Co.
United Nations Ind' Develop't Org.
Vantis Walkers. Middlesbrough.
Venture Capital Report.
Vickers PLC.
Virgin Group. Ltd.
Vosper Thornycroft (UK) Ltd.
Walt Disney Co.
Karl Watkin.
Western Group. Abu Dhabi.
Westinghouse Electric. London
Wise Speke. Newcastle & Stockton
Q. G. Wyvern-Batt.
Yorkshire Bank.
Yorkshire Fund Managers Ltd.
Yorkshire Venture Capital Ltd.

MINISTRY OF DEFENCE. Current in 1995.

Breeze. Overseas Trade. David Offer. (Head)
Defence Research Association. (DERA)
D.Lawrence.
Defence Sales Org. Whitehall.
DRA. Farnborough. Les Brett.
Pathfinder Schemes.
DRA. Chobham Lane Chertsey.
Testing, N.A.Warner.
DRA. New Ideas. Chris Lycldon.
Future Projects. Brian Pearson
Sea Systems. Dr Graham Segrott.
Sea Sector. Chris Stonehouse.
Small Boat Section. David Homes Peter Garner.
David Head
Hydrodynamics. Dr John Dering.
Marine Technology Dep't.
Dr John Williams.
MOD Bath. Mary O'Gorman.
MOD Logistic Vehicles. London.
Kevin Healiss.
Naval Architects. Bath.
Simon Rusling, Director of Design.

The response after many meetings in various MOD offices including those in Whitehall and the experimental base in Devon was positive. They were very interested, but all departments were seeking funds themselves. They expressed serious interest and were keen to be involved, if funding can obtained.

ACKNOWLEDGEMENTS:

Her Majesty the Queen.
HRH The Duke of Edinburgh.
James Blumer.
Frederick Barter.
Lord Carrington.
Irene Harris.
Robert James.
Lord Kingsland.
Lord Lofthouse.

Austin Mitchell MP.
Col. John.A.N.R.Royle. MBE DL
Alan Theakston.
Roger Tyrrell.
Michael Ware.
P & P Weegram.

And all the friends who encouraged me to write it.

LIST OF ACKNOWLEDGEMENTS - PRESS AND PUBLICATIONS.

AM. Aston Martin Magazine.
Autocar & Motor.
The Automobile.
Blandford Press.
Brooklands Books.
Bus and Coach Weekly.
Business Review.
Classic Cars.
Classic Car Mart.
Classic Cars Weekly.
Classic and Sportscar.
Classic and Thoroughbred.
Coach and Bus Week.
Daily Mail.
Darlington and S. Durham News.
Darlington Stockton Times.
Enterprise North East.
Eureka Innovative Engineering Design.
Engineering.
Eurofile.
Fawdingtons.
Inventors World.
Kit Car Magazine.
Markt Klassische Auto.
Motor Sport.
Newcastle Journal.
The News of the World.
North East Business.
Northern Echo.
The Observer.
Portrayal Press.
Royal Institute of Mech Eng.
Sage Publications.
Ship and Boat International.
Small Ships.
Sub Sea.
The Sun.
The Sunday Herald.
The Sunday Times.
The Times.
The Teesdale Mercury.
Workboat International.
Waterways World.
The Yacht Report.

AWARDS RECEIVED

- National Endowment for Science Technology and The Arts - Award and Fellowship. 2000.
- Spirit of Innovation - Companies Category. 2002.
- SMART Award. Department of Trade and Industry.
- Teesdale Enterprise Fund - Most Innovative Business. 2003.
- Innovation Action Fund. Innovation Award.

BBC/ITV TELEVISION

Various news items (on tape)
BBC2 Working Lunch (three programmes)
A mention on Jeremy Clarkson's car programme

EDITORIAL ARTICLES & ENQUIRIES RECEIVED FROM THE FOLLOWING MARKET SECTORS:

Financial Times	May 2000	Rescue and Flood Relief
Workboat Int.	Feb 1996	Commercial and passenger transport
Eureka	June 2000	Emergency Services
North East Business	July 1994	Public Transport
Northern Business Rev	Aug 1995	Marine Survey
Tec Talk	Sept 1995	Policing
The Northern Echo	numerous	Humanitarian Aid
The Daily Telegraph	numerous	Tourism
Darlington & Stockton Times	numerous	Military Transport
Teesdale Mercury	numerous	Ships Life Boat
Boat and Ship Int. RINA	Sept/Oct 04	Ferry for islands/ships/rivers/lakes
Subsea Diving magazine	1995	River authorities general transport
Bus and Coach	numerous	Customs and Excise
Coach and Bus	numerous	Para-Military
Waterways World Mag	Dec and Jan	Private transport/motor home
Enterprise NE mag	April 2004	Oil pollution control
Engineering	Sept 2004	Leisure activities, water skiing, racing.

ROYLECRAFT - COMMONLY HELD MISUNDERSTANDINGS
(Notes given to potential investors)

1. 'It is a start up' (and therefore disliked) - this is not correct, we had established a small temporary factory with full supply chain set up for all components. Now seeking funds for larger factory unit.

2. 'There is no management team' - not true, we have top class people standing by with whom we have already worked - used to big projects and international companies.

3. 'It is high risk' - no, the research and development is 95% complete, seventeen years work done. Ongoing plans for more adaptations using existing components as production proceeds to expand into further markets.

4. 'There is not a market' - not true, hundreds of enquiries and orders, see documentation from all over the world, visits and years of research confirm this.

5. 'Roylecraft are costly' - only when compared to second hand 62 years old DUKW's, but compared to GKN, Vickers and other new amphibians they are less than half price.

6. Are they profitable? - yes, 40% gross margin if built entirely in UK.

Up to 70% if built in the East. Potential £50 million profit in five years if small UK factory and worldwide licensing.

7. **Too difficult to create worldwide infrastructure** - no, plan is to productionise in UK factory then license to overseas companies already pressing us.

8. **'Untried technology'** - no, hundreds of hours of testing afloat and on the road in last sixteen years. Various sizes and types of prototypes tested.

9. **'Needs certification'** - Jet-Buses, yes, but much help from Minister of Transport directly with MCA and DTLR assistance. Jet-Trucks™ simpler than PSV Jet-Bus™.

10. **'Who needs them'** - many sectors of world markets; tourism, flood rescue, public and commercial transport - see substantial documents. Nobody else with our advanced technology.

11. **'Patents and IPR protection'** - yes, list of IPR in most industrialised countries of the world, patents, design rights, trade names -Jet-Bus™, Jet-Truck™ Roylecraft.

12. **'Recognition'** - yes, national and local awards, SMART, NESTA, IAF, etc. Plus many leading figures in industry, academia, etc.

13. **'Equity and participation'** - yes, in proportion with level of investment made with necessary expertise and experience respectively for participation.

14. **'Records and accounts'** - detailed and professionally prepared from 1988 to present day.

15. **'Purpose of funding'** - to re-establish, productionise and enlarge production. Good support ongoing from creditors, shareholders, directors.

16. **'Bad management - hence administration'** - no, appointed by Covelink's directors to freeze activity whilst funding organised. Newco is Cardox Ltd.

17. **'It is another converted motor vehicle'** - no, it is the only new purpose built amphibian, fast and efficient on water and land, designed expressly for marine operations and for use on the road. The first of their kind in the world.

18. **'It is far too risky'** - no, risks already taken. When proper evaluation is undertaken and there is a proper understanding, the risks are seen to be minimal.

19. **'UK manufacturing cannot compete with China'** - true, if product is price sensitive, but Roylecraft is entirely new technology and is not price sensitive, no equivalent competition. Substantial profits if UK built, more still when built in China and low cost economies.

20. **'Capital required is big sum'** - it is all relative, but minimum of £3.5 million is small sum for project and profits on this scale. Entry cost is 10% of normal capital required for these high value products.

21. **'Why has project taken so long'** - reluctance of institutions to invest in R & D, so project reliant upon piecemeal private sector funding.

22. **'Is there a forward plan?'** - yes, remained firm and the same for some years. Various printed business plans now out of date, need to be updated. New plan to be jointly made with new investor/partners, according to sums to be invested and rate of growth desired.

SYNOPSIS OF THE DESIGN AND DEVELOPMENT PROGRAMME OF THE AMPHIBIOUS TECHNOLOGY (Notes Circa 2005)

1986-1987	Initial technical research and preliminary design work. Private sector funding.
1988-1990	Company formed. Designs completed, first highspeed prototype built and successfully tested (1 8ft). Concept proved. Patents and IPR established.
1991	Dti R&D grants of £32,000 and £25,000 plus £2,000 for business plans. Also private sector funding. Market research - California west coast.
1993	Mk II water jet prototype built and tested (16 ft) Private sector funding. Market research continues.
1993-1996	Mk III prototype built and tested (22 ft) high speed, water jet propulsion, new hull design. Market research continues. Private sector funding continues.
1997-1999	Mk IV prototype tested + further development high speed (26 ft). Premier innovation award, NESTA £150,000. Private sector funding continues. Market research continues - South Korea, Germany. Second series IPR commences.
1999-2001	Mitsubishi of Japan asks us to design 40ft tourist bus. Visit Tokyo (British Embassy) Osaka development. Yen collapses. Private sector funding continues.
2001-2004	First tourist bus pre-production model built and tested (40ft). Period of British Waterways funding. Dedicated workshop set up. Video/DVD film produced (BBC) SMART award - £100,000, IAF Funding - £60,000. Private sector funding continues.
2004 to present	Private and public sector funding sources become fully expended. Project temporarily frozen. Directors dissolve company. New funding programme established (Cardox Ltd). Funding efforts continue.

APPENDIX

DAVID ROYLE'S 17 PAGE REPORT TO BRITISH WATERWAYS DIRECTORS AND DEFRA IN PARLIAMENT.

16.2.2005.

CONFIDENTIAL

INTRODUCTION AND OVERVIEW

ROYLECRAFT 12 METRE JET-BUS™
In Barr's colours

The attached report is intended to clarify and explain to the board of directors of British Waterways (BW) and to interested parties why the contract between British Waterways (BW) and David Royle's small company Covelink Marine Ltd (Covelink) failed, resulting in the appointment of administrators for Covelink on 20 October 2004. It covers the period commencing May 2001 through to the present day, February 2005.

At the time in 2001, there had already been fifteen years of intensive, successful work designing and building prototypes, proving and patenting the new amphibious technology. Now in 2005, Covelink continues to see a constant stream of potential orders for Roylecraft from around the world currently worth in excess of £100 million, but still being tied into the BW contract, have no means to supply them. It is important that the facts behind this serious predicament are made clear.

The report explains how the project was taken up by experienced and technically knowledgeable directors and management in British Waterways who could clearly

1

understand the benefits of 'Roylecraft' technology to BW's canal and river network and to overseas operators. It explains how David Royle had to take risks with estimating costs for the four buses wanted urgently for the remarkable BW Falkirk Wheel in Scotland. Everybody acknowledged that the time scales were tight and knew that costs were at risk.

Fully committed to the project six months before the contract was signed in January 2002, David Royle and his staff went to all possible lengths to expedite the preparatory work in the hope of meeting the date for the Royal opening at Falkirk in May. Having taken on staff at the new factory in February and March 2002 it was simply not possible to complete any of them in time for the scheduled delivery the same month. The report describes other contributing factors all of which were explained to BW in 2001. Matters were made more difficult by stringent financial controls and slower payments precipitating some delays at the factory.

Overall control of the BW project is later transferred away from the directors who had initiated it. Not surprisingly the payments to Covelink from BW stopped completely in August 2002 before the full contract price is paid and before the additional funds expected from the JV could be arranged. There were unfounded concerns that Covelink's financial controls and factory practices were unsatisfactory. Subsequently careful checks carried out by BW and independent engineers proved everything was in order and performance above average, but no further regular payments were made. Apparently occasional sums were paid to suppliers later on by BW direct to CML sub-contractors and suppliers without informing CML directors.

The anticipated immediate closure and winding up of Covelink did not occur at this time in 2002 as expected by the FD and the report explains how Covelink's directors and supporters kept the project going for a further two years by raising money from both the public and private sectors and by David Royle underwriting substantial loans to the company himself endeavouring to complete the four buses for BW and meet the contract.

The terms of the extensive contract willingly signed when the project was being controlled by the technical, experienced directors working in partnership, was now brought to bear, the assets were claimed by BW along with the substantial world wide IPR. The many costly and valuable patents, design rights and trade names are now seriously at risk since they may not be maintained whilst in the care and control of BW. For example, a valuable Chinese patent expires later this month. They are the result of many years of work and £2.5 million.

The partnership and proposed joint venture which were vital elements and agreed at the start with the BW directors were dropped leaving Covelink hamstrung and seriously disadvantaged. Covelink's planned funding was undermined and the company's weak financial position completely exposed due to the open books policy also entered into.

All negotiations with BW, Nesta, local government and potential investors were from then on, prejudiced by the open knowledge of Covelink's financial weakness and total reliance upon and subservience to BW and the all-embracing contracts. Subsequently David Royle had to fend off those who tried to take advantage of the company's weak financial position in order to prevent them taking large amounts of equity and control of Covelink. There were two separate attempts made by two other potential sources of funds working with BW to remove David Royle from control of Covelink and deprive him and the other thirty-five Covelink investors of the majority of the equity and financial benefits due to them. They are well documented.

The net result now is the potential loss of the £1 million spent by BW, the prevention of the completion of the buses, the loss to Falkirk of having no amphibians to service the visitor centre. The potential loss of the valuable international IPR through not being maintained by BW, the loss of £3.4 million now invested in the project by public and private sector investors in Covelink, the potential waste of 17 years work, the potential waste of a new technology and the inability to supply the potential incoming orders from around the world with a current value in excess of £100 million.

Taking the very substantial worldwide demand for Roylecraft (estimated variously at £500 million to a £billion) and their inestimable value for public transport and for humanitarian aid and flood relief in the disasters around the world and in the UK, this situation should not be allowed to exist. This small innovative company, Covelink Marine, has exhibited a remarkable dedication and perseverance over seventeen years in order to create a valuable new technology. A technology which is particularly beneficial and ideal for British Waterways operations. This company, its directors, shareholders and many supporters deserve better than the treatment received from BW.

(The figures discussed in the report are necessarily rounded but give the reader a realistic approximation of the facts. From late November 2003 my letters were not replied to and no information provided as to any payments made by BW direct to suppliers etc working outside my company's jurisdiction so the figures may be incomplete for 2004)

David Royle's involvement

It is important that the reader is aware of David Royle's total dedication and financial commitment to this project and the technology which he has created.

Due to the reluctance of institutional investors to be involved with R & D projects, the funding has largely been provided by David Royle and his specialist vehicle company.

Being on a large scale, the costs to him were such that he has, after seventeen years of intensive work, invested all his resources into the necessary work. Over 38,000 hours unpaid work involved prior to BW involvement. Having previously mortgaged his house, invested his pension fund and sold his most valuable moveable assets it was necessary for him to do it again when BW failed to continue their support, he again mortgaged his house, this time his workshops as well and in order to maintain his workforce he underwrote a government loan and bank facility over £200,000 on this occasion. In all he has provided £2.2 million out of the £4.4 million figure spent, leaving him with no money whatsoever and substantial debts.

Although he started work and formed Covelink Marine Limited in 1987 at the age of forty-seven he is now sixty-five and his main income is the state pension.

CONFIDENTIAL

Open letter and statement to:- The Board of Directors and Management of British Waterways and Interested Parties.

From:- David A C Royle Esq - the Inventor and Designer of the New Technology incorporated into 'Roylecraft' amphibians.

My respect for British Waterways (BW) and the good works involved in maintenance and the restoration of our canal system goes back to my childhood, I have early glass lantern slides and early post war 35mm movie film of the river Weaver and associated canals taken by my grandfather and my father, so to have the opportunity to supply the worlds first advanced amphibians to BW for the impressive and innovative Falkirk Wheel visitor centre was a great thrill and particularly satisfying even though in itself, the contract was not expected to be profitable.

For too long I have stood back allowing matters to take their course. The interruption in the funding and construction of the amphibious tourist buses for the Falkirk Wheel has been disastrous for my company, embarrassing for BW, seriously prejudicial to the new technology itself and all concerned with it.

My purpose in writing to you is to clarify the facts; explain the project and show that my duty of care to your organisation is and always has been unquestionable. It also explains the international importance of Roylecraft to transport generally which is evidenced with ample documentation.

Having now been obliged to appoint administrators for my small company, Covelink Marine Limited, it is important that all concerned are clear as to the reasons behind the current most serious and regrettable state of affairs.

The matters discussed here are generally in chronological order:-

For the first time in over half a century, there has been a major step forward in amphibious technology and British Waterways were ideally placed to benefit from it and to introduce it to the world transport systems.

2001 – initial discussions with BW - proposed JV and informal partnership based on open books policy.

Having won the 'No 1' and largest award for innovation from the National Endowment for Science, Technology and the Arts (NESTA) in 2000, (and many others since) the final Mk1V prototype was able to be completed by my two engineers and successfully tested. British Waterways were approached in April 2001 with a view to selling to the company our ten metre general purpose 'Roylecraft' vehicle. Being a shallow draft multi-role craft, I believed that it would be useful to BW as a workboat and service vehicle and also have uses in a number of other respects on their canals and river networks in the UK.

A meeting on 25 May 2001 resulted in BW showing more of an interest in our proposed tourist bus, the design of which had been previously created for and discussed with Mitsubishi in Japan, the collapse of the yen froze this project. Being twelve metres in length and a public service vehicle they are the most difficult challenge of all the amphibians due to the marine and road regulations being so extensive. The detail of design and construction therefore presented a more difficult challenge for us but the proposed order for four buses was still most welcome, it was the breakthrough into the market which the company needed and it benefitted from the same technology.

Early discussions with the Operations Director Stewart Sim and discussions with the other regional directors covering most of the areas of the country revealed that there was positive interest and a great deal of support to introduce our innovative, lightweight, shallow draft (and when required) high-speed machines onto the waterways of Britain.

There were however doubts expressed by Mark Smith the Financial Director and Robin Evans the Chief Executive Officer due to us being a very small company with little in the way of financial reserves. At this stage fourteen years of work and around £2.5 million had been spent, designing and building prototypes to test the principles and innovative mechanisms involved. This had drained the investors, me and my specialist motor company of their reserves leaving only £11,000 in the Covelink bank at that time.

In order to make progress and minimise the risks I wrote to Robin Evans and Stewart Sim on 31 May 2001 and 11 June 2001 respectively, suggesting that we build a single amphibious tourist bus to test this new model, it was the first of its kind in the world. I was confident however that it would operate satisfactorily since we had already built and tested our new technology in four prototypes with the mechanisms to be incorporated but wanted to be sure that the bus met BW requirements and have the opportunity to correct any faults which might appear. This suggestion was not taken up. It seemed that there was a need to press ahead ASAP and risk making the first four units for the Falkirk Wheel in one batch.

Later on in 2001, it was explained to us that it would be especially beneficial if one or two of the buses could be ready in time for the Royal opening at Falkirk by HM the Queen in May 2002. This was put to us at a meeting in Scotland on 20 July 2001 with George Ballinger the Chief Engineer Scotland and Ian Herbert the Falkirk Wheel manager. I said I would do my utmost to try to complete one or preferably two buses in time but could not promise. It was an extremely difficult challenge particularly as our existing facilities and funds were inadequate for 40ft 8 tonne vehicles.

Further discussions with Stewart Sim, Robin Evans and Mark Smith resulted in there being proposals for a joint venture between my company:- Covelink Marine Limited and BW. Due to a previous contract failure with a small company, the BW directors were concerned that it would not happen again and suggested that we provide an open books facility for BW so that a constant check could be maintained on our performance. I willingly agreed that we would provide any information required and that copy documents and certified invoices would be provided and inspections of the office systems and factory work could be made as and when required by BW. We have nothing to hide.

5

At the time, the contract with BW was to be conditional upon the JV, this was to provide BW with a commission on the anticipated sales of Roylecraft to canal operators around the world. At the same time taking equity in Covelink, BW would introduce the much needed capital into Covelink (see DVD film).

In discussions during 2001 I explained that David A C Royle & Co Ltd, my specialist motor design and restoration workshops, could not accommodate the proposed 40ft buses and that we would need to establish a dedicated small factory, buy machinery, employ staff and complete the design work before we could manufacture and supply the craft. Not having sufficient money to do this there was bound to be a shortfall, it was agreed that money would be paid for equity in the JV and also as we would be working in an informal with open books partnership, these arrangements would help with these costs. No fixed sum was agreed but the BW directors were aware that additional monies would be essential element in the funding programme and costs necessarily involved to build the four buses, set up the factory and maintain the IPR. In relation to the importance and costs involved, the additional funding was not considered a problem.

Naturally, the anticipated cost of manufacture was needed by BW before an order could be placed. Due to the bus design work being incomplete at that time, no quotations or costings could be provided to me by sub contract engineering suppliers for the new componentry so the price per completed bus unit could only be estimated. Being the first of their kind in the world with eight tonnes of innovative new mechanisms this was very difficult. A figure of £262,000 per vehicle was arrived at and given at the end of September 2001. This was said to be "high" by the directors of BW but it was accepted and the supply of four buses was to be made at a cost of £1.048 million. It should be noted that new amphibians built by Alvis, GKN and Vickers are three times this figure.

Whilst the formal decision to proceed was not made until September 2001 it was generally understood that an order would be placed, so to give us as much time as possible to progress the designs and components to try to meet the deadlines, I immediately cancelled my holidays for August 2001 and spent every available minute from July onwards designing the buses and all its major components and organising the production of the first four 'Jet-Buses™ as they have come to be called.

A first stage payment of 5% (£50,000) from BW was made on 27 Sept 2001. A great deal of work had already been undertaken and was ongoing with sub-contractors, pricing, planning the small factory, ordering substantial and costly components, setting up the supply chain, working with Newcastle university, ship designers, hull designers and builders, engineers and entering into discussions with the MCA and DTLR in order to establish the appropriate regulations. Liabilities of £150,000 work was already in hand with orders placed by me for the BW bus components before any monies were paid to cover the costs, such was my confidence in BW.

Whilst the bus designs were generally going to remain very much as originally conceived for Japan, there were a number of alterations and changes made as work proceeded in order to satisfy BW, the Falkirk Wheel requirements, the MCA, the DTLR and special requirements for the Queens visit. These include additional low level access doors with folding steps and wheelchair access, changes in air flow/cooling systems, fire prevention, bulkheads, etc. There being no legislation for amphibians, the PSV and marine regulations applied were those of a Class 5 ship and an M3 tourist bus.

There was and still is a considerable amount of help and support for this project by the Minister of Transport himself, the DoT authorities, people in business, academia, parliament and many technical organisations. A most encouraging relationship with BW developed but as with most boards of directors there was a division between those who enthusiastically supported the project and those who did not. The essential difference in attitude in my view was between those who were more involved and understood the technology and had faith in me and my staff and those who did not.

Those who had supported and progressed the contract had visited my workshops and assessed that my forty years of experience with every possible type of motor vehicle and water craft and with over 800 vehicles built, combined with my reputation for quality of work and honesty gave them confidence to proceed. This trust was a fundamental element in the partnership and for a successful outcome.

2002 – the contract, good progress, management change, financial support ceases, sponsorship, intensive search for money

When the time came to sign the contracts prepared by BW's lawyers, Eversheds, in January 2002, these were seen to consist of three separate 'books', an MF2 contract with a separate 'book' of amendments plus another 'book' covering the IPR. With Covelink having little financial capital the BW directors requested the IPR as security. I was happy to sign the contract in January 2002 and felt confident with the positive and enthusiastic BW team who were in control of the project and with whom we were now working.

I was aware that BW had complete control in every respect and was prepared to trust them with my project and the results of fifteen years of work. By having set up a small factory and planning to employ fifteen staff expressly for the contract and with more later, I was totally committed financially, commercially and personally. At that stage I had personally invested £2 million of the £2.5 million invested into the project which is all the money I had been able to raise and provide in the fourteen years of preparatory work.

I took great comfort from the fact that the BW directors involved were most helpful and considered us to be working in 'partnership' with them. This was stated many times in writing (eg. from S Sim 6 Dec (Nov 2002) but was described as being an 'informal' arrangement. This combined with the 'open books' facility for BW made it very much a joint team effort and gave me much comfort. Subsequently Mark Smith stated that there was no such arrangement between our companies.

As with virtually all statements I make in this document, there is ample written evidence to prove what I say to be true and factually correct, copies can be provided but are on your own files.

Jan 2002
Rapid progress had been made, the design work finished and sub-contract engineers appointed. The factory was fitted out with a small office, machinery, compressed air, and all necessary facilities were installed. It was a secluded low cost relatively new 4,000 sq ft

farm building convenient to my existing workshops. All this was made possible by the respect which our suppliers had for us and our confidence in the payments due to be made and being made to Covelink by BW.

The staff from my 'Royles' workshops carried out this preparatory work at the 'new' factory and the staff for Covelink were interviewed and inducted in February and March 2002 to build the Jet-Buses™ and assemble the major components which were beginning to arrive. Regular visits and meetings took place with BW management who oversaw the progress, all invoices were checked and authorised by BDN independent consultant engineers, and later by an engineer employed by Nesta and BW to oversee the work.

March 2002
Having started assembly of the first two buses with parts for all four vehicles being made and still being delivered, two factors were becoming clear:-
Firstly that having only taken on new staff in February and March (with more men in May), it was clearly impossible to manufacture them from scratch and supply them the same month. March had been the proposed date for delivery in good time for the Royal opening on the 24 May. Even to supply them by the opening day, which was eight to ten weeks away, was obviously not possible, even working overtime and six and seven days a week.

Due to the months taken by BW's solicitors to prepare the contract and in spite of its overbearing powers and delivery requirements, there was neither the time nor money to have our solicitors check or amend it. We were already totally committed in every respect to complete the work as soon as possible. Working so closely with BW and with an open books agreement, I did not believe that it would be necessary to inform them formally of this and did not for a moment expect that the recently signed contract to be used to close down this company a few months later for this reason.

Secondly, the costs were building up quickly, largely due to the urgency of supply of all the components being batch produced as ordered and anticipated. The JV was only progressing slowly at this time. As the opening event drew near, the Falkirk Wheel was sabotaged with flooding canal water which caused great difficulties for the BW engineers. With considerable effort and work the difficulties in the control room and mechanisms were overcome but this crisis caused a second one; BW had sponsors for the 'Roylecraft' buses and they were due to visit Covelink at this time. With all the commotion, the sponsors; Barrs Iron Brew, were not up to date with the situation and were surprised and disappointed to see that the buses were not going to be finished in time. They were not aware that the staff had only been employed two months earlier. I apologised to all BW personnel and to Barr's when I was criticised for not having the buses finished in time for the Royal opening. We all were very disappointed but could not have done more to speed the work through the factory.

In a letter to George Ballinger on 6 June 2002 I refer to Barrs having mentioned the possible launch of Roylecraft buses at Falkirk "in the spring of 2003," a much more likely possibility (I gather that Barrs would be sponsoring the original £million estimated cost of the buses). The letter also discusses "unknown development costs" and that the BW contract money allotted alone may not be sufficient. The situation was clear to all concerned.

8

During the early days of assembly, the hulls for the buses were painted in Barr's corporate colours then masked off, then painted again, altogether being re-painted three or four times for the purpose of Barrs confidentiality. Costs which Covelink bore along with all the other additional work mentioned above. We did not charge for any of this additional work neither for the spare parts ordered by BW, none were covered by any invoice. The total value of the contract would then have been around £1.2 million. Being in partnership I was not overly concerned since the JV investment by BW would cover this additional expenditure. It was however recorded and referred to by Ken Butcher the National Procurement Manager in his correspondence. It is clear that the project was also considered by BW staff to be a partnership or these costs would have been requested and paid for.

To those familiar with the project and with technical knowledge along with the shortage of time mentioned above and the ongoing delays in cash flow (see letters to BW requesting payments) due to the clerical checks and systems involved, the fact that the buses were not ready in time for the Queen was anticipated by those closely involved.

Independent engineering consultants confirmed later on that the efficiency of production was good and above average for the industry. In spite of the most successful progress resulting from the concentrated effort and total commitment to the project, the excellent performance and technical achievement were not appreciated and were overshadowed by Mark Smith's concern for the costs. A consultant, Colin McAusland, was employed subsequently to oversee the production and report on the progress. Although an experienced production engineer, he was able to do little to express completion since he had to work within the same constraints which we had.

Looking at the relevant correspondence, it seems that this was the time that control of the project passes to Mark Smith as Financial Director. The focus of attention moved away from the Falkirk Wheel and the technical aspects and centred upon the costs involved.

BW perceptions

The very considerable difference in the size, management and manpower of BW (up to 2,000 staff I believe) compared to the four people involved in the clerical work and management of Covelink meant that the demand for financial analysis, risk assessment reports and other documentation being made by London and Scotland could not be provided to the same standards as would be the case with a large organisation. This, I believe was interpreted as poor management and control. The BW directors now in charge do not understand how or believe that very small companies can operate satisfactorily without the documentation as circulated in large companies. The main difference being that with a small group of people working closely together, everybody is aware of what is going on.

Regrettably, without technical knowledge of the products there was no appreciation of the relatively low cost actually involved in the creation of our new advanced technology or of building the amphibious buses. Large companies had estimated costs in the region of £50 million for a project of this nature with selling prices for their amphibians in the region of £800,000. The very fact that the £262,000 cost originally estimated by me for each vehicle was perceived by the FD as being expensive clearly illustrates this. If the sponsorship is taken into account the final cost to BW was going to be relatively low in any event. Subsequently, the selling price of the Jet-Buses has been set at £350,000 which is commercially viable for civilian craft at the same time is profitable in production.

Although progress in the factory was very good, regular payment to Covelink ceased in August 2002. Between £900,000 and £1 million out of the contracted price of £1.048 million had been paid. With additional costs as previously mentioned the actual contract sum was £1.161 million. According to Ken Butcher £154,000 was still owing. The reason to withdraw support given being that Covelink was said to have breached the contract due to non-delivery in May, four months previously.

Having placed my faith and total commitment completely in BW, this retrogressive action was neither deserved nor beneficial to BW, their sponsors, Covelink, its investors or to me. Knowing our situation and with creditors owed £237,000 in early November 2002 Mark Smith said that he now thought that we would have no choice and he expected me to close down the company and said that the part completed buses would be uplifted to be finished by BW's own workshops further south.

This momentous decision by the BW directors now in charge of the project clearly illustrates the overall lack of understanding of the people involved, the technology and the history of the project. They also failed to take into account the benefits of the very substantial investments in time and money made in the fifteen years prior to BW involvement. They had completely misjudged the situation and our determination to succeed. The result, two and a half years later is an ongoing frustrating and costly business for all concerned.

The focus was upon the monies paid by BW at this point and the unfounded concerns that the costs were escalating were later shown to overshadow the quite remarkable progress and technical achievement made in the five months since the staff were employed at the small factory. The costs were in fact due to the supply of all the components for all the vehicles and were in line with our expectations, we emphasised earlier that the payments would need to be front loaded and that there would be a shortfall - hence the need for the JV and open books partnership.

As financial director of BW, Mark Smith is clearly responsible for the organisations control of its public purse, this is clearly understood. The success or failure of a project of this nature is entirely dependent upon the managements desire and determination for it to succeed or fail. This decision can only be based upon the perceived risks and costs when set against the benefits. In this case those originally evaluating the project, the people involved and the benefits, not only to BW but to the general public and transport in the UK and overseas, realised that the net costs likely to be involved for the public (BW) were low when compared to the very considerable benefits to transport and the public as a whole.

Comparable project costs

The only comparable project is that carried out by Alan Gibbs and his 'Aquada' sports car/speedboat. This man has copied most of my technical principles but in the process has spent £60 million on research and development. A sum more in line with the 'normal' commercial expectations of cost by large companies. He has failed to understand however the underlying theory behind our successful modern amphibious technology and also to properly investigate the market and how best the technology can be translated into useful and commercially viable machines. He may well find his project to be a costly failure in spite of having the funds to do it, the opposite to my own position. A comparison is made in the Royal Institute of Naval Architecture magazine "Ship and Boat" Sept/Oct 04 issue pages 52 and 53. Covelink are shown to be the most commercially viable machines in the world at this time between all current amphibious developments.

Due diligence positive – but negativity remains

Even though our costs are incredibly low, Mark Smith suspected poor financial control and inefficiency so BW carried out due diligence and in September of 2002, clerical management staff from BW Leeds office and independent engineers spent many days at Staindrop carefully investigating the accounts and office systems in Covelink and the progress, costs and technology involved at the factory respectively. The control systems and accounts were found to be efficient and in good order with no irregularities and the engineer also reported that the work at the Staindrop factory was efficiently carried out and at minimum costs. Any doubts as to a lack of financial control or inefficiency were expelled.

This information along with the fact that BW were also advised that their own workshops were not capable of dealing with the new technology involved or the work necessary to complete the buses meant that the entire project was now in limbo. We had no money coming in and BW could not complete the work. Important decisions had been taken without a detailed knowledge of the project.

None of the above information was directly relayed to me or our directors. It was only by word of mouth that this was discovered. Unlike Covelink's open books, BW provided little information in return; their 'books' have mostly been closed to me since August 2002. (even their minutes of directors meetings concerning CML are not published)

Determined to complete the contract to supply the four buses to BW even without any money coming in from them, I set out with the help of Covelink's directors and many people in all sectors of the industry, to raise the necessary money. Time was requested from BW so that this and the work to finish the buses could be done. Our duty of care continuing even in the face of great difficulties.

It must be remembered that the anticipated costs would be in excess of the contract price, this was discussed at the outset with Robin Evans, Stewart Sim and Mark Smith. Heads of Terms produced by BW management for the important JV which was to introduce the additional important capital to cover the factory set up costs and anticipated shortfall in building the buses, did not materialise from BW even though I believe that some were prepared by their staff.

One sided negotiations

Ongoing efforts by Covelink with the help of Peter Gordon, a mentor appointed by Nesta to put together an acceptable JV for BW were frustrated by increased expectations for control and large percentages of the equity in Covelink. Peter Weir had been newly appointed by BW to negotiate for BW. It is important to remember that any discussions or negotiations between BW and Covelink could not in any sense be equitable. From the start the open books relationship and Covelink's complete financial reliance upon BW presented an open, unbridled opportunity for those who sought to take control of Covelink and benefit from the fifteen years work (at that stage) and the very considerable investment made prior to the BW contract. (letter dated 9th July 2002 to Stewart Sim refers) The discussions demanded fair and reasonable suggestions, not hard commercial negotiations, the prevailing situation could not sustain a normal process.

The BW contract was such that Covelink's directors were now hamstrung, they could not build vehicles for anybody else, they could not sell the buses (letter dated 21 Nov 2001 refers) and the application of the contract terms resulted in the IPR being under their (BW) control. The advantage and control exercised by BW over Covelink was total. From the start Covelink's directors were reliant upon the informal partnership and co-operation of BW's directors and management. With their serious concern to ensure that BW money was controlled and with it being public funding, their caution was understandable but it has resulted in the present failure of the entire contract and this company. The losses being far greater than the costs and benefits of continuing. The new management misjudged Covelink and me and undermined the partnership and the project.

Problems raising money – but big market

From September 2002 onwards right through to the present day every effort has been made by Covelink to raise money from every possible source.
The original problems of raising money were now magnified by the fact that BW had withdrawn funding from the project. Mark Smith had also insisted that no publicity or website should be arranged until the supply of the buses to BW had been made. Having complied with these requests and demands, the result was that the majority of the city and other financial institutions approached for funding were especially reluctant to invest and to begin with had no knowledge of our existence or point of reference.

Finally in November 2003 in desperation, a small website was established. Not only did this put Roylecraft 'on the map' for investors, it also has resulted in a continuing stream of potential orders for hundreds of our Jet-Buses and multi purpose craft from all around the world currently worth over £100 million. No advertising or marketing has been done and this proves the demand. The many documents relating to this are here for inspection. The total world market is put at between £500 million and a £ billion.

Although conclusively proving the demand, all these orders are an embarrassment because we have no means to supply the vehicles and are still tied to the BW contract. This further damages the credibility of Covelink.

In 2003 ongoing requests were made to Nesta and BW but they would only provide further financial support if Covelink relinquished control of the company to Nesta and to them in another lengthy, overbearing joint contract which had been prepared by NESTA's director of innovation Mark White. This was out of character with both the CEO and Chairman of NESTA; Jeremy Newton and Lord Puttnam who had been most supportive throughout the life of Nesta. (see DVD) The existence of this contract was denied later by Mark Smith but we have copies on our files. Other organisations and investors were approached and during the next two years various local government departments and private investors introduced around £500,000, this was however after further attempts were made to take control of Covelink.

In April 2003 once again efforts were made to deprive me and the investors of Covelink of control and the benefits due to their company when BW, represented by Mark Smith, joined the Business Finance Team of One NorthEast at a meeting, held on 24 April at Stella House, government office. On this occasion funding of £199,000 by local government was to be provided, but was made conditional upon 60% and control of Covelink, equity being sold to a specified local group of businessmen for a disproportionately low price represented by the Chairman of the County Durham Development Company and that the Covelink board had to agree to this in forty-eight hours.

This assembly of people were aware of Covelink's urgent need for funding due to eight months (at this stage) having passed without any regular income from BW or outside source. Having a factory with fifteen staff and no income our position was dire. Having no option if the company was to continue and under duress, the Covelink directors had no choice but to convene not one, but two meetings in close succession to meet the substantially reducing offers being made by the local businessmen in order to sign the sale contract with Covelink board approval. This is fully recorded in writing by both parties.

Due to our very urgent need for this public funding to keep the factory running and the fact that time was passing, I had no option but to refer the matter to a higher authority, therefore shortly afterwards, our MP – Derek Foster, was informed of the situation and the money was immediately provided. (Letter dated 22 April 03 and 9 June refer) In the due course of time, no firm offer of money to buy the equity came from the businessmen and in spite of threats by local government to withdraw the loan guarantee, the contract was not enforced. In point of fact various banks and financial institutions had warned me against involvement with the key businessman involved.

Funding package failure – but good progress

Due to the ongoing urgent need for funding late in 2002 early 2003 it was agreed with BW and Nesta that if I would introduce further substantial capital of £110,000 (by mortgaging my house and workshops) they would also put in substantial sums. I did this and also additionally underwrote a government loan and bank overdraft and introduced sums with a total in excess of £200,000 to pay creditors and keep the factory running. Due to Covelink's directors not agreeing to pass control of the company to the specified party and with BW's strict controls with deadlines not being met due to unpredictable and insufficient funding, the £212,000 offered by BW and £75,000 from Nesta to make up the funding package at this time, was not forthcoming. Much lesser sums were provided piecemeal by them later in 2003 and 2004, when it was apparent that progress was still being made, in spite of their reluctance, albeit slowly.

In spite of the money being provided by me, which had to be borrowed, the full amounts were never paid by BW or Nesta to make up the agreed funding package.

The extreme financial difficulties which had to be faced during the last four months of 2002 with having no income, and indeed ever since, are difficult to describe. In spite of these, the first bus was still ready to be tested in water and on the road during this period in December 2002, nine months from the staff arriving at the factory. This is acknowledged to be a remarkable achievement for such a small and latterly underfunded company. A further request by BW to demonstrate a bus at Falkirk in early 2003 was also carried out much to the satisfaction of Edna Cunningham of Barrs and is recorded on video film. This was in spite of the known faults with the rear drive shafts and differential. BW and Barrs were informed of this in advance. They were discovered during the December 2002 tests. BW did pay the transport and other costs for this demonstration in Scotland which was most helpful.

Bad press -BW

As BW has published a damaging statement concerning technical problems with the first bus, in "Waterways World" page 44 May 2004 issue, it would seem that there is a desire within BW to excuse themselves from their responsibility for the failure of the contract. Quite clearly, having taken steps in August 2002 which would knowingly result in the winding up of Covelink, it is in BW's continuing interests to save 'face' by precipitating the failure of the company and its technology. So often we have seen potential investors who are seriously interested change their minds at the last minute and we can only presume that it is as a result of British Waterways failure to support the project.

Technical matters – exaggerated but no surprise

Whilst on the subject of technical problems I wish to clarify the facts behind this issue;-

Because of the urgency of supply of the first Falkirk buses discussed in 2001. It was thought by ourselves and our sub-contract supplier that the drive shafts, differential and gearbox previously designed for the 10 metre GP vehicles should be satisfactory for use in the 12 metre buses. These did work satisfactorily to begin with but more testing revealed that modifications would be needed to strengthen them. It was a risk taken to try to meet the BW deadline and minimise costs, it was not therefore a surprise or a serious technical problem.

Taking into account the important fact that these amphibians were the first vehicles of their kind ever to be built, it is not surprising that some development work in any event would be necessary. Indeed, George Ballinger said that we must anticipate some problems with 8 tonnes of new technology which had never before been tested. In fact the modifications were relatively straightforward in comparison to the overall cost of these highly innovative amphibious Roylecraft and the amount of new machinery involved. The none technical directors do not seem to understand that some developments are commonplace and are in this case relatively inexpensive to rectify in relation to the high value of the products; perhaps 5% of the project costs.

14

I believe that it was the fear of expensive development costs which led the directors of BW to make such serious decisions to cease their support for the company. Presumably they saw them as a never ending open door to expenditure.

Congratulations from Mark Smith were received as he saw the funding package coming together in 2003/2004. A total in excess of £700,000 was eventually raised excluding the expected sums due from the joint package agreed with BW and Nesta. As this amount was the original target estimated with BW needed to complete the buses for Falkirk, Mark Smiths compliments were understandable. Regrettably the rate at which the various sums raised were actually paid, extending over a two year period, were so slow, unpredictable and protracted that the factory overheads and wages absorbed most of the money as it came in. Little actual progress being made with the important development work.

Had there been the same level of confidence displayed by the BW financial directors in August 2002 as those directors previously in charge and the same regular sums of money provided as and when it was needed, at least two of the buses would have been in service during 2003 and at lower cost than the sums now expended. Remember that the first bus was driving and afloat in December 2002 and film exists showing it being driven in and out of the water at that time.

Disastrous results, potential losses – proposals for way forward

As a result of BW's withdrawal of the regular payments and the cancellation of the JV and partnership arrangements, Covelink, having used every possible reserve and facility, is now in administration and the project is at a complete standstill. The following facts speak for themselves:-

- BW has had to write off £1 million spent

- BW has ongoing costs at Falkirk for less suitable ordinary boats when Jet-Buses could by now have been in service.

- BW and Barrs have no benefit from the new technology designed to enhance and provide tourist facilities for Falkirk

- The possible loss of the opportunity for substantial sponsorship from Barrs

- The possible waste of a new technology and seventeen years work

- The possible waste of £3.4 million of private and public investment into the project excluding BW's contract

- The potential loss of a worldwide market estimated at over £500 million

- The loss of jobs and industry in the North East

- The waste of the years of positive support by many people in industry, academic institutions and parliament

- The potential loss of flood rescue vehicles for disasters and floods overseas as in the Tsunami in the Indian Ocean, Bangladesh, etc. the UK (eg. Carlisle)

- The imminent loss of the valuable worldwide patents and IPR which it now controls and may not be maintaining (eg. China 28 Feb see letter attached)

This list and the very fact that the BW board will not publish the discussions minuted at board meetings which concern Covelink, clearly shows that there are deep rooted concerns over this entire affair and that the decision taken to end the project is open to criticism.

Proposals

If BW does still support the project as has been said, then perhaps it will consider taking action to remedy the foregoing and begin by urgently ensuring that the patents and IPR are not lost, eg. China this week. See HGF patent attorneys correspondence dated 16 February 2005.

As a result of the difficulties encountered when trying to raise funding and with Mark Smith's reluctance to communicate with me, Richard Fletcher, Covelink's director who is often in London, met Mark Smith to see if anything could be done to resolve the deadlock. The result was that BW would cancel the contract and the claim on the patents, IPR and assets upon payments amounting to £350,000 to £450,000. This was not an unreasonable offer and is helpful (letter dated 27 April 2004 refers).

The minimum amount calculated to settle all the issues and set up a factory to start production is £3.5 million. My ongoing discussions with public and private sector sources of funding and capital are focussed upon this sum. Local government have indicated that seven figure amounts can be made available if we can also introduce private sector capital in seven figures.

Not having the necessary positive level of support from BW, we are still encountering resistance from large institutional investors. There have been occasions when, after lengthy negotiations even with agreed Heads of Terms, quite inexplicably, what was a keen interest is suddenly terminated overnight.

There is no doubt that the complete turnaround and lack of BW's positive support for this project has substantially impaired if not eliminated the possibility of attracting the necessary levels of investment to take this company into production to meet the orders coming in. It is now essential that BW takes whatever steps it can to revise this counterproductive view and negative attitude which prevails.

If this valuable technology is lost, the directors and shareholders of Covelink Marine Limited and David A C Royle & Co Ltd believe that they deserve an apology and financial consideration for their financial losses now amounting to £3.4 million (excluding BW's costs), the damage to their financial security and to their professional reputation achieved over many years.

What could be nationally and internationally a most successful project and technical achievement for the benefit of worldwide amphibious transport generally and for British Waterways and Covelink in particular, has deteriorated into an embarrassing, costly and hugely wasteful exercise. I regret to say that the decisions taken by BW are turning success into failure. The facts speak for themselves.

I suggest that the directors view the various DVD's and video tapes to remind themselves of the excellent Jet-Buses and Jet-Trucks and why so many people around the world wish to buy them. Compare them to the others on the market shown on other amphibious websites.

I strongly recommend that BW takes positive action now to rectify the situation and establish the City's confidence in Roylecraft and encourage potential investors especially in the private sector to provide the £1.5 million funding necessary to introduce the matched funding from local government. The directors and shareholders in my company have been most patient and tried to avoid confrontation with your company but under the prevailing conditions regret that this cannot continue. The matter must be brought into the public arena.

Signed

David A C Royle